P9-CLA-852

Please remember that this is a library book,
and that it belongs only temporarily to each
person who uses it. Be considerate. Do
not write in this, or any, library book.

# Psychology and American Law

# Psychology and American Law

Curt R. Bartol
*Castleton State College, Vermont*

with Anne M. Bartol

Wadsworth Publishing Company
Belmont, California
A Division of Wadsworth, Inc.

to Gina and Ian

Psychology Editor: Ken King
Production Editor: Hal Humphrey
Designer: Paula Schlosser

© 1983 by Wadsworth, Inc. All rights reserved. No part of this book may be reproduced, stored in a retrieval system, or transcribed, in any form or by any means, electronic, mechanical, photocopying, recording, or otherwise, without the prior written permission of the publisher, Wadsworth Publishing Company, Belmont, California 94002, a division of Wadsworth, Inc.

Printed in the United States of America
1 2 3 4 5 6 7 8 9 10—87 86 85 84 83

**Library of Congress Cataloging in Publication Data**

Bartol, Curt R.
    Psychology and American law.

    Bibliography: p.
    Includes index.
    1. Psychology, Forensic.   2. Criminal psychology.
I. Title.
KF9656.B38  1983        345'.001'9         82–8494
ISBN 0–534–01217–5        342.50019

345.0019
B292p

# ■ Contents

39572

# ■ Preface

☐ *Psychology and American Law* is intended to be a textbook for the behavioral science student who has limited knowledge about and minimal experience with the legal system. The text has three additional purposes.

First, the text tries to help the student to become skillful at discriminating between knowledge that is well supported and knowledge based upon "fireside induction" and folklore. This includes developing distrust of unverified statements presumed to be valid because they are offered by "experts."

Second, the text tries to help the student realize that scientific knowledge is not absolute in the sense of offering established fact or "ultimate truth." Rather, it is tentative, fallible, and developing.

Third, the text approaches psychology as fundamentally a scientific enterprise whose primary mission is to create or continually reconstruct testable theory, a process that allows psychologists to progress steadily toward understanding human behavior. Thus, the field of psychology and law should work toward systematizing and synthesizing valid and significant research findings about law-related behavior into viable, testable theory. Only when this is done will psychological knowledge become applicable to the problems facing the judicial system.

It would be unrealistic to claim that this text will bridge the enormous gap between psychology and law. Law is a practical, conservative, and traditional endeavor that is strongly influenced by moral, social, and political pressures. And, perhaps for good reason, law views the science of psychology with suspicion and skepticism, convinced that psychology must prove its worth in "meaningful" application before it can be accepted and trusted.

The text tries to cover as much of the judicial system as possible, but within the confines of available psychological research and current interest. The field is a rapidly developing one, and some of the material presented here may soon become dated. However, the principles and strategies of scientific psychology, and the need for unifying theoretical statements, will remain the same, regardless of the rate at which research evidence is reported.

Much of the research, reading, and thinking for this book occurred while the author was a National Endowment for the Humanities Fellow at the University of Wisconsin, Madison. The author is indebted not only to the NEH for its support, but also to the seminar group that met regularly under the tutelage of Joel Grossman. This outstanding group of young scholars, most of whom were political scientists, contributed to the atmosphere of intellectual inquiry, mutual respect, and camaraderie that helped the author to formulate the plan of this book.

I owe much gratitude to Ken King, Wadsworth psychology editor, who is a master at tolerating the whims of authors and motivating them toward project completion. Production editor Hal Humphrey and the production staff, who orchestrated the technical aspects of the book with remarkable precision, also deserve to be recognized.

Special thanks are also due Professors John Monahan, University of Virginia; Steve Penrod, University of Wisconsin; and George Bergen, Castleton State College; and the several anonymous reviewers, all of whom provided thoughtful, incisive, and invaluable comments and guidance. I wish also to acknowledge two of my students, Claire Durbrow and Judi Drazin, who carefully read and critiqued the manuscript from a student perspective. Librarian Jean Devoe was competent and most helpful in tracking down the numerous articles and books required in the research.

Curt R. Bartol

# 1

# Psychology and Law

☐ The focus of this book is the science of human behavior, specifically as this scientific enterprise is or can be applied to law and its supporting agencies. This focus will require some understanding of the basic philosophy and methods of the behavioral sciences and considerable delving into research findings applicable to the legal process. The student will find it increasingly apparent that there exists a desperate need for well-designed and well-executed psychological research directed at the many legal assumptions about human behavior. There is an even stronger need for psychological theories which encompass and explain the burgeoning data gained from this psychological research.

The American philosopher Charles Peirce outlined four general ways through which humans develop beliefs and knowledge about their world (Kerlinger, 1973). We will restrict our discussion here to how people develop beliefs about human behavior. First, there is the *method of tenacity*, where people hold firmly to their beliefs about others because they know them to be true and correct because they have *always* believed and known them to be true and correct. These beliefs are held to even in the face of contradictory evidence: "I know I'm right regardless of what others say or the evidence indicates."

The second way of knowing and developing beliefs is the *method of authority*. Something is so because individuals and institutions of authority proclaim it to be so. If the courts over the years have said it is so, it is so. If a well-recognized and respected legal scholar makes an argument in favor of or against a proposition, that scholar's name is cited as authoritative evidence for the proposition's soundness or unsoundness. Education is partly based on this method of knowing, with authority originating from teachers and the "great masters" they cite. Elementary school children often quote the authority of their teacher as indisputable evidence in support of an argument; college students often assert, "It says so in the book." Attorneys refer to the precedent of previous court decisions and the dicta therein to support the validity of their arguments.

The *a priori method* is a third way of obtaining knowledge. Evidence is believed correct because "it only stands to reason" and logical deduction; experience has little to do with it. "The idea seems to be that men, by free communication and intercourse, can reach the truth because their natural inclinations tend toward truth" (Kerlinger, 1973, p. 5). Early in the history of the American judiciary, it was believed that judges or legislators did not make law, but were merely discovering the already existing law of nature, which inherently communicated what was right and wrong (Carter, 1979). Therefore, through logical thought and reasoned deduction, one would ultimately arrive at the universal truths of "natural law." The "stands-to-reason" form of knowledge is used extensively throughout the judicial system today, although most participants in the system probably would not go so far as to call this "natural law" discovery.

The fourth way of obtaining knowledge is the *method of science*, which is the testing of a statement or set of statements through observations and systematic experiments. On the basis of these empirical tests, statements about natural events or processes are revised, reconstructed, or discarded. Science is an enterprise under constant change, modification, and expansion rather than an absolute, unalterable system full of facts. Science teaches us that there are few certainties in the natural world—only probabilities—and that we should base our decisions and expectations on "the best of our knowledge" at any particular time.

Scientific knowledge, because it is based upon observations, systematic experiments, and testable statements, places itself permanently at risk. It is constantly updated to account for observations and experiments, and it attempts to make predictions beyond our experience. Ultimately, it seeks the underlying order of nature. The method of science is a testable, self-corrective approach to knowledge that offers one of the most powerful sources available for the understanding of human behavior.

Common sense is an ingredient in each of the above methods, but it is most dominant in the *a priori* method. Common sense, in this context, refers to "a homespun awareness resulting from everyday experience, as opposed to the knowledge acquired from formal training in a technical philosophy" (Gordon, Kleiman & Hanie, 1978, p. 894). The relationship between common sense and science will be dealt with in more detail later in the chapter.

Peirce's four methods of knowing provide a rough framework for determining the source of one's knowledge, and they will be useful guides throughout the remainder of the book. They also offer a beginning argument for why psychology should be a scientific endeavor. With the possible exception of the method of tenacity, each method has its place in the accumulation of knowledge, as long as we recognize which method we are using to obtain our knowledge. Authoritative sources and reasoning both are valuable contributors to our beliefs and opinions. The method of science, however, provides us with additional information about the "soundness" of our authoritative and logical knowledge, and it promotes a critical and cautious stylistic way of thinking about our beliefs. This book will utilize, in some mixture, authoritative, logical, and scientific sources of knowledge, but the last will be stressed.

Many researchers in the behavioral sciences (perhaps in all sciences) conduct research in order to be competitive with their colleagues, to gain desired positions, and generally to be professionally "successful" rather than to advance the knowledge of mankind. As noted by Gordon, Kleiman, and Hanie (1978, p. 903), "Because of the pressure to publish, it seems that a substantial portion of the professional literature is comprised of articles and books prepared to serve the immediate needs of the researcher rather than to offer solutions to problems confronting society." For a variety of reasons, many individuals are simply not suited to conduct research which will lead to the idealistic "ultimate conclusion." Consequently, we have a plethora of published studies in scholarly and professional journals, and they vary widely in their contributions to knowledge. Some are methodologically sound but questionably relevant. Many appear to contribute more to the author's advancement than to the advancement of knowledge. Donald Hebb (1974, p. 71) observes: "The journals are full of papers that are very well done and will not be heard of again." While the method and analyses are solid, the inspiration these studies provide and their relevance to theory and existing knowledge remain in doubt. Far too often, the wide-sweeping conclusions of the authors hardly dovetail with the data.

The student of psycholegal research must be forever wary of the conclusions made by researchers, particularly when there are attempts to make firm conclusions on the basis of insignificant experiments. The educated person must be able to discern whether the hypothesis, design, and data warrant the conclusions (and convictions) of the author, and whether there is supportive evidence from other studies and replications. Otherwise, the reader will have to rely almost exclusively upon authoritative and logical sources of knowledge. Heavy reliance on these sources in studying the behavioral sciences will often yield contradictory statements and ambiguous conclusions, and this in turn may end in considerable disenchantment with what psychology has to offer. An understanding of the philosophy and methods of psychology will lead to a deeper understanding and appreciation of psycholegal research and the substantial contributions it can make to the judicial system.

Psychology students often complain about the need to become familiar with scientific methodology and concepts; they want only answers and interesting facts about the mind and about people. As we have seen, exclusive reliance upon authoritative and logical sources leads to confusion, especially when we are trying to understand the mysteries of human behavior. This statement, however, should not be construed as implying that empirical research is never contradictory or confusing. Science is rarely an objective progression toward truth or a steady, cumulative acquisition of data toward a unifying theory. During its early stages, scientific knowledge can be as contradictory and unclear as any knowledge acquired through authority or logic. Eventually, however, the scientific community chooses theoretical statements that can best account for research results and observations over those statements that do not account for the results and observations as well. In this sense, science should ultimately lead to a clearer and more consistent understanding of the phenomena under study than the other known ways of acquiring knowledge.

Though this text does not attempt to lay out the entire scientific blueprint advocated by the community of scientific psychologists, scientific principles and problems will be introduced bit by bit throughout the book as they pertain to specific issues. The text attempts to add to the reader's knowledge about psycholegal research, while cultivating scientific skepticism and critical thinking. We will begin by examining briefly the basic premises of scientific psychology and some of the key concepts that will be encountered with some regularity later on.

# ■ Basic Premises of Psychology

People hold many assumptions about human behavior, and the science of psychology tries to test the validity of these assumptions. Practically all forms of behavior have come under its scrutiny. An experimental or empirical psychologist studies organisms to understand, predict, and control (or, in the case of humans, to help them to control) their behavior, behavior being what organisms do, or how they act. The methods of study vary greatly, from simple, direct observation in natural environments to complex experimental manipulations in laboratory settings.

## THE EXPERIMENTAL METHOD

Many psychologists are convinced that human behavior can best be understood if researchers use the experimental method, which requires careful control and measurement of the phenomena being studied. Often, these experimental psychologists bring the phenomenon to be studied into the laboratory, where conditions can be manipulated or controlled with precise equipment and procedures, and where many possible extraneous factors can be discarded, minimized, or accounted for.

One such experiment was conducted by a group of experimental psychologists (Davis et al., 1975), who wondered how the size of a jury affected its final decision. Traditionally, juries in England, Canada, and the United States comprise twelve persons, who are usually required to arrive at a unanimous decision. However, some states are now experimenting with smaller jury sizes and with majority verdicts, especially in civil cases (Kalven & Zeisel, 1966; Wrightsman, 1977). Other countries regularly use trial juries of fewer than twelve persons (Saks & Ostrom, 1975).

Davis and his colleagues designed an experimental situation that simulated trial conditions, or a "mock trial" as it is called in the research literature. Various six- and twelve-person "juries" listened to a tape recording that contained an abbreviated version of the transcript of an actual trial. Some of the juries were instructed to come to a unanimous decision regarding guilt or innocence; other juries were told they must reach a two-thirds majority decision within the same time period. The twelve- and six-person juries generally arrived at the same decision (the defendant was found innocent) whether or not they were forced to unanimity. The differences between the two jury types were differences in group process rather than in the verdict itself. Unanimous juries needed a larger number of poll votes and longer deliberation time before reaching a verdict. On the basis of this experiment, the researchers concluded that jury size does not appear to affect the final verdict, but does affect the length of time and the manner of arriving at the final decision. Other researchers have been testing these findings by trying to replicate them. If additional studies reveal similar findings, valuable information about jury size will have been gained. One limitation of the Davis project—a limitation shared by many experimental designs—lies in the amount of generalization that can be made from simulated or experimental juries to actual juries.

## VALIDITY

When we ask to what extent results can be generalized to other persons and situations, we are inquiring about *external validity*. Usually, the degree of external validity is approximated by conducting further research using different populations, different situations, or both. Research on samples other than college students (usually sophomores) or research using situations that follow jury processes more closely would allow us to be more confident about the validity of the data applied to other but related conditions. By contrast, *internal validity* is concerned with how much confidence we can place in the results obtained in this particular experiment, using this particular procedure. Was the significant difference that was found due to some artifact in the design, or is it a naturally occurring difference? Both external validity and internal validity are important criteria to use in determining the value of psycholegal research, and we will encounter them repeatedly as we review the research throughout the book.

# ■ Research Strategies

## EVIDENCE

Rychlak (1968) noted that psychologists gather two types of evidence to help them arrive at knowledge and theories about human behavior. Evidence procured by using experimental methods like those in the Davis study is called *validating* evidence. It is the result of careful, controlled research that is time-consuming, often expensive, and complex, but also invaluable. A second type of evidence, most often gathered by applied and clinical psychologists, is called *procedural*. This is the information clinicians suspect to be correct based on their personal observations, assessments, and interpretations. Procedural evidence includes the elements of common sense, logic, and insight, and it results in a sense of conviction that a given hypothesis accounts for some observations and is useful. Clinicians have had considerable experience working with individuals in a clinical setting, and they use this expertise to form theory about human behavior. For example, police officers who have intervened in domestic disturbances have told clinicians it is wise to separate the disputants in a two-person confrontation (e.g., remove them to different rooms for a "cooling off" period). No wealth of precise validating evidence supports this practice, but there is ample procedural evidence to suggest that the method is effective for reducing conflict and tension between the parties.

The two types of evidence—procedural and validating—are interdependent in that they both contribute to our knowledge about human behavior. To reject one or the other severely limits the knowledge we can gain. Although it is sometimes difficult to draw a fine line between these two methods, because both may be methods of science, the distinguishing features between them are *replicability* and *control*.

**Replicability.** The method designed to gain validating evidence demands that the findings be potentially replicable, or able to be repeated by others. Replicability requires that the descriptions of the variables studied and the procedures used to study them be precise and objective enough so that it is clear what was tried. In some scientific circles this is called "operationalizing." For example, if researchers wish to study the effects of anxiety on test taking, they must be extremely clear about what is meant by anxiety and test taking, and precisely what procedures and measurements were used to examine the relationship. Clear, precise descriptions allow checks on both internal and external validity.

**Control.** Control refers to the attempts by the research to account for all potentially influential variables on the relationship being investigated. For example, in the test-taking anxiety study, the researcher must be certain that it is anxiety rather than some extraneous influence like intelligence, time, sex, age, or even room temperature that contributes to the test taking performance. These extraneous influences are called *secondary* variables. The researcher must also be careful to identify and measure the *independent* and *dependent* variables. Anxiety, in this example, represents the independent variable, whereas test-taking performance is the dependent variable. The independent variable in most scientific investigations is manipulated in a controlled fashion. In our example, the researcher might want to test the effects of three different levels of anxiety on test taking. This manipulation might require some procedure for inducing anxiety (however defined and measured), such as threatening the subjects with varying dire consequences for failing the exam. In one condition the subjects may be threatened with electrical shock for failure, whereas in another they may be threatened with public exposure of grades on the exam. A third condition might involve no threat or consequence (potentially a no-anxiety condition), and individuals in this group would be considered the controls. The first two groups would be the experimental groups. The dependent variable, of course, would be exam scores.

Procedural or clinical evidence may also be gathered in a similar manner, but in a majority of instances it is obtained with considerably less precise objective description and control. Its value rests principally in the hypotheses it generates. A hypothesis is a speculative explanation of behavior, and it implies prediction. In applied settings, hypotheses are referred to as psychological assessments or, more technically, as clinical judgments. Procedural evidence is also relied upon to some extent in the experiences of those working within the legal system and of those who formulate policy. Clinical psychologists and professionals in other applied disciplines, therefore, share common ground with participants in the legal system with reference to procedural evidence. This shared method of science explains, in part, why judges and lawyers often prefer the testimony of clinicians to that of experimentalists.

## CLINICAL JUDGMENT vs. STATISTICAL PREDICTION

The lines between procedural and validating evidence are often not as sharp as we have conceptually described here. This point can best be illustrated by the long-standing debate over the predictive accuracy of clinical judgment versus that of statistical or actuarial methods. Clinically based predictions of behavior make use of social history, interviews or other personal contacts, comments and recommendations from others, and information from various types of psychological tests. This clinical material is then used to form a clinical impression of what a person is like and how he or she might act in the future. The entire process is subjective, based more on common sense than on science, and it is a good example of use of procedural evidence.

The actuarial method employs statistics to identify certain parameters about the person's background and behavior that have been found to be related to the behavior being predicted. These parameters might include age, measurable past behavioral patterns, sex, scores on psychological tests, and occupation—as long as they have been found to have a significant relationship to the behavior in question. Once these parameters have been identified statistically, probabilities are offered or critical cut-off points are drawn relative to the person's future behavior. This process is independent of the evaluator's personal bias or clinical intuition. For example, the actuarial method might predict, on the basis of background and past behavior, that an individual being considered for parole represented a 75 percent statistical probability of committing another criminal offense within two years. If the parole board has established an objective criterion that anyone with a 60 percent or higher probability will be denied parole, the actuarial method dictates a decision against parole. In ideal form, the actuarial method is highly objective and mechanical in both data collection and application (validating evidence).

The conceptual demarcation between clinical judgment and the actuarial method disappears, however, when the data collection and application become mixed. For example, data collection may be objective and based on experimental data, but the prediction offered by the clinician may ultimately be based upon clinical experience and impressions. A psychological test may be carefully constructed and based on extensive research with accompanying statistical tables outlining accuracy probabilities in predicting recidivism (the committing of a new criminal offense after release from custody). Despite the availability of objective data, however, the clinician's decision-making may be swayed by clinical hunch. On the other hand, data collection may be clinical in nature, such as obtaining vague responses to inkblots and other ambiguous stimuli, but the decisionmaker may use specific objective criteria in prediction. For example, all subjects who see butterflies in an inkblot might be automatically classified obsessive-compulsive neurotics who are likely to commit a new crime within a two-year period—to use an absurd illustration.

The debate over which method (in pure form) is superior in accuracy of prediction has existed at least since the mid-1920s (Sawyer, 1966). More recently, Paul Meehl (1954, 1965) has brought the controversy to the forefront. Meehl incurred the ire of many clinicians when he concluded, after surveying approximately two dozen studies comparing statistical with clinical predictions, that the statistical methods were clearly superior in predictive accuracy. Subsequent reviews (e.g., Mischel, 1968; Goldberg, 1968, 1970) also found that clinical wisdom was faulty when compared to objective methods of arriving at overall prognostic or diagnostic decisions.

Studies have shown that people have a remarkable disregard for statistical data when they make judgments about others (e.g., Kahneman & Tversky, 1973; Nisbett et al., 1976), preferring hunches, intuition, and case-specific information over statistical base rates and tables. John Carroll (1980) points out that statistical predictive devices have been available to parole decisionmakers for over forty years, yet they are rarely used. Instead, it appears that parole decisionmakers rely on subjective impressions derived from case-specific information.

## THE CARROLL STUDIES

Carroll conducted a series of studies designed to determine to what extent parole decisionmakers will utilize statistical information to predict human behavior if that information is readily available. In his first study (1977), he presented both statistical and clinical material to individuals who were asked to make predictions of recidivism. Experimental subjects were 112 criminology students who received base-rate information on 100 offenders released from confinement two years previously. The base-rate information was the percentage of those 100 offenders who had committed a new crime during the two-year post-release period. For example, some subjects were informed, prior to reading brief case summaries of the parolees, that 25 percent of the population of these offenders had committed a new crime during the release period. Subjects were then presented with information on ten parolees of the 100 and asked to predict (actually postdict) which of the ten had committed another offense. The number selected represented the dependent variable. The information provided on each parolee was similar to that usually given at parole hearings.

Two sets of independent variables were manipulated during Carroll's study. One set involved base rates which were presented to the subjects prior to their reading the case summaries. Some subjects were told that the rate of recidivism for the parolee population was 75 percent, while others were informed the rate was 25 percent. The subjects were told that the case files of the 100 parolees had been examined, and it had been found that "$x$ percent of the group of 100 offenders committed another crime in the two years since release, while $(100 - x)$ percent did not commit another crime."

The second set of manipulated independent variables was the information given to the subjects about each parolee. Although the material was developed from real cases, it was "altered and recombined to give case descriptions which subjectively would be given a 50 percent chance of committing a new crime" (Carroll, 1980, p. 73). In addition, there were ten different descriptions of parolees.

The hypothesis was: "If high base rates for recidivism lead to predictions of more recidivists than low base rates for any types of base-rate information, it would show that subjects give some consistent weight to the base rates in making their judgments" (Carroll, 1980, p. 74). The results showed that subjects in the high base-rate conditions (70–75 percent) predicted that 50 percent of the cases had recidivated, while subjects in the low base-rate conditions (25–30 percent) predicted that 49 percent had recidivated. This suggests that the subjects paid little attention to the base rates in making their predictions and were more swayed by the case specific information given on each parolee. (Remember, each case description was written in such a way that it gave the impression of a 50 percent chance of recidivism.) The results, therefore, were in agreement with the previous research reporting that decisionmakers prefer descriptive, clinical information over the more pallid empirical data. However, Carroll had questions about the experiment's external validity, since only college students had been used as subjects. There were other concerns as well. For example, the artificial manner in which the base rates had been presented, combined with a brief sketch of the parolee, raised some doubts about the reality of the procedure.

In a second study, Carroll used actual expert decisionmakers from the Pennsylvania Parole Board, and the information was presented more realistically by using risk statements made by other experts (e.g., high risk, low risk, moderate risk). The results revealed that parole decisionmakers were influenced by the recommendations *and* clinical judgments embedded in the case summaries. These data indicate that parole decisionmakers are not influenced solely by their own inclinations derived from descriptive material; they also consider outside sources, provided these sources are experts offering clinical judgments.

In a third study, Carroll attempted to examine the implications of both studies by changing some of the procedures and manipulating the independent variables. He recognized the many shortcomings inherent in the two studies, especially in relation to making comparisons between the resulting data. Study 3 used the same case summaries as Study 2, but as in Study 1, criminology students were used as subjects. In addition, Study 3 presented base rates either as numerical percentages or as risk statements. In Study 1, numerical percentages were used as the major independent variables; in Study 2, only risk statements were used (e.g., high risk, low risk in terms of recidivism) as major independent variables. Study 3 included two conditions: one embedded either numerical or risk statements in each case summary; the other separated the statements from the body of the summary and labeled them "statistical risk predictions."

Results revealed that subjects used both risk statements and numerical statements in arriving at their predictions. Subjects in Study 3 used probability information, while those in Study 1 had not. It appears, therefore, that decisionmakers will use statistical, empirical evidence in making predictions, but only under certain conditions. What are those conditions? Although Carroll's research design does not lend itself to simple conclusions, one possible explanation centers on the difference in the way the information was presented. Because the statistical evidence in Study 1 was presented only once, before the subjects read the ten summaries, the subjects may have failed to make the causal connection between each case summary and probability statement. The numerical and risk statements in Study 3 were provided for each case, either embedded in the summary or separated from but related to that summary. Therefore, it was much easier for subjects in Study 3 to draw connections and integrate the statements into their judgments.

The data demonstrate that decisionmakers can use empirical or risk information if it is given in conjunction with a specific case, regardless of whether it is stated verbally or numerically. It also does not appear to matter whether the information is in the form of a risk statement made by another clinician or a probability ratio given by a computer, so long as the information is introduced into the description of the person.

The Carroll studies give some indication of how psycholegal research is conducted and what problems are encountered. The studies are far from conclusive; it is likely that considerable contradictory data will be found before the probability-information issue is settled. In fact, there is already research that offers contradictory results (e.g., Kahneman & Tversky, 1973). The external validity of the Carroll studies remains in question, since at no time were the subjects making actual decisions which would affect lives.

The studies also illustrate how difficult it is to maintain conceptual neatness between procedural and validating evidence. We used this artificial dichotomy early in this section to build a cognitive framework for ordering the material to follow. Reality often raises havoc with conceptual schemes and typologies.

## CLINICIANS AND EXPERIMENTALISTS

The evidence-gathering distinction between clinicians and experimentalists within psychology parallels differences in their work settings and, to some extent, in their goals. Experimentalists are generally affiliated with universities as professors and researchers, or with various research institutions and laboratories. Federal and governmental agencies and private companies, such as pharmaceutical or aerospace industries, employ experimental psychologists to conduct studies.

Although clinicians also may be affiliated with industry, often to offer consulting services in employee selection or counseling, most clinicians are in private practice or are associated with mental health agencies and social service institutions, such as hospitals and prisons. Clinicians who are specialists in various aspects of the law often call themselves forensic psychologists, while others who work closely with law enforcement prefer to be called police psychologists. Although many psychologists in academic settings who are principally researchers also prefer these titles, a majority of forensic and police psychologists are clinicians.

Clinical psychologists have a practical goal: to determine the nature of a problem and to develop an effective way of solving it. The police psychologist may be faced with developing a workable, valid method for the screening and selection of police candidates. The forensic psychologist may be asked by a law firm to advise its partners how to select a jury most favorably inclined toward their client.

Experimentalists, who are almost always psychologists at colleges and universities, have a more generalized goal, one common to all sciences: to amass enough knowledge about a phenomenon to be able to understand and predict it, with an accuracy rate substantially above chance. An experimentalist studying aggression in the laboratory tries to understand it enough to be able to predict when it will occur. Ideally, clinicians use the information obtained by the researchers, add it to their own procedural evidence, and also attempt to make predictions.

## RESEARCH AND THE JUDICIAL SYSTEM

Modern experimental-academic and clinical psychology both have much to offer the judicial system, as long as the information is presented accurately and with appreciation for the complexity inherent in human behavior. The judicial system, as we are using the term here, refers to courts and the legal process, law enforcement, corrections, and probation and parole. This perspective also will encompass peripheral areas like the personality of law enforcement personnel, stress, the causes and preventions of crime, and the treatment and rehabilitation of criminal behavior. Note, though, that a judicial system that operates in an organized, sequential, and coordinated manner between law enforcement, the courts, corrections, and probation and parole does not exist. The "system," realistically, is heavily plagued with disorganization, conflict, ambiguity, dilemma, and prejudice, and a deep-seated disenchantment emanates from all its segments. We use the word *system* only as a general term encompassing many facets; it is not meant to imply that there exists a smooth-running entity surrounded by continuity or logical processes.

This book is intended to be primarily a textbook designed to educate interested students about the contemporary psychological knowledge that is pertinent to the judicial system and process. It tries not only to point out existing fictions and misinformation about human behavior, but also to evaluate the limitations and the nature of psychological knowledge. The text's mission is to inform students about the relationship between psychology and law, to encourage critical thinking about the two disciplines, to communicate trends in psycholegal research, and to suggest how the two disciplines might better understand and relate to one another.

## PSYCHOLOGICAL THEORY

The reader is forewarned of a major shortcoming in psycholegal research: the paucity of theories behind which to rally. Often there is a hodgepodge of research in a given area with no unifying theme. Yet the basic aim of psychological research is theory development, not the unsystematic accumulation of facts. Thomas Kuhn (1970) notes that scientific history does not support the contention that science is doing research for its own sake without theoretical commitment. Scientific development depends upon at least "some implicit body of intertwined theoretical and methodological belief that permits selection, evaluation, and criticism" (Kuhn, 1970, pp. 16–17).

A theory is "a set of interrelated constructs (concepts), definitions, and propositions that present a systematic view of phenomena by specifying relations among variables, with the purpose of explaining and predicting the phenomena" (Kerlinger, 1973, p. 9). Psychological theory, therefore, explains and predicts human behavior. It provides a general explanation that encompasses and systematically connects many different behaviors. Moreover, "a theory which is not refutable by any conceivable event is nonscientific" (Popper, 1962, p. 36). Therefore, as a scientific explanation of behavior, a psychological theory must have falsifiability, or refutability, or testability. The terms in any scientific theory must be as precise as possible, their meaning and usage clear and unambiguous. Vague and imprecise theories generally are not falsifiable and hence cannot be tested scientifically. The advantage of vague theory is that it can live on, on borrowed time, without running the risk of being tested and found inadequate. Freudian and neo-Freudian theories are good examples. These ambiguous theories cannot be refuted by the methods of science, and their proponents can remain unchallenged by empirical data. Testable theories, on the other hand, draw heavy empirical scrutiny and critical comment; many fall by the wayside, and nearly all experience extensive revision.

In sum, then, we can say that scientifically powerful and heuristic theories which have the capacity to lead us toward explanations and predictions of behavioral phenomena are under constant revision and reconstruction. To the lay person, they appear fragmented and complicated, and they communicate excessive tentativeness and caution. Untestable theories, on the other hand, offer glib generalizations which appear to provide answers for human dilemmas, but they are little more than philosophical exercises.

The position taken in this book is that the avenue toward explanation and prediction is paved with scientific theory, which promotes experiments, evaluation, and criticism. The development of scientific theory represents the greatest challenge to psychologists studying the judicial system today.

The remainder of this chapter will be concerned with a review of what psychologists actually have been doing in the judicial system and of the nature of the problems inherent in the many roles they take. Prior to any discussion of these roles, however, it is important that the reader become familiar with the differences between psychology and psychiatry and their particular ways of viewing human behavior. It should be emphasized that the following presentation is an abbreviated sketch of the disciplines and their perspectives and calls for qualifications at almost every point.

## ■ Psychology and Psychiatry

The two main professions trained to provide services to persons with emotional or behavioral problems are psychiatry and clinical psychology. Psychologists, especially the clinicians, are often confused with psychiatrists in the public mind. The distinction between the two fields is an important one to make, because a difference in fundamental approach will mean that the same problem is viewed differently and that alternative solutions may be found.

Psychiatrists are medical doctors (MDs) who specialize in behavioral disorders rather than physical illness. The psychiatrist has experienced the rigors of medical school and all its requirements, and then has taken a psychiatric residency, with training in the handling of psychiatric patients. The psychiatric residency usually lasts anywhere from one to three years, depending on state, institutional, personal, and professional requirements. The training often combines a heavy reliance on drug treatment with the "medical model" approach to diagnosis and treatment, although the reliance upon the medical model is beginning to wane (Mechanic, 1980). According to the medical model, psychological abnormality is conceptualized as being analogous to physical disease, and like physical disease, it is classified and treated. While many practicing psychiatrists do not subscribe to this approach, there remains a sizeable number who accept some diagnostic categories as disease categories and treat the behaviors as symptoms of a mental disease, often through the use of psychoactive drugs.

The clinical psychologist generally has a PhD—an academic degree that usually requires from three to six years of full-time study in research methods, psychological theory, assessment, and psychotherapeutic techniques. In addition to academic training, the clinical psychologist typically experiences nine or twelve months of supervised internship in a clinical setting, where the theories and methods acquired in graduate training can be applied to human behavior problems. Psychiatrists believe that assessment and treatment are clinical arts gained through direct experience and a theoretical orientation, and that they involve many of the features of the medical model. Psychologists, in contrast, emphasize expertise in psychological theory and research as foundations for the scientific bases of assessment and treatment.

# ■ Psychologists in the Criminal Justice System

The criminal justice system is a bureaucracy comprising interacting parts or subsystems—the police, the judiciary, probation and parole, and corrections (Cole, 1975). It consists of all the institutions, agencies, and processes that deal with violations of the criminal law, and it is by far the most heavily studied component of the judicial system.

It is believed that psychologists are increasingly being used in the various segments of this criminal justice system, but exact statistics are difficult to obtain. Fortunately, the American Psychological Association (APA) has formed a Task Force on the Role of Psychologists in the Criminal Justice System, which has published results of an extensive survey of 203 psychologists principally employed in a criminal justice setting (Clingempeel, Mulvey & Reppucci, 1980). Most of the psychologists (67 percent) had doctorates and considerable postdegree experience (average of 10.9 years). The respondents were predominantly white males (98.4 percent). Most positions involved work with adults rather than with juveniles.

A majority of the psychologists surveyed offered indirect or direct services to correctional institutions (70 percent). Other services were offered to courts (46 percent), probation departments (41 percent), parole agencies (31 percent), community correctional agencies (25 percent), and police agencies (17 percent). Psychological assessment and treatment of offenders were the most frequently provided types of service (75 percent and 74 percent, respectively). Assessment might include testing, status appraisal, or prediction of dangerous or antisocial behavior. Other significant services included consultation to administrators (53 percent), personnel training (53 percent), and personnel screening and selection for the variety of criminal justice agencies (21 percent). From the data, it is clear that psychologists now working in the criminal justice system spend most of their time in corrections, evaluating and treating offenders.

## PSYCHOLOGY IN CORRECTIONS

Psychologists have been active in many facets of the correctional system for more years than in the courts or in law enforcement settings, but their track record of successful change has not been remarkable. This is partly due to the nature of the beast: the correctional system, particularly at the state and community levels, teems with overworked, underpaid, and undertrained personnel; its institutions are often outmoded and overcrowded; the working and living settings are depressing and hardly conducive to optimism and promise. Society, meanwhile, prefers to look the other way. The correctional "system" is composed of numerous variations in procedures, policies, and facilities, even within institutions in the same state or county. However, the problem for psychologists in that setting is more complex. Using psychological knowledge to intervene into the lives of others constitutes an imposition of one person's or one group's values onto some other person or group. Nowhere is this intervention more blatant than in the correctional system, where inmates have minimal choice concerning their situation or treatment.

One of the overriding concerns and conflicts faced by correctional psychologists is how to cope with the contrasting philosophies of the institution and their own profession. Should the psychologist be loyal to the institution and its custodial role, or to the client and his rehabilitation and treatment? Very often, the custodial nature of the institution and its restrictions on personal freedom work against helping an inmate to take control of his life and to make realistic decisions. Realizing the importance of this ethical dilemma, Brodsky (1972) proposed a typology that reflects how psychologists often deal with this primary conflict, positing that they elect to become either "system challengers" or "system professionals." The challengers align themselves firmly with the offender's needs and vehemently oppose the institution's custodial functions. Generally, the challengers leave the system after a short period of time and a long line of confrontations. The system professionals lean toward the institution's goals and resist becoming committed exclusively to the offender's best interest. They tend to remain at the job in a continuing effort to make difficult decisions in an educated manner.

Although Brodsky's typology has merit, like all typologies it must be accepted guardedly. The APA survey data cited above indicate that most psychologists in corrections place themselves somewhere between the two extremes: they express conflicting alliances to the offender, the institution, and society. In other words, the psychologists who responded to the survey appeared to be trying to balance their responsibilities and to please everyone.

The psychologists' responses also revealed a perceived powerlessness to effect genuine institutional or individual change. The majority seemed resigned to the impossibility of altering the system significantly under its present structure and process. Although the respondents indicated they had small successes, they doubted their ability to have a global or long-lasting effect on the correctional system.

In sum, there is a fundamental difference in philosophy between psychology and corrections, a difference that sometimes extends to law in general as well. The reality is that psychology will not be helpful unless this basic schism is recognized and modified. Brodsky (1980, p. 63) states this view very well: "Psychology tends to value trust; corrections values control. Psychology cherishes expert, scientific knowledge. Law and corrections value the common man, common sense, and pragmatics. Psychology pursues objectivity. Justice accepts more subjectivity and more personal than scientific insights."

Despite these differences in philosophy and method, psychology can make substantial contributions to corrections and to probation and parole. Psychology can pose questions and suggest responses, such as those we will deal with in Chapter 11. What do we know about the psychological effects of the prison environment on inmates and staff? Does our current knowledge about human behavior justify the correctional system's use of concepts like punishment, rehabilitation, and deterrence? Are psychologists, or any other behavioral scientists, able to assess and predict who will be dangerous several months or years into the future? What forms of treatment or rehabilitation have not succeeded, and why? Do any forms of treatment show promise? The reader will reencounter these questions later in the book.

## PSYCHOLOGY AND CRIMINAL BEHAVIOR

Crime repels and disgusts people, but it also intrigues them. The cause of criminal behavior is elusive to professionals and the public alike, and this elusiveness will be addressed in this text. A review of the major literature in criminology (the study of crime) reveals that, until recently, psychology was not integrated sufficiently into the approaches taken to crime prevention and treatment. The literature was predominantly sociological and psychiatric in perspective, the latter often being confused with psychological theory and research.

Psychology has been hesitant about defining its role in the judicial system, but it has been especially hesitant about making contributions toward the understanding of criminal behavior. While a good grasp of criminal behavior requires combined research from all interested disciplines and from the various schools of theoretical thought within those disciplines, there is little reason to leave the work primarily to sociologists, psychiatrists, anthropologists, and legal scholars. Psychology offers another dimension that can provide a clearer understanding of the scientific puzzle of criminal behavior. For example, psychology has the potential to help in the development of laws and policies concerned with crime prevention and appropriate sanctions once offenses have been committed. The cognitive-social explanation of crime will be emphasized in this book, not only because it offers a contemporary psychological viewpoint, but also because it recognizes the many complexities and variables involved in any human behavior.

## PSYCHOLOGY IN LAW ENFORCEMENT

Consider the following three scenarios:

- Police officers and their spouses are attending a workshop on police marriages and the stress that is unique to these relationships. Participants role-play situations they encounter in their marriages. A consulting psychologist leads the subsequent discussion.
- A staff psychologist in a metropolitan police department is summoned to talk with a person threatening suicide. Later in the day, the psychologist provides therapy for a police captain becoming increasingly disenchanted with his job and home life.
- A police chief decides not to hire a police officer candidate, partly on the basis of the results of psychological tests that pointed to potential behavioral problems.

The above examples all underscore some of the need for the services and skills of psychologists in law enforcement. Police are the first line participants in the judicial system. Some approaches to psychology and law neglect law enforcement, ignoring the fact that these officers are the agents who interrogate witnesses and suspects, gather a large portion of the legal evidence in criminal cases, and use their discretionary powers in making arrests and handling potentially dangerous situations. Moreover, police officials are more likely to be eyewitnesses to a crime, to influence society about the concept of justice in the legal system, and in general to have extensive impact on many elements of the judicial process. Psychology would be remiss if it failed to study the psychology of law enforcement with the goal of improving the quality of these first line participants in the legal process.

In the next two chapters we will examine the psychology of law enforcement, but the areas covered will be largely dictated by what psychologists have been interested in studying. Police psychologists have been most active in the areas of stress and its management and the psychological screening and selection of police candidates. We will give a substantial amount of attention to these areas, not only because of their relevance to law enforcement, but also because they are valuable to other aspects of the judicial system as well. For example, the effects of stress, discussed extensively in Chapter 3, are important to consider with respect to witnesses and victims of crime. Psychological assessment, the primary focus of Chapter 2, is a critical topic for courts and corrections.

## ■ Psychology and the Courts

The science of psychology, whose primary concern is the empirical study of behavior, has much to offer the judicial system. The reader must realize early, however, that psychology cannot provide absolute truths or easy answers. Instead, it has many partial, often tentative answers embedded in probabilities. Empirical psychology is *nomothetic* as opposed to *idiographic* in scope; it concentrates upon general principles, relationships, and patterns that transcend the single individual. Empirical psychologists are generally cautious in responding to questioners who demand simple, certain answers or solutions to complex issues. Moreover, the principles and theories proposed by psychology are confirmed only through the collection of consistent and supporting data, a process that not only is long and rigorous, but is also punctuated by debate and differing interpretations of the data. "History suggests that the road to a firm research consensus is extraordinarily arduous" (Kuhn, 1970, p. 15). Psychological theories or "truths" are arrived at primarily through experiments that employ methods emphasizing prediction, measurement, and controlled comparisons.

Courts, like psychology, are concerned with predicting, explaining, and controlling human behavior, but much of the relevant and extensive research available in psychology today is unknown to the legal system. Daniel Yarmey (1979, p. 10) notes that what Munsterberg wrote in 1908 about psychology and law continues to hold today. Munsterberg claimed:

> The court would rather listen for whole days to the "science" of handwriting experts than allow a witness to be examined with regard to his memory and his power of perception . . . with methods . . . of experimental psychology. It is so much easier . . . to be satisfied with sharp demarcation lines . . . ; the man is sane or insane, and if he's sane, he speaks the truth or he lies. The psychologists would upset this satisfaction completely.

Because of the complexity of human behavior and the nature of the scientific enterprise, psychology rarely can provide hard facts or certain conclusions to society. Human behavior results from a complicated and only partially understood interplay of personality and environmental factors. Therefore, the science of human behavior can only tease out trends, hypotheses, suggestions, probabilities, and ultimately sound theories. Courts, however, look for simple facts which are directly and specifically applicable to the case at hand and which rely more often than not on "common sense" (the *a priori* method of acquiring knowledge).

In a way, science and common sense are alike, since science is a systematic and controlled extension of common sense (Kerlinger, 1973). A common ingredient in both is some degree of logic, but the similarities drop out rapidly from that point. Science is a method and tradition which demands control, systematic variation, replication, and caution, and which is learned through the formal process of education. "Science is not natural to man at all. It has to be learned, consciously practiced, stripped out of the sea of emotions, prejudices, and wishes in which our daily lives are steeped" (Eiseley, 1973, p. 19). People seem to have a proclivity to resist science; maintaining subscribers to its fundamental philosophy and tenets is a fragile enterprise. People prefer "common sense" in their approach to problems, partly because it enables them to eliminate ambiguity and to order reality according to their beliefs and experiences.

However, the price one pays for commonsense approaches to problems is the vagueness, inconsistencies, faulty explanations, and lack of falsifiability the solutions carry. Debates based solely upon commonsense observations are likely to rage without resolution. Science provides an avenue for different perspectives and fresh approaches to these debates, with a promise for resolution.

The judicial process demands certainty, or at least the appearance of it, in the courtroom. Since scientific hypotheses and generalizations lack this conclusive certainty, they are held suspect by professional participants in the legal system. Authoritative experts and disciplines that can provide certainty and "facts" are much preferred over empirical psychology and its cautious approach. As we will find in Chapters 4 and 5, those psychiatrists and some clinical psychologists who are willing to make absolute statements and conclusions often are the parties invited to provide legal testimony. Many mental health practitioners too often have testified in line with the court's wishes, without emphasizing that caution and tentativeness are required in view of present knowledge.

## THE ADVERSARY MODEL

Empirical psychology, directed by theory, arrives at "truth" and scientific knowledge through the accumulation of data secured through experiments that emphasize precision, measurement, and control of an array of variables that potentially may contaminate outcomes. Law, on the other hand, arrives at truth through an adversarial process. The courts feel that the best way to uncover the facts in a case is to have proponents of each side of an issue present evidence most favorable to their position. The contenders confront one another in the courtroom, where truth is tested and refined through the "fight" theory of justice (Frank, 1949). Justice will prevail once each side has had the opportunity to present its version of the evidence to the decisionmaker—the judge or the jury. It is assumed that "objective" truth about human behavior cannot be acquired from only one version. Instead, different versions of the truth are sought which, when put together, allow for judgment within an acceptable margin of error.

The adversary model presents problems for empirical psychology, since it not only concentrates on one particular case at that particular point in time, but also encourages lawyers to dabble in and out of the data pool and pick and choose that segment of psychological information they wish to present in support of their position. The lawyer may select only part of a finding of an experiment and present the material out of context. This procedure allows distortion and misrepresentation of research findings, since the lawyer's main concern is to provide the decisionmaker with evidence that will be favorable to the lawyer's client. Therefore, by using legal skill—but without having to appreciate the goals of science—lawyers can apply almost any psychological data in the service of their position. The adversary model relies not necessarily on truth, but on persuasion (Haney, 1980). Adversary proceedings have the advantage of avoiding the dangers of unilateral dogmatism, but we cannot forget that the essential purpose of each advocate is to outwit the opponent and win the case (Marshall, 1972).

## ☐ FINDING COURT CASES

Students unfamiliar with law and legal research are often hesitant to approach legal materials, feeling deterred by the apparent "mystique" surrounding American law. Actually, locating information pertaining to many legal topics is a straightforward process. Most libraries have general source materials about the U.S. Supreme Court and the American judicial system, including excellent fundamental books on the structure of the courts. Many also have the publication *Words and Phrases*, which gives legal definitions for certain terms and refers the reader to those cases which helped define them.

Sizeable libraries list among their holdings *U.S. Reports* or the *Supreme Court Reporter*, both of which contain complete decisions of the U.S. Supreme Court. It is a simple process to locate a case, given its name (e.g., *Miranda v. Arizona*) and a cite (384 U.S. 436). The student has only to go to volume 384 of *U.S. Reports* and the case will be at page 436. The same principle is used to record lower court cases. Decisions of federal appellate courts are found in the *Federal Reporter* (e.g., 465 F.2d 496). The *Federal Supplement* holds federal district court cases. State court decisions are found in state reporters (e.g., 134 Cal. Rptr. 595) and in regional volumes (e.g., 159 S.W. 291).

Without the case name, and with only a general subject area to research, the process becomes more involved, but it is still manageable. In this situation, a

## PSYCHOLOGISTS AS EXPERT WITNESSES

Despite the wary attitude of empirical psychology and the judiciary toward one another, psychologists in general have become increasingly accepted as expert witnesses in recent years (Schwitzgebel & Schwitzgebel, 1980). Federal criminal courts have led this trend, but federal civil courts have been inconsistent (*U.S. v. Brawner*, 1972; *U.S. v. Riggelman*, 1969; *Williams v. U.S.*, 1962). In state courts, the acceptance of psychologists as expert witnesses varies from jurisdiction to jurisdiction. Chapters 2 and 5 will assess the validity of the methods used in psychological assessment, which is often the focus of courtroom testimony. We will also discuss the professional competence desirable for expert witnesses and evaluate the state of knowledge about free will and criminal responsibility, issues about which experts often must testify.

Closely related to insanity and responsibility is the question of dangerousness. Is it possible for an expert to predict whether an individual will display or repeat violent behavior in the future? At the present time the judicial system seems to believe it is, and psychologists, psychiatrists, and sometimes social workers are often called upon to do just that. Yet some research has suggested that the validity of expert testimony in the area of dangerousness depends on many factors often not considered by the courts.

---

student makes use of a limited subject index at the back of the case reporter or one of several special indexes, often called case digests.

The American Digest System, used in American law libraries, makes use of a "key number" system developed by West Publishing Company. Law is divided into seven main classes, each class into subclasses, and each subclass into topics. When a case is received for indexing, each point of law covered in the case is isolated and summarized in a headnote, which is then assigned a topic and a key number. Although the system sounds complex, it is relatively simple once the researcher has located the current digest, which will then refer him or her to appropriate cases on the subject of interest. Law libraries also carry other indexes or digests, including the *Supreme Court Digest*, which lists all cases heard by the U.S. Supreme Court, and a variety of specialized digests, including those of state and regional cases. The more sophisticated libraries, of course, subscribe to computerized data search services, including the legal LEXIS, simplifying the researcher's task even more.

It may help the student to keep in mind that cases heard by the U.S. Supreme Court follow the practice of listing the name of the loser at the lower court level (the petitioner) first. Thus, in *Miranda v. Arizona*, Miranda had lost his case in the lower courts and then petitioned the U.S. Supreme Court to hear his arguments against the state of Arizona. The case name does not hint at who won the ultimate U.S. Supreme Court battle, however.

Chapters 4, 7, and 8, therefore, will not only examine critically many assumptions now accepted by the courts, but will also explore the limitations of the behavioral sciences in this area.

Testimony is not limited to questions of mental competence. Psychologists may be asked to give opinions regarding opinion sampling, drug addiction, sex offenses, perceptual acuity, impact of media programming, employment testing procedures, testamentary capacity (e.g., whether someone was of sound mind while making a will), brain injury, and attitude formation, memory, and perception as they might affect eyewitness testimony.

Another area of increasing involvement is family law, especially when judicial determinations of child custody, adoption, and child welfare commitments are required. These decisions all require clinical judgment and predictions from the psychologists who are consulted. For example, child custody determination requires an assessment of the behavioral deficits and strengths of the child, intentions and adjustment level of potential caretakers, probable duration of relationships, and the total outcome of the relationship when the child reaches maturity. In most instances, clinical data collection and clinical judgment determine the prediction. Unfortunately, few longitudinal outcome studies of the accuracy of professional predictions have been undertaken. However, there is little reason to doubt that the research examining the validity of clinical collection procedures in other areas applies also to child custody, commitment, and adoption determinations. We will explore the validity of these methods in the next chapter.

Psychologists also consult directly with attorneys and judges in areas like jury selection, juror stress, jury dynamics and decisionmaking, and factors that can influence memory, recall, perception, and valid identification by victims and other witnesses. In some instances, psychological groups have filed *amicus curiae* (friend of the court) briefs stating a psychological position on an issue of great social importance. Psychologists have also conducted studies for prosecutors or defense attorneys, helping them to select jurors who would be most sympathetic to their client's case.

Only three to five percent of most crime in the United States is adjudicated by jury, however (Tapp, 1977). Psychological research, therefore, must also investigate judicial decisionmaking and the negotiating process between attorneys that settles a case out of court or before it is referred to trial. What factors influence judges to rule the way they do? What psychological factors help determine an attorney's success at plea bargaining or convincing a judge to dismiss a case? Although psychology until just recently has conducted very little direct research in this area, a considerable amount of partial information about individual decisionmaking and persuasion can be applied by the legal profession. This, too, will be discussed in Chapters 6 and 9.

## ■ Psychology and Law

Up to this point we have discussed some of the major perspectives and methodologies employed in psychology. As we go through the book we shall become better acquainted with these major positions. At this juncture, it would be worthwhile to outline psychology's relationships with law and the position this text will take. According to Craig Haney (1980), psychology can relate to law in three ways: psychology *in* the law, psychology *and* the law, and psychology *of* the law. Because Haney's analysis is relevant to the future of the psychology-law interface, it will be given considerable attention here.

## PSYCHOLOGY IN THE LAW

The psychology *in* the law relationship is the most frequent application of psychology to the legal system. In this situation, jurists use psychologists and their knowledge for specific cases, as by having them testify about a defendant's mental condition or consult with attorneys regarding jury selection. The important aspect to remember about this relationship is that the legal system brings psychology into the system only when it is to its advantage to do so. After gaining the psychologist's testimony or acquiring the relevant psychological knowledge (usually in favor of their position), lawyers dismiss the psychologist and the relationship is terminated. In this context, psychology is applied within the restrictions of standard legal categories and in the traditional course of the legal process. The law asks specific, narrow questions that psychologists are required to answer within a legal context. Thus the law not only controls the scope of the issue, but also translates the meaning of answers provided by psychology. The nature of this relationship permits psychologists to have very little impact on law and its beliefs about human behavior. "We'll call you when we need you," asserts the legal system, and that is the extent of the relationship. It is the kind of interaction that clinical or practicing forensic psychologists usually (but not invariably) find themselves in when dealing with the legal system, as chapters on mental health law and criminal responsibility will reflect.

## PSYCHOLOGY AND THE LAW

In the second relationship, psychology *and* law, neither psychology nor law dominates or dictates to the other. Rather, psychology is seen as a separate discipline analyzing and examining the legal system from a psychological perspective and developing psychological research and theory. Eventually, valid principles are adopted by the system. With the execution of well-designed studies and the thoughtful formulation of theory to tie the results of these experiments together, psychology can develop an impressive body of psychological knowledge relevant to the legal system. For example, are the numerous legal assumptions about human behavior empirically supported? Can the "courtroom psychology" used by lawyers be supported by psychological principles acquired through careful, well-designed scientific study? Are eyewitnesses, so heavily relied upon by the judiciary in the conviction of defendants, generally accurate in their perceptions and memory of the events surrounding a crime? In the psychology *and* law relationship, psychology tries to answer these questions. If the results are negative, and if the legal system chooses not to change its procedures and thinking in the direction of the scientific evidence, then educated members of society concerned about the ocean of psychological fiction in the judicial system may demand the change. Thus, psychology can be used to change legal doctrine as well as to alter the system in which law is developed and administered.

This book makes no pretense that legal reform built upon sound psychological principles will occur with ease. Law's practices are built upon a foundation of long traditions and rigidly conservative attitudes toward innovations. More importantly, law is highly skeptical about psychology, sometimes perceiving it as so much modern day witchcraft. However, it is precisely this mutually independent psychology and law relationship that holds promise for improvement in both disciplines.

### PSYCHOLOGY OF THE LAW

The third relationship, psychology *of* the law, concerns itself with law as a determinant of behavior. How does law affect society and how does society affect its laws? How successful are laws and the consequences for their violation in controlling and altering human behavior? Why are some laws tolerated and others not? What factors surround discretion in the enforcement of laws? The psychology of law poses and grapples with these questions. It studies social injustices and tries to understand why society allows legal fictions to proliferate or why society permits disastrously conceived policies to continue to exist. Although psychology of law can offer information about the most effective strategies for legal reform, it is essentially an abstract, nonempirical approach that will not be addressed to any great extent in the book.

## ■ Summary and Conclusions

This chapter has introduced readers to the plan and goals of the book and to psychology as the science of human behavior. We have seen that, with caution and with appreciation for the complexity of human behavior, the various segments of the judicial system can benefit substantially from psychological knowledge. Although the book will consider separately psychology's potential contributions to each sector—law enforcement, the courts, criminal behavior, corrections—much of the material can be applied interchangeably to the judicial system in general.

The judicial system is an assortment of poorly meshed components built primarily on the moral, social, and political perspectives of society. It is highly pragmatic, conservative, and traditional in outlook and process. The system generally views the science of psychology with suspicion and skepticism, and it occasionally utilizes segments of scientific or empirical findings only if advantageous. Therefore, it is unrealistic to expect that the scientific contributions of psychology, as outlined in this text, will be embraced eagerly. What we can hope for is a slow, gradual acceptance of some of the information psychology uncovers, reports, and consistently supports.

The three possible relationships between psychology and law were outlined. The psychology *in* law relationship, the one most typical today, will do little to advance and integrate psycholegal research into the system. Here, law dictates to psychology what it wants, when it wants it, and law proceeds to interpret the material as it wishes. Psychology *and* law, which presumes an equal partnership between the two disciplines, is best suited to the advancement of psychological knowledge in relation to the judicial system.

## ■ Key Concepts and Principles, Chapter 1

Four methods of knowing
Basic aims of psychology
Replicability and control
External and internal validity
Secondary, dependent, and independent variables

Two types of evidence
Adversarial process
Three relationships between psychology and law
Clinical judgment versus statistical prediction

# 2

# Psychological Assessment and the Law

☐ | Psychological assessment and psychological testing are not synonymous terms. The first refers to all the techniques used to measure and evaluate an individual's past, present, or future psychological status. The second refers specifically to the use of psychological measuring devices. Assessment usually includes interviewing, observation, and various measuring procedures which may include psychological tests. The emphasis in this chapter will be on psychological tests, although other assessment techniques will also be described.

Psychological assessment plays a significant role in the judicial system. In issues of criminal law, it is important in four major areas. First, when a defendant claims the insanity defense, evidence obtained from evaluations of his or her emotional status is crucial. Second, courts often inquire about specific mental states and processes of defendants, such as diminished responsibility, premeditation, and malice aforethought. Third, psychological assessment plays a major role in pretrial hearings where the defendant's competence to stand trial is examined. Finally, assessment is used to help courts determine a defendant's dangerousness to self and others, a topic to be highlighted in later chapters.

In civil cases, the oldest and most widespread use of psychological assessment centers around determinations of whether individuals are able to care for themselves or are in need of psychological treatment. Courts must make judgments about the need for confinement in a mental institution or for treatment services within the community, and to do so they turn to psychologists and psychiatrists for guidance. In other civil cases, various assessment procedures are frequently used to determine parental suitability for child custody, to appraise a person's ability and capacity to make wills, or to determine eligibility for federal and state benefits on the basis of mental or emotional incapacity.

Criminal justice agencies rely on psychological assessments to help administrators make screening, selection, and promotional decisions. Law enforcement candidates and already employed personnel are often given psychological tests designed to depict their intellectual and emotional functioning. Metropolitan police departments have so far been at the forefront in studying and adopting such procedures, but there is a growing nationwide trend toward using psychological assessment in smaller and rural departments. The psychological assessment of correctional officers is less common, although there is little doubt that it should be considered if corrections, especially at state levels, is to employ competent, adaptable personnel.

The assessment and classification of prison populations, a process with a history of mixed success (Gearing, 1979), is another example of assessment in criminal justice. Ideally, the psychological evaluation of prisoners should provide valuable insights into the development and treatment of criminal behavior and some understanding of the psychological effects of short-term and long-term imprisonment. Although large-scale assessments have been tried (e.g., Megargee, 1977), the realities of the prison systems have often interfered. These hindrances will be discussed later in this chapter and again in Chapter 11.

This partial list of the various uses of psychological assessment illustrates its pervasiveness throughout the judicial system. Generally, psychology's relationship with law vis-à-vis assessment is one of psychology *in* the law, where judges and lawyers use and interpret the information they have requested of the examiner. The relationship is one maintained for the most part by clinical and forensic psychologists and psychiatrists, seldom by experimentalists.

Lately, psychological assessment techniques have generated a spectrum of social concerns and considerable legal scrutiny, especially in civil cases involving unfair employment practices, discrimination, self-incrimination, and invasion of privacy. The primary purpose of this chapter is to acquaint the reader with the nature of the assessment-law relationship and the numerous concerns society has or should have about assessment methods. Misunderstanding about the strengths and weaknesses of tests and other procedures abounds; the intent here is to bring some clarity to the debate.

The reader will be introduced to basic concepts of psychological testing and will learn how to begin to evaluate specific tests. Some of the more provocative issues surrounding the use of assessment within the judicial system will be addressed. We have chosen to focus upon the screening, selection, training, and promotion of police officials, since law enforcement officers are first-line participants in the judicial system; however, the topics discussed in the chapter have relevance to all the judicial subsystems that use psychological assessment in some way.

At times the material presented will be dated, or drawn from past history. However, the problems and principles that drew the attention of psychologists eight or nine decades ago continue to haunt psychologists today. To fully appreciate current dilemmas in the assessment field, we must understand the trends and the errors made over the years. While there are new testing instruments on the psychometric market today, most of them represent new versions of old problems.

## ■ Psychological Testing

Psychological tests have many limitations and flaws, but they can be important tools to evaluate intellectual functioning, measure personality, and assess emotional or psychological status. The information about human behavior gained from such tests can be of value in law enforcement and corrections for selection, promotion, and research; in legal determinations of mental and emotional status; in predictions of dangerous behavior; and, generally, in appraisals of behavior related to legal questions.

Testing is a process of reducing the complexity of human behavior to a manageable set of variables, so that future behavior can be predicted. It is a complex process, and procedures vary widely according to the population being tested and the preferred methods of the examiner. Testing basically involves the quantification of a sample of behavior obtained under standardized conditions, with the level of quantification and the degree of standardization varying from instrument to instrument. Some tests require a well-trained examiner and must be administered under such highly controlled conditions that they are like scientific experiments. Other tests are less standardized and may be given by an untrained examiner, sometimes to large groups.

The three most important concepts to understand in psychological testing are *reliability*, *validity*, and *normative distribution*. Any test should be judged according to each of those concepts.

### RELIABILITY

Reliability refers to the consistency of measurement; a test is reliable if it yields the same results over and over again. A test's reliability may be measured in one of three ways. If different parts of the same test yield the same results, this is *internal consistency*. If the same test yields the same results when administered to the same person at two different times, this is *test-retest* reliability. If the test produces the same results when scored or interpreted by different clinicians or examiners, it is high in *interjudge reliability*.

A highly reliable test will meet all three criteria, but in reality, psychological tests rarely produce the exact-same results again and again. A mathematical index, known as a *correlation coefficient*, is computed to determine the degree to which a test comes close to producing the same results. The correlation coefficient is mathematical shorthand for the relationship one variable has to another. It may range from 0 to 1.00, with 1.00 being a perfect correlation—the identical test score is obtained every time. A zero correlation means there is no relationship; that is, a score obtained in one instance will most likely not be obtained in other instances.

Most examiners prefer to use psychological tests that have the highest correlation possible. A test-retest reliability correlation of .90, for example, is usually regarded as solid evidence that subsequent administrations to the same individual will yield essentially the same results. If the test is also high in interjudge reliability and in internal consistency, the test is well regarded.

When the attribute being measured is itself unstable over time, the correlation coefficient will be low. Compare, for example, measurements of intelligence and depression. Intelligence is expected to be a stable attribute over time. If an individual received an above average score the first time he or she took a test and a below average score the second time he or she took the same test a few weeks later, we would suspect that something was wrong with the testing instrument. If, on the other hand, we were trying to measure a relatively unstable personality attribute like depression, we would expect to find different scores from one testing session to another, depending upon what happens to the individual between testing dates. Therefore, we would expect a relatively high correlation coefficient in the first example and a lower coefficient in the second, because of the differing nature of personal attributes being measured.

## VALIDITY

The reliability of a test merely assures us that we have established a consistently accurate procedure of measurement. Before a test can be meaningful and useful, however, it must also have *validity*, which tells us whether it measures what it is supposed to measure. For example, if a psychological test is designed to predict how well applicants will perform in law enforcement, we must have evidence that it in fact does predict this. If not, the test is meaningless, even though it may have very high reliability. Like reliability, validity is usually expressed statistically through the computation of a correlation coefficient.

**Concurrent validity.** Among the more important forms or types of validity are concurrent and predictive, together called *criterion-related validity*. Concurrent validity is usually found by comparing one test with another, already established one. For example, suppose we wished to determine if a test we designed to predict success in law enforcement had concurrent validity. We would administer a test with a proven track record of criterion-related validity and our newly constructed test to a group of experienced police officers, and we would compare both scores received by each candidate. If the scores were similar, as determined by a high correlation coefficient (say, .80), we would be able to conclude that our test had a high level of concurrent validity. Concurrent validity also may be established by determining whether our psychological instrument can obtain the same results as other, nontest criteria. For example, can the test results differentiate between poor and satisfactory police officers as rated by their supervisors? In this situation, we would correlate test results with on-the-job ratings provided by the supervisors. If the resulting coefficient is high, our test has good concurrent validity for distinguishing "good" police officers from "bad" ones.

**Predictive validity.** The above comparisons do not tell us whether our instrument predicts performance in law enforcement. Whether we are concerned with performance in police work or the potential dangerousness of an inmate or defendant, it is important to be able to predict behavior with some degree of accuracy. *Predictive validity* is concerned with the degree to which a test predicts a subject's subsequent performance on the dimensions and tasks the test is supposed to measure. If an examination claims to be able to predict which candidates develop into good or outstanding police officers, its predictive validity should be high, discriminating those who eventually perform well in law enforcement from those who do not. If there is empirical evidence that the instrument does have predictive validity, a test is a powerful device for the screening and selection of law enforcement candidates prior to entry into law enforcement. Obviously, a device that could do this would save both the candidate and the agency valuable time as well as potential difficulty and embarrassment.

Good predictive validity in psychological tests, while a laudable goal, is often difficult to achieve. If we are trying to develop an instrument capable of distinguishing good from bad police candidates, we immediately face the problem of defining what constitutes success in law enforcement, an occupation requiring a wide assortment of skills, abilities, and temperament. A good police officer in New York City may not be a good police officer in Keene, New Hampshire. Also, establishing predictive validity requires performance ratings by persons who will be objective and reliable. It is sometimes difficult to decide whether immediate supervisors, peers, or clinicians knowledgeable about law enforcement should be chosen for this task.

**Content validity.** While psychometric (tests and measurement) experts have tried to perfect methods to establish criterion-related validity, courts have begun to address the issue of *content validity*. "Content validity involves essentially the systematic examination of the test content to determine whether it covers a representative sample of the behavior domain to be measured" (Anastasi, 1968, pp. 134–135). This type of validation is often used by nonexperts to evaluate aptitude and achievement tests. In law enforcement, for example, it is recommended that the test content be related to what the officer will encounter on the job, thereby supposedly tapping pertinent skills found in traffic investigation or judgment and reasoning needed to handle domestic disturbances. When emphasis is placed on content validity, the behaviors considered important must be fully described in advance, rather than defined after the test has been prepared. Further, successful behaviors specific to the various levels of law enforcement must be identified and delineated. Often, this approach eliminates the use of standard psychological tests and replaces them with made-to-order tests for law enforcement that may be high in content validity but untested as far as reliability and criterion-related validity are concerned. There are obvious advantages to strengthening content validity, but care must be taken not to sacrifice the other criteria of a test's strengths.

Very often, too, "face validity" is confused with content validity. Face validity refers not to what the test actually measures, but to what it superficially appears to measure (Anastasi, 1968). If a test "looks valid," or if it appears to measure what should be measured, it has face validity. In reality, there may be no empirical support for these assumptions. Face validity does have some value, because examinees believe the exam is at least pertinent to the job for which they are applying. However, unless other types of validity are also ensured, a test has little overall worth.

**Construct validity.** So far we have considered criterion-related validity (both concurrent and predictive) and content validity. Many other types of validity are discussed in psychology, including ecological validity, temporal validity, substantive validity, structural validity, and as we noted in Chapter 1, external and internal validity. Two things are important to note about validity and its relationship to testing. First, there is a common fallacy that a significant relationship between a test result and a criterion is sufficient grounds for claiming the test is valid. Second, concurrent, predictive, and content validity under close scrutiny begin to merge into one fundamental form of validity, called *construct* validity.

To what extent does the test measure a theory or theoretical construct? This is the question with which construct validity is concerned. Many scholars in the field of psychometrics argue that construct validity is the most important determinant of a test's validity. As Guion (1977, p. 410) asserts: "*All* validity is at its base some form of construct validity . . . It *is* the basic meaning of validity." Messick (1980, p. 1015) notes: "Construct validity is indeed the unifying concept of validity that integrates criterion and content considerations into a common framework for testing rational hypotheses about theoretically relevant relationships . . . [It] provides a rational basis both for hypothesizing predictive relationships and for judging content relevance and representativeness." In essence, Messick is arguing that empirical relationships found between a test score and some isolated criterion do little to advance our understanding of the human processes underlying these test scores. Test results and their relationships to specific criteria, such as job performance or academic achievement, must be linked systematically to theory. "The simple demonstration of an empirical relationship between a measure and a criterion in the absence of a cogent rationale is a dubious basis for justifying relevance or use" (Messick, 1980, p. 1017).

Therefore, some authorities in the testing field argue that in order for a psychological test to be valid, it must, in addition to demonstrating empirically established relationships between test scores and a behavioral criterion, be built upon theoretical constructs that explain the processes and personality structure it is attempting to measure. In addition to the empirical relationships found for concurrent, predictive, or content validity, therefore, true test validity requires the establishment of construct validity. The test should mean something. It should fit into a theoretical rationale and explanation. Impressive correlation coefficients, standing alone, are not enough.

## NORMS

*Normative distribution* is the third important concept to understand in psychological testing. A score in itself tells us little unless we know how other people have scored. If an individual has correctly answered seventy-one out of eighty-five items, it is impossible to conclude whether the subject has done well or poorly unless we know that most people have answered only fifty-five items correctly. Interpretation of results therefore requires that normative distribution—sometimes called norms—be developed before a test is put into general use. This is done by giving the test to a large and well-defined group of individuals, called a standardization or normative group. The statistical position at which an individual scores within this normative group may be expressed in various ways, such as percentile rank or standard score. We will elaborate upon normative distribution shortly.

The above discussion has been an attempt to familiarize readers with some of the dry essentials of psychological testing. It is necessary to understand these concepts, since they are basic in determining whether an examination or psychological test is "good" or "bad." All participants in the judicial system who have frequent contact with psychological testing should know whether a given test is reliable and valid and what the scores mean in comparison to the scores of others who have taken the test. It is one thing for a police agency to claim it uses psychological testing in its screening and promotion procedures, but quite another to say that the testing is an empirically valid and reliable procedure to use in that selection and promotion process. Likewise, when a behavioral scientist explains to a lawyer that given tests were administered to his or her client, the lawyer should have some knowledge with which to form an opinion about the validity of the tests.

# ■ Cognitive Assessment

When mental processes such as thinking, learning, perceiving, problem solving, and remembering are measured and evaluated, it is called cognitive assessment. Ideally, this is accomplished by some combination of interviewing, behavioral observation, and testing. The most common form of cognitive assessment, however, is intelligence testing, better known as IQ testing, and it sometimes stands alone in the assessment program adopted by agencies and groups within the judicial system.

### INTELLIGENCE TESTS

One of the first reliable and reasonably valid intelligence tests was developed by the French psychologist Alfred Binet. In 1904, Binet and psychiatrist Theodore Simon were asked to design a test that could identify mentally defective children, who could then be taught effectively at a different pace than normal children. The resulting scale, consisting of thirty problems arranged in ascending order of difficulty, was called the Binet-Simon Scale. The test, which was revised shortly thereafter to establish satisfactory validity, attracted worldwide attention and was adopted and translated into many languages. In 1914, German psychologist William Stern suggested that Binet scores be expressed as a ratio of tested age (mental age score) over chronological age (actual age), multiplied by 100. A ten-year-old with a mental age of 15 would have an IQ of 150 ($^{15}/_{10} \times 100$), for example. Thus was born the intelligence quotient, known today as the IQ.

In America, psychologist L. M. Terman revised and adapted the test to suit an American population and, since Terman was associated with Stanford University, it became known as the Stanford-Binet. The Stanford-Binet remained the most frequently used instrument to measure intelligence until clinical psychologist David Wechsler developed another group of intelligence tests, beginning in 1939. The first form of the Wechsler scales was known as the Wechsler-Bellevue Intelligence Scale, and it was primarily designed to measure the intelligence of adults. Later, Wechsler devised downward extensions of the Wechsler-Bellevue so that the intellectual functioning of children could also be measured. In 1955, the Wechsler-Bellevue was revised and renamed the Wechsler Adult Intelligence Scale (WAIS).

The WAIS measures a wider scope of intellectual functioning than does the Stanford-Binet, which is primarily a verbal measure of intelligence. The WAIS also taps both the verbal and behavioral components believed to be required in intellectual functioning. It consists of eleven subtests, each of which is assumed to measure a particular ingredient of intelligence. Six of the subtests relate to verbal intelligence, while five are designed to tap behavioral or performance intelligence. Together, the eleven subtests provide a Full Scale IQ. The examiner is thus able to determine the Verbal IQ, the Performance IQ, and the Full Scale IQ. This approach treats intelligence as comprising a number of different abilities, rather than as one generalized ability.

Both the Stanford-Binet and the Wechsler scales are individual intelligence tests, designed to be administered to one examinee at a time by a highly trained examiner. Trained examiners are needed both because the standard of administration is complex and because behavioral observations add substantially to the assessment. Administration time varies, but the test is usually completed within one hour. Scoring, interpretation, and report writing usually take an additional two to four hours. Individual intelligence scales accordingly require considerable time and expense, features that have helped stimulate the less expensive, more efficient group intelligence tests.

Group tests generally are paper and pencil instruments devised to be administered to small or large groups of people. The convenience and economy of group tests have led to their use in schools and employment offices, in the selection and promotion of law enforcement personnel, and in many other mass-testing situations. The Otis Self-Administering Test of Mental Ability and the Army Alpha and Army Beta, developed during World War I to classify soldiers, are examples of the more commonly used group tests. Administration, scoring, and interpretation usually do not require a highly trained examiner, and less interpretation and scoring time is needed than for individual tests.

While group tests provide an IQ score generally comparable to individual tests (concurrent validity), they do not yield the rich behavioral observation and interpretation so characteristic of individual tests. Also, because of minimal face-to-face contact, the examiner has much less opportunity to establish rapport, obtain cooperation, and maintain the interest of subjects, factors that may affect performance. Therefore, although group tests have undeniable advantages, their shortcomings cannot be overlooked. For thorough assessment, individual tests are more desirable, but because of their economy and practicality, group tests are administered more frequently.

Most IQ tests are designed to yield an average standard score of 100 and a standard deviation of about 15. A standard deviation is a statistical index that tells us how spread out the scores are around the average or mean score. An average of 100 and a standard deviation of 15 is based on the assumption that the population follows a normal distribution, where a majority of the examinees score somewhere around the middle and only a few score at the ends or poles of the distribution (see Figure 2–1). About 68 percent of the population falls between the IQ scores of 85 and 115. Approximately 95 percent scores between 70 and 130, and 99.72 percent between 55 and 145. A person who achieves an IQ score of 130 has scored higher than approximately 98 percent of the entire population.

# ■ Personality Assessment

The term "personality" means different things to different psychologists, but common themes run through their definitions. The definitions of most psychologists focus on some psychological attributes of the individual that are relatively enduring and that can generally differentiate one particular individual from others.

For example, almost all psychologists agree that some individuals are more anxious and tense than others across a variety of situations. Furthermore, it is commonly known in police work that some officers respond to stress and threat with greater levels of anxiety and agitation and take longer to return to their usual day-to-day anxiety

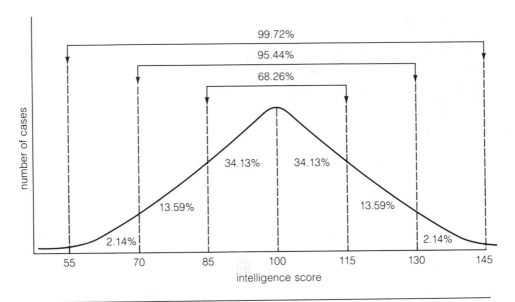

**Figure 2–1** ■ Distribution of intelligence scores in a normal curve.

levels than others. Moreover, they consistently react this way under stressful conditions. The personality variable in this instance is anxiety, more commonly called nervousness. For our purposes in this text, personality will be defined in accordance with Byrne (1974, p. 26) as "the combination of all of the relatively enduring dimensions of individual differences on which [the person] can be measured."

In general, the personality definitions adopted by psychologists can be divided into type or trait theoretical approaches. The type or typological approach assumes that people can be classified into distinct categories. A psychologist who subscribes to the typological approach might conclude that a given individual has a depressive or anxious type of personality. Today, few psychologists find typologies as helpful in describing people as the personality continuum used in the trait approach. While typologies assume discontinuous categories (depressed or normal, for example), the trait approach embraces continuous dimensions. Differences among individuals are arranged quantitatively by the degree of the quality possessed by the individual (for example, degrees of depression). Contemporary psychological measurements usually depict wide individual differences in the degree of a measured quality, although a few individuals do fall at either of the two extremes.

## PROJECTIVE TESTS

Personality measurement may be divided into two broad approaches: *projective* and *objective*. These two techniques are distinguished principally by the clarity of stimuli used to obtain responses from subjects. Projective tests are designed with the assumption that personality attributes are best revealed when a person responds to ambiguous stimuli such as inkblots. Since projective techniques were developed by psychodynamically oriented theorists interested in the hidden depths of personality, projective tests generally attempt to measure unconscious dispositions. Since there is no established meaning to the stimuli, it is premised that the responses of subjects reveal significant features about their personalities. Some of these personality features, perhaps even most of them, may be unknown to the respondent. Since psychodynamic theorists consider ambiguous stimulus material "the road to the unconscious," much of the material gained from projective tests is assumed to represent unconscious or subconscious components of the personality.

Some projective (ambiguous) test materials are very abstract, such as inkblots; others are more concrete, such as pictures of social situations. The most commonly used instrument representing the first category is the Rorschach, while the second category is represented best by the Thematic Apperception Test (TAT).

**The Rorschach.** Developed several decades ago by the Swiss psychiatrist Herman Rorschach, this test is administered by a trained examiner who presents the examinee with a series of ten bilaterally symmetrical inkblots and asks the person to describe what each inkblot resembles or suggests. The response characteristics are used by the clinicians as "signs" that reflect the individual's underlying personality dynamics. Scoring and interpretation are rather complex tasks requiring different phases of administration and different levels of interpretation. Using such information, some clinicians rate the subject on areas like anxiety, hostility, neurosis, organic brain damage, and psychosis.

**The Thematic Apperception Test.** At about the time the Rorschach was introduced, the American psychologist Henry Murray developed the TAT, which consists of twenty-nine pictures on separate cards and one blank card. The cards are presented one at a time, and the individual is instructed to make up a story suggested by each picture, complete with plot and characters. The respondent tells what the situation is, what has led up to the situation, what the characters are feeling and thinking, and what the outcome will be.

The Rorschach and the TAT both have been heavily criticized for their lack of objectivity in arriving at subject ratings. Anastasi (1968) strongly questions the validity of projective tests and suggests that they may be as much a projection of the examiner's biases, perceptions, and theoretical orientations as they are of the testee's personality attributes. Their usefulness in the judicial system is highly debatable, particularly where substantial criterion-related validation is required, as when predicting which candidates will perform well in law enforcement, or whether a defendant is dangerous. Extensive reviews of the research literature have failed to yield many encouraging signs for the empirical value or validity of projective tests (Maloney & Ward, 1976), and there is considerable evidence that other psychological instruments provide far more meaningful information for the assessment and prediction of human behavior.

## OBJECTIVE TESTS

The other personality measure frequently used in clinical practice is the objective test. Basically, a test is objective to the extent that scorers can apply a scoring key and agree about the result. When all steps avoid bias on the part of the examiner who administers, scores, and interprets the tests, objectivity is assured (Mischel & Mischel, 1977).

The vast majority of objective personality tests have a "self-report" format, meaning that the subjects are expected to respond "true" or "false" to brief statements or descriptions referring to their behavior or attitudes. Since self-report tests are by far the most widely and commonly used in the judicial system, it is important that the reader become familiar with their basic construction, which influences their predictive capabilities and general usefulness.

## PERSONALITY TEST CONSTRUCTION

The three most popular techniques for the construction of personality tests are the rational-theoretical, empirical, and factor-analytic methods. These procedures are not mutually exclusive, and some tests are constructed by using two or more approaches.

In rational-theoretical construction, the psychometrist designs test items that appear to be logically or theoretically capable of measuring certain personality attributes. The items may be based on common knowledge, existing theory, or the combined clinical judgment of a group of experts. A pool of items that seem to measure a personality variable—say, anxiety—is drawn and a group of experts in that area are asked to rate the appropriateness of each item to the variable. Those test items that receive the highest agreement among the judges usually are included in the final version of the test. Examples of rational-theoretical construction are the Edwards Personal Preference Schedule (EPPS) and the Goal Preference Inventory (GPI).

Empirical test construction is based on research results demonstrating that the responses to the test items are related to some clearly defined criteria. The focus is not on the content of test items, but on whether answers correlate significantly with desired behavior. For example, we might be interested in developing a test for law enforcement that can distinguish between police officers who perform well on the job and those who perform poorly. The standard procedure in empirical test construction is to design a pool of items and then ask groups of individuals who differ in some important way (the criterion) to respond to them. Items that differentiate the groups well are included in the test. In the law enforcement example, we would want to develop test items which distinguish "good" from "poor" officers. The items that do discriminate would be included on the test and presumably could be used to predict the performance of candidates prior to their entering police work. Of course, the above description oversimplifies the procedure. Test designers are faced with problems like choosing a pool of subjects and defining criteria for successful law enforcement performance. These and other issues related to law enforcement will be discussed in some detail later in this chapter. The two most widely known examples of empirically derived tests are the Minnesota Multiphasic Personality Inventory (MMPI) and the California Psychological Inventory (CPI).

Factor-analytic construction combines the rational-theoretical and the empirical methods. It is premised upon a complex and sophisticated statistical procedure that is beyond the scope of the present text. Basically, the factor-analytic method tries to discover relationships between several criteria and response patterns (empirical construction). Clusters of items that reflect a relationship with a certain criterion are subsumed under a common factor and then are named whatever appears logically sound or theoretically feasible (rational-theoretical construction). An excellent example of the factor-analytic approach is Cattell's Sixteen Personality Factor Test (16 PF).

Each of the three methods of test construction has certain advantages, depending upon the purpose of the testing program. In the screening and selection of personnel, however, the advantages of the empirically derived instrument outnumber the advantages of the other two methods. The empirically derived test lends itself more readily to criterion-related validity because it was constructed by demonstrating an empirical relationship between each of its items and some relevant criterion. Moreover, it allows for more valid answers, since the respondent cannot tell merely from the item content what is the "best way" to answer the items. In most cases, the factor-analytically derived instrument ranks second in advantages, primarily because of the subjectivity involved in deciding what attributes the test items are believed to be measuring.

## SPECIFICITY vs. GENERALITY OF PERSONALITY TRAITS

One of the active controversies in psychology today centers on the specificity and generality of traits: How stable are personality characteristics across time and place? If a person acts a certain way in one situation, will that person act in a similar way in a similar situation at a later time? This question is especially relevant to psychological testing, because most testing procedures are predicated on the assumption that the attributes being measured are highly consistent.

Personality traits can be understood only if both the person and the situation are considered. The expressions of a person's traits hinge on a given psychological situation (Mischel & Mischel, 1977; Bowers, 1973; Endler, 1973; Mischel, 1973). For example, a police officer may react with intense anxiety (trait of anxiety) in situations where alcohol is a significant factor, but he may not become anxious or may control his anxiety in incidents not related to alcohol. In this case, his anxiety is specific to the degree to which alcohol is involved in the situations he encounters.

It is a generally held tenet in psychology that behavior results from a complex interaction between personality predispositions (traits) and the situation. Therefore, the degree of consistency in personality partly depends upon the situation a person finds himself or herself in, a dependence called *cross-situational* or *trans-situational consistency*. Closely related is consistency across time, *temporal consistency*. If a person behaves a certain way now, will he or she behave essentially the same way a month or a year from now? Hence, there are two crucial aspects to address in determining personality trait stability—temporal and cross-situational consistency.

Consistency over time has never really been in dispute (Mischel & Mischel, 1977). Few psychologists seriously doubt that our lives have temporal consistency and coherence. Most people see themselves and others as relatively stable individuals who have continuity over time—at least in dealing with, or responding to, similar situations.

Cross-situational consistency is more involved. Some research suggests that a given person's actions are often highly specific to the particular situation and may in fact be unique to that situation. For example, a certain police officer may become assertive and dominant in dealing with women in traffic violation situations, but become passive and submissive dealing with women in family quarrels. Another police officer may react in opposite fashion. However, research focusing on traits has also reported much consistency across situations (Bem & Allen, 1974). In general, evidence indicates that people both discriminate and generalize their behavior as they interact with situations. Some people are consistent in some areas of behavior, but not in others; some are consistent on some traits. It is quite clear, though, that none are consistent on all traits (Mischel & Mischel, 1977).

The intricate interaction of personality and situation creates problems for personality assessment. Until recently, personality research and theory building emphasized the person to the exclusion of the situation. Traditional personality assessment theory (trait psychology or psychodynamics) assumed that stable personality traits or personality structures were the center of the universe; once these attributes were delineated, accurate prediction was almost guaranteed. Thus, to say an individual had an aggressive personality was to infer a corresponding list of behaviors, most of them negative. As we have just noted, however, the situation and the meaning of that situation for the person are crucial variables. Therefore, rather than relying on a global conclusion that a police candidate has an "aggressive personality," an agency would do well to try to determine how the candidate handles himself or herself in various situations. It is unwarranted to attach negative connotations to a personality label, which in fact tells us very little. In fact, aggressive behaviors are sometimes very necessary in some instances, while inappropriate in others.

The above discussion emphasizes that accurate assessment and prediction require not only an evaluation of the person (as advocated by trait and psychodynamic perspectives), but also an evaluation of the psychosocial environment within which the behaviors we are trying to predict occur. Failure to consider the context of the behavior is destined to result in sizeable inaccuracies and faulty conclusions. We will return to this issue in later chapters, but for now the reader should be forewarned to expect low accuracy rates in psychological assessment, particularly when trait or psychodynamic orientations are used.

# ■ Psychological Assessment in Law Enforcement

During the 1960s at least six different presidential commissions on law enforcement and crime emphasized the value of properly selected law enforcement officers. Implicit in these recommendations was the pressing need for reliable and valid instruments that would evaluate the intellectual capacity, emotional stability, and personality characteristics of police personnel. In 1967 the Task Force on the Police (President's Commission on Law Enforcement and the Administration of Justice) underscored the lack of adequate screening in most police agencies. Six years later, the National Advisory Commission on Criminal Justice Standards and Goals recommended that every police agency "employ a formal process for the selection of qualified police applicants. This process should include a written test of mental ability or aptitude, an oral interview, a physical examination, a psychological examination, and an in-depth background investigation" (Spielberger, 1979, p. xi).

Police selection has been traditionally based upon minimum (or maximum) standards of age, health, height, vision, hearing, physical fitness, weight, agility, or appearance. How these specifications related to actual job performance was generally unknown; the relationship was unexamined, but it was assumed. With the introduction of federal guidelines such as those of the Equal Employment Opportunity Commission (EEOC) into police selection of minorities, including women, many departments were prompted to reexamine their existing practices, to develop new ones, or to drop existing criteria of questionable validity.

Selecting capable police officers is a demanding responsibility for law enforcement administrators. The presence of even a few undesirable officers in a police department has enormous social and financial consequences and is potentially damaging to individuals in the population the agency serves. For example, one officer's over-zealous behavior, compounded by poor judgment, can result in psychological, social, and physical costs within the department and the community. Every new officer who is terminated because of misconduct, incompetence, or dissatisfaction costs each police agency thousands of dollars in training and equipment. It is crucial, therefore, that carefully designed and valid screening devices be available to weed out as many undesirable individuals as possible.

Psychological devices used without adequate validation very likely will literally have their day in court, forced to demonstrate their worth when lawsuits are filed by victims or by disgruntled police candidates claiming they were screened out of police work unjustifiably. To avoid costly litigation and embarrassment to the police agency, law enforcement must desist from using haphazard screening procedures and must support efforts to validate the methods it is using.

Recent research on law enforcement selection supports the value of four broad measures or procedures in the selection process:

1. Psychological tests, including measures of intelligence, aptitude, attitudes, interest, and personality
2. Situational tests, in which job behaviors are simulated or a candidate's behavior is observed in "test" situations, as in polygraph examinations
3. Background and physical data, including information about marriage, race, height, weight, and education
4. The interview, which includes oral boards and data gathered by a psychologist or psychiatrist

Each of these measures is discussed below.

## PSYCHOLOGICAL TESTING

Over the past three decades, various psychological devices have been tried in the police selection process. Lately, police agencies have shifted away from broad, largely unvalidated "intelligence" and "aptitude" tests or from projective personality instruments toward objective personality measures, usually of a paper-and-pencil variety given to police candidates in a group setting.

For instance, surveying assessment techniques used in metropolitan police departments, Narrol and Levitt (1963) found that 85 percent of the departments said they used objective tests specifically intended to assess aptitude for police work. However, the testing programs were described only vaguely, and the departments appeared to be using them as a symbolic gesture to appease society rather than as empirically conceived instruments of valid selection. Most of the tests were little more than un-standardized intelligence tests of questionable design or validity. Concurrent or predictive validity—the measures of how the tests actually related to performance—were unknown or not even examined by most departments. Only 22 percent of the departments reported using any of the four "personality measures" in their selection process, and only one department reported doing any original research to determine the validity of the tests it used.

In 1972, Murphy surveyed 258 local police agencies employing at least 100 officers and 49 state police forces. While his data indicated no significant shift in the percentage of departments using psychological exams, he found a substantial shift away from questionable aptitude, intelligence, or projective tests. Instead, departments were adopting more standardized and somewhat more valid psychological measures of personality and emotional status. About 44 percent of the local police departments used "psychological examinations" to screen police candidates, but only 13 percent of the state police agencies used them. Although this percentage is considerably lower than that found in the Narrol and Levitt survey (85 percent), it is important to note that Murphy's questionnaire was worded differently. It specified "psychological tests," whereas Narrol and Levitt asked to be informed of any type of examination.

Most of the tests reported in the Murphy study were objective, paper-and-pencil personality measures. The MMPI was by far the most common personality test used; 48.75 percent of the agencies used it alone or in combination with other tests. Murphy also learned that 41.25 percent of the agencies used a "psychiatric interview" in the screening procedure.

Although many different assessment techniques are currently used in the screening, selection, and promotion of law enforcement officers, it is usually not known whether these testing procedures are valid predictors of effective on-the-job police performance (criterion-related validity) (Spielberger, 1979). This is a sobering fact, since the use of any selection procedure should ultimately be validated. Empirical investigations evaluating relationships between initial selection standards (predictors) and the actual job performance of police officers should be undertaken, supported by attempts at determining construct validity.

One of the problems in using psychological tests as predictors of effective law enforcement performance relates to the diversity and complexity of behaviors required of police officers. Law enforcement personnel often must be adept not only at accident investigation and crime detection, but also at handling family disturbances and relating to the public. It is a maxim that the smaller the department, the more varied the responsibilities and duties to the community. It is not unusual to find a local, small-town police officer offering first-aid tips to an elementary school class and on the same day dealing with a violent domestic altercation. Specialization is a luxury very small departments cannot afford, and therefore it is very difficult to establish objective performance criteria upon which to base predictions. Some officers may perform very competently on some tasks while failing at others. The officer who relates exceptionally well to adolescents may perform poorly in crisis situations involving very young children.

To tap the heterogeneity of police activities, screening devices must contain a number of predictors based upon a multitude of behaviors, and few do this. In addition, police work differs substantially from one jurisdiction to another, so that a test that is adequate for a given department may not suffice elsewhere. Rural or small-town law enforcement requires different behaviors and talents from metropolitan or urban police work. Also, many states have sheriff's departments which often offer very different services from those of municipal or state police agencies.

Determining what precisely constitutes successful performance is another dilemma when psychological testing procedures are to be validated. Since interjudge agreement about performance ratings is often difficult to obtain, adequate predictors of success are elusive. What one supervisor or department considers superior performance in the field may be only average performance to another supervisor or department.

The wide scope of law enforcement, together with the urgent need for more vigorous and sophisticated methods of study, warn us that we should expect few solid conclusions in the research literature about what are adequate predictors of success or failure in police work. As expected, the literature is littered with inconclusive or mixed results. This does not mean that reliable and valid psychological assessment is beyond reach. Rather, we should stress the need for a clear understanding of what accurate screening of personnel entails, as well as for the awareness that a successful testing program may have to be tailor-made to the needs of a particular agency.

Below, we will examine research on the relationship between police work and intelligence and research concerned with personality and police performance. This will lead to the question: Is there a "police personality"—a personality pattern that differentiates police officers from the general population?

## ■ Cognitive Assessment in Police Selection

One of the first U.S. studies on police selection was conducted in 1917 by psychologist Louis M. Terman, who gave an abbreviated form of his Stanford-Binet Intelligence Scale to thirty applicants for police and firefighter positions in San Jose, California. He found that a large majority of the candidates were functioning near the dull normal range of intelligence; only three candidates obtained an IQ score over 100, the score considered average for the general population! Terman concluded that police and fire positions attracted men of exceptionally low intelligence. He recommended that all candidates who scored below 80 be eliminated automatically from further job consideration. He also urged police administrators to keep the IQ scores and compare them with later job performance, but apparently this was never done. As a result of Terman's project, 80 was established as an arbitrary score to indicate ability to perform police responsibilities.

A contemporary of Terman, psychologist Louis Thurstone, was also interested in the value of mental testing to police selection. Thurstone (1922) administered the Army Intelligence Examination (the Army Alpha) to 358 various ranking members of the Detroit Police Department. Officers at all ranks scored below average; in fact, the more experienced the police officer was, the lower was his intelligence. The average score for the 307 patrolmen was 71.44; the 34 sergeants averaged 54.71 and the 17 lieutenants 57.80. Thurstone concluded that law enforcement did not attract intelligent individuals. He also surmised that the more intelligent individuals who entered police service left for other occupations, where their ability and intelligence were presumably better recognized.

Fortunately, improvement in professionalism and in rewards of police work over the years began to attract significantly more intellectually capable law enforcement officers. In later studies, police officers obtained at least average intelligence scores (Matarazzo et al., 1964; Gordon, 1969; Kole, 1962). In a review of the literature, Poland (1978, p. 376) notes that "if police agencies can attract applicants with some college education, they have an applicant pool of above average intelligence." As encouraging as it may be to know that law enforcement personnel are not substandard intellectually, this tells us little about the relationship between intelligence level and actual job performance. Is high intelligence a predictor of superb or even satisfactory functioning as a police officer?

In general, intelligence and ability tests have been useful predictors of police academy performance, but less reliable for predicting how well an officer actually performs in the field (Spielberger, Ward & Spaulding, 1979; Henderson, 1979). Studies using general intelligence tests like the Army General Classification Test, the Wonderlic, and the California Test of Mental Maturity, typically report correlations between test scores and academy grades in the .35 to .70 range, with the most frequent correlations clustering around .50 (e.g., Dubois & Watson, 1950; Hess, 1973; Mills, McDevitt & Tonkin, 1966; Mullineaux, 1955). However, there are few parallel correlations between intelligence measure and field performance, or between academy and field performance. McKinney (1973) reports that the written examination used by the City of Phoenix in selecting officers has some value in predicting on-the-street job performance, although it has much better predictive power when applied to police academy performance. The Phoenix examination is one of the few tailor-made tests used, or at least reported, by an individual department.

# ■ Personality Assessment in Law Enforcement

### THE MMPI

Fortunately, police selection procedures in recent years have shifted from the use of poorly defined examinations of intelligence and vague assessments of personality dynamics to the more objective measures of personality that are able to provide criterion-related validation data. The most widely used personality inventory in American criminal justice today is the Minnesota Multiphasic Personality Inventory (MMPI) (Gearing, 1979), used as part of required entrance requirements in all federal and many state and local law enforcement agencies (Elion & Megargee, 1975). The MMPI is an extensive (550 to 566 questions) paper-and-pencil inventory that requires respondents to answer true or false to questions about themselves. The items delve into a wide range of behaviors, beliefs, and feelings.

**Scales.** Certain keyed answers to the items are grouped into ten "clinical" scales and four "validity" scales. Originally, the clinical scales were given psychiatric-sounding names like depression (D), psychopathic deviate (Pd), hysteria (Hy), and schizophrenia (Sc). However, research later revealed that these scales did not measure the disorders for which they were originally designated, so in more recent use the scale names have been replaced by numbers to prevent misinterpretation. The four validity scales indicate the number of items that the respondents:

1. Did not answer (? scale)
2. Answered in such a way as to suggest a deliberate, unsophisticated attempt to make themselves look good (L scale)
3. Answered in a highly unusual fashion (F scale)
4. Answered in a defensive manner so as to make themselves appear socially desirable (K scale)

The L and K scales are sometimes confused. The former, sometimes called the "lie scale," picks up attempts to deceive. Most people are willing to admit rather minor flaws and weaknesses, such as occasional fibbing or procrastination. If an examinee denies many such flaws, he or she will obtain an elevated L scale, suggesting some dishonesty. The K scale is more complex. It was developed as a subtle index of attempts by the examinee to deny psychopathology and to present himself or herself in a favorable light. It suggests resistance rather than outright dishonesty. A low K score, furthermore, may indicate a tendency to make oneself look bad, while a high K score can suggest an attempt to make oneself look good or a tendency to be defensive about revealing oneself. Because the K scale reflects unwillingness to admit to deviancy, a certain portion of the K score is added to some of the clinical scales to correct for this defensiveness. We will note shortly that the K score is one of the most consistent predictors of job performance in police officers.

**Interpretation.** The MMPI is intended for use with literate persons sixteen years of age or older who have at least a sixth grade education or an IQ of 80 (Maloney & Ward, 1976). MMPI scores are usually summarized and recorded in the form of a profile representing the individual's position on each scale. The profile is traditionally interpreted according to the pattern of unusually elevated or unusually low scores, a method called "profile analysis." From the extensive research done on the MMPI, it is clear that elevations on one scale are often not a sufficient basis for diagnosing or predicting. Rather, the configuration of the response patterns gained from scale combinations provides more accurate information than any one scale standing alone provides.

For various reasons, some clinicians are unhappy with the MMPI as it exists, although they are reluctant to abandon it in light of the vast amount of irreplaceable data accumulated on it over the years. Although some of the criticism is understandable, much of it appears unjustified and demonstrates misunderstanding about the instrument's design and intention. Since interpretation today is based on profile analysis, criticism focusing upon the validity of the scales as originally used seems misdirected. Attention should be directed at the validity of the new and developing profile analyses, rather than at the original intention behind any specific scale.

Furthermore, widespread misunderstanding of the original design and purpose of the MMPI has led to its faulty application in the criminal justice system. Maloney and Ward (1976) and Dahlstrom (1972) point out that both clinicians and researchers often confuse two types of assessment. The MMPI was designed specifically to differentiate abnormal persons (as defined by society during the late 1930s and early 1940s) from normal persons. It was not intended to be a personality measure which would provide information about personality traits. This misunderstanding has meant that experiments examining the MMPI's effectiveness to predict and discriminate have been poorly designed. Because it is frequently used in police selection, the MMPI has drawn the greatest amount of research attention of all psychological tests. But much of this research has assumed that the MMPI has the power to appraise both emotional status and normal personality traits. Psychopathological detection and personality description demand different methods of assessment, however. Tests that try to do both things seem destined for confusion and criticism; the MMPI is not such a test. The reader should keep this point in mind when he or she reviews studies that try to evaluate the MMPI's ability to depict police personalities, or even to distinguish good police officers from bad ones merely on the basis of MMPI scores.

**Research.** Almost all MMPI research has been of the concurrent validation variety, where the personality characteristics of already employed police officers are assessed. Typically, the test is administered to officers representing varying degrees of success in law enforcement work, with "success" determined by supervisor ratings. Thus, if a high percentage of successful officers answers true to a given question, that question is considered a good predictor of on-the-job performance. But research that examines individuals already on a police force ignores the potential and characteristics of officers who have dropped out because of hurdles along the way. It may miss significant segments of the applicant population, thereby curtailing its usefulness. We lose invaluable information when we do not include in our data bank personnel who dropped out or were forced out during the early stages of their careers, simply because one of the reasons for using any screening device is to discover the potential drop-outs or failures as soon as possible. Early detection saves large sums of money, time, and commitment.

Predictive validation, a more useful and vigorous research procedure, is rarely implemented because of the time it requires and the percentage of the police budget it swallows. Predictive validation demands longitudinal study to decide how well initial assessments and standards predict a candidate's success or failure as a police officer. In this method, the MMPI is administered to candidates and, several years hence, the researcher determines which of the candidates "succeeded" in law enforcement.

The concurrent validation and the few predictive validation studies of the MMPI's use in selection have been confusing and ambiguous in their hypotheses, designs, results, and conclusions. Clear, cogent, or unequivocal conclusions and recommendations are rarely found in the existing literature. Some researchers have reported good, even exceptional results, while others have found little in the way of encouraging data. However, it should be emphasized that there is much to be gained through testing programs founded on well-designed and well-executed research. Valid psychological measures hold great promise for the efficiency and accuracy of personnel selection.

The Los Angeles Police Department reported one of the earliest attempts to use the MMPI as a police selection tool (Rankin, 1959). The triggering event for this innovation was an incident in which police officers allegedly used unnecessary force and brutality toward prisoners in their custody (Gottesman, 1975). To answer public criticism and to reduce future incidents of this nature, the LAPD instituted a candidate screening program which included the MMPI, the Rorschach, and a psychological interview. Unfortunately, procedural and statistical details about the program, as reported by Rankin (1959), were not sufficient to permit generalizations to other departments. Rankin said he rejected a substantial number of potentially "unsuitable" police officers on the basis of psychological test results. He posits that 11 percent of the 2,000 applicants screened over a six-year period were rejected for "psychiatric reasons." However, there is a basic flaw in Rankin's claims: How do we know that a person labeled as having "psychological problems" necessarily makes a poor police officer, unless the person has been given an opportunity to try police work? It is possible that "neurotics" or people who had problems with their mothers might be highly capable, competent officers. More importantly, it should be realized that clinical diagnostic labels are subjective opinions of someone's behavior; there is nothing objective, let alone scientific, about contemporary diagnostic labeling of human behavior.

Matarazzo and his colleagues (1964) reported that police candidates often try to impress others with their good psychological health, undoubtedly in order to appear acceptable for police work. The candidates in the Matarazzo study were also impulsive, sociable, opportunistic, and had high levels of activity. However, while these results are similar to those reported by Rankin, both studies only report the chief characteristics of police candidates, not experienced police officers. The information is of limited value to police departments trying to determine which candidates will be most successful in carrying out the duties of a police officer. Again, a connection must be made between the candidate and the eventually successful officer.

Jay Gottesman (1975) undertook one of the more ambitious projects designed to assess the value of the MMPI in police selection. Subjects were 203 police applicants who had successfully completed and passed all of the screening and selection procedures for a northern New Jersey urban police force. The control group consisted of male veterans who reported to the Veterans Administration for educational counseling. Unfortunately, the project involved only new recruits and not experienced officers, and there was no follow-up. Still, important information about the MMPI was obtained.

Gottesman found strong evidence of distinctive personality differences between urban police recruits and the control group. The police recruits were more defensive and guarded about revealing themselves (as demonstrated by elevated K scores), but generally "healthier" than the control group. This observation is highly similar to Rankin's and Matarazzo's conclusions about candidates. The police group also scored significantly lower on seven of the ten clinical scales and higher on the validity scale. These differences suggest that the MMPI may be a powerful device in the screening and selection of police candidates.

Despite the scope of the Gottesman study, it too tells us little about predictive validity. The data provide some information about how urban police candidates with no police experience scored on the MMPI, but they offer no clues as to who among this group performed above average, average, or below average once in the field. Several other concurrent validation studies report a significant relationship between certain MMPI scales and serious misconduct of police officers (Blum, 1964) and between MMPI scales and frequency of auto accidents in the line of duty as active police officers (Marsh, 1962; Azen, Snibbe & Montgomery, 1973).

One of the most consistent findings reported in the research literature is the tendency of police officers, especially those considered successful by their superiors, to present a good front and "stiff upper lip" both in taking psychological examinations and in working in the field. This attribute is usually reflected by a high K scale and moderately high L and Hy scales. This frequently reported feature suggests that both society and police colleagues expect officers to deny psychopathology, feelings of insecurity, and inadequacy. Moreover, the tendency to present a good front probably accounts to some extent for the repetitive observation in the recent criminal justice literature (see Lefkowitz, 1975) that police officers appear well adjusted and present few indicators of psychopathology.

The MMPI should be a useful aid in the screening and selection of criminal justice personnel, because it samples over 550 self-report behaviors; because it is the prototype of personality testing; and because it has stimulated nearly 4,000 research articles examining its strengths and weaknesses. According to Maloney and Ward (1976, p. 342), "Problems, critics, and rivals notwithstanding, the MMPI will probably continue to be a dominant force in the field. This is primarily due to the vast wealth of accumulated data and 'wisdom' that it possesses."

Recently, this author has completed a series of studies on rural and small-town law enforcement personnel, using the MMPI as a principal preemployment measure of attitudes and personality attributes (Bartol, 1982). The project involved a six-year follow up of police officers, sheriffs, and game wardens who had originally taken the test. Police chiefs and supervisors were asked to rate the performance of the officers, using a behaviorally anchored rating of eleven relevant law enforcement behaviors as developed by Farr and Landy (1979).

The ratings, in conjunction with scores on the various subscales of the MMPI, have enabled us to employ a decision theory of personnel assessment (Wiggins, 1973). Using only the Hs scale, we are able to "hit" those most suited or unsuited for law enforcement 73 percent of the time. If we also examine the scores on D, Pt, and Pd, we are able to identify 92 percent of those most suited or unsuited for rural law enforcement. The project has convinced us of the utility of the MMPI in personnel selection and screening, and cross-validation studies using other police departments should provide additional support for the MMPI. However, we still need to establish construct validity and a theoretical framework within which to interpret the empirical relationships.

## OTHER SCREENING DEVICES

**The CPI.** The California Personality Inventory (CPI) is patterned substantially upon the MMPI, but whereas the MMPI is keyed to detect psychopathology, the CPI describes normal personality patterns. Constructed between 1956 and 1960, the CPI consists of fifteen scales that measure such personality dimensions as achievement via conformance, dominance, responsibility, and sociability. Three validity scales measure test-taking attitudes. The test has 480 items that require a true or false answer, and the item content is less distasteful to the respondent than that of the MMPI, which occasionally asks for very personal information, as about bodily functions or sexual attraction.

The CPI has not been extensively used in the screening and promotion of law enforcement, partly because the instrument has received mixed reviews (Sherman, 1979). Criticism has been directed at the large number of scales it contains; essentially, they provide too much data for a clinician to integrate effectively. Moreover, there are no suggested standards for interpreting CPI profiles and response patterns. Finally, several of the scales are repetitive, measuring similar personality characteristics.

Some researchers have reported good success with the CPI (Spielberger, Spaulding & Ward, 1978) and have suggested it should be considered for use in screening programs. Hogan (1971) examined the personality characteristics of three classes of police cadets and state police officers with one year's experience. Staff and supervisory ratings served as the criterion measures. Hogan cross-validated the concurrent "prediction" of the supervisory job-performance ratings with scores on the CPI and found that the CPI scales related to intelligence, self-confidence, and sociability discriminated highly rated officers from those less highly rated. As a relatively new screening instrument, the CPI holds promise and should be explored in future research.

**The interview.** The interview, in any form, has not been found to be a particularly valid device for discriminating or predicting which candidates will become successful police officers (Stotland & Berberich, 1979; McDonough & Monahan, 1975; Landy, 1976). In fact, contrary to what would be expected in view of its widespread use, the interview is not a particularly helpful tool for making screening decisions, even outside law enforcement (Fisher, Epstein & Harris, 1967; McKinney, 1973; Smith & Stotland, 1973; Ulrich & Trumbo, 1965). Interviews probably test the potential compatibility of an employer and a prospective employee rather than subsequent job performance per se. Indeed, some researchers have suggested that, if it is to be used to screen police candidates, the interview should be considered a rapport builder and an educating medium for the candidate, rather than an evaluating device (McDonough & Monahan, 1975). Moreover, reliability between oral interviewers (the degree to which the interviewers agree with one another about an applicant's ability to succeed) is also poor (Stotland & Berberich, 1979). Despite these facts, oral examinations or interviews continue to be among the most commonly used police candidate selection methods.

### SITUATIONAL TESTING

Because psychological tests in law enforcement lack predictive validity, some psychologists have constructed test situations that resemble as closely as possible the working conditions actually encountered in police work. Proponents of such situational tests argue that paper-and-pencil intelligence and personality testing procedures do not require candidates to do anything that approximates actual police work. Tests attempting to simulate actual job situations and to elicit behaviors that would be required in those situations were used extensively by German, British, and American military during World War II to select officers and special services personnel. Although there are few data to support the value of these situational tests in predicting success (Murray et al., 1948), they have a strong intuitive appeal and remain popular.

Chenoweth (1961) was among the first to suggest that situational tests be used for the selection of police officers. Later, Dillman (1963), R. B. Mills and his colleagues (1966, 1969, 1976), and Tagatz and Hess (1972) began to explore the use of such tests through research.

Dillman (1963) reported the first application of situational tests to police screening in a study involving a police force in Albuquerque, New Mexico. He devised two situations typical of police work in that city, one requiring an officer to interview an uncooperative hit-and-run suspect, the other requiring the officer to deal with a man stopped for speeding in the process of driving his pregnant wife to the hospital. Police academy recruits were used as subjects. In each situation, the recruit's responses were taped and rated by a group of judges, who scored the responses for both frequency and dominance. Frequency referred to the actual number of responses made by the recruit, and dominance to the overriding or "repetitive theme" of the recruit's response pattern. As a criterion measure, the recruits were ranked by the commandant of the academy according to their potential as police officers. The relationships between frequency and dominance of responses and the commandant's ratings were highly significant for the first situation, but considerably less so for the second.

In view of the inconsistent relationship between academy performance and field performance frequently reported in other studies (e.g., Spielberger, 1979), the usefulness of this situational study to the selection of police officers is questionable. It is not even known whether frequency and dominance of responses contributes to successful police work. Also, it is unwise to rely on one person's assessment (the commandant's, for example) of who will and will not become a successful officer.

The only other published attempt to apply situational tests to police selection was reported by Robert Mills and his colleagues in Cincinnati. The Mills group constructed scenarios of a variety of situations commonly encountered in some aspect of police work. The overall results were discouraging and did not support the value of situational tests for selection of police officers.

Major drawbacks to situational tests are the time and finances they consume. Technical and professional assistance and skill are required, resulting in heavy costs for the agency. Situational tests also demand special equipment and space, luxuries often not available. More importantly, there is little guarantee that the tests, though apparently job-related, have any value in predicting who will succeed in law enforcement and who will not. On the contrary, there is evidence that paper-and-pencil exams are more accurate than situational tests in assessing and predicting good police officers. Finally, the notion that test content which appears job-related increases the validity of the test is misguided. Unfortunately, this favorable attitude toward job-related content is not uncommon in personnel selection.

## OTHER SCREENING MEASUREMENTS

Other assumed predictors of performance have fared no better in the research literature. For example, there are notable inconsistencies in studies evaluating the validity of minimum and maximum age limits, both of which have traditionally been used in law enforcement selection (Cross & Hammond, 1951; Levy, 1967, 1971). Few studies have investigated sex or race as predictors of successful job performance, and these studies have been inconclusive. While some researchers have tried to compare racial groups (ususally whites and blacks) (Baehr, Saunders, Froemel & Furcon, 1971; Spencer & Nichols, 1971; Cohen & Chaiken, 1972; Snibbe, Fabricatore, Azen & Snibbe, 1975), the overall results remain equivocal.

In an extensive study, Ruth Levy (1967) found that certain life-history background characteristics are significantly related to subsequent nonretention in law enforcement. During a ten-year period, she examined the personnel records of 2,139 former law enforcement officers who separated from their departments, either voluntarily or for cause. Levy found that the fired officers were usually younger at the time of appointment, had more years of education, more than one marriage, shorter work histories, more citations for vehicle code violations, and in general tended to present a life pattern of "greater mobility and uncontrolled impulsivity." She also reported that failure in law enforcement, regardless of locale, often stems from inability to suppress retaliatory aggressive behavior and that such behavior was characteristic of the individuals even before police employment.

## CONCLUSIONS

In the early 1970s two writers concluded that with few exceptions the quality of research pertaining to police selection was poor and of limited usefulness (Kent & Eisenberg, 1972). The same conclusion, again with some exceptions, can be offered today. Predictive (as opposed to concurrent) and construct validation for police selection are desperately needed. Research examining personnel already on the police force must be evaluated cautiously, for such concurrent studies ignore the potential and characteristics of applicants who dropped out because of the hurdles along the way. A theory to explain why given behaviors are predictive of good performance while others are predictive of unsatisfactory performance is also desirable.

It is clear that no one procedure or variable, by itself, is powerful enough to predict on-the-job performance. This includes the most commonly used instrument, the MMPI, although it has more support in the empirical literature than any other single test. Furthermore, the task of predicting, or even identifying, successful police performance is complicated, because police duties are multidimensional and highly variable from one agency to another. As a result agencies often become discouraged and eschew predictive validation methodology, shifting to job-related tests or content validation. This last trend was noted by Kent and Eisenberg (1972) and continues today.

In selecting screening devices, police administrators should look for testing instruments that are able to predict the probabilities of success in law enforcement prior to entry. It is probably unrealistic to expect administrators to evaluate construct validity also, but they can inquire about it. The administrator should also be aware of the percentage probabilities—the number of "hits" an instrument can make compared to "misses." The hits come into two categories: those that allow rejection of poor candidates and those that allow the retention of good ones. Misses also come in two categories: those that missed identifying poor candidates and those that rejected potentially good candidates. When cost considerations are important, it is more crucial that an instrument be able to identify as many poor candidates as possible, while still not rejecting a large number of potentially good candidates. There is no fast rule about which cut-off score to use in selection. This is an administrative decision that hinges upon the social, psychological, and material costs the agency is willing to risk.

## ■ Psychological Assessment of Corrections Officers

Corrections officers have the unenviable task of maintaining control of inmates, who are sometimes hostile and dangerous, in a psychologically adverse environment. The ideal prison guard relies on appropriate judgment, poise, and leadership and is able to manage the stress generated from fear and from exceedingly boring conditions. If correctional personnel lack the necessary personal attributes and coping skills—and they so often do—the consequences can range from mere ineptitude on the job to severe exacerbation of tension, risks, disruptions, and violence. Thus, an effective program of psychological assessment to obtain suitable candidates for these working conditions is crucial.

Not long ago, Goldstein (1975) surveyed requirements for corrections officer positions in the fifty states. Forty-two of the forty-six responding states indicated they screened applicants "to identify those emotionally and psychologically unfit for corrections work." The states reported a wide variety of screening procedures, including personal interviews, medical exams, written examinations, background checks, and interviews. Few of these procedures were validated. In fact, according to Inwald, Levitt, and Knatz (1980, p. 2), "less than a dozen studies have been done analyzing the relationship between predictor measures and subsequent performance (in the correctional system), and, for a variety of reasons, the results have been less than enlightening."

Inwald and her colleagues (1980) launched a comprehensive attempt to screen correctional guards in the New York City Department of Corrections and follow up their job performance. The guards were evaluated on the basis of a number of procedures, including the MMPI; an overall rating by an experienced corrections officer/interviewer; and an interview by a counseling psychologist. The general results demonstrated that strong negative psychological evaluations can predict eventual on-the-job difficulty. The results also revealed a "trouble variable," identified by the presence of one or more of the following: a) at least one disciplinary action; b) at least one corrective interview; c) at least three or more separate absences; d) three or more separate times late to work. Inwald and her colleagues concluded that if one or more of the above behaviors appeared, the officer would probably have some difficulty working in a correctional institution.

Inwald discussed several political and practical realities that hinder empirical studies in the correctional setting. She also noted that there is a high attrition rate among corrections officers (one out of six leave within ten months after being hired) and considerable pressure for departments to maintain full staffs. Therefore, supervisors or peers are reluctant to evaluate negatively; even if officers are performing at a substandard level, their supervisors prefer to keep them on the job. This need to give officers every chance to succeed develops into an internal code of solidarity and mutual protection among officers and supervisors. Inherent in this internal code of expected conduct is the assumption that an officer who "blows the whistle" on another will eventually encounter problems of his or her own, with no backup support. This internal code, together with the usual suspicions toward mental health personnel, often prevents the researcher from obtaining performance data.

# ■ Educational and Occupational Discrimination

The above presentation of psychological assessment methods in law enforcement has highlighted problems frequently encountered in the evaluation process and has touched upon the nature of police employment. In the next chapter we will discuss psychological characteristics of policing in more detail. Psychological assessment also pervades the judicial process, however, and the judicial system is, in turn, beginning to examine it. Although we will deal with assessment procedures in various contexts in subsequent sections of the text, it is not too early to mention some of the legal issues relating to testing in admission, educational placement, hiring, promotion, transfer, and termination practices. These issues reflect in the large part the courts' increasing examination of the limitations and potentials of psychological testing, an examination particularly centering on discriminatory practices.

There is considerable controversy today about the use of psychological tests as selection devices for educational and occupational opportunities. In the Civil Rights Act of 1964, Congress addressed the broad spectrum of discriminatory practice in its many forms—Title VII of the Act forbidding discrimination on the basis of race, color, religion, sex, and national origin. Psychological tests which lacked adequate validation data or which based classification and cut-off scores on norms developed from a culturally advantaged population were particularly susceptible to lawsuits. Many psychological tests, especially of the mental ability (IQ) variety, came under heavy social and legal attack.

## TESTING IN EDUCATION

Testing affects most of us in some way, but it is most pervasive in the American educational system. More than 250 million commercial standardized tests designed to measure ability and perceptual, achievemental, emotional, and social competencies, as well as interest patterns, are administered annually in our schools (Bersoff, 1979).

For years, the use of these educational and psychological tests went unchallenged. Prompted by various interest groups, in the 1960s the courts began to scrutinize the cultural and social validity of a wide range of testing practices in both the educational setting and the employment policies of various private companies and public agencies. Psychologists were hard-pressed to justify and document the validity of the lack of discrimination in their testing instruments.

One landmark case, *Hobson v. Hansen* (1967), questioned the propriety of using standardized tests to place a disproportionate number of minority children into the lower academic tracks and middle-class white children into higher ones. In *Hobson*, the federal appellate court condemned the practice of rigid, poorly conceived group classifications on the basis of group tests lacking sensitivity to minorities. The court found that the skills measured by the test instruments were not innately intellectual but rather were acquired through cultural experience gained in home, community, and school. Once labeled, the child would carry this label throughout his or her school years, perpetuating the classification and leaving little opportunity to alter it.

Bersoff (1979, p. 50) writes, "With one blow Judge Wright's decision in *Hobson* severely wounded two sacred cows, ability grouping and standardized testing." Perhaps the gravest blow came from the court's insistence that educational grouping must be based on tests that measure innate ability. However, the quest for culturally fair tests or tests that measure innate ability has not been successful. Behavior is a result of the ongoing interaction between cultural-social experience and neurophysiological predisposition and capacity. One component cannot be isolated and measured independently of the other. Therefore, this jurisprudential demand could not be met, and psychological testing within the nation's school systems faced the possibilty of elimination.

Controversy swirled and psychologists tried to educate the public and the courts about what psychological tests can do. For example, psychologists argued that standardized tests are useful to some extent in predicting future learning. The correlation coefficients of validity between test scores and academic performance are modest, but they are significant and generalizable. Moreover, achievement tests generally demonstrate good content validity and do measure how well students have acquired the skills taught in the school system.

Another landmark case, *Larry P. v. Riles* (1972), questioned the use of individual intelligence tests and the existence of special classes for the academically or intellectually handicapped. In 1971 the parents of black children attending San Francisco schools filed a suit charging discrimination in the educational placement of their children into special educable mentally retarded (EMR) classes on the basis of a score of 75 or lower on an individual intelligence test. The parties filing the suit (plaintiffs) presented affidavits from black psychologists who had retested the children and found them to score above the 75 cutoff point. The black examiners, while administering the same tests as the previous white examiners, tried to establish rapport during the testing and reworded test items in a way which was consistent with the children's social and cultural background. Of course, altering the testing procedure contaminates the internal validity of the test results, rendering the scores questionable for comparison purposes. Yet, the point made by the black examiners cannot be ignored.

The court decided that the defendants (the San Francisco School System and the

California Department of Education) could meet the challenge initiated by the suit by showing "a minimally reasonable relationship between the practice of classification and the goal of placement" (Bersoff, 1979, p. 72). The problem now becomes: What constitutes a "reasonable relationship"? What correlation coefficient would satisfy the court's expectations? As noted by Donald Bersoff, validity correlations that psychologists find acceptable (often around .30 to .40—lower than the reliability coefficients they find acceptable) may not satisfy the expectations of the courts. In *Merriken v. Cressman* (1973, p. 920), for instance, it was ruled that "when a program talks about labeling someone as a particular type and such a label could remain with him for the remainder of his life, the margin of error must be almost nil." "Nil" implies an unusually high correlation, probably ranging between .90 and a perfect correlation of 1.00. Few if any psychological tests demonstrate any type of validity of this magnitude.

*Riles*, which was ultimately resolved by the California Supreme Court, became a long and difficult case because of the numerous important issues raised about testing and its potentially discriminatory classification and labeling properties within the educational system. The case took over seven years to settle. Some analyses of the case divide it into two phases, *Riles I* (1972) and *Riles II* (1979) (e.g., Bersoff, 1979). *Riles I* was only concerned with the propriety of a preliminary injunction to suspend classification on the basis of existing methods of testing the children. *Riles II* ruled in favor of the plaintiffs and against the California State Department of Education. *Riles II* required that the tests used for classification purposes be shown to have clear validity and be appropraite for use with minority children. For example, "tests would have to be correlated with relevant criterion measures; that is, IQ scores of black children would have to be correlated with classroom performance" (Bersoff, 1981, p. 1048). Bersoff (1981, p. 1048) states that given the stringent criteria outlined by the court, "it is unlikely that any of the currently used intelligence tests are valid, which casts doubt on the continued utility of traditional evaluations using psychology's storehouse of standardized ability tests." *Riles II* found the intelligence tests used for classification were culturally biased in favor of whites and therefore were discriminatory. Even recent restandardizations of the Wechsler and Stanford-Binet Scales using a representative population of black children have failed to satisfy the court's standard of validity.

The conclusions reached in *Riles II* reflect considerable misunderstanding and ignorance of psychological testing and psychometric theory (Bersoff, 1981). But even more unsettling is the case of *PASE v. Hannon* (1980), where, in opposition to *Riles*, the court ruled that intelligence tests do not discriminate against black children. The unsettling aspect of that decision is the highly subjective and unscientific manner in which it was made. The judge cited each question on the Wechsler and Stanford-Binet Scales and then cited every acceptable response to each item. He decided for himself on the basis of this "analysis" which items were culturally biased. In his judgment, only eight items on the WISC/WISC-R and one item on the Stanford-Binet met his "criterion" for nonbias.

The ultimate resolution of the status of psychological testing and its utility in educational and occupational selection and classification appears far down the road. However, the remaining confusion is at least partly due to the lack of knowledge about testing and psychometric theory which pervades the judicial system and to some extent psychology itself.

## TESTING IN EMPLOYMENT

The judicial and legislative branches of government have both demanded clarification and revision of employment testing procedures. The Office of Federal Contract Compliance (OFCC) and the Equal Employment Opportunity Commission (EEOC) have established guidelines which pertain to any test designed to facilitate personnel decisions for purposes of selection, transfer, promotion, training, referral, and retention. These guidelines encompass educational opportunities as well as employment practices. Two major U.S. Supreme Court decisions, *Griggs v. Duke Power Company*

## ☐ EMPLOYMENT DISCRIMINATION CASES

The issue of employer discrimination in the use of psychological tests was first addressed by the U.S. Supreme Court in 1971 in *Griggs v. Duke Power Company*, when thirteen of fourteen black employees at a steam station owned by Duke Power Company brought a class-action suit. Prior to the Civil Rights Act of 1964, the Company had openly discriminated against blacks, assigning them only to the labor detail, where the highest-paid laborer earned less than the lowest-paid white worker in other departments. To comply with the Act, the Company allowed blacks to transfer, provided they had a high school diploma and could pass two psychological ability and aptitude tests, the Wonderlic Personnel Test and the Bennet Mechanical Comprehension Test. Neither test was designed to measure the ability to learn to perform a particular job. New employees, furthermore, were required to score satisfactorily on two additional aptitude tests.

The petitioners contended that these requirements made a disproportionate number of blacks ineligible for a better job. Lower courts rejected their claims, because there was no proof of a discriminatory intent on the part of the Company.

The U.S. Supreme Court said in part that

good intent or the absence of discriminatory intent does not redeem employment procedures or testing mechanisms that operate as "built-in headwinds" for minority groups and are unrelated to measuring job capability . . . Congress directed the thrust of the [Civil Rights] Act to the *consequences* of employment practices, not simply the motivation. More than that, Congress has placed on the employer the burden of showing that any given requirement must have a manifest relationship to the employment in question.

The *Griggs* case was cited frequently in *Albemarle v. Moody*, where again a class action suit on behalf of black employees was initiated. Albemarle, a company that transformed wood into various paper products, had been administering the Wonderlic Personnel Test and the Revised Beta Exam to prospective employees at skilled-labor jobs. When the *Griggs* decision was announced, Albemarle hired an industrial psychologist to study the job relatedness of the testing program. Although the psychologist performed a concurrent validation between the tests and present employee performance, the

(1971) and *Albemarle Paper Company v. Moody* (1975), have supported the guidelines and had extended impact on psychological testing procedures (see box).

In *Griggs*, black employees challenged the legality of general ability exams used by an employer to hire and promote. The tests had a disproportionate impact on minorities by encouraging the hiring and advancement of a substantially greater portion of whites than blacks. The Court found fault with the testing practices of the private company and reminded it that the EEOC required that the employment tests used must be predictive of important and relevant job behaviors.

In *Albemarle*, the Court found a concurrent validation study done by an industrial

---

U.S. Supreme Court questioned his procedure.

Noting that the EEOC had established guidelines for test validation that were based on guidelines of the American Psychological Association, the Court found the psychologist's validation study defective. First, it did not validate the test for all of the jobs. Second, the procedure relied on subjective, vague supervisory ratings. There was no way of knowing what criteria of job performance were being considered. The Court was also concerned that data for minority groups were not available.

Thus, the Court gave the message very clearly that it was not enough for an employer to say that a testing program had been validated. Companies can expect that the very validation process will be scrutinized.

In a case heard just a year later, however, the Court seemed to qualify its stance on employment testing. Here, in *Washington v. Davis*, black applicants for police officer positions argued that a written personnel test was racially discriminatory and violated the due process clause of the Constitution.

The Court majority ruled that the respondents had failed to show a racially discriminatory purpose, since a sufficient proportion of other black applicants had passed the test. Furthermore, the test had been validated by the showing of a positive relationship between it and performance in the police training program. "It was thus not necessary to show that Test 21 was not only a useful indicator of training school performance but had also been validated in terms of job performance—'The lack of job performance validation does not defeat the Test, given its direct relationship to recruiting and the valid part it plays in this process.'" The Court then agreed with a lower court, which had ruled that there was no proof the department was qualifying officers on the basis of skin color rather than ability. The minority dissent criticized the majority's reasoning and argued that the *Griggs* and *Albemarle* cases required proof of a positive relationship between tests and actual performance.

These three decisions have received much critical commentary from civil libertarians and from experts in the measurement of ability. There is widespread disenchantment with the Court's view of test construction and validation (e.g., Bersoff, 1981), but there is also widespread recognition that the legal scrutiny will continue.

psychologist faulty and incomplete. The study had supported the employment test used by a private company, but the Court criticized the study for not analyzing "the attributes of, or the particular skills needed in, the studied job groups" (p. 432). Implicit in the Court's complaint was the lack of construct validity of the employment test used.

However, in a later U.S. Supreme Court case, *Washington v. Davis* (1976), the Court altered its previous decisions and failed to advance standards for employment testing. In *Washington*, the plaintiffs maintained that a personnel examination (used throughout the federal government) discriminated against black applicants for positions in the District of Columbia Police Department. The case was litigated under the equal protection clause of the U.S. Constitution rather than the EEOC guidelines (Title VII), which had been used by plaintiffs in *Griggs* and *Albemarle*. A divided Court ruled that the EEOC guidelines required that tests be "validated" in relation to job performance, and that this was a rather rigorous standard under the Constitution. The Court held that the employer need only demonstrate a rational basis for the tests used. In addition, it was not necessary to show a relationship between test results and actual job performance. A significant relationship between training performance (in this case, the police academy) and test scores would meet the validity requirement.

It should be mentioned that the EEOC guidelines do not reject the use of properly validated tests designed to help place people into positions requiring certain skills. They do reject the use of tests that involve unfair discrimination in determining access to educational and occupational opportunities. For example, an employer may promote an employee after she has scored higher than others on a valid skills test. An employer may not, however, limit a training program to individuals who have scored high on a mental ability test, unless the employer is certain the test has been validated with reference to performance in that program. In other words, "A test may discriminate between individuals or groups but may not discriminate *against* them" (Schwitzgebel & Schwitzgebel, 1980, p. 122).

Many of the legal problems encountered in testing could be eliminated, or at least reduced, if test designers and users understood and systematically described the behaviors they were measuring, the tasks to which those behaviors were demonstrably related, the conditions for the instrument's proper use, and the known distortions and potential risks involved (Schwitzgebel & Schwitzgebel, 1980). Before concluding that a test measures "intelligence," one should know the precise behavioral definition of intelligence one wishes to adopt for that instrument, the specific behaviors included, what tasks or performance the behaviors are related to, and the inherent dangers and possibility of approaching discriminatory practices. This would presuppose knowledge about a test's reliability and validity, the methods used to establish its norms, and the standardization procedures. In addition, there must be a continual realization that a test samples a very small segment of behavior under restrictive and artificial conditions. It is unfortunate that a large portion of existing published tests would fail to meet many of these guidelines.

This does not mean that all tests, including IQ tests, are meaningless and useless. We must know what a test can and cannot do, and we must apply it to appropriate populations with a very cautious and scientific attitude. With this approach, we can use valid psychological tests to our advantage and that of the population we are assessing. Shortcuts entail a myriad of potential social damages to consumers in the same manner that a hastily marketed drug may harbor potential physiological damage.

One last area needs attention. Judicial concern about the discriminatory potentials of testing in the educational and employment fields has focused almost exclusively upon ability or intellectual testing, both group and individual. Personality testing has yet to be challenged seriously, although its susceptibility to challenge is extremely high. Personality testing is plagued by vagueness and excessive levels of subjective interpretation backed by little empirical support. This form of testing appears to be a good candidate for legal attention in the near future, and it may well be that solid construct validation would best offer its salvation.

# ■ Summary and Conclusions

The goal of psychological assessment is to reduce the complexity of human behavior to a manageable set of variables so that present behavior can be appraised and some parameters of future behavior can be predicted. As such, assessment can be a valuable tool to the psychologist consulting with courts, law enforcement, and correctional personnel. This chapter has focused on testing services provided to police agencies, specifically with reference to the screening and selection of personnel. To some extent, services provided to corrections were also discussed. Psychological assessment as it relates to the judicial system will be discussed in a later chapter.

An understanding of the basic principles of reliability, validity, and normative distribution is crucial if one is to evaluate any testing program. Too many police departments have initiated testing programs without any evidence that the instruments they are using are valid or reliable.

The primitive state of the art of test validation in law enforcement and, in particular, in corrections, must be emphasized. To date, the data are inconclusive. There is a great demand for predictive validation studies: those that will help administrators detect, prior to hiring an individual, whether that person is likely to succeed as a police officer. At present the very definition of "success" in law enforcement is open to interpretation. The importance of construct validity as the unifying concept and fundamental rationale for psychological assessment must also be stressed.

Various screening devices are available, with varying limitations and strengths. In view of the inconclusive nature of the research in this area, it is important to note that, as yet, no one test or variable is powerful enough to predict on-the-job performance. At present the most frequently used device is the MMPI, but the traditional methods of using that test have been no more validated than methods of using other tests.

The quality of present selection and promotional procedures in law enforcement is substandard and in need of more careful scrutiny from psychologists. Lack of interest on the part of psychologists partly explains the poor quality. Other factors include the limited available research upon which to base decisions and plan programs and a general ignorance about assessment validation.

Finally, the legal questions about psychological testing practices in both educational and employment screening and placement remain unsettled and are likely to crop up repeatedly in future litigation. Many of them can be eliminated, however, with better understanding of what psychological tests can and cannot do and with empirical study to determine whether the instruments are doing what they are designed to do.

## ■ Key Concepts and Principles, Chapter 2

Reliability
Internal consistency
Test-retest reliability
Interjudge reliability
Correlation coefficient
Validity
Criterion-related validity
Concurrent validity
Predictive validity
Content validity

Construct validity
Norms
Individual and group testing
Projective and objective testing
Rational, empirical, and factor-analytic
    test construction
Cross-situational and temporal
    consistency
MMPI and CPI

# □ | 3

# ■ | The Psychology of Policing

□ | This chapter will examine some of the law enforcement areas in which psychology has been most active. We begin by exploring the empirical evidence for the so-called police personality, mentioned in Chapter 2. Does law enforcement, in fact, attract personnel with distinguishable behavioral patterns or personalities? Next, we will examine discretionary behavior and how "occupational socialization" affects this behavior. Finally, the remainder of the chapter will focus upon the many dimensions of stress and its relationship to law enforcement. Stress has an important influence upon the attention, memory, and decisionmaking not only of first-line participants in the criminal justice system—the police—but also on the participants at all levels of the judicial system. Neither witnesses, plaintiffs, defendants, judges, nor lawyers are immune to its effects. Although we will concentrate upon stress as it affects law enforcement officers, the material covered is generalizable to human beings in a variety of occupational and social situations.

## ■ The Police Personality

The public's perception of police officers ranges over a broad spectrum of images. Some people associate them with the rigid, dogmatic institutions that perpetuate social injustices in favor of the financially, politically, and socially powerful. Others feel that the police are unappreciated, caring individuals trying to protect the community from the onslaughts of crime. Some academicians have zealously promoted the image of the typical police officer as an authoritarian, politically conservative, socially and psychologically insensitive person, who is not very bright or creative. By contrast, the entertainment media have been instrumental in encouraging images of free-wheeling, unorthodox cops who, in the face of political and organizational pressures, unrelentingly pursue criminals to the end, even if it means losing their jobs. Often, novice officers model these media characters, but they soon learn through the socialization process that this image is unrealistic.

What, then, is the "police personality?" Is there such a thing? Does law enforcement attract certain types of people?

## RESEARCH TRENDS

To provide a framework for our discussion, we will adopt the classification scheme proposed by Lefkowitz (1975), who identified and evaluated two trends in the theoretical writing and existing research on the police personality. He labeled these trends to reflect the personality theme or "trait syndrome" being examined by the researchers.

Trait Syndrome I includes behavioral indicators of social isolation and secrecy; defensiveness and suspicion; and cynicism. It is based upon the common observation that police officers generally associate with their "own kind" and develop values and interests that correspond closely to those exhibited by their in-group. Law enforcement officers are often said to party, go fishing, and attend sports events together. This promotes social isolation from individuals outside police-related occupational groups and encourages secrecy about police work. It is unclear whether this socio-occupational isolation results from pressures encountered in police work or the police training program, or whether it is a feature of the personality structures of the people drawn to law enforcement. That is, would these individuals be just as socially isolated if involved in different occupations? Whatever the origin, isolation and secretiveness seem to promote mutual misunderstanding between the police and the public (Lefkowitz, 1975).

Trait Syndrome II encompasses behaviors that generally carry the label "dogmatic" or "authoritarian." The authoritarian personality is displayed by a rigid adherence to and an overemphasis upon middle-class values; uncritical acceptance of authority figures; a firm belief in strong punishment and discipline for those who violate social values and laws; and a generalized tendency to think in rigid, oversimplified categories that generate black-and-white answers for social and psychological problems. Authoritarian personalities are hypothesized to show a strong desire to associate themselves with powerful people, to be cynical about the motives and purposes of others, to be superstitious, and to disapprove of free emotional lives or displays of emotion (Adorno et al., 1950).

## TRAIT SYNDROME I

Lefkowitz cites research indicating that police officers not only feel misunderstood by the public, but also that they rate this as one of the major problems they face (e.g., Olson, 1973; Opinion Research Corporation, 1968). On the other hand, research surveying the public has found that police officers are not viewed as negatively as they think they are (Lefkowitz, 1975, 1977).

Police personnel, it seems, are suspicious of citizens (Matarazzo et al., 1964; Mills, 1969; Rhead et al., 1968; Roberts, 1961; Verinis & Walker, 1970) and of each other (Westley, 1956). However, the factors contributing to this high level of suspiciousness are a mystery. As with isolation, it is not known whether suspicious personalities are drawn to police work or whether suspicion develops as a consequence of the job experience.

Niederhoffer (1967), who studied New York City police officers, decided that cynicism was one of the most salient features of their personalities. He saw cynicism as a way of adapting to frustration, which results from diffuse feelings of hate toward citizens, envy, impotent hostility, and a "sour grapes pattern." Police develop a belief that most people are basically evil and would commit crimes if they knew they could get away with it, and this belief results in feelings of hate, Niederhoffer suggests. Impotent hostility springs from personal feelings of inability to express hostility against society; a police officer must remain calm, even when spat upon. The "sour grapes" behavior pattern refers to the feelings of police officers that desired but attainable goals are really not all that important or valuable. For instance, college-educated patrolmen may find that their expectations of promotion do not become fulfilled, and they may try to convince themselves that promotion really does not mean all that much to them. On the other hand, non-college-educated officers may rationalize that higher education is not necessary.

Niederhoffer contends that cynicism—which comprises any or all of the above elements—is discernible at all levels and in all fields of law enforcement. In addition, he sees two kinds of cynicism: one kind is directed against life, the world, and people in general; the other is aimed at the police system and its flaws.

Niederhoffer reports that police cynicism passes through four distinct stages of development. The first stage, which he calls "pseudo-cynicism," is most recognizable among recruits at the police academy. Although they express cynical attitudes, they can barely conceal the idealism and commitment they actually feel. "Romantic cynicism," the second stage, is reached during the first five years of the police career. Although the precise behavior is not defined, it appears that the most idealistic, young members of the force are the most disillusioned by the reality of police work and hence most vulnerable to this type of cynicism. The third stage, "aggressive cynicism," usually occurs around the tenth year. According to Niederhoffer, it corresponds to a resentment which is best expressed by the catch phrase, "I hate citizens," and it results in a diffuse resentment and hostility toward society and the department. The fourth stage, "resigned cynicism," occurs during the last few years of a police career. It is demonstrated by acceptance of the job situation and capacity to come to terms with the flaws of the criminal justice system. This final stage is viewed by Niederhoffer as the successful culmination of a career marked by much dissatisfaction and conflict.

Niederhoffer observes that, for the first few years of a police career, cynicism increases in proportion to the length of service. It then tends to level off sometime during the fifth and tenth years of service. Cynicism is learned as part of a socialization process typical of the police occupation, a process estimated to take about five years.

Reiser (1973) has hypothesized a similar process, the "John Wayne syndrome," which begins early in the career of a police officer and lasts for three to four years. This behavior pattern is characterized by coldness toward others and emotional withdrawal, authoritarian attitudes, cynicism, overseriousness, and a black-or-white, dogmatic approach to life.

Niederhoffer's theory and the twenty-item scale of police cynicism he developed have received considerable attention, but supportive research is minimal (Lefkowitz, 1975). Most of the research has examined cynicism scores of police officers at various stages of their careers, and generally, it has failed to support Niederhoffer's observations (Rafky, Lawley & Ingram, 1976; Lefkowitz, 1973; Regoli, 1976).

## TRAIT SYNDROME II

Research examining Trait Syndrome II is also unsupportive. Although components of the authoritarian personality often exist in many police officers, the existence of a pervasive authoritarianism as outlined by Adorno and his colleagues (1950) has not been substantiated.

Authoritarianism is usually measured by an attitudinal scale called the California F-Scale. After reviewing the literature in the area up to 1974, Lefkowitz (1975, p. 11) concluded: "Policemen have scored, almost without exception, as not particularly authoritarian or dogmatic on the F-Scale, D Scale, and modifications of same." Research done since that time continues to lend support to this conclusion (Conser, 1980).

## REPRESENTATIVE RESEARCH

A study by C. Abraham Fenster, Carl F. Wiedemann, and Bernard Locke (1977) is representative of much of the traditional research on the police personality. Over 700 male subjects were divided into four groups, depending on whether they had police experience or a college background. All were comparable in age (with an average age in the late 20s). A variety of group mental and personality tests were administered to all subjects, and comparisons were made between the scores of the four groups. However, as in most studies on the police personality, little theoretical rationale was offered as to why these particular tests were selected, nor was validity information described. Several of the tests used have notoriously questionable validity and weak theoretical bases for their construction. Therefore, at the outset the investigators began their study on rather shaky grounds.

Results showed that police personnel demonstrated significantly lower neuroticism scores (reactivity to stressful events) than the nonpolice groups. In addition, police obtained lower authoritarian scores and slightly higher intelligence scores. The authors concluded that this police sample "may represent a *superior* subsample of the general population" (p. 104), and that the police were better adjusted psychologically than the nonpolice groups. Overall, there was little evidence for particular police personality traits.

A more recent study by Carol Mills and Wayne Bohannon (1980) illustrates a trend toward better research design and a more vigorous attempt to link test scores with theory. The Mills-Bohannon project tried to identify those personality characteristics associated with supervisory ratings on leadership and overall suitability for police work. Further, the study was designed to test two predictive models of police effectiveness and leadership (viz., Hogan, 1971; Gough, 1969).

The measuring instrument used to delineate personality characteristics was the empirically constructed California Personality Inventory (CPI). Forty-nine male

Maryland state police officers with one year's experience served as subjects. Each subject was rated by two supervisors on a 7-point scale for leadership and "overall suitability for police work." There was a good amount of interjudge reliability (.78) between the two supervisory ratings for each subject.

The results showed that the Hogan model of police effectiveness was significantly better able to predict leadership than Gough's model. Hogan's model (repression equation) uses the four CPI personality variables of social presence, self-acceptance, achievement via independence, and intellectual efficiency to predict police performance. "Social presence" refers to the personality trait of being poised and self-confident in personal and social interaction. "Self-acceptance" refers to a tendency to feel competent, combined with a capacity for independent thinking and action. "Achievement via independence" denotes motivation to achieve in settings where autonomy and independence are encouraged. "Intellectual efficiency" refers to the ability to think clearly and planfully.

The results of the Mills-Bohannon study suggest that the personality requirements for successful police leadership are the above described four traits in combination, although caution is advised when generalizing to other police agencies in other states. Also, the vagueness of the personality traits remains troublesome and susceptible to multiple interpretations. For example, what precisely does "the ability to think clearly and planfully" mean, and in what context?

There is some evidence to suggest that police personnel in general tend to be conservative, conventional, and concerned with maintaining the status quo (Lefkowitz, 1975). Hence, at least one component of the authoritarian personality is supported in the research literature. This conventional outlook appears to be fostered by militant regulations and rules of conduct expected by the police agencies. Beyond this conservative aspect, the "average" police officer seems to display personality characteristics similar to those of the "average" population—normal and free of pathology.

Very little research has been directed at motivations for pursuing a police career (Stotland & Berkerich, 1979; Lefkowitz, 1975). One frequent conclusion is that job security is the greatest attraction of police work (Gorer, 1955; Niederhoffer, 1967; Reiss, 1967). This motivation seems to be more characteristic of white candidates than of members of minority races (Hunt, 1971).

It should not be surprising that the research on the police personality continues to be equivocal and inconsistent. As we learned in Chapter 2, individual behavior (personality) and situational context intermingle. The search for consistent behaviors must consider what kind of consistency (temporal or cross-situational) is being measured, and in what context. The fact that some researchers report police officers to be authoritarian or cynical while others do not underscores this interaction. Some police agencies, through peer pressures, expect their officers to assume an authoritarian role, while others do not. Some agencies look for applicants who already "fit the mold," while others anticipate that the young officers will acquire appropriate roles through peer pressure or occupational experience. It is entirely possible that police behavior is shaped more by the agency-appropriate roles the officer is expected to assume than by the officer's own personality variables. In other words, the occupational socialization process may override individual differences or personality styles.

In conclusion, it does not appear productive to search for global police personality traits that characterize, even in part, the person who becomes a police officer. It is more appropriate to limit one's research conclusions to the specific police agency in which the subjects are employed. In this sense, research findings about the "personality" of police officers may prove to reveal more about the characteristics and expectations of the police agency than about the personnel therein.

# ■ Police Discretion

"Discretion involves the ability to act on the basis of personal judgment, uncontrolled by prearticulated rules of law" (Nimmer, 1977, p. 257). It is the central ingredient in the day-to-day activities of the police officer, who deals directly and frequently with the public. Discretion is more important in the lives of local police agents than federal agents, because procedures and rules are more clearly spelled out at the federal level (Bennett-Sandler et al., 1979).

Most students and participants in the judicial system realize that discretion is an indispensable element that is both impossible and undesirable to eliminate. It is a reality at all levels of the system (Cole, 1975). "Squeeze out discretion here and it will emerge there!" (Wilkins, 1979, p. 46), is an observation that would meet minimal challenge from observers and participants in the judicial system.

The discretionary behavior of police officers depends upon a number of factors, including the nature of the offense at issue. Generally speaking, the more serious the act the less latitude there is for discretionary action by the police officer (Gallagher, 1979). Although the official limits of an officer's actions appear to be strictly proscribed (Lefkowitz, 1977), all experienced personnel acknowledge there is wide discretion in minor matters. Thus, the police have considerable discretion in handling moving traffic violations, minor juvenile offenses, exhibitionism, drunkenness, and family disturbances, but very little when homicide, aggravated assault, rape, or robbery are involved.

Discretion is also influenced by community concerns. If the community places great pressure on police to eliminate prostitution in a given area of the city, or to keep intoxicated persons off the streets, the scope of discretionary behavior is somewhat narrowed.

Other limiting factors are the officer's frame of mind at the time he or she investigates the offense and the perpetrator's reaction to the officer (Gallagher, 1979). If the officer has encountered recent personal difficulties, he or she is apt to be less generous in handling minor violations. If the offender is hostile to the officer, an escalation effect may occur, where each challenging remark or action is met with increased action by the other party.

### AN ARCHIVAL STUDY

In a recent study, Sarah Berk and Donileen Loseke (1980–81) examined some of the characteristics of police discretion in handling domestic disturbances. The method of data collection was *archival*, in which events previously recorded are adopted for study. In the Berk-Loseke study, the data were drawn from police reports of domestic disturbances forwarded to the district attorney's unit of the Santa Barbara (California) Family Violence Program.

To increase internal validity, the researchers analyzed only those 262 police reports which had enough detailed information to convey a relatively complete picture of the domestic incident. However, by increasing internal validity the researchers lost some external validity. That is, by using only the most complete police reports in their analysis, they neglected a sizeable portion of the total reports available. This limits the extent to which the results can be generalized to police discretion in other domestic disputes.

"Domestic" was defined as those incidences "where the principals were adults involved in a heterosexual 'romantic' or conjugal relationship prior to, or at the time of, the incident" (p. 326). Therefore, two kinds of relationships qualified for analysis: (1) legal ones, as indicated by marriage, separation, or divorce; or (2) relationships which constituted a sharing of a residence, such as a common-law marriage or a live-in arrangement. "Disturbance" was defined by the police reports. Various events qualified, but most included physical violence or threats of violence, property damage, and verbal arguments.

The researchers were primarily interested in determining what specific characteristics found in domestic disturbances contributed to the police decision to arrest one of the parties. In the reports, a wide variety of notations were made by the police in describing each incident. The notations were assumed to identify the critical dimensions of police decisionmaking and, therefore, formed the basis of a police discretion model proposed by Berk and Loseke.

The dependent variable in this study was whether an arrest was made. The independent variables were determined on the basis of demographic and notation material earmarked and coded for statistical analysis.

Results indicated that four variables exerted a significant effect on police arrest. The strongest was whether one party (always female) was willing to sign an arrest warrant against the other party. Thus, if the woman refused to sign, arrest on any grounds was unlikely. Two other significant variables were whether the male was intoxicated and whether there was an allegation of violence by the female. However, these two independent variables were significant only when both parties were present at the time the police arrived on the scene.

The fourth variable exerting a significant effect on the officers' decisionmaking was whether the female party or someone else called the police. If the female alerted the police to the disturbance, the probability of an arrest decreased. The researchers speculated that the person or party who alerted the police was an index of the severity of the disturbance. If neighbors, friends, or social service personnel called police, the disturbance had probably got out of hand and represented a more serious incident. If the female party called the police, the incident was less likely to be serious.

This project demonstrates how police discretion can be studied in a realistic setting through archival study. (We will return to the many advantages of archival research in a later chapter.) However, the degree of generalizability of this study to police decisionmaking in other domestic disturbances is limited because of the attention given to internal validity over external validity. Therefore, the study suggests the influence of some variables on decisions to arrest in cases where a detailed and full report is filed. Potentially, other variables may also exert powerful effects on decisions to arrest if we analyze all police reports, including the less informative ones.

## A FIELD STUDY

Another example of police discretion research using a different methodology was conducted by Donald Black (1971). In this study, arrest was again the dependent variable, but it was related to a much broader scope than domestic disturbances. The independent variables included the suspect's race, the legal seriousness of the alleged crime, the evidence available in the field setting, the complainant's preference for police action, and the social relationship between the complainant and the suspect. The research intent was to discover which of the independent variables emerged as significant factors in the officer's decision to arrest or not to arrest.

The data were collected through "systematic observation" of police-citizen transactions in three major cities during the summer of 1966. Therefore, while the Berk-Loseke study was archival and not contaminated by any obtrusive measure or observer, the Black investigation utilized a data collection method which could potentially affect the results. That is, the presence of observers might potentially alter the event being investigated. The Black field study used thirty-six observers who recorded observations of encounters between patrolmen and citizens. The observers' training and supervision was approximately the same in all three metropolitan locations. The observers accompanied the police officers on all work shifts, but most of the observation time was spent when police activity was highest, especially on weekend evenings.

Over 5,700 incidents were observed and recorded, but only about 5 percent of them were used in the study analysis. Again, as in the Berk-Loseke study, a concerted attempt was made to insure internal validity, somewhat to the detriment of external validity. Incidents in which there was no opportunity for an arrest—situations in which the suspect had left the scene prior to police arrival or in which no apparent crime had been committed—were deleted from the analysis. Traffic encounters and incidents that could "invisibly distort or otherwise confuse the analysis" were also excluded. The final data were gathered predominately from encounters with blue-collar adults suspected of criminal conduct, and they represented only a small amount of the total encounters observed.

Although caution and scepticism are advised, the data do provide some clues about the discretionary decisionmaking of police officers working in metropolitan police departments. Results revealed that a majority of the police-citizen encounters were *reactive* rather than *proactive*. Specifically, most encounters were citizen initiated rather than police initiated. On an average evening shift, for example, there were six citizen-initiated encounters for every one police-initiated contact. These results suggest that a major portion of criminal-law enforcement activity depends upon citizens, not the police.

Arrest practices also depended heavily on the preferences of citizen complainants. In situations where a citizen's immediate testimony linked a suspect to a crime, an arrest resulted in fully three-fourths of the cases in which the complainant specified a preference for an arrest. On the other hand, when the complainant preferred that no arrest be made, the police went along with this request 90 percent of the time. One conclusion which can be drawn from these data is that the complainant's preference may be a more powerful situational factor for arrest than the evidence itself.

Results also revealed that the probability of arrest increased as the intimacy of the relationship between the complainant and the suspect decreased. The more familiar the complainant and the suspect were to one another, the less likely was it that the suspect would be arrested. Further data showed that the probability of an arrest also increased when a suspect exhibited disrespectful behavior toward police. In legally serious crimes (felonies), police arrested 40 percent of the respectful suspects compared to 69 percent of the disrespectful suspects. In less serious crimes (misdemeanors), the police arrested 43 percent of the well-mannered and 71 percent of the disrespectful suspects.

The Berk-Loseke and Black investigations provide some information about the discretionary behavior of police officers in making arrests. There is little doubt that much more data collection must be done, using different research approaches and samples of behavior. The two projects illustrate two different methodological approaches to the study of police behavior, archival and field study, which are the most common methods of studying police behavior.

## DISCRETION IN THE CONTEXT OF THE LEGAL SYSTEM

Along with the factors already mentioned, police discretion is influenced by the feedback the officer receives from the legal system itself. Regardless of other situational factors and of how strict or lenient the officer is in dealing with incidents, the bottom line is how peers, supervisory personnel, the prosecuting attorney, the judge, and other agents of the system react to the discretionary behavior. As Saks and Miller (1979, p. 74) have noted, "It is the behavior of other actors in the system that regulates the behavior of any given actor, not the written law."

The prosecuting attorney's strategy in handling a case is often dictated by the anticipated behavior of judge and defense. Judges make decisions that often serve as messages to the police and prosecutors about how to handle future cases. Prosecuting attorneys also give messages to the police about what will "go" in court and what is a legitimate case. Among these messages is one that excessive vigor in arresting and charging perpetrators of minor offenses will overload the system. Such behavior may also generate public outcry against the zealousness of the police over minor infractions. The public will clamor, "Catch the criminals and stop harrassing the citizens."

An officer usually learns how to use discretion by modeling the more experienced officers within the agency. Heavy peer pressure about the "right way" to do things and handle incidents appears to be continually exerted, and excessive deviance from the norm is usually not tolerated. The officer who uses discretion in an atypical way may be inviting occupational and social sanction from colleagues, occupational termination, or even prosecution. Alternately, his or her actions may be neutralized by the actions of others, like a supervisor or the prosecuting attorney.

Behavior that stays within the limits of the police officer's legally and departmentally defined role will be interpreted as legitimate discretion (Saks & Miller, 1979), while behavior that exceeds these limits will be considered deviant. Therefore, discretion is partly based on the judgment of the individual, but also partly (perhaps even largely) based on the department's code of expected conduct. Experienced officers show the rookies strategies to use in handling incidents, and the rookies model the veterans. In many instances, the "war stories" of the veteran cop offset the training and strategies presented by the police academy; in most instances, instructors who are also well seasoned officers are given greater credibility than college professors. It is occupational socialization, therefore, which probably has the most influence on the development of discretionary behavior at the gateway to the legal system.

Inexperienced police officers who become system challengers and who do not respond well to this occupational socialization process are usually not tolerated by peers or supervisory personnel. Serpicos and Dirty Harrys are pariahs in most police departments, and supervisory personnel typically evaluate their performance below average or poor. These syndromes are tolerated in the first year, but they are expected to be eradicated with experience.

The discretionary behavior of each police officer, then, is partly dependent upon the strategies and codes adopted by each particular department, and sometimes it is independent of the written law. In the larger departments, the strategies and codes to be adopted may be dictated more by the subgroups within the department than by any efficient organizational unit. These unwritten rules are in turn partly determined by behavior of other participants in the judicial system, such as the prosecuting attorneys, the defense attorneys, the trial judge, the appellate judge, and even the probation and parole officers. In some cases the capacity of the correctional system dictates the discretion used by the first-line participants. An officer who knows the local jail is overcrowded may hesitate to arrest a belligerent reveler and detain him overnight. When traffic court dockets are full, an officer may issue a stern warning rather than send a motorist before the judge.

In sum, the judicial system functions with interdependence among its components, and the discretionary behavior used by one component affects other components. In addition, as Saks and Miller (1979, p. 79) have observed, "actors closest to the borders of a system are least influenced by the system's norms and sanctions. It may therefore be predicted that judges have the least ability to deviate; police have the most."

We noted earlier that most students of and participants in the judicial system believe that discretion is a necessary and integral part of the legal operations. Justice must be tailored to the individual case, not applied inflexibly to the crime. In an incisive probe of whether the judicial system is an open or closed system, Saks and Miller (1979) argued that discretion provides the flexibility necessary for the effective functioning of a system that could be described as relatively closed. A closed system is one which allows very little input from the external environment, whereas an open system invites such input. The American judicial system considers itself relatively closed, but able to adapt cautiously to changes. Saks and Miller (1979, p. 77) note: "It is possible that in less adaptable, less open systems discretion serves the purpose of improving the system's response capacity. The formal system cannot track environmental changes quickly enough; so discretionary functions may develop to respond to changes in the environment until the formal structures catch up."

We will encounter discretion and its many facets again in the chapter on the psychology of lawyering. For now, it is important for the reader to realize the importance of the built-in mechanisms that advocate and limit police discretion, since this discretion operates at the gateway to the criminal justice system. In other words, it is often the discretion exercised by the police officer that determines whether a case will enter the judicial arena.

# ■ Psychological Stress in Law Enforcement

Police work is believed to rank among the top of all occupations in the amount and variety of stress it promotes (Selye, 1978; Kroes, 1976). But stress is not only germane to law enforcement; it is also pertinent if we seek to evaluate eyewitness testimony and victim accounts of traumatic incidences. Also, any empirical elucidation of criminal behavior requires some attention to stress. In this section we will examine what stress is; how it develops and intensifies; how it affects behavior; and what procedures for stress reduction and control may be used. Although the focus will be upon the stress faced by law enforcement officers, the principles outlined could be applied to all other actors in the judicial system.

### DEFINITION

"Stress" was first used as an engineering term referring to any external force directed at a physical object (Lazarus, 1966). It was introduced into the life sciences in 1936 by endocrinologist Hans Selye (Appley & Trumbull, 1967), who has since become one of the world's leading researchers on biological stress. Selye directed most of his attention to effects of biological stress on the physiological and biochemical functions of the living organism. He defines stress as "the nonspecific response of the body to any demand" (Selye, 1976, p. 15). Thus, the bodily reaction is presumed to be generalized, with the whole body system as a unit engaged in reducing or eliminating "agents" which cause stress. The agents, which Selye called *stressors*, may be external to the organism (exogenous) or within the organism (endogenous), and they may develop from a virus, physical injury, or disease-causing agent.

It is perhaps unfortunate that the life sciences adopted the term stress from the physical sciences, because it is extremely difficult to measure "forces" being exerted on living organisms the way physical science can measure force directed at inanimate objects. Selye may have realized this, because he replaced engineering's "force" with the life sciences' "response."

For our purposes here, we will suggest that psychological stress occurs when a stimulus initiates a response which does not lead to greater perceived or actual control over the stimulus. The behavioral pattern of the person involved is relatively unique, but it typically involves sympathetic activity in the autonomic nervous system and a restriction in the range of cue utilization to guide behavior. In other words, stress as a response involves physiological arousal and a reduction in the ability to use environmental guides (Easterbrook, 1959). The stimuli which prompt physiological arousal or a stress response are called stressors. To keep our discussion short, we will focus attention briefly on the input-output factors and skip the behavioral strategies for coping, unless they relate directly to law enforcement.

The input elements are the stressors or the stimuli which a person considers stressful—the stimuli or events which are evaluated as threatening, frustrating, or conflicting. The output element is the person's reaction or response. In psychology, the most common response is called *anxiety*, a term often used interchangeably with *stress reaction*. Anxiety is an unpleasant emotional state marked by worry, fear, anger, apprehension, and muscular tension, and manifested in behavior. Thus, the anxious person may stammer or display other speech disturbances, may chainsmoke, display irritability, avoid a situation, or assume any number of other behavioral postures, all of which may be responses to stressors.

We should distinguish briefly here between two types of anxiety (Spielberger, 1966). *State anxiety* is an emotional reaction to a specific situation and is a common human occurrence. We have all been anxious in the face of certain stressors. If we are anxious in many or most situations, however, anxiety is labeled a trait and thus is regarded by behavioral scientists as a personality variable. In *trait anxiety*, the person consistently or frequently perceives threatening situations.

## MEASUREMENT OF STRESS

To conduct effective research on stress and bring it out of the realm of speculation, it would be helpful if behavioral scientists were able to measure it. Ideally, this calls for methods of discovering both how much stress a person is going through at a particular time and how much cumulative stress the person has faced. Measuring physical stress forces or vectors (in the field of engineering) is now no problem to physicists; instruments to measure biological stress reactions are also available. There is yet no satisfactory, objective way to measure psychological stress, however. We can measure only some of the behavioral responses and physiological reactions to stress.

Physiological reactions encompass a wide range of bodily changes, including changes in blood pressure, muscle tension, brain activation, skin conductance, heart rate, blood biochemistry, urinary levels of epinephrine, fatty acid mobilization, and hormone levels. Sophisticated equipment can monitor accurately any changes in these variables when stressors are introduced. Some psychobiological and physiological psychologists argue cogently that these physiological indices are the most quantifiable and therefore the most precise procedures for measuring the effects of psychological stress, and consequently much of the contemporary research concerned with stress factors has used these measures. The measures have two general shortcomings, however. First, they consider, in large part, only the immediate stress reaction; the cumulative reaction, which would be more reflective of the amount of stress a person is experiencing, is largely out of reach. Second, in working with human subjects, researchers generally deal with stress that is artificial, in the sense that it is induced in a laboratory setting. This lab-induced stress must also be restricted because of ethical considerations.

Some researchers have relied on *subjective reports* to attempt to measure stress. In this method, the person tells the experimenter what feeling he or she is experiencing or has experienced, what is believed to have precipitated it, and in some instances what is being done to adjust to it. However, due to individual differences in how one appraises stress conditions, comparable, quantifiable data are often difficult to obtain unless the researcher sets up objective, standardized questionnaires limiting the variety of responses.

A number of standardized questionnaires have been developed recently in an attempt to measure subjective appraisal of psychological stress elicited by various stimuli and everyday events. The best known is the Social Readjustment Rating Scale (SRRS) designed by Thomas H. Holmes and his colleagues (Holmes & Rahe, 1967; Holmes & Masuda, 1974), who identified forty-three events that most people experience as stress situations (stressors). Groups of subjects then rated each situation according to the amount of change or adaptation needed to adjust to it. The intensity and duration of change accompanying the event, rather than how desirable or undesirable the event itself was, determined its rank value. For example, marriage earned a high rating while a minor traffic accident, though presumably less desirable, did not require much change. Thus, each event in the SRRS is assigned a numerical value, called a Life Change Unit. Individuals asked to respond to the SRRS indicate whether or not each event has occurred in their lives and if so, when.

Life Change Units (LCUs) are summed, and when their values add up to 150 or more over a one-year period, the person is said to have "life crises." Holmes and Rahe (1967) have hypothesized that the greater the magnitude of LCUs the greater the probability that physical or psychosomatic disease will result from the stress that results from readaptation.

Although some research on the SRRS is suggestive of promising results (e.g., Rahe, Mahan & Arthur, 1970; Holmes & Masuda, 1974), the scale is not an accurate predictor of stress reactions. Some behavioral scientists (see Brown, 1974) have been its strong critics and have pointed out numerous methodological and conceptual flaws in its design and development. One of the major shortcomings is its inability to take into account individual differences in subjective appraisal of the stress in life's events. A $30,000 mortgage is unlikely to be of equal stress to everyone who assumes it.

In summary, stress is measured by assessing the person's appraisal of and response to a class of stressors. Most current research has focused upon immediate physiological reactions to specific stressors in humans, studied under laboratory conditions. The long-term effects of stressors are still unknown. Attempts to rectify this have prompted the development of standardized questionnaires to determine the effects of life event changes on adaptation and illness, but as yet conclusive data have not emerged. Behavioral measures, usually subsumed under the heading "anxiety," have lost some popularity, but the term anxiety remains very much in vogue as a catch-all category to signify a generalized response pattern to stress.

## OCCUPATIONAL STRESSORS IN LAW ENFORCEMENT

Persons in many occupations may argue that they face more physical danger than police officers. Construction workers, miners, stunt pilots, and demolition workers are all exposed to potential death and physical injury more consistently than law enforcement personnel. However, few occupations encounter the same variety of stressors, amply reported in the research literature. Stressors, the reader will recall, are the first elements or stimuli in stress conditions, and police officers face them in abundance. The possibility of physical danger is only one of many.

It has been suggested that one of the predominant stressors confronting police officers is alienation (Niederhoffer, 1967). Jirak (1975) found that alienation due to perceived lack of support from political groups, the press, courts, and the public was a dominant stressor for New York City police. He also found that feelings of alienation usually increased throughout an officer's career, reaching a peak about the fifteenth year of service, at which point they decreased, apparently due to anticipated retirement. This trend was also reported by Lotz and Regoli (1977).

Police-community relations are presumed to be important contributing factors to this alienation (e.g., Banton, 1964; Cain, 1973; Skolnick, 1973). In a survey study by Chappell and Meyer (1975), only two percent of U.S. police officers polled believed the public held them in high esteem. Related to this is the often reported role conflict between what police officers think they should be doing (e.g., crime detection and arrest) and what the public believes they should be doing (e.g., protecting citizens, settling family disputes, chasing unleashed dogs) (Wilson, 1968).

Caplan and his colleagues (1975) surveyed 111 police officers with an average of sixty-three months on the job and found that four stressors occurred very frequently: lack of support from supervisors, role conflict, inability to use skills and abilities to the fullest, and the complexity of the job. This last stressor referred to the variety of skills needed in police work and the inherent unpredictability of the job.

Other stressors identified by behavioral science research include problems with the courts (Kroes, Hurrell & Margolis, 1974) and poor equipment, the latter implying to the officers that others don't care (Margolis, 1973; Eisenberg, 1975). Many police officers feel court appearances are excessively time consuming, and they are often frustrated over judicial procedures, inefficiency, and court decisions. Other surveys have reported shift work as a major occupational stressor (Eisenberg, 1975; Hilton, 1973; Kroes, 1976; Margolis, 1973). Shift work not only interferes with sleep and eating habits, but also with family life. Moreover, irregular hours often preclude social get-togethers and family activities, a fact that socially isolates the police officer even more.

Some occupational stressors confront virtually every police officer, while others are unique to certain types of departments or certain job specialties. For example, several recent studies have focused on the rural law enforcement officer, who has been too long neglected by behavioral and social scientists. One such study (Sandy & Devine, 1978) identified four stressors faced by rural police which their urban counterparts do not encounter. The first, lack of security, referred to the isolation rural officers experience on a daily basis. Help is often a considerable distance away, and officers rarely work in pairs. It is also commonly assumed that many rural homes contain firearms, which are potential hazards. A second stressor identified by the study was social relationships. Rural officers cannot be anonymous in the community, and they frequently socialize with the people they protect. Dealing on an authoritative basis with persons they know well is often stressful. Working conditions accounted for a third stressor; salaries are substantially lower in small departments and training is limited because of lack of funds. Finally, rural police are especially susceptible to boredom and inactivity, and there is good reason to expect that boring, tedious work may be as stressful as the more exciting, urban police work.

By contrast, the organizational structure of large police departments often promotes office politics, lack of effective consultation, nonparticipation in decisionmaking, and restrictions on behavior (Cooper & Marshall, 1976). Niederhoffer (1974) reports a change in class structure among police candidates over the past twenty years, with more professionally-oriented middle-class recruits appearing on the scene. Apparently, this has precipitated interdepartmental conflict about issues like professionalism and resentment toward officers with college degrees (Lewis, 1973).

Police administrators report their own unique occupational stressors. Being the "man-in-the-middle" in the organizational structure is apparently a major problem (Kroes, Hurrell & Margolis, 1974). The administrator is responsible for his or her own actions and for the conduct and efficiency of subordinates. The responsibility is both to the community and to upper police echelons.

Other stressors also develop from an officer's emotional state or from marital or other interpersonal problems off the job. In fact, interpersonal conflicts (especially family and marital ones) appear to be important and persistent stressors for law enforcement personnel. In the Kroes, Margolis, and Hurrell (1974) survey, seventy-nine of the eighty-one married police officers interviewed felt that the nature of their work had an adverse effect on their home life. More specifically, the officers thought that police work gave a negative public image to their family, that their spouses worried regularly about their safety, that they took the tremendous pressures of the job home, that it made them less able to plan social events, and that the job inhibited nonpolice friendships. Another survey of 100 police wives (Rafky, 1974) revealed that nearly one-fourth were dissatisfied with their husbands' careers and that particular aspects of the job resulted in frequent family arguments.

Although criminal justice literature frequently mentions exceedingly high divorce rates and general marital unhappiness among police officers, documentation is very difficult to obtain. One extensive study by the National Institute of Occupational Safety and Health (NIOSH), however, does reveal some evidence that the divorce rate is high for police officers and that marital problems are a chief reason for leaving the force. The NIOSH study (cited by Blackmore, 1978) polled 2,300 officers in twenty-nine departments around the United States and found that 22 percent of the police officers in the sample had been divorced at least once (compared to a national divorce rate of 13.8 percent among urban white males (1970 census)). The NIOSH study also revealed a 26 percent divorce rate for officers married before joining the force, compared to an 11 percent rate for those who married after joining. Officers also reported that marital problems are the prime cause of quitting the force before retirement.

Hageman (1978) found some evidence that as length of service increases marital unhappiness and discontent also increase. Since no comparison was made with marriages in the general population, it is not clear whether the increasing disenchantment was directly due to length of service. However, the study did report that increasing "emotional detachment" of the officer was one of the primary factors in marital conflict.

In view of the above data, it is not surprising that police departments are increasingly hiring full-time psychological, counseling, or psychiatric consultants who are available not only to consult on cases but also to offer their services to individual officers. In addition, many family support groups are appearing throughout the country, frequently at the instigation of police spouses who band together to discuss and solve common problems (Brandreth, 1978).

With the exception of extreme and sudden life-threatening situations, it is reasonable to assume that no stimulus is a stressor to all individuals exposed to it (Appley & Trumbull, 1967). Whether stress develops depends greatly on how the person perceives and appraises the stimulus, in combination with other personality variables. Therefore, the above occupational conditions are not invariably stressors for all law enforcement personnel. Also, the same individual may enter into a stress condition in response to one presumably stressful situation and not to another. Accordingly, a great variety of different environmental conditions are capable of producing a stress state. Not only are there differences in the ways persons perceive and appraise the stimulus, but also differences in the various strategies they use to adapt to stress, as we shall be noting throughout the remainder of the chapter.

## WHEN ADAPTATION FAILS

In this section we will consider some of the more common maladaptive patterns found among the general population and related to law enforcement personnel. The reader should be forewarned that law enforcement is one of the most difficult professions about which to gather information regarding failures to adapt. Although it is generally assumed that the field has higher levels of stress because of its peculiar demands, consistent and valid statistics on maladaptive behavior are lacking. Unfortunately, most of the data are based on anecdotal or incomplete clinical or agency information. This procedural information is valuable, but it should be balanced with validation evidence in the form of experimental studies, which are to this point lacking.

**Alcoholism.** It has been reported by various sources, but not confirmed, that approximately 20 percent of law enforcement personnel have a serious drinking problem (Somodevilla, 1978), that this approximate figure is on the increase (Shook, 1978), and that it is more common in the older, more experienced police officer, over age 40, with fifteen to twenty years of service (Unikovic & Brown, 1978). Although some police departments would concur with these statistics, many others would deny them. Despite the quibbling about the incidence rate of alcoholism and the denial that it is a major problem, that it does exist is not in question.

**Depression.** Behavioral scientists often divide depression into two major categories: endogenous and reactive. The first refers to features which are believed to be precipitated by some biochemical or physiological imbalance. It is commonly held that a predisposition to this is transmitted genetically. Drugs such as Lithium have been successful in rectifying this imbalance and in substantially alleviating the depression. Endogenous depression, however, is believed to account for only a small proportion of depressive features. In recent years, there has been a good deal of criticism of physicians and psychiatrists who almost blanketly prescribe drugs for depressive reactions.

Reactive depression, which is due to stress from a traumatic event or a series of negative events, is far more common. Loss of a loved one, loss of a job, loss of self-esteem, or a series of small failures can all precipitate reactive depression, which appears to have no fundamental physiological cause. Reactive depression, then, is essentially a psychological phenomenon directly related to psychological stress, and it affects law enforcement personnel (and the general population) far more often than endogenous depression does. When we refer to depression henceforth, it will be considered a maladaptive response to psychological stress rather than an illness.

We often think of depression as a mood disorder, and in fact its symptoms do include apathy and disinterest, sometimes verbally expressed. It is also often cognitive, in the sense that a person has thoughts and feelings of helplessness or hopelessness ("What's the use of trying," "Life is not worth living," and so on). Although these mood-cognition symptoms are probably the most important indicators, other things also signify depression. There are, for example, behavioral and somatic manifestations. The depressed person may withdraw socially, may procrastinate at tasks, may overeat or undereat consistently, may not be able to perform his or her role. There also may be gastrointestinal disturbances or sleep problems.

Any or all of the three modes—somatic, mood-cognition, and behavioral—may exist in the individual. Note, however, that the degree or severity of the depression is not necessarily indicated by the number or frequency of behavioral or bodily symptoms. Thus, it is possible for a person to be very severely depressed and only manifest it cognitively. In fact, recent research by Martin Seligman (1975) has indicated that how people feel about themselves and their competence in relation to their environment (especially the social environment) appears to be the most crucial indicator of how widespread and intense their depression will be.

**Antecedents of depression.** There is growing support for the view that reactive depression is partly due to a learned reaction to life events. One of the most crucial antecedents of depression seems to be a lack of mastery over one's environment, or a feeling that one has little control over what happens to oneself (Seligman, 1975). With successive failures over an extended period of time, a person "learns" that his or her behavior does not seem to have any or much effect on events in his or her life. This learned helplessness may begin as early as childhood, since children are especially susceptible to feelings of not being able to control their lives. If the child is not provided with sufficient opportunity to exercise some decisionmaking and competence building skills, that child may be unable to achieve the mastery expectations that are so important in later life.

Acquisition of social skills is another important element for gaining control of one's situation. Conversing with others on a give-and-take basis without monopolizing the discussion is an example of a social skill for which the person receives approval from others. Lack of social skills reduces the opportunity for the child—and later the adult—to receive recognition, while allowing more time to be preoccupied with negative personal thoughts.

Thus, in some instances the antecedents of depression occur in childhood, where the individual has first learned helplessness and inability to adapt to stress. The helplessness may become a pattern continued into adulthood. Depression, therefore, happens as a result of poor social skills and adaptation skills, and not vice-versa. However, depression does not always begin in childhood. The adult who meets a long series of personal failures which seem to accent personal incompetence may have sufficient cause to encounter feelings of helplessness and depression.

Depression is also often preceded by difficulty in adapting, not only to major stress events (which require "coping" and which may occur very rarely), but also to less dramatic but routine stressors. For example, among the most consistently reported stressors as antecedents of reactive depression are consistent arguments with a spouse or otherwised disturbed interpersonal relationships. McLean (1976) calls these sources of small, repetitive personal and social frustrations *microstressors*. He theorizes that the basis for much reactive depression is an accumulation of these microstressors, which may be present in the lives of many people. That is, depression may not be primarily a result of a heavy or serious failure or loss (called a macrostressor), but rather of an accumulation of many small failures and frustrations. McLean cites six specific sources of microstressors:

1. *A reduction in behavioral productivity.* A retiree with nothing to do can experience considerable strain. Sometimes activity is deliberately reduced because there seems little reward for undertaking it. A housewife may reduce her domestic output because no one appreciates or even notices her efforts, for example.
2. *Lack of interpersonal communication.* Communication with others allows us to obtain personal feedback, essential for our self-esteem. Thus, the macrostress which invariably occurs with the loss of a loved one can be compounded by the microstress that can occur if the surviving mate becomes isolated from other personal contacts.

   Law enforcement officers often complain that only other police personnel understand the nature of their job. It is not uncommon to find in many cases that their after-hours contacts are restricted to a close circle of friends who are occupational colleagues. Part of this is also due to the reinforcement they get from one another. The nature of the law enforcement job often produces interpersonal isolation from other members of society, however. This lack of communication with others, especially with spouse or family, is potentially a good foundation for depression.

   Many police personnel are familiar with the "John Wayne syndrome" mentioned early in this chapter, named after the strong law-and-order image that actor portrayed. New and naive officers are especially likely to display characteristics of the syndrome, which include overseriousness, emotional withdrawal, coldness, cynicism, authoritarian attitudes, and a heavy reliance on peer group identification. The syndrome usually lasts three or four years, and it is believed to help the new officer adapt to the demands of the job. Because of the tendency to take the work so seriously, however, and the almost complete identification with the police role, officers with that syndrome are often distant and cold toward spouse and children (Chandler & Jones, 1979). The John Wayne syndrome, then, can produce considerable microstress.

3. *Lack of goals in one's life.* It is important for all of us to set attainable and realistic goals. Not having such goals formulated can be a source of considerable discomfort.

4. *Inadequate social interaction, distinguished here from the interpersonal communication factor mentioned above.* Here McLean is referring to inadequacy in dealing with others. If a person is brusque and offensive toward others, for example, that person's interactions will be unsatisfactory, and microstress will probably result. This differs from lack of communication in the sense that one may have adequate social interaction skills but may not have achieved a satisfactory communication relationship with others.

5. *Decisionmaking and problem solving difficulties.* When people are unable to make adequate decisions or solve small everyday problems, this becomes a stressful situation.

6. *Lack of cognitive self-control.* If the person ruminates frequently about failures or shortcomings, microstress will likely occur.

If we accept McLean's theory, the above are all sources of microstress and may eventually produce depression. Whether a person does indeed become depressed as a result of these series of microstressors appears to depend on at least three factors: 1) the degree, chronicity, and pervasiveness of the stress experiences; 2) the adaptation skills available to the person to reduce the stress; and 3) the nature and number of compensating positive experiences under the individual's control. In this connection, it is important to remind ourselves that law enforcement officers are very likely bombarded with both macrostressors and microstressors. Whether the officer actually perceives them as stressors has much to do with how chronic they will become. In many instances, the stress situations are built into the job. Therefore, it is especially important that adaptation skills and compensating positive experiences be available, else depression may set in.

Depression appears to develop in four discernible stages (McLean, 1976). First the individual faces repeated goal frustration in a variety of significant areas and/or a series of minor but consistent stressors. Second, lacking satisfactory adaptation skills, the individual feels little control over the environment. Third, because lack of control is habitual, the individual anticipates more of it in the future; there is no reason for him or her to think otherwise. At this point, the depression has set in. Finally, it is manifested in the somatic, mood-cognition, or behavioral symptoms discussed earlier.

The ultimate behavioral manifestation of depression is suicide, to which we now turn our attention. Although other factors can lead to suicide (e.g., terminal illness, killing oneself for a cause), the bulk of suicide appears to be precipitated by feelings of hopelessness and helplessness (Bedrosian & Beck, 1979).

**Suicide.** Statistics in this area are misleading, because it is often difficult to tell whether a person's death was suicidal or accidental. For example, car accidents and drownings are sometimes suspected to be self-induced, but the theory is impossible to prove. There are probably many suicide attempts that are thwarted by relatives or friends and that go unreported. Taking these facts into consideration, experts estimate the number of suicides in the U.S. to be anywhere from 25,000 to 60,000 a year; attempts are believed to number another 20,000 per year (Mears & Gatchel, 1979). When successful suicide rates are examined, the following facts emerge:

1. The male rate is three times greater than the female (Mears & Gatchel, 1979). However, more women than men attempt suicide.
2. Men commonly kill themselves by violent and lethal means, especially with firearms (Haas, 1979). Women most commonly use drugs, especially barbiturates (Haas, 1979). This may explain to some extent why men are more successful at suicide than women.
3. Suicide deaths increase linearly with age (Haas, 1979). That is, there continues to be far more death among the aged, even though there are reported increases in adolescent suicides.

When we narrow the statistics to police suicide, which is of particular interest here, we find that data are extremely difficult to obtain. To date only six published studies are available. Kroes (1976) suggests that many departments fail to report police suicides because of the stigma (the blot on the police image). Survivors do not report them because of possible loss of insurance benefits. There are frequent assertions in the literature that the actual rate is two to six times higher than the rate for other occupations (Stratton, 1978; Blackmore, 1978; Somodevilla, 1978). In an often cited, but unfortunately outdated study, police officers in 1950 were found to have the second highest suicide rate of thirty-six occupations in the United States, with only self-employed manufacturing managers and proprietors having a higher rate. The actual rate for police officers was 47.6 per year per 100,000 officers (Labovitz & Hagedorn, 1971).

The most heavily cited research was conducted by Friedman (1967), who studied in detail the cases of ninety-three New York City officers who were believed to have committed suicide between January 1, 1934 and January 1, 1940. He concluded that the annual suicide rate during the six-year period was 80 per 100,000. Heiman (1975) reports rates during the same years of 48 per 100,000 in Chicago; 51.8 per 100,000 in San Francisco; 17.9 per 100,000 in St. Louis; and 0 per 100,000 in Denver.

More recent data reported by Heiman (1975) for the period 1960–1973 was a New York rate of 19.1 per 100,000, a substantial decrease from the figures reported above. Danto (1976) reported only twelve suicides among Detroit police officers from 1968 through 1976.

Dash and Reiser (1978) compared incidents of police suicide with a national rate which in 1975 was about 12.6 per 100,000, including both males and females. Studying the Los Angeles Police Department over a seven-year period, they found a rate of 8.1 per 100,000. That figure was also below the California average, which was 16 per 100,000 for both sexes together during the same year.

What do these statistics tell us? Very little in the way of definitive information. In spite of assumptions or sketchy reports of high suicide rates among police officers, there is little research evidence to support this. Recent evidence, in fact, suggests that the rates may be lower than the national average for males. Any conclusions we make can only be speculative, except for the conclusion that more detailed research and better reporting systems are needed.

If suicide rates for law enforcement personnel are indeed lower than in the past, this may be due to a number of factors, such as a more sophisticated screening procedure and rigorous evaluation at times of hiring, increased use of stress-awareness training, greater use of psychological or psychiatric consultants in police departments, and better police training, enabling officers to feel more competent at their jobs. On the other hand, the few studies available may show decreasing rates because police suicides are too often unreported by departments and by families.

## PSYCHOPHYSIOLOGICAL DISORDERS

The symptoms of psychophysiological disorders are highly similar to those of physical diseases. The basic distinction between the two is made on the basis of cause. Psychophysiological disorders are caused primarily by psychological factors, such as psychological stress, while physical illnesses are caused by non-psychological agents, such as viruses or faulty diet. It should be realized, however, that recent research has indicated that almost all physical illnesses are either caused, exacerbated, or prolonged to some extent by psychological factors (Mears & Gatchel, 1979).

While recent literature on law enforcement often asserts that there is a high rate of psychophysiological disorder among police officers, documentation and well-designed research to substantiate the claims are noticeably lacking. Much of the information, again, is based on procedural evidence alone. For example, it is not unusual to find statements such as "Cardiovascular disorders and other health problems are very frequent and psychosomatic illnesses in general are rampant in police work" (Somodevilla, 1978, p. 111) or "The increase in emotional problems, heart trouble and other physical ailments related to job stress among police is alarming" (Hagerty, 1976, p. 9). Neither source cites a research project to validate the observations.

Certainly, if law enforcement is a highly stressful occupation, we should expect a relatively high incidence of psychophysiological disorders as a result of the chronically high stress. Available research addressed at examining this issue is sketchy, fragmented, and often poorly designed. Nonetheless, the few studies that have emerged do *suggest* a positive relationship between job stress and psychophysiological disorders. Jacobi (1975) reported that police officers in his survey submitted disability claims at a rate six times greater than other employees. Fifty percent of the claims involved high blood pressure and another twenty percent lower back pains. Studies by the Los Angeles County Sheriff's Department and the U.S. Department of Health, Education and Welfare suggest that police officers are among the highest occupation in stress related to physical disorders, when compared with other occupational groups of similar age (Thomas, 1978). The Los Angeles study revealed that the three leading causes of nonaccidental disability retirement among police officers were cardiovascular disorders, back disorders, and peptic ulcers. It will be instructive, therefore, if we examine more closely some of the more commonly reported disorders of law enforcement personnel, together with the available research.

The categories of psychophysiological disorders commonly reported in the general population include:

1. Skin disorders, such as hives, acne, eczema, and an assortment of other rashes

2. Musculoskeletal disorders, such as tension headaches, muscle cramps, and some forms of arthritis
3. Respiratory disorders, such as bronchial asthma
4. Cardiovascular disorders, such as hypertension (high blood pressure), heart attacks, paroxysmal tachychardia (palpitations of the heart), vascular spasms, migraine headaches
5. Gastrointestinal disorders, such as peptic ulcers, chronic gastritis, colitis, and indigestion

Musculoskeletal, cardiovascular, and gastrointestinal disorders appear to be the most commonly reported among law enforcement officers, and we will pay closer attention to them. However, before we do, the reader should be aware of several considerations about psychophysiological symptoms.

First, it is often believed that persons afflicted with psychophysiological symptoms are not actually suffering physical ailment or discomfort, but that the symptoms are "all in the mind." The assumption is that the person is imagining or malingering. This is a misconception. Psychophysiological disorders differ from physical illnesses only in cause, as we mentioned above. They may be accompanied by pain, tissue damage, and in many cases they may cause permanent physical handicap, tissue alteration, or death.

Second, the formation of psychophysiological disorders appears to be extremely complex, with physical, social, and psychological factors interacting in a complicated way with organic and neurological predispositions. Although it is hypothesized that certain stress factors acting on some part of the body over a long period of time might develop symptoms of a particular psychophysiological disorder, it is quite well established that there are wide individual differences in what part of the body shows the disorder, to what intensity, and for how long (Ursin et al., 1978). Some individuals, because of their biological makeup and personality, may be particularly susceptible to ulcer formation under stress, while others may be highly prone to develop cardiovascular disorders.

Third, psychoanalytic or psychodynamic theory concerning psychophysiological disorders in years past offered numerous leads about cause and treatment. For example, it was theorized that repressed rage led to high blood pressure, repressed dependency to peptic ulcers, and repressed chronic anger to migraine headaches. Extensive and intensive psychobiological research in recent years has failed to support these hypotheses (Ursin et al., 1978). However, one factor which continually appears in literature is the general issue of helplessness and lack of personal control. Conditions of helplessness and lack of control in experimental animals have often precipitated an assortment of psychophysiological disorders (Seligman, 1975; Weiss, 1968, 1970, 1971; Ursin et al., 1978). Obviously, setting up similar experimental conditions with human subjects would not be condoned. However, if we are allowed to generalize the findings to the human organism, we find the strategy of mastery to be an especially important one.

Finally, the studies reported in the next section only suggest a potential relationship between the psychological stress found in police work and physical disorders which might be psychophysiological, in that a portion of the cause is not strictly organic or biological. Psychological stress does not necessarily cause physiological disorders in police officers. For example, physical stress brought on by job activity such as sitting in a patrol car for extended periods, poor eating habits, and little opportunity for rest might be a more potent cause of the reported physical ailments. Much more work needs to be done before we can conclude that the psychological stress inherent in law enforcement employment often leads to psychophysiological disorders.

**Cardiovascular disorders.** These are all the disorders related to the heart and blood vessels. In this section we shall consider briefly only three: coronary heart disease (CHD), high blood pressure, and migraine headaches. As is true for all psychophysiological disorders, the relationship between them and the occupational stress of law enforcement has only been minimally examined. Research does consistently show, however, that the cardiovascular system is highly susceptible to stress in relation to its reactivity and activation. In fact, Selye (1976) comments that psychological stress is among the most frequent causes of cardiovascular disease.

Selye further notes that many studies have demonstrated a relationship between hypertension and tensions and threats arising from interpersonal relationships in the family or at work, whereas acute, intense "mental arousal" is often involved in cardiac failure. He comments: "There appears to be little doubt that emotional stress is one of the most frequent factors in the development of high blood pressure, congestive heart failure or cardiac infarction in predisposed patients" (1976, p. 768). Moreover, cardiovascular dysfunction appears to be closely related to the organism's available options for adaptation strategy (Seligman, 1975). That is, if the organism appraises the situation as hopeless, the likelihood of cardiovascular dysfunction may be greatly increased.

In recent years behavioral scientists (e.g., Friedman & Rosenman, 1974; Glass, 1977) have carefully studied the relationship between CHD and certain personality types. These personality types have been simply labeled A, B, and C. The Type A personality pattern is competitive, achievement-oriented, driving, constantly preoccupied with job deadlines, and has a high sense of time urgency and restlessness. Type A is believed to be a style of responding designed to assist the individual to adapt to stressful life events which could threaten his or her sense of environmental control and mastery (Glass, 1977). Type B individuals manifest the opposite pattern of behavior and generally respond to life in a less hurried, relaxed fashion. Type C is characterized as having the same features as Type B, but with an added element of chronic anxiety, which promotes over-reaction to stress. As you might expect, Type A is hypothesized to have the higher susceptibility to cardiovascular disorders. However, although research has shown Type A to have an unusually high cholesterol level, a shortened blood clotting time, and some tendency for CHD (Selye, 1976), the recent, extensive research findings of David Glass (1977) indicate the relationship is much more complex than that. Personality variables are not the only element to consider when seeking causal factors for CHD. Situational variables, for example, such as the frequency and intensity of stressful life events, appear to play a very crucial role.

Do law enforcement officers have Type A personalities? Research by Caplan and his colleagues (Caplan et al., 1975) indicate they do not, if we can generalize from his small sample of 111 police officers. Few other research projects have closely examined this personality variable with police officers, and thus generalizable statements cannot be made.

Do law enforcement officers tend to be plagued by high levels of cardiovascular problems? Richard and Fell (1975) report that police officers are admitted to hospitals for cardiovascular disorders at a much higher rate than other occupations. Kroes et al. (1974) cite some evidence that hypertension is the second most frequently reported major health problem among police officers. Grenick (1973) also reports several findings of import:

- A survey of heart index found that one-fourth of the officers studied were in a category of medium to high risk for coronary heart disease.
- 15 percent of the officers had levels of cholesterol which rendered them twice as prone to coronary heart disease as persons in the general population.
- The onset of coronary strain appeared to occur early in the officers' careers.

A more recent LEAA-funded study showed that officers under 30 years of age tended to be of average risk for coronary heart disease (Gettman, 1978), while middle-aged officers were of higher than average risk.

The available research, therefore, does suggest a relationship between CHD and hypertension, but the nature of this relationship and how it compares with other occupational groups and the population in general when age and other related variables are controlled remains unanswered.

**Migraines.** At least fifteen categories of headaches were delineated in 1962 by the Ad Hoc Committee on Classification of Headaches. Among the most frequently experienced headaches are migraine and muscle-contraction or tension headaches (Bakal, 1975). The tension headache will be discussed in the musculoskeletal section.

Migraines are characterized by aching, throbbing pain, often coincident with the pulse beat, and usually on one side of the head. Migraine headaches occur with regularity within families, which suggests that they may be hereditary to some extent (Bakal, 1975). In addition, they tend to be more common in females, with the female-male ratio ranging from 1.7:1 to 4:1 (Refsum, 1968).

The physiochemical basis of migraine appears to center on the constriction and dilation of of blood vessels. It is generally accepted that migraine is associated with blood-vessel constriction in the brain during the preheadache and vessel expansion in the brain during the headache phase (O'Brien, 1971, 1973; Dalessio, 1972). Moreover, there has been good success in treating migraines with procedures emphasizing blood-vessel volume changes, such as biofeedback of finger temperature (Bakal, 1975). Through biofeedback, finger temperature can be raised during the headache phase, thereby increasing the blood volume to the peripheral regions (fingers and toes) and reducing the blood volume (vasodilation decrease) in regions of the brain.

Both migraines and tension headaches appear to be principally triggered by psychological stress (Bakal, 1975). The relationship between migraines and the occupational stress of law enforcement has received minimal attention, however. Kroes (1976) reported that headaches were the second most frequently listed minor health problem mentioned by police officers in an interview survey, but it is impossible to tell whether these were migraine or tension headaches, or both. Blackmore (1978) observed that police officers are plagued by unusually high rates of migraine headaches. However, hard data are again difficult to obtain and, as was reported for all other psychophysiological disorders, conclusions cannot be drawn. Despite the paucity of research available, the frequency of reported migraines in law enforcement in comparison to other stress-inducing occupations leads to the suspicion that the problem is a very real one.

**Peptic ulcers.** These are usually caused by excessive flow of the stomach's acid (especially hydrochloric acid), which eventually destroys portions of the stomach lining or the upper part of the small intestine or duodenum. Causal agents may include diet, various diseases, and psychological stress, but stress, working in combination with physiological neurological predispositions, is believed to be a principal factor (Lazarus, 1966; Coleman, 1976).

Ulcers, common in the general population, may be "quiet" in the sense that they cause no pain or discomfort and remain unnoticed (Mears & Gatchel, 1979). Most often, though, people feel discomfort ranging from a burning sensation to severe pain accompanied by nausea and vomiting. If the ulcer involves damage to blood vessels in the walls of the stomach, vomiting of blood may occur. If this becomes excessive, there is the possibility of hemorrhaging and even death.

Contemporary research strongly indicates that ulceration is most likely to occur under stress, when people feel events are unpredictable or aversive and out of their control (Seligman, 1975; Weiss, 1968, 1970, 1971; Ursin et al., 1978). Thus, persons who feel they have little influence over their fate are more likely to develop peptic ulcers than those who perceive themselves as more in control of their lives. However, we must continue to keep in mind the added factor of biological predisposition, without which stress probably will not be manifested in an ulcerative condition.

Since the job demands of police work are often unpredictable and ambiguous, especially for the less trained officer, we would expect a high incidence of ulcers. After studying 2,300 officers in twenty departments, Blackmore (1978) reported that police officers are among the highest of all occupations in reporting stomach disorders, especially ulcers. Kroes, Margolis and Hurrell (1974) found that 32 percent of police officers interviewed reported gastrointestinal disorders and that police officers suffer from ulcers at a significantly higher rate than the general population.

This is hardly enough information to conclude that the situation is representative of police officers as a whole, however. More data are needed. Specific figures remain unavailable, and we know little about the course of the reported ulcerations. Such factors as length of time on the job before the ulcers occurred and personality and background characteristics of the individuals must be uncovered. Until this is done, we face the quagmire of suspecting something must be true without having validating evidence to confirm the suspicion.

**Musculoskeletal disorders.** There is little doubt that stress causes muscular tension (Selye, 1976). In fact, muscular tension is a component of the reaction to stress clinically referred to as "anxiety." Chronic or sustained muscular tension is directly related to a wide variety of muscular aches and pains, including tension headaches and backaches.

Tension or muscle-contraction headaches appear to arise from sustained tension of skeletal muscles about the face, scalp, neck, and shoulders (Martin, 1972). It is usually experienced as sensations of tightness and persistent band-like pain located bilaterally in the back or front of the head or both (Bakal, 1975).

Back pain arises from a wide variety of causes, one of which may be muscular tension in reaction to stress. This is especially true for low back pain (Gentry, Shows & Thomas, 1974), a problem apparently encountered frequently in law enforcement (Kroes, 1976).

Unfortunately, no published studies are available that have examined tension or musculoskeletal disorders in law enforcement compared to other occupational groups. Most of the claims of high incidence are reported informally or anecdotally and are often subject to multiple interpretations.

## ■ Summary and Conclusions

Although it is a commonly held assumption that police officers are conservative, rigid, dogmatic, or insensitive, the existence of any "police personality" has yet to be supported. Police officers as a group exhibit personality characteristics not unlike those of the general population. There is evidence that many officers display one component of the authoritarian personality—namely, conservatism—but it is unclear whether this feature is developed on the job or whether police work attracts individuals with a conventional, cautious approach to the world.

Police officers are the first-line participants in the judicial system, and as such, they often determine what cases will encounter the rest of the system. Their ability to exercise discretion effectively becomes an important aspect of their work. We saw in this chapter that discretion, especially with respect to minor offenses, is both encouraged and shaped within the police network. This occupational socialization, which teaches each officer the acceptable way to exercise his or her judgment, is one of the implicit realities within criminal justice. Discretion is also affected by the acts of other participants in the system, like the various attorneys, the judge, supervisors, and even the perpetrator of a given crime.

Since psychological stress seems to appear with more intensity in law enforcement than in other occupational groups, much of this chapter was devoted to examining that phenomenon. We first adopted a definition for stress that encompasses 1) the initial perception of a stimulus as potentially harmful and 2) the strategies an individual adopts to adapt to the resulting discomfort. There is no completely satisfactory, objective way to measure psychological stress, although physiological and subjective methods are often used. In general, an attempt is made to measure the individual's appraisal of a situation and his or her response to it.

Stress in law enforcement can develop from a variety of situations, some seemingly minor (microstressors) and others far more taxing (macrostressors). It is a generally accepted maxim that a series of microstressors can be as debilitating as one major catastrophe. Alienation from society, police community relations, role conflict, job unpredictability, and interpersonal relationships were all listed as possible sources of microstress. Just because an officer experiences these difficulties, however, does not mean he or she will be confronted with stress to the point where it inhibits adequate job performance. Situational and personality variables help determine the severity of the stress. Often, a person's general feelings of competence or motivation to overcome a crisis will lessen the intensity of stress. Individual differences in nervous system characteristics also account for the differential effects of stress-producing stimuli.

We discussed examples of what can occur when an individual fails to adapt satisfactorily to stress. Alcoholism, suicide, depression, and psychophysiological problems were examined individually. It is important to note that, although police officers are often assumed to exhibit these failures to adapt, there are not enough data to support this assumption. Although it is difficult to obtain information about police alcoholism, depression, suicide, and psychophysiological problems, we have no reason to believe they occur more frequently in law enforcement than in the general population.

# ■ Key Concepts and Principles, Chapter 3

Discretionary behavior in law

Psychological stress and its role in the judicial system

Stressors

Occupational socialization in law enforcement

Open and closed judicial systems

State and trait anxiety

Ways of measuring stress

Psychological and physiological indicators of stress

Microstressors

John Wayne syndrome

Authoritarianism

Type A versus Type B personalities

# 4

# Criminal Law, Civil Law, and Mental Health Law

☐   In this and the following four chapters we will begin to apply psychology to the problems and administration of the courts. To give some structure to the discussion, we will focus upon three major phases of the judicial process: pretrial procedures, trial, and sentencing (although not always in that order). What can and cannot contemporary psychology contribute to each of these areas? In the pretrial phases, psychological assessment is often used as evidence in competency hearings, or psychological consultation is sought by attorneys preparing to select a jury. During the trial phase, psychologists testify on matters like criminal responsibility, eyewitness testimony, or the emotional stability of a litigant. In the sentencing phase, judges often use the recommendations of psychologists and other social scientists to help them choose from alternatives like prison, suspended sentences, probation, or some form of treatment.

The above highlights reflect the major and traditional roles of the forensic and clinical psychologist in the courts, but they do not include all the roles. Increasingly, forensic and clinical psychologists are becoming involved with social action research and research evaluation, family law, custody dispositions, crisis management in forensic settings, and efforts to understand criminal behavior before, during, and after the trial process. Although we will not direct much attention to these areas in this chapter, some will be covered in later sections of the text.

A primary objective of this chapter is to differentiate the basic philosophies and processes characteristic of criminal law, civil law, and mental health law. This will require a clear understanding of the distinction between police power and *parens patriae* power, two doctrines which have long been the philosophical underpinnings of court decisions when the mental or psychological status of defendants or affected persons are questioned. The chapter will also introduce the reader to the court system and to issues surrounding dangerousness and expert testimony.

# ■ Organization of the Courts

The United States Constitution provides for the existence of two major court systems, federal and state. Federal courts, sometimes called federal constitutional courts, have authority over matters arising from violations of federal laws, including violations of rights believed to be explicitly or implicitly guaranteed by the Constitution. There are three major levels of the federal court system: the United States district or trial courts, the United States (circuit) courts of appeals, and the United States Supreme Court. State courts often parallel these three levels, but there are wide variations in number and jurisdiction, especially at the lower court levels.

## THE FEDERAL COURTS

The federal district courts carry most of the workload in the federal system. There are ninety-four U.S. district courts, with some states having two or three to handle the higher frequency of litigation, but at least one federal district court exists in every state. Three states—California, Texas, and New York—have four district courts each. Included among the ninety-four courts are district courts located in Puerto Rico, the Canal Zone, Guam, and the Virgin Islands.

Each federal district has from one to twenty-seven judges, depending upon the volume of cases which must be decided. Each district also has a clerk's office, a U.S. Marshal's office, one or more bankruptcy judges, U.S. magistrates, a U.S. Attorney's office, probation officers, and court reporters.

The United States is also divided into eleven geographically defined jurisdictions or circuits. Each sector has a U.S. Court of Appeals, consisting of between three and fifteen judges, depending upon the amount of work required in the circuit. The judge with the longest service, who has not reached his or her seventieth birthday, is chief justice. The primary purpose of the Court of Appeals is to review decisions made by the district courts within its jurisdiction. Unsatisfied litigants in a district court usually have a right to have the decisions in their cases reviewed by the Court of Appeals in their circuit. In addition to reviewing district court decisions, Courts of Appeals frequently review cases heard by tax courts and the various federal administrative agencies to correct possible errors of law.

The highest court in the land, the U.S. Supreme Court, consists of nine Justices appointed for life by the President, with the advice and consent of the U.S. Senate. One Justice is designated the Chief Justice, and the Court is usually referred to collectively by the name of that chief—the Burger Court or the Warren Court, for example.

The Supreme Court begins to meet on the first Monday of October each year and usually continues in session until June. Although what the Court may hear is defined by Congress, the Justices are given nearly complete control over what they choose to hear and review, within that framework. The cases the Justices select are usually those of litigants who are not satisfied with decisions rendered by federal or state appellate courts and which the Court believes address important, unanswered questions. An unsuccessful litigant or defendant may request review of his or her case by filing a writ of *certiorari*, a legal document summarizing the facts of the case, the decision of the

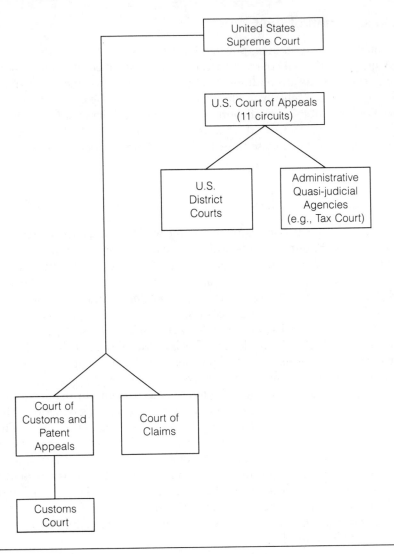

**Figure 4–1** ■ Federal judicial system.

lower court, and setting forth an argument as to why the Court should hear the case. About 5,000 appeals are filed each year, but most are disposed of by the brief decision that the subject matter is either not proper or is not of sufficient importance to warrant full Court review. On the average, the Court decides to hear about 150 to 200 cases each year. At least four of the nine Justices must vote to hear a case, a decision known as granting *cert*.

In addition to the pyramid of courts presented here, the federal system includes other courts of limited jurisdiction which handle only certain kinds of cases (Figure 4–1). For example, the U.S. Court of Claims handles lawsuits against the U.S. government, while the U.S. Tax Court deals with cases arising from disputes concerning the Internal Revenue Code.

## STATE COURTS

State courts follow roughly the same pyramidal structure as the federal courts—trial courts, intermediate appellate courts, and a state supreme court. The process and administration of these state courts vary widely from state to state, as do the state laws under which they operate. In fact, state court systems are so varied that they may justifiably be considered fifty different systems.

State courts have a general, unlimited power to decide almost every type of case, subject only to the limitations of state law. Therefore, state courts are the place where most of the legal business of American society begins and ends. A case begins in the lower or trial court, as dictated by statute—statutes being laws enacted by a legislative body and set forth in a formal document. The higher or appellate state courts are created to deal with questions of law which arose in the lower court, often during the trial process. These questions are presented in the form of appeals, and they typically take one of two forms: a trial *de novo* (a new trial), or a more limited review of specific aspects of a trial proceeding. For example, a defendant might argue that his case received unfair publicity and seek a new trial. Another defendant may seek a review of certain procedural irregularities he claims were inherent in his trial. Most state appellate courts have great discretion in deciding whether or not to handle an appeal, whereas the U.S. Courts of Appeals must consider all cases properly presented for review.

Whether a case should be introduced into the federal or state court system is often a matter not easily settled. Disputes which can be resolved by federal courts are set forth in Section 2 of Article III of the U.S. Constitution.

> The judicial Power shall extend to all Cases, in Law and Equity, arising under this Constitution, the Laws of the United States, and Treaties made, or which shall be made, under their Authority;—to all Cases affecting Ambassadors, other public Ministers and Consuls;—to all Cases of admiralty and maritime Jurisdiction;—to Controversies to which the United States shall be a Party;—to Controversies between two or more States;—between a State and Citizens of another State;—between Citizens of different States;—between Citizens of the same State claiming Lands under Grants of different States, and between a State, or the Citizens thereof, and foreign States, Citizens or Subjects.

Therefore, it appears that the federal courts cannot decide every case which arises, but only those which the Constitution and the laws enacted by Congress allow. However, Section 2, Article III is ambiguous enough to engender considerable disagreement about appropriate jurisdiction, so that in many instances litigants choose either the state or federal system.

# ■ Types of Law

Laws are often classified according to their content or origin. Legal scholars frequently try to make a distinction between *substantive* law and *procedural* or adjective law, but the lines of separation are difficult to draw.

Broadly, substantive laws define the rights and responsibilities of members of a given society as well as the prohibitions of socially sanctioned behavior. For example, substantive criminal laws prohibit homicide, rape, assault, arson, burglary, and other crimes against personal safety and property security. The Constitution sets forth many of the fundamental rights of U.S. citizens. These Constitutional proclamations are sometimes called "substantive due process" rights.

Procedural laws outline the rules for the administration, enforcement, and modification of substantive laws in the mediation of disputes. In short, procedural law exists for the sake of substantive law. It is intended to give litigants or disputing parties the feeling that they are being fairly dealt with, and that all are given a reasonable chance to present their side of an issue before an impartial tribunal (James, 1965).

Another common classification distinguishes between Constitutional law, case law, statutory law, and administrative law. *Constitutional law* provides the guidelines for the organization of national, state, and local government, and it outlines the limitations on the exercise of government power. *Case law* usually refers to "judge-made" law developed through precedents set in previous judicial decisions of cases not covered or addressed directly by statute. Thus, case law is based on the earlier decisions of courts, and these decisions are directly applicable to the dispute at issue. The principles outlined in the written decision become precedent under the doctrine *stare decisis* (stand by past decisions). The principles are perpetuated unless a court can show "good cause" for overturning or repudiating a decision or a principle in later cases. *Stare decisis* is more a matter of policy than a rigid rule to be mechanically followed in subsequent cases dealing with similar legal questions.

*Statutory law* refers to written laws (statutes) or acts whose exact words have been drafted and approved by a federal, state, or local legislature. Statutes are what most citizens mean when they refer to "law." They outline what crimes will be considered felonies or misdemeanors, for example, or what factors entitle a person to initiate a civil suit.

*Administrative law* is created by administrative agencies of national, state, or local governments in the form of regulations, orders, and decisions. Zoning law, public education regulations, and licensing and utilities regulations: all are typical subjects of state and local control. At the national level, hundreds of volumes of the Code of Federal Regulations contain rules made by federal agencies pursuant to the rule-making power delegated to them by Congress. The Internal Revenue Codes that spell out what is allowed and not allowed in income tax deductions are good examples of administrative law.

Although it is wise for students to be familiar with the above classifications, the distinction we are most interested in making here is that between civil, criminal, and mental health law, each of which may be found in the four major classifications outlined above. For example, crimes may be defined by statutes or by administrative agencies, civil actions may be based on administrative rules or state laws, and the relatively new concept of "mental health law" encompasses deprivations of rights guaranteed by the Constitution, or challenges to existing administrative procedures. Mental health law may be regarded as an offshoot of civil law, but it has enough unique characteristics to merit a separation, as we will discuss shortly. For the moment, it is important to distinguish between civil and criminal law.

# ■ Civil and Criminal Law

The distinction between these two types of law rests primarily on the subject matter of a case. A dispute between private persons or organizations becomes a case at civil law. Criminal law is concerned with crimes against the public order and the appropriate punishment for such violations.

Essentially, civil law governs the relations between individuals and defines their legal rights. Examples of civil cases include breach of contract suits, libel suits, divorce actions, or various other actions where one or both parties seek legal redress for an alleged wrong. Cases at civil law are often complex and difficult, and judicial discretion plays a major role in their disposition. Moreover there are few statutes defining violations. Therefore, enforcement of the solution is often nonexistent, or at best difficult to guarantee. Because most cases reaching the courts are civil rather than criminal, the backlog of civil disputes is very high, and the process of achieving settlement is tedious.

A case at criminal law is invariably brought by or in the name of some legally constituted government authority at either the federal, state, or local level. In bringing a criminal law case to court, the proper government authority (called the prosecution) accuses a defendant (or defendants) of a specific violation of law as defined by statute. Like civil cases, criminal cases are backlogged, but the courts are expected to handle them as expeditiously as possible to insure that the due process rights of the defendants are not abridged.

## THE LEGAL PROCESS

The legal process in a criminal case begins when a crime is reported and evidence begins to accrue. For major federal crimes and for some state violations, grand juries are used to weigh evidence and decide whether an individual should be formally charged with an offense. In the absence of a grand jury, a suspect may be brought before a lower court judge and arraigned. The arraignment is the legal proceeding during which the individual is formally charged with an offense. The judge then asks if the person understands the charge and informs him or her of the right to counsel. At this point, it is not unusual for minor offenders to plead guilty and receive an immediate fine or sentence.

If the defendant pleads not guilty, the judge must decide whether to set bail, confine the person, or release him or her on his or her own recognizance. This decision is made after consideration of the nature and circumstances of the offense, the accused's background, and recommendations from the prosecutor or other relevant individuals. If a bail amount is set and cannot be posted, the person is placed in or returned to jail.

The not-guilty plea sets the trial process in motion. The next step is one or more pretrial preliminary hearings, where some witnesses, arresting officers, and other parties may present evidence. The judge also decides at this point what evidence may be admissible at the time of the trial.

During the preliminary hearing or hearings, and between these and the trial, extensive negotiating and plea bargaining often take place, with the result that cases rarely get to the trial stage. An estimated 90 percent of the defendants charged with major offenses either plead guilty at the outset or change to guilty pleas during the hearing stages or between the preliminary hearings and the trial date (Williams et al., 1976; Miller, McDonald & Cramer, 1978). It is interesting that inmates at major correctional facilities freely speak of the dangers of going through the actual trial process ("blow trial") and admit to active attempts at plea bargaining at any point prior to the trial. We will discuss the trial process later in this chapter and again in Chapter 5, when we cover expert testimony and determinations of criminal responsibility.

The legal process in civil cases has very few parallels to the above. When one citizen sues another, there are no formal charges, preliminary hearings, indictments, or pleas. Like criminal cases, however, civil suits involve extensive negotiation between parties before they see the inside of a courtroom; often, the cases are settled well before the trial date.

## FUNDAMENTAL PURPOSE

Criminal law also differs from civil law in its fundamental purpose. Civil law is designed to settle disputes, or to make the "victim whole" through monetary awards or injunctive relief (a court order to one party to cease some activity, such as harassing another). Criminal law is designed to punish those who violate rules and regulations created to preserve the public safety and order. Thus, while civil law tries to be remedial in nature, criminal law inflicts penalty.

## CRIMINAL RESPONSIBILITY

Most crimes require the commission or omission of some specified act. However, the commission or omission of an act designated criminal, standing alone, is usually not a punishable crime unless it can be shown that the persons accused of committing criminal acts conducted themselves in a manner through which the law would hold them responsible. This requires proof that actions were deliberate and that a particular state of mind existed. Therefore, punishable crimes usually require an act (*actus rea*) and a specified state of mind (*mens rea*).

We have used "usually" in the above paragraph in describing the two requirements of a punishable crime because there are several exceptions to this rule. For example, traffic violations only require the existence of the act and not the intent. However, the more serious the crime, the more likely the requirement of a specified state of mind before the accused can be held responsible or culpable. It should also be recognized that the act and the mental state or intent must exist simultaneously. The California Penal Code is representative of this: "In every crime or public offense there must exist a union, or joint operation, of act and intent, or criminal negligence." In most instances, therefore, the law will not punish someone for committing prohibited acts unless it can be shown that the necessary mental elements or *mens rea* existed at the time the act was committed. In other words, the person is held criminally responsible if it can be shown that the accused had "evil" or "criminal" intent during the commission or omission of an act.

A bewildering array of terminology exists in the area of criminal responsibility or culpability. For example, the words culpability, criminal intent, excuse, state of mind, criminal negligence, recklessly, knowingly, *mens rea*, intentionally, willfully, and maliciously are used with regularity and often interchangeably. The confusion is especially apparent in the state statutes. We will confine our discussion to the Federal Criminal Code, which has been in the process of development over the past fifteen years (S. 1437; Criminal Code Reform Act of 1977).

The Code recognizes four culpable mental states, classified by degree. Guilty persons have either acted intentionally, knowingly, recklessly, or negligently, and their sentences presumably reflect these degrees of culpability. An act is considered *intentional*, performed with the highest degree of culpability, if it was the individual's "conscious objective or desire to engage in the conduct (or cause the result)." That is, if the act was done on purpose, it was done intentionally. The second degree of culpability is *knowing*, a mental state which exists when accused persons are aware of the nature of their conduct, or if they are aware or believe that the conduct is substantially certain to cause the result. The distinction between acting intentionally and acting knowingly is a narrow one, but the distinction enables the judiciary to assess criminal responsibility in particular crimes. The court's chore is to assess the main direction of a person's conduct versus the anticipated side effects of that conduct. For instance, a landlord who burns down his apartment building for the purpose of collecting insurance does not necessarily desire the death of the occupants, but he is substantially certain the death will occur. The main direction of his act is to collect insurance, not to murder, but a sidelight is his full realization that the fire will result in death and injury. He *intended* to set the fire to collect insurance and *knowingly* murdered the occupants.

The third culpable mental state is *recklessness*. A person is reckless if he or she is aware of but disregards the risks involved in a situation, and "the disregard of the risk constitutes a gross deviation from the standard of care a reasonable person would exercise under the circumstances" (Criminal Code Reform Act of 1977, p. 60). Recklessness involves conscious risk taking and the awareness that there is some probability (not substantial certainty) that damage or injury will result from the behavior. If the landlord set fire to the building during school vacation, believing his tenants were away, he would likely be acting recklessly.

The fourth culpable mental state and that which represents the lowest degree of criminal responsibility is *negligence*. A person's state of mind is negligent "if he ought to be aware of a risk that a circumstance exists or that a result will occur and his failure to perceive the risk constitutes a gross deviation from the standard of care a reasonable person would exercise in the situation" (Criminal Code Reform Act of 1977, p. 61). A negligent act, unlike an intentional, knowing, or reckless act, does not involve a state of awareness. Rather, it occurs when the accused should have been aware of the substantial and unjustifiable risks involved in the act. Any reasonable person would have known of the risk, and the act therefore represents a "gross deviation" of conduct.

Proof of which if any of these mental states existed at the time of the offense is often difficult to obtain. In most cases, the fact finders are allowed to presume or infer the accused's state of mind at the time he or she committed the act. A judgment is made about the accused's mental state, based upon what was allegedly done and said and all the circumstances surrounding the act. We will consider the validity of determining mental states through clinical judgment in Chapter 5.

## PUNISHMENT

States are free to call criminal violations by any name they choose and to impose whatever punishment for violation they wish, providing the punishment does not infringe upon rights guaranteed by the Eighth Amendment, prohibiting excessive bail, fines, or cruel and unusual punishments. Most jurisdictions make a distinction between felonies and misdemeanors, but the bases for the distinction vary. Some states make the demarcation on the basis of whether the imprisonment takes place in a maximum security state prison or a minimum security local jail. Other jurisdictions consider the length of imprisonment allowable for the crime. If the maximum sentence is one year or less, it may be labeled a misdemeanor; all offenses which carry a minimum of one year and a maximum of life may constitute felonies. Some jurisdictions use a combination of both approaches to define felonies and misdemeanors.

The Federal Criminal Code labels offenses by the length of sentences allowable. A misdemeanor is represented by a prison sentence ranging from thirty days to one year. A felony authorizes terms ranging from three years to life. A third category of crimes, infractions, carry a maximum sentence of five days. Disobedience of an order issued by a public servant or a law enforcement officer to move, disperse, or refrain from specified activity is an example of an infraction. Failure to move away from the scene of a fire is a more specific example. Short sentences are believed appropriate for some offenders because of the "shock value" they possess; it is presumed that a brief period in a prison setting will have a significant deterrent effect. In addition, brief imprisonment may be the only available punishment for "indigents" under some circumstances.

The reader should be aware that whether a crime is a felony or a misdemeanor is governed in federal law by the *maximum* punishment that can be imposed by the courts, and not by the punishment that is actually imposed. The fact that an offender receives a suspended sentence and probation rather than the prescribed maximum penalty of ten years does not make the crime any less a felony.

The courts have considerable freedom in the nature of the sentence handed out to a convicted offender. At the federal level, the criminal code permits forfeiture, restitution or reparation, public notice, and the more commonly used fines, probation, or imprisonment. The practice of forfeiture was abolished by Congress in 1790, but it was reinstated in 1970 as a penalty for certain organized crime cases. The provision gives law enforcement authorities greater latitude to deal with organized crime by separating the leaders from their sources of economic power and influence. For example, if a defendant is found guilty of racketeering, part of the penalty may be to forfeit any property constituting his interest in the racketeering syndicate or enterprise involved in the illegal activity. Consequently, property used for the purpose of conducting illegal criminal activity may be confiscated by the government and sold, although the law does not permit confiscation of the offender's personal property.

The court may also order the offender to make restitution or reparation to aggrieved parties for actual damages or loss caused by the offense. For example, a court may require an offender to repay all or part of the money acquired through an embezzlement scheme. In certain cases the criminal code also permits the court to give notice or explanation of a conviction to a segment of the public affected by the conviction or financially interested in the subject of the offense. For example, if an industry is found guilty of fraudulent claims which caused property damage, the court may decide to make the nature of the offense widely known in order to expedite lawsuits by affected parties.

The above sentences are rarely handed down; sentences more commonly involve fines, probation, confinement, or some combination of the three. Fines are specified as an authorized form of sentence for virtually all offenses, but they are most often imposed upon corporations and other organizations, including government agencies, when it is difficult to accuse any one person. However, the amounts are hardly in keeping with inflation or equivalent in severity to incarceration. Probation involves the suspension of an imposed sentence, but with the requirement that the person remain in close contact with law enforcement authorities. Probation can be administered for all offenses except those which are punishable by death or life imprisonment. The maximum term allowable for a probation is five years. Confinement is most often the most severe penalty for criminal behavior, and most offenses carry a provision to incarcerate as an appropriate punishment if the court deems it just. Confinement and its psychological effects will be discussed in more detail in Chapter 11.

At this point, we will turn our attention to an area that appears to straddle the line between criminal and civil law, contains elements of both, and is a rapidly developing component of the judicial process—mental health law. It is also the area that psychologists are most apt to encounter in their dealings with the courts, particularly the civil courts.

# ■ Mental Health Law

In almost every area of civil and criminal law, individuals believed to be mentally disordered are treated differently from those regarded as normal (Morse, 1978a). In general, society and the legal profession think that "normal" people have considerable freedom of choice and personal control over their lives, while disordered people, because of "mental illness," presumably have limited or no control over their behavior. The legally relevant behavior of the disordered is believed to be a product of their illness and not of their free, rational choice.

When a state exercises its power to deprive individuals of liberty and compel them to accept treatment, either in their own best interest or for society's protection, this is called involuntary civil commitment. States wishing to assert this power must first develop commitment statutes that articulate standards and procedures to be followed prior to and during commitment. Most such statutes require proof of the existence of a mental illness, defect, or disorder and some showing that there will be negative consequences of the disorder.

Because the mentally abnormal are believed to have less free choice than the normal, these special legal rules, collectively called *mental health law*, can be applied. The term covers all forms of involuntary commitment, including that following an insanity plea; incompetence to stand trial; a determination that a person is a "sexual psychopath" or "defective delinquent"; and the civil finding that a person, by reason of "mental illness," dangerousness, alcoholism, or other drug abuse can be confined for treatment or social protection or both against his or her will (Monahan, 1977). At least two of every five persons admitted to mental hospitals are classified as involuntary commitments, and it is difficult to know how many of the others chose to enter voluntarily because of the threat of commitment (Stone, 1975). All fifty states and the District of Columbia provide for involuntary civil commitment to mental institutions (Developments, 1974).

Definitions and standards vary widely from state to state, as do the procedures, which range from detailed judicial proceedings to highly discretionary administrative hearings. In most states, the commitments include two categories of confinement: emergency detention and long term involuntary commitment. Emergency detention is intended to protect individuals from serious harm to themselves or to prevent injury to others. The short-term confinement provides a "cooling off" period, during which the person recovers from immediate psychological agitation or during which arrangements are made for permanent disposition of the case. While due process and other individual rights are often suspended temporarily in these emergency situations, the second kind of confinement, involuntary commitment, must be justified with attention to more stringent standards. There is a trend in recent statutes toward limiting involuntary civil commitment to the dangerous mentally ill and a parallel trend toward restricting the type of harm that must be shown to support a finding of dangerousness (Bartol, 1981). We will return to this issue shortly.

In general, proceedings for involuntary civil commitment do not follow the format of criminal proceedings, where the adversary process is usually employed with some care. Commitment hearings are often informal and hinge around opinions of medical or psychiatric practitioners, who may or may not be present. Family members, social workers, employers or friends may also testify, but in most cases the judge makes a decision based solely on testimony or written reports from medical, psychiatric, or psychological experts. Rarely are juries present, and due process often may not be a consideration. In some jurisdictions the affected person does not attend, under the rationale that his or her condition will be aggravated by the proceedings.

When a judge allows the civil commitment, the affected person is confined for an unspecified period, until the disorder is alleviated or corrected to the satisfaction of the expert or the court or both. Statistics reveal that the average length of stay in a mental institution for all types of confinement, including voluntary and emergency, is short (Stone, 1975). An individual facing involuntary civil commitment, however, is susceptible to lifelong deprivation of rights and liberties in most states.

To evaluate the rationale behind involuntary civil commitments, we should consider some fundamental issues revolving around freedom and responsibility. Although the philosophical debate that has always raged about free will is no closer to being tamed, it must be addressed at this point. Keep in mind, during the following digression, that patients who are committed involuntarily to mental institutions have neither been charged with nor convicted of crimes against the social order.

# ■ Free Will vs. Determinism

Law is a normative enterprise that considers nearly all persons completely responsible for most of their behaviors and often for the natural and probable consequences of those acts (Morse, 1978a, 1978b). Both criminal and civil law are rooted in the concept that individuals are masters of their fate, the possessors of free will and freedom of choice. As one federal appellate court put it, "our jurisprudence . . . while not oblivious to deterministic components, ultimately rests on a premise of freedom of will" (U.S. v. Brawner, 1972, p. 995). Thus, law adheres to a common-sense psychology that behavior is simply a matter of choice and that persons in most situations freely choose their actions. Law does acknowledge that individuals are influenced to some extent by various biological, psychological, and environmental forces, but these forces do not determine how individuals behave.

*Psychological determinism* is the belief that antecedents—prior experiences or situations—determine present behavior. According to this thesis, human behavior is governed by causal laws and free will is undermined. Determinism in its extreme form, radical psychological determinism, asserts that all behavior is determined by antecedent stimuli or events and that all human behavior, therefore, is lawful. If the relevant laws are understood, behavior is also highly predictable. Although radical determinists are in the minority, almost all psychologists subscribe to the view that some degree of determinism plays a role in human behavior. In fact, a majority believe determinism plays a major role in governing human behavior.

The free will–determinism debate will be discussed again in the next chapter. However, the reader should realize at this point that while law—especially criminal law—embraces free will, psychology—especially experimental psychology—is steeped heavily in the deterministic tradition. In this sense, criminal law places total blame on a "mentally normal" person who commits a criminal act with intent, whereas most psychologists would argue that the person's past and present social environment play a major role in the criminal action. The psychologists thus raise disturbing questions about which members of our society function with the greatest "free will."

# ■ Parens Patriae

Though it is quite apparent that mental health law encompasses a wide variety of statutes and behaviors, three primary behavior components are shared by all commitment laws: need for treatment, dangerousness to others, and dangerousness to self (Morse, 1978a). The first component is based upon a *parens patriae* philosophy, the second concerns police power, and the third involves elements of both.

The concept *parens patriae* (literally, "parent of the country") has had a long and ambiguous history, dating as far back as ancient Roman law, where it was applied when the state considered the head of the family incompetent and in danger of wasting his estate. The state was then vested with the power to declare him *non compos mentis* and commit him and the estate to the care of curators or tutors designated by the praetor. *Parens patriae* was a doctrine applied selectively to persons who had valuable property holdings and other wealth, rather than to the general population.

The concept was adopted from Roman law in the eleventh century by the Anglo-Saxon king Aethelred II and developed and expanded during the early years of Edward I's reign (1272–1307) (Kittrie, 1971). The doctrine was first codified in 1324 during the reign of Edward II in the statute *Prerogativa Regis*, and it gave the king the power to protect the lands and profits of "idiots" and "lunatics" until their mental restoration (Cogan, 1970).

Researchers have debated whether *parens patriae* has been used throughout its history as a humanistic concept (Cogan, 1970) or as primarily a state fiscal policy to protect wealth and property (Halpern, 1974). Cogan (1970) notes, however, that even in *Prerogativa Regis* care was taken to limit the king's rights to the lands. For example, the king had *guardianship* of "natural fools," a term which referred to those mentally incapacitated from birth. He had only *unprofitable care* of "lunatics," those who lost their "wit" sometime after birth. Cogan (1970, p. 157) surmises that the distinction was made to prevent "enemies of the King from being declared lunatics and having the profits of their lands added to the King's treasury." However, in a well-reasoned dissertation in *State ex rel Hawks v. Lazaro* (1974), Justice Neely found that *parens patriae* was a state fiscal policy "conceived in avarice and executed without charity." Moreover, Neely asserted, "while well-meaning people frequently attempted to operate under it [*parens patriae*] for the benefit of their fellowmen, it has often been used as a justification for greedy actions on the part of relatives or for the removal of unwanted or troublesome persons." We shall see in this chapter that the statement continues to ring true.

Though *parens patriae* has been used in various contexts in American law, it has usually referred to the role of the state as the sovereign or quasi-sovereign guardian of persons under some form of legal disability. Thus it authorizes the state to substitute and enforce its decisions about what is believed to be in the best interest of persons who presumably cannot or will not protect themselves, even when these affected individuals are causing no direct harm to others. Therefore, *parens patriae* power has been used as the basis of many statutes which protect the interest of minors and establish guardianships, as well as of those which provide for the involuntary commitment of the "mentally ill" (Developments, 1974).

The *parens patriae* rationale eventually came to be used to commit both criminal and noncriminal individuals to mental institutions against their will. This development can be traced to the so-called cult of the asylum (Rothman, 1971) and cult of curability (Deutsch, 1949) periods, somewhere between 1810 and 1844 (Dershowitz, 1974). The legal and medical professions perpetuated the widespread belief (and myth) that the safe, protective, and nonstressful environment of the asylum offered the best treatment that society could offer to "lunatics." Medical superintendents claimed 90 to 100 percent cure rates for insanity (Deutsch, 1949; Dershowitz, 1974) and this prompted courts to commit involuntarily an outrageously high number of those they considered insane, even if only marginally so. As Dershowitz (1974) notes, although the asylum may be viewed in terms of humanitarian reform, had it not been invented many people would have remained at liberty without negative consequences to themselves or to society.

State legislatures traditionally have taken very seriously their duty to do something about noncriminal deviants. Consider, for example, New York State's insanity statute, enacted in 1842, barely six years after the state legislature authorized the building of the Utica asylum. "All lunatics, not only the dangerous ones, were to be confined; and they were to be confined immediately upon the occurrence of the disease. Moreover, it became the statutory 'duty of the assessors in each town' to make 'diligent inquiry' and ascertain with accuracy the number and names of all insane persons and forward their lists to the asylum at Utica" (Dershowitz, 1974, p. 808). Therefore, the statute not only allowed authorities to incarcerate the insane accused of committing deviant acts, but also urged them to "seek out the quiet insane as well so that they might be cured of their disease" (Dershowitz, 1974, p. 808). In addition, the law required confinement for at least six months. More alarmingly, this New York statute became a model for other states and reflected a shift from confinement of the "dangerous" insane to medical "treatment" of the "harmless" insane. Thus, "institutional confinement, regarded as a last resort in the eighteenth century, was emerging as a first resort in the nineteenth" (Dershowitz, 1974, p. 803).

One of the earliest American court cases illustrating the full implementation of *parens patriae* power was an 1845 decision of the Massachusetts Supreme Judicial Court, *In re Oakes*. Josiah Oakes, a 67-year-old widower and wharf builder from Cambridge, was committed by his family to McLean Asylum because he was laboring under a "hallucination of mind." His wife had died after a lengthy illness, and the court record notes that on that occasion Mr. Oakes did not demonstrate the emotions which could be expected from a person in his right mind: he did not appear perturbed. Moreover, he had begun to "manifest a change in character" about six years earlier when he began seeing a young woman of "bad character," causing anxiety in his family. His conduct at his wife's funeral showed a "perversion of mind," according to the record. It was also noted that his persistence in his intention to marry the young woman and his refusal to believe the evidence of her bad character were indicative of this perversion.

There was no record of a trial during the initial commitment process, and Oakes petitioned the court for release, claiming that his family had committed him illegally. In January 1845 the Massachusetts court sat for two days to deliberate the case. Chief Justice C. J. Shaw, considered an "enlightened liberal" (Zilboorg, 1944), delivered the opinion, which kept Oakes confined and set considerable legal precedent (see box).

Deutsch (1949, p. 422) referred to the Oakes case as "one of the most important decisions affecting the civil insane in the history of American jurisprudence." It defined for the first time in American law the justification and limitations implicit in common law concerning restraint of the insane. Not only did it specify that public and personal dangerousness were necessary but, more importantly, it also asserted the power of the state to detain individuals for remedial treatment against their will. Kittrie (1971, p. 66) comments that the Oakes case represents the "cornerstone of the full-fledged modern therapeutic state."

The Oakes opinion sheltered the *parens patriae* doctrine under the formidable guise of the "great law of humanity" logic in American jurisprudence. *Parens patriae* was now based on the benevolent assumption that someone must act as a substitute decisionmaker in the best interest of an individual evaluated incapable of making sound, rational decisions concerning his or her life and treatment (Developments, 1974). Although this may not have been intended by Chief Justice Shaw, the court opinion relied heavily on English common law and drastically eroded constitutional due process for persons believed to be lacking free will and decisionmaking capacities.

Due process is a paramount consideration in any form of involuntary commitment, because the commitment entails the loss of liberty, dignity, life style, job, living arrangements, and social relationships, and it often carries the social stigma of incompetence and emotional weakness. Due process is the right of a person to be present before the court examining his or her case; to be heard, by testimony or otherwise; and to argue or dispute any evidence brought up against him or her. Due process also suggests that a court must have proper jurisdiction and evidence to proceed with a case. It is the cornerstone of the fair distribution of justice under the criminal law and most areas of civil law.

Due process is very often superseded by *parens patriae* philosophy, however, be-

---

## ☐ IN RE OAKES

The 1845 *Oakes* case was a landmark decision in mental health law because it set precedent in at least five areas. First, according to Chief Justice Shaw, "the right to restrain an insane person of his liberty is found in the great law of humanity, which makes it necessary to confine those whose going at large would be dangerous to themselves or others." Thus, the court said it is an inherent right for society to confine "crazy" persons against their will, if it is determined that they pose a danger to society or to themselves. Second, the court asserted that insane people simply do not have free will and thus cannot decide for themselves what is in their best interest. "It is a principle of law that an insane person has no will of his own." Third, the involuntary commitment may last for as long as the "physician of the asylum" finds necessary. "The restraint can continue as long as the necessity con-

tinues. This is the limitation, and the proper limitation." This judgment probably set precedent for the current practice of indeterminate sentencing in involuntary civil commitment. Fourth, the court emphasized the distinction between civil and criminal proceedings, even where insanity was at issue. "The same rules do not apply to the same extent in this case, which apply in the case of a person who has committed a crime, and is sought to be excused on the ground of insanity." Finally, the *Oakes* case firmly entrenched the *parens patriae* rationale. "The restraint should last as long as it is necessary for the safety of himself and of others, *and* until he experiences relief from the present disease of mind . . . *and* (as long as) the care which he would meet with at the hospital, would be more conducive to his cure than any other course of treatment" (italics added).

cause it is assumed that the affected individual is not functioning with freedom and rational decisionmaking capabilities as a result of his or her mental illness. Since the illness robs the individual of free will, he or she would be unable to benefit from due process procedures. In the best interest of the person, therefore, decisionmaking about what is best for recovery is left to a normal, rational guardian appointed by the state.

Involuntary civil commitment based upon a *parens patriae* rationale increased during the late nineteenth and well into the twentieth centuries, due to the discovery of the asylum and the growth of the cult of curability. This paralleled the emergence of psychiatry, which quickly introduced itself and its self-proclaimed treatment effectiveness to the commitment process (Rothman, 1971). These developments stimulated an attitude toward civil commitment that focused upon status, or person-oriented jurisprudence, rather than behavior or act-oriented jurisprudence (Stier & Stoebe, 1979; Fuller, 1969). That is, the law in civil commitment began to emphasize what a person was like, or was likely to do, rather than what he or she had already done. The diagnosis "mental illness" alone was sufficient to justify confinement and involuntary treatment; it need not be accompanied by a criminal or antisocial act.

## ▪ Police Power

*Parens patriae* and police power can be compared on several points. Whereas *parens patriae* is used to protect individuals who presumably cannot or will not protect themselves, police power refers to the inherent obligation and responsibility of the state to protect the public from danger and harm to persons or to property. It encompasses the state's power to make laws and regulations for the protection of public health, safety, welfare, and morals (*Jacobson v. Massachusetts*, 1905, p. 24–25; Comment, Police Power in Illinois, p. 158). *Parens patriae* relates to protection of the individual and involves remedial, therapeutic, and care-giving responsibilities; police power relates to protection of society. *Parens patriae* focuses on the individual's ability to make appropriate decisions concerning his or her welfare; police power revolves around issues of dangerousness or the individual's potential threat to others. Only police power is used in criminal law, which is based upon defined standards and elaborate procedures designed to establish the occurrence and conditions of an act. Mental health law, by contrast, uses both *parens patriae* and police power rationales.

When incarceration or confinement of an individual is used to vindicate a social interest rather than to further the interest of an individual, it constitutes an exercise of police power. If this power is to be upheld as a valid action, it must protect the public interest from harm, and the means used must be reasonably necessary for the accomplishment of the purpose, not unduly oppressive to individuals. The reasonableness of an action is best determined by weighing the imposition upon the affected person against the benefits to society. Thus, if society's interest is sufficiently compelling to outweigh the deprivations imposed upon a person, the person's rights to liberty, autonomy, and freedom may be restricted under a police power rationale.

The distinction between *parens patriae* and police power becomes nebulous in situations where a person's actions are considered dangerous only to him or herself and not to society as a whole. If individuals are believed unable to make decisions in their own best interest (or are lacking free will), involuntary commitments might be undertaken with *parens patriae* power. If, on the other hand, competent but suicidal persons wish to take their own life, then commitment would likely involve a police power rationale (dangerousness to self). The distinguishing feature between the two situations appears to be the level of competence and personal freedom possessed by the person, as determined in most cases by medical experts (physicians and psychiatrists). It is difficult to justify a police power rationale in cases involving a person believed dangerous only to self, because the law chooses which allegedly dangerous behavior to discourage. For example, society permits overworking, overeating, and excessive smoking, but often does not permit riding motorcycles without helmets or using proscribed drugs.

Another difficulty in using a police power rationale to justify involuntary confinement and treatment for competent but suicidal individuals relates to predictability. The evidence is clear that the medical and mental health professions are notoriously poor predictors of who will commit suicide. Thus, experts would by far prefer to use a *parens patriae* rationale to confine individuals rather than a police power standard, which would require precise justifications. The law, however, strongly prefers that involuntary commitments be based on police power standards. So strongly did the editors of the *Harvard Law Review* feel about this that they recommended substantial restrictions on the use of *parens patriae* power. They also asserted that a competent individual's refusal to seek treatment should be considered "strictly a private concern and thus beyond the reach of all governmental power" (Developments, 1974).

## ■ The Concept of Dangerousness

Criminal law is based on a need to procure compelling evidence that a person performed a certain behavior in violation of a criminal code. As we have seen, the illegal act must have been committed, a condition referred to as *actus rea*, before legal action can be taken. However, before the person can be found guilty and punished, a second element, intention, must also be established. The individual must have intended to perform the criminal act, or it must be established that the person was of the state of mind (*mens rea*) to have evil intent.

While criminal law is based upon such past actions, mental health law is based upon both past and future actions, but especially the latter. Mental health law is more concerned with what a person might do to himself or others sometime in the future than with past behavior. Although the concept of dangerousness is an important ingredient in deciding how to deal with individuals convicted of a crime, it is *the* ingredient in mental health law when police power is invoked, since society fears individuals who are potentially dangerous to themselves or others.

There is usually little argument against state intervention when someone is decidedly "dangerous" to society. So compelling is that concept as a justification for involuntary commitment that most states specifically authorize the institutionalization of mentally ill persons who have the misfortune to be considered dangerous. There is also a statutory trend favoring the restriction of involuntary civil commitment to the dangerously mentally ill (Developments, 1974; Schoenfeld, 1977). At first glance, this trend appears to be reasonable, but closer examination reveals its ambiguity. Should the legal definitions include psychological or cognitive harm as well as physical harm?

How frequent or how severe should the harm be before legal or police intervention are justified? Is potential harm to property rather than to a person valid reason to confine an individual against his or her will? John Monahan (1981, p. 43) suggests that the term "violent behavior" is preferable to dangerousness, because it can be more clearly defined as "acts characterized by the application or overt threat of force which is likely to result in injury to people." In this sense, of course, he is recommending that we narrow our focus to include only acts designed to injure others physically.

The belief that dangerousness should be limited to acts intended to do physical harm to others is not held by the courts, however. The Maryland Court of Appeals, in *Director of Patuxent Institute v. Daniels* (1966), ruled that "one who is a menace to the property of others fits within the definition of a danger to society." Society holds that potential harm to property may be considered dangerous, although of less magnitude than potential harm to body. Although some states have rejected property harm as a ground for dangerousness, a majority still include harm to property as an indicator of such dangerousness (Developments, 1974).

Definition is not the only problem, for even if an acceptable standard of dangerousness were found, there would still be the problem of accurate prediction. The ability to predict human behavior is often a crucial focus of legal inquiry, since such prediction will influence decisions about the disposition of a case. Prediction of future violence or harm is often used as the fundamental rationale for police power and state intervention.

## CLINICAL JUDGMENT

Since prediction is a critical activity of psychologists working within the judicial system, a careful examination of clinical judgment is warranted. In Chapter 1, we indicated throughout the discussion of accuracy in predicting human behavior that the evidence was overwhelmingly in favor of the superiority of actuarial or statistical methods over clinical judgment. In this chapter, we intend to focus specifically upon clinical prediction as it relates to the concept of dangerousness. In the next chapter, we will direct attention to the problems of clinical assessment in general and to why these problems exist.

The law supposes that professional decisionmakers, such as clinical psychologists, are generally more accurate in their judgments of human behavior than are lay persons or those without certain psychological training. This presumed accuracy and expertise in understanding and predicting others is based upon the special qualifications professionals have acquired through training, experience, and the development of rules for interpreting human data. These human data serve as the input information from which interpretations and decisions are made, and they include various parameters of emotional (affective), cognitive, situational, demographic, and behavioral indicators. These input data are referred to as *predictor variables*, while the behaviors targeted for prediction are called *criterion variables*. The predictor variables are most often information gained from psychological tests, background data, and face-to-face contact from observation and interviewing. They may include age, sex, and occupation. The criterion variables may be any number of behaviors targeted for prediction; in this case, the critical variable is the global behavior of dangerousness.

Discouragingly, the available research (e.g., Wiggins, 1973) does not support the legal assumption of a direct relationship between training (or experience) and accuracy in clinical prediction. Highly trained and experienced clinicians are often no more accurate in their predictions concerning a variety of human behaviors than nonclinicians or less trained and experienced clinicians. Even in those instances where highly experienced clinicians did demonstrate greater judgmental accuracy than totally experienced laypersons, brief supplementary training of the inexperienced tended to drive their level of performance to that of the highly experienced (e.g., Goldberg, 1968).

Paul Meehl (1954, 1957, 1965, 1977) has argued convincingly and has illustrated without mercy the poor accuracy of clinicians in predicting various behaviors. In 1954, Meehl found only twenty studies which had compared the accuracy of clinical judgment to that of statistical or actuarial methods. The criterion variables included success in academic or military training, recidivism and parole violation, and recovery from psychosis. Eleven of the twenty studies showed relative superiority of statistical methods over clinical judgments in accuracy of prediction. Eight were classified as ties; neither clinical judgment nor statistical prediction was superior. The results of one study were unclear, but further examination revealed that this investigation, too, qualified as a tie. Of the twenty studies reviewed, there was not a single example of clinical judgment exceeding statistical methods in the accuracy of predicting human behavior.

In 1957 Meehl was able to review twenty-seven additional studies on the issue. Seventeen showed superiority of statistical methods over clinical judgment. Ten were evaluated as ties. Again, not one study revealed superiority of clinical judgments over the statistical methods which could be used by a clerical worker or computer in making predictions.

By 1965 Meehl was able to evaluate fifty studies. The criterion variables now included continuance in psychotherapy, response to shock treatment, psychiatric diagnosis, job success and satisfaction, and even medical diagnoses. The box score now read thirty-three in favor of statistical methods, seventeen ties, and one in favor of clinical judgment. However, the study showing the superiority of clinical judgment was later determined to be also a tie. The results clearly support the superiority of statistical methods, or at the very least, their equivalence to clinical judgment.

Clinical and applied psychologists maintain, however, that the research designs of the studies Meehl evaluated were faulty (many were) and that only fragments of the total data available to psychologists working in the field were used. The clinical psychologist Robert Holt (1958, p. 1) commented: "Clinical students in particular complain of a vague feeling that a fast one has been put over on them, that under a great show of objectivity, or at least bipartisanship, Professor Meehl has actually sold the clinical approach up the river."

Implicit in the concerns of the clinicians is that the prediction of human behavior requires, ultimately, the human ingredients of integration, cognitive processing, and judgment of a wide range of input data. Essentially, it takes humans to predict and understand the complexity of humans. Humans are able to take into account the unique, the unexpected, and the mysterious workings of other human minds. Computers and statistical tables based on mathematical probabilities cannot possibly take into consideration individual differences to the same degree. Computers and actuarial methods are based on patterns of groups (nomothetic) and not individuals (idiographic). Despite these arguments, however, clinical judgment has yet to be redeemed; it has not demonstrated its superiority over actuarial methods in any criterion variable targeted for study. The fact remains that when the same input data or predictor variables are given to an individual using statistical tables or formulae and to a clinician, and when each is asked to make specific predictions, the clinician continually fails to achieve a higher "hit" ratio than the person using the statistical procedure.

In recent years, the research has shifted from studying accuracy of prediction to the process of prediction. That is, what data combination rules or strategies do clinicians use in making their judgments? Are the data combinations of clinicians qualitatively and quantitatively different from computer or statistical models? Many practicing clinicians argue, however, that clinical processing is inaccessible or private, and therefore not subject to logical or empirical analysis. They argue too that the process is so complex that they are unable to verbalize the cognitive operations that enter into data combination. They claim, therefore, that these cognitive operations do not lend themselves readily to empirical formulation or to computer analogues.

The process clinicians use in arriving at predictions is not well understood, but available research suggests that they use far less data and are much more simple in their data combinations than even they believe (Wiggins, 1973; Goldberg, 1968; Jones, 1977). Moreover, the instruments and methods for obtaining human data or predictor variables are, as we discovered in Chapter 2, often not designed to uncover the behavioral indicators that are àpropos to the criterion variables. Also, the interpersonal skills and prejudices of the clinicians may be as much a limitation of data collection as the instruments employed (e.g., Truax & Mitchell, 1971; Mischel, 1981).

Clinicians use these limited data to estimate a person's status with respect to given hypotheses and then use their favorite theoretical model as a basis for prediction. In most instances, the practicing clinicians base their inferences on "regularities" that have been observed in the past between predictor variables and the criterion variables, and this process tends to be an art more than a science. That is, clinicians rely too heavily on intuition and the "unusual case," and this violates the statistical rules of prediction in systematic and fundamental ways (Kahneman & Tversky, 1973).

## PREDICTIONS OF DANGEROUSNESS

Research literature consistently concludes that behavioral scientists and clinicians are unable to specify the type or severity of harm an individual may cause, or to predict with reasonable accuracy the probability of harm even occurring. Statistical techniques fare no better with reference to legal standards of reasonable accuracy. According to Alan Stone (1975, p. 33),

> It can be stated flatly on the basis of my own review of the published material on the prediction of dangerous acts that neither objective actuarial tables nor psychiatric intuition, diagnosis, and psychological testing can claim predictive success when dealing

with the traditional population of mental hospitals. The predictive success appropriate to a legal decision can be described in three levels of increasing certainty: Preponderance of the evidence, 51 percent successful; clear and convincing proof, 75 percent successful; beyond a reasonable doubt, at least 90 percent successful.

Stone asserts that mental health professionals have failed to prove their ability to predict dangerousness by even the lowest criterion, a preponderance of the evidence.

Accepting Stone's quantification, Cocozza and Steadman (1976) conclude that "any attempt to commit an individual solely on the basis of dangerousness would be futile if psychiatric testimony were subjected to any of these three standards of proof" (p. 1101). They add that the research has demonstrated "clear and convincing evidence of the inability of psychiatrists or anyone else to predict dangerousness accurately" (p. 1099).

The ability to identify persons who will engage in what may be termed dangerous or violent behavior may be expressed in several ways. One frequently used index is the ratio of *false positives* to *true positives*. False positives refer to those persons who are labeled dangerous, but who do not engage in dangerous behavior after release from custody, or during a specified period of time. True positives refer to persons predicted to be dangerous and who show the prediction to be correct. Thus, if a clinician predicts all ten persons of a selected population will demonstrate dangerous behavior—defined as violent behavior—within a two-year period, and six of the ten follow the prediction, then we have a 60 percent rate of true positives and a 40 percent rate of false positives.

We may also have a ratio expressed as *false negatives* to *true negatives*. In this case, we are dealing with persons predicted not to engage in a specified or criterion behavior. False negatives refer to those persons predicted not to engage in dangerous conduct, but who do. True negatives, on the other hand, refer to those persons predicted not to engage in dangerous conduct who do not (see Table 4–1). Therefore, if a clinician predicts that none of the population of ten will exhibit dangerous behavior over a period of time, and six do, we then have a 60 percent rate of false negatives and a 40 percent rate of true negatives.

It is obvious that it is more to the advantage of the clinician to predict that people will engage in violence than not predict it. More specifically, clinicians who fail to warn and protect the community by not detecting those persons who eventually do engage in violence will pay a heavy social and professional price compared to clinicians who overpredict to the point of asserting that most of a certain population will be violent after release. Not surprisingly, then, most studies indicate that current techniques for predicting dangerous behavior result in overprediction (Monahan, 1976, 1978; Wexler & Scoville, 1971). At a minimum, the most sophisticated methods yield 60 to 70 percent false positives (people said to be dangerous who were not) (Rubin, 1972; Kozol, Boucher & Garofalo, 1972; Wenk, Robison & Smith, 1972).

For example, in an effort to predict violent recidivism among parolees, the California Department of Corrections Research Division in 1965 tried to develop a violence-prediction scale based on predictor variables such as age, commitment offense, number of prior commitments, opiate use, length of imprisonment, and institution of release. Ernst Wenk, James Robison and Gerald Smith (1972) describe three studies

criterion behavior

| | | Did | Did Not |
|---|---|---|---|
| predictions | Will | true positive | false positive |
| | Will Not | false negative | true negative |

Table 4–1 ■ Four possible outcomes of predictions.

which resulted from this massive project. In the first study, predictor variables were used to divide the parolees into groups. This classification scheme resulted in the isolation of about three percent of the parolee population as the most violent. However, it was found that only 14 percent of these most violent individuals actually violated parole by engaging in a violent or potentially violent act, compared to a 5 percent violation rate for parolees in general. Although the most violent group was considered nearly three times more likely than the other groups to break parole by involvement in violence, it should be emphasized that a majority (86 percent) of those high-violence parolees did not actually engage in violent activity while on parole. Of course, it is entirely possible that many of the violent group did become involved in violence but were not detected or recorded as such.

In the second study sponsored by the California Department of Corrections, Parole and Community Services Division, all parolees released were classified into one of six categories, according to past aggressive behavior. Categories ranged from the most serious aggressive category (those who committed one or more acts of major violence) to the lowest level of aggression category (no recorded history of aggression). These classifications were based on offender histories and psychiatric evaluation of violence potential. This procedure revealed that those parolees evaluated as most potentially aggressive (two highest aggressive groups) were no more likely to be violent than the less potentially violent groups (two lowest aggressive groups). The rate of actual violence for the potentially aggressive groups was 3.1 per thousand, compared to 2.8 per thousand for the potentially least aggressive groups—an insignificant difference.

In the third project, Wenk and his colleagues (1972) followed a sample of 4,146 youthful offenders admitted to the Reception Guidance Center at Deuel Vocational Institute, California, during the years 1964 and 1965. The study was primarily aimed at determining which background data were most useful in predicting violence during a fifteen-month parole period following the young parolee's release from confinement. During the follow-up period, 104 (or 2.5 percent) of the youthful offenders had been involved in a violation of parole because of violent (assaultive) behavior.

In an effort to discover the predictive variables of dangerousness (violent behavior), Wenk et al. (1972) combined and divided the background data in a variety of ways. One analysis revealed that general recidivism (any violation of parole) and violent recidivism (violation of parole by violence) were highest for youthful offenders who had been admitted to the correctional facility on several occasions (multiple offenders). In another analysis, offenders who exhibited a history of "actual" violent behavior (which may or may not have resulted in legal custody or confinement) were three times more likely to be involved in violent recidivism during the fifteen-month parole period. Although this is an impressive finding, the authors admonish that if they were to make predictions based on the same background data, they would be accurate only once in twenty times (95 percent false positives), since only a tiny proportion of the parolees with violent backgrounds had a violent violation during parole.

It appears, therefore, that with our present ability to predict dangerous behavior, at least two out of every three persons predicted to do harm on the basis of predictor variables will not engage in dangerous activity during the period of prediction. The moral and social question then becomes: How many false positives—how many harmless men and women—are we willing to sacrifice to protect outselves from one violent individual? As Monahan (1976, p. 182) pointedly asks: "If, in the criminal law, we say that it is better that ten guilty men go free than one innocent man suffer, how can we reverse this ratio when it comes to mental health law?"

Three major factors contribute to overpredictions of dangerousness. First, the base rate of dangerous behavior is very low. That is, it occurs so rarely that "hits" or accurate incidents of dangerous behavior will be relatively low, even with sophisticated prediction methods.

Base rates, in this context, refer to the proportion of persons within some specified population who engage in a criterion behavior during some period of time. For example, if the base rate is 10 per 100 persons (or 10 percent), this means that ten out of every 100 persons of some group would exhibit the criterion within a specified time frame. The base rate for violent behavior tends to be exceedingly low in that few persons commit violent acts within a certain time frame (say one year). Therefore, it is not unusual to find one or two violent episodes occurring within a targeted population of 100. Furthermore, trying to predict with reasonable accuracy from this situation approximates finding needles in a haystack.

A second major factor contributing to the overprediction of dangerousness is that psychiatrists and psychologists will be less likely to be criticized or held responsible for any damages suffered during confinement than for releasing people who turn out to be dangerous. In essence, it becomes a choice between being accurate and being safe from social sanction. Clinicians could be more accurate if they predicted that all persons would not be dangerous, but they would not be protected from lawsuits and the wrath of society if they allow even one person out of confinement and that person later becomes violent. Therefore, clinicians prefer to be safe than right, or worse, wrong.

A third factor contributing to overprediction is the unclarity of the concept of dangerousness. No one is able to agree on precisely what behaviors should be included in the term dangerousness. Courts have tried to limit it to a propensity to "attack or otherwise inflict injury, loss, pain, or other evil" (Steadman, 1976, p. 57). In addition, it is often believed that the dangerous act must occur in "the community in the reasonably foreseeable future" and that any prediction of dangerousness must be based on a "high probability of substantial injury" (Rubin, 1972, p. 399). Steadman (1976) observes that these judicial terms are insufficient for legal application and, more distressingly, that the courts rarely press expert witnesses to explain and document the reliability or validity of their measuring instruments. If courts did press, they would likely find that many psychiatrists and psychologists rely on hunches, speculation, vague clinical judgment, and theoretical prejudice.

# ■ The Psychologist as Expert

In order for a defendant to be convicted of a crime, *mens rea* must be established by credible evidence, beyond a reasonable doubt in the minds of the jurors or a judge. Intention or state of mind is also crucial in civil wrongs committed against persons or their property and in the interpretation of contracts and wills. The legal system requires knowledge of mental states both to determine guilt and to dispose of a case. If an individual commits a legally forbidden act with evil intent, guilt is established and the appropriate punishment is meted out by the court. The decisionmakers in this process are the jurors and the judge, who sometimes rely on the advice of relevant experts.

If the trial is by jury, a significant portion of the case's disposition rests in the hands of the defendant's peers. This is especially true if the case is straightforward and involves minimal consideration of the mental or psychological status of the defendant. However, if the case demands such an appraisal, the pretrial assessment and trial testimony of the research or psychiatric expert become significant.

Persons testify in court to provide useful and relevant information which will help judges and juries make legal decisions. In most jurisdictions, lay witnesses can testify only to events that they have actually seen or heard firsthand. Opinions and inferences are generally not admissible (Schwitzgebel & Schwitzgebel, 1980). On the other hand, the opinions and inferences, speculations and conclusions supplied by experts are not only admissible, but are also often sought by the courts. Theoretically, anyone with skill, training, or experience not possessed by the general public in some science, art, or trade can serve as an expert witness. In reality, however, there is heated debate about who qualifies as an expert on a given issue. It is especially troublesome when the law decides what members of which professional group qualify as experts in questions involving the diagnosis, prediction, and treatment of mental illness or disease.

### THE BATTLE OF THE EXPERTS

Psychiatrists and other medical practitioners have traditionally been the principal expert witnesses in matters of mental illness, disease, or defect, thereby influencing legal decisions on criminal responsibility, civil commitment, or competence to stand trial. Slowly, this tradition is beginning to change, and psychologists are testifying increasingly on a wide variety of legal questions concerning mental states and behavior. They are also consulted in many other legal areas. As Schwitzgebel and Schwitzgebel (1980, p. 239) note: "Behavioral scientists may be asked to give opinion regarding child custody, copyright or trademark infringement, opinion sampling, drug addiction, sex offenses, perceptual acuity, impact of media programming, employment testing procedures, testamentary capacity . . . etc."

The increased courtroom status of psychologists has been a hard-fought and hardearned achievement, because psychiatrists and medical experts in general have not wanted to relinquish their very powerful influence on the legal-judicial process. A joint resolution adopted in 1954 by the American Psychiatric Association, the American Medical Association, and the American Psychoanalytical Association discouraged courts from allowing psychologists to testify on questions of mental illness or disease (Miller, Lower & Bleechmore, 1978). As a result, many courts adopted an approach reflected in the following comment by a California judge: "Here is a man [a psychologist] that comes in, glib of tongue, hasn't had a day's medical training at all, and he is going to qualify as an expert on insanity, when a part of the mental condition of legal insanity, as we know it in California, is a medical proposition: and I would like to see the Supreme Court tell me I am wrong." In _People v. Davis_ (1965), the California Supreme Court did tell the judge he was wrong.

A precedent-setting U.S. court of appeals decision announced in 1962 promoted wider acceptance of psychologists as expert witnesses. In _Jenkins v. U.S._ (1962) the American Psychiatric Association and the American Psychological Association both filed amicus curiae (friends of the court) briefs to delineate their positions (see box).

Petitioner Jenkins had pleaded insanity in the face of charges stemming from a sexual assault. Although three psychologists for the defense testified that he was mentally disordered at the time of the offense, the trial judge instructed the jury to disregard their testimony because they had no medical training in the area of mental disease. "A psychologist is not competent to give a medical opinion as to a mental disease or defect. Therefore, you will not consider any evidence as to the effect that the defendant was suffering from a mental disease or a mental defect . . . according to the testimony given by the psychologists" (_Jenkins v. U.S._, 1962, p. 643). The court also cited the joint resolution of the psychiatric, psychoanalytic, and medical associations.

The U.S. Court of Appeals for the District of Columbia, probably the most influential of the courts of appeals, reversed the lower court and remanded the case for a new trial, and subsequent court cases have followed that precedent. Judge David Bazelon stated that a psychologist's lack of a medical degree did not automatically disqualify him or her from testifying on the mental state of an individual. Other courts have asserted that properly qualified psychologists can diagnose mental disease and may elaborate on the probable influence of disordered mental states either in relation to past, present, or future behavior. Today, all federal criminal courts have accepted psychologists as expert witnesses, but federal civil courts have been inconsistent (Schwitzgebel & Schwitzgebel, 1980). Psychologists are also allowed as expert witnesses in many state courts, providing they meet state legal requirements, which vary from state to state. In general, licensing or certification and a doctorate in psychology appear to be highly desirable assets to qualify as an expert in most jurisdictions (Miller, Lower & Bleechmore, 1978). The battle to allow psychologists to testify as expert witnesses is still in progress, however (Perlin, 1977). Lawyers' and trial judges' statements about the lack of medical qualifications of psychologists are offered with discouraging frequency.

The "expert" problem in the courts often stems from a fundamental confusion about the differences between psychology and psychiatry. We referred to these differences in Chapter 1, noting in particular the training emphasized by each profession. Compounding the problem is the fact that psychology is a broad discipline that encompasses widely diverse specialties. There are child psychologists, developmental psychologists, physiological psychologists, industrial psychologists, and social psychologists, to mention but a few. Clinical or forensic psychologists qualify best as expert witnesses, but other specialists can qualify equally well if the legal questions posed relate to their area of expertise. In most cases, the doctoral level clinical and forensic psychologists have been trained in assessing, diagnosing, treating, and researching mental illness or behavior problems at a level comparable to the psychiatrist. In some cases, the training has been superior to psychiatric training—superior even relative to the effects of certain drugs on behavior (psychopharmacology). The training received by doctoral level psychologists also often includes the assessment and diagnosis of brain damage and other neurological dysfunctions.

## SURVIVING THE WITNESS STAND

"The courtroom is a place best reserved for those who are brave, adventuresome and nimble-witted." This comment (Schwitzgebel & Schwitzgebel, 1980, p. 241) summarizes very well the perils inherent in cross-examination and the discomfort almost guaranteed the expert witness. The professional literature contains ample advice for psychologists daring enough (some say foolhardy enough) to approach the witness stand. Poythress (1979), for example, suggests that good preparation for the psychologist intending to be an expert witness should include thorough experiential learning in mock trial situations, observations of experienced expert witnesses, and specific course work or field placements in forensic settings.

Courtroom testimony, if punctuated by vigorous cross-examination, can be a punishing experience even when the expert witness is fully prepared. This is especially true in the behavioral sciences, where complexity compounded by incomplete information is rampant. Conflicting testimony by two psychologists or two psychiatrists or by one of each confuses the courts and the public and can undermine the credibility of both professions (Yarmey, 1979).

Differences of opinion between and within professions should not necessarily be interpreted as error or misinformation. The "collision of experts" is partly due to the complexity and ambiguity of the issues about which they are commenting. Problems and inconsistencies may also be due to differences in training and philosophies. In some cases, the confusion arises when medical and psychological testimony is so replete with professional jargon and with esoteric, empirically unsupported speculation that the testimony is nearly, if not completely, useless to the court. In other cases, problems stem from inadequate preparation or poor communication between the expert witness and the lawyer who has called that witness to testify. Also, as any experienced judge or trial lawyer knows, it is often easy to obtain psychiatric or psychological testimony to support either side of a case (prosecution or defense). In such cases, the so-called battle of experts is not even remotely edifying (Meehl, 1977).

Because psychologists represent the science of behavior, they would be well advised to be highly familiar with the behavioral research literature directly related to the legal issue upon which they will testify. They should also be prepared to substantiate the reliability and validity of any assessment instruments and procedures used in arriving at their conclusions. Writing about "survival on the witness stand," Brodsky (1977) notes that this preparation is essential. When experts are able to defend their specific theories, methods, and conclusions, their testimony becomes much more credible.

# ■ Summary and Conclusions

The major theme of this chapter, and an underlying theme of the chapter to follow, is that the dual system of justice now used in American courts—criminal law and mental

---

## ☐ JENKINS v. U.S.

### Selected Amicus Curiae Briefs

The brief submitted by the American Psychiatric Association in *Jenkins* emphasized the extensive medical training of psychiatrists, training which made them uniquely qualified to offer diagnoses of the presence or absence of mental illness. By contrast, the psychiatrists told the court, psychologists may be highly trained, but they are competent in a very specialized area, which does not include mental illness. They also suggested that the role of the psychologist was to be a helpmate to the psychiatrist.

The American Psychological Association emphasized that psychology is an established science. The brief delineated the ethical responsibilities and the intraprofessional standards that psychologists are expected to embrace. Like the brief of the psychiatrists, the APA brief expanded upon the years of training that culminate in the PhD, in particular the PhD held by clinical psychologists.

Following are excerpts from each of the briefs.

*American Psychiatric Association*

Psychiatrists traditionally have been called upon by our Courts to give expert medical testimony concerning mental illnesses, the productivity thereof and their effects.

The question of whether a person *not* trained in medicine, *not* a Doctor of Medicine and *not* a doctor trained as a specialist in the diagnosis, treatment and care of the mentally ill, can qualify as a *medical* expert and give expert *medical* opinions concerning the diagnosis of specific mental diseases and the *medical* effects thereof is of grave concern to psychiatrists and their Association. . . .

The clinical psychologist, like "teachers, ministers, lawyers, social workers and vocational counselors," all utilize their skills as aids only to the psychiatrist in his medical diagnosis, care and treatment of the mentally ill. . . .

Reduced to simple terms, clinical psychology "remains simply one of the possible methods" to be selected by the psychiatrist in evaluating and treating a specific mental illness. Its use in any specific case is for the psychiatrist to determine. . . .

While they (psychologists) are skilled in psychology, this does not qualify them to diagnose or to prescribe treatment and care for a specific

health law—is confusing and in many respects unjustified. Persons being processed through courts under mental health law are often deprived of due process, under the misguided rationale that the system operates in their best interest.

Criminal law, which holds individuals responsible for their illegal actions, operates under a police power rationale that eventually results in punishment if an individual is judged guilty. Mental health law operates under the opposing philosophy that some individuals are not responsible for their actions, whether deviant or illegal or both, and that the state must therefore step in and assume the role of benefactor, meting out not punishment but treatment. Yet the treatment dispensed under this *parens patriae* rationale is, by its very nature, often punitive, and it often deprives individuals of due process rights. More importantly, it often does not work.

The issues surrounding *parens patriae* are complex, but they are treated simplistically by the judicial system. It is assumed, for example, that free will either exists or it does not; the more realistic approach that free will exists on a continuum and ac-

---

mental illness. Traditionally, ultimate medical diagnosis, care and treatment for the mentally ill is reserved to the psychiatrist. . . .

The American Psychiatric Association recognizes the clinical psychologist as a highly trained person in a special field of psychological examination. He can provide important relevant data, such as the result from M.A. and I.Q. tests, to the psychiatrist who has the final responsibility for medical diagnosis. But the psychologist, not being a qualified Doctor of Medicine with special training in the mental health field, cannot qualify as a medical expert in the diagnosis, treatment and care of the mentally ill.

### American Psychological Association

From a scholarly discipline and science developed mainly in university centers, the result of psychological effort has become recognized as capable of application in many fields of activity. . . .

The foundation stone, however, of all developments of the field continues to be a rigid adherence to the principles of science, to a belief in the value of empirical evidence and verification, and to the development of appropriate theory. These are some of the processes which differentiate the sciences from other approaches to the understanding of human behavior. . . .

It is submitted that psychology in its present state of development is clearly an established science and . . . psychologists are clearly engaged in the practice of an established profession. It would obviously be foolish to assert that any psychologist is testimonially competent to express an expert professional opinion upon all questions relating to the science of psychology. In fact, the Association would oppose any such rule as being contrary to the professional standards to which it and its membership adhere. It is submitted, however, that a psychologist is clearly competent under well-established rules of evidence, to testify as an expert upon matters within the scope of his professional experience. . . .

In the diagnosis of mental disease and mental defect, including the formulation of professional opinions as to causal relationships between mental disease or defect and overt behavior, a principal tool of the clinical psychologist is found in psychological tests. . . .

Infallibility is not claimed for any psychological test, and no professional psychologist would assert that he could reach a valid diagnosis upon the basis of test results alone. However, the use of test results, in conjunction with a review of a person's history and evaluative interviews, can be extremely useful to the clinical psychologist in reaching informed opinions as to the nature and existence or nonexistence of mental disease or defect in a given subject and as to the causal relationship or lack thereof between such mental disease or defect and the subject's overt behavior.

cording to situational and personality factors is not addressed. We will return to this point in Chapter 5. *Parens patriae* also assumes that clinicians can predict dangerous behavior and, more crucially, that they have at their disposal the magic formula to make such behavior disappear. We have seen, however, that clinicians are no more adept at these predictions than the rest of the population; in fact, if they are in doubt clinicians are more likely to diagnose persons dangerous, rather than diagnose them not dangerous and incur the wrath of the public if their diagnosis is proved wrong. A comment made recently by Stanley Brodsky (1981, p. 12) is revealing in this context. Discussing the pressures to provide predictions of violence or dangerousness, he said, "Many clinicians are legally mandated to make such judgments, and psychiatrists, psychologists, and other mental health professionals do continue to predict violence. Without doubt, their attitudes have become questioning, sometimes bitter and cynical. Yet out of occupational requirement or personal belief in what they do, they continue." This statement illustrates one of the many abuses of the psychology *in* law relationship. It is impossible for psychology to maintain its integrity under such conditions and unlikely that a coequal partnership with law will develop.

Finally, we discussed the role of experts in the courtroom and the pitfalls inherent in cross-examination. The comparison between criminal and mental health law in this arena is sobering. Experts in involuntary civil commitment hearings are rarely challenged, whereas in criminal proceedings, they are often ridiculed. The very question of who qualifies as expert is important in criminal law; in mental health law, it is seldom at issue.

## ■ Key Concepts and Principles, Chapter 4

*Parens patriae* and police power
Substantive and procedural law
Constitutional law
Case law
*Stare decisis*
Statutory law
Administrative law
Civil versus criminal law
*Actus rea* and *mens rea*

Misdemeanor and felony
Mental health law
Free will
Determinism
Dangerousness
Accuracy of clinical judgment
False and true positives
False and true negatives

# □ | 5

# ■ | Criminal Responsibility, Competence, and Mental Illness: A Psychological Perspective

□ | Two areas of criminal law, competence to stand trial and criminal responsibility, often confound behavioral scientists working with the courts. In this chapter we will examine each of these concepts, learn how they are used in the judicial system, and point out fallacies associated with this use. Later in the chapter we will return to mental health law, free will and determinism, and the *parens patriae* rationale, since each of these areas is intricately associated with competence and insanity.

## ■ Competence to Stand Trial

"Criminal responsibility" and "competence to stand trial" refer to a defendant's mental capacities at two different points in time (Schwitzgebel & Schwitzgebel, 1980). In issues of criminal responsibility, the legal question asked is, "What was the state of mind of the defendant at the time the alleged offense was committed?" In competence, the question becomes, "What is the state of mind of the defendant at the present time, or at the time of the trial?" Specifically, competence is concerned with the individual's capacity at the time of the trial preparation and actual trial to understand the charges and legal proceedings and to communicate with legal counsel. A ruling that an individual is "incompetent to stand trial" (IST) means that, in the judgment of the presiding judge, the defendant is so intellectually or psychologically impaired that it would be a farce to initiate or continue the trial process.

Incompetence and criminal responsibility are not interrelated and must be viewed as two separate determinations. An individual who was mentally disordered at the time of an offense may have regained mental stability before or during pretrial procedures to the point of understanding the charges and proceedings and helping in the preparation of a defense. On the other hand, a person may be of "sound mind" during the offense, but may later become disoriented and distressed and be evaluated IST.

Most statutes dealing with incompetence allow psychological or psychiatric examination of the defendant either at the request of the prosecution, the defense, or the presiding judge. The incompetence question may be raised at any time during criminal proceedings (*Pate v. Robinson*, 1966). It is interesting that prosecutors raise the issue of competence more often than the defense (Slovenko, 1977). When the initiative is taken by the prosecutor, the process is called "preventive detention." When the defense raises the competence question, it is generally termed seeking immunity from trial.

It should shock the reader to learn that, until recently, incompetence to stand trial could mean a lifetime of confinement in a mental institution. Competence evaluation required that defendants first be confined to a security institution for a lengthy psychological-psychiatric assessment (usually lasting from sixty to ninety days). Following this assessment, a court would hold a hearing. If, on the basis of written or oral assessment reports, the court found the defendant unable to understand the charges or the judicial proceedings or to help counsel, the defendant would be committed involuntarily to a security hospital for an indefinite period of time, supposedly until rendered competent. Theoretically and realistically, since there were no standards to determine what constituted competence, lifetime confinement was a real possibility. Some studies have reported that about 50 percent of those found incompetent under these procedures spent the rest of their lives confined to a security hospital (Hess & Thomas, 1963; McGarry, 1971). Note that there are parallels between this procedure and involuntary civil commitment of persons for noncriminal, but deviant, actions.

In 1972 the U.S. Supreme Court ruled that a person may be involuntarily confined only for the reasonable period of time necessary to determine whether there is a substantial chance of his or her becoming competent enough to stand trial (*Jackson v. Indiana*, 1972). Moreover, the evaluation and confinement do not have to take place in a security institution, but can be undertaken on an outpatient basis. If the defendant is not likely to gain competence in the foreseeable future, standard civil commitment proceedings must be initiated. It is left to each state to determine what are reasonable amounts of time and how to evaluate likelihood of change. Unfortunately, individuals committed involuntarily for deviant but noncriminal behavior have the benefit of no such Supreme Court-imposed time limit.

Competence evaluations occur far more frequently than determinations of criminal responsibility (Kanno & Scheidemandel, 1969), which we will discuss shortly. Estimates of the number of IST's in security mental hospitals or "wings for the criminally insane" before the 1972 *Jackson* decision ranged from 40 percent (Steadman & Cocozza, 1974) to as high as 90 percent (Committee on Psychiatry and Law, 1974). Thus, over one-third and perhaps as many as nine out of every ten of the persons involuntarily confined in security hospital-prisons were only charged with (not convicted of) a crime and were ordered by the court to be confined to an institution for an indefinite period until somehow found or rendered "competent." The extent to which the 1972 Supreme Court ruling changed these statistics is not known.

## PSYCHOLOGICAL ASSESSMENT OF COMPETENCE

The methods used to assess competence depend upon the clinician's training and theoretical orientation, and there are a wide variety of approaches. Some assessors prefer to use only the interview, while others choose the interview in combination with projective or objective testing instruments. Still others use a complete assessment procedure, including psychological tests, interview information, observation, and extensive background information and social history.

Regardless of the specific procedures or techniques used, the psychological assessment directed at questions of competence should strive for three major goals. First, the clinician must have a thorough understanding of the referral: Who made it and why? What specific questions did the referring agent pose? Were there questions about the intellectual or neurological functioning of the defendant, or was the referring agent concerned about the person's personality characteristics and emotional stamina to face trial? Second, the information must be collected with reliable and valid instruments that will hold up under cross-examination or judicial scrutiny. Third, the clinician must be able to establish a nexus between the data collected and the referral questions and to communicate the relationship clearly to the court. The report must be free of psychological jargon and extraneous material; it should be concise, contain behavioral referents, and it should set forth interpretations and conclusions.

Researchers at the Harvard Laboratory of Community Psychiatry (1974) have developed two instruments specifically designed to direct clinicians toward relevant defendant behaviors. One instrument, the Competency Screening Test (CST), allows a summative score of competence to stand trial. The defendant is asked to complete twenty-two sentences (Example: "When I go to court the lawyer will . . . "), and each response merits a 0, 1, or 2 score. A total score below 20 usually raises questions about the defendant's competence. The instrument's major advantage is its ability to screen out quickly the clearly competent defendants, so that more time-consuming examination can be directed at those defendants whose competence is questionable.

The second instrument, the Competency Assessment Instrument (CAI), is designed to assess all possible legal grounds for a finding of incompetence. The instrument consists of thirteen "ego functions" or behavioral functions related to a defendant's ability to cope with and understand the trial process. Each of the thirteen functions is scored on a scale ranging from 1 (total incapacity) to 5 (no incapacity). There is no recommended minimal score, so each assessor is left to make his or her own decision about the defendant's competence.

# ■ Criminal Responsibility

The public is acquainted with the concept of criminal responsibility in criminal law primarily through its absence, for the absence of responsibility is what most people know as "insanity." To paraphrase a key federal case, if a person chooses to do evil through the exercise of his or her free will, that person is exercising criminal responsibility (U.S. v. Brawner, 1972). Insanity is the legal term which refers to an "excusing condition" from criminal responsibility. Thus, if a person was "insane" at the time of an illegal action, in most states he or she would not be guilty of the crime.

In at least one state, California, a "bifurcated trial" process exists, whereby a defendant is tried in two phases. During the first phase, it is determined whether the defendant is guilty or innocent of having committed the illegal act. The defendant is "conclusively presumed" to be sane, and any evidence of insanity is generally not admissible. If the defendant is found guilty, he or she has the option of pleading insanity, and a second trial phase determines whether the individual was indeed insane at the time of the crime. It has often been recommended that the federal court system adopt this same bifurcated rule, which would allow perpetrators of crimes to be found insane, but also guilty.

Insanity pleas often receive extensive press coverage, but they are rare compared to the total number of criminal cases tried. Valid estimates cite defendants pleading insanity in only about 4 percent of all United States criminal cases (Steadman & Cocozza, 1974; Kanno & Scheidemandel, 1969). It is estimated also that insanity acquittals comprise only about 2 percent of all cases terminated (U.S. v. Brawner, 1972, p. 989).

There is an erroneous public tendency to consider insanity identical to mental illness or crazy behavior. Insanity is not a medical, psychiatric, or psychological phenomenon; it is the legal term for an excusing condition which, in most jurisdictions, must consist of both the existence of "mental illness" and an incapacity of mind due to that illness. Both must be present at the time of the alleged offense.

Realistically, insanity is not a complete defense, since acquittal will be accompanied by forced confinement for "treatment," which can be considered a form of punishment. In fact, defense attorneys rarely use the insanity defense, because success would not free their clients. In virtually every case involving an insanity plea, there is little question that the defendant committed the act; the contention is that evil intent was not possible because of the individual's aberrational state of mind. Thus, if the court determines that the person was insane at the time of a serious offense, it almost invariably will commit the individual for treatment. In minor offenses, the court may dictate either commitment or some treatment regimen advocated by a medical or mental health expert. If a court rules that the person was guilty but not insane at the time of the offense, and is not mentally disordered at the time of the trial (IST), then punishment in the form of prison confinement (or the death penalty) will very probably be ordered.

Standards or tests to determine insanity vary widely among the states, but they usually center around one of three general models of criminal responsibility. These are the M'Naghten Rule, the Durham Rule, and the Model Penal Code Rule, each of which will be discussed below.

## M'NAGHTEN RULE

This most frequently used rule to determine legal sanity is derived from the "wild beast" test pronounced by the English courts in 1724 (Marshall, 1968). It held that an individual was not responsible for his or her actions "if he could not distinguish good from evil more than a wild beast" (Leifer, 1964, p. 825). The ability to reason distinguished humans from beast, the test implied. In 1760, the words "right and wrong" were substituted for "good and evil" (Sobeloff, 1958).

The origins of the M'Naghten Rule as we know it can be traced to mid-nineteenth century Britain. In 1843 one Daniel M'Naghten believed he was being persecuted by the Tories, England's right-wing political party, and he identified his major persecutor as none other than English Prime Minister Robert Peel. Traveling to London for the sole purpose of assassinating Peel, M'Naghten proceeded to shoot into the Prime Minister's carriage. His plan would have succeeded but for the fact that Peel had chosen that day to ride in Queen Victoria's carriage. His secretary, Drummond, died from the bullet intended for Peel. Thus, M'Naghten shot and killed Drummond in error.

There was no question that M'Naghten had committed the act, but the issue raised at the lengthy trial was his mental state at the time of the homicide. On the basis of new psychiatric insights gained from the classic work on mental illness by the psychiatrist Isaac Ray, M'Naghten was found "not guilty by reason of insanity." The decision was not based on the traditional right-from-wrong moral test in use at that time, but based on a presumption of a defect of reasoning due to mental illness.

Queen Victoria's ire was raised by the decision, and she demanded that the House of Lords and the criminal judges of the common law courts reexamine the acquittal. The Queen had good reason to be upset, since there had also been three attempts on her own life, although not by M'Naghten. After considerable debate and pressure from the Crown, Lord Chief Justice Tindal wrote an opinion for the fifteen judges of the common law courts. It reaffirmed the sixteenth century right-from-wrong test of morality and found that M'Naghten could not be excused under that standard. It is this test upon which the present M'Naghten Rule is based.

Throughout the years the Rule has been interpreted and clarified by courts. It is now generally recognized to state that a defendant is not responsible if he or she committed an unlawful act "while labouring under such a defect of reason, from disease of the mind, as not to know the nature and quality of the act he was doing; or, if he did know it, that he did not know he was doing what was wrong" (Brooks, 1974, p. 135). The rule emphasizes the cognitive elements of (1) being aware and knowing what one was doing at the time of an illegal act, or (2) knowing or realizing right from wrong in the moral sense. The test recognizes no degree of incapacity. The jury's only choice is to decide whether the defendant knows right from wrong or knew what he or she was doing at the time of the offense (U.S. v. Freeman, 1966). This apparent simplicity may be a key to understanding why the M'Naghten Rule continues to be popular in most states.

For a time, the Rule was accepted as the principal standard of criminal responsibility in virtually every American jurisdiction (Saks & Hastie, 1978). However, it was also attacked by several schools of psychiatric and psychological thought, because it was too narrow and not in keeping with psychiatric-psychological theory and clinical practice.

## THE DURHAM RULE

In 1954, apparently motivated by widespread discontent with the restrictiveness and moral tone of the M'Naghten Rule, U.S. Court of Appeals Judge David Bazelon drafted what was to become the Durham Rule (*Durham v. U.S.*, 1954). Bazelon hoped that the new rule's broad definition would give psychiatrists the latitude to talk freely about the defendant, where before they had had to testify piecemeal within the stricter confines of M'Naghten. Psychiatry had been asserting that, if responsibility for illegal conduct was framed solely in terms of cognitive impairment, it was impossible to convey to the judge and jury the full range of information that had been obtained by assessment of the defendant's responsibility. By bringing the rule for criminal responsibility up to date with psychiatric theory, it was assumed that the ascription of responsibility was made more "scientific."

The Durham Rule states that "an accused is not criminally responsible if his unlawful act was the *product* of a mental disease or mental defect" (Brooks, 1974, p. 176). Hence, the rule is concerned with mental illness itself rather than with the cognitive elements of knowing or realizing the rightness or wrongness of a specific action. The Durham Rule was later clarified in *Carter v. U.S.* (1957), which held that mental illness must not merely have entered into the production of the act, it must have played a necessary role.

Soon after the Durham Rule was adopted, its broad scope became its major shortcoming and eventually its downfall. Since definitions of mental illness are extremely vague and broad, the Rule promoted widespread variability in the discretionary power of psychiatry. Definitions of mental illness can be broad enough to include the mental condition of most (if not all) offenders, since any antisocial act may be viewed as a product of mental illness. Applied in this way, the Durham Rule could be and was used to exculpate large numbers of offenders who had previously been held responsible. Thus, moves to delimit and redefine the Rule began in earnest—moves made by legal scholars, clinicians, and social and behavioral scientists who tried to define "mental disease" or "defect" and to determine what acts were "products" of such conditions.

The Durham Rule also created confusion about expert testimony. Upon whose testimony should courts rely? Would experts agree? The professional jargon and ambiguity characteristic of psychiatric testimony often resulted in an irony: one of the purposes of the Durham Rule was to insure that the legal, social, and moral decisions regarding responsibility were to be made by the jury, yet the expert testimony became so technical and abstruse that the jury was often left with little choice but to go along with the expert. In sum, the Rule became so unmanageable that it was eventually discarded by most of the jurisdictions that had adopted it. Some states replaced it with the Model Penal Code Rule and its very close relative, the Brawner Rule, while others returned to some variant of M'Naghten.

## THE ALI AND BRAWNER RULES

In 1972, in *U.S. v. Brawner*, Judge Bazelon himself ended eighteen years of unhappy experiment with the Durham Rule by adopting in large part the 1962 draft of the Model Penal Code Rule formulated by the American Law Institute (hereafter referred to as the ALI Rule). "A person is not responsible for criminal conduct if at the time of such conduct as a result of mental disease or defect he lacks substantial capacity either to appreciate the criminality (wrongfulness) of his conduct or to conform his conduct to the requirements of the law" (*U.S. v. Brawner*, 1972, p. 973). While adopting this ALI Rule, however, Judge Bazelon also expanded it, by specifying that "mental disease" or "defect" must be a condition which substantially (a) affects mental or emotional processes or (b) impairs behavioral controls. Therefore, *Brawner* permits exculpation based on either cognitive or control incapacity. This "control incapacity" component is a derivative of the so-called irresistible-impulse test which is based upon the defendant's alleged inability to control behavior, whatever might have been his or her cognitive capacity.

The Brawner Rule recognizes the ALI Rule's "caveat paragraph," which asserts: "The terms 'mental disease or defect' do not include an abnormality manifested only by repeated criminal or otherwise anti-social conduct" (American Law Institute Model Penal Code, 1962, Section 4.01, p. 160). The purpose of this provision was to exclude insanity defenses by psychopaths, whose lawyers argued that theirs was a mental abnormality.

The Brawner Rule also allows a judgment of "partial responsibility," which simply means that a defendant can be held responsible to some extent, even though he or she was laboring under a mental disease or defect. This partial responsibility aspect is most often used in first degree murder trials, where it is often determined that the accused was suffering from some mental illness at the time of the offense. The mental illness factor allows courts to convict for a lesser crime, such as second degree murder. Whereas some insanity defenses only allow a decision that the defendant is responsible or not responsible, the partial responsibility test encourages a middle-ground approach.

The ALI Rule and the Brawner Rule have done little to improve the insanity defense and, in the view of many critics, do not vary from M'Naghten in any significant sense. Each criminal responsibility defense now available suffers from the lack of concise definitions of terms that may be clearly related to observable behaviors. As noted earlier, the M'Naghten Rule remains the most commonly used insanity rule in the United States today, although it is sometimes used in conjunction with the "irresistible impulse" test. The Durham Rule is currently used in very few states (at this writing, only one). The ALI-Brawner Rules are used in several states (about seven) and in most federal courts.

## ■ The Label "Mental Illness"

Diagnosing abnormal behavior is little more than labeling a pattern of behavior that deviates from some norm, presumably because of some mental, attitudinal, or motivational defect or faulty learning experience. In most diagnostic classifications, the norm is a sociocultural one; any deviation from what is socially appropriate or culturally expected is considered abnormal. If, upon entering an elevator, you stand facing the back of the elevator wall rather than turn around to face the door, your behavior is "abnormal" according to most social standards or expectations. Whether a behavioral pattern is considered seriously abnormal to the point of generating a diagnostic label (e.g., psychotic, neurotic, or personality disorder) usually depends upon two factors, both of which rely on clinical judgment. First, what are the motives behind the behavior? Second, to what extent does the unusual behavior cause distress to the individual or to those around him or her? Therefore, the perspective and clinical discipline (e.g., psychology, psychiatry, social work, psychiatric nursing) of the labeler often determine what behavioral, emotional, or thought patterns will be designated abnormal and determine also their alleged etiology.

Historically, and especially during the past century, determining what constitutes abnormal behavior has been a medical enterprise dominated almost exclusively by

## ☐ U.S. v. BRAWNER

### Excerpts

*U.S. v. Brawner*, the 1972 federal appellate decision that rejected the *Durham* product rule in favor of an expanded version of the ALI rule, was seventy pages long. The following are some of its key points.

A principal reason for our decision to depart from the Durham rule is the undesirable characteristic . . . of undue dominance by the experts giving testimony. . . . The difficulty is rooted in the circumstance that there is no generally accepted understanding, either in the jury or the community it represents, of the concept requiring that the crime be the "product" of the mental disease.

When the court used the term "product" in Durham it likely assumed that this was a serviceable, and indeed a natural, term for a rule defining criminal responsibility—a legal reciprocal, as it were, for the familiar term "proximate cause," used to define civil responsibility. But if concepts like "product" are, upon refinement, reasonably understood, or at least appreciated, by judges and lawyers, and perhaps philosophers, difficulties developed when it emerged that the "product" concept did not signify a reasonably identifiable common ground that was also shared by the nonlegal experts, and the laymen serving on the jury as the representatives of the community.

The doctrine of criminal responsibility is such that there can be no doubt "of the complicated nature of the decision to be made—intertwining moral, legal, and medical judgments . . ." . . . jury decisions have been accorded unusual deference even when they have found responsibility in the face of a powerful record, with medical evidence uncontradicted, pointing toward exculpation. The "moral" elements of the decision are not defined exclusively by religious considerations but by the totality of underlying conceptions of ethics and justice shared by the community, as expressed by its jury surrogate. . . .

There is, indeed, irony in a situation under which the Durham rule, which was adopted in large part to permit experts to testify in their own terms concerning matters within their domain which the jury should know, resulted in testimony by the experts in terms not their own to reflect unexpressed judgments in a domain that is properly not theirs but the jury's. The irony is heightened when the jurymen, instructed under the esoteric "product" standard, are influenced significantly by "product" testimony of expert witnesses really reflecting ethical and legal judgments rather than a conclusion within the witnesses' particular expertise. . . .

The experts have meaningful information to impart, not only on the existence of mental illness or not, but also on its relationship to the incident charged as an offense. In the interest of justice this valued information should be available, and should not be lost or blocked by requirements that unnaturally restrict communication between the experts and the jury. The more we have pondered the problem the more convinced we have become that the sound solution lies not in further shaping of Durham "product" approach in more refined molds, but in adopting the ALI's formulation as the linchpin of our jurisprudence.

The ALI's formulation retains the core requirement of a meaningful relationship between the mental illness and the incident charged. The language in the ALI rule is sufficiently in the common ken that its use in the courtroom, or in preparation for trial, permits a reasonable three-way communication—between (a) the law-trained, judges and lawyers; (b) the experts and (c) the jurymen—without insisting on a vocabulary that is either stilted or stultified, or conducive to a testimonial mystique permitting expert dominance and encroachment on the jury's function. There is no indication in the available literature that any such untoward development has attended the reasonably widespread adoption of the ALI rule in the Federal courts and a substantial number of state courts.

Our ruling today includes our decision that in the ALI rule as adopted by this court the term "mental disease or defect" includes the definition of that term . . . as follows:

(A) *mental disease or defect includes any abnormal condition of the mind which substantially affects mental or emotional processes and substantially impairs behavior controls.*

psychiatrists. Although many psychiatrists believe that abnormal behaviors in no way describe true disease conditions, most do subscribe to a disease or medical model to explain and diagnose the varying conditions of abnormal behavior. Because of the enormous success of the "medical model" approach in dealing with physical disease—obtaining symptoms and diagnosis and providing treatment based on that diagnosis—it was deduced that classification and treatment schemes employed in dealing with physical disease would work equally well to describe behavior and mental problems. Thus, the terms "mental illness," "mental disease," "patient," "mental hygiene," "sick," "treatment," "mental hosptial," "mental health," and "diagnosis" permeate even the scientific study of abnormal psychology. The public, the courts, the media, and the behavioral and social scientists and practitioners all use these terms with regularity. Abnormal behaviors are called "symptoms" and are allegedly due to some internal malfunction or disease. The disease or medical model continues to influence our present theories, classifications, and treatment of abnormal or deviant behavioral patterns, often with the implicit understanding that only medicine has the expert knowledge to classify and treat illness and disease, physical or mental, medical or psychiatric.

The radical psychiatrist Thomas Szasz (1960, 1968) contends that mental illness is a myth and that the standards by which persons are defined as mentally sick should be psychosocial, ethical, and legal, but not medical. In Szasz's opinion, only confusion results from the use of "mental illness" to characterize both disorders of the brain and deviations of behavior, thinking, and emotion due to nondisease related causes. More soberingly, thinking of mental abnormality as illness promotes abuses by psychiatry and the use of medical terminology to deprive persons of their civil liberties through involuntary hospitalization, confinement, incarceration, or other coercive techniques. "Mental illness" erroneously justifies the use of various medical "psychotherapeutic" techniques, like drug therapy, psychosurgery, and electroconvulsive therapies, Szasz argues. Furthermore, he believes the medical-psychiatric profession has held on to the inaccurate and scientifically unsupported concept of mental illness to control and dominate the assessment, care, and disposition of the unfortunate many whom it labels "mentally ill."

Szasz is not alone. A similar conclusion was reached by Hardisty (1973), who believes that psychiatry still employs the words "mental illness" to achieve social purposes and maintain power in influencing legal determinations of mental states. Donald Mazer (1978, p. 98) adds, "The concept of mental illness gives psychiatrists the power to determine who is normal and who isn't, to dictate how persons ought to think, feel and behave in different situations." Although these are minority opinions in the field of psychiatry, they have been voiced cogently and with enough fervor to prevent their abrupt dismissal.

In contrast to psychiatry, mainstream psychology views abnormal behavior as principally due to faulty learning experiences. The abnormal behavior reflects an attempt by the person to cope or adapt to the environment. Emphasis is generally directed at observable behavior and at what factors maintain that behavior. This contrasts with the traditional psychiatric approach of looking for unconscious and conscious motivational states or biochemical imbalances. However, psychology and psychiatry both embrace within their own ranks divergent views of the causes and maintenance of abnormal behavior. Therefore, it should be realized early in this discussion that there is no scientifically agreed upon definition of abnormal behavior among representatives of either discipline.

Like Szasz, the author believes the process of deciding who is normal and who isn't is largely a social, moral, and legal one and not principally a scientific or medical procedure. Stephen Morse, also adopting this point of view, has recommended (1978a) that the legal system use the term "crazy behavior," since he believes it is a far more accurate and communicative concept for legal purposes than the medical jargon now surrounding "mental illness" and its many variants.

Whether we are referring to a mental disorder, crazy behavior, mental illness, or abnormal behavior, the terms all refer to unusual behavior expressed through either thinking processes (cognitions), feelings (affect), actions (behavior), or a combination of these. Abnormal behaviors are elusive primarily because individual behavioral patterns are unique and resist neat classifications. Normal or abnormal behavior is a product of an elaborate interaction between the person's biological and psychological predispositions and the enormous variety of environmental factors that act upon that person. Contemporary behavioral and social research continually underscore the infinite complexity and uniqueness of human behavior, even to the point of raising the serious question: Can even broad generalizations of personality be meaningful? (Mischel, 1973). It appears that the most realistic approach to describing human behavior is to examine each person's behavior in relation to his or her particular context. Moreover, the best source of the individual's behavioral patterns is the individual himself or herself, a source free from the prejudicial hunches and speculations of clinicians (Mischel, 1968).

The legal system has become increasingly disenchanted with the terminology, concepts, and methods surrounding "mental illness." After 25 years of experience on the U.S. Court of Appeals, Judge Bazelon (1974, p. 18) said: "My experience has shown that in no case is it more difficult to elicit productive and reliable expert testimony than in cases that call on the knowledge and practice of psychiatry." This statement is especially revealing considering Judge Bazelon's long-time reputation as a friend of psychiatry and his past presidency of the American Orthopsychiatric Association. As you will recall, it was Bazelon who responded to the continual complaints of organized psychiatry relative to the M'Naghten right-from-wrong test by initiating the Durham product rule for determining insanity.

Another judge-advocate of psychiatry, Judge Samuel P. King of Hawaii, concluded: "The overriding consideration behind recent cases . . . has been the personal freedom [that] is involved. A close second consideration has been that the diagnosis and treatment of mental illness leave too much to subjective choices by less than neutral individuals" (*Suzuki v. Quisenberry*, 1976, p. 1130).

As noted earlier, studies that have examined the ability of highly trained and experienced clinicians to diagnose or even characterize persons have consistently failed to demonstrate even minimal interjudge reliability (e.g., Spitzer & Fleiss, 1974; Goldberg & Werts, 1966; Golden, 1964; Little & Schneidman, 1959; Soskin, 1959; Kostlan, 1954; Meehl, 1959). There is some evidence that clinicians are no more talented in the diagnosis of abnormal behavior than nonclinicians (Luft, 1950), and that psychological diagnosis and stereotyping have a great deal in common (Jones, 1977).

The literature is littered with assertions that clinicians are not making medical or scientific judgments when they diagnose and prescribe treatments; they are making moral and social judgments that reflect the values of the dominant class (Greenaway & Brickley, 1978). This becomes evident in testimony given both in the criminal and civil courts. Shaffer (1973, p. 369), commenting on psychiatric testimony in involuntary civil commitment cases, states that "the commitment decision is a process of social definition, of rejection by society, of deviance from norms of behavior; there is nothing honestly scientific, let alone medical, about it." He notes that the poor and the powerless are at least twice as likely to be involuntarily committed as the rest of society. Finally, Shaffer concludes, "America has mental hospitals because it wants them."

A series of intriguing studies by Dorothea and Benjamin Braginsky provide strong support for the position that the diagnosis of mental illness is a value judgment (Mazer, 1978, p. 98–100). Interested in whether a patient's political attitudes would affect a diagnosis, the researchers videotaped two simulated interviews between a clinician and a bogus mental patient. Each tape consisted of four segments: (1) the presentation of the psychiatric complaints; (2) expression of the patient's political philosophy; (3) expression of political tactics for change; and (4) the patient's attitude toward mental health professionals. The psychiatric complaints in both interviews were identical, and they were constructed to depict mildly neurotic problems (e.g., fatigue, irritability, listlessness). The second and third segments reflected either moderate or radical views. In the fourth segment, both bogus patients criticized mental health professionals, but the radical patient called them "handmaidens of a repressive society," while the moderate accused them only of destroying traditional values and encouraging permissiveness.

Each videotape was played for different groups of trained and qualified psychiatrists and psychologists. The tape was stopped after each segment, and the clinicians were asked to rate how "mentally ill" the patient was.

After the first segment, both patients were rated as having mild problems. When the other segments were shown, however, the "radical" patient became progressively more deviant to the clinicians, whether psychologists or psychiatrists. The researchers wrote, "When the new left radical discusses his political philosophy, has aired his political tactics, he is seen as being twice as disturbed as his moderate counterpart, whose rating stays the same as he voices his political attitudes" (Mazer, 1978, p. 99). When the patients criticized mental health professionals, the mental illness ratings of both increased substantially. Both were suddenly seen as "severely and psychotically disturbed."

The Braginskys conducted a later study in which the "radical" patient had nothing but praise for mental health professionals. New audiences rated the first three segments comparably to their colleagues in the first study. When the patient praised the professionals, however, his sickness was drastically reduced and he was seen as a sensible and rational individual. "If insults are the illness, then flattery is the cure," the researchers quipped (Mazer, 1978, p. 100).

Despite the clinical, theoretical, and empirical problems in determining precisely what mental illness or abnormal behavior is, society and the legal system continue to believe that the bizarre or crazy behavior they cannot understand is psychologically sick, frightening, and often dangerous. It is generally reckoned that crazy people cannot help themselves make rational decisions or control their own behavior (Morse, 1978a). Mental illness, it is assumed, robs people of freedom of will and renders them legally nonresponsible in that they are not free to choose "sensible" behavior or legally correct alternatives.

These beliefs are readily apparent in the special legal rules applied to the mentally ill. Law, remember, is a normative enterprise that treats nearly all persons in all situations as responsible for their actions and often for the nature and probable consequences of those actions (Morse, 1978a). In most cases, law adheres to the common-sense view that behavior is a matter of free choice; it is the actor's act. However, when there is a suspicion of mental defect, law provides special consideration for acts which may have been the product of that defect and hence out of the actor's control and choice; the mental disease is responsible and the actor is its victim. Is this special consideration valid?

There is little empirical evidence to support the assumption that mental illness robs an individual of control and free will (Morse, 1978a). In terms of our present knowledge, there is also little reason to believe that any behavior, non-crazy or crazy, is even irresistible. Crazy people behave normally most of the time and in many ways. In addition, between crazy periods crazy people are not reliably distinguishable from normal people. In fact, there is evidence that individuals whom society and medical experts are likely to evaluate as crazy may, in many cases, have substantially more control and freedom over their lives than persons living under poverty or deprived conditions (Prentky, 1979; Easterbrook, 1978).

## ■ Psychological Assessment in the Judicial System

A leading critique of the clinical field of assessment and prediction is a monograph by Walter Mischel, *Personality and Assessment* (1968), which raises incisive questions about the tendency of clinicians to use a small number of behavioral signs to categorize people into fixed slots. Mischel demonstrates that the assessor's favorite theoretical biases enter very clearly into appraisals of other people's functioning. These status determinations in turn are used to predict specific behaviors (such as dangerousness) and to make important decisions about others' lives. Mischel's justified concern was that even highly trained and experienced clinicians infer, generalize, and predict too much from too little information, and they do so in a way that is disconcertingly similar to the personal judgment of nonclinicians. In addition, the "expert" judgments of clinicians—like everyone else's judgments—are subject to strong biases that often produce serious distortions and oversimplifications in their conclusions about behavior. For example, studies by Katz and his colleagues (1969) found that different clinicians not only see different cues in the same patient, but also use the same cues to infer differing things.

### HOW CLINICAL TRAINING AFFECTS ASSESSMENT

As noted in Chapter 4, clinicians also very often attribute causality to a person's personality rather than to the circumstances in which the person acts. This well-ingrained clinical proclivity for underestimating the importance of situational determinants and overestimating the importance of the actor's personality was noted as long ago as 1943 (Ichheiser, p. 151) and has received renewed empirical attention in recent years (e.g., Ross, 1977; Mischel, 1979).

The fact that clinicians often subscribe heavily to dispositional or personality determinants of behavior probably reflects the nature of their training. Research and theory in personality have been guided by four major theoretical models: trait psychology, psychodynamics, situationism, and interactionism (Endler & Magnusson, 1976). Of these four models, trait psychology and psychodynamics are representative of the long-standing, traditional theoretical perspectives taken toward human behavior. The trait model has been one of the most dominant forces in psychology, especially in the study of personality, whereas psychodynamics has been the corresponding force in psychiatry. According to trait psychology, personality consists of clusters of "traits," which are abstract terms for tendencies or predispositions to respond (Allport, 1937). They are considered general and enduring from situation to situation, and their various combinations are what make up individual differences between people. Psychodynamics, by contrast, assumes the existence of a basic personality core which serves as the predisposition to respond in various situations.

We have not done justice either to trait or psychodynamic theory by this cursory treatment, but the point to be advanced is that both perspectives rely extensively on individual internal predispositions as the causal links to behavior. The situation or environment are not considered powerful determinants of behavior. Clinical training has been highly steeped in the dispositional or personality approach, which most likely colors clinical assessment and prediction. However, this one-sidedness allows only a partial understanding of behavior and increases the likelihood of inaccurate prediction.

Situationism is a relative latecomer to clinical and applied professional programs (but not to experimental psychology), and many traditional programs have yet to accept this perspective. Situationism regards the situational stimuli or the situational factors as the basic determinants of individual behavior. Internal states and factors are deemed superfluous in the understanding and prediction of behavior. This perspective is often referred to as S-R (stimulus-response) psychology or as behaviorism.

Interactionism emphasizes the importance of person-situation interactions and the continuous interplay between individuals and the situations they encounter. According to Endler and Magnusson (1976), four main features characterize interactionism. First, behavior is believed to be a function of a continuous, mutual interaction between the individual and the environment. Second, the individual is seen as an intentional, active agent in that interaction. Third, the person's cognitive processes are considered essential determinants of behavior. And fourth, the psychological meaning of the situation for the individual is also viewed as a crucial factor in determining behavior.

Trait psychology and psychodynamics focus upon individual factors, situationism emphasizes the environment, and interactionism looks at the interaction of both. Given the difference, it is clear that the training and theoretical orientation of the evaluator will greatly influence the psychological assessment and behavioral predictions that are made. Trait and psychodynamic psychologists assume an underlying basic stability and continuity of personality, and therefore assume the existence of trans-situational consistency. Once the basic personality structure is determined, one should be able to predict behavior across situations. Situationism, on the other hand, concentrates on the particular stimuli of the external environment which provoke relevant responses or behavioral patterns. Interactionists analyze the constantly changing mutual interplay between individuals and their environment and develop assessments and predictions which consider both determinants.

The trait and psychodynamic perspectives have only been marginally successful in predicting behavior across situations. Some traits allow better predictions than others. For example, intelligence, as well as Eysenck's (1967) extraversion, are two traits which have demonstrated some trans-situational consistency, although there is substantial room for improvement in predictive accuracy even for these two examples. Situationism also has shown some trans-situational accuracy by focusing exclusively on the set of stimuli to be encountered by an organism. That is, by determining the typical response pattern in the presence of a particular set of stimuli, the predictor gains accuracy regardless of the personality features of the individual. However, the best predictive accuracy of behavior is gained by considering the person × situation interaction (Bowers, 1973; Argyle & Little, 1972; Endler, 1975). More specifically, the research data indicate that predictive accuracy is improved substantially by assessing each individual's criterion behavior within the context of specific situations. This observation further suggests that greatest accuracy can be achieved through idiographic (individual-based) analysis rather than through nomothetic (group-based) analysis.

## OTHER FACTORS INFLUENCING ASSESSMENT

There also appears to be a curious need for humans, including clinicians, to favor subjectively vivid but unreliable data over more complete empirical but pallid information, regardless of theoretical leanings (Mischel, 1979; Kahneman & Tversky, 1973; Nisbett & Borgida, 1975). A personal account of one's feelings is considered more revealing than actually observed behaviors. This preference for subjective information over objective data is reflected in the continuing popularity of inkblots and other projective instruments for use in clinical practice, in spite of extensive data showing them to be unreliable and fundamentally invalid (see Jones, 1977, Chapter 3). Researchers cautioning their clinical colleagues about these instruments are often ignored or are told that public pressure forces clinicians to address stressful but complex problems and provide at least a semblance of a solution.

The expectations of the referral source also potentially influence the accuracy of clinical judgment. For example, referrals from the court may communicate to the assessor, explicitly or implicitly, some desired direction or conclusion. It is possible that a sizeable number of clinicians slant their assessments to some extent to meet the expectations of the court. If the court expects a finding of competence to stand trial because of community pressure, it is possible that this expectation will be communicated to the evaluator in some manner and may influence the report delivered.

The foregoing discussion should not be construed as asserting that accurate assessment and predictions about human behavior are impossible. It does warn about the severe limits on the range and level of assessment and prediction that can be expected in view of our present knowledge about human behavior. Contemporary psychological research (e.g., Kenrick & Stringfield, 1980; Bem & Allen, 1974; Mischel, 1979) indicates that people have some consistency across situations, but it is an error to assume that even most of their behavior is consistent. In fact, research suggests that behavior is inconsistent across diverse situations but consistent across time (temporal consistency) in highly similar situations (Mischel, 1973). That is, people are apt to act the same way when the situations are very similar; in different situations, though, much behavior is not consistent. Therefore, any notion that generalities can be offered about persons based on traditional personality types or traits is misplaced. As Endler and Hunt (1969, p. 20) remark, behavior "is idiosyncratically organized in each individual."

Outside observers, like psychiatrists and clinical psychologists, cannot possibly conduct a brief interview and administer a battery of psychological tests and thereby understand the meaning of the individual's past and present behavior and accurately predict future occurrence. Yet it is not unusual for psychiatric and psychological examinations of persons alleged to be mentally ill, dangerous, and proper candidates for involuntary civil commitment to take about ten minutes (Schoenfeld, 1977); there are also many cases in which psychiatrists have certified as mentally ill and dangerous persons whom they have not even seen (Scott, 1976).

The unreliable status assessments and the inaccurate predictions so frequently offered by clinicians, their years of training notwithstanding, may also be due in part to the limited access to a small, nonrepresentative sample of behavior during an artificial, stressful interview or testing session. The best source of information about a person's past, present, and future behavior appears to be the person himself or herself (Mischel, 1968; Kenrick & Stringfield, 1980; Bem, 1967, 1972; Monson & Snyder, 1977). The person has more data at his or her disposal, along with direct access to the publicly unobservable affective and cognitive elements that affect and instigate that behavior. A secondary source of information is someone who knows the subject well and has had the opportunity to observe the person in a variety of situations (Kenrick & Stringfield, 1980). These persons, often family members or close friends, can corroborate the information provided by the subject. However, they are usually not aware of what behaviors the subject considers consistent or inconsistent.

Therefore, the accurate assessment and prediction of human behavior appears to require careful study of the interaction of the behavior of interest and the psychosocial environment in which it occurs. The best source for this analysis is the person, but other good sources are those who have had the opportunity to observe the person extensively. Accurate assessment and prediction also require, of course, a good understanding of the contaminative influence of personal biases and hunches, along with a heavy reliance on statistical and empirical data developed on the criterion behavior. The advancement of our understanding of human behavior depends upon the empirical study of the interactions of persons and their psychosocial environment.

# ■ Free Will

In the previous chapter we discussed the concept of *parens patriae*, which rests on the belief that the mentally ill are unable to make decisions that are in their best interest.

Whereas the criminal justice system assumes that criminals are responsible for their behavior, the mental health system assumes that the mentally disordered lack free will.

Recall that the fundamental rationale for state intervention in individual lives under the doctrine of *parens patriae* is that some people cannot (or will not) make "appropriate" decisions in their best interest. Appropriate decisionmaking and best-interest criteria usually reflect social attitudes filtered through the legal system. In the case of mental illness or disturbingly bizarre behavior, the social assumption is that the actor is unable to make appropriate decisions because the mental disorder has substantially reduced or completely eradicated the ability to exercise free will. In short, mental health law is based on a supposed lack or reduction of free will, whereas criminal law operates on the assumption that freedom of will is intact. Therefore, it is imperative at this point that we examine the validity of the free will concept as a viable psychological construct.

## PSYCHOLOGICAL DETERMINISM

The concepts associated with free will and their polar opposites—subsumed under the term "determinism"—have been extensively debated in religious, philosophical, and legal arenas. In an 1884 address at the Harvard Divinity School, psychologist-philosopher William James remarked, "A common opinion prevails that the juice has ages ago been pressed out of the free will controversy, and that no new champions can do more than warm up stale arguments which everyone has heard" (James, 1962, p. 145). Although James considered this argument faulty then, he did little to decimate it during his lifetime. In fact, with the emergence of Freudian determinism around the turn of the twentieth century and the rapid rise of Watsonian determinism shortly thereafter, questions of free will in psychological study fell from grace and became alien to mainstream psychological and psychiatric thought. Freud (psychodynamic theory) believed that humans were born with primitive, animal-based urges which, together with early stages of psychosexual development, determined their personality, in large part, for life. Watson (situationism) argued that people were born neutral and were determined by their conditioning and reinforcement history, possessing virtually none of the free will assumed by philosophy and religion. The medical profession of psychiatry embraced Freudian and Neo-Freudian views of human behavior, while a large segment of psychology adopted the Watsonian perspective.

While scientific psychology, with its strong deterministic orientation, dominated academe and the psychological literature, psychiatry influenced legal publications about human behavior and mental states. To repeat, psychology and psychiatry are often confused, much to their mutual resentment. Psychiatry, whose roots and basic platform were developed by Freud and his psychodynamic and psychoanalytic ways of conceptualizing human behavior, is a clinical-based profession with a strong deterministic orientation. Although there are several schools of psychiatric thought, a majority hold that humans are fundamentally driven by some combination of instinctive, biological or psychic (unconscious) forces or urges. Psychology, on the other hand, is a scientific enterprise built principally upon situationism.

In criminal justice, an expanding group of advocates are subscribing to what has become known as the "behavioral position" (Packer, 1968; Wootton, 1963). This position argues that free will is an illusion, because human action is determined by environmental forces beyond the control of the individual; the position qualifies as "radical" situationism. The notion of personal or moral responsibility is untenable, since behavior is beyond a person's control or responsibility. The social environment and society are the culprits in criminal action, not the individual. Carrying this one step further, the behavioral position argues that punishment and social sanction for such determined behavior, even if it is illegal behavior, are not useful or valid processes or procedures for changing behavior. Rather, behavior that is in conflict with society's rules and expectations must be changed through scientifically validated techniques of behavioral change and psychotherapy. Instead of incarcerating people in prison as a means of punishment and social sanction, society should treat and rehabilitate them, using the knowledge of social scientists, behavioral scientists, and mental health or behavioral clinicians.

The behavioral position outlined above should not be confused with psychological positions in general. There is a wide variety of psychological theory in the area of free will and personal responsibility, some of which will be discussed below.

Situationism (or behaviorism) generally views human behavior from a deterministic perspective, where there are no free actions; all actions are caused and predictable with reference to known causal laws. If we have enough information about the causal laws operating in a particular situation, we should be able to predict with nearly absolute accuracy what a person will do.

## RENEWED INTEREST IN FREE WILL

Recently, psychology has shifted away from this strong mechanistic point of view and has focused upon whether or not the individual perceives or thinks he or she possesses free will and freedom of action. In light of a substantial body of research, it is now apparent that *perceived* freedom is one of the most important variables in the understanding of human social behavior (Harvey & Smith, 1977; Baron & Byrne, 1981). Therefore, rather than becoming entangled in the web of the centuries-old philosophical question, "Is there or isn't there free will?" the psychological study of freedom has been asking, "What effect does a belief in one's free will (or an illusion of free will) have on one's behavior?"

Other recent psychological attempts to define and stimulate renewed interest in free will (e.g., Easterbrook, 1978; Rychlak, 1979; Rottschaefer & Knowlton, 1979) emphasize two basic components: behavioral choice and proaction. The choice component refers to the number of possible alternate behaviors available or thought to be available to an individual in any given situation. In simplest terms, it is assumed that the greater the number of choices a person feels he or she has in a situation, the greater is the perceived freedom.

The *proactive* component refers to the argument that a person has more freedom when performing a behavior for the sake of some plan, goal, or reasoned purpose. In *reactive* behavior, by contrast, an individual automatically responds to or reacts to a stimulus or an array of stimuli present in a situation (situationism). The person, therefore, is controlled (or feels controlled) by the stimulus, which not only initiated the behavior in question but also dictated much of the subsequent response pattern.

Proaction indicates that the person performed an act for a thought-out purpose and plan, not simply in reaction to a stimulus.

Choice and proactive components both depend upon competence, which is the end product of a matrix of variables, the more important being those outlined by the social-learning theorist Mischel (1973) and, to some extent, by Easterbrook (1978). Mischel maintains that six factors contribute to the development of competence:

1. Structure and predictability of the environment
2. The individual's learning experiences
3. Successes in mastery (efficacy)
4. General ability, like intelligence and cognitive encoding strategies
5. Subjective values
6. Goals, plans, and self-regulatory systems

The six are not independent entities; they overlap and influence one another. For example, learning experiences are strongly affected by learning ability (and vice-versa), and subjective values often depend upon mastery of the environment. Readers interested in learning more about the six major factors involved in the development of competence and how they contribute to choice and proaction are referred to Mischel's influential article (1973).


## THE PERSONAL FREEDOM CONTINUUM

If we accept the existence of interacting factors like the above, we are compelled to conceive of free will as existing on a continuum: at the one end, absolute determinism; at the other, absolute free will. Therefore, persons are responsible for their actions in degrees. Individual competencies and individual situations preclude an all-or-none approach to personal freedom, although this approach is often taken when the law assesses mental illness, insanity, or competence to stand trial. Psychological data emerging from social learning studies strongly suggest that most individuals fall somewhere between the two extremes of the perceived personal freedom continuum. Moreover, their place on the continuum changes when they are placed in different situations.

Learning experiences are garnered from the richness and variety of daily encounters with events. Presumably, the more experience an individual has with a wide set of circumstances, the greater the range of alternate behaviors available in the person's repertoire. However, not everyone can acquire, store, categorize, and retrieve the information gained from these experiences. Those who can have a significant advantage in developing and generating alternate behaviors.

The above capacities are subsumed under the rubric of "ability," and despite the tenuous status of the concept of IQ, there is little question that people do differ in cognitive processing, organization, and storage. In addition, the person who feels the ability to master and control what happens over a wide variety of situations has a subjective interpretation of more choices and hence feels less restricted by his or her predicament. It is these subjective interpretations and anticipations about events that social learning theorists call *expectancies*.

Proaction strongly depends upon the presence of self-developed standards, goals or plans, and self-regulatory systems. Persons who set goals, have plans to reach those goals, and possess (or feel they possess) the ability to control their behavior in a variety of circumstances experience greater freedom than those who lack these characteristics. In other words, people who regulate their own behavior by self-imposed standards and self-produced consequences, even in the absence of external contraints and social monitors, experience greater control over their lives than people who feel victim to external control and standards. Moreover, such personal standards specify the kinds of behavior appropriate under particular situations, the performance levels (goals) which the behavior must achieve, and the consequences (positive or negative) of attaining or failing to reach these standards (Mischel, 1973).

Therefore, in the broadest terms, relatively free persons are those who believe themselves to be generally competent, who strive to master and control their environment in accordance with subjective values, and who recognize responsibility for their behaviors (Easterbrook, 1978). They have, in most situations, a wide variety of perceived alternate behaviors at their disposal and generally act (or feel they act) in a proactive manner. Note that it is not necessary that choices actually exist; if the individual feels there are choices, he or she is relatively free. The relatively unfree person, on the other hand, yields to forces and structures that he or she perceives to be acting upon him or her in most situations, regardless of personal ideals and standards. The unfree person also denies responsibility for action or inaction. Again, most individuals fall somewhere beteen these two extremes on a perceived personal freedom/determined behavior continuum.

## IMPLICATIONS FOR THE LEGAL SYSTEM

When society makes legal determinations about free will, responsibility, intent, and mental illness, the social learning position argues that it must consider a person's competencies and each situation. Personal freedom cannot be assessed on an all-or-none basis; it must be assessed along a relative continuum of perceived responsibility.

Research indicates that all mentally disordered persons function with some degree of perceived free will and choice (Morse, 1978a; Easterbrook, 1978; Rychlak, 1979). In fact, many mentally disordered individuals function with more freedom of choice than most "normal" persons (Prentky, 1979). Many "normal" persons do not have a repertoire of choices open to them in day to day living. Therefore, the simple generalization that mental illness, schizophrenia, or psychosis robs a person of free will and decisionmaking ability appears unjustified and empirically unsupported.

There is no conclusive evidence that as a group individuals labeled mentally ill are any less free than other nondeviant members of the society. It might even be said that individuals regarded deviant by society may in fact perceive themselves as more free than normal or nondeviant persons, who generally conform to society's expectations rather than to their own. There is nothing to indicate that the mentally ill are less free than individuals living under poverty, deprivation, or powerless conditions in the various segments of society.

There is also little psychological evidence to support the functioning of two different legal systems—criminal law and mental health law—on the basis of freedom of will (Morse, 1978a; Monahan, 1977; Easterbrook, 1978). Monahan argues that the goals of both criminal law and mental health law are the same, though the procedures diverge. The four most frequently cited justifications for imposing the criminal sanction, he notes, are

1. Rehabilitation, which is designed to help the offender improve his or her quality of life
2. Special deterrence, intended to protect society by keeping offenders out of circulation
3. General deterrence, meant to protect society by using the offender as an example
4. Retribution, which is concerned with exacting a price from an offender for having trespassed against society

Presumably, mental health law shares the first two justifications. It attempts to rehabilitate or cure those believed to be disordered, for their own benefit, and it attempts to change them for the benefit and protection of society, so that they will no longer flout its laws and customs. Though the goals are the same, criminal law encourages due process and trial by peers; mental health law encourages discretion and trial by experts. Criminal law is concerned with past acts; mental health law with future actions. Criminal law assumes freedom of will and individual responsibility; mental health law assumes determinism, and it attributes responsibility to the so-called mental disease. Yet we have seen that the concept of mental illness is nebulous, that expert testimony and discretion are based on a profession which is largely a clinical art rather than a science, and that the prediction of future behavior is at a primordial stage of development and is often inaccurate. Moreover, free will and determinism are best conceived of as opposite ends of a continuum; very few individuals in society fall at the extremes, as criminal and mental health law would have us believe.

Treatment and rehabilitation in both corrections and mental institutions have not been successful, partly because they are parceled out on an institutional, wholesale basis with little consideration for differential treatment needs, and partly because we understand so little about human behavior. Thus, the first goal of criminal and mental health sanctions—rehabilitation—is rarely attained.

The goal that both criminal and mental health law accomplish is that of special deterrence. The primary purpose of mental health law is not to treat individuals under a *parens patriae* rationale, but rather to keep those who are likely to be dangerous or unduly bothersome out of the family, out of the community, and off the streets, using a police power rationale. As Ralph Slovenko (1977, p. 176) has remarked, this purpose remains "the hidden agenda. The consequence of a decision is often the unarticulated major premise of the decision."

## ■ Should the Insanity Plea Be Abolished?

There is increasing support for the argument that insanity is an empirically unsupported and socially unjustified concept (Monahan, 1973). Thus, whether the insanity plea should be abolished still represents one of the hottest issues in criminal law today.

Those who support the status quo contend that the insanity defense symbolizes and reinforces the average citizen's belief in personal responsibility, and that this belief is an important determinant of each citizen's law-abiding behavior. Eliminating the insanity defense, they say, would adversely affect the basic assumptions of free will upon which contemporary criminal law is built.

In a cogent presentation of the issues concerning abolition of the insanity plea, John Monahan (1973) posits that two separate issues are involved in efforts to justify the defense. If two questions can be answered affirmatively, the insanity defense is acceptable. First, does a belief in responsibility for one's actions really have an effect on one's behavior? If yes, does the existence of an insanity plea in the criminal justice system contribute to the individual's belief in personal responsibility?

## BELIEF IN PERSONAL RESPONSIBILITY

A good amount of psychological research clearly indicates that belief in personal responsibility does significantly affect one's behavior. While several theoretical positions and their supporting research evidence attest to this, we will concentrate for illustration purposes on three: locus of control, reactance, and attribution.

**Locus of control.** Also called internal-external control of reinforcement, this theory of personality was formulated by Julian Rotter (1966) and expanded by other social learning theorists (e.g., Phares, 1976). The theory deals with personal expectancies about the relationship between one's own behavior and outcomes. Locus of control represents the extent to which, in a variety of situations, individuals believe they have personal control over what happens to them. *Internal control* refers to "the perception of positive and/or negative events as being a consequence of one's own actions and thereby under personal control" (Lefcourt, 1966, p. 207). On the other hand, *external control* refers to "the perception of positive and/or negative events as being unrelated to one's own behaviors" (Lefcourt, 1966, p. 207) and therefore beyond personal control. A solid body of research (e.g., Rotter, Chance & Phares, 1972; Phares, 1976) demonstrates that people who perceive themselves as responsible for their actions behave very differently from persons who believe that they lack responsibility.

**Reactance theory.** As developed by Jack Brehm (1966; 1972), this theory hypothesizes that people view themselves as possessing a set of free behaviors or freedoms, any one of which they usually can engage in at any given time. When any of these behavioral freedoms is reduced or threatened with reduction, psychological reactance is aroused. Reactance is a motivational state directed toward restoring or safeguarding the threatened freedom. Generally speaking, the more important the threatened freedom, the greater the reactance aroused.

Reactance can be conceived of as an increased desire to act contrary to the force that is constricting one's freedom. Thus, if people feel they are being prevented from doing something, they will want to do it more than before; if they feel they are being forced to do it, they will want to do it less than before. Psychological reactance will be generated only if the person perceives an interference with his or her freedom, however. Reactance theory provides interesting possible explanations for certain violations of law and opposition to new laws restricting what people believe to be their freedom of movement. Busing, zoning regulations, and antidrug laws are good examples; prohibition, of course, is a classic one.

**Attribution theory.** A third example of the theoretical and research support for the significant effect that belief in personal responsibility has on behavior is attribution theory (Heider, 1958; Kelley, 1967). When we make judgments and interpretations about our own internal states and those of others on the basis of outward behavior, we are engaging in the attribution process. We are telling ourselves (or others) what causes certain behavior.

Attribution theory recognizes two possible types of cause—internal and external. Internal causality is the attribution of responsibility for events to an individual's personal qualities; external causality is the attribution to environmental circumstances or forces of nature existing outside the individual. Do people become criminals because of inner psychological deficiencies or problems (internal causality) or because of forces from the social environment, like peer pressures and poverty (external causality)? Should an individual be responsible for his or her behavior, or should society be held accountable?

Studies suggest that for the most part we tend to view internal factors as accounting for other people's behavior (Duval & Wicklund, 1973; Storms, 1973; West, Gunn & Chernicky, 1975). Our own behavior, however, is controlled by outside forces.

The amount of perceived freedom an observer attributes to the behavior of others also enters into attribution theory. Did a person who acted a certain way have a choice? If the person is seen as having freedom to act, the course of action will likely be attributed to the actor rather than to the environment.

According to attribution theory, judges and juries make decisions about blame and about guilt or innocence partly on the basis of the above factors. If the research is correct, there is a tendency to attribute the behavior of defendants to their own personal qualities (internal causality), rather than to outside forces. However, few data are available regarding the perceived freedom element. Research to date is in substantial agreement, however, that the attribution process plays an extremely important role in determining or at least ascribing responsibility to the actions of oneself or others (Harvey & Smith, 1977).

## NEED FOR THE INSANITY DEFENSE

While we have solid research support to answer affirmatively Monahan's first question concerning the behavioral effects of belief in responsibility, we have very little empirical support in either direction for his second question. Will citizens become more responsible if the need for responsibility is emphasized by the existence of the insanity defense?

Monahan himself finds little logical or empirical support for the argument that citizens need the insanity defense, but he does find compelling justification for asserting that the law needs it. To function adequately, our present system of legal principles requires the free will concept, rather than a strict adherence to the deterministic position advocated by behaviorists. Specifically, Monahan contends that the elimination of the insanity defense would lead to the complete acquittal of increasing numbers of abnormal offenders and would eventually result in a legal system based upon nonexistent treatment procedures and unfounded faith in our ability to predict dangerousness. A legal system of this sort would leave the citizen at the mercy of politically chosen "experts" with full *parens patriae* power. In sum, "the consequences are too uncertain and too potentially disastrous to recommend abolition" (Monahan, 1973, p. 738).

# ■ Summary and Conclusions

This chapter has assessed critically the judicial system's assumptions with regard to issues of insanity and competence to stand trial. We have also reargued the position, introduced in the previous chapter, that mental health law, presumably based upon a solicitous *parens patriae* rationale, often treats individuals less fairly than does criminal law, with its strong emphasis on due process.

Far more individuals are affected by competence to stand trial determinations than by the insanity defense. Defendants are judged IST when, because of present mental functioning, they are either unable to help their attorney mount a satisfactory defense, unable to understand the judicial process in which they are enmeshed, or both. Insanity focuses on the individual's functioning at the time of the alleged illegal act. Because the plea of insanity is often an admission to *actus rea* and because persons found insane are usually committed to institutions for lengthy, unsuccessful treatment, attorneys avoid the plea whenever possible. Thus, only a very small percentage of persons going through the criminal courts plead the insanity defense.

Guidelines most often used in assessing IST and insanity were covered. The predominant insanity rules, Durham, M'Naghten and the ALI/Brawner rules, were covered separately and evaluated.

Considerable emphasis was placed on the concept of mental illness, how it evolved, and to what extent it is justified. As with predictions of dangerousness, diagnoses of mental illness are often arbitrary and based upon insufficient information. Too often abnormal behavior—behavior deviant from that of the rest of the population—is frightening and therefore considered dangerous. More importantly, however, this abnormal behavior is not distinguished from the abnormal behavior associated with a heinous criminal act. Both are believed out of a person's control and, in both situations, the person is not responsible.

The concept of free will as a viable psychological concept was examined from a social learning viewpoint. All individuals, including the mentally ill, have free will to some extent. The relatively more free are those who see themselves as competent and able to control their environment. From this perspective, a person inhibited by poor social environment, who perceives himself as having little choice, has less free will than the supposedly mentally ill person who brutally murders children. Therefore, determinations of free will and ultimately of responsibility should be based, not on the presence or absence of mental illness, but on the degree to which a person feels choices are available.

Although attempts to abolish the insanity defense because of its obtuseness and inconsistent applications occur with regularity, the legal system does not appear ready to forego the defense. The chapter concludes with the question, "Should the insanity defense be abolished?" The reader is left to arrive at his or her own conclusion.

## ■ Key Concepts and Principles, Chapter 5

Competence
Insanity plea
M'Naghten Rule
Durham Rule
ALI and Brawner Rules
Mental illness and criminal
    responsibility

Trait psychology
Psychodynamic psychology
Situationism
Interactionism
Free will

# ☐ 6

# ■ The Psychology of the Jury

☐     The jury is one of the most powerful components in the American system of justice, with authority to take away freedoms and autonomy from the accused, bestow them, or settle suits and declare financial liability. The jury is one of the few channels through which ordinary citizens can impose on society their own standards or biases concerning what is morally or socially right and wrong behavior. Although in some jurisdictions judges are the final decisionmakers, only rarely will they overrule a jury's decision. The jury's responsibility is sobering, therefore, and there is good evidence that citizens take the judicial process seriously and try to provide what they believe is the best decision for the case at hand.

The Sixth Amendment of the U.S. Constitution guarantees the right to a jury trial in both criminal and civil matters where the penalty for an offense is greater than six months' imprisonment (*Duncan v. Louisiana*, 1968; *Baldwin v. New York*, 1970). The Seventh Amendment extends this right to federal civil cases where the damages are above a certain amount, usually $500 (*Ross v. Bernhard*, 1970; *Curtis v. Loether*, 1974; *Pernell v. Southall Realty*, 1974). Despite these guarantees, however, participants in the judicial system are under social, political, and economic pressure to settle a case before it gets to the trial stage. Trials, especially by jury, are time consuming, expensive, and unpredictable, and their unpredictability often prompts even the most experienced attorneys to avoid them if possible. Thus, each case is submitted to a filtering process, replete with discretionary maneuvers which may include plea bargaining, dismissal of charges by the court, or a mutually agreeable settlement by the parties in a civil suit. Throughout American history, most criminal cases have been disposed of through plea bargaining, a procedure in which the defendant pleads guilty to a lesser charge (Alschuler, 1979; Heumann, 1978). In fact, the vast majority of civil and criminal cases today are settled or dismissed before they take the tedious journey through the entire judicial sequence.

When cases do proceed to the trial stage, juries are used in about half of the criminal and civil cases in federal district courts and in less than 10 percent of all cases (both civil and criminal) in state trial courts (Vago, 1981). This discrepancy is explained partly by the fact that state courts are most often the setting for civil suits and that juries are used most often in criminal cases.

In general, criminal cases are the major consumers of jury trials (Jacob, 1972), perhaps because there is a strong tradition in favor of being judged by a jury of one's peers when one is prosecuted for a criminal offense. The technical complexity inherent in many civil matters also accounts for some of the discrepancy between criminal and civil use of juries, however. The judiciary discourages the use of juries in many civil cases because the litigation revolves around issues that are believed too complicated for the average person to comprehend (e.g., engineering patents or trade secrets). Often, therefore, with the exception of personal injury cases, civil cases are tried before a judge, if tried at all. More often, they are settled before approaching the trial stage. For the above reasons, most of the discussion in this chapter will relate to juries in criminal cases.

Psychology's interest in jury behavior centers around questions like the following: Does the jury render verdicts based upon evidence presented in the courtroom irrespective of the characteristics of the attorneys, the litigants, witnesses, or the jurors involved, or do these extra-evidentiary factors play a significant role in the decision-making process? Are jury decisions based on whim, sympathy, or prejudice, or on rational, logical foundations? Are there procedures or variables that help predict verdicts prior to the trial? Can jurors be significantly influenced by events prior to the trial, as by extensive pretrial publicity? How do members of the jury influence one another, both during the trial itself and during the deliberation process?

Answers to these questions are elusive, partly because empirical investigations of jury behavior are hampered by legal restrictions relative both to the jurors themselves and to the jury process. Deliberations are shrouded in secrecy, and the courts resist any infringement upon the jurors' privacy. Therefore, psychologists and other social and behavioral scientists have resorted to *simulation research*, where some segment of jury selection or trial process is acted out in a way that approximates the real process, or where subjects read or listen to portions of trial transcripts or tapes. Findings from simulation research must be interpreted in a very guarded manner, however, as will be explained later in the chapter.

Experimentation is only one way psychology can help us understand jury behavior. Psychological theories and information on group decisionmaking, attitude change, attraction, and persuasion, although not directly related to legal matters, can shed light on events that transpire in the courtroom as well as in the privacy of the jury deliberation chamber. This chapter will summarize and evaluate the jury research that has been done to date, assess it critically, and consider some of the relevant psychological theories. First, we will give some attention to procedural and structural features of the jury: how it is chosen, how large it should be, and what its responsibilities are.

# ■ Jury Selection

Jury composition is influenced at two stages of selection, *venire* and *voir dire*. In the first stage, the venire (which literally means "to come when called"), a pool of prospective jurors is drawn from an eligible population presumed to be representative of a local geographical area. Usually, the prospective jurors are drawn from voting lists by a clerk of courts. In some jurisdictions, a "key man" system is used: outstanding or model citizens are asked to submit names of individuals they think would be good jurors. It has been suggested that both of these traditional ways of accomplishing the venire are imperfect, if not plagued by biases and prejudices (Abraham, 1968), despite the fact that the U.S. Supreme Court has consistently ruled that jury pools must represent a cross section of the community or general population. Even though the voting list method appears to afford random representation, in reality it is not difficult to be excused from jury duty, and certain occupational groups (e.g., teachers, police officers, attorneys) are virtually untouchable for jury duty in many jurisdictions.

The logic of fireside induction leads us to believe that the most impartial juries will be demographically representative of the community at large. However, Gordon Bermant and John Shapard (1981, p. 89) have suggested that "achieving demographical representativeness for any or all recognizable groups will not automatically, or even necessarily, move us closer to the major goal of eliminating bias." In fact, there is a distinct possibility that the most impartial juries will, in general, be demographically unrepresentative of the entire population.

Several stages are involved in the process of jury selection. Names of persons chosen through the venire appear on a list of potential jurors for a given period, and those individuals are eligible to participate in the next stage of jury selection, the voir dire. This process allows the judge and attorneys to question the prospective jurors and possibly disqualify them from jury duty. It is at this juncture that "common-sense psychology" as espoused by attorneys as well as findings from the research are likely to be applied. During voir dire, attorneys can apply their own hypotheses about people in an attempt to generate the jury that could be most sympathetic to their client.

The defense and the prosecution (in civil cases, the litigants) each have two options for challenging the impanelment of a prospective juror, *peremptory* and *for cause*. The peremptory option lets a lawyer request the removal of a prospective juror by "fiat," without giving reason. "The essential nature of the peremptory challenge is that it is one exercised without a reason stated, without inquiry and without the court's control. . . . The peremptory permits rejection for a real or imagined practility that is less easily designated or demonstrable" (Justice White, *Swain v. Alabama*, 1964, p. 220).

The number of peremptory challenges allowed an attorney is restricted by statute or by the presiding judge, who sets the rule in a pretrial conference. In some jurisdictions, the defense in a criminal trial may be allowed more peremptory challenges than the prosecution. For example, in a federal criminal trial where the final jury size is twelve, the prosecution has six peremptories and the defense has ten. On the other hand, in a federal civil trial where the jury size is six, each side has three peremptories.

A challenge for cause is exercised whenever it can be demonstrated that a would-be juror does not satisfy the statutory requirements for jury service (e.g., age, residence, occupational requirements), or when it can be shown that the prospective juror is so biased or prejudiced that he or she is not likely to render an impartial verdict based only on the law and on evidence presented at the trial. Challenges for cause based on bias may be subdivided into those claiming a specific bias and those claiming nonspecific bias (Bermant & Shapard, 1981). A nonspecific bias refers to expected bias due to the fact that a prospective juror is a member of some group or class similar to that of the litigant or defendant. For example, socioeconomic or racial class may be grounds for disqualification in some cases. A specific bias refers to situations where the prospective juror has a blood relationship to one of the litigants, ties through marriage, or linked economic interests to the case.

The idealized purpose of voir dire is to eliminate potential jurors whose biases may interfere with a fair consideration of the evidence presented at the trial. Bermant and Shapard (1981) refer to this as the "probative purpose" of voir dire, probative in that the lawyer or the judge are able to "probe" in order to discover reasons to exercise challenges for cause or peremptoriness. However, lawyers often use voir dire to gather information and to indoctrinate or ingratiate themselves to jurors (Blunk & Sales, 1977). This strategy to influence the jury is referred to as the "didactic purpose." There is some evidence that 80 percent of voir dire time is used to persuade the jury panel to be sympathetic to lawyers' clients (Broeder, 1965), although a more recent study indicates that the percentage is closer to 40 (Balch, Griffiths, Hall & Winfree, 1976).

In 1977 the Federal Judicial Center (Washington, D.C.) gathered information about current voir dire practices and opinions of federal district judges (Bermant, 1977). Completed questionnaires from 365 active federal judges and 55 senior judges were used in the analysis. Approximately 70 percent of the judges said they conducted the voir dire examinations themselves in both civil and criminal trials, although they would accept additional questions suggested by counsel. Between one and two percent said they conducted the voir dire completely by themselves, rarely seeking or accepting additional counsel from attorneys. Bermant (1977) concluded from earlier data that federal judges are increasingly taking over the voir dire, leaving little room for lawyer participation.

About three-fourths of the judges stated that insuring an impartial jury was the primary purpose of the examination. Eighty percent of the judges felt that there was considerable variation among lawyers in conducting the voir dire. These data contrast with the opinions of judges about the skills of lawyers during trials. Judges have stated in previous surveys that in about three-fourths of the cases they have heard, the lawyers were about equal in skill (Kalven & Zeisel, 1966; Partridge & Bermant, 1978). This difference is difficult to reconcile with existing data, but it does suggest that although judges believe lawyers vary widely in voir dire skills, these skills do not significantly affect the overall quality of advocacy during the trial process.

Another area of interest concerning voir dire centers around methods of juror challenge. There are two major methods or strategies by which one may challenge the suitability of a prospective juror (Bermant & Shapard, 1981). One is the *struck jury* method, whereby the judge rules on all challenges for cause before the parties claim any peremptories. In a second method, called *sequential*, the lawyers exercise their challenges without knowing the characteristics of the next juror to be interviewed. In this method, overexercise of challenges may result in a challenged juror being replaced by someone even more objectionable. Preliminary research using mathematical models has shown that the struck jury method may be superior in eliminating bias to the sequential method (Bermant & Shapard, 1981), but much more research is needed before firm conclusions can be offered.

# ■ Scientific Jury Selection

The possibility that individual juror personality characteristics might affect final verdicts has led some attorneys to experiment with new techniques for the voir dire. Of course, lawyers have always used their assumptions about human nature to help them select juries. For example, if one's client is a self-made businessman who holds traditional and conservative values (even though he may have "slipped" and allegedly poisoned his business partner), one does not want radical political activists on the jury. Sometimes, enterprising lawyers have used more than assumptions to choose jurors. At a 1981 meeting of the American Trial Lawyers Association, attorneys were advised to hang around the favorite bars of potential jurors, quizzing their friends whose tongues were loosened by liquor (see box).

The traditional hunches, guesses, and amateur (sometimes professional) detective work are now being supplemented by the time-consuming and elaborate procedures of social scientists in the employ of attorneys. The process, alternately called scientific jury selection (Saks & Hastie, 1978) or systematic jury selection (Kairys, Schulman & Harring, 1975), was launched in the early 1970s, when the defense in the Harrisburg Seven conspiracy trial hired a group of psychologists and other social scientists to help them choose jurors who would be most sympathetic to their clients.

The defense reasoning was understandable. The defendants were antiwar activists who were accused of sabotaging a government installation. The conservative community in which the trial was being held, coupled with the money the state was funnelling into the prosecution, made acquittal unlikely. The social scientists gathered background and demographic information on each potential juror, as well as measures of attitudes, interest patterns, and possible personality characteristics. All of the information was obtained indirectly, since the researchers could not contact members of the venire or the jury itself. After the trial, which acquitted the alleged co-conspirators,

---

## □ LAWYERING TACTICS

Effective trial lawyers make jurors seethe with anger and squirm with vicarious pain, and they dress to please the upper-class tastes of the presiding judge. And, as indicated by reports about a 1981 meeting of the American Trial Lawyers' Association, they are always ready to learn new tricks of their trade.

According to a *New York Times* news item (July 28, 1981), a common theme at the week-long conference was that courtroom victories require much more than dry exposition of facts.

"Juries vote based on their impressions, their feelings, their biases, and their prejudices, not the facts of the case," the *Times* quoted one of the speakers. Another advised his colleagues to "get each juror to think [about a 'guilty' client], 'there's a reasonable doubt because he's a nice guy and I like him.'"

The lawyers also received advice about posing a final question to a prosecution witness:

"Put the cold steel between their eyes and drive it in and leave them twisting in the wind as you sit down."

the defense publicly credited its victory in large part to the extensive help of the social scientists.

Since then, a growing number of sociologists and social psychologists have been refining and expanding scientific jury selection techniques. Along with the attitude and behavioral scales, elaborate statistical procedures and mathematical probability formulae are being applied to provide attorneys with an educated guess about whether a given individual will be the juror they want for their client. Sometimes, even after a jury is seated, the behavioral scientists continue to help attorneys by offering opinions regarding the nonverbal behavior of witnesses or jurors during the trial.

Do behavioral scientists belong in the courtroom in this advisory role? How helpful are their suggestions regarding the voir dire procedure? Opinions and findings regarding these scientific methods vary (Suggs & Sales, 1978). There is some evidence that scientific jury selection is slightly superior to random selection (Padawer-Singer, Singer & Singer, 1974) or even to the traditional selection methods used by attorneys (Zeisel & Diamond, 1978). Overall, we must remember that few juror characteristics have been found to predict with any consistency the outcome of the trial. Thus, the persuasiveness and nature of the evidence appear to outweigh strongly any personality or specific characteristics of individual jurors. However, when the evidence is ambiguous or poorly presented, the characteristics of the jurors might carry greater weight in the decisionmaking process, although it appears that group dynamics, rather than individual differences, play the substantial role.

The weight that jurors give to evidence is not surprising if we remember that most people are not familiar with the judicial process and, in fact, are awed by it. Thus jurors tend to be more strongly influenced by the judicial context than by their own personality and attitudes. Within the judicial context, "jurors adopt a role of 'fairness' and 'objectivity' which may be as extreme as they ever have had or will have in their lives" (Saks & Hastie, 1978, p. 70). The jury box and the courtroom itself may exert powerful situational pressures that mitigate the individual differences of the jurors.

## ■ Jury Size and Decision Rule

Whether by historical accident or some unknown logic, the traditional jury in Great Britain, the United States, and Canada has consisted of twelve persons who must come to an unanimous decision. Winick (1979) suggests that the English dislike of the decimal system and an affinity for the number twelve (e.g., twelve pennies in a shilling) account for the system, which originated in 14th century England (Saks, 1977). In 1966, England began to require that only ten out of twelve jurors had to agree on a verdict (Saks, 1977), and soon after that lawyers in the United Sates also began to challenge the traditional system. As a result, *decision rule*, which refers to the proportion of the total number of jurors required to reach a verdict, is no longer always unanimous, since some jurisdictions now allow agreement among fewer individuals (majority or quorum rule). Nor is the twelve-person jury now a universal phenomenon.

Beginning in the late 1960s and early 1970s, the U.S. Supreme Court permitted states and federal courts to experiment with both jury size and decision rules, in the interest of economy and efficiency. Twelve-person juries were expensive, and they consumed too much time. The experimentation, however, has resulted in considerable controversy over the merits of changing the traditional jury structure and process.

## SIZE

In two landmark decisions, *Williams v. Florida* (1970), which dealt with state criminal trials, and *Colgrove v. Battin* (1973), dealing with federal civil trials, the Court claimed that reduction in jury size would not alter trial results significantly. A six-person jury does not violate a person's constitutional right as laid down by the Sixth Amendment, the Court said in *Williams*, since that amendment mandates a jury "only of sufficient size to promote group deliberation, to insulate members from outside intimidation, and to provide a representative cross-section of the community" (*Williams v. Florida*, 1970, p. 100). Nor does a smaller jury size violate the Fourteenth Amendment, which guarantees the right of trial by jury in all state nonpetty criminal cases, the Court said.

Although the Justices cited social and behavioral research to support their assertions, immediate responses decrying the logic of the two decisions erupted from some social and behavioral science representatives, who were concerned about the Court's misguided and inappropriate use of empirical data (e.g., Walbert, 1971; Zeisel, 1971, 1974; Saks, 1974, 1977). One statement in *Colgrove* generated particular foment by noting that "four very recent studies have provided convincing empirical evidence of the correctness of the *Williams* conclusion that 'there is no discernible difference between the results reached by the two different sized juries'" (*Colgrove v. Battin*, 1973, fn. 15, p. 11). Most of the "experiments" cited by the Court were not experiments or empirical evidence at all, but the common-sense observations and opinions of individuals with experience in the judicial system. The experiments which the Justices relied upon were permeated with critical methodological flaws to the point of producing poor, or at best unconvincing scientific evidence. Saks (1974) even finds that some of the studies reported in *Colgrove* actually reported data opposite to the interpretation made by the Court.

In *Ballew v. Georgia* (1978), the Supreme Court once again broached the jury size issue, this time drawing a line at the minimum number of jurors to be allowed. Georgia statutes permitted a five-person jury to decide a criminal case, and the petitioner, tried on an obscenity charge, claimed that this law deprived him of due process rights. Since the Court had thus far avoided establishing a constitutional minimum, the Justices apparently decided that a more enlightened ruling was necessary to prevent possible erosion of the jury system.

Arguing that a minimum jury size must be established, the opinion written by Justice Blackmun cited social and psychological research supporting the position that anything below six members violated the Sixth and Fourteenth Amendments. This time, the Court used the available research accurately and carefully, and the Justices somewhat improved their reputation in the eyes of the research community (see box).

Common sense and information gleaned from the few empirical studies of jury size tell us that there are advantages and disadvantages to both small and large juries. Small groups allow more active participation from all members, because people are usually less inhibited in expressing their opinion in a small-group discussion. How-

## ☐ BALLEW v. GEORGIA

### Excerpts

Eight years before the U.S. Supreme Court heard this case, in *Williams v. Florida*, it had been established that a jury of six members was not unconstitutional. Two years later, in *Johnson v. Louisiana*, the Justices referred to a "slippery slope" of decreasing jury size but did not indicate when this "slope" would become too steep. Now, in *Ballew*, they were ready to be more specific. "We face now, however, the two-fold question whether a further reduction in the size of the state criminal trial jury does make the grade too dangerous, that is, whether it inhibits the functioning of the jury as an institution to a significant degree, and, if so, whether any state interest counterbalances and justifies the disruption so as to preserve its constitutionality."

The opinion written by Justice Blackmun made extensive use of empirical research to address and answer several concerns, including the following:

First, recent empirical data suggest that progressively smaller juries are less likely to foster effective group deliberation. At some point, this decline leads to inaccurate fact-finding and incorrect application of the common sense of the community to the facts. Generally, a positive correlation exists between group size and the quality of both group performance and group productivity. . . .

Second, the data now raise doubts about the accuracy of the results achieved by smaller and smaller panels. Statistical studies suggest that the risk of convicting an innocent person (Type I error) rises as the size of the jury diminishes. Because the risk of not convicting a guilty person (Type II error) increases with the size of the panel, an optimal jury size can be selected as a function of the interaction between the two risks. . . .

Third, the data suggest that the verdicts of jury deliberation in criminal cases will vary as juries become smaller, and that the variance amounts to an imbalance to the detriment of one side, the defense. . . .

Fourth, . . . the presence of minority viewpoint as juries decrease in size foretells problems not only for jury decisionmaking, but also for the representation of minority groups in the community. The Court repeatedly has held that meaningful community participation cannot be attained with the exclusion of minorities or other identifiable groups from jury service. . . .

The Justices also referred to methodological problems in some studies that claimed no differences in the decisions of juries of varying sizes. Noting that there were a substantial number of individual cases which were significantly affected by jury size, Blackmun concluded that aggregate data, or averages, "masked significant case-by-case differences that must be considered when evaluating jury function and performance."

While we adhere to, and reaffirm our holding in *Williams v. Florida*, these studies, most of which have been made since *Williams* was decided in 1970, lead us to conclude that the purpose and functioning of the jury in a criminal trial is seriously impaired, and to a constitutional degree, by a reduction in size to below six members. We readily admit that we do not pretend to discern a clear line between six members and five. But the assembled data raise substantial doubt about the reliability and appropriate representation of panels smaller than six. Because of the fundamental importance of the jury trial to the American system of criminal justice, any further reduction that promotes inaccurate and possibly biased decisionmaking, that causes untoward differences in verdicts, and that prevents juries from truly representing their communities, attains constitutional significance.

ever, it has also been shown that small groups, to avoid upsetting the group balance, sometimes inhibit expressions of disagreement among participants (Slater, 1958; Bales & Borgatta, 1955). The mere opportunity to speak is greater in a small group, however.

Larger groups have a number of advantages that are important to note if jury size is being considered. Large groups tend to provide the greater variety of skills and knowledge that may be necessary to arrive at a decision in a complex issue. Large juries appear to remember testimony given during the trial, although small juries have been shown to be better at recalling the arguments presented (Saks, 1977). Also, as jury size increases, a more representative cross section of the community is obtained, thereby assuring minorities a better opportunity to be represented (Zeisel, 1974).

Larger juries increase the probabilities of two kinds of minorities being represented: racial, subcultural, or other demographic groups and opinion minorities. This second type of minority, which refers to those persons within a decisionmaking group who resist or go against the majority, has significant implications with regard to jury size. We will give this topic greater attention by referring to the recent research of Robert Roper (1980).

Roper tested a number of hypotheses, but only two directly concern us here. One predicted that juries with *viable minorities* will "hang" (fail to reach a verdict) more often than juries without viable minorities, a term which refers to juries with at least two members not in agreement with the majority. Social psychological research initiated by Solomon Asch (1952) found that in group situations, one minority member with even one ally greatly increases his or her resistance to persuasion by the majority. On the other hand, one minority member lacking an ally is substantially less likely to resist the majority of three or more.

The second relevant hypothesis tested by Roper predicts that larger juries will hang significantly more often than smaller ones. This hypothesis is built upon the observation that viable minorities have a great probability of occurring in larger juries, an observation for which Roper found convincing support in analyzing his own data.

Roper used a simulation design with a strong attempt at establishing external validity. One hundred ten mock juries ranging from six to twelve members were selected from jury rolls of Fayette County, Kentucky. A videotape of a trial was presented in a courtroom, and the juries were then permitted to deliberate for an unlimited amount of time to reach a verdict. The verdict could take one of three forms: guilty, not guilty, or hung. Juries that initially reported they were deadlocked were sent back twice to try to reach a decision. If they returned a third time without a verdict, a hung jury was declared.

As predicted, juries with viable minorities were more likely to end up hung than juries with nonviable minorities. In addition, the larger the jury, the more likely it was that a viable minority would emerge—hence the more likely that the jury would be hung. The conclusions from the Roper study indicate that viable minorities are more successful at resisting conformity pressures exerted by the majority. Furthermore, larger juries over the long haul will result in significantly fewer convictions, a point which presents an interesting dilemma.

Juries always have the possibility of making either a Type I or Type II judicial error. A Type I error is made when an innocent person is convicted; a Type II error when a guilty person is released (see *Ballew v. Georgia* box). Roper's results suggest that, if the judicial system and society wish to avoid making Type I judicial errors, they should encourge twelve-member juries. On the other hand, if Type II errors are to be avoided, six-member juries should be instituted. The dilemma, of course, is deciding which of the two we want least: the occasional conviction of innocent persons or the occasional release of the guilty.

Arguments about jury size can be tempered somewhat by the fact that most of the cases handled by the judicial system are clearcut, where any number of individuals would probably reach the same verdict. The sensational cases we encounter in the media, where juries deliberate for long periods, represent only a small percentage of all trials ushered through the courts. It has been estimated that small and large juries would disagree in no more than 14 percent of all verdicts (Lempert, 1975), although as a nationwide figure this represents many defendants. And although it appears that the jury-size issue has been settled temporarily in view of the Court's ruling in *Ballew*, states would be well advised to examine the psychological evidence and to consider which judicial error they can least tolerate before deciding to opt for small juries.

## DECISION RULE

The U.S. Supreme Court began to deal with decision rule at about the same time as jury size, addressing the question: Is it constitutionally permissible to allow a less than unanimous decision to convict defendants or to resolve civil matters? Two key cases, *Johnson v. Louisiana* (1972) and *Apodaca, Cooper and Madden v. Oregon* (1972) are relevant. Noting that there was no existing law or judicial precedent, the Court concluded in both cases that nonunanimous verdicts are acceptable and reasonable, especially in view of the fact that such majority or quorum verdicts would presumably result in fewer hung juries.

Unfortunately, the research evidence examining the differences between majority and unanimous decisions is sparse. The few data available have suggested that quorum juries (those which do not have to have a unanimous vote to convict) demonstrate better recall of the arguments and display more communication among members (Saks, 1977). However, it has also been found that quorum juries often stop deliberating the moment they reach the requisite majority (Kalven & Zeisel, 1966; Saks, 1977), thus providing less opportunity for a minority member or dissenter to argue a position or even be heard at all. Therefore, unanimous juries probably have the advantage of allowing greater minority participation. Moreover, since the first vote of quorum juries generally becomes the final verdict, it appears that it is primarily in unanimous juries that the minority can effectively alter the course set by the majority. On the other hand, unanimous juries also are more likely to block verdicts or to result in hung deliberation. In their classic work *The American Jury* (see box), Kalven and Zeisel (1966) cite data that, in jurisdictions requiring unanimous verdicts, 5.6 percent of juries were hung. This figure compared to 3.1 percent in jurisdictions that required quorum verdicts.

The available research does not allow us to conclude whether the quorum or the unanimous jury is more advantageous. Regardless of which jury type is chosen, we lose some of the desirable features of the unchosen. It appears, however, that concerns that quorum juries deprive a defendant of due process are unjustified. Although unanimous juries, when convicting, seem more certain of a defendant's guilt, they apparently do not render verdicts significantly different from those rendered by quorum juries (Saks, 1977).

# ■ Jury Dynamics

During a trial, jurors are expected to remain passive, in the sense of having no direct involvement in the proceedings, but they are also expected to be attentive. They must listen to testimony and arguments, pay attention to demonstrations, scrutinize exhibits, and form their impressions. Much of the information must be acquired and retained through hearing and auditory memory, since jurors are usually prohibited from taking notes. The trial follows three phases: the opening arguments, the presentation of evidence, and the closing arguments. In criminal trials, the prosecution has both the first and the last word.

The role of the presiding judge is to enforce rules of procedure in the courtroom by controlling the manner in which evidence is presented, by ruling on objections, and by choosing between the procedural arguments of attorneys as to the proper process to be followed. It is also the judge's prerogative to control the courtroom by threatening and imposing contempt citations for disturbances or other interference with courtroom procedure.

### JURY INSTRUCTIONS

The judge often instructs the jury about the respective roles of judge and jury during the course of the trial; these are usually called *preliminary instructions*. At some point during the trial, the judge also gives *substantive law instructions* about the substantive law that should guide the jury in weighing the evidence and reaching a decision. In many jurisdictions, some of the substantive law instructions are included in the preliminary instructions and later repeated at the end of the trial.

The preliminary instructions usually include comments about the jurors' conduct during the trial, their responsibility to avoid representatives of the media, their need for impartiality, and their duty not to discuss the case with other jurors or other persons during recess. The substantive instructions in most jurisdictions occur at the end of the trial and include information about the law as it applies to the particular case. These instructions further outline the possible verdicts the jury can return, reexplain whether there must be a unanimous or a majority verdict, and explain what standard of proof is required. An example of standard of proof is the requirement that jurors must be satisfied "beyond a reasonable doubt" that the defendant is guilty before returning a conviction.

With regularity, research has found that jurors find jury instructions technical and confusing (Elwork, Sales, & Alfini, 1977; Forston, 1970; Jacob, 1972; Strawn & Buchanan, 1976). Providing substantive law instructions at the very end of the trial appears to be a poor procedure for enhancing juror understanding of what is expected of them. Elwork, Sales, and Alfini (1977) and Kassin and Wrightsman (1979) report evidence that the jury is far more likely to understand the substantive law it is expected to rule on if the substantive instructions are read at the beginning of the trial as well as at the end.

Bruce Sales and his colleagues (Sales, Elwork & Alfini, 1977) have analyzed the semantics of the instructions and their presentation in terms of their usefulness as learning devices. For instance, many jurisdictions have the judge read instructions to jurors without providing them with a written copy. The evidence from the learning research indicates that the jury would be better able to comprehend and remember the law if the instructions were both heard and read. We will comment further on legal language in Chapter 9.

## DELIBERATION

At the end of the trial, jury members are ushered to special quarters, where they are expected to deliberate in complete privacy until they reach a verdict or believe they are hopelessly deadlocked. No outside participants or information that might contaminate the deliberation are permitted in the jury room.

When a jury begins its deliberation, one of its first decisions is to select a foreman

---

## ☐ THE CHICAGO JURY PROJECT

The University of Chicago Jury Project, which officially began in September 1952, was financed through a $1.4 million grant provided by the Ford Foundation. The principal architect of the venture was legal scholar Edward H. Levi, Dean of the University of Chicago Law School, who later became Provost of the University. The project's broad goal was to further research in the law and the behavioral sciences by focusing upon the jury system, commercial arbitration, and income tax law. The project leader was lawyer-academician Harry Kalven, Jr., who worked closely with Professor Hans Zeisel, former President of the American Statistical Society, and Professor Fred Strodtbeck, an expert on the behavior of small groups. Others associated with the project, whose names you will find cited throughout this text, included lawyer and professor Dale Broeder, who did extensive interviewing research with jurors, and Rita James Simon, who investigated, among other things, the jury's handling of the defense of insanity.

Numerous articles and several books resulted from the data collected during the seven-year project. Among the best known books are *The American Jury*, by Kalven and Zeisel (1966), *Delay in the Court*, by Zeisel, Kalven and Buchholz (1959), and *The Jury and the Defense of Insanity*, by Rita James Simon (1967).

The project was plagued by numerous problems in the collection, analysis and write-up of the data. Lawyers had trouble understanding social and behavioral scientists, and social and behavioral scientists had difficulty understanding lawyers (Broeder, 1958).

At one point, the project's research approaches toward the jury resulted in a national scandal, complete with a Senate subcommittee investigation. Researchers had recorded, via videotape, jury deliberations in five civil cases in the federal district court in Wichita, Kansas, without

who will lead subsequent discussions and oversee the votes. Not surprisingly, research has shown that this foreman is most likely to be male, middle-aged, of high status in the community, and from a managerial or professional occupation (Strodtbeck, James & Hawkins, 1957; Strodtbeck & Mann, 1956). The place where a person chooses to sit at a rectangular table in the deliberation room also appears to influence the possibility that he or she will be chosen; individuals who sit at the end of the table have a substantially higher probability of being picked than those persons who locate themselves along the sides (Strodtbeck & Hook, 1961; Nemeth & Wachtler, 1974). Of course, it is also expected that high status males would be most likely to seat themselves at the head of the table as a matter of habit. The person who speaks first in the group is also more likely than others to be chosen foreman.

It appears that the influence of the foreman on the jury's decisionmaking is minimal, however. The research has shown that he or she usually takes the position of moderator rather than advocate and tends to be more concerned with procedural rules than with any given position (Saks & Hastie, 1978).

---

the knowledge of jurors, but with the consent of the trial judge and counsel. This infringement upon the traditional privacy of the jury generated a public outcry, public censure by the United States Attorney General, hearings before the Subcommittee on Internal Security of the Senate Judiciary Committee, the enactment of statutes in some thirty-odd jurisdictions prohibiting jury-taping, and widespread editorial commentary and news coverage by the national press.

Among those leading the public charge was then Assistant Attorney General Warren E. Burger, who at a regional meeting of the American Bar Association stated he was "shocked" by the actions of the University researchers. He also claimed that the project had originally planned to include "surreptitious eavesdropping" on 500 to 1,000 federal juries (New York Times, Oct. 13, 1955). On October 12, 1955, Senate subcommittee counsel Julius Sourwine devoted most of his questioning to an attempt to link Dean Levi and Professor Kalven to subversive or communist causes, implying that the pro-

ject was a communist plot designed to undermine the freedom of secret jury deliberation.

Dean Levi and Professor Kalven tried to defend the methodology of "eavesdropping" on the jury by arguing that the only way to improve the jury system was to collect data on the actual processes which occur within the secrecy of jury deliberation. This call to science did little to mitigate the furor that had been engendered. Impeachment of the federal judges who permitted the eavesdropping was entertained, though not carried through, and statutes prohibiting similar eavesdropping were adopted.

The data collected during the taping of the Wichita civil jury deliberations were never used by the Chicago Jury Project, but the data collected through other means (e.g., interviews and surveys of jurors and judges) resulted in one of the most extensive jury studies ever completed by social scientists. The material gained from the project will be cited frequently throughout the text.

Once settled in the deliberation chamber, jurors may only request clarification of legal questions from the judge or ask to look at items of evidence. In some cases, they have received permission to visit or revisit the scene of a crime or accident. If a verdict has not been returned by late evening of the first day, the jurors are given overnight accommodations and continue their deliberation the next day, sometimes continuing for weeks.

The evidence suggests that most juries in criminal trials do not involve themselves in lengthy deliberations. Kalven and Zeisel (1966) found that, for trials lasting one or two days, 55 percent of the juries took one hour or less to reach a verdict, and 74 percent of the juries completed their deliberation in less than two hours. Most juries take a vote soon after settling into their deliberation chamber. The University of Chicago Jury Project (Broeder, 1958; Kalven & Zeisel, 1966; see box) found that in 30 percent of the cases jurors reached a unanimous decision after only one vote. In 90 percent of the cases, the majority on the first ballot usually won out, regardless of who sat on the jury or who constituted the majority and minority. Lengthier deliberations appear not so much to change a predominant opinion as to bring about consensus.

James (1959) examined the specific content of simulated jury deliberations and found that about 50 percent of the discussion was devoted to personal experiences and opinions. Another 25 percent was devoted to discussions of procedural issues, 15 percent to actual testimony, and 8 percent to the instructions provided by the judge. Another study found that the more highly educated they were, the more jurors emphasized procedure and instruction. Jurors with only a grade-school education were more likely to focus on opinions, testimony, and personal experiences (Gerbasi, Zuckerman & Reis, 1977).

As part of the extensive Chicago Jury Project, researchers sent questionnaires to judges throughout the country who had presided over a total of 3,567 criminal cases. The judges were asked to record general information about each case, the verdict of the jury, and what they would have decided in the absence of the jury. If they disagreed with the jury, they were asked why the jury probably decided as it did.

Judges agreed with juries in 75.4 percent of the cases, both believing that 13.4 percent of the defendants should be acquitted and that 62 percent of the defendants should be convicted. Although the judges disagreed with juries in about 25 percent of the cases, most of this disagreement occurred when a defendant had been acquitted. In fact, judges agreed with jurors in fewer than half of the acquittals. Hence, juries appear to be more lenient than judges, who were bound by official legal rules. The judges indicated the jurors were influenced by "sentiments" about law and about defendants, extralegal factors that did not enter into the judges' own decisions. Extralegal factors have received a great deal of attention from psychologists studying the jury process, and we will encounter many of them throughout the rest of this chapter.

# ■ Psychological Studies of the Jury Process

The jury may be studied either from a molecular approach, where specific variables about individual jurors are examined, or from a molar perspective, where the group as a whole is studied. Psychologists thus far have been drawn to the molecular approach, focusing on several characteristics of individual jurors, usually within one experiment. Although group processes are well represented in psychological experiments, rarely do these experiments deal directly with juries or even simulated juries. Exceptions will be noted later in the chapter.

Almost all the psychological investigations of the jury have been conducted under simulated or "mock jury" conditions, since the costs of carrying out studies in a real setting—not to mention obtaining the requisite judicial approval—are beyond the reach of many researchers. We will find, however, that most simulation studies do not approximate the real jury situation.

Very few psychological investigations of the jury process were conducted prior to 1969 (Weiten & Diamond, 1979), but since then simulation projects have increased dramatically. Although there are critical methodological flaws in many of the studies, rendering their applicability to the jury process questionable, the reader should become familiar with some of the frequently cited work to understand what has been attempted.

Anyone reviewing jury simulation literature is confronted with a bewildering array of experiments, using a wide range of methods to investigate an assortment of jury variables. We will attempt to put some order in the disarray by presenting the studies and their findings by topic area and by trying to tie them together through a few theoretical themes. The failure to relate the data to some systematic theory that could enable an organized summary of the results is one of the major problems of jury research. The topic areas covered in this section are those that experimental psychologists (usually social psychologists) have isolated. The following presentation by no means covers the constellation of possible variables that can be studied, nor does it describe all of the experiments in the areas discussed. The intent is to provide the reader with highlights and trends of the data, to help him or her appreciate the problems faced by investigators, and to suggest future research directions.

## THE EFFECTS OF DEFENDANT AND VICTIM CHARACTERISTICS ON JURORS

**Physical attractiveness.** Social psychological research has shown that most people believe that good-looking people, compared to physically unattractive people, possess socially desirable traits and lead more successful and fulfilling lives (Dion, Berscheid & Walster, 1972). In other words, "beauty brings its own rewards." Moreover, transgressions or violations of the social code are more highly tolerated when they are committed by a physically attractive person (Dion, 1972; Efran, 1974). This may account in part for why convicted felons are appraised as being "uglier" than most people (Cavior & Howard, 1973).

When Michael Efran (1974) asked subjects (college students) if they felt physical appearance should play a role in jury decisions, 93 percent said it should not. Efran then simulated a jury situation, drew different subjects from that same college student population, and asked them to evaluate guilt or innocence and to mete out punishment. Subjects were shown photographs of the "defendants." The physically attractive defendants were believed less guilty and deserving of less punishment than unattractive defendants accused of the same offense (cheating).

Several qualifiers must be attached to the Efran results. First, female subjects always evaluated male defendants and male subjects female defendants. This pairing of opposite sex probably accentuated a possible attractiveness variable. Second, the significant results occurred because male subjects responded favorably to female defendants. Female "jurors" were not as strongly influenced by the male attractiveness. Third, a juror's decision was not made after group discussion (deliberation), but individually and without any influence from others. We do not know whether group influence would have mitigated a possible attractiveness factor.

A study by Sigall and Ostrove (1975) suggests that a defendant's physical attractiveness does not always lead to leniency by individual jurors; sometimes the nature of the crime overrides. Subjects (sixty male and sixty female undergraduates) were presented trial information about a female defendant accused of either burglary or a swindling scheme. Attractiveness was manipulated by showing the "jurors" photographs of the defendant. There was also a neutral defendant condition, with no photographs shown. The burglary was a breaking and entering and grand larceny of $2,200 in cash and merchandise. In the swindle, the defendant allegedly induced a middle-aged bachelor to invest $2,200 in a nonexistent corporation. Hence, the experimenters not only manipulated the attractiveness of the defendant, but also created a condition under which the defendant used that attractiveness to perpetrate her crime.

Attractive defendants in the swindle scheme received longer sentences than un-

## ☐ SIMULATION RESEARCH

Simulation research is an attempt to bring some scientifically relevant aspect of the "real" world into the artificial world of the laboratory. Therefore, simulation is a representation of reality that is examined in simplified form within the controlled setting of an experiment, or quasi experiment. Its usefulness in advancing knowledge about the real world depends heavily upon how closely the simulated condition mimics the essential components of the reality it represents.

Simulations in psychological research may be divided into three broad categories: person-to-person designs; person to machine or to bogus person designs; and computer simulation. Computer simulation has generally focused upon two topics: cognitive processes, as

exemplified by models of juror or judge decisionmaking; and social processes, such as models of jury deliberation.

The person to bogus person or machine simulation occurs when the subject interacts, knowingly or unknowingly, with a bogus, programmed respondent. For example, in a bargaining or negotiating paradigm, the computer or bogus subject responds to offers or counteroffers in a pre-established sequence in order to discover the strengths and weaknesses of theories and theoretical models.

The two-person simulation condition is most often encountered in various bargaining-game paradigms. The most popular in recent years has been the "prisoner's dilemma" situation. The game follows the following sequence:

attractive defendants for the same offense. On the other hand, attractive defendants in the burglary situation received substantially *less* severe punishment for the same offense. Therefore, the results support the hypothesis that good looking criminals are generally treated better, as long as they have not capitalized on their looks to commit their crime.

Physical attractiveness also emerged as a significant factor in a study using a simulated civil case involving personal damage suits. Stephen and Tully (1977) report that mock jurors were more inclined to award larger amounts of money for damages when the plaintiffs were attractive. Also of interest was the finding that male mock jurors awarded the male plaintiff the largest amount of money and the female plaintiff the smallest amount. There was no difference in the awards given by female jurors on the basis of sex. In general, sex of defendants has not been found to influence mock jurors in criminal cases (Weiten & Diamond, 1979). Other demographic variables like socioeconomic status or race have been marginally important or not significant at all (Weiten & Diamond, 1979).

Research results thus far suggest that physical attractiveness could be of considerable significance in the courtroom, especially in criminal cases. However, in view of group dynamics and the effects of evidence itself, we must remain extremely skeptical in making inferences about the total impact in a majority of cases.

---

Two suspects are taken into custody and separated. The district attorney is certain that they are guilty of a specific crime, but he does not have adequate evidence to convict them at a trial. He points out to each prisoner that each has two alternatives: to confess to the crime the police are sure they have committed, or not to confess. If they both do not confess, then the district attorney states he will book them on some very minor trumped-up charge . . . and they will both receive minor punishment; if they both confess they will be prosecuted but he will recommend less than the most severe sentence; but if one confesses and the other does not, then the confessor will receive lenient treatment for turning state's evidence whereas the latter will get the book slapped at him [Luce & Raiffa, 1958, p. 95].

In the above dilemma, maximum joint gain is derived if neither subject confesses. However, if one prisoner confesses and the other does not, the second prisoner gets the book, and the confessing prisoner gets favorable treatment. Of course, subjects do not actually receive prison sentences, and this represents the major disadvantage of simulation research. Success depends upon the degree of subject involvement that the experimental situation can engender. If the subjects become deeply involved, the situation may approximate real life scenarios. However, regardless of the approximation of reality, the simulation taps only what subjects might do, not necessarily what they would do.

Simulations do have the advantage of testing theory in areas that are extremely difficult or impossible to examine experimentally, such as jury or judge decisionmaking. However, generalizations made on the basis of simulation procedures alone should be cross-validated with generalizations derived from other methods before conclusions are offered with confidence.

**Social attractiveness.** Many of the investigations focusing upon social attractiveness have weighted that variable heavily by manipulating several characteristics of a person at the same time. For example, marital status, work history, age, and occupational status have all been used to contribute to overall attractiveness. Therefore, it is difficult to know whether any one characteristic outweighed the others, or how combinations of them may have affected the total picture. Mock jurors are usually given descriptions of defendants that include several positive or several negative attributes. The crime is always identical, regardless of the defendant's description. The object of the experiment is to discover whether the socially unattractive defendant will be judged more harshly than the socially attractive one.

One of the earliest such empirical projects was a two-part study designed by Landy and Aronson (1969) that examined both victim and defendant social attractiveness. In the first experiment, the hypothetical victim of a drunken driving accident was presented as either of high or low social status, and there was no manipulation of the defendant's attractiveness. Jurors were harsher when defendants had killed the high status victim. In the second experiment, the two levels of victim status were maintained, but the researchers introduced three levels of defendant status (high, neutral, low). Here, high and neutral status defendants were given less harsh sentences than those of low status, even though the offense was identical.

The Landy and Aronson experiments have been criticized on several fronts. The researchers have been accused of stacking the cards by making the victims or the defendants overly attractive and of examining too many variables. Age, past criminal record, occupational status, previous personal tragedies, and friendliness were all included as variables, thus making it difficult to determine precisely which variable or combination of variables affected sentencing. Davis, Bray, and Holt (1977) claimed that neither experiment, by itself, showed an effect for victim attractiveness; it was only after pooling scores across the two studies that an effect emerged. Davis and his colleagues argued that this method is of dubious validity, since the studies differed in samples and procedures.

The Landy and Aronson study stimulated a rash of additional research, because the suggestion that a relationship exists between social attractiveness and decision-making by juries was too provocative to ignore. Many of the subsequent studies have provided at least partial support for the hypothesis that defendants who are perceived as socially positive and as responsible members of society receive more lenient treatment than persons seen in a less positive light (Berg & Vidmar, 1975; Kaplan & Kemmerick, 1974; Reynolds & Sanders, 1973; Nemeth & Sosis, 1973; Friend & Vinson, 1974; Izzett & Fishman, 1976; Izzett & Leginski, 1974; Sigall & Landy, 1972; Dowdle, Gillen & Miller, 1974; Kulka & Kessler, 1978; Solomon & Schopler, 1978). To date, studies regarding victim attractiveness have been less definitive.

**Attitudinal attractiveness.** Is it any surprise that people tend to like those who agree with them and to dislike those who disagree (Baron & Byrne, 1981)? People who have many of the same attitudes as we do are viewed more positively than people whose attitudes are largely dissimilar. The proportion of similar attitudes expressed by the other person is critical, however (Byrne & Nelson, 1965). If a person only agrees with us on twelve out of twenty-four topics, he or she is not liked as much as another who agrees with us on four out of six topics (Byrne, 1971). If a juror perceives a defendant (or any litigant) as having many of the same beliefs and attitudes as that juror, might he or she be more inclined to view the defendant favorably and to be more lenient in judging the person's behavior? Like physical and social attractiveness, attitudinal attractiveness has been subjected to empirical study under simulated conditions in an attempt to answer this question.

Griffitt and Jackson (1973) tested the attitude-similarity hypothesis and found that the more similar the defendant's attitudes were to the mock jury's attitudes, the more likely jurors were to find the defendant attractive and the less inclined to find him guilty. When they did find him guilty, jurors recommended that the attitudinally similar defendant be given a more lenient sentence.

Mitchell and Byrne (1973) also report some support for the attitude-similarity hypothesis. Their study looked at the relationship between juror-defendant attitude similarity and authoritarianism and how that relationship affected ratings of guilt and sentencing. The results suggested that personality of the juror may play an important role. Only jurors high in authoritarianism were significantly influenced by attitude similarity; they considered a dissimilar defendant more guilty and recommended a more severe sentence than for a defendant they believed more similar to themselves. Jurors low on authoritarianism, however, were not influenced by attitude similarity.

As a whole, studies like these indicate that defendants who are physically and socially attractive or who are attitudinally similar to mock jurors will probably receive some degree of leniency. If these results were generalizable to actual courtroom situations, it would mean that defense attorneys could engender sympathy for their clients by emphasizing these attractiveness variables to the jury. On the other hand, an opposite effect might be produced by varying levels of the victim's attractiveness. However, we cannot say with assurance that the results can be applied so readily. As emphasized at the beginning of this section, empirical psychologists investigating attractiveness have concentrated upon a molecular approach, where the judgments of individual jurors are reported. A molar approach, emphasizing group deliberations, has produced less definitive answers.

An experiment by Izzett and Leginski (1974) suggests that group deliberation reduces the tendency of individuals to give severe sentences to unattractive defendants, but that the effect on the sentencing of attractive defendants is negligible. Kaplan and Miller (1978) suggest that group deliberations tend to mitigate individual juror biases. On the other hand, Rumsey and Castore (1974) (cited by Davis, Bray & Holt, 1977) found that mock jurors were lenient toward an attractive defendant both before and after group discussion. At this point, we can only state that attractiveness appears to play a significant role in influencing the judgments of individuals, but the effects of group deliberation remain equivocal.

Many of the studies on the relationship between attitudinal attractiveness and jury decisionmaking have been conducted by social psychologists testing Byrne's (1971) reinforcement theory of attraction, which predicts that the perception of similarity is rewarding and the perception of dissimilarity is nonrewarding, or even punishing. Byrne argues that similarity leads to liking, because it gives people independent evidence for the correctness of their own interpretation of social reality. While this theory has solid support (Clore & Byrne, 1974; Lott & Lott, 1974), it does not explain why jurors would respond favorably to physically or socially attractive defendants, who may not be similar to the jurors themselves. Below, we will examine two theories that may help account for this leniency or for juror harshness: the just world theory and the theory surrounding the authoritarian personality.

# ■ Just World Hypothesis

Psychologists have observed that many people believe the world is a just place, where one gets what one deserves and deserves what one gets (Lerner, 1970). This simplistic belief may help to explain why juries sometimes make the decisions they do, and it should be examined more carefully in future research. In a just world, fate and a person's merit are closely aligned, "good" people are rewarded, and "bad" people are punished. Believers in a just world perceive a connection between what people do, are, or believe in and what happens to them. Over the past decade, these observations have been shaped into a hypothesis which is getting and should continue to receive considerable research attention.

According to the just world hypothesis, for the sake of cognitive consistency, many people cannot believe in a world governed by a schedule of random reinforcements or events. The suffering of innocent or respectable people—those who have done nothing to bring about their own grief—would be too unacceptable and unjust (Lerner & Simmons, 1966). Thus, when tragedy strikes, believers in a just world tend to blame the victims, concluding that these victims must have deserved their fate in some way. Conversely, there is also a strong propensity to attribute good fortune and luck, like winning a lottery, to having done something good or positive (Rubin & Peplau, 1973). An important qualification, however, is that just-worlders tend to attribute causality or blame to the victim only as a last resort, preferring to blame another person or an obvious cause whenever possible.

Researchers examining the hypothesis have found that belief in a just world is positively related to belief in God and religiosity (Staub, 1978; Zuckerman & Gerbasi, 1977); authoritarianism (Rubin & Peplau, 1973); political conservatism and adherence to traditional values (Lerner, 1977; Staub, 1978); trust (Rubin & Peplau, 1975); the "protestant ethic" (hard work brings just rewards) (Zuckerman & Gerbasi, 1977); and a tendency to admire and respect political leaders and powerful institutions (Rubin & Peplau, 1975). Believers in a just world are also presumed to be hostile and unsympathetic toward victims of social injustice, especially when their suffering cannot be easily alleviated (Lerner, 1970; Lerner & Simmons, 1966). Moreover, a just world orientation encourages an adherence to the rules and laws that are intended to guide conduct and control the nature of a society as a whole (rather than a benevolent attitude toward individuals and their specific welfare).

Just-worlders use two dimensions to decide whether others deserve their fates—actions and attributes (Lerner, 1980). To just-worlders, certain acts, like cruelty, unfriendliness, stinginess, hostility, or antisocial behavior, deserve a range of negative consequences. However, attributes like physical attractiveness, intelligence, taste in dress, social status, or social power and influence also determine just-worlders' (as well as many other people's) impressions and judgments.

Attractiveness, whether physical or social, is assumed by many people to be deserved. That is, attractive people have earned their attractiveness by being good, positive persons. It follows the same logic as that proposed by Dion, Berscheid, and Walster (1972), that "what is beautiful or socially desirable must be good." Therefore, we would expect jurors who are just-worlders to consider attractive defendants as being basically good and deserving of lenient treatment. To the author's knowledge, this hypothesis has yet to be tested.

The just world hypothesis has been examined, however, in relation to victims of criminal actions or accidents. Jones and Aronson (1973) investigated several hypotheses, including the counterintuitive prediction that a socially attractive victim of a crime is perceived as more at fault than a less socially attractive victim. Mock jurors were 234 college undergraduates who read a brief case account of either an actual rape or an attempted rape, involving victims presumed to differ in social respectability: a married woman, a virgin, and a divorcée. The subjects were presented with descriptions of the crime, the defendant, and the victim, and they were asked how many years the defendant should be imprisoned and how much the victim was at fault.

The first hypothesis predicted that more fault would be attributed to a respectable victim than to a less respectable one. This is in accordance with the just world belief that something tragic does not happen to persons with good character; somehow, they must have done something to bring their fate upon themselves. A second hypothesis predicted that a defendant who injured a respectable person would be punished more severely. The researchers had distributed a pretest questionnaire which indicated that married women and virgins are more highly regarded in society than divorcées. As a third hypothesis, Jones and Aronson predicted that an actual rape would be more severely punished than an attempted rape.

The results were generally in the direction of the predictions. Regardless of their own sex, subjects did feel that the married woman and the virgin (high respectability) were more at fault for the rape than the divorcée (low respectability). In assigning punishment to the defendant, the subjects gave more severe sentences when an actual rape had occurred. The second hypothesis was only partially confirmed, however. Although stiffer sentences were meted out when the victim of an actual rape was married, the jurors drew no distinction between virgins and divorcées; similar punishments were given in both cases. For attempted rape, however, the culprit received approximately the same sentence whether the victim was married or a virgin and received substantially less punishment if the victim was a divorcée.

In general, the results of the Jones-Aronson study lend support to a just world hypothesis concerning the misfortunes of victims, if we assume, as Lerner (1980) does, that most people are just-worlders. Jurors persisted in attributing fault to women of high respectability who, because the world is just, somehow must have done something to bring the attack upon themselves. This attribution of fault did not affect the severity of punishment given the defendant, however.

Although there are many unanswered questions regarding the results of the above study, they are striking enough to make a just world interpretation worth pursuing.

Research is needed to explore the just world phenomenon in depth. Is it a near-universal attribute? If not, is it present in a significant percentage of the population? Had Jones and Aronson administered a just world scale to their jurors, the results might have proved more intriguing.

## AUTHORITARIANISM

Authoritarianism is the term used to describe an ideology or an attitude system holding that one should unquestionably accept authority from recognized powerful people and institutions. Since authoritarianism is present in people in varying degrees, it is possible to speak of high or low authoritarians. The former conform strictly to conventional social norms and exhibit black-or-white thinking, rigid prejudice toward those who are different or do not embrace their point of view, and hostility toward those who deviate from established social norms. On jury panels, high authoritarians are hypothesized to be intolerant and to have a tendency to condemn, reject, and punish those who violated conventional wisdom and laws. Therefore, we would expect high authoritarians to convict frequently and to render severe punishment for deviants. On the other hand, it is hypothesized that authoritarians would be more accepting and lenient toward those individuals whom they perceive as sharing their own values.

Low authoritarians demonstrate opposite attitudes. Authority is not inherently respected, but must earn respect. Low authoritarians do not place great value on conventional norms, and they have more tolerance for those who deviate. Sometimes called egalitarians, people low in authoritarianism are believed to be more objective in making jury decisions.

A number of jury simulation studies have examined the authoritarianism continuum and have contrasted persons at both poles. As expected, the research has reported that high authoritarian jurors are more inclined to perceive guilt and give more severe punishments when the defendant is described as attitudinally dissimilar from themselves or as having a negative character (Berg & Vidmar, 1975; Mitchell & Byrne, 1973; Boehm, 1968). It has also been reported that authoritarians are more in favor of the death penalty than egalitarians are (Jurow, 1971) and are especially punitive toward low status defendants (Berg & Vidmar, 1975).

Authoritarians seem to be more strongly influenced by the judge (Bandewehr & Novotny, 1976), but they are also more likely to ignore a judge when told to disregard testimony about a defendant's character. Egalitarians, presumably because they are open minded, recall more evidence about the crime (Berg & Vidmar, 1975). High authoritarians have also been found to be "source oriented" and nonauthoritarians to be "message oriented." That is, authoritarians pay comparatively little attention to arguments and testimony and base their responses more readily on the attributes of the sources (Johnson & Steiner, 1967).

Might group interaction limit the impact of an authoritarian personality? Several researchers have addressed this question. Boehm (1968) contended that authoritarians reach their verdicts early in a trial and resist changing their verdict in the face of new information. Egalitarians, on the other hand, presumably resist making early judgments until they are given all the information about a case. Other social psychological research, however, has found that authoritarians are more susceptible to influence than egalitarians are (e.g., Kirscht & Dillehay, 1967; Bray & Noble, 1978).

In an attempt to obtain further information on the effects of group interaction on authoritarians, Bray and Noble (1978) conducted a simulation study in which forty-four six-person juries listened to a 30-minute audiorecording of a murder trial based on an actual case. After hearing the tape, subjects entered into group discussion to simulate the jury deliberation process. A verdict could be returned only if five of the six jurors agreed on a decision within 45 minutes; failure to do so resulted in a hung jury.

Prior to the experiment, the subjects were administered psychological scales to determine their level of authoritarianism. In addition, measures of the individual juror's judgments about guilt were made prior to and after the deliberation. The experimenters were interested in both individual juror decisions and in the six-member group jury verdict.

The results revealed that authoritarian jurors and juries reached guilty verdicts more often and imposed more severe punishments than egalitarian ones did. The latter finding is consistent with other studies (e.g, Berg & Vidmar, 1975; Jurow, 1971; Mitchell & Byrne, 1973) and has some potential implications for trials involving capital punishment. Authoritarians were more likely than egalitarians to say they would convict when death was a potential penalty.

The data also showed that predeliberation to postdeliberation verdict shifts existed for both authoritarians and egalitarians, although authoritarians exhibited significantly more such shifts. This finding lends credence to the possibility that authoritarians are influenced substantially by group interaction. The direction of the shifts differed: Authoritarians gave more severe sentences after group deliberations, while egalitarians demonstrated a trend toward more lenience. These shifts reflected the choice initially favored by the jurors and provide support for the group-polarization effect to be discussed below.

Although we must be cautious about making generalizations from simulation to actual jury decisionmaking, it does appear that authoritarianism is an influential factor in the jury process. Ellison and Buckhout (1981) conclude that authoritarianism is a common syndrome in American citizens and very likely plays a significant role in the legal judgments made by juries. According to these researchers, scores on the authoritarian scale have been the best predictors of conviction they have encountered. Also, like Bray and Noble, Ellison and Buckhout found that authoritarians are consistently in favor of the death penalty.

This leads to an important issue, one that comes in the realm of the psychology *and* law relationship discussed in Chapter 1. Some researchers have suggested that authoritarians are undesirable as jurors and should be eliminated in the voir dire. But American law is a social and political enterprise developed from the moral fabric of society. If authoritarianism is a common ingredient of American culture and presumably of American juries, and if a democratic system is based on the attitudes of its citizens, shouldn't authoritarians be impaneled representatively? If attorneys are to reject prospective jurors on the basis of personality type, the rejections should be made via established judicial procedures of peremptory and for-cause challenges. A policy decision that would preclude authoritarians (or just-worlders or "neurotics") from being seated on a jury would be ill advised.

# ■ Group Processes

### POLARIZATION

James Stoner (1961) discovered that when people got together in a group they were more daring or "risky" in their decisionmaking than when they made decisions as individuals. This heuristic phenomenon, eventually called the risky-shift effect, stimulated the interest of numerous investigators who generated a collection of studies to test it. As so often happens in psychological research, however, what appeared to be simple was discovered to be highly complex. "Risky shift" was a misnomer that did not portray accurately the effects of groups on individual decisions (Myers & Lamm, 1976). Subsequent research illustrated that group deliberation may produce cautious decisions as well as more risky ones, depending upon the context, and thus was born the group-polarization hypothesis.

The hypothesis states: "The average postgroup response will tend to be more extreme in the same direction as the average of the pregroup responses" (Myers & Lamm, 1976, p. 603). That rather complicated maxim simply means that group interaction tends to draw the average individual pregroup decision more clearly in the direction in which it was already leaning. Hence, if individual members of a group were leaning toward a not-guilty verdict, the group interaction would increase their commitment toward a not-guilty verdict even more. If, on the other hand, individual members tended to believe a defendant guilty, group discussion should encourage a stronger commitment toward a guilty verdict. In civil cases, an individual juror's belief that a plaintiff deserved a substantial award for damages might be reinforced in group discussion, and the ultimate group decision would award even higher damages. Thus, polarization refers to the shift toward the already preferred pole.

Myers and Kaplan (1976) presented subjects with case materials that clearly made defendants in eight hypothetical traffic felony cases appear either guilty or not guilty. If the subjects found the defendant not guilty, they were also expected to recommend punishment. The guilty–not-guilty judgments were made on a scale ranging from 0 (definitely not guilty) to 20 (definitely guilty), and the punishment recommendation was given on a scale ranging from 1 (minimum punishment for the infraction) to 7 (maximum punishment).

Myers and Kaplan found that group discussions (deliberations) polarized the initial response tendencies associated with a case. Mock jurors who evidenced reactions toward guilty verdicts and punishment became harsher following deliberations. Those with lenient initial judgments became more lenient after deliberations. When jury deliberations were not allowed, however, judgments did not change from the first to the final rating.

Walker and Main (1973) compared the civil liberties decisions of individual federal district court judges to the decision of three-judge panels in the same cases. Initial individual views were mildly pro–civil liberties, so it was anticipated that group interaction would magnify (polarize) these views. This hypothesis was supported, as the group condition engendered more pro–civil liberties decisions than the single-judge condition (65 percent compared to 30 percent).

A number of other experiments using simulated jury conditions have demonstrated the shift from prediscussion tendency to postdiscussion certainty (Bray & Kerr, 1979; Kerr, Nerenz & Herrick, 1979; Bray et al., 1978; Kaplan, 1977). It appears that group discussion, at least under simulated conditions and with college students as mock jurors, does in fact polarize already existing opinions or beliefs.

## INFORMATION INTEGRATION MODEL

Martin Kaplan and his colleagues (see, generally, Kaplan & Schersching, 1980; 1981) have tried to work *information integration theory* into the jury deliberation process with some success. The theory is a model that demonstrates how individual jurors combine information about an object or person in reaching a judgment. Each bit of information or impression about a judged object is assigned a scale value, which "refers to the quantitative expression of the belief on the judgment dimension" (Kaplan & Schersching, 1981, p. 236). For example, if we are talking about a guilty–not-guilty dimension, and the defendant matches a witness' description, we would conclude that this bit of information has high scale value in determination of guilt. However, if other evidence indicates that the defendant was hundreds of miles away at the time of the crime, the descriptive information would have lower scale value for establishing defendant guilt.

The first step in the information integration model, then, is for a juror to assign cognitively an impression or scale value to each bit of information which relates to the judgment. These separate scale values must be integrated into a unified impression or judgment. Obviously, all pieces of information will not contribute equally to the judgment to be made. For instance, discovering that a defendant had a good motive for committing the crime may not be as informative as finding out that the defendant was at the scene of the crime.

The information integration model, therefore, theorizes that each belief has two quantifiable features: a scale value on the judgment continuum and a weight (or importance) for the judgment. These weighted scale values are then integrated into an overall judgment concerning a defendant or other relevant object. This integration process is hypothesized to follow a simple algebraic rule in each juror's head.

For illustrative purposes let us examine how the model might account for the polarization effects described above. Polarization effects, remember, are specific to group deliberations, and if the model is to account for them it must explain what transpires within the "cognitive algebraic processing" of each juror during the group deliberation. It is assumed that a preliminary judgment has already been made by each juror prior to deliberation. According to the polarization hypothesis, this preliminary judgment becomes more extreme after discussion. Kaplan makes the theoretical assumption that the preliminary or predeliberation judgment will not be as extreme in guilt-value as warranted by the evidence provided during the trial. This theoretical assumption can be supported by a weighted-averaging model: When a "neutral" initial impression possessed by most jurors is averaged in with the evidentiary information received during the trial, the predeliberation judgment will be less polarized than might be expected strictly from the evidence. In other words, the initial impression will tend to dampen the overall judgment, at least until the jury deliberates.

During the deliberation process, information received during the trial is exchanged among the jurors. While all the information that is exchanged was available to each juror during the course of the trial, each juror, due to his or her attention and cognitive restraints, chose only segments of the total informational pool. Therefore, each juror based his or her initial or predeliberation judgment only on a segment of the total information, which was also dampened by a neutral initial impression. During discussion with other jurors, a larger amount of trial information is acquired. The information integration model predicts that increasing the amount of nonneutral informational elements (trial information) relative to the more neutral initial impression will move the judgment closer to the information value, which essentially represents the polarization effect.

The information integration model hypothesizes that other influences occur during deliberation, but these lie at too great a theoretical tangent to our main topic for consideration here. However, Kaplan's model does strongly support the value of a twelve-person jury compared to a six-person jury because of the information sharing which occurs. Even more important from a psychological perspective, however, is the considerable theoretical value the model has for integrating our knowledge about the jury process and for stimulating further research.

## ■ Jury Simulation: Critiques and Conclusions

Jury simulation studies that attempt to understand both individual and group decision-making are being conducted at a steady pace, but doubts about their external validity persist. Can an experimental situation even approximate a real life encounter? Studying the jury process is a formidable task. Even if researchers were allowed to observe or manipulate actual jury proceedings, there would be such an annoying myriad of independent variables that experimental control and precise measurement would be nearly impossible. More importantly, of course, such experimentation would border on the ethical, social, and legal issue of what is "just."

The simulation studies to date have had other problems, summarized bluntly by Neil Vidmar (1979). "It is argued that much jury simulation research, especially that involving investigation of the effects of defendant character on juror-jury decisions, can be fairly described as marked by (a) legal naivete, (b) sloppy scholarship, and (c) overgeneralization combined with inappropriate value judgments" (Vidmar, 1979, p. 96).

Vidmar's first criticism refers to the lack of legal sophistication and knowledge displayed by research psychologists relative to the judicial system. Thus, their experimental designs are flawed by the inclusion of unrealistic scenarios or instructions. For example, many studies have required subjects to determine the amount of punishment a defendant should receive (sentencing), when in actual practice juries are rarely involved in sentencing. Some researchers have been known to confuse criminal and civil trials, as by presenting subjects with criminal trial materials and asking them to award damages! More subtle gaffes have occurred when researchers have not been familiar with statutes, with what is permissible evidence, or with what are legally acceptable jury instructions. Sometimes, courtroom procedures have been presented out of sequence, or researchers have failed to provide subjects with clear definitions of what constitutes guilt or innocence.

Researchers commonly ask subjects to determine degrees of guilt (as on scales from one to ten) rather than simply return a guilty or not-guilty verdict. In defense of this practice, we must note that simple guilty or not-guilty verdicts are difficult to analyze statistically. They result in a "dichotomous" variable—one that has only two possibilities. For ease of analysis and sensitivity to differences, researchers prefer a continuous variable denoted by different degrees, since such a variable allows a more sophisticated computer analysis.

As an example of sloppy scholarship, Vidmar notes a frequent, unwarranted practice on the part of researchers to cite inaccurately the findings of Kalven and Zeisel's *The American Jury* and to align their own results with those of that classic study. In essence, Vidmar argues, many investigators are not justified in claiming similarity between their study and the Kalven-Zeisel project, because their results simply do not correspond. Some researchers are just as lax with respect to other studies, inaccurately citing results or misunderstanding the theoretical positions of other scholars. This laxity builds pyramids of inaccuracy and misinformation into the research literature.

Vidmar's third criticism pertains to grandiose assertions by researchers that their studies will help solve the problems of the judicial system. "Researchers have tended to puff up the potential importance of their findings without taking into consideration all the other factors that might offset them in a real world trial" (Vidmar, 1979, p. 100).

It is debatable whether jury simulation studies, as they have thus far been designed, can make significant contributions to understanding courtroom procedures, primarily because of the artificial and dissimilar conditions under which they are conducted. No matter how much the simulation approaches authenticity, subjects still realize they are playing a role devoid of all the stresses and anxieties that deciding the fate of another human being can generate. As we learned in Chapter 3, stressful conditions can substantially affect judgment and decisionmaking.

It is likely also that researchers overvalue the extra-legal influences and biases of jurors. Although these factors can influence some of the proceedings, in most cases the evidence is presented in such a way that it is quite clear and straightforward what the verdict should be. Researchers also cannot forget that there are various legal procedural safeguards that reduce bias. Attorneys can mitigate prejudice during the voir dire, although the extent to which this is done varies widely with the competence of the attorneys. Regular participants in the judicial system are fully aware of the numerous subjective irregularities and biases that are part of the adversary process, and they consider this feature a part of the game.

Several other problems undermine the quality of the research and limit its applicability to the judicial system. An often repeated criticism questions the use of college students as mock jurors. Students are usually middle class, well educated, intelligent, young, and liberal in ideology—hardly representative of the population at large from which juries are typically drawn, although with increases in continuing education and reentry programs, this problem may be attenuated. Nevertheless, the sophistication, skepticism, and intellectual abilities of college students may be significantly different from those of persons who are available and willing to serve on jury panels.

Still another problem pertains to the presentation of materials. In over half of the studies on jury decisionmaking, subjects have been presented with written case materials that are often extremely brief and simplistic summaries of usually hypothetical cases (Bray & Kerr, 1979). In about a third of the experiments, audio presentation has been used, and it too was of short duration (thirty to ninety minutes). These time limits and modes of presentation in no way reflect the intricacies of courtroom trials. True jurors receive trial information in uneven, sometimes lengthy time-intervals through all the sense modalities. By and large, the information is received by hearing or through auditory channels. Jurors rarely read case materials while trials are in progress.

Another fundamental problem is that most jury simulation research has focused on individual juror decisions rather than on collective jury decisions. Those projects that have included group discussion or group-derived verdicts have had unreasonable time restrictions (e.g., a verdict must be reached within thirty minutes) and have used an exceedingly small number of "jurors." They have rarely been asked to return a final group verdict; rather, individual verdicts after group discussion have been sought (Weiten & Diamond, 1979).

Some researchers believe that studying individual jurors is a valid approach. Citing the Kalven and Zeisel data, they argue that the first ballot in deliberation is a strong prediction of the final outcome, even without group discussion. Although the first vote often does predict the eventual verdict, some group interaction has occurred prior to the vote, sometimes pertaining to evidence, sometimes to opinions about a wide range of issues. By preventing at least some group interaction, some researchers have altered significantly the conditions they are trying to simulate. We have no basis for assuming that group decisionmaking parallels individual decisionmaking.

Finally, the subjective values of the behavioral and social science researcher have entered frequently into their studies' conclusions. As Vidmar notes (1979, p. 101), if it were up to psychologists, the jury "would be an elitist body composed primarily of liberal ('nonauthoritarian'), well educated persons. . . . Potential jurors who are conservative in their sociopolitical attitudes are assumed to be less competent as jurors." This position is hardly in keeping with the scientific objectivity espoused over the years by experimental psychologists.

## CONCLUSIONS

The problems discussed above are some of the major flaws making generalizations from laboratory to courtroom risky. While the foregoing may make one wonder if any of the research on jury simulation is of value, it is important to remember that one of the hallmarks of science is to be skeptical of interpretations and to seek alternative explanations and approaches. The behavioral sciences move in a spiral fashion, becoming more sound both in theory and in method as the pioneer approaches are critiqued and improved. We must also keep in mind that a great majority of the jury simulation studies have occurred only since 1970.

Some researchers argue that the simulated jury approach still offers the best alternative to research using real juries, which is seldom tolerated by the judicial system. Of course, it is possible to study the product of the jury—the verdict—and to obtain demographic and personality characteristics of the jurors, as well as their personal accounts, after their decision has been rendered. The major problem with this product approach is that the nearly endless list of possible contributors is difficult to disentangle. It is much more advantageous to investigate before and during the decision-making process.

However, the simulation research done so far hardly approximates the reality of the jury process in a number of crucial variables. Theories developed from these studies have a high risk of being inadequate in accounting for the actual jury process. Although empirical psychology is self-corrective in the long run, a premature conclusion by researchers that they have discovered the psychological secrets of the jury process through simulation study may do more harm than good. Theories and hypotheses developed within the confines of the artificial atmosphere of the psychological laboratory must be tested against the actual natural event before some tentative conclusions can be advanced. This may require archival and case-by-case analysis of actual trials. In any event, results acquired from simulation research should be treated with great caution and skepticism.

# ■ Models of Juror and Jury Decisionmaking

One of the most recent trends in jury research is the development by psychologists of cognitive-behavioral, mathematical, and computer models of juror (and jury) decisionmaking. The models try to describe the operations which human beings use to make decisions and judgments based both on preconceived notions and on information gained through the trial process. Some of these decisionmaking models are extremely elaborate and technical; those of the mathematical and computer variety, for example, often employ algebraic combinations, weights, constants, and intricate formulae. They are designed to take into consideration relevant, quantifiable variables; to combine these variables by means of mathematical logic; and to produce an end result which should approximate decisions actually made by human decisionmakers.

The numerous models now being tested are too complicated, new, and incomplete to present here. Considerable work remains to be done before they are ready to apply to the judicial process. The reader is referred to Penrod and Hastie (1979) and Pennington and Hastie (1981) for a complete assessment of the mathematical and computer models germane to juror and jury decisionmaking.

The mathematical and computer models do raise an issue which merits some discussion. Let us assume that one of the mathematical models were developed to such a point that it could accurately predict (99 percent of the time) the verdicts juries delivered. The prediction track record eventually becomes so impressive, in fact, that it generates the suggestion that the model should replace the jury. After all, it would probably be much more cost efficient. The question then becomes, "Should it?"

In an influential *Harvard Law Review* article in 1971, law professor Laurence H. Tribe was extremely critical of the potential use of scientific mathematical techniques in place of the more "intuitive tools" traditionally used in the trial process. Specifically, he asserted that the use of mathematical analyses and models in legal decisionmaking should be banned. The trial process and juror decisionmaking should be based on intuition and humanness rather than on quantifiable variables, in keeping with the long tradition of Anglo-Saxon law. Legal "truth" can be garnered from the "soft quantifiable variables" inherent in the human reliance on values and justice, Tribe added. The institution of the jury and the human involvement it ensured should be preserved because of the social, political, and psychological benefits it affords society. Humans should be judged by other humans, not by mathematics and computers, he said.

But let's take our "impressive model" one step further and assume that not only does it predict jury decisions, but it also produces its own accurate decision about guilt or innocence. Moreover, its decisions are accurate 98 percent of the time, while jury decisions are accurate 90 percent of the time. We are assuming, of course, that an acceptable definition of accuracy has been adopted by the legal system, an assumption which makes this discussion purely an intellectual exercise. Nevertheless, given greater decisionmaking accuracy by a model, do we substitute our model for human jurors? Should the symbolic function of the trial be more important than accurate fact-finding?

Saks and Kidd (1980–81) suggest that mathematical models are more accurate in general decisionmaking than the information processing of humans. They apply "the same logic, while the human decision maker fluctuates, being over-influenced by fortuitous, attention-catching pieces of information that vary from time to time, and processing a too-limited set of variables. Unaided individuals tend to have great difficulty incorporating quantified variables, give excessive weight to bits and pieces that happen for whatever reason to be salient, base their decision on less information (often the less useful information) than do mathematical models, and apply their decision policies inconsistently" ( Saks & Kidd, 1980–81, p. 147). The models fail to capture the realistic cognitive functioning of human beings, Saks and Kidd add, and it is precisely for this reason that they are considered undesirable. The judicial system, as Tribe argues, prefers the imperfect, but human element.

Saks and Kidd (1980–81) do present an argument in favor of *cognitive-behavioral* models of human decisionmaking (such as the Kaplan information integration model covered earlier) in contrast to the mathematical models. However, regardless of whether a model is cognitive, behavioral, or mathematical, the bottom line is to what extent it provides answers about human decisionmaking and offers grist for theory development. The goal of mathematical models is not to predict jury decisionmaking with total accuracy and thus take the job of trying facts away from the citizenry. Rather, inasmuch as the model predicts the decisionmaking of each juror or of the group, it accounts for some of the processes operating in the jurors' minds. Understanding leads to prediction, and both lead to theoretical development, the ultimate goal of the science of psychology.

## ■ Summary and Conclusions

Wallach Loh (1979, p. 166) observes that the relationship between psychology and law is marked by recurrent cycles. "Initially, optimistic views regarding the contribution of psychology to law are presented. These are met with skeptical rejoinders from the academic legal community that dampen further interest. A period of silence and inaction follows. The lessons are soon forgotten and a new cycle of optimism-skepticism-silence is repeated."

At first glance, the behavioral science research on the jury appears to promote additional legal skepticism resulting in another period of silence. Jury research is inconclusive, some of it perhaps lacks validity, and much of it can stand substantial improvement. If psychology perceives its relationship with law to be one where lawyers and other judicial actors are entitled to answers from the psychological community to the legal questions they pose, then the behavioral science community should be concerned. Based on jury research so far, psychology will again encounter skepticism and silence. But it is a mistake to conceive of the relationship in this way; it is taking a psychology *in* law rather than a psychology *and* law approach.

Psychological research should not be dictated by what law wants but by what psychologists find interest in studying. The ideal empirical approach functions relatively independently of social demands, even if the grim reality may be that the impact on society—in this case, on the judicial system—is minimal. The scientific enterprise operates in spiral fashion, with contradictory findings, debates, disagreements, and further experimentation advancing the process. Methodology is improved and data are collated into systematic theory. At present, jury research may be too new, too incomplete, and too fragmented to be of much value to the judicial system; its worth may lie predominantly in its attempts at theory building. The expansion of jury research should not be stunted simply because the legal community finds it lacking. Researchers should continue to seek a systematic theory that will help integrate the confusing array of data. This is needed more desperately than increased sophistication of methodology or more realistic simulation techniques.

Research psychologists should not be too eager to attach their investigations to the legal system or to state conclusively that legal scholars and participants must attend to the reported results. It is more important and effective to proceed with research seeking theoretical development and posing heuristic questions for subsequent research. In the end, sound theory backed by an impressive body of research is very apt to creep into the judicial system.

# ■ Key Concepts and Principles, Chapter 6

Simulation research
Venire
Voir dire
Peremptory and for-cause challenges
Probative and didactive purposes of voir
   dire
Decision rule
Type I and II errors and jury size
Jury size and decisionmaking
Chicago Jury Project

Jury dynamics
Effects of various kinds of attractiveness
   on jury
Authoritarianism
Group polarization
Information integration model
Problems with jury simulation research
Mathematical models and jury
   decisionmaking

□ | 7

■ | # The Psychology of Evidence: Eyewitness Testimony

□ | The testimony of a witness can be the most influential parcel of evidence delivered in the courtroom, particularly if the witness claims to have personally seen the legally relevant event, object, or person. The impact of eyewitness testimony is especially great if other kinds of evidence (e.g., weapon or fingerprints) are sparse or unavailable. Loftus (1979) notes that jurors have often been known to accept eyewitness testimony at face value, even when it is heavily contradicted by other evidence. People are more apt to believe someone who was at the scene of an incident, despite what experts may assert about the evidence. Even judges, attorneys, and law enforcement officials tend to accept the observations of witnesses as legally relevant facts of a case.

Eyewitness evidence, in fact, often has even greater legal status than other kinds of evidence in the eyes of the judiciary. Experienced trial attorneys have long known that visual identification is one of the most cogent forms of evidence they can present to jurors and judges. They also fully realize that the quality of eyewitness testimony often determines the outcome of a case, no matter how logically tight and persuasive the arguments presented to the jury are. In her excellent review of eyewitness research, Elizabeth Loftus (1979, p. 19) summarizes the impact of witnesses on the court when she states: "All the evidence points rather strikingly to the conclusion that there is almost nothing more convincing than a live human being who takes the stand, points a finger at the defendant, and says 'that's the one!'"

The strength of eyewitness testimony can be partially explained by the legal profession's traditional reliance on common-sense generalizations about human behavior. Paul Meehl (1971) refers to this legal proclivity as "fireside induction," which is "those commonsense empirical generalizations about human behavior which we accept on the culture's authority plus introspection plus anecdotal evidence from ordinary life. Roughly, the phrase 'fireside induction' designates . . . what everybody (except perhaps the skeptical social scientist) believes about human conduct, about how it is described, explained, predicted, and controlled" (Meehl, 1971, p. 66). Thus, "everybody knows" that an eyewitness's account is the best piece of evidence that can be found to assure justice in the courtroom. This is especially true if the person who recalls and identifies the legally relevant information does so with conviction and confidence. Hence, fireside-induction logic holds that the more confident the witness appears, the more accurate is the recall of the event.

Eyewitness testimony is also powerful because of a belief in the ultimate accuracy of observation and human memory. Throughout its long history, law has had to be highly dependent upon what people saw and what people said they saw. Recreations of crime scenes were almost exclusively dependent upon human memory, which was considered to be occasionally fooled, sometimes purposely distorted, but basically accurate. Today, sophisticated technology that can recreate crime scenarios and provide forensic evidence to the smallest detail is being increasingly made available to the courts, but belief in the accuracy of human perception and memory persists.

How reliable is such eyewitness testimony? Most psychologists will answer, "It depends." Eyewitness testimony may be highly reliable under some conditions and extremely unreliable in other settings. However, the psychological research on perception and memory over the past 100 years underscores the discouraging fact that in most cases eyewitness testimony is partially unreliable and highly susceptible to numerous influences.

In this chapter we shall examine this psychological research and theory and discover how closely the findings approximate the numerous fireside inductions inherent in the judicial system's near total acceptance of eyewitness testimony. A large segment of the research on eyewitness testimony lacks a well-integrated theoretical goal, but the reader should keep in mind that the general purpose of applied eyewitness-testimony research "is to generate scientific knowledge that will maximize the chances that a guilty defendant will be justly convicted while minimizing the chances that an innocent defendant will be mistakenly convicted" (Wells, 1978, p. 1546). Therefore, even though an all encompassing theoretical framework has yet to be developed, there is enough research literature to begin closely questioning the judicial system's reliance on the accuracy of eyewitnesses.

The problems we encountered in the last chapter pertaining to the study of the jury process will not reappear here. Simulation studies are more able to approximate real life witnessing than real life jury decisionmaking. In addition, eyewitness research has the benefit of methodologically sound data about human perception and memory which have been developed by empirical psychologists for nearly a century. These traditional works offer a solid foundation for the study of eyewitness observation. The contributions psychology can make in this area are substantial, and they warrant the careful attention of participants in the judicial system.

# ■ Human Perception and Memory

When a person recalls and identifies legally relevant events, objects, and persons, two fundamental but exceedingly complicated mental processes are at work: perception and memory. In the first, sensory inputs (what one sees, hears, smells, touches, tastes) are transformed and organized into a meaningful experience for the individual. In the second process, the transformed inputs are stored in the brain, ready to be called up when needed. Each operation will be looked at in more detail in the following paragraphs.

## PERCEPTION

Perceptions are reports of what a person sees or senses at any particular moment. Seeing is only a part of the process of perceiving; in fact, what one perceives is not always what one sees. The eye does not relate to the brain like a camera operates on film. The eye communicates by electrochemical "blips" along neural pathways to other neuron cells and eventually to processors in various sections of the brain, specifically in the cortex. Once these blips (neural impulses) reach the cortex, they may be further coded, reorganized and interpreted, or they may be left undeveloped. Neurophysiological researchers have not yet discovered exactly what happens in the human brain to incoming information, although there are several theories. It is clear, however, that the perception of stimuli and the person's reaction to them depend upon past experiences, especially with similar stimuli. If you were once the beneficiary of a very painful hornet sting, you perceive those insects in a far different way than a friend who has never had such an experience. Perception, then, is an interpretive process, and it appears that our senses are not only physical organs, but social ones as well (Buckhout, 1974).

There is ample evidence in the research literature that people are not consciously aware of the perceptual processes that determine their perceptions or the perceptual content of their senses. Yet, these nonconscious perceptual processes are extremely important in the representation of events or objects and therefore are crucial determinants of what occurs on the witness stand. Researchers also know that the end products of these perceptual processes are often incomplete, inaccurate, and highly selective. Much external information is either not attended to, lost in the filtering and selection of information, or misinterpreted. Past experience or learning, expectations, and preferences all determine how this partial or incomplete information will be synthesized. Yarmey (1979) reminds us that we should also not forget that many individuals have sensory deficiencies, like visual defects of depth perception, color blindness, failures in adaptation to darkness, and lack of visual acuity. Even before the stimulus information is synthesized at the higher levels of perceptual interpretation, these individual defects may contaminate the information. Human sensory mechanisms are far from perfect, and this basic frailty should not be overlooked in the search for potential errors in eyewitness testimony.

## MEMORY

Memory, the second fundamental process with which we are concerned, is usually studied in three stages—acquisition, retention, and retrieval. Acquisition, also called the encoding or input stage, is intimately involved with the perceptual process, and a clear demarcation between the two is difficult to make. The point at which perception registers in the various areas of the cortex and is initially stored is the point of acquisition. Retention (also called the storage stage) is when information becomes "resident in the memory" (Loftus, 1979). In the retrieval stage, the brain searches for the pertinent information, retrieves it, and communicates it. Any one of these three processes may not function properly, and the result, then, is a failure to remember (Klatzky, 1975).

Eyewitness research has continually found that memory is highly malleable and easily subject to change and distortion (Yuille, 1980). Apparently, humans continually alter and reconstruct their memory of past experiences in the light of present experiences, rather than store past events permanently and unchangingly in memory (Leippe, 1980; Yuille, 1980). That is, people rebuild past experiences to fit better their understanding of the stream of events. Memory, especially for complex or unusual events, involves the integration of perceptual information with preexisting experiences, as well as with other subjective relevant information that may be introduced later. In this sense, memory is very much a reconstructive, integrative process, developing with the flow of new experiences and thoughts. It would not be economical to add a fourth memory stage, reconstruction, although a strong case probably could be made in its favor.

As is true for the perceptual processes, people are unaware of their memory processes. They are aware of the products or content of memory, but there is every reason to believe they are not aware of the transformations that have occurred during acquisition, retention, and retrieval. While eyewitnesses may remember an event or person, they are not conscious of the complex encoding, decoding, organizing, storing, interpreting, and associating that preceded the final memory of that event or person. Moreover, there are ample opportunities for witnesses to encounter additional information after the event and then integrate it unknowingly into their original memories. Therefore, even the most well-intentioned eyewitnesses may err and unconsciously distort their recall and identification. In part, this explains the radically different accounts of the same event that are provided by witnesses who are "absolutely positive" about what they saw.

Human beings forget easily and quickly, and they especially forget visual information. Information becomes less available as the time interval increases between the first witnessing of an event and later attempts to retrieve it (Loftus & Loftus, 1980). Based on the available research, we can say that the unretrieved information is in large part lost forever, regardless of the method used to try to retrieve it. Claims that hypnosis brings back "old forgotten" memories are unsubstantiated. Forgotten or partially remembered events become reconstructed and embellished as the person gains additional information. Imagination plays a part in this reconstruction, sometimes to the point of letting the person exaggerate aspects of initial events or perceptions. Many people are surprised when they return as adults to a childhood home. The "large, almost majestic" house is actually a small, unpretentious cottage, with very few of the stately features they "remembered."

This reconstructive-process theory cannot account for all the aspects of forgetting; interference theory also offers an explanation. According to this theory, forgetting is caused by both interference from material learned previously (called by cognitive psychologists "proactive interference") and interference from material learned afterward ("retroactive interference") (Bournes, Dominowski & Loftus, 1979).

In the following sections, we will discuss characteristics of the situation, the witness, and the defendant which are believed to be influential in determining the accuracy of eyewitness testimony. Although this classification may seem unfair to the interaction that occurs between the variables in determining eyewitness accuracy, it does promote a more organized presentation.

## ■ Situational Factors of Eyewitness Testimony

### TEMPORAL FACTORS

The judicial system is most interested in learning details about events that are generally fast moving, unusual, chaotic, and threatening to the observers. In most instances, the legally relevant incident produces a "stimulus overload," where too many things are happening too quickly and under less than ideal conditions for careful scrutiny. Thus far the study of situational variables as they relate directly to eyewitness accounts has been a relatively neglected area, but the research to date agrees with many common-sense observations about the effects of these variables.

Not surprisingly, the less time a witness has to observe something, the less complete the perception and recall will be. Obviously, studying a topic for a long time will mean a better exam grade, provided that the student was concentrating. There is abundant literature in the field of cognitive psychology and memory to demonstrate that the longer a subject is exposed to material, the more accurate the recall (e.g., Loftus, 1972; Loftus & Loftus, 1976; Klatzky, 1975). Some researchers have found that the longer subjects had to inspect slides of faces, the more accurate they later were at recognizing a given face from photographs (Laughery, Alexander & Lane, 1971). In addition, Laughery and his colleagues found that the smaller the number of photographs the subjects had to search through, the more likely the subjects were to be accurate. The researchers suggested that law enforcement agencies might keep this in mind when having witnesses look through mug shots for criminal identification. Fewer mug shots might result in more accurate recognition.

Closely related to the duration of eyewitness exposure time is frequency of exposure. The more often a witness observes an event or person, the more accurate his or her description or recognition should be. Although there is substantial support for this in the experimental literature, dating as far back as Hermann Ebbinghaus's work in 1885, frequency of exposure has not been examined in studies of eyewitness testimony. Loftus (1979) suggests that perhaps the relationship is such a commonsensical one that it has failed to draw the attention of eyewitness researchers.

Another temporal factor that is likely to influence witness accuracy is the rate at which things happen. Fast-moving events are more difficult to process and thus to remember than slow-moving events, because of the limited processing capacity of human beings and their selective attention mechanisms. Therefore, incidents surrounded by complex activity tend to confuse, even when witnesses have a reasonably long opportunity to observe the occurrence.

It has repeatedly been found that witnesses frequently overestimate the time a criminal incident takes (Buckhout, 1974, 1977; Marshall, 1966; Johnson & Scott, 1976). While Ellison and Buckhout (1981) suggest that some witnesses may consciously lengthen time estimates to strengthen the validity of their descriptions, there is abundant laboratory evidence to indicate that humans generally think unpleasant events last longer than they really do (Loftus, 1979). It appears also that if people feel especially anxious or threatened during an incident, they tend to overestimate its duration even more (Sarason & Stoops, 1978). Therefore, in obtaining evidence from witnesses, it is important to try to determine how long and how often the person observed the incident and how much activity was present. It is important also to realize that the witness very probably is overestimating the event's duration.

## DETAIL SIGNIFICANCE

Not all details of a scene are equally remembered, because certain novel, complex, ambiguous, or arousing features draw more attention than others. Blood, masks, weapons, and aggressive actions are more likely to be noticed than clothing, hair style, or background features in a crime scene. A gun pointed at a person is likely to be studied more intently than other features impinging on the person at that moment. People are quite certain about whether a gun or a knife was threatening them, but they are perhaps less certain of an assailant's clothes or facial characteristics. This phenomenon, known as "weapon focus," will be discussed again when we examine witness characteristics.

The tendency to focus on some details to the exclusion of others is well illustrated by a study in which unsuspecting subjects sat in an anteroom waiting to participate in an experiment (Johnson & Scott, 1976). A no-weapon condition and a weapon condition were used. Subjects in the no-weapon condition overheard a conversation from the experimental room concerning equipment problems, after which an individual entered the waiting room, holding a pen in greased hands. The individual, who was part of the experiment (a confederate or "stooge"), made a brief comment and then exited quickly. In the weapon condition, subjects overheard an angry confrontation, accompanied by sounds of bottles breaking and chairs crashing. The confederate bolted into the waiting room, holding a bloodied letter opener in blood-stained hands. As in the no-weapon condition, the confederate muttered something and then left.

Subjects were interviewed about the scenario either immediately or one week later. Nearly every subject in the weapon condition described a weapon, while very few of the no-weapon subjects could describe the pen. More importantly, the presence of a weapon (weapon focus compounded by emotional arousal) reduced the ability of the subjects to identify the confederate from a set of fifty photographs. Apparently, the witnesses focused their attention primarily on the weapon rather than on the culprit's features. However, it should be emphasized that in both the weapon and no-weapon conditions, the confederate was only in the presence of the witnesses for about four seconds. A longer exposure time might have dissipated weapon focus.

Another aspect of the situation that may influence eyewitness accuracy is that persons in the midst of a crime do not always perceive that something significant is happening. People have often been present during the commission of a crime and have failed to realize it. Baron and Byrne (1977) cite the tragic sniper incident on the University of Texas campus in 1966 as an example. Disgruntled student and veteran Charles Whitman managed to gain access to the top of the 307-foot tall University tower with an arsenal of weapons and began firing at passersby below. Some heard the shots, noticed bodies falling, and immediately ran for cover. A surprising number of people simply continued along their way without perceiving the seriousness of the situation, and many of them became victims. Some individuals later said they interpreted the event as a fraternity stunt and did not take it seriously.

Social psychologists (e.g., Darley & Latané, 1968) have studied the phenomenon of "bystander apathy," where people sometimes fail to come to the aid of a victim of an accident or assailant. The researchers have found that in a significant number of cases the observers simply did not interpret the event as serious. (It is possible, of course, that the bystanders told the researchers this to save face.) Therefore, it would seem prudent for law enforcement officers to learn how far the crime had progressed before a witness realized the incident was significant enough to warrant attention. Some witnesses may conclude that a crime is taking place only near the end of the sequence and may embellish the beginning so as not to appear too foolish.

Perceiving the seriousness of an event is as important as perceiving its significance. Leippe, Wells, and Ostrom (1978) staged a theft in front of a group of students waiting to participate in an experiment. The item stolen in one condition was a $50 electronic calculator (high seriousness); in another it was a pack of cigarettes (low seriousness). In both conditions one of the waiting subjects (actually a confederate) grabbed the item, dropped it to assure that everyone present noticed the theft, and quickly left the room. There was no doubt that all the waiting subjects recognized that a theft had happened and knew the relative value of the stolen item.

After the theft, subjects were told individually that it had been planned as part of the experiment, and they were shown six photographs and asked to identify the thief. In the high-seriousness condition, 56 percent of the subjects made an accurate identification, whereas in the low-seriousness condition only 19 percent made accurate identification. These results suggest that the perceived seriousness of a crime may be a powerful determinant of accurate offender-identification.

The researchers in the above experiment suggested two possible hypotheses for the increased accuracy as a result of crime seriousness. First, perceived seriousness may prompt witnesses to make full use of selective attention and acquisition processes during the event. Second, the perceived seriousness may have motivated the witnesses to rehearse the event in their memory, which would have improved the retrieval of the information at a later time. Of course, what was considered "serious" in this experiment would probably be considered "borderline serious" by most people. Even in the 1970s, fifty dollars was no amount to lose sleep over. However, the researchers did make the point that the amount approximates the sums involved in such common crimes as shoplifting and purse snatching, and as such the study may have implications for petty crimes.

## VIOLENCE LEVEL OF EVENT

Crimes differ in the amount of emotional arousal they generate in both victim and witnesses, probably ranging along a continuum of arousal or generation of stress. Generally speaking, increases in violence produce a corresponding increase in arousal, probably to a point where further increases in extreme, terrifying violence no longer

affect arousal because the observer chooses not to watch any longer. It has been suggested that the recall and recognition abilities of witnesses (and victims) reflect a negative relationship to that violence-arousal spectrum (Clifford & Scott, 1978). That is,
the higher the violence of the crime, and hence the higher the emotional reaction to
the incident, the lower the accuracy and completeness of the testimony of witnesses
and victims. Clifford and his colleagues have been the leading proponents of the high-
violence–low-accuracy hypothesis; it is worthwhile reviewing two of their experiments
designed to test it.

Clifford and Scott (1978) found that persons who watched violent events on videotape were significantly less able to recall the incidents than those who watched
nonviolent versions. In the nonviolent scenario, two police officers searched for a
suspect, found him, and entered into a verbal exchange with the man. The exchange
culminated in some "weak restraining movements" by one of the officers. In the violent episode, the same situation escalated into a physical confrontation, with one of
the officers hitting the suspect four times.

In addition to the finding that witnesses demonstrated poorer recall of the violent
incident, the study also discovered that females were significantly less accurate than
males in their recall of the violent film. There were no significant sex differences in
recall of the nonviolent version.

In a more recent investigation of the effects of violence on eyewitness accuracy,
Clifford and Hollin (1981) learned that accuracy depends not only on the level of
violence observed, but also on the number of perpetrators. Violent incidents were less
well remembered as the number of perpetrators increased, while nonviolent incidents
yielded no such difference. The results suggest that, in violent events involving more
than one offender, the accuracy of eyewitness testimony can be expected to be poorer
than in violent events having only one perpetrator. In fact, the Clifford-Hollin data
revealed that almost three-fourths of the witnesses observing the violent scenes were
incorrect in their identification of the key perpetrator. Apparently, no significant sex
differences emerged, since the researchers made no reference to this effect in their
report. It seems, therefore, that the influence of violence on the recognition and recall
ability of males and females remains equivocal. This is one area in obvious need of
further investigation.

The results from the Clifford studies imply that the criminal justice system must
be especially careful in its reliance on the testimony of eyewitnesses to a violent episode, especially in cases where violence is high and there are several perpetrators. At
the very least, the data certainly counsel against any fireside induction that violence
leads to accuracy in testimony.

# ▪ Witness Factors: Perceptual and Acquisition Influences

## WITNESS AROUSAL AND STRESS

Most criminal incidents precipitate some continuum of stress and emotional
arousal in both victims and other witnesses. However, the effects of this emotional
arousal on eyewitness testimony have baffled the legal system for many years (Katz &

Reid, 1977). Some jurists believe that stress increases the accuracy of witness observation and subsequent testimony. Others think stressful incidents generate so much
nervousness that they promote unreliability in witnesses.

An example of the first position is a very old but often cited appellate court opinion quoted by Wall (1967). Two men were accused of torturing and killing a husband
and wife, based on the oral dying declaration of the husband. In affirming the conviction and commenting about the victim's ability to identify the accused, the court stated
that "every peculiarity of each of the murders . . . must have been literally burned
into the memory" of both the husband and his wife (Commonwealth v. Roddy, 1898).
In another case (State v. Lanegan, 1951), a man and his wife had been awakened by
an intruder pointing a firearm in their faces and demanding money. The court found
these to be "circumstances calculated to impress [the defendant's appearance] upon
their minds." In still another example (U.S. ex rel. Gonzalez v. Zelker, 1973), the
U.S. Court of Appeals defended the validity of a robbery victim's identification by
asserting that "the robbery unquestionably made a deep impression on Mrs. D'Amora,
who was obviously terrified by Gonzalez when he pointed the gun at her and announced the holdup." However, as Katz and Reid (1977) have observed, the court
demonstrated its confusion about the effects of stress by also stating that the same
victim should be excused for her inaccurate initial description since "she was understandably nervous at the time of the robbery."

Few judicial decisions have dealt with the effects of stress on eyewitness or victim
accuracy, and any decisions handed down have left the issue vague, confused, and
largely unresolved (Katz & Reid, 1977). If a position could be teased out of legal
precedent up to this point, it would be the fireside induction that stress or fear increases witness and victim testimonial accuracy.

According to psychological research, does arousal strengthen or weaken memory?
Not surprisingly, empirical investigations have found that it sometimes facilitates perception and memory and sometimes hinders these processes. In many instances, the
relationship between arousal and performance can be best represented by an inverted
U-shaped function: very low or very high levels of arousal reduce perceptions and
inhibit memory, while moderate levels faciliate them.

This hypothesized relationship is known as the Yerkes-Dodson principle, first proposed in 1908. The relationship depends not only on the existing level of arousal, but
also on the difficulty or complexity of the task. If the task is relatively simple, high
arousal will improve the performance. If the task is complex, high levels of arousal
will decrease performance and moderate levels will improve it.

The eyewitness's task in recalling events or persons qualifies as an extremely complex one, requiring perceptual and memory components. We can expect, therefore,
that the high arousal which is presumably typical of witnesses' reactions to violent
crimes causes a spectrum of inaccuracies and incomplete information in testimony.

The reader will recall the experiment by Leippe and colleagues (1978) in which
either a package of cigarettes or a $50 calculator was stolen. The calculator theft pro-
duced more accurate descriptions of the perpetrator, very likely because it generated
more arousal than the cigarette theft. Moreover, the arousal generated would be moderate, rather than high—just right to improve performance or identification of the
offender. On the other hand, the experiment conducted by Johnson and Scott (1976),

which involved a weapon condition (bloody letter opener) and a no-weapon condition (greasy pen), apparently produced such high levels of arousal in the weapon condition that it interfered with accurate recall and recognition of the perpetrator. The Yerkes-Dodson principle indicates that persons who are extremely frightened or emotionally upset during an incident are not the most dependable witnesses to that incident.

Research has also demonstrated that high arousal prompts people to reduce the attention they pay to information in the environment and to narrow their attention (Easterbrook, 1959). Persons in a high arousal-provoking crime situation are concerned more about their own safety (and that of their loved ones) than about what they consider to be nonessential details in the environment. When highly agitated and aroused, a person will focus intensely on some of the personally relevant cues in the environment, as on a weapon, but the person will miss other elements. Loftus (1979, p. 175) explains it this way: "When a person witnesses a crime involving a weapon, that weapon captures a good deal of the witness's attention, takes a portion of the witness's processing time, and leaves less time available for focusing on other details." Weapon focus is one phenomenon that the criminal justice system must take into consideration with reference to the interrogation of witnesses and victims.

In summary, there is considerable evidence from the psychological laboratory that extreme arousal interferes with eyewitness accounts of violent scenes. In petty crimes, like shoplifting or even purse snatching, arousal is significantly lower and eyewitness accounts probably are more accurate.

## EXPECTANCIES AND STEREOTYPES

A powerful determinant of what a person perceives is what he or she expects to perceive in any given situation. Every hunting season is replete with tales of hunters mistakenly shooting other hunters, cows, or horses, in the belief that they are game. Hunters who shoot at these nongame targets typically have high expectations of seeing their deer (or pheasant, squirrel, or rabbit) at any moment. In addition, the hunt traditionally is at its best at dawn and early dusk, because these are times when wildlife is most active in its movement toward feeding areas. These are also times when visibility, particularly at long distances, is poor. Any movement in the meadow at this time can be quickly embellished with antlers (or feathers) by the tense and expectant hunter intent on finding prey.

Many sightings of unidentified flying objects, Loch Ness monsters, Bigfoot, Lake Champlain's own "Champ," and other unusual creatures may be explained by expectations of the observers. Psychologists have found that eyes do indeed play tricks. Expectancies shaped by previous experiences and learning (including tales and legends) form cognitive templates to which unusual experiences are compared. Any out-of-the-ordinary sight may be interpreted in such a way that it will fit these cognitive templates. Thus unusual ripples in a lake at dusk can easily become a highly publicized, unexplained creature.

Incidents of crime, particularly violent ones, are highly unusual events to most persons and are especially susceptible to distortions consistent with expectancies. If we have learned that robbers often carry .38 revolvers, we may see a .38 in our assailant's hand when it is actually a hammer. However, while there is abundant collateral research clearly and convincingly demonstrating that expectancies influence descriptive accuracy, none has tested the expectancy hypothesis in relation to eyewitness testimony in a simulated judicial setting. The substantial body of research already available on related issues, though, would lead us to agree with Loftus (1979, p. 48) that "one thing is clear and accepted by all: expectations have an enormous impact on what a person claims to have seen."

Stereotypes—which are a form of expectancy—are cognitive shorthand devices that allow us to simplify and organize the vast array of social stimuli present in a complex society. We all use them to some extent, and as long as they do not promote social injustices, they tend to be effective and harmless psychological adaptations that help manage our implicit personality theories about others. However, stereotypes can distort our perceptions and subsequent identifications of others. There is evidence that some people may in fact incorporate their stereotype of "criminal" in their identification of suspects. Shoemaker, South, and Lowe (1973) asked subjects to select from a set of twelve facial photographs the person most likely and least likely to have engaged in one of four "deviant behaviors" or crimes: homosexuality, murder, robbery, or treason. None of the persons in the photos had actually engaged in these behaviors. Subjects tended to categorize the photos into deviant-nondeviant or criminal-noncriminal stereotypes, and they also tended to stereotype which faces belonged to what type of behavior. The researchers discovered that males were more likely than females to use facial stereotypes in judging guilt or innocence. The study suggests that many people have stereotypes about how "deviants" and criminals are supposed to look. These stereotypes could influence an eyewitness's selection of a perpetrator, especially if that witness observed the incident under intense stress or other less-than-ideal viewing conditions.

## WITNESS MEMORY: RETENTION FACTORS

Witnesses, of course, generally must recall events weeks, months, or even years after they occur. Yet cognitive psychology has firmly established that people are less accurate and complete in their accounts of events after a long interval has elapsed between the event and the recall than after a short interval. Part of this inaccuracy stems from the higher probability that new information will be received and processed by the person during the longer interval.

Elizabeth Loftus has designed numerous experiments demonstrating that postevent experiences, such as exposure to additional information, can substantially affect a person's memory of the original event. She showed, for example, that the simple mention of an existing object in an interview significantly increased the probability that the object would be recalled by the witness later on (Loftus, 1975). For example, asking an eyewitness to a traffic accident, "How fast was the car going when it ran the stop sign?" will enhance the recall of the stop sign, even if the witness failed to notice it in the first place. Similarly, casually mentioning an object that did not actually exist in an accident scene increases the likelihood that a witness will later report having seen that nonexistent object (Loftus, Miller & Burns, 1978).

Loftus (1975, 1977) also found that witnesses compromised their memory when they learned of new information that conflicted with an initial observation. For example, if a witness thought she noticed a red car passing in the wrong lane, but the investigating officer mentioned a green car, the witness would be likely to recall an off-colored green or blue-green car in a later report. If a witness thought a vehicle was traveling at eighty-five, and the investigating officer mentioned the speed of sixty-five, the witness would later report the speed to be somewhere between sixty-five and eighty-five, probably closer to sixty-five. The witness might be aware of the compromise, but it might also be an unconscious phenomenon attributable to perceptual and memory processes occurring outside awareness.

The above studies imply that police officers or attorneys can manipulate a witness's memory by feeding relevant information. However, there is evidence that this is more difficult to do with important or even noticeable factors than with less important details (Loftus, 1979). Furthermore, data also suggest that misleading information provided to witnesses sometime after the event and just before a recall test will have greater impact than misleading information given immediately after the incident (Loftus, Miller & Burns, 1978). Therefore, if an unscrupulous interviewer or interrogator wished to introduce misleading information into eyewitness memory, he or she would find it more effective to mention the information sometime after the relevant incident and close to the time when the witness was to testify. On the other hand, an interviewer merely wishing to maintain a consistent description of the initial incident would be wise to obtain the information immediately after the incident and then reiterate the material before and as close as possible to the time of courtroom testimony.

## WITNESS CONFIDENCE: RETRIEVAL FACTORS

Persons given to fireside inductions about eyewitness testimony believe that the more confident witnesses are about what they saw, the more accurate their observation and memory. As a result, testimony presented assertively and positively is generally treated with deference by the judicial system; it is believed to be accurate and truthful (Deffenbacher, 1980). For example, in *Neil v. Biggers* (1972), the U.S. Supreme Court ruled that eyewitness confidence is a valid criterion upon which to judge the trustworthiness of eyewitness testimony.

The confidence-accuracy relationship assumed by judges, attorneys, and jurors is far more complicated than they suppose. In fact, Yarmey (1979) concludes from his research that, with reference to the identification of faces, the confidence-accuracy relationship is exceedingly weak or virtually nonexistent. Leippe (1980) asserts that recognition accuracy has little to do with witness confidence, primarily because people are usually unaware of the inaccurate mental operations that lead to their conclusions. According to Leippe, the conditions under which witnesses observe an incident may affect recognition accuracy but not confidence. Thus, witnesses may be just as confident of what they see under poor observing conditions as they are of what they see under excellent observing conditions.

Wells, Lindsay, and Ferguson (1979) found that the confidence of witnesses, whether measured by the witnesses themselves or through jurors' estimates, was unrelated to accuracy in identifying a thief from a six-person picture gallery. In other studies (Lindsay, Wells & Rumpel, 1981; Clifford & Hollin, 1981; Clifford & Scott,

1978) the confidence-accuracy relationship was also found wanting. In conclusion, the judiciary's belief that accuracy can be assumed merely on the basis of the confidence expressed by eyewitnesses is untenable, given the present state of psychological knowledge.

## WITNESS AGE

There is a widespread belief among participants in the judicial system that the information acquired through the interrogation and testimony of children is permeated with far more distortion and inaccuracy than that acquired from young and middle-aged adults (Cohen & Harnick, 1980; Marin et al., 1979; Yarmey & Kent, 1980; Yarmey, 1979). The age at which children may testify as credible and competent eyewitnesses in criminal and civil proceedings has long been a controversial issue. For reasons which are unclear, many jurisdictions stipulate that fourteen is the minimum age for delivering competent testimony; exceptions can be made after a judicial inquiry into the child's mental and emotional capacity. Other jurisdictions regularly allow ten-year-olds to qualify as competent witnesses.

There is evidence to suggest that younger children (age nine) have poorer memories for relevant details of petty crimes than older children (age twelve) (Cohen & Harnick, 1980). The researchers attributed the difference to the developmental maturity of older children and their ability to give more attention to detail than their younger friends.

An interesting project by Marin and her colleagues (Marin et al., 1979), however, documents that young children can be as accurate in eyewitness accounts as adults, under certain conditions. Much depends upon the nature of the questioning and the type of memory retrieval that is required. Marin's subjects were divided into four groups: kindergarteners and first graders, third and fourth graders, seventh and eighth graders, and college students. When recall memory was requested by open-ended questions ("What happened?"), older subjects were able to report more material than younger ones. The younger the subject, the less detailed was his or her description of an incident. Nevertheless, the younger subjects were accurate in the incomplete information they reported. When Marin's task demanded recognition memory (identifying photographs or answering yes and no or multiple choice questions), younger subjects were just as accurate as the older groups. Furthermore, they were no more easily misled by leading questions than the older subjects.

Other studies indicate that a similar situation exists for older subjects (ages 65–90) in comparison to younger subjects (ages 15–26). Older subjects are as accurate in recognition memory (Yarmey & Kent, 1980), but less complete in verbal recall of the incidents. Yarmey and Kent also noted that the older witnesses were more cautious and less confident in their responses than younger subjects. As we saw earlier, however, high witness confidence should not encourage us to conclude that accuracy exists.

The strategy for obtaining comparatively accurate testimony from young children and elderly witnesses, therefore, involves tapping recognition rather than recall memory. This may be done by using objective prompts or cues, which might include closed-ended questions requiring yes or no answers. Asking witnesses to identify suspects through photographs or carefully conducted lineups also calls for recognition memory.

We should be wary about making generalizations to real-life violent incidents, however. None of the simulated experiments involved terrifying depictions of violence. We would anticipate that frightening crime scenes would result in different responses from children and possibly from the elderly. In fact, Dent (1977, cited by Yarmey, 1979) observed that children aged ten and eleven appeared nervous, embarrassed, and frightened by the stress produced in making identifications from live lineups in comparison to slides or photographs. This gives us a clue that the arousal-provoking violence scenarios could inhibit even the recognition memory of very young children.

## ■ Identifying Characteristics of the Offender

### THE FACE

Are witnesses who have observed a face once, perhaps only for a brief moment and often under conditions of stress or poor visibility, able to remember the face well enough to recognize it correctly sometime later? The legal system apparently believes that recognition memory for a face seen only once is comparable, even equal, to recognition memory for a face seen many times (Goldstein, 1977). The studies accumulated in this area, however, demonstrate that the accurate recognition of a relatively unfamiliar face is an extremely complex and error-ridden task. A consistent finding in the research literature is that the average person trying to identify a face seen once and for a short time will be accurate about 70 percent of the time (Goldstein, 1977). Rarely do studies report more than an 85 percent accuracy rate (see box).

Psychological experiments examining face recognition usually follow a two-step paradigm. Subjects are first shown live people, films, photographs, or face illustrations and are then given either a recognition or recall task to test their memory of the faces. Although the number of faces to study, the length of time allowed, and the time interval between study and test vary from experiment to experiment, the results have been surprisingly consistent.

In one of the earliest such experimental projects on face recognition, Howells (1938) discovered that faces were more difficult to recognize when the lower sections of the face area (middle of the nose down) were covered than when the upper sections were covered. In contradiction to this pioneering study, however, more recent experiments have reported with consistency that the upper portions of the face are decidedly better recognition cues than lower portions (Yarmey, 1979), although it is unclear which upper facial features are most important.

The current research also indicates that the relative importance of facial cues depends upon the particular face being evaluated. For reasons which are unknown, some faces are easier to discern and elicit more accurate identifications than others. Highly unique faces are better recognized than plain or average faces (Going & Read, 1974; Cohen & Carr, 1975). Faces high and low in attractiveness also are easier to recognize than faces judged to be of medium attractiveness (Shepherd & Ellis, 1973).

There is some evidence to suggest that most people concentrate more on the right side than on the left when looking at a human face (Gilbert & Bakan, 1973; Liggett, 1974).

## UNCONSCIOUS TRANSFERENCE

Some witnesses have mistakenly identified as offenders persons they have seen at some other time and place. This phenomenon, which Glanville Williams (1963) called unconscious transference, occurs when a person seen in one situation is confused with or recalled as a person seen in another situation. A witness may have had limited exposure to a face (e.g., on a subway) and, upon seeing the face at a later time, conclude that it is the offender's. Loftus (1979) theorizes that unconscious transference is another feature of the integrative, malleable nature of human memory, where earlier input becomes tangled up with later input. As we learned above, perceptual and memory processes are unconscious, and the mixtures produced by them often range widely on a continuum of transformation and potential distortion.

The phenomenon of unconscious transference illustrates that it is highly possible that a store clerk, who is witness to a robbery, might incorrectly finger an occasional customer who may have some of the features of the actual culprit. However, for unconscious transference to take place, the previous encounters with the innocent face

---

## ☐ PLACE THE FACE

On a December evening in 1974, viewers of a New York City news show were "eyewitnesses" to a simulated purse-snatching incident. They saw a young woman confronted by a leather-jacket-clad man, who grabbed the woman's purse and struck her down. The entire incident lasted twelve seconds, and for one or two seconds the perpetrator ran toward the camera. Immediately after the incident viewers saw a lineup of six men who resembled the assailant. They were told that the attacker might or might not be in the lineup, and they were asked to call in and indicate whether they recognized the assailant.

The real attacker was indeed in the lineup, but only 14.1 percent of the 2,000 viewer-witnesses who called in correctly identified the attacker. The data produced the striking figure of 1,843 mistaken identifications (Buckhout, 1975). This is the same result as would be expected if the witnesses had been merely guessing; that is, according to probability theory, someone who had not even seen the incident would have one chance in seven of picking the correct person. Men and women witnesses did not respond differently from one another.

The above "experiment" illustrates a dilemma that the legal system cannot ignore. Witnesses who have observed a face once, perhaps only for a brief moment and often under stressful conditions, usually cannot remember that face well enough to identify it correctly sometime later. Yet, the law expects witnesses and victims to make such identifications—indeed, the law encourages them to do so.

---

must have been brief. Continual, relatively prolonged encounters, even with nameless faces, would be unlikely to result in incorrect identification.

Unconscious transference may also come into play when witnesses are asked to glance through a series of mug shots. The unconscious perceptual and memorial processes may prime the witness to identify a suspect seen later on the basis of mug shot exposure rather than on the basis of observation at the scene of a crime (Laughery, Alexander & Lane, 1971; Laughery et al., 1974).

The pioneering Howells study (1938) suggested that subjects who were most accurate in the recognition test for faces were the least accurate in verbally recalling details of the faces. This hints that visual recognition of faces and their verbal recall may be two separate processes. More recent studies have supported the Howells data (Goldstein & Chance, 1970; Chance & Goldstein, 1976; Malpass, Lavigueur & Weldon, 1973). This indicates that accuracy of facial recognition is more dependent upon visual encoding than upon verbal processes of memory (Yarmey, 1979). Law enforcement officials who ask witnesses to describe the offender are tapping a very different and perhaps less accurate perceptual process than when they ask them to pick out an offender from a lineup or series of mug shots. One task calls for recall memory, the other demands recognition memory.

Recall demands a different kind of retrieval operation, requiring a reproduction of the initially seen object or event. Recognition is an operation which requires a subject to note whether he or she has seen an object before. An illustration from a typical campus nemesis—testing—will make the point. Multiple choice exams normally tap recognition memory; essay exams usually involve recall memory, called "memorization" by students, who often resist such tests, claiming that they fail to help them understand the material. The resistance is partly due to the fact that memorization is a more demanding task than recognition. Students find themselves resorting to cue words or acronyms, like "pabble," where each letter represents a key concept. By doing this, students are altering their task to a process more in line with the easier recognition operation. It will come as no surprise that a long series of experiments in cognitive psychology have confirmed the observation that people find recognition tasks far easier than recall tasks (Klatzky, 1975).

During the initial interview, law enforcement officials should not expect a great wealth of information if they ask the witness to describe the perpetrator. If conditions permit, it would be a better tactic to pose questions jarring recognition memory. This is especially true if young children or the elderly are witnesses.

## RACE

The comment so frequently made about people of other races, "They all look the same to me," appears to have validity. People do seem to be better able to discriminate between faces of their own race than other races. In one of the first laboratory studies of racial identification, Roy Malpass and Jerome Kravitz (1969) asked twenty black students and twenty white students to examine twenty slides of black and white faces for about two seconds each. The subjects were asked to identify the faces they had initially seen from eighty slides (sixty new faces, twenty old ones). The researchers discovered that white observers were more accurate with white faces than with black

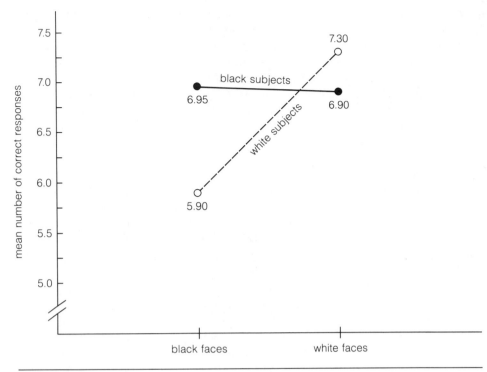

**Figure 7–1** ■ Relationship between the average number of correct responses to black and white faces by black and white subjects. [Figure developed from the data reported by Malpass and Kravitz (1969).]

faces. Black observers gave equally correct responses for both white and black faces, however (Figure 7–1).

These results were later replicated by Cross, Cross, and Daly (1971), who found that whites were more accurate in recognizing faces of their own race (45 percent correct) than black faces (27 percent correct). However, again black subjects were about as accurate with white faces (40 percent correct) as they were with black faces (39 percent correct). Chance and colleagues (1975) reported that while whites recognize white faces best, they are even worse at recognizing oriental faces than black faces. Blacks, on the other hand, were more accurate in recognizing black faces, second best with white faces, and least accurate with oriental faces.

A similar pattern appears to exist for children (Yarmey, 1979; Feinman & Entwisle, 1976). White and black children are more adept at recognizing faces of their own race. There is also some evidence that recognition accuracy increases with age (Goldstein & Chance, 1964).

There are several possible explanations for this other-race recognition effect. One of the more popular, called the differential experience hypothesis, argues that individuals will naturally have greater familiarity or experience with members of their own race and will thus recognize its features. That is, individuals are typically raised in social environments that require the perceptual skills to recognize own-race faces, beginning at a very early age.

Although some researchers (e.g., Loftus, 1979) dismiss the differential experience hypothesis as a valid explanation for the other-race recognition effect, much of the research supports the theory, at least as a partial explanation (Elliott, Wills & Goldstein, 1973; Yarmey, 1979). Yarmey (1979) suggests a clarification that may help the opposing parties reach a compromise. The experience presumed to be a significant factor in recognition must be distinguished from mere exposure, he says. Growing up in an integrated neighborhood does not necessarily allow one to discern other-race facial characteristics accurately. Rather, it is the frequency of meaningful and positive contacts with other races that engenders perceptual skill in accurate facial discrimination. For example, having close friends of other races is more likely to promote facial discernment than having frequent but superficial exposure.

Additional support for the differential experience hypothesis is provided in studies showing that training in face familiarization dissipates the other-race effect (e.g., Elliott, Wills & Goldstein, 1973; Lavrakas, Buri & Mayzner, 1976). In the Elliot project, white observers' recognition of unfamiliar oriental faces significantly improved as a result of training in a learning task (paired associates) which increased their attention to identifying features of oriental faces. In another experiment (Ellis, Deregowski & Shepherd, 1975), white observers from Scotland were found to concentrate more on such features as hair color and texture and color of eyes when looking at white faces. On the other hand, black observers from Rhodesia, looking at black faces, attended more to facial outline, hair style, eye size, whites of eyes, eyebrows, ears, and chin. These results suggest at least two possible explanations for differences in race identification. People may develop specific strategies based on certain discriminatory cues of the human face to identify same-race members. Or, in view of the Ellis data, blacks may process a greater number of useful facial cues than whites when discriminating own-race members. It is, of course, entirely feasible that blacks use both strategies in facial recognition.

If the strategies used by individuals in identifying same-race members can be delineated, it is possible that the discernment of eyewitnesses may be improved prior to any identification procedure of other-race suspects. However, how crucial initial observations of suspects are and whether they might be improved by employing after-the-fact strategies remains an unanswered question.

A second hypothesis (in contrast to the differential experience hypothesis) pertains only to white observers. It contends that other-race recognition is a result of the fact that faces in other-race groups are more homogeneous than white faces and therefore less discriminable. White faces have more variability in hair, skin, and eye color than black faces and are therefore more discernible. In a series of experiments designed to test this hypothesis, Goldstein and Chance (1976, 1978) found that white subjects did not perceive oriental faces to be more homogeneous or alike than white faces. This outcome suggests that the explanation of the other-race effect lies not so much in the facial characteristics of the person being observed as it does in the observer.

In sum, the literature is consistent in concluding that people have difficulty recognizing unfamiliar persons of other races. This other-race effect is obviously a crucial aspect in the identification accuracy of suspects by eyewitnesses. The most valid explanation for the phenomenon at this point appears to be the differential experience hypothesis, which implies that substantial, meaningful interactions with members of a different race may promote strategies for facial discrimination.

# ■ Pretrial Identification Methods

The identification of suspects by witnesses begins as soon after the offense as possible. Police usually obtain verbal descriptions of the perpetrators from witnesses or show photographs to obtain a preliminary identification. In some instances, the police will have witnesses scan mug shots of individuals with previous arrest records, either to identify the specific offender or to obtain an approximation of the offender's appearance. Some police agencies routinely ask witnesses to examine a group of photographs (photoboards) fairly well matched to the physical characteristics described, including the person the police suspect to be the guilty party. The validity of these photo identification techniques has been addressed by the nation's highest court in a number of cases.

On February 27, 1964, two men entered a Chicago savings and loan association office. One man pointed a revolver at a teller and demanded that she place money into a sack. Soon afterward, the FBI apprehended two suspects, after tracing a motor vehicle described by one of the bank employees. The FBI then obtained group photographs from relatives of the suspects and showed them to five bank employees. The group pictures included the suspects, and all five witnesses identified one of the suspects (Simmons); three identified the other.

After its route through the lower courts, the case was heard by the U.S. Supreme Court as *Simmons v. United States* (1968). Simmons asserted "that his pretrial identification by means of photographs was in the circumstances so unnecessarily suggestive and conducive to misidentification as to deny him due process of law" (*Simmons v. U.S.*, p. 381). The Court, however, felt otherwise. The Justices ruled that the photograph procedure used by the FBI was appropriate under the circumstances, and they elaborated: "convictions based on eyewitness identification at trial following a pretrial identification by photograph will be set aside on that ground only if the photographic identification procedure was so impermissibly suggestive as to give rise to a very substantial likelihood of irreparable misidentification" (p. 384). An example of an "impermissibly suggestive" procedure would be where a black suspect is shown to eyewitnesses among five white persons, or where a perpetrator described as short is shown among tall foils (known innocent persons).

Just prior to *Simmons*, the Supreme Court heard three cases dealing with pretrial identification abuses (*U.S. v. Wade*, 1967; *Gilbert v. California*, 1967; *Stovall v. Denno*, 1967). In *Wade* (see box), the Court recognized the many problems inherent in pretrial identification, especially lineups, and it ruled that suspects have the right to have counsel present to assure an unbiased procedure. In *Gilbert*, the Court found the defendant was denied due process of law when he was identified in a large auditorium by 100 witnesses to several different robberies which he had allegedly committed. The Court was concerned about the possible effect of group suggestion on the identification of the defendant.

In *Stovall*, the defendant was brought to the hospital room of the victim, who had been stabbed eleven times. It was one day after major surgery to save the victim's life. The black defendant was handcuffed to one of the five escorting white police officers, who were also accompanied by two staff members of the District Attorney's office. This motley contingent descended upon the hospital room to request victim identification. In criminal justice circles, this procedure of parading one person in front of a witness or witnesses is called a "one-man show-up." The badly injured victim did affirm that Stovall was the offender.

The Supreme Court ruled that, under the unusual circumstances and because of the possible death of the sole witness, the procedure was *necessarily suggestive* and hence not improper. "The practice of showing suspects singly to persons for the purpose of identification, and not as part of a lineup, has been widely condemned. However, a claimed violation of due process of law in the conduct of a confrontation depends on the totality of the circumstances surrounding it, and the record in the present case reveals that the showing of Stovall to Mrs. Behrent in an immediate hospital confrontation was imperative" (Justice Brennan commenting, p. 292).

In all three of the above cases, the Court acknowledged the inherent dangers of bias in pretrial identifications and concluded that "counsel is required at all confrontations to promote fairness" (p. 298). The cases specified some of the conditions under which certain identification procedures were permissible and recognized that pretrial identification is extremely critical in the proceedings against defendants.

## IDENTIFICATION BIASES

Pretrial identification methods are especially susceptible to a wide spectrum of biases, running from very blatant practices to more subtle innuendo. A police investigator suggesting to the witness that he look closely at "the third one in from the right" is subtle innuendo when compared to other practices. Psychologists are beginning to examine more closely the psychology of the lineup and its ramifications for the criminal justice system.

Since the witness will look for a suspect in the lineup or photoboard who fits the description given the police, the physical makeup of the members of the lineup is a crucial factor. Individuals being viewed should have as many of the relevant characteristics remembered by the witness as possible. Age, physical stature, race, hair style, and manner of dress—especially if described by the witness—should be approximately the same for all members of the lineup. If the witness remembered the offender as a six-foot-tall individual with blond, wavy hair and a moustache, the lineup is obviously biased if only one person in six follows that description. No matter how many foils are standing in the line, the test is effectively limited to the number of participants who resemble the suspect. We refer to this condition as *composition bias*.

Composition bias has been analyzed in a number of studies, but two which appear especially relevant are those of Wells, Leippe, and Ostrom (1979) and Doob and Kirshenbaum (1973). Using the previous work of Doob and Kirshenbaum, Gary Wells and his colleagues developed a concept they call the "functional size" of a lineup. This refers to the number of lineup members who resemble the suspect in physically relevant features. By contrast, "nominal size" refers to the actual number of members within the lineup, which theoretically may include some very dissimilar foils.

In a typical lineup of six persons, the functional size decreases as the physically dissimilar members of a lineup increase. For a lineup to be considered fair, its functional size should approximate the nominal size. If by employing various measures and statistical tests it is determined that all the members of a six member lineup have equal probability of being selected on the basis of crucial characteristics, the functional size is six. If only three resemble the suspect, the functional size is four and the nominal size is six.

## ☐ WITNESS IDENTIFICATION CASES

*United States v. Wade, Gilbert v. California,* and *Stovall v. Denno* form the trilogy of cases dealing with the effects of prejudicial lineups and witness identifications of accused persons. The following excerpts are from *Wade,* but they make reference to the critical aspects of the other two cases relative to the suggestive manner in which witness identification was carried out by the police.

The Government characterizes the lineup as a mere preparatory step in the gathering of the prosecution's evidence, not different—for Sixth Amendment purposes—from various other preparatory steps, such as systematized or scientific analyzing of the accused's fingerprints, blood sample, clothing, hair, and the like. We think there are differences which preclude such stages being characterized as critical stages at which the accused has the right to the presence of his counsel. . . .

But the confrontation compelled by the State between the accused and the victim or witnesses to a crime to elicit identification evidence is peculiarly riddled with innumerable dangers and variable factors which might seriously, even crucially, derogate from a fair trial. The vagaries of eyewitness identification are well-known; the annals of criminal law are rife with instances of mistaken identification. . . .

A commentator has observed that "[t]he influence of improper suggestion upon identifying witnesses probably accounts for more miscarriages of justice than any other single factor—perhaps it is responsible for more such errors than all other factors combined." . . . Suggestion

can be created intentionally or unintentionally in many subtle ways. And the dangers for the suspect are particularly grave when the witness' opportunity for observation was insubstantial, and thus his susceptibility to suggestion the greatest.

Moreover, "[i]t is a matter of common experience that, once a witness has picked out the accused at the line-up, he is not likely to go back on his word later on, so that in practice the issue of identity may (in the absence of other relevant evidence) for all practical purposes be determined there and then, before the trial." . . .

The lineup in *Gilbert* . . . was conducted in an auditorium in which some 100 witnesses to several alleged state and federal robberies charged to Gilbert made wholesale identifications of Gilbert as the robber in each other's presence, a procedure said to be fraught with dangers of suggestion. And the vise of suggestion created by the identification in *Stovall* . . . was the presentation to the witness of the suspect alone handcuffed to police officers. It is hard to imagine a situation more clearly conveying the suggestion to the witness that the one presented is believed guilty by the police. . . .

Since it appears that there is grave potential for prejudice, intentional or not, in the pretrial lineup, which may not be capable of reconstruction at trial, and since presence of counsel itself can often avert prejudice and assure a meaningful confrontation at trial, there can be little doubt that for Wade the post-indictment lineup was a critical stage of the prosecution at which he was "as much entitled to such aid [of counsel] . . . as at the trial itself." . . . Thus both Wade and his counsel should have been notified of the impending lineup, and counsel's presence should have been a requisite to conduct of the lineup.

Obtaining theoretical and statistical indices about composition bias is an interesting academic exercise for researchers, but we also must consider the reality or "ecological validity" of this approach. Police officials and prosecuting attorneys remind us that there are problems in including lineup members who closely resemble the suspect. First, it is often difficult to find persons (outside of members of the police department) who are willing to participate and who resemble the suspect in salient features. A volunteer might be identified as the guilty party! This is particularly a problem for medium-sized city or small-town police departments, where the subject pool is already limited. Second, police officials worry about the possibility that a high level of similarity between lineup (or photoboard) members may confuse the witnesses and distract from the accurate identification of the primary suspect.

On the other side of the ledger, it can be argued that the quality of the evidence is enhanced when suspects are selected from lineups possessing high functional size. Lindsay and Wells (1980) provide evidence that high similarity compared to low similarity lineups reduce correct identification of perpetrators. Their research found low similarity lineups produced correct identifications 71 percent of the time, whereas high similarity lineups produced it 58 percent of the time. However, the researchers contend that the reduction in correct identification is compensated by the assurance that the identifications presented to the court are stronger evidence and less open to counter-argument.

A more subtle form of composition bias enters in with respect to who constructs the lineup. As we have learned, people have trouble discriminating the faces of other races, presumably because they do not attend properly to discerning features. If the suspect is black, the lineup constructor is white, and the witnesses are white, we have a situation with much potential bias. This possibility is suggested by John Brigham (1980), who bases his observations on accompanying research. Brigham notes that witness accuracy should be the greatest when the constructor and the lineup members are of the same race and the witness of a different race.

Another area of pretrial identification which must be closely examined is *commitment bias*. When a witness has initially identified a face, even an incorrect one, he or she will be more likely to choose the face again. This phenomenon is an offshoot of the foot-in-the-door technique long studied by social psychologists (Vander Zanden, 1977). It has been demonstrated in several simulated experiments on eyewitness testimony (Brown et al., 1977; Gorenstein & Ellsworth, 1980).

Commitment bias is most operative in conditions where witnesses want to please police investigators and also presume that the police have good evidence against someone in the identification proceedings. Because of commitment bias, a witness who initially identifies a suspect, but with some doubts, is more likely to identify the suspect in subsequent exposures with greater conviction. Each subsequent identification promotes greater confidence because of the public and private commitment that "he *is* the one."

Thus, a witness may begin the identification sequence by saying, "I think maybe he is the one."

The police officer inquires, "Are you sure?"

The witness replies, "Yes, I'm pretty sure."

The police officer inquires further, "*Pretty* sure?"

The witness affirms, "Yes, I'm sure."

Between the time of this identification procedure and the trial, the witness replays the scene in his or her mind, thereby strengthening the commitment. This is done repeatedly as the trial date approaches.

When the prosecuting attorney asks this key witness during the trial, "Are you sure this is the man?" the answer becomes, "Yes, I'm absolutely positive."

There are many other sources of bias inherent in pretrial identification procedures, but those delineated here have received the most attention from psychologists in recent years. Another source, one relatively unstudied, is police bias. This refers to the use of police officers as foils or to the questioning techniques used by the police investigator.

The use of officers as foils in a lineup is a practice fraught with potential bias. Certain nonverbal cues, like frequent glances in the direction of the suspect by the foils, could easily contaminate an independent judgment by the witness. Leading questions directed toward the witness and the quality of the questioning directed at lineup members by the police investigator can also produce biased results from witnesses who are sensitive to cues from the police.

## ■ Police as Witnesses

Are police officers more keen and accurate observers of what goes on around them than the general population? More accurate in remembering characteristics of suspects? The evidence is sparse, but the half-dozen studies we have available on this subject clearly indicate that police officers are no more accurate than ordinary citizens (Clifford, 1976; Yarmey, 1979). In fact, police officers are more likely to misinterpret events and see suspicious behavior where it does not exist (Verinis & Walker, 1970). Part of the problem stems from inadequate training. Existing police knowledge is outdated, often misguided, and too often based on working hypotheses about the nature of reality (Clifford, 1976). It is also likely, however, that some police officers are so intent on upholding the law and finding perpetrators of crime that they commit themselves to identifying suspects with more conviction than others.

## ■ Summary and Conclusions

The material presented in this chapter illustrates that evidence obtained through traditional procedures of eyewitness interrogation and legal testimony is replete with potential inaccuracies and misconceptions, regardless of the avowed certainty of the witness. Human perception and memory are like unexplored labyrinths where original input becomes altered, partially lost, and transformed into an arrangement that fits our expectancies, experiences, and sometimes the disguised needs of others. Situational, witness, and offender factors intermingle to produce an output which may barely resemble the incident as it "actually" occurred.

On the other hand, eyewitness information has been, is, and will continue to be the principal source of evidence in both criminal and civil case law. This book by no means advocates the elimination or reduction of witness testimony as evidence in the judicial process. The research evidence does suggest, however, that the judicial system should carefully examine some of the widespread fireside inductions about eyewitnesses and perhaps even entertain some small but critical changes in procedures.

Gary Wells (1978) divides eyewitness research into examinations of two sets of variables—estimator variables and system variables. Estimator variables are those situational, witness, and offender variables present at the scene of a crime or incident. For example, violence level, speed of events, the age of the witness, and the race of the perpetrator are all estimator variables. No matter what strategy or procedure the criminal justice system employs, it is unlikely to have major impact on this set of variables. The criminal justice system and the experimental psychologist can have little control over the occurrence and mixture of these variables. Research on them, as presented in this chapter, can be used to estimate, post hoc, the likely accuracy of a witness. It can also be used to alter beliefs and attitudes about eyewitness testimony. But it will have little influence on legal strategy and procedure.

In contrast, system variables are under the direct control of the legal system and do lend themselves to changes in strategy and procedure. Examples of system variables include lineup procedures and guidelines, witness interrogation techniques, and the length of time between the initial event and subsequent testimony. Research data on system variables do apply to methods presently employed in the judicial system, most particularly criminal justice.

The research evidence on eyewitness testimony is backed by eight or nine decades of data accumulation and increasing methodological sophistication, factors we did not find in jury research. It is in eyewitness research that we best see an independent psychology *and* law relationship—and perhaps a meeting of the two disciplines in a mutual acceptance that they are coequals.

## ■ Key Concepts and Principles, Chapter 7

| | |
|---|---|
| Fireside induction | Yerkes-Dodson Principle |
| Perception and accuracy | Expectancies and eyewitness reports |
| Memory stages and accuracy | Retention factors and eyewitness reports |
| Reconstructive process | Recall and recognition memory |
| Temporal factors on eyewitness testimony | Memory characteristics of faces |
| | Unconscious transference |
| Detail significance and memory | Race and face recall and recognition |
| Violence level and memory recall | Composition bias |
| Witness arousal and recall | Commitment bias |

□ | # 8

■ # Psychology of Evidence and Related Issues

□ | Now that the shortcomings and unreliability of some of the information obtained from eyewitnesses have been covered, it is time to give some attention to the information provided by accused persons themselves. Although courts have repeatedly told law enforcement personnel that individuals may not be forced to testify against themselves, to confess, or otherwise to provide evidence that may be damaging to their cases, these warnings have not been interpreted to mean that defendants may not plead guilty or provide evidence. Neither do the court rulings mean that law enforcement officers cannot interrogate suspects and witnesses to gather evidence. At issue are the methods of questioning and the conditions under which interrogations are conducted.

We will begin this chapter with an overall look at psychological information that may be of use to criminal justice personnel in the process of gathering evidence, specifically when they interview suspects or other persons believed to be connected with a crime. We will evaluate some of the myths about nonverbal behavior and various methods "guaranteed" to detect lying. Methods of interrogation, including the use of hypnosis, will also be discussed. Later in the chapter we will redirect attention to the jury in an attempt to decide whether and to what extent jurors can be influenced by "evidence" of guilt or innocence provided outside the courtroom setting.

## ■ Methods of Interrogation

Convictions based on "coerced" confessions have been overturned consistently by the U.S. Supreme Court, although lively debate has surrounded the question of what conditions define coercion (Shapiro & Tresolini, 1979). Prior to the 1950s, courts accepted arguments that some methods employing physical restraints, prolonged physical discomfort, beatings, and a wide variety of physical abuses were, not surprisingly, coercive and not to be tolerated. Gradually, courts also began to acknowledge the existence of more subtle forms of "psychological" coercion.

In the landmark case *Escobedo v. Illinois* (1964), the U.S. Supreme Court ruled that the petitioner's confession should not have been admissible in the state court because it was rendered only after Escobedo had repeatedly asked for and been denied counsel. The Court also found that the interrogation methods used by the police had so emotionally upset the man that he was impaired in his capacity for rational judgment. The best way to prevent potential injustice of this sort, the Justices said, was to allow subjects to be interrogated in the presence of their attorneys. Therefore, the Court held that once a police interviewing process shifts from an investigatory to an accusatory focus, or once its purpose is to elicit a confession, the individual must be permitted to have counsel present.

Two years later the Court heard the famous (or infamous, depending upon one's perspective) *Miranda v. Arizona* (1966) (see box). Chief Justice Earl Warren, delivering the opinion of the Court, commented extensively on the pressure tactics of interrogation and made several references to the powerful effects of psychological coercion inherent in that process. "We stress that the modern practice of in-custody interrogation is psychologically rather than physically oriented. As we have stated before . . . 'this Court has recognized that coercion can be mental as well as physical, and that the blood of the accused is not the only hallmark of an unconstitutional inquisition'" (p. 448).

The Court felt it was paramount that the accused have counsel present during interrogation and be able to consult during the process. The majority contended that the presence of an attorney, combined with clear warning delivered to the individual at the moment of arrest, would enable an accused, under compelling circumstances, to tell his or her story without fear, and in a way that eliminates "the evils in the interrogation process."

The interrogation process continues to be a powerful and commonly practiced method of securing evidence and obtaining confessions. In fact, in spite of the Supreme Court's position, police classroom instruction and texts continue to advocate the psychological tactics which traditionally have been applied. For example, in reaction to the Supreme Court's dicta, Inbau and Reid (1967, pp. 213–214) commented,

> interrogations . . . must be conducted under conditions of privacy and for a reasonable period of time; and they frequently require the use of psychological tactics and techniques that could well be classified as "unethical," if we are to evaluate them in terms of ordinary, everyday social behavior. . . . We are opposed . . . to the use of force, threats, or promises of leniency—all of which might well induce an innocent person to confess; *but we do approve of such psychological tactics and techniques as trickery and deceit that are not only helpful but frequently necessary in order to secure incriminating information from the guilty, or investigative leads from otherwise uncooperative witnesses or informants* [italics added].

How can these methods be advocated and used, even after *Miranda*? The answer may lie in a number of decisions by the Burger Court that significantly reduced the scope of that decision (Shapiro & Tresolini, 1979). Although the more conservative

Burger Court has not overturned *Miranda*, it has allowed some indirect use of statements from persons who had not been warned of their rights to have attorneys present or to protect themselves from self-incrimination. For example, in *Harris v. New York* (1971), the Court ruled, although in a badly split decision, that statements made by a defendant without Miranda warnings could be used if the defendant took the stand in his or her own defense, giving evidence contradicting what he or she had already told police. In *Michigan v. Tucker* (1974), the Court allowed prosecutors to use a statement from an unwarned suspect to locate a witness against that suspect. Still later, the Court refused to extend the requirements of the Miranda warning to grand jury witnesses,

---

## ☐ MIRANDA v. ARIZONA
### Excerpts

We dealt with certain phases of this problem [custodial police interrogation] recently in *Escobedo v. Illinois*, 378 U.S. 478 (1964). There, as in the four cases before us, law enforcement officials took the defendant into custody and interrogated him in a police station for the purpose of obtaining a confession. The police did not effectively advise him of his right to remain silent or of his right to consult with his attorney. Rather, they confronted him with an alleged accomplice who accused him of having perpetrated a murder. When the defendant denied the accusation and said "I didn't shoot Manuel, you did it," they handcuffed him and took him to an interrogation room. There, while handcuffed and standing, he was questioned for four hours until he confessed. During this interrogation, the police denied his request to speak to his attorney, and they prevented his retained attorney, who had come to the police station, from consulting with him. At his trial, the State, over his objection, introduced the confession against him. We held that the statements thus made were constitutionally inadmissible. . . .

Our holding will be spelled out with some specificity in the pages which follow but briefly stated it is this: the prosecution may not use statements, whether exculpatory or inculpatory, stemming from custodial interrogation of the defendant unless it demonstrates the use of procedural safeguards effective to secure the privilege against self-incrimination. By custodial interrogation, we mean questioning initiated by law enforcement officers after a person has been taken into custody or otherwise deprived of his freedom of action in any significant way. As for the procedural safeguards to be employed, unless other fully effective means are devised to inform accused persons of their right of silence and to assure a continuous opportunity to exercise it, the following measures are required. Prior to any questioning, the person must be warned that he has a right to remain silent, that any statement he does make may be used as evidence against him, and that he has a right to the presence of an attorney, either retained or appointed. The defendant may waive effectuation of these rights, provided the waiver is made voluntarily, knowingly and intelligently. If, however, he indicates in any manner and at any stage of the process that he wishes to consult with an attorney before speaking there can be no questioning. Likewise, if the individual is alone and indicates in any manner that he does not wish to be interrogated, the police may not question him. The mere fact that he may have answered some questions or volunteered some statements on his own does not deprive him of the right to refrain from answering any further inquiries until he has consulted with an attorney and thereafter consents to be questioned. . . .

Again we stress that the modern practice of in-custody interrogation is psychologically rather than physically oriented. . . . this Court has recognized that coercion can be mental as well as physical, and that the blood of the accused is not the only hallmark of an unconstitutional inquisition.

even though they could become potential defendants (*U.S. v. Mandujano*, 1976). And the Court would not accept the argument that a juvenile's request to see his probation officer required police to stop questioning him (*Fare v. Michael C.*, 1979).

## INTERROGATIVE TACTICS

The student of psychology and law should be aware of some of the methods of evidence-gathering through the psychological strategies used in custodial interrogation. Belief in the effectiveness of these strategies is based on procedural evidence and personal experience rather than any validating evidence gained through systematic experimentation. Still, most police officials swear by their usefulness in solving crimes and they employ the strategies whether or not the suspect is accompanied by counsel. The reader should be reminded that experienced interrogators make certain that the rights outlined in *Miranda* are read and understood by the subject. Proof of this is usually obtained by having the subject sign a brief, clearly written document attesting to that fact. If the accused does not request an attorney, the interrogation can proceed.

The interrogative tactics to be sketched below have been culled from a variety of sources, mixed with the author's personal experience in the training and application of these tactics in police academy instruction programs. The most well-known source materials on interrogation are Inbau and Reid's *Criminal Interrogation and Confessions* (1962); Gerber and Schroeder's *Criminal Investigation and Interrogation* (1962); O'Hara's *Fundamentals of Criminal Investigation* (1970); and Aubry and Caputo's *Criminal Interrogation* (1965).

Interrogation as discussed here will be limited to those situations involving suspects or defendants. It is a procedure conducted to obtain either an admission of guilt or clarification and elaboration of certain facts under coercive, but not too coercive, conditions. Precisely what constitutes too much coercion is often unclear to police officials, who are usually instructed to read the *Miranda* case when in doubt. Interviewing, in contrast to interrogation, is designed to obtain clarification and elaboration of relevant facts from witnesses, potential witnesses, victims, or informants. It involves different principles and approaches, which will not be discussed here.

Three general psychological principles are emphasized in most interrogation techniques. The first pertains to psychological control; the interrogator communicates to the subject that he or she has total control over both the subject and the interrogative situation. The second principle involves the use of methods designed to induce tension or guilt in the subject, with the assumption that this will break down the subject's defenses. The third principle is that the interrogator must appear confident and in command throughout the interrogation process.

**Setting.** Most outlined procedures for interrogations specify the most conducive setting. In general, a setting which ensures isolation from the psychological security of friends or familiar surroundings is advocated. The value of a special interrogation room which deprives the suspect of psychological advantages usually gained from familiar places is strongly emphasized. The setting should be private enough to guarantee no interruptions or distractions that would interfere with the flow of information or contaminate the control and tension-induction methods. This requires a room that is sparsely decorated, with no pictures or other items to encourage a breakdown in concentration or divided attention.

**Conduct.** The three psychological principles of control, tension-induction, and confidence are clearly evident in the conduct the interrogator is recommended to adopt. The interrogator should stand while the subject sits, a method intended to communicate control. A subject's request to smoke should be refused, not only to communicate control but also to preclude the tension-reduction gained from smoking behavior. When the subject is answering questions, it is suggested that the interrogator "violate" the subject's personal space by standing close to him or her so as to induce discomfort and tension.

Psychological control is also communicated through the calm, patient, and systematic approach exhibited by the interrogator throughout the interrogation process. Virtually all manuals and classroom instructors tell the interrogators that time is on their side and that extreme patience, combined with persistence and repetition, will eventually "break" most guilty subjects. Psychological control is also gained when the interrogator is fully informed of all the known facts about the case and all the possible motives. Inconsistencies and distortions are, of course, more likely to be detected by the carefully prepared, informed interrogator.

While control and tension-inducing procedures are being initiated, interrogators should simultaneously communicate sympathy for and understanding of the subject's predicament. Most manuals recommend that interrogators use only language that can be understood by the subject and that is permeated with the communication, "We are only seeking the truth." Almost all manuals dictate that the subject should be treated with respect, regardless of the nature of his or her alleged offense. It is also advocated that paper and pencil should be kept out of sight except to record names, dates and addresses, because extensive notetaking tends to inhibit "free" exchange.

The presence of weapons on the interrogator is discouraged, because these objects not only inhibit communication but also may instigate hostility on the part of the subject. If the suspect is not "interrogation-wise," that is, if the subject has not been questioned in the past, it is suggested that the interrogator sympathize by saying that others in similar situations might have done the same thing. In some instances, manuals suggest that it might be effective to reduce the subject's guilt feelings temporarily by minimizing the moral seriousness of the offense.

**Questioning.** Certain general rules are offered to get the subject to talk about himself or herself. The interrogator is advised to open by asking background questions and general, nonthreatening questions that the subject can answer without having to deceive. Most instruction urges the interrogator to observe the mannerisms and behaviors of the subject while he or she is responding. Does the subject appear calm or nervous, intelligent and educated, arrogant, humble? These observations can provide information about what specific strategies to employ, although it is not wise to make conclusive judgments based on such nonverbal behavior, as we shall see later in the chapter.

Question content and form are given considerable attention in interrogation training. Questions should be directed at gaining specific information about details of an incident rather than at seeking a global confession. The interrogator should focus upon chipping away at the subject's resistance, since few persons are eager to incriminate themselves and since immediate confessions will not likely be forthcoming. It is also emphasized that questions be worded in relatively innocuous terms, so that they do not connote a specific offense like "rape," "kill," "shoot," or "molest."

Manuals warn interrogators against becoming personally involved to the point where they might get upset, angry, or otherwise demonstrate lack of control over the process. A subject will welcome the impression that the interrogator has lost confidence in the direction of the conversation. Patience, control, and confidence on the part of the interrogator are essential.

Beyond these general points, specific strategies for dealing with certain types of offenders or kinds of offenses may be outlined. Inbau and Reid (1967) offer a dichotomy based upon the emotionality of offenders. They posit that emotional offenders typically commit crimes against persons, and because they often have strong feelings of remorse are particularly responsive to the "sympathetic" approach. Nonemotional offenders are more likely to commit crimes for financial gain, highly resistive to being detected and convicted, and more responsive to common sense reasoning.

Inbau and Reid also make a division based on whether or not the suspect's guilt is quite certain or questionable. They suggest that, when guilt is certain, the interrogator should make known this belief to the subject from the outset. However, the interrogator is warned not to ask questions which require the subject to repeat a denial of guilt, since repetitive denials render the subject less likely to admit guilt later. The interrogator is told to ask direct questions of the "why" variety, rather than to ask "whether" the person committed the crime.

**Cues.** Interrogators should be alert to a number of physiological indicators of anxiety and stress. This is especially recommended in the case of emotional offenders who are strongly suspected. Sweating, blushing, dry mouth, shaking hands, elbows close to the body, are all nonverbal cues of tension that should be brought to the subject's attention.

The interrogator is further instructed to be alert to deception indicators, such as the subject's avoidance of eye contact, frequent hand to face contact, or even frequent trips to the bathroom. Signs of deception are also claimed to be inherent in the way the subject says things. For example, the interrogator is told to be suspicious of statements that are prefaced by "I swear to God I'm telling the truth" or "I'll swear on a stack of bibles." Suspicion is also drawn to the "spotless record, religious man" routine: "I've never done anything illegal in my life," or "I'm a deeply religious, church-going person." The interrogator is advised to be especially suspicious of the "not that I remember" comment, because it is often used by lying subjects. Therefore, it is implied that deception cues help to establish the guilt or innocence of the interrogation suspect. There is a danger in being too quick to adopt these suggestions, as we will discuss shortly in the section on deception.

**Role playing.** The sympathetic approach frequently advocated combines tension-induction strategies with humanistic gestures. A pat on the shoulder, a grip on the hand, a proferred cigarette or soft drink or sandwich—all are intended as symbolic gestures of understanding and compassion. Experienced interrogators claim that this is an effective strategy to use with younger subjects or first-time offenders. Some police agencies use the Mutt and Jeff routine, or the unfriendly-friendly role play. Here, an interrogator plays the role of the gruff, insensitive cop who threatens and cajoles the subject. Then, a friendly, sensitive, compassionate officer arrives on the scene, advises his colleague to "take it easy," and speaks gently to the subject. The effectiveness of this method is believed to stem primarily from the accent placed on the friendly officer, which ultimately improves the sympathetic approach.

**Other strategies.** There is no dearth of suggested alternative strategies in the interrogation literature. Have the suspect tell his or her story a number of times, in backward sequence. Then, have the suspect explain the discrepancies that are likely to surface. Or propose a hypothetical situation: "It doesn't look as if you were involved in this crime, but if you had been, what would you have done? What techniques would you have used?" This presumably forces a suspect to propose a modus operandi that may give the interrogator clues to the crime under investigation. Another suggestion is directed at investigations of white-collar crimes. The interrogator is advised to enter the interrogating room armed with official looking papers and to proceed to examine them periodically, sometimes frowning or shaking his head. This procedure assumes that white-collar offenders are impressed with the power of documents and are apt to become anxious in the face of possible evidence.

If the subject's guilt is uncertain, interrogators must decide whether to treat him or her as guilty or innocent, or to assume a neutral role without implying either. Most experienced interrogators believe it is most effective to take a neutral position until some clearer determination of guilt or innocence can be made.

It is often recommended that investigators discover early in the process whether subjects are lying by asking questions to which answers are already known. Alternatively, the interrogator may present fabricated data about the case and notice how the subject deals with it. Any tactic that catches the subject in a lie not only will provide valuable information about the subject's integrity but also will give the interrogator the upper hand, once the subject realizes he or she has been caught fabricating.

Although we have outlined some of the commonly used methods of interrogation, the reader should realize that there are numerous other approaches which various agencies claim are highly effective. All, however, have the three basic ingredients of psychological control, tension induction, and confidence and persistence on the part of the interrogator. To what extent psychological manipulation and trickery should be allowed remains problematical. Police officers claim that any further limitations on interrogation procedures would hinder seriously any attempt to solve crimes. However, many civil libertarians are concerned about the infringement of individual rights and psychological dignity that occur when deceit, trickery, and psychological pressures are employed.

### COERCIVE PERSUASION

Coercive persuasion, or "brainwashing," follows many of the strategies incorporated in interrogation except that they are carried out to extremes. Control over the victim is total, including complete social isolation and control of all channels of information and communication (Schein, 1971). Physiological debilitation, such as an inadequate diet, insufficient clothing, and poor sanitation not only underscore the degree of control by the agents in charge but also lower physical and psychological resistance by promoting weakness and lowered self-esteem. In many strategies, continual threats of death are often used to increase the tension and anxiety levels. Other strategies employ persistent peer pressure to confirm to and adopt the group's convictions, or repetitive symbolic acts of self-betrayal.

In recent years the issue of coercive persuasion has drawn interest in legal circles along two major lines of inquiry: (1) the legal-constitutional issues revolving around the coercive methods used by certain religious cults to gain active members; and (2) the extent to which brainwashing tactics used by third persons mitigate the culpability of an allegedly brainwashed person who engages in illegal conduct.

The first issue involves psychological servitude resulting from indoctrination and membership in an extremist religious cult. The servitude is so extensive that people concerned about the welfare of indoctrinated members become convinced that they are no longer functioning of their own free will. Therefore, measures are taken to remove cult members forcibly and against their will from the coercive environment. However, to remove individuals forcibly because of their religious persuasion and to restrain them against their convictions conjures up serious infringements of an adult's freedom of choice of religion. Also, any charges leveled against a religious conversion practice may be challenged because religious groups merit the protection of the First Amendment (Delgado, 1977).

The second legal concern—criminal culpability under duress initiated and maintained by a third party—is as complicated an issue as religious conversion. Although it has been attempted as a criminal defense (e.g., *United States v. Hearst*, 1976), coercive persuasion or "transferred culpability" has yet to be successful (Delgado, 1978). However, as social conditions conducive to terrorism and other methods of psychologically controlling behavior continue, the likelihood of brainwashing as a viable defense will increase. Richard Delgado (1978) makes the first cogent argument for the introduction of coercive persuasion as a defense. In a rejoinder, however, Joshua Dressler (1979) argues that it is logically impossible to frame a coercive persuasion defense that is both consistent with present criminal law and jurisprudential doctrine and morally acceptable.

Experimental psychologists have not been drawn to brainwashing as an empirical field of study, partly because of the enormous ethical dilemmas inherent in any coercive persuasion experiment. Therefore, scientific psychological answers to legal questions in this area are not currently available.

# ▪ Deception

Deception is behavior that is intended to conceal, misrepresent, or distort truth or information for the purpose of misleading others. It is most commonly found in the criminal justice system when one or more individuals are suspected of having committed an illegal act or of having relevant information about an illegal act. Under these conditions, the goal of the system is to discover which suspects, if any, are being deceptive. Three methods are commonly used to uncover such deception: interpretation of nonverbal behavior, the polygraph, and voice-stress analysis.

## NONVERBAL INDICATORS OF DECEPTION

The criminal justice system is replete with folklore and procedural evidence concerning how to discern whether someone is lying. Interrogation procedures in particular often have referents to nonverbal signs of deceit and guilt, as we have seen in the preceding section. Inbau and Reid, for example, assert (1967, p. 34): "When a subject fails to look the interrogator straight in the eye, or when he exhibits a restlessness by leg swinging, foot-wiggling, hand-wringing, finger-tapping, the picking of fingernails, or the fumbling with objects such as a tie clasp or pencil, it is well for the interrogator to get the idea across that he is aware of such reactions and that he views them as manifestations of lying." Other nonverbal behaviors believed to be indicative of guilt or lying include pulsation of the carotid artery in the neck, excessive activity of the Adam's apple, dryness of the mouth, and wiggling of the ears!

Over the past three decades many empirical studies have probed the relationship between nonverbal behavior and deception. Nonverbal cues like facial expressions, body posture, and movements of the legs and feet and arms have drawn the greatest attention. One general observation emerging from early scientific inquiry took researchers aback: Individuals who wish to deceive are also aware of the common folklore, and consequently they try to control the so-called indicators of lying. For example, people who are trying to deceive do not have more frequent eye shifts than truthful communicators (Mehrabian, 1971). Deceitful communicators also may smile more often than truthful communicators (Mehrabian & Williams, 1969), have longer eye contact (Mehrabian, 1971), or in some conditions maintain a more placid expression (McClintock & Hunt, 1975).

The above features all indicate an attempt, or even an over-attempt, to control the normal channels of nonverbal communications. Channels normally used in communicating emotions and feelings, such as facial expressions and eye contact, are held in tight check by the deceiving communicator. Thus, empirical study has found that deceit is not so much communicated through shifty eyes, decreased eye contact, or "evasive" facial expression, but rather through channels that typically are not used in expressing oneself. These more covert nonverbal modalities are called "leaky channels" by researchers (Ekman & Friesen, 1969, 1974), because they leak information not intended by the communicator.

The placid expression, longer eye contact, and tendency to smile are therefore often examples of leaky channels. In further attempts to control communication, deceitful individuals may speak at a slower rate, speak fewer words, but produce more speech errors (Rosenfeld, 1966; Kasl & Mahl, 1965). Their posture often is rigid and stiff (Mehrabian, 1971), and they display very little head nodding (Rosenfeld, 1966). Hand gestures are kept to an unusually low level (Ekman, Friesen & Scherer, 1976), but there is considerable movement and shifting with feet and legs (Ekman & Friesen, 1969). There is also evidence that deceitful speakers make exceedingly few factual statements, but many sweeping statements (Knapp, Hart & Dennis, 1974).

A wide variety of communicative cues may accompany deception, but the fact is that they also may not, or may accompany truth. In addition, most studies have found that observers have difficulty distinguishing liars from truth-tellers; the accuracy rate of observers is slightly better than chance (Bauchner, Brandt & Miller, 1977; Littlepage & Pineault, 1978; Knapp, 1978; Ekman & Friesen, 1974). It is not wise, therefore, to make assumptions about truthfulness or deception strictly on the basis of nonverbal cues. It is especially foolhardy to accept the prevailing folklore in the area. If anything, the cues associated with deception may be better behavioral indicators of stress and anxiety than they are signs of lying.

Witness credibility is a highly critical feature of courtroom trials. Jurors and judges not only consider the material presented in the courtroom but also evaluate its veracity. Regardless of the completeness or consistency of the testimony, if the decisionmakers perceive the source as less than honest, the value of the testimony is severely undermined. Veracity in the courtroom is largely based on the manner in which the testimony is presented. More fundamentally, veracity is primarily determined by the conventional wisdom linked to certain nonverbal cues.

Gerald Miller and his colleagues (1981) conducted several experiments to replicate some previous findings reported in the deception-detection literature; at the same time, they tried to recreate critical aspects of the courtroom in an effort to improve external validity. The Miller studies were designed to examine the following three major questions (Miller et al., 1981, p. 149):

1. In general, how accurate are jurors in detecting deception?
2. What effect(s) do variations in the mode of presentation of a trial (live, televised, audio only, transcript only, and, in the televised case, color vs. black and white) have on jurors' abilities to detect deception?
3. What sources of information facilitate a juror's ability to distinguish between deceitful and truthful testimony?

The basic experimental paradigm of the Miller studies was modeled after Ekman and Friesen (1974). In that project, motivated subjects were told to lie or to tell the truth about a stressful or nonstressful film they had just seen. The subjects' descriptions of the film were videotaped. Observer-subjects then viewed these videotapes and were asked to decide which narrators were telling the truth and which were lying. Results indicated that observer-subjects were not much better than chance at depicting who was lying and who was not.

Two of the Miller studies deserve our close attention. In the first, a similar paradigm to the one described above was used. However, the videotaped subjects were not only asked to lie or to be truthful about the stimuli they had seen, they were also questioned about the facts of the events they had viewed. Therefore, both emotional and factual content were included in the design, allowing the experimenters to measure accuracy in depicting lying in both emotional and factual testimony. In addition to videotapes, audiotapes and transcripts of the interview were also made to determine the influence of verbal cues compared to visual cues in detection of deception. Furthermore, the individuals interviewed were videotaped in both color and black and white, with sound. Lastly, to determine what bodily, nonverbal cues might best communicate deception, camera shots included either (1) head only, (2) body only, or (3) head and body.

Nineteen male and four female criminal justice undergraduates (seniors) served as the taped interviewees. To insure a reasonably high level of motivation, all the subjects—who were planning careers in law enforcement—were told that the School of Criminal Justice would receive information concerning their cooperation and performance in the experiment.

The observer-subjects who judged the videotapes were 719 undergraduate students enrolled in introductory communication classes and 193 adult residents from the local community. The primary dependent variable was the observer-subject's accuracy in identifying interviewee veracity. Each observer-subject was expected to make sixteen accuracy judgments, eight based upon identifying the veracity of statements by means of emotional content and eight by means of factual content.

The results revealed that people are no more accurate than chance in identifying deception. The results also indicated that judgments of witness veracity were not influenced by the use of color as opposed to black and white videotape. More surprisingly, the data suggest modification of Ekman and Friesen's (1969) leaky channel theory. It appears from the Miller study that nonfacial cues are the most reliable cues to deception when lying involves the deceiver's emotional response to events or situations. However, facial cues seem to provide the best information for making judgments about factual veracity. Hence, the leaky channel theory may hold for emotional deception but not for factual deception. It must be remembered, however, that regardless of the source or message content, people tend not to be accurate decipherers of deception.

Results from the transcript-only condition, the audio-only condition, and the visual-only condition also cast serious doubts on the assumption that detecting deception is enhanced by the presence of nonverbal behavioral cues. Observer-subjects in the transcript-only condition were as accurate as subjects in the audio-only condition when detecting deception dealing with factual information. Furthermore, audio-only and transcript-only subjects were more accurate than visual-only subjects, suggesting that nonverbal behavioral cues are less dependable sources for determining factual veracity than oral or verbal ones. Relative to detecting deception in expressing emotion, there were no significant differences in accuracy in visual, audio, or transcription sources.

Study II parallelled Study I in design except for four changes. First, in order to more closely approximate actual courtroom procedures, the interviewed subject in Study II was seen or heard live by the observer-subjects. Second, an attempt was made to control for possible sex differences in deceptive behavior by having equal numbers of male and female interviewees. Third, the researchers tried to have the interviewees more ego-involved in their deception by offering monetary prizes. Fourth, while in Study I interviewees acted out both deceptive and truthful conditions, in Study II they were assigned to only one condition.

Observer-subjects either saw, heard, or read interviews, made a judgment as to whether the sources were lying, and specified the amount and type of information used in making their judgment. Those observer-subjects assigned to the live condition watched the interview through a one-way mirror or listened to it.

Again, as in Study I, the results indicated that people are poor judges of the veracity of testimony and can detect deception no more often than chance. Moreover, it does not seem to make any difference in the type and amount of information they receive; they still make poor judgments about veracity. Further, it makes little difference whether the information is live or videotaped. Although much still needs to be resolved, it does seem that the average juror is unable to distinguish between deceptive and truthful testimony. And it does not seem to matter whether the deception is based on factual issues or feelings or emotions about stressful or exciting events.

## VOICE DETECTION

Some law enforcement agencies have been examining voice characteristics in an effort to identify suspects or to detect deception. In the identification procedure, it is assumed that each individual has a unique, personal style of speaking due to anatomical, structural differences in the speech mechanisms and the manner in which tongue, lips, and teeth are used. "Voiceprints" are oscillographic representations of spoken sounds that identify these unique elements of vocalization.

Both the scientific community and the judicial system have guardedly accepted voiceprints as an adequate means of identification under certain conditions. Courts adjudicating several criminal cases have allowed voiceprints as evidence (*U.S. v. Franks*, 1975; *U.S. v. Baller*, 1975; *Commonwealth v. Lykus*, 1975; *State v. Andretta*, 1972). However, the courts have attached limitations. For example, courts have ruled that voiceprints could be used only as collaborative evidence, or without contradictory expert testimony or evidence, or to justify an arrest warrant (Schwitzgebel & Schwitzgebel, 1980).

The value of voiceprints as discriminators between deception and truth has yet to be accepted by science or law. Proponents argue that a deceptive speaker's voice changes under stress and that these stress-related changes are reflected through minute vibrations or microtremors. The physiological changes are recorded and analyzed by instruments specifically designed for this purpose.

A number of commercial firms have marketed various pieces of hardware claimed to detect stress, and ultimately lying, from live or recorded segments of speech. Dektor Counterintelligence and Security Corporation of Springfield, Virginia, has developed the Psychological Stress Evaluator (PSE), for example, which is specifically designed to measure deception-induced stress in the human voice. Other less well-known instruments include the Mark II voice analyzer, marketed by Law Enforcement Associates, Inc.; the Voice Stress Analyzer (VSA), produced by Decision Control, Inc.; the Psychological Stress Analyzer (PSA), developed by Burns International Security Services; and the Voice Stress Monitor, offered by Security Specialists Marketing Group. The level of sophistication and complexity in instrumentation differ widely from one piece of equipment to another.

The most extensively marketed and researched instrument is Dektor's PSE. In marketing literature, Dektor claims that the PSE is 95 to 99 percent accurate in discriminating liars from truthtellers. This claim has yet to be substantiated in the published scientific literature, and Dektor fails to support it with any cites of replicable research (Hollien, 1980; Yarmey, 1979). Research projects testing the PSE have consistently found that it does no better than chance at identifying deception through voice-stress analysis (Hollien, 1980; Podlesny & Raskin, 1977; Kubis, 1973; Yarmey, 1979). In fact, none of the voice analyzers to date have been able to distinguish deception from truthfulness in the scientific laboratory.

The basis of the PSE's discriminatory power supposedly rests on its sensitivity to slight tremblings (microtremors) that occur in the voice mechanism, apparently in the small laryngeal muscles. However, available research demonstrates that while microtremors do exist in the large muscles, especially in the extremities, they do not appear to exist in the small muscles of the larynx (Hollien, 1980; Bachrach, 1979). Miron (1980) has suggested that the microtremors detected by the PSE might be located in the network of the large, slow-acting muscles that support the laryngeal mechanisms. Considering the extremely high level of sensitivity required to measure even known microtremors in the large muscles using sophisticated laboratory equipment, it seems that the PSE may be based on some voice-stress principle other than microtremors.

In summary, there is little scientific evidence to support the reliability and validity of instruments that attempt to detect deception by means of voice analysis. In light of our present knowledge, reliance on this equipment by industry and by the judicial system is risky at best.

## THE POLYGRAPH

Often called the "lie detector," the polygraph does not really detect lies or deception, but only the bodily responses that accompany emotions and stress. Presumably, when one tries to deceive, there are telltale bodily or physiological reactions that can be measured with sophisticated equipment.

Variants of the modern polygraph have been used in the psychological laboratory for nearly a century, and much cruder versions of its components existed as far back as 300 B.C. (Trovillo, 1939). Development of the modern field polygraph equipment and technique is generally credited to Larson and Keeler (Barland & Raskin, 1973). The field polygraph is a portable instrument that records on a paper chart changes in respiration (pneumograph), skin conductance (galvanometer), and blood volume and pulse rate (cardiophysmograph or, more accurately, an occlusion plethysmograph). The polygraph is not designed to measure blood pressure, as many professionals mistakenly believe. Some of the standard commercial field polygraphs only measure two physiological reactions, usually respiration and cardiovascular activity (blood volume and pulse rate). Many standard field polygraphs lag behind those used in laboratory settings by two or three decades in sophistication. However, despite their simplicity in instrumentation and design, with proper calibration and maintenance standard field polygraphs can accurately measure gross physiological activity.

Laboratory polygraphs are usually far more sophisticated and sensitive and can record simultaneously a great number of physiological indices. Moreover, they are often linked to a computer system which allows monitoring, "hard copy," and technical or statistical analysis of the relevant physiological dimensions. Most of the empirical research on the polygraph has used these more advanced instruments.

The field polygraph is used in two major areas—the interrogation of criminal suspects and the selection of personnel in American industry. It is estimated that several million such polygraphic exams are administered annually by at least 3,000 professional examiners (Lykken, 1974). The examiners are usually licensed or certified after being trained at a school of polygraphy, but most do not have psychological or research training.

Psychophysiologists conducting laboratory studies have consistently and continually reported that skin conductance, called either the skin resistance response (SRR) or the skin conductance response (SCR), can discriminate between truth and deception at a higher level of accuracy than any of the other physiological measures traditionally used (Podlesny & Raskin, 1977; Barland & Raskin, 1973). Although there have been fewer experiments in field settings, the little research done has also supported the value of the SRR. In fact, "virtually no reported experiment has failed to find significant discrimination between truth and deception, using measures of SCR and SRR" (Podlesny & Raskin, 1977, p. 791).

Nevertheless, field polygraphers often consider skin responses to be the least effective discriminators and prefer measures of respiratory and cardiovascular activity, even though there is a paucity of empirical evidence to support this preference. A strong proclivity on the part of the polygraphers to favor procedural (clinical) evidence over validating (experimental) evidence may account for this practice. It is of course also possible that polygraphers are unaware of the laboratory evidence in favor of skin conductance data.

SRR (or SCR) is a measure of how easily an imperceptible, small amount of electrical current passes through the skin. Although the exact physiological mechanisms involved remain largely unexplored, the sweat glands are understood to play a major role. These glands are highly sensitive to changes in arousal and emotional reactions, and they readily secrete sodium chloride, albumin, urea, and other compounds (sweat) at the slightest change in arousal. These compounds increase the electrical conductivity of the skin.

The standard procedure for measuring skin conductance (or skin resistance) is to attach electrodes (small metal discs) to the fingers of the unpreferred hand, or to one finger and the wrist. The active electrode sends a very small, painless electrical charge through the skin, and the current flow is picked up by the neutral electrode attached to the skin somewhere in the vicinity.

Respiration rate is measured through the use of one or two corrugated pneumatic tubes positioned about the chest or upper abdomen (Abrams, 1977). Changes in tube size produce vacuums in the tube, which then cause a recording pen to move on the recording chart. Changes in blood volume and pulse rate are recorded by use of a blood pressure cuff around the upper arm and over the brachial artery.

**Accuracy.** The typical experimental paradigm for the study of psychophysiological measures of deception has subjects engaging in mock crime; thereafter, the polygrapher tries to discover deception in the subjects' responses. Therefore, a majority of the studies on the polygraph have followed a simulation procedure.

Laboratory investigations have reported that the polygraph can detect deception, with rates ranging from 64 percent (Horvath, 1977) to 96 percent (Raskin & Hare, 1978), against chance rates of 50 percent. Accuracy hovers between 70 and 85 percent in most research; chance expectancies fall between 20 and 50 percent. Professional field polygraphers, however, have claimed extraordinary accuracy rates: 92 percent

(Bersh, 1969), 99 percent (Arther, 1965; MacNitt, 1942; MacLaughlin, 1953), and 100 percent (Kubis, 1950). The professional polygraph literature also reports with regularity that the trained polygrapher errs not more than 2 percent of the time, and often less than 1 percent (Barland & Raskin, 1973). Most psychophysiologists find these statistics hard to believe. In addition to occasional arithmetical errors, none of the published reports give any details of the methods and procedures used, nor of criteria used to decide accuracy rates. David Lykken (1974) was so disbelieving of the many claims of professional polygraphers that he asserted (1974, p. 738): "claims of 95%, 98%, and even 100% validity are so implausible, they should be taken seriously only if accompanied by unusually clear, well-replicated empirical evidence. Such evidence is wholly lacking."

There is little doubt, however, that the empirical evidence does conclude that the polygraph can distinguish deception from truth with an accuracy rate much higher than chance (e.g., Raskin & Hare, 1978; Barland & Raskin, 1973; Cacoukian & Heslegrave, 1980; Podlesny & Raskin, 1977). David Lykken (1979) is cautious in his conclusions, reporting accuracy of 64 to 71 percent (against a chance expectancy of 50 percent). He also stresses that subjects can be taught various methods to foil a researcher looking for deception.

**Examination techniques.** The field polygraph examination typically consists of four separate phases: data collection, pretest interview, test administration, and posttest interview (Abrams, 1977). In the data-collection stage, the examiner gathers all the relevant information concerning the area under investigation as well as known information about the subject. The pretest interview is intended to establish some rapport with the subject and to explain some of the questions and procedures that will be used during the examination. Often during the pretest interview, questions to be asked on the examination are devised with the cooperation of the subject, so that nothing will be surprising and ambiguities may be cleared up prior to the exam.

Several techniques are used by polygraphers and psychophysiologists to determine deception or truthfulness during the examination. Three of the more common ones are the "control-of-question" approach, the "peak-of-tension" test, and the "guilty-knowledge" approach.

The control-of-question approach is the most commonly used by professional polygraphers (Abrams, 1977). This method uses a variety of questioning techniques and three basic types of questions: (1) irrelevant or neutral questions; (2) relevant questions; and (3) control questions. Irrelevant questions are those posed about neutral topics, like date of birth, name, age, height, and birthplace. They usually occur at the beginning and end of an examination, but they may be interspersed between other questions to bring the subject down to a normal physiological baseline following questions that generate stress.

The relevant question probes whether the subject committed the crime or behavior in question. For example, "On August 26 at approximately 9:00 p.m., did you break down the door at Mr. Brown's residence?" It is recommended that emotion-laden words not be used, since the respondent may respond more to the word than to the question itself.

The control question is as important in determining deception or truthfulness as the relevant question. It is based upon either an assumed or a known lie. An assumed lie is denial of a behavior that most people would readily admit to. For example, "Did you ever steal anything when you were between the ages of five and fifteen?" "Did you ever take advantage of a friend?"

The subject is asked the control question during the pretest interview; if he or she answers no, deception is assumed. This assumed lie might then be used as a control question during the actual examination. The examiner compares the physiological reaction to this assumed lie with physiological reactions to relevant questions. A control question developed from a known lie is based upon a subject's denial of a fact that the examiner knows from a background check is true.

The peak-of-tension (POT) test consists of a series of five to nine questions which are worded almost entirely alike. The subject is asked to answer no to each question. The test is repeated several times. The critical question is usually placed somewhere near the middle of the series, and always in the same place. Because of the repetition, the subject learns to expect the critical question. For example, if a murdered woman was killed with a .357 magnum revolver, the questioning might go like this:

Do you know whether Sara Smith was killed with a .38?
Do you know whether Sara Smith was killed with a .45?
Do you know whether Sara Smith was killed with a .44?
Do you know whether Sara Smith was killed with a .357?
Do you know whether Sara Smith was killed with a .22?

The innocent subject presumably does not know the weapon caliber and therefore should exhibit a similar physiological reaction to each question. The guilty party, however, should demonstrate a significantly different response to the crucial question, particularly in the repeated series, because he or she will begin anticipating the crucial question at the beginning of each series. Anxiety (tension) should build, peaking near the critical question and declining after it has been asked.

The "guilty-knowledge" test (GKT) has been strongly endorsed by the psychologist and polygraphy expert David Lykken as the most powerful procedure for determining deception or truthfulness. The examiner uses detailed, publicly unknown knowledge about a crime to construct questions that can be answered only by someone who was present at the scene. The answers are offered to the subject in a multiple-choice format. For example (Lykken, 1974, p. 726):

> The man we're looking for held up a loan office in Manhattan. If you're the guilty party, you will recognize the name of the loan company. I'm going to name a few loan companies that have offices in the vicinity; you just sit there quietly and repeat the names after me as you hear them. Was it the Ideal Loan Company? . . . Was it the Continental Loan Company? . . . Was it the Guarantee Loan Company? . . . Was it the Friendly Loan Company? . . . Was it the Fidelity Loan Company?

Since the GKT assumes that the guilty subject will recognize the significant alternative, consistent physiological reactivity to this "correct" answer would indicate deception, regardless of the verbal content of the subject's answers. And since the questions are derived from information not reported in the press and not generally known by the public, innocent subjects rarely give physiological reactions to "correct" items.

There are many other approaches recommended by polygraphy advocates, but the above three are the most commonly used. Surprisingly, considering its potential accuracy and the probability of detecting deception, the GKT is the least used by professional polygraphers.

The procedure used often dictates the posttest interview conducted between polygrapher and subject. Depending upon the examiner's school of thought, the subject may be told the results or may be told that the results will be given to investigators or to the defense attorney when they become available. Some strategies call for some limited interrogation of the subject if the results suggest deception or guilt, and some approaches recommend further interviewing in the case of inconclusive results. The U.S. Army Military Police School recommends that the examiner never accuse the subject of lying, under any conditions.

## ■ Legal Status of the Polygraph

Courts have rarely allowed polygraph results as evidence in a case, although laboratory research has established that a properly functioning polygraph administered by a competent examiner is highly valid. The precedent of inadmissibility of polygraph evidence was established in 1923 in U.S. v. Frye. An appellate court ruled that information acquired from polygraphic examination was unacceptable because the scientific community did not endorse it. Since then, most courts have continued to reject the results of the polygraph whether they have been submitted by the defense or the prosecution as evidence of guilt or innocence (Schwitzgebel & Schwitzgebel, 1980). In recent years, some jurisdictions have admitted polygraphic evidence if the examinee has given full cooperation and an established test procedure was used, and then only with a list of stipulations.

While many courts continue to cite the precedent-setting Frye case as a basis for rejecting polygraph information, other reasons have also been given. Some courts have commented upon the lack of scientific recognition of the instrument and the paucity of qualified examiners (Langley, 1955). Others note the presence of too many variables that would cause excessive courtroom debate (e.g., U.S. v. Urquidez, 1973); undue influence upon the jury (People v. Davis, 1949; People v. Sinclair, 1942); an undermining of the credibility of witnesses (Richardson, 1961); the lack of soundness of polygraphic theory (State v. Bohmer, 1971); and infringement upon the freedom and privacy of the mind (Silving, 1956; Westin, 1967).

Even so, psychophysiologists and professional polygraphers are baffled by the courts' continued rejection of polygraphic testimony and information. The polygraph is now accepted as a scientifically reliable and valid instrument by the scientific community; therefore it is unjustified to continue to rely on Frye. Its ability to discriminate between truth and deception is outstanding, particularly if SRR or SCR measures are used. It is especially baffling when we consider that courts generally do accept evidence gained through other scientific methods with significantly less-established validity, e.g., psychological tests, psychiatric interviews and diagnoses, handwriting analyses, and eyewitness testimony. In fact, in a recent study, the polygraph was found to be the most accurate investigative tool, when compared with other methods of identification like fingerprint analysis, handwriting analysis, and eyewitness testimony (Widacki & Horvath, 1978). Therefore, the criteria for admissibility do not appear to rest upon the empirical support for the polygraph's accuracy (Cavoukian & Heslegrave, 1980).

It is most likely that legal resistance comes from viewing the polygraph as an information-gathering device that runs counter to legal philosophy about the legal process. Not only does the polygraph bring into the courtroom an aura of absolutes, but it also infringes upon the privacy of the mind. In essence, it forces people to testify against themselves. Their most hidden secrets and intimate transgressions may be exposed for public judgment, whether or not they have engaged in criminal conduct. Therefore, the polygraph may go too far as an invasion of privacy measure and as a self-incriminatory device. It probes individual beliefs and desires and violates a sense of personal autonomy, without the individual being able to exert any control over this probing. In psychological tests and in the information provided to psychiatrists and psychologists, individuals still perceive that they have control over revelations and actions, regardless of the subjective or "scientific" interpretations made by the clinical expert. The experts cannot prove that individuals lied or are guilty, no matter what level of the unconscious they feel they have tapped. However, the polygraph presents "proof" of lying and dishonesty, even though it may not be accurate in every case.

In addition, the more reliable, valid, and accurate the polygraph becomes, the more it undermines the traditional judicial process, its adversarial nature, and the fact that the system thrives on debate and uncertainty. Awesome power will be given to the polygraphic examiner who becomes directly involved in decisions of guilt or innocence, a prerogative traditionally reserved for the judge or jury. Although Cavoukian and Heslegrave (1980) report simulation evidence that the impact of polygraphic testimony can be reduced if the examiner stresses the room for error in the report, its potential dangers still remain. Participants in the judicial process and legal scholars still resist its implications.

## ■ Facial Composites in Criminal Identification

Composites are considered indispensable aids to criminal investigation by most police agencies. Composites are reconstructions of faces through memory, and they are built either with the help of an artist's sketching skills or by using the various commercial kits available to law enforcement. The latter include an assortment of photographed or drawn facial features, which witnesses move about like pieces of a jigsaw puzzle to reconstruct a face.

Some law enforcement agencies claim that face-memory reconstructions by artists based upon eyewitness verbal descriptions are superior to other composite reproductions, but few hard data to support these claims are available. As we learned in the previous chapter, accurate memory for faces is already difficult to achieve. Composites require one person to transform his or her perceptions to memory to verbal description, at which point another person continues the process, involving another set of perceptions, and finally, motor reproduction by the artist. The likelihood of misrepresentation and inaccuracy throughout this transformation process is very high.

Harmon (1973) asked an artist with experience in drawing police composites to describe verbally a facial image he had seen to another artist with similar police sketching experience. Subjects who knew the verbally described person were able to identify the drawing in only 50 percent of the cases. On the other hand, when an artist sketched faces from photographs, the subjects correctly identified the drawing 93 percent of the time. These data suggest that artist sketches based upon verbal descriptions—a common way of obtaining composites—are subject to considerable error.

In the usual reconstruction procedure, both the artist and the witness make repetitive attempts at getting facial features "just right." It would appear, therefore, that repeated inaccurate constructions of the feature in question could bias the witness's memory to the point where the witness could not discriminate between the reproductions created by the artist and his or her memory of the offender's face (Yarmey, 1979). Related to this point, we can also assume individual differences in the ability to describe facial features, in that some people have a knack for transforming visual perception and memory into descriptions displaying verbal precision while others lack this ability. In addition, it is likely that certain facial features draw more attention and accuracy than others, which would suggest that people are more accurate with specific facial features than with others.

Most law enforcement agencies, especially those in small cities and towns, rely on commercial composite kits to reconstruct faces from witness accounts, since skillful, experienced artists are not always readily available. The designers of composite kits assume that the world's faces can be reduced to a manageable set of commonalities. All chins, for example, can be reduced to types which approximate all imaginable configurations. Theoretically, therefore, all facial parts can be classified into categories. Consequently, their combinations should be able to produce the vast majority of human faces. Most kit designers recognize that the facial reproductions will not be exact, but only close approximations.

All of the kits require witnesses to select individual features from groups of alternatives. Some of the kits use line drawings of the possible features, while others use photographed features from actual faces. Davis, Ellis, and Shepherd (1978) have reported data that the photographic approach is superior to systems using line drawings. There appears to be more information in photographs than in line transcriptions, no matter how much detail is provided in the drawings.

Research by Kenneth Laughery and his colleagues (Laughery & Fowler, 1978; Laughery, Durval & Fowler, 1977) has reported evidence indicating that composite kits using line drawings are inferior to photographs or even artist sketches. It appears, however, that neither photographed nor line-drawing composite kits nor artist sketches can compare with the information and accuracy provided by actual photographs of the suspects. Law enforcement agencies that use composite facial kits are advised to treat composites, and especially line drawings, with extreme caution in identification of suspects by witnesses. Even if composites are not used as evidence, their danger lies in the possibility that a witness will so painstakingly describe a face that the subsequent composite will replace the actual face in the witness's memory. This can lead to the misidentification of an innocent person who happens to resemble the composite.

## ■ Hypnosis

Hypnosis has long been used as entertainment, as a method of psychotherapy, as a procedure in several branches of medicine, and as a means of enhancing the memory of eyewitnesses and victims in the criminal justice system. At least 2,000 police officers and detectives in the United States have received various levels of training to allow them to use hypnosis to help individuals recall events they saw or were involved in. How valid is the evidence obtained under these conditions? To answer this question, we will have to understand what hypnosis is and how it is induced.

Relaxation is usually the primary goal of hypnosis. Subjects are sitting or lying down, and the hypnotist continually emphasizes quietness, calmness, and drowsiness. The subject, asked to concentrate only upon some object and the hypnotist's voice, is encouraged to drift to sleep, all the while hearing what the hypnotist is saying. The hypnotist generally will suggest different behaviors to the subject, and with each behavior the subject falls deeper into a trance, or at least becomes increasingly convinced that the hypnotism is in effect. About 10 percent of the general population cannot be hypnotized, and 5 to 10 percent are highly suggestible (Hilgard, 1965). Most people fall somewhere between those two extremes.

Despite its long history, hypnosis is still at a relatively low level of scientific development, and its application far exceeds our scientific knowledge about the phenomenon. We still do not know precisely what hypnosis is. We have little knowledge of why one person is readily susceptible and why another is not. We do know that hypnosis has no significant physiological effect upon bodily functioning other than those that occur in physical relaxation. We know also that hypnosis is not the same as sleep or the same state as that found during sleepwalking. But we know little more than this.

While hypnosis lacks scientific elucidation, there are two major theoretical perspectives directed at explaining the mechanisms behind its effects. The most widely accepted perspective, generally referred to as the "hypnotic trance" theory, assumes that hypnosis represents a special state of consciousness that promotes a high level of responsiveness to suggestions and changes in bodily feelings. Under this special state of consciousness (some argue that it taps the unconscious), the subject may be able to regress to childhood and vividly remember or act out events that have been repressed, or at least put on the back burner of memory. While in the trance, subjects may be instructed to feel little or no pain, or to perform acts that they are unable to do when not hypnotized. Individuals can be instructed to sense, feel, smell, see, or hear things not normally possible outside of hypnosis; even memory can be enhanced and drastically improved in some situations. Generally speaking, the deeper the "hypnotic trance" the more intense, detailed, and vivid a scene becomes to the subject. The chief spokesperson for this position has been Ernest Hilgard.

The second position advanced to explain hypnosis is the cognitive behavioral viewpoint, which maintains that the subject is not in a special state of consciousness when he or she appears hypnotized. Rather, hypnosis is a product of certain attitudes, motivations, and expectancies toward the "hypnotic state"—not a mysterious alteration of consciousness. Specifically, people who have a positive attitude toward hypnosis are motivated to be hypnotized, and expect to be hypnotized. They play the role suggested to them by the hypnotist; when the hypnotist suggests to them that they feel relaxed, they will try and probably will feel relaxed.

Theodore X. Barber, the chief advocate of this perspective (Barber, Spanos & Chaves, 1974) has postulated that the good hypnotic subject is one who not only has the proper mixture of attitude, motivation, and expectancy, but also has the ability to think and imagine with the hypnotist. The good hypnotic subject is like the person who watches a motion picture and feels the emotions and experiences of the persons on the screen. Intense and vivid experiences are suggested by the communication; Barber argues that hypnosis is, in most respects, a highly similar experience.

Orne (1970) has hypothesized a similar viewpoint, suggesting that role playing accounts for much of the so-called hypnotic phenomenon. That is, subjects act the way they think a truly hypnotized individual would act. Additionally, Orne has found in his research that the material described under so-called hypnotic trances is often inaccurate and embellished with many intervening events that occur between the initial incident and the hypnotic session. It appears that hypnotic subjects may be as susceptible to distortions, suggestions, and leading questions as the eyewitnesses described in the previous chapter. Particularly if the interrogator is a police officer convinced of the powers of hypnosis, he or she is apt to inadvertently suggest events or details that were not present at the crime scene. The hypnotized witness or victim, eager to please the interrogator, can easily imagine a scene decorated with subjective fantasies and thoughts in line with the suggestions of the questioner. Under these conditions, the hypnotized subject may begin to be convinced of the accuracy and power of hypnosis to the same degree as the hypnotist. Furthermore, the subject also may become convinced of the accuracy of his or her account of the imagined scene.

When hypnosis is used as a tool to aid the recall of events that may be either several hours or several years old, the fundamental assumption is that human perception and memory functions like a videotape camera. All the events and details are stored accurately and simply must be recalled or brought to consciousness. We have seen, however, that this assumption is faulty. Human perception and memory are flawed and permeated with inaccuracies and distortions. The frailties of perception and memory, combined with the highly suggestive medium under which hypnosis is conducted, provide a situation where critical inaccuracies have a high probability of occurring.

Courts have been reluctant to admit testimony acquired through hypnosis as evidence (Schwitzgebel & Schwitzgebel, 1980). Considering the present scientific knowledge about hypnosis, particularly with relation to the accuracy of memory under its influence, court resistance appears wise. Until hypnosis and its applicability to courtroom questions receives substantially more empirical scrutiny, it is good for the law to be extremely guarded in allowing hypnotic evidence to be used in legal decision-making.

## ■ Extraevidentiary Factors

The evidence obtained by law enforcement officers in the investigation of a case and later admitted into trial proceedings is not the only "evidence" a jury considers. Ideally, jurors should attend to testimony, exhibits, arguments, and the instructions of the judge, and they should resist influence from sources outside the courtroom, or in some cases within the courtroom as well. Jurors are warned not to allow prior information about a case or prior sentiments to enter into their decisionmaking. They must decide cases solely on the evidence before them and on relevant law, as explained by the presiding judge. Realistically, we know that a variety of factors can have an effect upon jurors, including their own biases (e.g., about race or political affiliation), the opinions of persons they respect, and community sentiments.

Although jury decisionmaking was introduced in the previous chapter, the subject will not be closed until we consider two influences on jury deliberation that have received extensive attention of late, both from the judicial system and, ironically, from the media. They are the electronic coverage of jury trials (called the cameras-in-the-courtroom issue) and the alleged influence of extensive pretrial publicity upon subsequent jury decisions. The latter is referred to by the press as the free press/fair trial dilemma and by the judiciary as the fair trial/free press problem. The topics are introduced here because of their relevance to the psychology of evidence. Pretrial publicity allegedly bombards jurors with so much evidence before the actual trial that they are presumably rendered unable to make a fair decision. Cameras in the courtroom may interfere with the presentation of evidence to the jurors.

## PRETRIAL PUBLICITY

Courts have often addressed the issue of extensive publicity and whether it prejudices the outcome of a trial. When especially flagrant, inflammatory publicity has been involved, courts, including the U.S. Supreme Court, have sometimes overturned a conviction. Such was the case of Dr. Sam Sheppard, whom the media hounded mercilessly from the time his wife was murdered up to and during his trial. The Sheppard decision, *Sheppard v. Maxwell* (1966), focused upon both the courtroom atmosphere during the trial, which the Supreme Court characterized as "bedlam," and upon press reports of material that never was mentioned on the witness stand. The trial judge, however, bore the brunt of the Court's criticism. The Justices severely chastised the judge for not controlling his courtroom or enacting measures to insure fairness.

The case of *Irvin v. Dowd* (1961) also resulted in a reversal due to media coverage. Irvin, whom the press at one point called a "mad dog," was said to have confessed to six murders in a small Indiana community. Reporters and editors, aided by law enforcement officials, made use of screaming headlines, street corner interviews ("He should be hanged"), and background stories revealing previous felony convictions. During the voir dire, two thirds of the jurors said they believed Irvin was guilty, although all said they would be fair and would consider the evidence impartially. About this, the Supreme Court said, "No doubt each juror was sincere when he said he would be fair and impartial to petitioner, but the psychological impact requiring such a declaration before one's fellows is often its father. Where so many, so many times, admitted prejudice, such a statement of impartiality can be given little weight."

Flagrant media coverage by respectable publications is the exception today, at a time when many journalists are conscious of their obligations to the public. Still common, however, are extensive stories about a person's background, interviews with persons who knew him, reports of evidence taken during investigations, and testimony during pretrial suppression hearings.

The free press/fair trial problem is troublesome because it represents an apparent clash between the first and sixth amendments, the one guaranteeing press freedom and the other granting the right to a speedy and public trial by an impartial jury.

Defense attorneys have argued consistently that it is impossible for their clients to be judged by an impartial jury if those jurors have read extensive information prior to the trial, particularly if the coverage damns the defendant, is sensational, or includes information that may later be inadmissible during the trial. During the late 1960s and early 1970s many judges agreed, and they enjoined the press from printing material about a case. Sometimes these injunctions were very general, restricting reporters from informing the public about newsworthy information.

The U.S. Supreme Court severely restricted such "gag orders" in 1976, with its landmark *Nebraska Press Association v. Stuart* decision (see box). Guessing that extensive, prejudicial publicity doubtless had some effect on jurors, the Court said that such restraints were nevertheless the least tolerable infringement upon the press's first amendment right. The Court stressed that it was the presiding judge's responsibility in each case to seek out and employ alternatives to gagging the press. Included among these alternatives were extensive voir dire questioning to determine whether the jurors had been influenced; changing the location of the trial; sequestering the jury; postponing the trial. Regarding the effect of the publicity, the Court said that the presiding judge "could . . . reasonably conclude, based on common human experience, that publicity might impair the defendant's right to a fair trial. . . . His conclusion as to the impact of such publicity on prospective jurors was of necessity speculative, dealing as he was with factors unknown and unknowable."

The important consideration here is whether factors about jury prejudice are indeed "unknown and unknowable," and whether the claims about jury prejudice have

## ☐ NEBRASKA PRESS ASSOCIATION v. STUART

After a multiple murder in a small Nebraska town, population 850, appellate judge Stuart acceded to the request of prosecuting and defense attorneys that he restrain all journalists, print and broadcast, from publishing information strongly implicative of the accused, one Erwin Charles Simants. The implicative information included a past criminal record, alleged confessions, statements made to other persons, and certain aspects of the medical testimony given at a preliminary hearing. Although the Nebraska Supreme Court modified Stuart's order, it remained in effect until the beginning of Simants' trial, at which point the jury was sequestered.

The Nebraska Press Association, through its attorneys, engaged in a spirited volley of appeals and counterappeals with the judicial system, including at one point the association's seeking and obtaining the direct intercession of U.S. Supreme Court Justice Harry Blackmun. Meanwhile, the case against Simants was readied and went to trial. Thus, by the time the Supreme Court heard the association's petition, the defendant's trial was over and he had been convicted. The Court nevertheless heard the petition because of the likelihood that the press-bar conflict would be repeated.

validity. Psychologists, sociologists, legal scholars and communication researchers, sometimes in collaboration, have conducted experiments to attempt to answer this and to suggest possible ways of reducing bias, if it does occur. In general, studies have indicated that, although it cannot be said that no prejudice results from publication of certain information, neither can it be said that jurors will be prejudiced.

The most realistic research study yet reported was the interdisciplinary Fair Trial Project conducted by a group of sociologists, psychologists, lawyers and journalists at Columbia University (Simon, 1980). The researchers chose subjects from an actual jury pool and conducted their project with cooperation of the judiciary, the bar, and the local media. Subjects listened to audiotapes of an actual jury trial, after having seen newspaper clippings that were either "neutral" or "prejudicial." Final results indicated that more jurors exposed to prejudicial publicity convicted than jurors not exposed to such publicity. Unanimous verdicts of "not guilty" were reached only by nonprejudiced juries. Of particular impact were newspaper stories which revealed that a defendant had a previous criminal record or had allegedly confessed and then retracted.

The researchers noted that much research is still needed to determine the relative effects of group influence during the decisionmaking process or other factors that might mitigate prejudicial publicity. They noted also that many defendants in recent years have been exposed to massive unfavorable publicity, but have nonetheless been found not guilty. "This leads one to speculate that different kinds of unfavorable publicity may have different outcomes, whether because of the political or nonpolitical

---

After commenting at length on the value of press freedom and the unconstitutionality of government interference with what the press published, the Court addressed, but very briefly, the effect of pervasive publicity. The relevant quotes are scant:

Our review of the pretrial record persuades us that the trial judge was justified in concluding that there would be intense and pervasive pretrial publicity concerning this case. He could also reasonably conclude, based on common human experience, that publicity might impair the defendant's right to a fair trial. He did not purport to say more, for he found only a "clear and present danger that pre-trial publicity *could* impinge upon the defendant's right to a fair trial." (Emphasis added.) His conclusion as to the impact of such publicity on prospective jurors was of necessity speculative, dealing as he was with factors unknown and unknowable. [pp. 562–563]

Later, the Court added:

Reasonable minds can have few doubts about the gravity of the evil pretrial publicity can work, but the probability that it would do so here was not demonstrated with the degree of certainty our cases on prior restraint require. [p. 569]

The Court cited no studies to support its dicta that some pretrial publicity is bound to affect juror decisionmaking in a way that is unfair to the defendant. The Justices did not ask for empirical evidence, as they seemed to do in a later case (*Chandler v. Florida*). Rather, they relied on fireside induction to conclude that prejudice must result, in some cases.

nature of the cases or the national-versus-local type of publicity, among many other factors, and that methods of screening and instructing jurors to avoid prejudice do exist" (Padawer-Singer & Barton, 1975, p. 136). Until more information is obtained from well-designed study, it appears unwarranted to assume that extensive publicity—barring the unconscionable tactics of the media in some isolated cases—will preclude a fair trial for defendants.

## ELECTRONIC COVERAGE OF TRIALS

The cameras-in-the-courtroom issue focuses not only on the jury but also on the effect of electronic coverage on all participants in a trial. It is often assumed that broadcast equipment will adversely affect the judicial process, that participants' conduct will be unnatural, and that the trial will not be fair. When broadcast technology was in its infancy, this argument was persuasive, so much so that it was accepted by the U.S. Supreme Court in the Billie Sol Estes case (*Estes v. Texas*, 1965). The Court ruled, in a 5–4 decision, that broadcasting was a punishment in itself, turning the courtroom into a "stadium setting." Furthermore, there was such a probability of prejudice (although no prejudice need be shown) that the defendant had been de-

---

## ☐ CHANDLER v. FLORIDA

Two police officers were convicted of conspiracy to commit burglary and grand larceny and breaking and entering into a popular Miami restaurant. The trial had been partially broadcast over television and radio stations. The convicted men appealed the decision, claiming that the presence of the electronic equipment hampered the defense in its presentation of the case and deprived the defendants of an impartial jury. A Florida appellate court did not agree, and the Florida Supreme Court denied review.

The U.S. Supreme Court ruled 8–0 in favor of the state, which had been experimenting with televised trial coverage. The Justices refused to declare an all-out ban on electronic coverage, as petitioners had urged. They did rule, however, that in some cases, prejudicial broadcast accounts of pretrial and trial events could impair the ability of jurors to decide guilt or innocence. It was up to the defendants in each case to demonstrate that the media coverage in that particular instance was unfair and "compromised the ability of the particular jury that heard the case to adjudicate fairly."

Noting that "any criminal case that generates a great deal of publicity presents some risks that the publicity may compromise the right of the defendant to a fair trial," the Court repeated its admonitions to judges to be "especially vigilant" in guarding the rights of defendants. The Justices then turned to the subject of "psychological prejudice," which had been raised in the *Estes* case in 1964.

As we noted earlier, the concurring opinions in *Estes* expressed concern that the very presence of media cameras and recording devices at a trial

prived of due process. "The heightened public clamor resulting from radio and television coverage will inevitably result in prejudice. Trial by television is, therefore, foreign to our system." The Court added that "the distractions, intrusions into confidential attorney-client relationships and the temptation offered by television to play to the public audience might often have a direct effect not only upon the lawyers, but the judge, the jury and the witnesses."

Nearly twenty years later, a different Supreme Court again addressed the question of cameras in the courtroom, in *Chandler v. Florida* (1980), and this Court did an about-face. Noting the sophistication of broadcast technology today, the Justices remarked that there was no inherent prejudicial effect due to the presence of electronic equipment.

The petitioners in *Chandler* argued that television coverage of their robbery trial had deprived them of due process safeguards (see box). Florida, like numerous other states, had been experimenting with allowing broadcasters to cover trials, even when the participants objected. In general, the state rules require broadcasters to notify the court prior to the trial that they are interested in covering it, and it is left to the court's discretion whether or not to grant the request.

Noting that the court record revealed only "generalized allegations of prejudice"

---

inescapably gives rise to an adverse psychological impact on the participants in the trial. This kind of general psychological prejudice, allegedly present whenever there is broadcast coverage of a trial, is different from the more particularized problem of prejudicial impact discussed earlier. If it could be demonstrated that the mere presence of photographic and recording equipment and the knowledge that the event would be broadcast invariably and uniformly affected the conduct of participants so as to impair fundamental fairness, our task would be simple: prohibition of broadcast coverage of trials would be required.

The Court noted that television technology had advanced substantially since the time of Estes, and noted also that safeguards had been built into the experimental programs to protect defendants' rights. "Florida admonishes its courts to take special pains to protect certain witnesses—for example, children, victims of sex crimes, some informants, and even the very timid witness or party—from the glare of publicity and the tensions of being 'on camera.'"

The Court noted that the data now available do not support the thesis that electronic media presence interferes with trial proceedings. Nevertheless, further study was recommended.

It is clear that the general issue of the psychological impact of broadcast coverage upon the participants in a trial, and particularly upon the defendant, is still a subject of sharp debate. . . . [Briefs submitted by the American Bar Association and the American College of Trial Lawyers had indicated that, although data were not available, "actual experience" bore out the fact of negative psychological impact on trial participants.]

Whatever may be the 'mischievous potentialities . . . for intruding upon the detached atmosphere which should always surround the judicial process' [citing *Estes v. Texas*] at present no one has been able to present empirical data sufficient to establish that the mere presence of the broadcast media inherently has an adverse effect on that process.

because of the cameras with no empirical evidence to support these charges, the Court said that the risk of juror prejudice in some cases did not justify an absolute ban on news coverage of trials. Nevertheless, "the general issue of psychological impact of broadcast coverage upon the participants in a trial, and particularly upon the defendant, is still a subject of sharp debate."

The Court appears to be implicitly inviting researchers to study the effects of broadcast equipment upon trial participants. This issue raises a number of thought-provoking questions. It is unlikely that the sophisticated, relatively unobstrusive cameras available to broadcasters today will distract participants in the way that the wires, lights, and whirring noises inevitably accompanying television crews in the 1950s and 1960s did. The closed circuit cameras often positioned in rooms where official proceedings take place testify to the sophistication of today's media. In fact, many judges will not allow cameras in their courtrooms unless they are stationary and unobtrusive, and they attach the stipulation that jurors may not be filmed.

Nevertheless, questions remain. Will the knowledge that the trial is being televised force lawyers to "play" to cameras more than they now play to the presence of print reporters? How will cameras affect the decisionmaking process of judges? It can be argued that the legal actors will do a better job in the face of such intense scrutiny, but there is no evidence to that effect as yet. What of the emotional effect upon witnesses? Although most state guidelines allow the presiding judge to prevent reporters from televising the testimony of certain witnesses, this does not guarantee that the other witnesses are unaffected. Following the *Chandler* decision and with the increasing dominance of electronic journalism over print, it is very likely that judicial proceedings will be televised with more frequency. Psychological researchers must look for creative research designs to study this growing phenomenon.

# ■ Summary and Conclusions

We have continued our concentration upon evidence brought before the courts by discussing in this chapter the psychological research related to specific types of evidence gathering. Interrogation, the custodial questioning of criminal suspects or unwilling informants in an effort to persuade them to confess or to gain more information about a crime, is a process fraught with psychological implications. Although students of psychology and law must be aware of what courts have allowed in relation to custodial interrogation, they must also know what methods are effective in eliciting information and what methods are still used by criminal investigators in interrogatory procedure. Information gathering in nonaggressive situations—such as interviewing witnesses of crimes or taking depositions in criminal and civil cases—was not covered in this chapter.

Another crucial evidence-gathering talent for criminal investigators to possess is the ability to detect deceptive responses. Here, law enforcement is sometimes aided by mechanical devices, such as the polygraph or voice-stress analyzer, but most often investigators look for nonverbal indicators that an individual is being less than truthful. As we have seen, the surest way to detect deception is to use a valid laboratory polygraph device. Nonverbal behaviors can be misleading, especially if the investigator has swallowed the prevalent myths about shifty eyes, fumbling behavior, or restlessness.

Sophisticated suspects may well have mastered the "dead giveaways." If the investigator is determined to use nonverbal indicators, he or she should pay attention to the so-called leaky channels, those not typically used in communication. Even so, nonverbal indicators are by no means conclusive evidence of deception. Ironically, the most valid indicator of deception, the polygraph, is generally not admitted as evidence in courts. The judicial system is much more willing to accept expert testimony offered without proof of validity or the error-prone testimony of eyewitnesses.

We warned about the use of hypnosis, voice-stress analyzers, and facial composites in gathering evidence. Manufacturers of stress analyzers have been able to offer no empirical evidence to support their claims, and the connection of voice stress with deception is a specious one. Facial composites, though they may give investigators clues as to the general description of a perpetrator, have the danger of imprinting the wrong face into a witness's memory. Hypnosis is too much of a scientific unknown to be used as an accurate method of eliciting memory recall.

The chapter ended with some consideration of the effects of extraevidentiary factors on courtroom participants. Prejudicial publicity, which defense attorneys abhor and insist is detrimental to their clients, has received a good share of attention from researchers conducting simulation studies. Although evidence has indicated that jurors may be unfavorably disposed toward defendants who have received media attention, juror prejudice in such situations is not inevitable. Furthermore, it is impossible to control other sources of influence on a juror, such as his or her value system, comments from respected persons, community rumors, or even his or her attraction to the prosecutor.

The effects of increasing broadcast coverage of criminal trials, and their probable extension to many other judicial proceedings, is an area demanding research attention. With the recent Supreme Court decision supporting the rights of states to allow such coverage, it is likely that broadcast cameras will find their way into many more courtrooms.

## ■ Key Concepts and Principles, Chapter 8

Custodial interrogation
Three psychological principles of
    interrogation
Coercive persuasion
Nonverbal indicators of deception
Facial and nonfacial cues of deception
Emotional and factual veracity
Voiceprints
PSE

Polygraph
SRR and SCR
Control-of-question approach
Peak-of-tension approach
GKT
Composites
Hypnosis and eyewitness accuracy
Extraevidentiary factors

# 9

# The Psychology of Lawyering

☐   The iconoclastic Clarence Darrow, who swayed juries and stirred the imagination of budding attorneys, or the acerbic but sagacious Perry Mason, who kept television viewers mesmerized week after week, have few counterparts in the legal profession. If the well-respected Kalven-Zeisel project (1966) accurately captures courtroom dynamics, the total impact lawyers have on the trial process is minimal.

Judges surveyed by Kalven and Zeisel concluded that prosecution and defense lawyers were equivalent in skills and in impact in slightly over three-quarters of the 3,567 criminal cases they heard. Even when there was superior performance by one or the other lawyer, the jury's decision did not necessarily reflect it. In general, the nature of the case and the evidence presented, not the advocacy skills or the personality of the lawyers, accounted for the final verdict.

Trials, however, are avenues of last resort, and they occur only when the respective attorneys have met an impasse in negotiations and bargaining. There is little doubt that most of what attorneys do on behalf of their clients in both criminal and civil cases is bargain and negotiate. In fact, many lawyers believe that the effective advocate, especially in civil disputes, is one who achieves a favorable settlement rather than ends up in courtroom litigation. Therefore, much of what a lawyer does is hidden from public scrutiny.

In an effort to conceptualize the character of the lawyering process, Henry Hart and Albert Sacks (1958) talked about the "great pyramid of legal order," and Marc Galanter (1974) the "legal iceberg." Each of the writers described the billions of disputes and charges that are settled through informal or formal negotiation, without ever reaching formal litigation or adjudication in the courts. Lawyers, therefore, practice their profession primarily outside courtroom settings.

# ▪ Lawyers

There are approximately 500,000 lawyers in the United States, and it is estimated that there will be 600,000 by 1985 (Vago, 1981). Preparation for legal practice usually requires four years of undergraduate college and three years of legal education (full time) in a law school, although some states make provision for a clerking procedure by which individuals can try to pass bar exams after intensive study under the supervision of practicing attorneys. About 170 law schools are approved by the American Bar Association, all now empowered to confer the first degree of law, the Juris Doctor (JD) (American Bar Association, 1979). Law schools originally awarded the Bachelor of Laws (LLB) as the first degree, and the JD was reserved for special curricular and educational activity. The master's degree (LLM) can be obtained after a one-year educational program of course work and research beyond the JD. The Doctorate of Juridicial Sciences (SJD) is a graduate academic research degree awarded on the basis of substantial advanced scholarly work.

Like all professions, law implicitly recognizes a social hierarchy of status and prestige, but perhaps more than other professions it is also oriented toward socioeconomic status and credentials. A law degree from an elite school (e.g., Harvard, Yale, Columbia, Chicago, Stanford) is the first step on the way to a partnership in a prestigious law firm. The large, urban firms often woo the top students in elite schools, usually while evaluating the social and family backgrounds of these potential associates. Two-thirds of the attorneys associated with Wall Street law firms are graduates of Harvard, Yale, or Columbia schools of law (Vago, 1981; Smigel, 1964). This heavy orientation toward credentials and status and the tendency to equate them with competence and authority is often reflected in a lawyer's choice of expert witnesses in trials. The more degrees, preferably from elite schools, the more credible the witness, at least from a legal perspective.

The social hierarchy that pervades the legal profession is also reflected in the specialization each lawyer chooses. John Heinz and Edward Laumann (1978) conducted an extensive survey of the social structure of the legal profession, by personally interviewing 777 Chicago lawyers. They found that the legal profession is to a very great degree shaped and structured by its clients. Despite the fact that the American Bar Association officially endorses a holistic approach by its members (that is, it encourages them to be generalists), twenty-five different specialties could be delineated on the basis of client needs. The specialties clustered into two major groups, corporate and personal, and there were six subgroups: large corporate, regulatory, general corporate, political, personal business, and personal plight.

Heinz and Laumann learned, not surprisingly, that services to individual clients with modest or limited finances were rarely intellectually challenging or stimulating to the attorneys in their sample. The legal needs of these clients were straightforward. Services to the socioeconomically elite and powerful not only paid better, but they also offered far more interesting and complex legal challenges. "If the stakes are high, the problems can become very complex; if the client lacks money, his problems are likely to be routine" (Heinz & Laumann, 1978, p. 1117). It is obvious, therefore, that the more competent and intellectually "bright" lawyers from the elite law schools gravitate to clients with "deep pockets" and challenging problems, although there are certainly exceptions. In general, the three most prestigious fields of law were within the large corporate group, particularly in big business litigation, antitrust, and securities.

At the bottom of the legal social hierarchy, Heinz and Laumann found, was the personal plight group, especially lawyers specializing in personal injury suits, divorce or matrimonial disputes, general family practice, and criminal defense. Attorneys who habitually initiated personal injury suits were regarded as opportunists on the lookout for cases with which to threaten or cajole frightened respondents (defendants of suits). Divorce cases, also low in status, were seen as emotionally demanding, unpredictable, petty, and distasteful encounters where neither party is satisfied with the final property settlements or child custody and visitation arrangements. Lawyers often considered their clients in criminal cases the "dregs of society" and found their cases undemanding and intellectually unrewarding. Other writers have also commented on these perceptions, noting that criminal clients are often hostile and rarely thankful for services rendered (e.g., Platt & Pollock, 1976). Moreover, criminal defendants often do not have the financial resources to hire attorneys. Therefore, most criminal cases are handled by the public defender's office.

Criminal prosecutors—called state or district attorneys—have significantly higher status than criminal defense counselors. The prosecutors are local, municipal, state, or federal government employees who coordinate evidence and litigation in criminal cases on behalf of the citizens in their jurisdiction. Although they represent a corporate interest (the government) they are still regarded by their fellow lawyers as servers of the "personal plight" group. Prosecutors also are often assumed to be using their office and its visibility as a stepping-stone to higher political appointment or position.

The civil rights group is difficult to classify on the status ladder, because many civil rights cases are handled without fee as a public service (*pro bono publico*) by attorneys who have attended elite law schools and sometimes have even been affiliated with a large, prestigious law firm. Although the cynic would see this as a "do-gooder" conscience-saving involvement, it is also plausible that a less questionable motive is operating. Civil rights cases exemplify the type of legal work that deals with personal liberty and freedom, the philosophical underpinnings of American law (Heinz & Laumann, 1978). A lawyer presumably dedicated to these principles will be drawn to defend them, even gratis. Closely related to civil rights law is public interest law, a specialty which emerged rapidly during the 1970s and which also drew some high-powered attorneys to litigate for various interests or environmental groups against the ills of a powerful political system (Rabin, 1976). The publicity surrounding the Alaska Pipeline case (*Wilderness v. Morton*, 1973) was especially instrumental in bringing public interest attorneys into the national limelight.

Although some legal specialties thrive on courtroom encounters (e.g., prosecuting and defense attorneys in major criminal cases and attorneys in extended antitrust cases), the bulk of legal practice occurs outside the court. Some lawyers spend their professional time almost exclusively interviewing and advising clients, drafting legal documents such as wills, trust agreements, debentures, and contracts, and bargaining with their colleagues over the phone or at a local pub. Clearly, lawyering consists of a wide assortment of tasks and skills, and much of what transpires, while dictated by client needs, comprises a hidden "legal iceberg" (Galanter, 1974).

To cover the psychology of lawyering and its many facets would require a volume. To anchor our topic to some manageable segment, we will concentrate upon those areas in the legal process that have received the greatest amount of empirical inquiry and scholarly comment. Psychology's contributions to date have focused upon negotiations and decisionmaking in a variety of settings and, to a limited extent, on persuasion in the courtroom. Most of the work has been done with reference to the criminal justice system and its principal actors—the defense lawyer, the prosecuting attorney, and that specialized attorney, the judge. The remainder of the chapter will reflect this emphasis.

# ■ Plea Bargaining

Plea bargaining, "the explicit or implicit exchange of reduction in charge for a plea of guilty" (Feeley, 1979a, p. 200), is a negotiation or bargaining process found in many variations and disguises within the criminal justice system. Usually, plea bargaining occurs between the prosecuting attorney and the defense attorney in consultation with their respective clients. In the conventional meaning of the term, it is implied that, in exchange for a plea of guilty, the defendant gains concessions from the prosecuting attorney, either in the form of reduced charges or sentence recommendations. In addition to these typical inducements, there are other bargaining "carrots," like place of confinement (local jail versus maximum security institution).

## PAST AND CURRENT PRACTICES

Plea bargaining in this country is believed to have originated at least as far back as the late nineteenth century (Friedman, 1979). Its history and form are difficult to trace, because it has never been officially recognized as an acceptable form of legal settlement within the criminal justice system. Although the participants and actors within the system accept plea bargaining as a common ingredient, and although the U.S. Supreme Court perceives it as "an essential component of the administration of justice" (Santobello v. New York, 1971), its unofficial status precludes the keeping of systematic statistics. The extent of plea bargaining is usually inferred from the rates and circumstances of guilty pleas, particularly when past practices are examined and analyzed. When pleas are changed from innocent to guilty of a lesser charge, the plea bargaining that occurred is obvious. An alternative procedure for determining the occurrence of plea bargaining is to interview or survey system participants.

Lawrence Friedman (1979) notes that it is likely that the character and strategies of plea bargaining have changed over the years, but it is difficult to know what procedures were previously used. Some of the current practices were not dominant at the turn of this century. "Overcharging," for instance, where prosecutors charge the defendant with more criminal counts than are warranted by the evidence to allow flexibility in subsequent negotiations, was rarely in evidence.

"Implicit" plea bargaining is a term suggested by Heumann (1975) to describe circumstances in which there is no actual bargaining, but defendants realize it is in their best interest to plead guilty in hopes of avoiding the punishment of a heavy sentence. This is understood by all the participants. If the defendant is naive or inexperienced in the judicial process, the defense attorney will pass the word to the client, who will plead guilty with the impression that the court will be more lenient in sentencing. This form of plea bargaining is especially difficult to document, and the extent of its usage in the past as well as the present is unknown.

Friedman asserts that a high number of guilty pleas in any jurisdiction is a barometer of plea bargaining, explicit and implicit. "After all, why should a defendant plead guilty unless he expects to get something out of it? He has given up any chance to go free; even in an open-and-shut case, there is always a chance of acquittal" (Friedman, 1979, pp. 254–255). The alternative offered to the defendant—the deal—must be made more attractive than outside possibility of acquittal.

After carefully observing lower criminal courts in an extensive field study, Malcolm Feeley (1979b) concluded that plea bargaining can be analogized to shopping in a modern supermarket, where prices for various commodities have been clearly established and labeled in advance. Thus, there is little haggling, concession, and exchange, as one would find in a "middle eastern bazaar," he observes. Feeley notes that very little genuine negotiating takes place in the great mass of small criminal offenses in lower criminal courts. The limited bargaining that takes place usually centers on the nature of the crime and the quality of the concomitant evidence. Once the interpretation and value of the case are established, the case is priced at a "going rate," which is not fixed, but which fluctuates with the mood, significant events, and interpretations of the relevant world. The "plea market" fluctuates with higher court rulings, community moods, and other relevant decisions in a given jurisdiction.

Some drug possession cases are illustrative of this market process. As courts have adapted to the upsurge of marijuana usage at all levels of the community and have become acquainted with the research literature, the going rate of criminal charges for its possession has steadily declined. A community outcry would probably bring the going rate up again, however, as would decisions handed down by the jury or judges in a number of cases. "Because communication is rapid in the small world of the courthouse, it only takes a handful of such cases—perhaps only one—to establish a new 'going rate'" (Feeley, 1979b, p. 463).

Therefore, most of what prosecutors and defense attorneys insinuate to be plea bargaining may be little more than a charade to appease society and the defendant. Obviously, minor tradeoffs and concessions are made in the interest of maintaining reasonable exchanges between the prosecutor and the defense attorney for future interactions, but active negotiations for major concessions are, in a majority of cases, virtually nonexistent. Deals offered to the defense are in actuality the going rate for the particular offense. The defense attorney is well aware of the going rate but gives the client the impression that he or she has bargained for the best deal possible under the circumstances.

Critics of plea bargaining contend that it should be abolished from the criminal justice system for a variety of reasons, although their arguments generally focus upon one of two issues. Some critics believe that criminals are inappropriately sentenced, sometimes too harshly, but more often too leniently. This belief is rooted in the notion that prosecutors and judges make socially unfair concessions for administrative expedience (Church, 1979). Thus, plea bargaining is thought to result in criminals "getting off easy" for their crimes. Other critics believe plea bargaining infringes upon the constitutional rights of individual defendants to waive their right to a trial. Related to this argument is the position that plea bargaining is destructive to the lawyer-client relationship because it encourages a lawyer to disregard a client's interest (Alschuler, 1975). In addition, the prosecutor in plea bargaining situations becomes an administrator, an advocate, a judge, and a legislator (Alschuler, 1968). Consequently, he or she is given tremendous power to manipulate and control the defendant's fate, whereas in the trial process the power of the prosecutor is more limited.

## PLEA BARGAINING STUDIES

In view of misgivings and the potential injustices in plea bargaining, several behavioral scientists have examined the effects of procedural modifications of this negotiation process on defendants' perceptions of "fairness." LaTour (1978) reported evidence suggesting that defendants who feel they have participated in the plea bargaining process or in dispute resolution perceive a greater sense of justice than individuals who are not allowed to be participants. In another study, Houlden, LaTour, Walker, and Thibaut (1978) confirmed this discovery.

Pauline Houlden (1980–81) conducted a simulation study designed in part to replicate previous findings and also to shed new light on what types of plea bargaining modifications would provide greatest satisfaction or sense of fairness to defendants. Two procedural modifications were tested. One allowed the defendant to participate directly in the plea bargaining process; the other introduced a third-party mediator who played an active role in the negotiation. Several additional independent variables were considered. One was mediator background, where the third party was either a state-paid person or a community volunteer. Other variables pertained to the defendant, including whether he was guilty or innocent, and whether the state's evidence was strong or weak. Subjects themselves were either college undergraduates or inmates in a detention center awaiting trial or sentencing. Thus the experiment included five two-level variables.

Subjects read one of four stories about a person who drove his motor vehicle over a business partner. They were asked to consider themselves the central figure, who was charged with first-degree murder. The stories were designed so that the central figure was either innocent or guilty as charged and the evidence against him was either weak or strong. The subjects then read descriptions of six different plea bargaining procedures, after being told they were to think about which procedure they would want to be involved in if caught in that situation. The various procedures either did or did not allow the defendant to participate in the plea bargaining process and either did or did not include a mediator. If present, the mediator was described as either a community volunteer or a state-paid official.

As might be expected, the results were complex, and we will consider only the data highlights at this point. One overriding result was that all "defendants" preferred plea bargaining procedures which included them directly in the negotiation process, a finding consistent with those reported by LaTour (1978). There were, however, two interactions that bear mentioning. Preference for participation was especially strong among undergraduates when they believed themselves guilty and facing strong state's evidence. Inmates who imagined themselves in a similar situation (guilty and strong evidence) were apparently convinced that little could be gained by procedural modifications in a situation so dire. This viewpoint probably reflected their personal experiences with the criminal justice system.

"Guilty" defendants, however, were not fond of situations which did not allow their participation or where there were no mediators. This type of situation, of course, represents much of the current practice within the judicial system. If a mediator was to be included in the plea negotiations, undergraduates preferred a state-paid person, while inmates preferred a community volunteer. This may reflect a proclivity for inmates to perceive state-paid agents as motivated to convict.

These studies represent a good beginning of an empirical investigation of plea bargaining. However, theoretical integration and development must also be undertaken, in conjunction with empirical study, before there can be substantial progress toward an understanding of plea bargaining and its effect upon defendants and the justice system as a whole.

We will now turn our attention to the psychology of negotiation and bargaining as, in reality, it is used by lawyers, especially in civil disputes.

# ■ Legal Negotiation and Bargaining

Most civil disputes and some minor criminal cases are settled by the legal negotiation process. Among the best-known types of civil disputes in which attorneys negotiate on behalf of their clients are divorce settlements which must distribute property or determine child custody arrangements. The impetus behind attempts to reach agreement through negotiation is presumably the ultimate threat of a trial, a threat directed more at the defendant or litigants than at the negotiating lawyers. Defendants and litigants envision heavy financial, social, and psychological costs arising not only from attorney's fees and personal emotional investment, but also from possible public exposure of their problems. In some instances, attorneys feel that their professional reputation is on the line, particularly when they are dealing with unpredictable cases, and they strive for a reasonable out-of-court settlement or for a plea bargain agreement.

It should be mentioned that there are gradients of court-oriented settlements or bargains, especially with respect to criminal proceedings. Criminal violations are seldom settled between private parties in the same manner as civil disputes are. If the prosecutor or private citizen decides to press charges, court involvement must result. Hence, various court-oriented settlements may result, an example of which is the plea bargaining process. Dismissal of the case by the presiding judge is another possibility. If no court-oriented settlement occurs, the case will proceed to actual adjudication, which refers to formal decisionmaking by a jury or trial judge (Galanter, 1974). A trial then, especially in civil cases, is a process of last resort when negotiators have reached an impasse in their attempts to reach an agreement.

Roughly 10 percent of both civil and criminal cases reach the trial stage, requiring adjudication (Williams et al., 1976; Adelstein, 1978; Lachman & McLauchlan, 1977; Miller, McDonald & Cramer, 1978). This often-cited percentage is only a nationwide approximation, since practices vary widely from jurisdiction to jurisdiction. For example, in some jurisdictions trials may be merely "slow pleas of guilty" to appease the community that justice is being served or to maintain adequate statistics of judicial activity. In other jurisdictions, some prosecutors maintain tough stances toward plea bargaining and prefer formal adjudication. In still others, statutes require a court appearance for certain civil disputes, even though a dispute may have been settled agreeably between the parties.

Given that a major portion of legal problems are processed through bargaining rather than formal litigation and adjudication, it is surprising to find that books on effective lawyering and law school courses are disproportionately concerned with the trial process rather than bargaining (Saks & Hastie, 1978). Part of the reason may be that trial skills are considered more necessary and more difficult to develop. In this sense "attorneys who are unwilling or unable or afraid to go to trial will be unable to bargain successfully" (Saks & Hastie, 1978, p. 120). The lawyer who has not learned effective trial skills is at a disadvantage during the negotiation process, because the knowledge that one's opponent can perform well in the courtroom is an incentive to settle out of court.

Nevertheless, empirical literature on the psychology of bargaining* abounds. Much of the research has followed a simulation paradigm, where game situations, like the prisoner's dilemma game, the Parcheesi coalition game, the Acme-Bolt trucking game, or the bilateral monopoly game, are used. Another common simulation paradigm involves asking a subject to interact with a bogus adversary, who responds with pre-planned strategies. Simulated negotiation research suffers from the same limitations that characterize simulated jury research, however. Generalizations from negotiation strategies and theory that are tested in laboratory settings should be treated with caution.

Suprisingly little research attention has been directed specifically at legal negotiation. This neglect is due partly to the fact that there are few formal rules in legal negotiation. Also, most legal negotiation sessions are held confidentially between the mediating attorneys and hence are not accessible to study by the usual research methods (Williams et al., 1976). A professional code, both overt and covert, develops within the legal profession in a given community and what transpires between the attorneys during the bargaining process is often a localized professional secret, unknown even to clients. Even so, it is worthwhile to examine some of what is known about the psychology of negotiation and bargaining, since both scholars and experienced negotiators have supported the validity of most of the findings and hypotheses to be reported here.

## PSYCHOLOGY OF NEGOTIATION

An effective negotiator plans strategy beforehand, with the realization that it will probably have to be modified somewhat to accommodate the opponent's strategy. Each planned strategy includes an initial or opening offer, a target and a resistance point,

---

*The term *bargaining*, although sometimes reserved for a process where selling and buying are the central themes, is used here as synonymous with *negotiation*.

and the ideal number, timing, and size of concessions or compromises. *Resistance point* refers to the lowest or minimal offer the negotiator (or client) will accept without terminating the bargaining. The *target point* is the best offer that the negotiator hopes to attain. *Aspiration level*, similar to the target point, refers to the level of accomplishment that would satisfy the negotiator's or client's best expectations.

Although many hypotheses concerning negotiating strategies have been tested, early research in social psychology has focused on three—the aspiration level, reciprocity, and independent hypotheses. The *aspiration level hypothesis*, first proposed by Siegel and Fouraker (1960), predicts that a consistently tough or hard stand by one negotiator prompts the other negotiator to lower his or her aspiration level and make eager concessions. Conversely, consistently large concessions by a negotiator encourage the other negotiator to raise his or her aspiration level and to make smaller concessions. The *reciprocity hypothesis* predicts the opposite effect, namely, that each negotiator will respond in kind to each other's responses. Hence, small concessions will promote small concessions from one's adversary and large concessions will generate large concessions. The *independent hypothesis* is based upon the belief that effective bargaining is produced by a predetermined, fixed strategy that is not affected by the opponent's responses (Yukl, 1974).

While each of these hypotheses has received some research support, the aspiration level hypothesis decidedly has gained favor in recent years, particularly with reference to situations where there is little trust and cooperation, or where no prior relationship exists between the negotiators. Research testing the hypothesis has looked at how a bargaining outcome is affected by the size of the initial offer; speed, frequency and size of concessions; and information known about the adversary.

The initial or opening offer is a crucial phase in any transaction or bargaining process, since it provides valuable information about how "tough" (high demands) or "soft" (low demands) the bargainer intends to be. Experienced negotiators communicate to their adversaries that the bargaining is going to be tough by opening with an offer that is considerably higher than their aspiration level. Hence, the attorney for a plaintiff in a negligence suit will attach an exorbitant amount of money to the claims, partly to communicate toughness and partly to allow considerable flexibility in reaching a satisfactory figure in the final settlement. According to the aspiration level hypothesis, the party to whom the suit is directed will lower his or her aspiration levels and will be willing to concede more. Is this indeed what happens?

Extensive research by Otomar Bartos (1970) demonstrates that in most bargaining situations it is better to be tough by beginning with high demands and conceding little. After examining a variety of simulated bargaining situations, Bartos found that toughness generates softness in one's opponent and softness generates toughness. In the long run, tough negotiators received higher payoffs at settlement time than either moderate or soft ones.

The size of the concessions is also an extremely important factor. A high initial offer quickly loses its impact when it is followed by rather large concessions. Large and frequent concessions communicate weakness and vulnerability, which has the effect of encouraging an adversary to increase aspiration level and to become less flexible and less open to compromise. In fact, the negotiator who tries to be fair and cooperative in reaching a "just agreement" by making concessions and by providing information to an adversary seems to invite exploitation rather than to elicit trust and cooperation (Black & Higbee, 1973; Shure, Meeker & Hansford, 1965). Exploitation is especially likely to occur in situations where one adversary is unconditionally cooperative and it is expected that there will be no further interaction between the negotiators in the future (Marlow, Gergen & Doob, 1966). Negotiators who make irregular or unpredictable concessions are perceived as tough, and they often elicit large concessions from their opponents (Chertkoff & Conley, 1967; Pruitt & Johnson, 1970). On the other hand, a negotiator who presents regular, predictable, and consistent concessions is seen as weak and often one to be taken advantage of (Komorita & Brenner, 1968). Summarizing the studies on negotiation, Worchel and Cooper (1979, p. 484) concluded, "'nice guys finish last' and are often exploited."

In general, it appears wise to make highly discrepant offers or strong demands in the beginning of the negotiation and to make small and infrequent concessions. This strategy is especially effective when strong time-pressures or deadlines are present (Komorita & Barnes, 1969). Time pressures reduce aspiration levels and precipitate an eagerness to reach an agreement before time runs out. Concessions, even small ones, made under time pressures are interpreted by opponents as more representative of the approximate resistance points of their adversary (Holmes & Miller, 1976).

Much of the bargaining process can be said to be a search for the resistance point of an adversary in the first place (Tedeschi & Lindskold, 1976). Initial offers and concessions thus become probes to determine the adversary's resistance point, and to establish one's own realistic level of aspiration from what transpires during each step of the negotiation. If both sides of negotiating proceedings know each other's resistance points, then ploys and probes from both sides are unnecessary and perfunctory.

Indeed, negotiation follows a different pattern when information about an adversary's strategy and resistance points is known or when the negotiators have confronted one another in the past. The aspiration level hypothesis fails to make accurate predictions in this context because the process is less ambiguous, and the parties are less likely to manipulate aspiration levels. Of course, any negotiator has considerable leverage if the adversary's position is known but his or her own position is unknown, a situation that is quite rare. The knowing negotiator can then stake a claim, assert demands near the opponent's known resistance point, sit back, and control the process without conceding much more than symbolic points.

## NEGOTIATION IN CRIMINAL CASES

In most legal negotiating, the attorneys know one another, or at least are aware of each other's professional reputation. In addition, they are often playing dual roles, requiring both competition and cooperation. For example, cooperation between the defense attorney and the prosecuting attorney is a very necessary ingredient in the criminal justice system. Each must bargain for pleas, bail, changes in charges, and sentencing. Furthermore, to some extent they must elicit the cooperation of other legal participants, such as the judge, police officers, the probation officer, and even the court clerk or other clerical personnel who are in control of the court calendar.

Cooperation in the criminal justice system is not only required, it is also usually beneficial to participants. Defense and prosecuting attorneys typically have had numerous contacts in the past and expect to continue these contacts in the future. The defense attorney, who often specializes in criminal cases, wants to keep a positive relationship with prosecutors, in order to maintain a "paying" practice for future criminal cases. More importantly, since the prosecutor has considerable legitimate power in dealing with criminal cases, a positive working relationship will allow the defense better access to evidence gathered by the police and prosecutor's office, access to the defendant who is in jail, and concessions or favors in bail setting. Reasonable settlements in future criminal cases are also more likely to be assured.

The prosecution also depends upon the cooperation of defense attorneys and does not want to alienate those adversaries. Long drawn-out, well-publicized trials have the potential to tarnish the prosecutor's public image, and they often can be avoided only with cooperation from the defense. In the long run, it is more likely that defense attorneys will have uncooperative, hostile clients than problematical professional adversaries (Saks & Hastie, 1978).

The professional cooperation between defense and prosecution must be nurtured by some sharing of information and by trust that each party is bargaining in "good faith." A lawyer who fails to abide by these professional codes may find the prosecutor's office uncooperative and to some degree may be ostracized by members of the inner circle of regulars at the criminal court. For a vast majority of criminal attorneys, who are in a specialization which serves mostly indigent clients, being shunned in this way is a "kiss of death." What little income they can make is reduced when the word gets around that they are not willing to play the game their colleagues long ago established rules for. Except for high-powered criminal attorneys who have acquired a reputation by successfully handling cases drawing heavy media coverage, or who specialize in white collar crimes like income tax evasion or computer fraud, criminal lawyers are not well paid. Clients are often poor, powerless, and emotionally distraught, and the defense attorney often must rely on a defendant's family to meet legal costs.

In sum, cooperation, mutual trust, and information sharing are prerequisites for resolving most criminal cases. Frequent contacts between the respective attorneys assure that negotiation and concession strategies are understood and anticipated. Therefore, bluffs, deceptions, or other symbolic actions are unnecessary and probably used primarily by inexperienced, novice criminal attorneys not yet socialized to the system.

This suggests that the aspiration level hypothesis does not apply to the majority of criminal cases. Its major relevance appears to be in civil dispute cases, particularly where large claims are mediated by seasoned attorneys. Labor negotiations, class-action suits against large corporations, and divorce actions which involve large property settlements are examples of litigation which follows the strategies and bargaining processes outlined above, where negotiators probe for resistance points and settlements in their client's (and their own) best interest. In contrast, the nature of the relationship between the defense and the prosecuting attorneys in the criminal justice system suggests that the reciprocity hypothesis discussed earlier is relevant.

### INTEGRATIVE BARGAINING

In recent years Dean Pruitt and his colleagues have conducted research having particular relevance to the negotiation process practiced in the criminal justice system.

They have coined the term *integrative bargaining* to refer to cooperative, trusting negotiation and information sharing (Pruitt & Lewis, 1977). In such a process, bargainers locate and adopt options that satisfy their collective needs and produce agreements of high joint benefit.

Empirical study on integrative bargaining has revealed three types of negotiation tactics—distributive tactics, heuristic trial and error, and information exchange. *Distributive tactics* employ threats and arguments to convince the other party to concede; they are aimed at pressuring the opponent. Available research has found that this approach is usually ineffective in arriving at satisfactory joint gains (Carnevale, Pruitt & Britton, 1979; Pruitt & Lewis, 1975; Pruitt et al., 1978), suggesting that pressure tactics employed by either the prosecution or the defense will not result in a mutually satisfactory settlement.

The *heuristic trial and error tactic* involves one or more of the following strategies (Kimmel et al., 1980):

1. Frequent changing of an offer or of concessions
2. Seeking the other party's reactions to each offer
3. Making larger concessions on items or issues of lower priority
4. Systematic concession making, where a negotiator explores the various alternatives available at one level before proceeding to another

In essence, this tactic relies on making systematic proposals and concessions in order to discover the other party's reactions and counterproposals. It is a testing process designed to determine whether the other party is willing to concede or offer options on certain items.

In the *information exchange tactic* the bargainers request and provide valid information about their positions and aspirations. Providing information about one's needs and priorities helps the other negotiator locate a mutually satisfying alternative or agreement. This tactic, or course, requires a high level of trust on the part of the negotiators.

Pruitt and Lewis (1977) report that when the goal is to locate a mutually acceptable agreement with maximum cooperation and trust, both information exchange and heuristic trial and error are likely to be employed, the former less frequently. A negotiator who provides information about his or her needs and priorities helps an adversary locate the resistance point; the informing party is then committed to a barely acceptable position if the opposing negotiator does not reciprocate. Not surprisingly, therefore, bargainers prefer the heuristic trial and error strategy. In some instances, when a negotiator is especially fearful of revealing information (high aspiration and low trust conditions), the negotiator resorts to distributive tactics like threats, competitiveness, and pressure methods (Kimmel et al., 1980). The research by Pruitt found that negotiators who did rely on these distributive strategies did not improve their positions, however.

Two qualifiers should be advanced concerning the information exchange tactic. Information exchange appears most effective when the negotiators exchanging positions are high in cognitive complexity (Pruitt & Lewis, 1975). Second, a recent study (Kimmel et al., 1980) has reported evidence that information exchange may occur explicitly, such as when negotiators communicate clearly their priorities, or implicitly, where negotiators report nothing about their priorities but allude to them by indicating the issues on which they seek favorable action from the other party.

The first qualifier—concerning cognitive complexity—refers to the well-researched finding that people differ in the complexity of their cognitive constructions of reality. Some people perceive most events as complex and shaded in grays, while others view the world in simplistic fashion. If negotiators are high in cognitive complexity, which is linked positively to intelligence, information exchange helps them arrive at a mutually satisfactory joint agreement. However, negotiators low in cognitive complexity apparently do not utilize the information exchange to any great benefit.

In summary, of the three major hypotheses advanced to explain the bargaining process, two have found considerable support, each under different conditions. The aspiration level hypothesis appears relevant in civil disputes, particularly when attorneys have limited information and contact and when their dealings with one another are infrequent. Since government officials and government attorneys change positions with some regularity, and since these changes are accompanied by corresponding changes in philosophy, focus, and strategies, the bargaining procedures of the aspiration level hypothesis are more likely to occur. Corporate attorneys engaged in big-business or antitrust litigation often meet different, unfamiliar adversaries, and therefore probably also rely on aspiration level strategies. On the other hand, attorneys engaged in practices that involve repetitive contacts with the same actors, such as in some sectors of criminal justice, probably depend more on a reciprocity bargaining orientation. The third hypothesis, which predicts that bargaining strategy is not affected by the opponent's position, has received little research support.

# ■ Persuasion in the Courtroom

Attitude change and persuasion are two of the most extensively studied topics in social psychology. The zeitgeist in the area was first promoted by psychologist Carl Hovland, who directed the Yale Communication Program initiated shortly after World War II (Hovland & Janis, 1959; Hovland, Janis & Kelley, 1953). During the 1950s and 1960s the research activity probing the many facets of persuasion was impressive. Since then, the theoretical development and empirical interest has waned, primarily because inconsistent data accumulated and the emergence of each new study revealed unanticipated complexity about the topic being studied (Jaccard, 1981). Also, since psychology is a science always in search of a frontier, it too often fails to explore each area in detail.

Many fields of inquiry fade with complexity, but the persuasion literature has demonstrated an uncanny knack for survival. This is probably due in great part to its great potential for applicability to society's needs. The extensive amount of research interest during the past decades has prompted a splintering of the persuasion field into seven major theoretical camps, all of which may be classified both classical and contemporary (Petty & Cacioppo, 1981). The interested reader is urged to consult Petty and Cacioppo's excellent volume, *Attitudes and Persuasion: Classic and Contemporary Approaches.* Despite the mass of data and the inconsistency often found therein, the following section will try to offer some cautious generalizations.

Persuasion research has focused on three major categories of variables:

1. Characteristics of the source or communicator of a message
2. Characteristics of the communication, involving what is spoken or written, how, and in what context
3. Characteristics of the audience which receives the message

Below we will consider only those variables which appear especially relevant to courtroom lawyering. Furthermore, we will concentrate on the variables associated with the source and with the communication itself, since we discussed the audience, the jury, in an earlier chapter.

## THE SOURCE

Common sense dictates that the more credible the source of a communication the greater the persuasion, and research has consistently supported this fireside induction. Two factors appear to be of great importance in source credibility: (1) level of expertise and (2) the communicator's intentions in communicating (Baron & Byrne, 1981). Sources who are regarded as having high expertise in a given area tend to be believed more than sources with lower expertise, according to a number of experiments (e.g., Bochner & Insko, 1966; McGinnies & Ward, 1974; Aronson, Turner & Carlsmith, 1963). These findings confirm the observation that juries (and judges) are more inclined to believe the testimony of an expert well trained and well credentialed in the topic at issue. Thus, experienced trial attorneys will prompt their experts to list their training and experience, often in impressive detail, before asking them specific questions concerning the case. On the other hand, each attorney will try to discredit the expert offered by the opposing party by challenging credentials or devaluing them.

Expertise does not invariably persuade, however. If the information the expert is providing is not understood by the audience, the string of credentials will matter very little. Technical, esoteric jargon may give the impression the expert is trying to dupe or make the audience feel inferior, producing the opposite effect from that intended. Another important consideration is the perceived motivation of the communicator. If the audience perceives a blatant attempt to persuade, the credibility of the source is reduced (e.g., Mills, 1966; Mills & Jellison, 1967). It is crucial, therefore, that any witness appear as objective as possible in presenting expert knowledge. Witnesses are not persuasive if their audience believes they have much to gain personally from the testimony. Conversely, if the audience believes a witness has nothing to gain, credibility is maintained or even increased.

We must emphasize that attorneys have immense power and control over witnesses in a courtroom, particularly when evidence is ambiguous or of poor quality. Within broad limits, attorneys are able to direct and redirect testimony, making it appear credible or questionable. Even though lawyers have this kind of impact within only a narrow range of cases, this small percentage of cases still affects thousands of defendants.

It is the jury or the judge whom the attorneys must persuade. "Hard sells" and strong persuasive appeals are likely to prove counterproductive. Not only does this approach damage the credibility of the communicator, but it also may precipitate psychological reactance (Brehm, 1966, 1972). When individuals sense or perceive that their freedom of choice is being threatened or forced, they often become aroused and motivated to restore their freedom. Under these conditions, people often resort to making decisions opposite those desired by the communicator. Therefore, a lawyer who implies that jurors have no choice other than to absolve his or her client may soon learn that the jurors do indeed have an alternative.

### THE CONTENT

Variables surrounding the content of the communication have received continual research scrutiny, sometimes yielding surprising results. Common sense would tell us that distractions from the content of a presentation would reduce the effect of the message. Michael Saks and Reid Hastie (1978) describe with apparent relish one of the tactics sometimes employed by the legendary Clarence Darrow to distract the jury from his opponent's closing arguments. "Darrow would insert a wire inside his cigar so that when he smoked it the ash would grow long without falling. He would smoke it during his opponent's closing, and as the ash grew increasingly long, the jury (it is said) would become increasingly fascinated and not be able to attend to the opponent's arguments" (p. 105). As Saks and Hastie correctly point out, however, there is evidence that distraction during presentation may actually increase the influence of that presentation (e.g., Festinger & Maccoby, 1964; Allyn & Festinger, 1961). Thus, common sense must yield to the research evidence. However, it also has been shown that distraction is most effective when the communication content is simple rather than complex (Regan & Cheng, 1973). Darrow's ploy would have been potentially destructive to his case if the opponent's arguments were involved and demanded the intense concentration of the jury.

In the summation of the case, is it more effective to present both sides of an argument or only one side? That is, should a prosecutor summarize his or her arguments and the defense attorney's and try to persuade the jury in the state's direction? Research in social psychology suggests that we must look at several characteristics of the audience before answering. Presenting one side of an argument is the best strategy if the jury is already convinced of that side; then, the summation reinforces an already held position. If the jury is undecided, or if the jury is above average in intelligence, the lawyer would be wise to present both sides, but should carefully offer strong counterarguments to the opponent's position. This tactic is similar to what William McGuire (1964) called *inoculation*, a strategy of exposing the audience to arguments against the communicator's position and following them with strong arguments in favor of the communicator's position. This approach, McGuire asserted, may serve to inoculate the audience against later persuasive appeals.

## ■ Legal Language

Recent research by Allan Lind and William O'Barr (1978) reveals that the type and style of communication that occurs in the courtroom has great influence on the participants. They observed and recorded the speech of numerous criminal trials in a North Carolina Superior Court, and they concluded that certain common expressions and mannerisms used by witnesses and lawyers communicated status, power, and control over listeners.

First, using a model of speech characteristics developed by Lakoff (1973), Lind and O'Barr divided speech into "power" and "powerless" modes. "Powerless" speech includes the frequent use of intensifiers (i.e., so, very, too); empty adjectives (e.g., divine, charming, cute); hyper-correct grammar (e.g., never a split infinitive); hedges (you know, kind of, I guess); and rising intonation. Lakoff had observed that the speech pattern characterized by these words and phrases was not a very convincing form of communication.

Lind and O'Barr discovered that professionals used these forms of speech less frequently than persons who had low social prestige and occupational status. With these speech data from the courtroom, they then conducted a simulated experiment using various levels of powerful and powerless testimony. "For both the male and female witnesses, the power speech testimony produced perceptions that the witness was more competent, attractive, trustworthy, dynamic, and convincing than did the powerless speech testimony" (p. 72). These data suggest that rather subtle speech characteristics can communicate status, credibility, and competency to jurors.

The researchers also explored the length of a witness's response to the attorney's questions. As Lind and O'Barr noted, lawyers are often advised (e.g., Keeton, 1973) to encourage their own witnesses to provide long answers while demanding that opposition witnesses respond briefly. Although the evidence was complicated, in general it showed that this advice is basically correct, since longer answers generate more favorable evaluations of a witness.

Lind and O'Barr explored a third dimension, hostile interchanges between the lawyer and the person on the witness stand. Mock jurors heard a lawyer cross-examining a witness; at several points during the cross-examination, lawyer and witness spoke simultaneously. When this happened, one or the other would persevere, or continue to talk, and this was the measure of hostility.

Distinct sex differences emerged in the results. Male subjects considered the witness more competent and more likeable when he or she persevered than when the witness acquiesced; attorneys who persevered were considered more skillful by the male subjects. Thus, perseverance was definitely a positive characteristic in the eyes of the male subjects. Female subjects reacted in opposite fashion. They evaluated witnesses as less competent and likeable, and lawyers as less skillful, when each persevered rather than when they acquiesced.

Overall, the Lind and O'Barr project suggests that the type of speech used in the courtroom may have substantial impact on a juror's perceptions of witnesses. In the eyewitness chapter, we discovered that the way a witness is questioned can have considerable influence on how the witness answers. The many dimensions of speech appear to offer exciting possibilities for future research on its application and persuasive capacities in the courtroom.

## THE PLAIN ENGLISH MOVEMENT

In recent years, considerable interest has focused upon the relationship between language and law outside the courtroom, in such matters as lawyer-client communication, contracts, and other document language (see Danet (1980) for an excellent, comprehensive review). For example, are contracts and legally relevant documents, such as warranties and consumer-loan forms, written so that consumers can understand them? Or are they purposely ambiguous and incomprehensible to protect manufacturers and enable them to deal with each particular case as it occurs?

A barometer of this interest is the "Plain English Movement" outlined by Danet (1980). In 1971 the American National Council of Teachers of English created a Committee on Public Doublespeak, whose primary activity was to cultivate a critical attitude toward the way English is used today. During the 1970s a number of "pop" books on the English language appeared (e.g., Edwin Newman's A Civil Tongue (1976) and Strictly Speaking (1975)), which were highly critical of the speaking and writing skills of Americans. Shortly after his election, President Carter issued an executive order requiring "clear and simple English" as a means of improving government regulations. The Plain English Movement extended not only to written and spoken forms of communication found in state and federal government agencies, but also to the private sector, involving the legal documents used by banks and insurance companies. In the late 1970s the Document Design Center was established in Washington, D.C., to conduct research and provide advice about the writing of legal and bureaucratic documents.

Over twenty states now have laws specifying standards and procedures for the readability of insurance policies and other types of consumer contracts, several other states have laws pending, and at least ten have regulations or directives dealing with the issue (Danet, 1980). New York has passed a "Plain English Law" which mandates that all consumer credit contracts be written in a nontechnical, coherent, and meaningful way. On a larger scale, the Employee Retirement Income Security Act of 1975 requires lucid explanations of employee benefits, and the Magnuson-Moss Warranty Act requires that consumer warranties be written in clear and simple English.

Do such changes in the readability of legally relevant documents change the practices of both consumers and industry? While there is little empirical evidence with which to answer this question, Davis (1977) reports some preliminary data which suggest that when readability is improved on consumer contracts only low-income consumers benefit. Levels of comprehension remain about the same for other consumers.

Danet (1980) warns that attempts to reform legal language should not be construed as rejections of legality and legal documents, but rather as attempts to make the language more understandable to the lay person. However, she asks pointedly, "Will more people read contracts if they are written in Plain English? If the conditions remain the same, will customers benefit because the language is comprehensible?" (p. 489). In her review, Danet is pessimistic about the extended impact of the Plain English Movement. She concludes, "In short, much of the thinking behind the Plain English movement is naive, both about the complexities of language and about the extent to which linguistic reform can change sociolegal realities" (p. 490).

In similar fashion, some legal commentators argue that the legal language should remain vague to accommodate legal flexibility (e.g., Christie, 1964), and others contend that the legal terms promote efficiency (since they function as a shorthand for legal participants) and maintain the cohesiveness of the profession (e.g., Friedman,

1964; Steuer, 1969). Others argue that to modify or alter the existing legal jargon would create professional disharmony, because legal words are precise and have withstood the test of time.

On the other hand, critics maintain that legal language is embraced by the legal profession to promote the "illusions" of authority (Gusfield, 1980), consistency (Arnold, 1935), certainty (Edelman, 1977), or power and control (Bloch, 1975). Others feel that legal jargon is a barrier to lawyer-client communication (Zander, 1978) or a source of mystification and confusion intended to convince people that they need legal counsel (e.g., Pei, 1973).

## FIVE STYLES OF ENGLISH

Despite the fact that there is little systematic, empirical study on the relationship between language and law, it will be beneficial at this point to tie legal language to some theoretical mooring. Martin Joos (1961) has delineated five basic styles of English along a continuum from formal to informal. The styles are frozen, formal, consultative, casual, and intimate, and only the first four are relevant to legal situations. Joos also identifies three basic modes—written, spoken-composed, and spoken-spontaneous. The written mode includes anything in written form, such as legal documents, briefs, and statutes. The spoken-composed mode refers to those spoken words with prior preparation and internal (cognitive) rehearsal. A spoken-spontaneous style characterizes those oral communications with minimal preparation or prior cognitive rehearsal.

Frozen style, the most formal type, is designed for print or declamation, where the reader or listener cannot question the speaker, but the text is available for analysis and review. An example of frozen style in a written mode is a legal document, such as a will or lease. Examples of frozen style in the spoken-composed mode are witness oaths, marriage ceremonies, indictments, verdicts, and some portions of the instructions to the jury.

The formal style is intended to inform in a comparatively detached manner. Examples of formal style within a written mode includes statutes, briefs, and appellate opinions. The cross-examination of witnesses, opening and closing arguments, and expert-witness testimony are courtroom examples of the formal style in a spoken-composed mode. Direct examination of witnesses usually entails more prior rehearsal and therefore may be considered a better illustration of formal style, that is, closer to the formal end of the continuum (Danet, 1980).

The consultative style is characteristic of communications where a speaker is providing a listener with desired information. This style is most often limited to either the spoken-composed mode, as found in lay witnesses' testimony, or the spoken-spontaneous mode, as found in lawyer-client interactions or bench conferences. The casual style is most characteristic of lawyer-to-lawyer conversations and conferences among the "in-group," and it most often occurs in the spoken-spontaneous mode.

The Joos conceptual scheme of legal language is presented here primarily as a learning device to demonstrate an approach to analyzing legal language. The fate of its accuracy rests ultimately with empirical study and continued adaptation to the data. Realistically, a sizeable portion of legal communication is likely to consist of some mixture of these styles and modes, and merely locking communications into some category may not be wise. At this point we have little empirical data with which to confirm or disconfirm the Joos analysis, but it does illustrate a systematic attempt to order legal language into a meaningful structure.

### PSYCHOLINGUISTIC RESEARCH

The field of psychology presently most concerned with studying legal language is psycholinguistics. At this stage of its topical development, psycholinguistics is mostly interested in the relationship between mental processes involved in the acquisition and use of language. In an effort to bridge the gap between the highly active science of psycholinguistics and law, Bruce Sales and his colleagues (Sales, Elwork & Alfini, 1977) examined the research findings in psychololinguistics in relation to the comprehensibility of the instructions to the jury. The analysis sheds light on the frozen style, spoken-composed mode of legal language.

Instructions given to the jury about what is expected of them have become of critical importance in determining the fairness of a trial and the justice inherent in the verdict or decision. In fact, error in instructing the jury often has been cited as the single most frequent cause of reversal on appeal (Sales et al., 1977). Lower court judges, realizing that the language in the instructions must be acceptable to the appellate court, have often emphasized the legal accuracy of the instructions to the neglect of clarity. This has prompted the adoption by a majority of states of patterned jury instructions, which are intended to be uniform, concise, error-free instructions, intelligible to the average juror. However, extremely few empirical studies have been conducted to determine the comprehensibility of patterned instructions. Moreover, few of the committees appointed to draft them have sought the aid of experts to ensure that the instructions were clearly worded.

Drawing on the psycholinguistic literature, Sales and his colleagues (1977) note that drafters of patterned instructions fail to realize that high frequency words (those most commonly used in the media and in everyday speech) are better understood and learned than low frequency words; or that concrete words, contrasted with abstract words, are remembered better, are more meaningful, and are therefore better comprehended; or that synonyms are often misunderstood and have a debilitating effect on comprehension. These are only examples of Sales' numerous observations, and interested readers are advised to consult the source.

In sum, psycholinguistic research has yet to make direct, substantial contribution to the field of law, but it is rich in relevant material. Since law is based primarily on the power and communicative properties of words, the future relationship between the two fields should be profitable, provided that the linguists communicate their findings to the lawyers.

## ■ Adversary Procedures and Lawyering

Although countries throughout the free world employ different legal procedures, two principal forms can be identified. The inquisitional or nonadversary procedure is used in various forms in continental European countries (e.g., France), and the adversary procedure is used primarily by the English-speaking world. The two procedures use lawyers and judges in decidedly different ways. In the inquisitional method, one party files a grievance or claim, and the judge—with the help of court investigators or lawyers—actively seeks out the evidence before making a decision. Judges in these settings are afforded awesome power in their search for evidence. They may commission experts to investigate and report on special aspects, they may badger witnesses, and they may call as many witnesses as they deem necessary. The witnesses testify for the court rather than for the opposing parties. If a judge permits, contending parties may ask clarifying questions or submit additional evidence for the judge's consideration. After hearing the final arguments from each side, the judge makes the ultimate decision.

In the adversary process the disputants and their attorneys develop their own evidence, which traditionally includes preparing and interviewing witnesses, both in and out of the courtroom. The extent and quality of the evidence is the responsibility of the parties, while the judge remains relatively passive, acting primarily as a referee or an impartial arbiter deciding the flow of the information and, occasionally, its direction.

The respective advantages and disadvantages of each system have been debated for well over a century (Sheppard & Vidmar, 1980). An often-cited extensive investigation (Thibaut & Walker, 1975) found considerable evidence that in many ways the adversary approach was "clearly superior" to other modes of legal evidence gathering. Although the methods and logic used by Thibaut and Walker were carefully critiqued by Robert Hayden and Jill Anderson (1979), a recent theoretical collating of the data presents an even more convincing argument, also in favor of the adversary procedure (Thibaut & Walker, 1978; Lind & Walker, 1979).

The Lind-Thibaut-Walker group delineates three arguments in favor of the adversary procedure. First, Lon Fuller (1961) has suggested that adversarial approaches reduce decisionmaker bias, since a two-sided presentation of information induces the decisionmaker to reserve judgment until all of the facts are in. In general, the evidence supports this position (Lind & Walker, 1979). Second, Freedman (1970) contends that attorneys will search more diligently for facts about the case if they are working within the context of adversarial procedures. This diligence presumably will yield more accurate information, which is then presented to the decisionmaker. The available evidence supports the contention that attorneys do work more diligently under adversary conditions, but they do not necessarily present more accurate information to the decisionmakers (Lind & Walker, 1979). Instead, they will present material in support of their client's position but will not present information potentially damaging to it. This especially appears to be the case for attorneys with Machiavellian personalities (Sheppard & Vidmar, 1980), a characteristic that deserves some attention here.

Niccolo Machiavelli lived in sixteenth-century Italy and wrote about the use and abuse of power in interpersonal relationships (e.g., *The Prince* and *The Discourses*). Machiavelli was cynical about human behavior, believing that people are basically selfish, ungrateful, and strongly oriented toward their own personal needs. "Machiavellianism" is now a personality dimension that can be measured by a questionnaire called the Mach Scale, which was fashioned from Machiavelli's views of power (Christie & Geis, 1970; see box). Individuals who score high on the Mach scale are likely to have a cool, detached, and manipulative approach toward others. Sheppard and Vidmar (1980) reasoned that Machiavellian lawyers are likely to handle cases significantly differently than lawyers low on Machiavellianism. In their research, high Mach "attorneys" (actually students who role-played attorneys) were more effective under adversarial conditions in biasing witness testimony in a direction favoring their case. They appeared more motivated and generally more persuasive in their advocate roles than low Mach subjects. A guarded generalization from these results may be that adversary procedures favor Machiavellians who are not only more masterful at manipulating others but also may be more diligent in seeking out facts.

Proponents of the adversary system also argue that it promotes greater satisfaction in the disputants (Adams, 1974; Noonan, 1966). In research reported by Lind and Walker (1979), subjects who participated in adversary procedures were more satisfied and considered the verdicts more fair than those who participated in nonadversary conditions. This result underlines some interesting issues. The Lind-Walker-Thibaut research indicates that the adversary procedure promotes a perception of "fairness" and "justice." However, because lawyers distort or at least leave out information that is unfavorable to their client's position, it does not directly serve the cause of "truth." In contrast, truth-oriented conflicts appear to be best resolved by nonadversary procedures. Justice may best be served by the adversary process; truth may best be served by a nonadversary procedure.

## ☐ MACHIAVELLIAN PERSONALITIES

The name of Niccolo Machiavelli (1469–1527), the political theorist of the Italian Renaissance, has become associated with a personality pattern demonstrating exploitative and manipulative tactics in dealing with others. Machiavelli's protagonist in *The Prince* (1532) used guile, deceit, and opportunism in interpersonal relations. More than four centuries later, those who view others as weak, manipulable, and to be used to advance their own purposes and causes are "Machiavellians."

Richard Christie and Florence Geis (1968, 1970) converted Machiavelli's precepts into statements that could be used to construct a paper-and-pencil opinion survey known as the Mach (pronounced "mock") Scale. The scale includes a number of statements, and respondents are asked to agree or disagree with each. Examples:

*The best way to handle people is to tell them what they want to hear.*

*Barnum was probably right when he said there's a sucker born every minute.*

*Some people attempt to manipulate others.*

*Anyone who completely trusts anyone else is asking for trouble.*

*It is safest to assume that people have a vicious streak and that it will come out when they are given a chance.*

Researchers during the 60s and 70s tried to discover the relationship between scores on the Mach Scale and behavioral

# ■ Legal Decisionmaking

The judicial system is permeated with decisionmakers with discretionary power at every juncture. The police and the prosecutor's office decide whether to pursue a case; the probation department decides whether there was violation of probationary status; the parole board decides the fate of an inmate; the jury decides guilt or innocence or what is just settlement for a civil case; the judge decides whether and how to set bail, guilt or innocence, what sentence to impose, and how to dispose of civil matters. None of the system's actors, however, have more discretionary power than the judge, who directly or indirectly influences every component of the judicial system.

In this section we will concentrate on the two important decisionmaking points of bail and sentencing in an attempt to discover what cognitive-psychological factors contribute to the decisionmaking equation. The reader should be forewarned, however, that the available evidence is fragmentary and often not related to any systematic theoretical framework. Often, researchers computerize large arrays of variables in hope that something meaningful will emerge. One of the more interesting studies reported in this section is a series of projects by Konečni and Ebbesen (1979) on bail and sentence decisionmaking; it reveals that the research findings on these two processes are highly dependent on the particular research method used. Variables which emerge as important in the decisionmaking process differ according to the research method

patterns and background data. No significant correlations were found between Mach scores and psychopathology, political ideology, or social class. High scorers (high in agreement with Machiavellian philosophy) tended to be males from urban backgrounds and clustered in people-oriented professions (e.g., psychiatry, clinical psychology, business administration) (Wrightsman & Deaux, 1981). In general, it appears that persons with high Mach scores have greater success in meeting the demands of American society and getting ahead in their chosen profession. The research also suggests that high Machs operate best under highly structured situations and in face-to-face encounters. They also tend to be quite accurate in their views of others' weaknesses, and they are rarely out-maneuvered by others.

High Machs also tend to be characterized by emotional detachment and the ability to depersonalize relationships, at least with those persons they try to manipulate and control. Machiavellians keep their cool under stress and in emotionally arousing situations. Research also indicates that high Machs tend to be better negotiators and administrators.

It appears, therefore, that we could expect the more successful attorneys to score significantly higher on the Mach Scale than less successful attorneys, or that they at least will be substantially more inclined to accept Machiavellian principles in the course of their professional exchanges. At this point, though, there is little evidence with which to accept or refute these assumptions concerning lawyering.

used; they cannot be predicted by any one decisionmaking model or equation. This important finding underscores the need for students of the judicial system to be ever suspicious of any particular finding that has not been cross-validated through different methods and approaches.

## BAIL DECISIONMAKING

John Goldkamp and Michael Gottfredson (1979) have suggested that bail decisions can be best analyzed in relation to three major themes or dimensions—rationality, equality, and visibility.

**Rationality.** Rational decisionmaking in criminal justice requires that a decision be based upon some substantiated and reasonable purpose. In theory, the sole purpose of bail is to guarantee the appearance of a defendant at subsequent proceedings against him or her (Kaplan, 1973; Jacob, 1972). Presumably, once an individual posts the cash or collateral specified in the bail bond, it is far more likely that that person will appear rather than forfeit the money or property. The criminal justice literature continually reports that whether a judge releases or detains a defendant or sets a bail depends primarily on the seriousness of the crime and the defendant's past criminal record. However, in order for the judge's decision to be based on rational considerations, there should be a significant relationship between the likelihood of a defendant's fleeing the area and the seriousness of the crime, or between likelihood of fleeing and the defendant's past criminal record.

The research shows no such relationship. In fact, legal commentary concludes that a great majority of defendants appear for hearings or for trial; bail seems irrelevant. Defendants usually believe it is more to their advantage to appear than to run, probably for three convincing reasons (Kaplan, 1973). First, the average defendant realizes his chances of being caught again are very high. Second, most defendants also understand that any attempt to leave town will work against any favorable disposition of their case. Third, "almost every adult defendant going to trial nurtures in his heart the hope, however faint, that he will somehow either be acquitted or given a suspended sentence, and his very optimism helps to assure his appearance" (p. 298). A fourth reason why defendants choose not to flee may be that they have limited resources or skills and cannot simply begin a new life elsewhere, or have family ties they do not wish to sever.

**Equity.** Bail decisions are also supposedly based on equity, a concept that centers on issues of fairness and requires individuals in similar situations to be treated equally. Yet criminal justice research and commentary repeatedly stress the wide disparity in bail and sentencing decisions. While there are inputs from other actors within the judicial system, decisions to release, detain, or set bail are highly discretionary and are made ultimately by judges who have very few official guidelines or standards to follow. The spectrum of available options ranges from release on own recognizance to incarceration without bail until the conclusion of a trial—a detainment that could take many months. The hardships imposed on defendants by bail decisions can be almost as extensive as sentencing after conviction.

Equity demands that persons in similar circumstances receive similar treatment, but how does one define "similar circumstances"? More specifically, how do we judge whether defendants have situational parity? Should the nature of the charge, socioeconomic background, criminal and conviction history, race, or age be a determining factor? Or should "similar circumstances" be represented by some combination of these variables? Most judges and prosecutors contend that the deciding variables on bail decisions are the seriousness of the crime and conviction history (Konečni & Ebbesen, 1979). This observation implies that equity in bail decision hinges on the charge and on previous charges and convictions. Despite what court officials say, do these factors really determine "equity" in actual bail decision practice? And, from a societal viewpoint, should they?

**Visibility.** The third major theme outlined by Goldkamp and Gottfredson is visibility. Bail decisions generally have low visibility, and criteria used and goals intended are often the hidden agenda. Thus, bail negotiations and bail decisions are difficult to study, because the criteria used to make decisions are unavailable. It is possible, for instance, that some bail decisions which result in pretrial detention are intended as punishment. The evidence against the accused is faulty, but the decisionmaker is convinced that "he did it." Certainly, pretrial punishment has been a factor when courts have dealt with rioters and demonstrators, and where the charges were questionable. Pretrial custody also can be used to instigate pressure on the defendant to plea bargain, especially if the judge and prosecutor have the power to delay trial proceedings for an uncomfortably long time.

### RESEARCH

To gain insight into these three themes, Goldkamp and Gottfredson (1979) analyzed judge decisionmaking in an extensive project using the Philadelphia courts. The researchers noted that there were three possible alternatives available to the judges:

1. To grant release of the defendants on their own recognizance (ROR)
2. To detain defendant under custody without bail
3. To set a specific bail amount

Dispositions of 3,592 cases were studied. Background data on the cases were obtained from court records and from the pretrial services agency of the court.

Results revealed that 47 percent of the defendants were granted ROR, 1 percent were detained without bail, and 52 percent had bail amounts set upon release. Whether a defendant was granted ROR depended mostly on the seriousness of the current criminal charge, but also, to a lesser extent, on the most serious prior arrest and the seriousness of all prior convictions. The less serious the current charge, prior record, and prior conviction, the more likely the defendant was to be granted ROR. The 1 percent of the defendants detained without bail were accused of murder or serious assault. In this sense, the second alternative decision was also related to the seriousness of the crime.

Possession of a weapon at the time of a crime significantly influenced the third decision, how much bail to set. To a lesser extent, this decision was also influenced by the number of complaints against the defendant. Higher bail amounts were set for defendants who used a weapon in the commission of the current crime and for defendants who had many complaints (transcripts) lodged against them.

In general, except for detention without bail, the relationships between all the relevant variables and the judge's bail decisions were weak. Thus, the primary factor or factors which may determine the judge's decisions to grant ROR or to set the amount of bail remain a mystery. Possibly, the major determinant of judge bail-decisionmaking is nothing more than whim, a fact that would undermine any pretension of equity.

The data also do not lend themselves to the "rationality justification," which requires bail decisions to be based on some substantiated rationale or explicitly expressed goal—usually, to prevent defendant flight from the area. There was no indication from the data that this was the purpose.

The data do support the visibility theme somewhat, because bail decisions appear to be dominated implicitly by the nature of the current offense and the prior record of convictions or arrests. Goldkamp and Gottfredson suggest that if a large proportion of the bail decisions are decided on the basis of some combination of these factors, their impact on the decision should be acknowledged in written, explicit guidelines. Once these explicit guidelines are established, they can be refined and policy can be improved.

Ebbesen and Konečni (1975) investigated the third of the bail decision alternatives, setting a bail amount for those defendants not granted ROR. Two research paradigms were used: simulation and naturalistic observation of actual courtroom proceedings.

In the simulation design, eighteen San Diego County judges were used as subjects. They were seen separately in their chambers and presented with eight fictitious case summaries, which were designed to simulate information typically available in bail hearings. All cases described a young male who had been charged with robbery and who had entered a plea of "not guilty." Imbedded in the case summaries were four factors assumed to be influential in bail setting decisions: (1) prior criminal record of the defendant; (2) local ties in the community (length of time in the community, marital status, number of children, and employment status); (3) defense attorney's bail recommendation; and (4) prosecutor's bail recommendation. The judges were asked to recommend bail in dollar amounts in each case.

The simulation results showed that judges set higher amounts for bail when there were longer prior records, weaker local ties, and stronger recommendations from prosecuting attorneys. Local ties emerged as the strongest variable associated with bail amount. That is, persons with weak local ties were significantly more likely to be tagged with higher bail amounts before being allowed back into the community. Not surprisingly, there was no relationship between the defense attorney's recommendation and the judge's bail decision.

Unfortunately, these results cannot be compared to the Goldkamp and Gottfredson data because the seriousness of the crime was held constant (robbery). Moreover, in the jurisdiction studied in the Goldkamp-Gottfredson project, neither the probation department nor the prosecutor's office made bail recommendations as a matter of court policy. However, the results reported by Ebbesen and Konečni are reasonably consistent with reports by other researchers regarding factors that apparently play an important role in bail decisions.

Next, Ebbesen and Konečni had assistants unobtrusively observe and record the actual courtroom bail setting behavior of five of the eighteen judges who had been subjects in the simulation. In this natural observation design, neither prior record nor the local ties were related to the bail amounts. Instead, it was discovered that judges relied heavily on the recommendation of the two attorneys in making their bail decisions, most particularly those of the prosecuting attorney. Severity of the crime played only a minor role. Interestingly, many defendants with strong local ties had to post higher bails than defendants charged with similar crimes but having weak local ties.

The facts that severity of crime, prior record, and local ties played relatively minor roles in determining the judges' bail decisions were highly inconsistent with previous findings and commentary. What judges say they do does not jibe with what they actually do in the courtroom.

Also, the finding that strong local ties proved detrimental to many defendants flies in the face of "rationality justification," which is grounded on the notion of flight prevention. Logically, we would expect that weak local ties would be more likely to precipitate high bail amounts, since the fundamental rationale is to keep the defendant around until time of the trial. In addition, to predicate judicial decisions primarily on the recommendation of the prosecutor rather than the deliberate wisdom of the judge hardly fulfills the theme of equity. And, in relation to visibility, it appears that explicit policy is based on prior criminal record, local ties, and severity of current crime; implicit policy is rooted in the recommendations of the prosecuting attorney.

## ■ Sentencing

In most jurisdictions, a sentencing judge has wide discretionary powers in selecting the type and duration of a sentence, with no clear guidelines or rules to follow. The sentence in both the state and federal court systems may cross fine lines between minimum or maximum amounts, a period of probation, a suspended sentence, any period of imprisonment up to the statutory maximum for that offense, or some combination of the above. Wide latitude in sentencing is a built-in mechanism for allowing defendants to be treated according to the specific characteristics of their offense, but this latitude also results in inexplicable disparities in what judges prescribe for persons in highly similar circumstances.

It should be mentioned that sentencing is not the sole prerogative of the judge in all jurisdictions. In more than a dozen states, sentencing for certain noncapital offenses is performed by juries.

Three major forms of sentencing are traditionally found in the criminal courts— the definite, the indefinite, and the indeterminate sentence (Kaplan, 1973). In *definite sentencing*, which is also called determinate, flat time, fixed, or presumptive sentencing, a specified length of time for incarceration is dictated. An *indeterminate sentence* is a term with neither minimum nor maximum limits, such as from one day to life or "at the pleasure of the government." Actually, it is no sentence at all since it simply turns the guilty person over to the care of prison officials. An *indefinite sentence* has a fixed maximum and, usually, a fixed minimum (e.g., five to twenty years).

## SENTENCING DISPARITIES

Much of the research on sentencing has been directed at what appear to be the inexplicable disparities between the sentences imposed on defendants in similar circumstances and for similar offenses. In one district, a person may be placed on probation for passing bad checks, while in another district a person may receive ten years imprisonment for the very same violation.

Judges typically do not have the time (or interest) to consider all of the surrounding circumstances and special characteristics of a defendant prior to sentencing (Cole, 1975). This is especially true with respect to minor criminal violations, where the judge routinely pronounces a sentence for crimes within given classifications of offenses. Minor offenses are often dispatched immediately after a plea of guilty, with no evidence that judges have considered extenuating circumstances.

Sentencing disparities occur both among different judges (interjudge disparity) and within the individual judge, who may be inconsistent in sentencing for similar offenses (intrajudge disparity). Interjudge disparity may be a result of differences in practices in jurisdictions, statutes and local precedents, community and administrative pressures, or differing perceptions and interpretations. Intrajudge disparity is probably more a result of the judge's social values and personal interpretations of the causes and prevention of criminal action, or what he or she believes the goals of social sanctions to be.

It is unnecessary for us to canvass the numerous positions and several studies on sentencing disparity, because from a psychological perspective we are more interested in discovering how judges arrive at their decisions. It will be instructive at this point to examine a series of studies by Konečni and Ebbesen (1979) designed to uncover factors playing crucial roles in the sentencing decision. The Konečni-Ebbesen data will provide an important conceptual framework to use in discussing the remaining material in this section.

## FACTORS IN THE SENTENCING DECISION

The Konečni and Ebbesen project used six different data collection methods, all designed to discover relevant factors in sentencing. These differences in methodology yielded the most heuristic finding of the study.

In the interview method (also called the journalistic approach), eight San Diego Superior Court judges were interviewed by teams of students and asked which variables they felt influenced their sentencing decisions. The researchers noted that much of the public's knowledge about the criminal justice system is arrived at through this method, since interviewing is by far the most common information-gathering device used by the media. Conclusions from the interview method were that (1) there were many factors involved in the sentencing decisions; (2) decisions were highly complex; and (3) every case was different. The judges told their interviewers that each case was evaluated uniquely according to the nature of the offense and the background and status of the defendant. After a myriad of crucial elements were carefully weighed, they said, a decision was handed down. This "ideal" sentencing procedure is probably what the public expects of its judiciary.

The questionnaire or "sociological" approach was a second research method used. Superior Court justices again served as subjects, but this time sentencing behavior was measured by a structured questionnaire, distributed to and completed by sixteen judges. The questionnaire listed twenty-five factors presumably considered by the sentencing judge, including the defendant's age, sex, religion, family status, race, political views, military record, education, economic situation, prior criminal record, severity of the current crime, and whether a weapon was used in connection with the offense. The judges were asked to rank the importance of each factor. Almost all the judges weighted heavily at least four different variables: (1) severity of the current crime; (2) prior criminal history; (3) family situation; and (4) employment status. The judges did not feel that the recommendations of the defense or prosecuting attorneys or of the probation department played a major role in their decisions.

In a third study, eight judges were asked to rate eight presentence factors and place them on a continuum of importance, from 0 (totally unimportant) to 10 (extremely important). Results showed that severity of current crime, prior criminal record, and family situation were rated as most important. These data corroborated the questionnaire data, but in contrast to the questionnaire study, the defendant's employment status was now rated as totally unimportant.

As part of this third study, questionnaires and rating scales were also administered to thirty-three San Diego defense attorneys who had an average of seven years' experience in criminal law and who had handled numerous felony cases. The attorneys' ratings were similar to those provided by the judges in only two factors—severity of crime and prior criminal record. The lawyers believed these two factors were the most important determinants in making sentencing decisions. However, the third and fourth most important factors from the defense attorneys' perspective were the race and income of the defendant.

The fourth study of the Konečni and Ebbesen project involved simulation. Twelve judges and twenty-two probation officers were given brief descriptions of fictitious felony cases which differed on important factors about the defendant. Judges were asked to impose one of three sentences: (1) prison; (2) probation with time in custody; or (3) straight probation. Probation officers were also asked to make a sentence recommendation, choosing among the same three options given the judges.

The judges imposed harsher sentences on defendants who had committed more severe crimes, had more extensive criminal records, had received a harsher recommendation from the probation department, and who had been convicted through a trial process (as opposed to pleading guilty). Family or job situation of the defendant were not considered important. A further analysis of the data revealed that judges' decisions were influenced primarily by only two factors—severity of the crime and prior criminal record.

The recommendations of the probation officers were most affected by the defendant's prior criminal record, followed by the severity of the crime, family and job situation, and "remorse" variables, which refer to defendant expressions of regret for having committed the offense. Whether the individual pleaded guilty or went through the trial process did not enter into the probation officers' recommendations.

A fifth study employed the natural observation research technique. Four hundred actual sentencing hearings were observed between 1976 and 1977. (It was noted that these hearings seldom lasted more than five minutes.) Prior to the hearings, researchers developed an elaborate coding system for the relevant variables to be observed; this was to assure sophistication in the statistical analyses to be carried out following the observations.

Results of this study were discouraging, since no factors emerged as statistically significant. The researchers lamented (pp. 58–59),

> One could presumably spend many years sitting around courtrooms and coding the sentence hearings without being able to isolate any strong predictors of the sentences imposed. . . . when all these facts are coupled with the speed with which the sentencing hearings are carried out, the mumbled sentences and the incoherent speech of the participants, and the general clamor that characterizes courtrooms (in sharp contrast to the air of dignified silence that the public typically associates with them) . . . these "public hearings" . . . are, for all practical purposes, merely a smoke screen for the actual decision-making process.

The sixth and final study of the Ebbesen-Konečni project involved archival analysis of court files, a procedure requiring scrutiny of court documents in over 1,000 cases. Despite extensive coding of the numerous factors which the researchers thought might be important, very few emerged as possible predictors of the sentencing process. Only four factors proved to have a significant relationship with the sentence given: (1) type of crime; (2) the extent of the defendant's prior criminal record; (3) the bail decision; and (4) the probation officer's sentence recommendation. Following a careful analysis of all the data, the probation officer's recommendation emerged as the most powerful predictor of sentencing.

This finding suggests that the factors of severity of crime and prior criminal record periodically emerged in the previous studies because the probation officer's recommendation usually considers those factors. In other words, the judge may rely heavily on the recommendation of the probation officer because it is assumed that severity of crime and previous criminal record have been taken into account. Therefore, when judges say they take these factors into account, it is because they obtain the material from their primary source of information about these factors, the probation officer's report.

The results of these six studies demonstrate convincingly that discovering what factors play a significant or crucial part in judge decisionmaking is highly dependent upon the research method used. No two methods by Konečni and Ebbesen produced identical results in relation to type, number, and importance of various factors in the decisionmaking of judges. Factors which were found important in one study often were found less important in another. For example, what judges tell us they look for and what behaviors are noted in the courtroom may not accurately reflect what actually transpires. If the researchers had been content to gather information only from interviews, questionnaires, or rating scales, they would have concluded with conviction that severity of crime and criminal history are the most crucial components in the decisionmaking process of judges. Other methods and research designs, however, revealed other factors of equal or even greater importance, such as the probation officer's report.

The time-consuming, mundane task of sifting through court files may be an extremely valuable method of studying judicial decisionmaking, judging by the above data. The archival method taps the official, written record of what happened, and in this sense measures real-world legal decisions. Also, the written court record contains a large array of variables and potential predictors usually not available through other methods. Moreover, archival researchers are unobtrusive; their presence does not interfere with the legal process or generate a "front" from legal participants wanting to be on their best behavior. Finally, the written case materials follow defendants throughout their careers in the criminal justice system and consequently may serve as a valuable source of information prior to each actual sentence.

As noted earlier in this book, humans are limited processors of information, and they continually try to simplify memory content. Despite the popular belief that clinicians are highly complex decisionmakers, for example, actually they use very little information in making their assessments. Additionally, biases, values, and learning experiences strongly sway their diagnoses and treatment plans. The legal decisionmaking process is also often believed to be complex, an assumption judges clearly encourage. "Most experts, legal judges or otherwise, feel that their decisions are byzantine inferential masterpieces" (Saks & Hastie, 1978, p. 33). The journalistic interview portion of the Ebbesen-Konečni project confirmed this. In practice, however, even though human behavior is complex, human decisionmakers rely on pathetically little information and simplified cognitive templates. In the following sections we will look more closely at the legal decisionmakers who wield so much power in the judicial system.

# ■ Judges

Judges are the central actors of the judicial system, with extensive indirect and direct power over all agencies within the system. Their robes, honorable title, restricted and discreet interpersonal contact, the high level of the courtroom bench, and the expected societal respect they receive all attest to and reinforce their lofty status and power.

In 1975 there were 5,640 general jurisdiction judges in the fifty states and the District of Columbia (Committee on the Judiciary, 1977; Law Enforcement Assistance Administration, 1979a). There were also 339 full-time judges assigned to courts of last resort (state Supreme Courts) and 442 to intermediate appellate courts. In 1977 there were 397 authorized active federal district judges (Committee on the Judiciary, 1977). Selection procedures for state judges vary from state to state; some states elect judges, while in others judges are appointed by the governor, and in still others a merit selection procedure is used. A federal judgeship is a lifetime presidential appointment, which must be confirmed by the U.S. Senate.

Judges are fundamentally political creatures whose position is often due to involvement in local, state, or national politics. In a survey of 306 state supreme court justices, Glick and Vines (1973) reported that they had attained their positions only after years of activity and occupancy of a variety of political offices. As a group, state judges had held two or more offices at state or national levels before gaining their judgeships. More than half had held judicial posts, such as state's attorney, local district attorney, or state attorney general. Only about a half of the newly selected judges had had any prior courtroom experience; even those with such experience had little background in criminal cases (President's Commission, 1967). The Glick-Vines survey also revealed that about ten percent of the state supreme court judges did not have law degrees.

Many writers have commented upon the conservative orientation of judges. John Kaplan (1973, p. 486) observes that "viewed as a group, the people who enter upon service as trial judges are somewhat elderly, more experienced than most lawyers in litigation, almost totally unencumbered by learning or experience relevant to sentencing, and inclined by temperament and circumstance toward the major orthodoxies." Stuart Nagel (1969) administered a modified version of the Eysenck Liberalism Questionnaire to 118 state and federal supreme court justices and found a significant trend toward an association with the interests of the upper or dominant groups in society. Resistance to long-run social change was also evident. Judges who scored high in conservatism showed a history of siding with the prosecution in criminal cases, with business concerns in business regulation cases, with the party being sued (generally an insurance company) in motor vehicle accident cases, and with employers in workmen's compensation cases.

There is little doubt that the decisional and policymaking activity of judges is related to certain features of their social background, educational experiences, and past political affiliation. Conservatism in legal matters is taught by law schools and is strongly reinforced by colleagues and in legal practice. Increasing age may also be an element in the conservative orientation, as most judges are appointed or elected at an advanced age.

Research data on the relationship between personality features and decisionmaking styles are scant. Many judges remain unflattered when social and behavioral scientists express interest in their personal backgrounds, personalities, cognitive processing, and decisionmaking or judicial style. Furthermore, the traditional aloofness often expected of those serving on the bench reinforces this reluctance to talk about themselves.

Earlier in this text we noted that behavior is a result of a reciprocal interaction between situational and individual or personality factors. A compelling argument could be advanced that judges play a role largely dictated by legal socialization. They have acquired experiences that affect and crystallize their image of what justice should be. The legal socialization of a judge encompasses all the heroes or role models he or she tries to emulate and the constant feedback received from playing that role. The interjudge and intrajudge disparities so often cited in the literature may be a result of judges' individual perceptions of their judicial roles. Judges are to a great extent political actors affected by personal, political, and judicial-system forces.

## ■ Summary and Conclusions

This chapter has tried to integrate data from the psychological laboratory into the realities of lawyering. This task is not an easy one, as almost none of the indirectly relevant psychological research has examined the legal process, and therefore any fit between lawyering and the data represents only an approximation. We have hypothesized, for example, that the aspiration-level theory of negotiation is relevant to civil disputes, whereas legal negotiation within the criminal court is more likely to follow a reciprocity-bargaining orientation. We have touched upon the psychology of persuasion and its value in the courtroom, noting that interest in the topic has waned in recent years. Also, as with other issues in lawyering, psychologists involved in persuasion research have not expressed much interest in its application or relevance to legal proceedings.

We have also made leaps in logic in speculating that the adversarial process is more likely to promote a greater sense of justice within the participants than it is to bring truth into proceedings. Finally, we have followed closely the work of Konečni and Ebbesen as it relates to legal decisionmaking to illustrate how various research methods influence the final results. The primary intention here was to encourage skepticism and a critical style of thinking on the part of students of psychology and law, and to underscore the need to evaluate carefully the methodology on which far-reaching conclusions are based.

Perhaps more than any other, this chapter has stressed that psycholegal research and theory is a young, uncharted area with promise of exciting possibilities. The real danger lies in the tendency of a few psychologists to promote "truths" on the basis of studies conducted in the artificial setting of the laboratory and to sell the wares to the wary discipline of law.

In a recent article, Konečni and Ebbesen (1981) note that a very large proportion of all psycholegal research falls into only three categories—jury decisions, eyewitness identification and testimony, and legal procedural issues concerning the adversarial process. Of these three, jury decisionmaking leads in its degree of visibility and in the number of studies it includes. Approximately 90 percent of the research in the three categories has been conducted in artificial laboratory settings, rendering the utility of the findings questionable. While we strongly advocate a psychology *and* law relationship, it is important to realize that psychology's equity will be advanced only by careful consideration of the reality of the legal process and the development of a body of research data with a good probability of meaningful, direct application. Cautious, skeptical attitudes should be cultivated at all times.

Caution and skepticism are important not only because of the dangers of selling faulty goods to the legal system, but also because the realities of lawyering demand this approach. The legal system and its participants can be perceived as a social network where rules and policies only provide very broad guidelines and limits for action. Professional relationships, often difficult to detect and measure, informal agreements, and discretion provide the lubrication for the legal machinery. Psychology must be sensitive to these undercurrents, and its researchers must develop ingenious methods to study them. Only then will psychology reach equity with law in the psycholegal realm.

# ■ Key Concepts and Principles, Chapter 9

| | |
|---|---|
| Plea bargaining | Reciprocity hypothesis |
| Overcharging | Independent hypothesis |
| Implicit plea bargaining | Integrative bargaining |
| Aspiration-level hypothesis | Heuristic trial-and-error tactics |

Distributive tactics
Information-exchange tactic
Cognitive complexity
Legal language
Plain English Movement
Five styles of English
Inquisitional and adversary processes
Machiavellianism

Bail decisionmaking
Definite, indeterminate, and indefinite
    sentencing
Journalistic method
Sociological approach
Scale method
Natural observational research
Archival research

# 10

# The Psychology of Criminal Behavior

☐ Criminology, the multidisciplinary study of crime, can be psychological, sociological, anthropological, political, psychiatric, or even economic in emphasis. To a large extent, however, it has been dominated over the years by sociology. Sociological criminology traditionally has emphasized the effects on crime of social-group and such situational variables as age, race, sex, interpersonal relationships, and social class. For example, sociological criminology provides us with data on the age, race, sex, and socioeconomic trends of various offender groups. This approach has allowed us to draw such conclusions as the one that homicide is committed disproportionally by young black males from the low socioeconomic class. The sociological approach also probes the social conditions that are most conducive to criminal action—the time, place, and circumstances surrounding crime or even the kinds of weapons used. Homicides, for instance, often occur after considerable alcohol has been ingested by either the offender or the victim; the weapon most often used is a firearm; and in most cases, the offender and victim have known one another, frequently as relatives or friends.

Psychological criminology is often confused with psychiatric criminology, which has dominated the individual perspective of the study of crime. The psychological perspective views criminal behavior in ways that are drastically different from the mainstream psychiatric position, however. Psychiatric criminology is steeped in the Freudian-psychoanalytic-psychodynamic tradition. It subscribes to the theory that overt behavior represents symbolic distortions of underlying unconscious structures which make up the personality (e.g., Sadoff, 1975; MacDonald, 1976; Abrahamsen, 1960). Psychiatric criminology, also called forensic psychiatry, holds that criminal behavior springs from unconscious urges and conflicts. Moreover, in accordance with the medical model, the criminal is believed to be mentally ill or sick, and hence in need of treatment.

This is a necessary oversimplification of the diverse positions found in forensic psychiatry. Not all psychiatrists believe that criminals are emotionally sick, nor do all contend that criminal behavior is a package of disguised symbols of underlying unconscious or even preconscious processes. We are using the term *psychiatric criminology* to label the view that criminals are sick and driven by unconscious processes or urges. Some psychologists and many forensic psychiatrists subscribe to this theoretical stance, which has had a powerful influence on the individual perspective of criminology since psychiatrist Isaac Ray first propounded it. Psychiatric criminology continues to exert considerable influence on criminology and criminal justice today, although its persuasive power is diminishing.

Psychiatric criminology has developed on the basis of clinical experience, observation, and anecdotal data. It places its clinical material within the framework of the medical model, diagnosing illness and treating the cause. Criminals, as a group, must be psycho-treated as individuals to alleviate their conflicts and purge their unconscious urges. Some therapists believe that the criminal's superego must be strengthened and helped to gain mastery over the selfish properties of the id.

In identifying problems and explaining criminal behavior, the psychiatric criminologist has a notable tendency to rely on post hoc explanations of unconscious motivations, which are typically cloaked in terminology that is difficult for both the lay person and the professional to understand. Concepts used are frequently abstract, refer to intangible "dynamic forces," and require equally abstract, complicated, philosophical, and vague interpretation.

Psychological criminology, by contrast, also focuses upon the individual as a subject of study, but it emphasizes the social context of behavior as well. Where the psychiatric perspective uses clinical data (procedural evidence) for the development of criminal theories, the psychological viewpoint relies heavily on empirical investigations and laboratory experiments (validating evidence). The price paid for the reliance on validating evidence is that it becomes impossible to offer all-encompassing theories of criminality or empirically sound proposals for the eradication of crime. Science requires patience and a high tolerance for conflicting, contradictory data which can be subjected to multiple interpretations. Scientific knowledge is gained slowly, and there are no glib answers or easy solutions, even when they are so often demanded by political and societal forces.

Nevertheless, psychiatric criminology often has brazenly claimed to have answers and has dictated what needs to be done, and to a much lesser extent, so have psychology and sociology. One solution for the reduction of crime is to offer treatment for individual disorders; situational forces and social environment play a minor role in the psychiatric scheme. The sociological perspective, however, strongly disagrees with this position. Often, persons holding this view assert that the environment plays the major role in the development and provocation of criminal behavior (e.g., Gibbons, 1977). Changes in the system and in society as a whole are of paramount importance in reducing criminal behavior, and individual factors play a minor role.

Psychological criminology lies somewhere between these two polar regions of an individual-situational continuum: It stresses the reciprocal interaction of individual and situational factors. Reciprocal interaction refers to the continual process of the person influencing the situation and the situation influencing the person. Thus, victims of homicides or aggravated assaults sometimes play a crucial part in their own misfortune.

It should be stressed that sociologists, criminologists, psychiatrists, and psychologists fall along various points of the individual-situation continuum. Not all psychiatrists subscribe to the position that individual behavior and individual factors are the only things to consider (e.g., Halleck, 1967), nor do all psychologists belong to the reciprocal-interaction group. It can be stated, however, that when representatives of these professional groups study criminal behavior, they are likely to cluster at opposite regions of the proposed continuum.

Psychological criminology is the science of determining how criminal behavior is acquired, evoked, maintained, and modified. It assumes that various criminal behaviors are acquired by daily living experiences, in accordance with the principles of learning, and are perceived, processed, and stored in memory in a unique fashion for each individual. Criminal behaviors depend upon how each individual perceives and interprets a situation and upon what he or she expects to gain by acting in a certain way. An analysis of a given criminal behavior requires inquiry into the perpetrator's experiential history and expectancies and into how these interact with the situation and the social environment. Before continuing further with this topic, however, it is necessary to define criminal behavior.

## ■ Defining Crime

Crime is commonly defined as "an intentional act in violation of the criminal law (statutory and case law) committed without defense or excuse, and penalized by the state as a felony or misdemeanor" (Tappan, 1947, p. 100). Criminal behavior, therefore, refers to the broad span of behavior which violates the criminal code. This expansive definition does not suit our purposes, because it is not specific enough. If we abided strictly by Tappan's definition, we could refer to most of the U.S. population as, in some sense, "criminal." Have you, the reader, never engaged in some action that could be regarded as criminal according to the above definition? Have you ever committed a behavior that could justifiably be considered a felony and carry with it a possible jail sentence? Illegal drug usage certainly qualifies. Theft or damage (vandalism) over a certain amount ($50 in many jurisdictions) also qualifies as felonious conduct. Driving while intoxicated is another example of behavior in violation of criminal codes.

In a dated but relevant self-report survey of criminal conduct (Wallerstein & Wyle, 1947), approximately 1,700 persons were asked to indicate on a list of forty-nine criminal offenses which, if any, they had committed. The list excluded traffic violations but included both felonies and misdemeanors. Fully 91 percent of the respondents admitted they had committed one or more offenses for which they might have received jail or prison sentences.

Therefore, unless we plan to include a conservative 90 percent of the population in our criminal sample, we should give our definition more specific limits. Other proposed definitions may be just as troublesome, however. For example, for research purposes a criminal is typically defined as one who has been detected, arrested, and legally convicted. However, legal determinations are dependent upon what society, at some point in time, considers socially harmful or, in some cases, morally wrong. Societies differ in their criteria for criminal behavior; states differ; and the same society or the same state, over time, may change the criminal code and its perceptions of what constitutes illegal or criminal conduct.

Restricting ourselves to convicted persons to help us define crime is also troublesome because of the discriminatory practices of each culture. Each judicial system perceives and processes violators of the criminal code with some discrimination, so that offender background, social status, personality, motivation, age, sex, race, and even the offender's choice of lawyer may affect the judicial process along with the circumstances surrounding the crime itself. Accepting this legal definition, therefore, would mean that our definition of criminal behavior would be contaminated with the biases and discriminatory practices inherent in the system.

Defining criminal behavior, therefore, is no easy task, and precise, operational definitions often fail to include all possible violations or relevant behavior. Since almost all the available data on crime are based on arrest or conviction records, the chapter's research content will be directed at this population. The theoretical discussion will be expanded to include criminal behavior, broadly defined as any behavior that violates prevailing codes of conduct and for which penalties or fines may be imposed.

## ■ Crime Statistics

Official crime statistics kept by law enforcement agencies, such as those found in the annual FBI *Uniform Crime Reports*, are strongly influenced by the social, moral, and political climate at the time they are reported. Generally, however, the official law enforcement reports underestimate the total actual crimes committed—a total known as the "dark figure."

In recent years, victimization surveys have shed further light on crime statistics. Based on representative sampling of households, these surveys provide information about the victim's experiences with crimes, both those which were reported to the police and those which were not. Information obtained from victims yields data about the details of the criminal events, the circumstances under which they occurred, and the effect of the crimes on the victim. The surveys tap crimes that for a variety of reasons were never reported to police and therefore provide information as to why certain criminal acts go unreported.

According to the National Crime Survey (NCS) program (LEAA, 1979c), the surveys have proved most useful in estimating crimes against victims who understand what happened to them, how it happened, and are willing to report what they know. The surveys have yielded particularly valuable data on rape, robbery, assault, burglary, personal and household larceny, and motor vehicle theft. Murder and kidnaping are not covered, because these serious criminal offenses are almost always reported to the authorities. Also, they occur so infrequently that statistics are not worth compiling. The so-called victimless crimes, such as drunkenness, drug abuse, and prostitution, also are normally excluded from victimization surveys.

In order to provide the reader with some knowledge about the frequency and nature of criminal offenses, we will focus our attention on the NCS conducted in 1977 (LEAA, 1979c). The information gathered for this survey was derived from interviews with approximately 136,000 occupants of some 60,000 housing units, which were statistically selected and which represented all fifty states and the District of Columbia. The survey received a high degree of cooperation, with 96 percent of the housing units responding.

By treating this project in some detail, we will provide the reader with definitions of the variety of possible crimes as well as the conventional classification schemes for criminal behavior. Furthermore, the National Crime Survey is a good example of the information that can be gained through methodologically solid field surveys. Finally, the program gives a good estimate of the various crimes in American society that cannot be compiled through traditional record-keeping by the nation's police agencies.

## NCS PROCEDURES

In the NCS project, each interviewer's first contact with a housing unit was in person; if it was not possible to have interviews with all eligible members of the household during this initial visit, interviews by telephone were permissible thereafter. Although a series of interviews was conducted with each subject, the primary purpose of the initial interview was to "bound," or to establish a time frame to avoid duplicative recording of data on subsequent interviews. This procedure was designed to correct for the potential flaws in the memories of criminal events by the victims. More specifically, it was assumed that crime victims often have a tendency to recount incidents occurring outside (usually before) the designated time frame to be covered by the survey.

Subjects were interviewed once every six months over a period of three years, and subjects who for a variety of reasons left the housing units were replaced by other subjects on a rotating basis until they were interviewed over a three-year interval. This field survey divided crimes into two major divisions: (1) crimes against persons; and (2) crimes against households. Crimes against persons were further subdivided into (1) personal crimes of violence (rape, personal robbery, and assault) and (2) personal crimes of theft.

The most serious crime against persons was rape, defined as carnal knowledge through the use of force or the threat of force, regardless of whether the act was completed or attempted. Statutory rape (sexual relations with a minor female) without force was excluded. Personal robbery was defined as the taking of an object or property from a person by force or the threat of force. The force used may be a weapon (armed robbery) or physical power (strong-arm robbery). Personal assaults referred to those incidents where the objective was to do physical harm to the victim, and they were classified as aggravated or simple. An aggravated assault was one carried out with a weapon, regardless of the degree of injury, if any. An assault carried out without the use of a weapon, but where serious injury occurred, also qualified as aggravated assault. Simple assault occurred when the injury, if any, was minor and no weapon was used.

Personal crimes of theft (larceny) might or might not bring the victim into direct contact with the offender. Personal larceny with contact included purse snatching, attempted purse snatching, and pocket picking, all done without force or threat of force. Personal larceny without contact involved the stealing of cash or property anywhere outside the home or immediate surroundings. For example, the theft of a raincoat from a restaurant, a portable radio from a beach, a bicycle from the playground, or an automobile from a parking lot would all be classified as personal larceny without contact.

The second major division involved crimes against households. The three crimes included in this category—burglary, household larceny, and motor vehicle theft—do not involve direct contact with the offender. A personal confrontation qualified as a personal crime rather than a household crime. Burglary in this project referred to the illegal or attempted entry of a structure with the apparent purpose of committing a crime, usually theft. Entry might be by force, such as breaking a window or a lock, or it might be through an unlocked door or open window. In addition, the act need not have been directed only at the home structure to qualify as burglary; it also may have been illegal entry into a garage, shed, or any other structure on the premises.

Household larceny referred to acts where cash or property was removed from the home or immediate vicinity without personal confrontation. Theft of motor vehicles as a specialized form of household larceny is self-explanatory.

## NCS RESULTS

From the results of the NCS, it is estimated that 40.3 million victimizations occurred in this country during 1977. The personal crimes of violence (rape, personal robbery, and assault) accounted for 15 percent of this total. Personal and household larceny accounted for 65 percent of the total and, therefore, it was by far the most frequent criminal activity reported. The remaining 20 percent of the crimes included motor vehicle thefts and household burglaries.

An index usually employed to gauge the incidence of specific crimes in relation to the general population (age 12 and over) is the victimization rate, expressed by the number of victimizations per 1,000 potential victims. In relation to personal crimes, this index is expressed per 1,000 potential individuals, whereas for household crimes it is expressed per 1,000 households. The data collected by NCS are extensive, and we will consider only the highlights, especially those characteristics relating to violent personal crimes. The interested reader is encouraged to examine the original source for additional information.

The personal crimes of violence statistic was highest against males, the young (ages 16–19), blacks, Hispanics, the divorced or separated, the poor, and the unemployed. Household crimes were more difficult to characterize. Blacks were more likely to be victims of household burglary or motor vehicle theft, but there were no differences between blacks and whites for household larceny. The poor were the most likely victims of burglary, but the least likely victims of household larceny or motor vehicle theft.

During the five years the NCS project has analyzed victimization data, males have been far more likely to be victims of personal robbery (8.7 per 1,000) and assault (37.5) than females (4.0 and 16.9, respectively). With regard to crimes of personal larceny, the sex differences also were slightly in favor of males (107.9 versus 87.5 per 1,000).

Rape affected between one and two women for every 1,000. The most likely woman to be raped was one who was separated or divorced (2.8 per 1,000), followed by victims who never were married (1.7), those married (0.3), and those widowed (0.6). The age group most frequently raped was 16–19 (5.3); the least frequently raped was 50–64 (0.1). Of the three violent personal crimes, rape was most likely to have happened inside victims' homes. Furthermore, approximately as many rapes occurred inside or near victims' residences as in outdoor areas away from their dwellings.

For personal crimes of violence and personal crimes of theft, NCS discovered that the age bracket 12–14 sustained the highest victimization rates, and the elderly (ages 65 and over) had the lowest. Actually, persons under age 25 had a violent crime rate three times higher than that for persons aged 25 and older, and the rate difference between these two age groups for crimes of theft was approximately 2 to 1. These characteristics were especially true for young males.

Minorities (blacks and Hispanics) reported the highest victimization rates when it came to violent crime. This finding has been reported consistently in sociological literature, especially as it pertains to blacks. For example, in his classic investigation of 588 homicides in Philadelphia between the years 1948 and 1952, Marvin Wolfgang (1958, 1961) found that about 73 percent of the offenders and 75 percent of the victims were black. In almost all the reported cases (about 94 percent), blacks killed blacks, or whites killed whites, indicating that violence is largely an intraracial affair. In a more recent study examining violent crimes in Chicago between 1965 and 1974, Richard Block (1977) found this intraracial relationship to be nearly identical to Wolfgang's data.

Stranger-to-stranger offenses comprised 63 percent of all personal crimes of violence, ranging from 59 percent for assaults to 75 percent for personal robberies. In terms of victimization rates, 21.4 per 1,000 victimizations were a result of stranger-to-stranger contact, compared to 12.6 per 1,000 victimizations being a result of contact with acquaintances, friends, or relatives. In addition, approximately one-half of all personal robberies were carried out by two or more offenders. Also, multiple offenders were more likely to engage in more serious assaults (aggravated assault) than in the less serious simple assaults.

The NCS found that the extent to which a crime was reported to the police depended on the type or seriousness of victimization, and there was a good deal of consistency in the reasons given by victims for not notifying the police. Altogether, only 30 percent of all personal crimes were reported, compared to 38 percent for household crimes. This implies that about two out of every three crimes go unreported. The highest report rate was associated with motor vehicle theft (88.6 percent), while the lowest was associated with household larcenies amounting to less than $50 (14.4 percent).

Among the violent crimes, slightly more than half of the rapes were reported

(58.4 percent) in 1977, and two-thirds of the robberies with injury were reported. Only about a quarter of the personal larcenies were reported, varying, of course, with the amount stolen.

The two most common reasons victims gave for not reporting crimes were (1) that nothing could have been done; and (2) that the offense was not important enough to warrant police attention. Inconvenience and fear of reprisal were rarely mentioned as reasons. It is important to note that both rape and assault victims were more likely than robbery victims to view their victimizations as a private or personal matter. This was especially true when the offender was an acquaintance, friend, or relative. Rape and assault appeared to represent a serious infringement upon the victim's self-esteem and general feelings of worth.

We will now turn to some psychological theories of criminal behavior. There are not very many, and the research has focused upon aggression and, to some extent, moral development. Later in the chapter, we return to a more data-based and statistical treatment of crime when we examine rape, both from a sociological and psychological perspective. At this point, let us begin with neurophysiological positions on criminal behavior.

## ■ Physiological-Genetic Influences on Crime

Psychological criminology is concerned with the person (personality) as he or she interacts with the environment. It is logical, therefore, to begin by examining the major dimensions of personality. Personality refers to a person's unique experiential history, which is a mélange of physiological and genetic properties interacting with cognitive processes. What follows is a brief presentation of the physiological-genetic variables that may be intimately involved in the development of criminal behavior.

American criminologists have been all too eager to bury any notion that neurophysiological or genetic factors play influential roles in the development of criminal behavior. Cesare Lombroso (1836–1909), an Italian physician and self-termed criminal anthropologist, is perhaps the best known classical advocate of the position that genetic-biological properties determine criminal behavior, at least in part. Lombroso believed that such behavior was an atavism, an evolutionary throwback to primitive and savage propensities of the human animal. In essence, he believed that criminals (later, he relented to say "some criminals") were genetically and evolutionarily retarded and were not in biological step with the evolutionary mainstream of modern man. Criminologists immediately attached the "born criminal" stigma to Lombroso's work and concluded derisively that his theory was simply misguided and basically foolish. Although the ghost of the Lombrosian theory occasionally haunts criminology texts, nearly all criminologists consider it exorcised. Any modern attempt to revitalize the concept of biological ingredients as influential factors in criminal behavior is quickly labeled "born-criminal theory" and dismissed.

Despite the American criminologist's strong bias against biological causation in favor of social causation, some researchers (mostly from other countries) have begun to accumulate data implicating neurophysiological and genetic factors in the development of criminal behavior. We will introduce this material briefly and classify it into three leading research areas: twin and adoption studies, Eysenck's theory of personality, and research on the psychopath.

## TWIN AND ADOPTION STUDIES

To determine what role genetics plays in criminality, some researchers have compared the incidence and types of crimes committed by identical and fraternal twins. Fraternal twins (also called dizygotic twins) develop from two different fertilized eggs and are no more genetically alike than ordinary siblings. Identical (monozygotic) twins develop from a single egg and, therefore, are always the same sex and share the same genes.

The twin paradigm assumes that the environment exerts different influences on each twin's growing-up process. Thus it can be argued that any strong similarities can be traced to the influence of genetics. This argument is especially powerful when twins have been raised apart from one another. The interested reader is referred to H.J. Eysenck's *Crime and Personality* (1977) and A. Mednick and K.O. Christiansen's *Biological Bases of Criminal Behavior* (1977) for elaborate discussions of these issues.

The concept of concordance is an important one in genetics. Concordance is the degree to which related pairs of subjects show a particular behavior or condition, and it is usually expressed in percentages. For example, suppose we wished to find the concordance of "intelligence" between twenty pairs of fraternal twins and twenty pairs of identical twins. Suppose further that "intelligence" was determined by scores on a given standarized test. Twins received similar scores when they were plus or minus five points within each other's score. Assume that we found ten pairs of identical twins obtaining similar scores and five pairs of fraternal twins obtaining similar scores. In this example, our concordance for identical twins would be 50 percent (ten out of twenty pairs); our concordance for fraternals would be 25 percent. Therefore, the concordance for identicals would be twice that for fraternals, suggesting that hereditary or genetic factors played an important role in intelligence.

Numerous twin studies using this concordance method have strongly indicated that heredity is a powerful determinant in intelligence, schizophrenia, depression, neuroses, and alcoholism (e.g., Claridge, 1973; Rosenthal, 1970, 1971; McClearn & DeFries, 1975; Hetherington & Parke, 1975; Eysenck, 1973, 1977). In relation to criminal behavior, the concordance rate for identical twins as reported in many studies (beginning in 1929) is nearly three times the concordance rate reported for fraternal twins (Bartol, 1980). If one twin is involved in criminal activity, and he or she is a member of an identical couplet, the probability that the other member of the pair is or will be engaged in criminal activity is nearly three times higher than it would be if the twins were fraternal. Of course, these results should be treated with caution and scientific scepticism, but they do suggest a possible hereditary link in criminal behavior.

In less convincing fashion, adoption studies have also uncovered genetic links to crime (e.g., Hutchings & Mednick, 1977). In the typical adoption paradigm, adopted children with biological parents possessing criminal convictions are discreetly followed and compared to adopted children whose parents were not criminal. Although these types of projects often have many methodological shortcomings in experimental design, their results imply that adopted children are more likely to engage in criminal behavior if their parents had criminal records.

Together, twin and adoption studies suggest that heredity is a component of behavior that should be reckoned with if we are trying to advance explanations of crime. To date, the research merely points to a relationship between crime and biology; it does not detail much beyond the reported statistical correlations. The next question becomes, how might heredity influence criminal behavior?

## THE EYSENCKIAN THEORY OF CRIMINALITY

Perhaps the best answer to the above question can be found in the theory and experimental work of the German-born British psychologist, Hans J. Eysenck. Eysenck (1977) has proposed an interactionist theory of criminality, where criminal behavior is the result of environmental conditions and inherited personality traits. He argues that we must explore the biological makeup and socialization history of the individual in order to develop a comprehensive and useful theory of criminality.

Eysenck does not suggest that individuals are born criminal in the Lombrosian tradition. Rather, he proposes that some individuals are born with nervous system characteristics that are significantly different from those of the general population and that affect their ability to acquire social expectations and rules. Armed with an impressive body of research support, Eysenck has conceptually isolated certain features of the central and peripheral systems to account for a substantial portion of the differences found in personality. He finds that particular functions in the reactivity, sensitivity, and excitability of these two subdivisions of the nervous system account not only for differences in behavior, but also for predispositions to antisocial behavior.

The most commonly used measurements to determine Eysenckian dimensions are self-report personality questionnaires developed by Hans and Sybil Eysenck. In addition, there are various physiological (e.g., sedation thresholds), perceptual (two-flicker thresholds), and behavioral measures which may be used. The reader should be aware that the self-report measures have revealed no major sex differences. Therefore, the personality traits mentioned below will refer to both male and female subjects.

Eysenck's personality dimensions also refer to "traits" which have been derived through statistical methods, most prominently through factor analysis. Remember, traits are clusters of behavioral patterns describing individuals typically. They do not represent distinct categories requiring each member of each category to possess all of its defining features.

Eysenck rests his theory of criminality upon three concepts—cortical excitation, conditionability, and drive. Each of these will be explained in some detail below.

**Cortical excitation.** This concept refers to hypothesized properties of the cerebral cortex, that part of the brain responsible for many human cognitive functions such as memory, association, and thinking. The cerebral cortex is the central core of the central nervous system. Eysenck theorizes that everyone seeks an optimal level of cortical excitation, and this search for a just-right level in part explains human behavior. Furthermore, cortical excitation is a function of the amount of stimulation input we receive from our environment.

According to Eysenck, some of us find that our cortical arousal level is too high (e.g., too much noise or commotion), and we avoid environmental stimulation by taking time away from others, reading a book by the fireplace, or taking a nap. Other persons are often at a low level of cortical arousal and they actively seek excitement from the environment by frequenting loud parties or places of amusement or by seeking thrills and excitement. Most of the population falls somewhere between needing constant avoidance and constant seeking of stimulation.

Eysenck labels these behavioral patterns along a continuum called extraversion-introversion. Stimulation seekers who are frequently cortically underaroused are labeled—for research convenience—extraverts; stimulation avoiders who are frequently cortically overaroused are called introverts. The majority of the population, falling between these two polar regions, are called ambiverts.

Why are there individual differences in cortical excitation or arousal? The explanation rests ultimately with the functioning of a complicated neurological structure located within the brain stem and known as the reticular activating system (RAS). The hypothesized properties of the RAS are believed to be inherited. This means that part of everyday behavior can be traced back to the inherited neurophysiological substrata of the central nervous system, most particularly the RAS.

Eysenck posits that criminal behavior is partly determined by two properties of the RAS and the functioning of the nervous system. First, those individuals who are chronic stimulation or excitement seekers are more apt to run afoul of the law. That is, they are more likely to be impulsive, out looking for a good time, and involved in risk-taking behaviors. In essence, they are trying to increase their cortical arousal to the optimal level. This aspect is the first of the three major concepts of criminality outlined by Eysenck.

**Conditionability.** Second, and related to Eysenck's second major concept in his theory of criminality, extraverts condition less readily than either introverts or ambiverts (Eysenck, 1967). Conditioning is one of the three primary processes of learning as proposed by learning researchers. The other two are instrumental or operant learning and cognitive social learning, which will be elaborated upon later in this chapter.

The reader with a background in introductory psychology will recall the Russian physiologist Ivan Pavlov and his famous experiments with dogs that learned to salivate at the sound of a bell. Pavlov discovered that pairing a naturally neutral stimulus (in this case a bell) with a significant stimulus (for example, food), would result in the dogs' eventually learning to associate the sound of the bell with food. The response which indicates that the association has been acquired is the dog's salivation, a response normally associated with food and not with bells. The process of learning to respond to a formerly neutral stimulus (bell) which has been paired with another stimulus that already elicits a response (salivation) is known as *classical* or *Pavlovian conditioning* (Bourne & Ekstrand, 1976). In the classical example, when the dog begins to salivate to the bell even when food is not forthcoming, classical conditioning has been established. It should be emphasized that conditioning is basically a descriptive term for learning through paired experiences; it is not an explanation of how learning takes place.

Introverts, and to a lesser extent ambiverts, condition more easily than extraverts. Eysenck (1977) presents a compelling argument, well grounded in the research literature on conditioning, that the fundamental reason why more people do not engage in criminal activity has to do with individual differences in conditionability. Through the long and sometimes tumultuous process of childhood socialization, people generally acquire, in an uneven way, the *association* between "bad" or inappropriate conduct and some form of punishment. Pavlov was able to condition his dogs to connect bells with punishment. That is, when a bell was closely followed by an aversive stimulus, such as an electrical shock to the left front paw, the dog quickly learned to associate the bell with pain and began lifting its paw to the sound of the bell, even if the electrical shock did not always follow the bell. Eysenck contends that the socialization process that discourages antisocial conduct operates essentially in the same manner. The child who immediately receives a handslap for inappropriate behavior will eventually associate that particular behavior with aversive events (contiguity without reinforcement). Therefore, Eysenck believes that conscience, pangs of guilt, and even the superego are all results of classical conditioning.

Since extraverts condition less readily than introverts or ambiverts, they are less likely to develop the constantly haunting conscience or to fear the consequences of antisocial or illegal behavior. Extraverts, therefore, would be more likely to be involved in criminal actions, not only because of their higher risk-taking and general neurophysiological needs for stimulation, but also because of their less developed conscience and their lack of concern for anticipated consequences of their actions.

**Drive.** Extensive psychological research has found that neurophysiological activity and reactivity "propel" the individual to demonstrate certain behaviors. Eysenck has called this cluster of behaviors "neuroticism" or "emotionality." He postulates that they spring from the reactivity and sensitivity of the peripheral nervous system, specifically the sympathetic subdivision of that nervous system. This is also an inherited characteristic of the human neurological mechanism.

Like extraversion-introversion, neuroticism is hypothesized to represent a continuum, with most persons falling at the midpoint. Individuals who demonstrate most of the characteristic behaviors of this trait are called, again for experimental purposes, "neurotics," while persons displaying few of the relevant behaviors are referred to as "stables." Persons exhibiting "neurotic" behaviors overreact to stress and take an unusually long time to recover from stressful events. In many ways, neuroticism is similar to the clinical concept "anxiety." However, anxiety has more surplus meanings than neuroticism; it also appears to encompass many of the same behaviors as extraversion-introversion.

Neuroticism functions like a drive, pushing an individual to perform existing habits or well-learned behaviors. Let us suppose a neurotic extravert has not been properly conditioned to avoid stealing. Because of its rewarding attributes in the acquisition of material goods (or social status), stealing becomes a well-learned habit, and neuroticism is likely to be the impelling force encouraging the individual to steal.

According to Eysenckian theory, therefore, a large percentage of criminal behavior is committed by persons who demonstrate extraverted behaviors and also are highly emotional (or driven).

This discussion has, of necessity, simplified a very complex theory of criminality. The many intricacies of Eysenck's position have not been examined. In order to maintain clarity in the presentation, we also have not described a fairly recent addition to the theory, the dimension of psychoticism. However, the essential details of Eysensk's theory have been presented, illustrating how a genetic component may enter into explanations of criminal behavior without drawing fire from the critics of "born criminality."

The research designed to test Eysenck's theory has disclosed mixed results (Passingham, 1972; Allsopp, 1976; Feldman, 1977). The trend is in support of some aspects of the theory; however, as a general explanation of criminality, the theory needs considerable refinement. For example, while the theory appears to hold for European whites convicted of property crimes, it does not hold for American blacks convicted of violent offenses (Bartol & Holanchock, 1979). Also, the theory is not sensitive enough to take into account the differences in motives and situational forces demonstrated by various offender groups. For example, individuals who commit a once-in-a-lifetime homicide have very different expectations and socialization processes from those who pursue a lifetime of lucrative burglaries.

Despite these problems, Eysenck's theory of criminality does offer the promising possibility of a generalized, testable theory of criminal behavior based on the interactions of biological factors and learning processes. Perhaps its major weakness lies in its heavy reliance upon conditioning as the primary learning process. Other forms of learning—like operant and observational learning—also appear to be interwoven in the development of antisocial or criminal behavior.

## THE PSYCHOPATH

The clinical or diagnostic group of individuals who offer the most promise as a support base for Eysenck's theory are the psychopaths. While it is always wise to be cautious in cataloging humans into neat diagnostic packages, the clinical entity called the psychopath does have some validity as a distinguishing behavioral pattern.

Psychopaths should not be confused with "sociopaths." In common usage, sociopath refers to a person who is continually socially deviant and repetitively in conflict with the law and who has no apparent capacity to learn from past experiences. The psychopath, on the other hand, may or may not demonstrate antisocial or criminal behavior. He or she does exhibit certain behavioral patterns that appear to have their basis in differences found in the functioning of the nervous system.

The characteristic behaviors of the psychopath are most ably described by Hervey Cleckley (1976) in a book, *The Mask of Sanity*. Two main features include superficial charm and average to above-average intelligence, both of which are especially apparent during initial contacts. Psychopaths appear friendly, sociable, outgoing, likeable, and alert. They often appear well-educated, knowledgeable, and interested in a wide variety of things.

Although some psychopaths may be involved in socially deviant behaviors, they generally do not exhibit behaviors that would qualify as clinical descriptors of neurosis or psychosis. Under even the most stressful conditions, the psychopath is likely to remain cool and calm, demonstrating few of the typical indicators of anxiety. He or she appears emotionally flat, with few mood swings, and displays few signs of a genuine sense of humor.

In many ways, the psychopath is unreliable, irresponsible, and unpredictable, regardless of the importance of the occasion or the consequences of impulsive actions. This pattern is cyclical, however. For extended periods, the psychopath may appear responsible and may have outstanding achievements. Then, without warning, the psychopath will do something that jeopardizes his or her status. For example, the psychopath may open a window and scream obscenities at the crowd below a third-floor executive suite, go on a drunken spree, steal a car, or drive off into the sunset. Because of this cyclic pattern, psychopaths rarely pursue consistent, successful criminal careers. Rather, they are more likely to participate in capers or hastily planned crimes for immediate satisfaction.

Other typical behaviors include extreme selfishness and inability to love or give affection to others. They are unable to learn from past mistakes and become vulgar, domineering, loud and boisterous under the influence of alcohol. The cardinal trait of the psychopath appears to be an unusually high need for stimulation. Most of their behavior seems to be a result of attempts to satisfy their insatiable requirement for excitement and stimulus input. In this way, they are very similar to the extremely extraverted individuals described by Eysenck.

People who display a large percentage of the behaviors described above also show neurophysiological functions that generally reflect underarousal (Hare & Schalling, 1978). Extensive research investigation has reported notable differences in peripheral and central nervous system functioning between individuals who fit the behavioral description of the psychopath and those who do not (e.g., Hare, 1970; Lykken, 1957, 1978; Hare & Schalling, 1978; Bartol, 1980). Although additional research is needed, the data do suggest that neurophysiological factors may predispose certain individuals toward antisocial or criminal behavior.

It is important that we underscore the predisposition factor. Whether a person neurophysiologically predisposed ultimately engages in criminal behavior depends upon the person's learning history, cognitive expectancies, and the situation at hand. Theoretically, if the person has learned to meet needs for excitement and stimulation in ways that run counter to society's rules, and if socialization (conditioning) has done little to generate anxiety when codes are violated, then antisocial behavior is likely to result.

## ■ Psychosocial Factors of Criminal Behavior

As mentioned earlier, one of the weaknesses of Eysenck's theory of criminality is his failure to account for possible effects of operant or instrumental learning and observational learning, relying instead almost exclusively on classical conditioning. Behavior that enables us to obtain rewards or avoid punishing circumstances is likely to be repeated when similar conditions recur. The rewards may be physical (e.g., money, material goods), psychological (e.g., feelings of control over one's life), or social (e.g., improved status). Even behaviors that are considered antisocial or criminal may bring rewards that are worth the psychological risks and costs.

In psychological parlance, rewards are termed *reinforcements*. The acquisition of positive items is called positive reinforcement; the successful avoidance of negative or aversive events is called negative reinforcement. Avoiding a painfully boring meeting by malingering provides negative reinforcement and is likely to be repeated if the ploy is successful.

The concept we have been referring to is instrumental learning, a process which offers the most easily grasped explanation of criminality. People who commit crimes are seeking to gain or avoid something. A person may wish to terminate a nagging or abusive spouse (negative reinforcement) or may hunger for the cash deposits at the local liquor store. The reinforcements may seem fairly straightforward, but they also can be deceptively complex. Some antisocial behavior may be directed at gaining the social approval of a significant subgroup, or the psychological feeling of personal control over one's plight, and it may be independent of the obvious material gain promised by the successful completion of the crime. Or the behavior may be intended to gain some mélange of all three reinforcements.

If the eventual reinforcement makes the investment worthwhile, the behavior is likely to be repeated. Therefore, criminal behavior will continue to be practiced if it is materially, socially, or psychologically lucrative. But this is only part of the story, since the establishment of criminal action can also occur under observational learning, or more broadly, cognitive-social learning.

## COGNITIVE-SOCIAL LEARNING THEORY

Julian Rotter (1954, 1966, 1972) is a major contributor to cognitive social learning theory because of his emphasis on the cognitive, mediating aspects of human learning. Cognition refers to structures and processes within the brain which make up mental activity, including thinking, planning, deciding, wishing, organizing, reconciling, and mental transformation. Cognitive psychology, the study of the above processes, is the dominant force in academic psychology today.

Cognitive psychology emphasizes the internal, "mind" representations of the external world. Generally, it contends that behavior is a function of the subjective world as transformed and represented by the person's mind. That is, people behave in accordance with their subjective thoughts and interpretations about the world rather than in reaction to how the outside world objectively or "really" is.

The traditional learning theories of classical conditioning and instrumental learning fail to take into careful consideration what goes on between the time the organism perceives a stimulus and responds or reacts to that stimulus. Cognitive-social learning posits that this classical view is too simple and too general to allow complete understanding of human behavior.

**Expectations.** Rotter stresses the importance of the individual's cognitive expectations about the consequences of behavior and the rewards that will be gained from the behavior. In other words, before responding to a given set of circumstances, an individual evaluates: "What has happened to me before in this situation, and what will I gain if I do this?" This self-questioning process may occur very rapidly or may take place with much deliberation. According to Rotter, the probability of a specific behavior occurring depends upon the individual's expectancies regarding the outcomes of the behavior and the subjectively perceived gain that will result. Therefore, behavior is a function of the person's relevant expectancies, acquired from past experiences, and the perceived importance of the rewards gained by the behavior. Over the long haul of daily living, the person will develop "generalized expectancies" which tend to be stable and consistent across relatively similar circumstances (Mischel, 1976).

**Modeling.**  With reference to criminal action, we can posit that the individual expects or anticipates the action to be effective in the acquisition of status, power, affection, material goods, or generally positive living conditions. The specific behavior chosen (and its concomitant expectancies) need not have been directly reinforced previously, however. An individual may obtain the cognitive imagery of a particular behavior simply by observing another person perform the action. This is known as *observational learning* or *modeling* (Bandura, 1973). Consider, for example, the use of a gun. Although many individuals have never directly fired a gun, almost everyone knows how to do so. Although there are technical aspects of the firearm which may cause difficulty, like the safety catch and loading mechanisms, the overall general behavioral pattern is familiar to most: point the barrel and pull the trigger.

Albert Bandura (1973) postulates that much of our behavior is acquired initially by watching others, who are known as models. Moreover, the more significant and meaningful these models are to us, the greater the likelihood that the observed behavior will be imitated. Models may be parents, teachers, siblings, friends, peers, and even symbolic figures like television or film characters or the protagonist in a favorite novel.

The observed behavior may be copied immediately or at a future time deemed most appropriate by the observer. Once tried, its continuance depends substantially upon its consequences. If the new behavior delivers gain or reinforcement, it will probably be used again. Therefore, although initial cognitive representation may be gained through observation, its maintenance usually depends upon the nature of its reinforcement return.

Although we have outlined cognitive-social learning theory in relatively simple terms, it would be a mistake to assume that the observer simply mimics the behavior of the model. The observer also notes if, how, and when the model is rewarded, disregarded, or punished. Adults in particular also evaluate the consequences in relation to their own position and capacities. Hence, the observer assesses self-evaluative components as well as external outcomes. "People do not indiscriminately absorb the influences that impinge upon them" (Bandura, 1974, p. 862). They evaluate and consider, and once they have decided to behave a certain way, they expect something.

Criminal behavior is intended to gain something that is subjectively useful or meaningful to the acting person. In this sense, criminal behavior may be perceived as *subjectively adaptive* rather than simply deviant or emotionally sick. It may be antisocial or deviant in reference to society's rules and values, but for that particular person, at that particular time, in the particular psychological state, the conduct is perceived as the best choice possible.

Thus far, we have discussed neurophysiological predispositions to conditioning, instrumental learning, and cognitive-social learning as psychological factors that help explain crime. The reader may be wondering at this point, "Which is the culprit?" Criminal behavior appears to be due to a varying composite of all of these factors. People who engage in crime, however defined, do so for a variety of subjective reasons stemming from their learning history, their neurophysiological predispositions, and their cognitive styles and competencies. Therefore, antisocial or criminal behavior can best be regarded as subjectively adaptive, even if socially deviant, behavior.

## RECIPROCAL DETERMINISM

Thus far, however, we have also emphasized the individual and neglected the situation. Cognitive-social learning theory tries to accommodate both personal (or dispositional) and situational factors. It analyzes behavior in relation to reciprocal interaction or determinism (Bandura, 1974, 1977). "Determinism" in this context signifies "the production of effects by events, rather than in the doctrinal sense that actions are completely determined by a prior sequence of causes independent of the individual" (Bandura, 1978, p. 345). Reciprocal determinism refers to the hypothesis that behavior is influenced by the environment, but also that the environment is partly of a person's own making. By their own actions people create their social milieu; the social milieu, in turn, affects their actions. Therefore, from a cognitive-social learning perspective, criminal behavior is a result of a continuous reciprocal interaction between behavioral, cognitive, and environmental influences.

Reciprocal determinism needs further elaboration before the reader can obtain a clear understanding of the interaction between person and environment. According to Bandura (1978), "interaction" has been used in three fundamentally different ways— unidirectional, partially bidirectional, and reciprocal interaction.

In unidirectional interaction, the person and the situation are conceptualized as independent entities that combine to produce behavior. The person finds himself or herself faced with a set of circumstances, remembers previous, similar circumstances, and responds accordingly. Therefore, neither the person nor the situation affect one another.

In the partially bidirectional conception, the person and the situation are considered interdependent causes of behavior. The person's behavior influences the situation, and the situation in turn influences the behavior in reciprocal fashion.

What is missing from both of the above interpretations is cognition, an element which Bandura's third type of interaction—reciprocal determinism—takes into account. In psychological functioning, cognitions influence both behavior and the situation, and these, in turn, influence cognitions.

**Deindividuation.** Any complete understanding of criminal behavior from a psychological perspective requires an analysis of the reciprocal interaction which occurs. A vivid illustration can be found in the literature on deindividuation, a process whereby a group can activate behaviors, including antisocial and brutal ones, in individuals not normally so inclined (Festinger, Pepitone & Newcomb, 1952). Crowd violence, looting, vandalism, gang rapes, and crowd panic are all examples of this phenomenon.

Deindividuation is dependent upon an interplay between each individual's perceptions of himself or herself (cognitions), his or her behavior (individual behavior), and the actions of the crowd (situation). The process usually follows a sequence. First, the presence of many other persons prompts one to begin to feel part of a group, or at least personally diffused in the group, so that he or she cannot be singled out or easily identified. In this phase, the behavior of others influences a person's cognitions and self-awareness, and the person's behavior in turn begins to influence the actions of others in the group, in reciprocal fashion. During the second phase, the behavior of the group is imitated, usually cautiously and tentatively. Once begun, the antisocial or violent behavior is found rewarding and pleasurable, bringing physiological arousal into play. The behavior is providing the cognitive component of the triad with feedback, and the cognitive component in turn interacts with the behavioral component, "urging it on." Meanwhile, of course, the person is still receiving and providing behavior and cognitive cues (attitudes and values about the behavior) from and to the crowd.

In the third and final deindividuation phase, the behavior of the individuals and the collective crowd reaches a crescendo of violence, brutality, and destruction. All three components are involved in reciprocal interaction. Once the group action has reached this stage, very little can be done to terminate it until there is a change in the state of the group (e.g., people become fatigued or injured), a change in the state of victims (e.g., they lose consciousness or die), or a change in the weapons used (e.g., bullets are expended). Because the crowd has reached the final stage of deindividuation, and because individuals are melded into the group, appeals to reason are unlikely to be effective. In these situations, police have sometimes used the method of photographing the crowd or confiscating identification papers. Realizing that they are to be singled out, individuals are led to disperse. This method is especially effective when the group action was unplanned.

**Escalation.** Escalation is another psychological process which illustrates triadic reciprocal determinism. Here, one offended or humiliated person resorts to salvaging self-esteem by "going one better" and insulting his or her humiliator. Thus, two people become caught up in an escalating conflict, since exchanges of barbs will continue until one person decides to stop or must stop. Verbal insults become pushes, pushes become punches, and ultimately, lethal weapons may be used. However, during each step of the escalation, each individual is continually appraising the conflict, the other person's behavior, the situation, his or her own behavior, the antecedents, and the consequences. In the beginning of the scenario, neither party may have wished for the final outcome. The nature of the conflict, the context, and the cognitive appraisals of the actors at each progressive step determined the ultimate action. Many homicides and aggravated assaults follow this escalating pattern.

## PREDICTION

Since person-situation reciprocity indicates that the factors involved in crime are dynamic, ever-changing, and complex, can we make predictions about the likelihood of anyone engaging in criminal behavior? Can we talk about criminal "personalities" with any degree of confidence? Cognitive-social learning theory certainly casts doubt upon the validity of the long-standing search for the personality of the murderer, the rapist, the skyjacker, or the child abuser. However, examining a particular individual's response pattern under certain conditions allows some predictive power. Past behavior is perhaps one of the best predictors of future behavior we have available. A repeat offender who has engaged in a string of burglaries is predictable to some degree. But any predictive equation will have to examine the individual's competencies, expectancies, and other relevant behavioral patterns, as well as the specific conditions which activate the behavior or burglary. Even after careful study, the predictive equation will likely result in only a rough estimation of behavioral occurrence within a certain time frame.

The concepts of cross-situational and temporal consistency should also help in any analysis of criminal behavior. As the reader will recall, cross-situational consistency refers to the degree to which behaviors or traits generalize from one situation to another dissimilar situation. Temporal consistency refers to the degree to which behaviors are consistent over time, in similar situations. Research has found that individuals in general reflect greater temporal consistency than cross-situational consistency. Therefore, criminal behavior that has been reinforced in a particular context is more apt to recur in a similar context than across a wide variety of situations. Thus, a person who has engaged in a lifetime of burglary is more likely to burglarize again if surrounded by familiar situations. On the other hand, if his or her environment has changed substantially (e.g., long-time partner in crime has died; person is now living in Lubec, Maine, instead of Boston, Massachusetts), it is less likely that the criminal activity will continue.

Psychologists have often remarked that their discipline helps them to predict some of the people some of the time (Bem & Allen, 1974). Actually, we can be more optimistic and say that we should be able to predict most people's behavior much of the time if we apply the principles this chapter covers (Kenrick & Stringfield, 1980).

It is also important to take note of a recent "discovery" several psychologists have brought to light (Kenrick & Stringfield, 1980; Mischel, 1973, 1976). A valuable resource in helping psychologists improve their predictive power is the information people provide about themselves. The best clues to understanding people are the traits and behaviors they say they have, and people are surprisingly willing to reveal such information. Rather than dismiss such reports because they are self-serving, psychologists are listening more carefully and applying these comments to their evaluations. A person who admits he is often hostile, loses his temper, and feels like physically abusing others, and who has a history of assault convictions, would probably merit careful monitoring. On the other hand, without these self-reported behaviors, the predictive power is less convincing.

In sum, full appreciation of criminal behavior requires analysis of the triadic reciprocal system, the situation, and the "personality" (expectancies, learning history, competencies, subjective values, cognitive structures, and the self-regulatory systems and plans). We make no pretense that this is a simple task. It is often more appealing to advance dogmatic, simplified generalizations that are more manageable cognitively than to tackle the immense problem of understanding, predicting and changing criminal behavior.

# ■ Aggression

Psychology, especially social psychology, has made its most sizeable contribution to the understanding of criminal behavior in the area of aggression. The historical line of inquiry and theory on aggressive behavior can be traced from the earlier instinctive-biological perspectives to the more contemporary learning position, most notably cognitive-social learning theory (Bandura, 1973; Baron, 1977; Johnson, 1972; Goldstein, 1975). Within the context of our present knowledge, the experimental data dictate that the cognitive-social learning theory best accounts for the development and maintenance of human aggression and offers the most promising leads for its reduction. The interested reader is referred to any of the excellent books cited above.

Statistics invariably show that the United States is the most violent of the stable, democratic countries in the world (e.g., Goldstein, 1975). Violence in America appears to be increasing at a rate faster than the rate of population growth. Part of this violence can be attributed to the predominance of aggressive models in our society, models found not only in the entertainment media but also within the numerous subcultures of the various socioeconomic classes. Violence is found most notably, but certainly not exclusively, within the lower socioeconomic class, where aggressive behavior has been traditionally used as a way to gain rewards and avoid aversive circumstances and feelings of powerlessness. Aggressive behavior also is acquired, activated, and maintained, like all other behavior, through the other forms of learning outlined earlier in the chapter. Therefore, it is not only aggressive models that contribute to violence; the extent of violence in American society indicates that violence is also rewarding for a sizeable segment of our population.

Although the cognitive-social learning theory appears to account best for most of the research findings on aggression, considerable revision of that theory will be required as additional data are obtained. This, of course, is true of all testable theories. In fact, there is a good possibility that social learning theory will be replaced by a more attractive theory in the future. Its greatest threat at this point is the possibility that a lack of interest on the part of researchers will lead to its demise. The theory is becoming highly complicated, and this complexity may discourage further research. The triadic reciprocal system described above suggests that behavior is not regulated only by the reciprocal influence of antecedent and consequent acts (original social learning approach), but that behaving persons are also cognitively appraising the progression of events. The task of predicting behavior, therefore, necessitates analyzing each person's unique triadic system under specified conditions. Until we have an alternative proposal that does not merely categorize individuals or make unwarranted generalizations, cognitive-social learning will remain the wisest path to follow.

# ■ Mental Illness and Crime

It is a common misconception that some crimes, particularly heinous, violent acts such as brutal and "senseless" slayings, are almost always committed by person who are mentally ill. That misconception, perpetuated by the news and entertainment media and generally accepted by the judicial system, has become ingrained into

American society to the point that the "crazy" person is feared and often confined for society's protection. There is little doubt that there are some mean and vicious people who do some extremely cruel things to others. This does not mean, however, that they are emotionally disturbed in the clinical or psychological sense. They certainly may be described as deviant in a societal or cultural sense, and their acts may defy common understanding. But to label these individuals mentally ill is incorrect and it does an injustice to those persons who do have clinically defined psychological problems.

We do not mean to imply that emotionally or mentally disordered individuals never commit heinous, brutal crimes. Bizarre crimes have been committed by mentally disordered persons. Overall, however, there is no evidence that "crazy" persons are any more likely to engage in criminal behavior than the general population (Lunde, 1976; Brodsky, 1972, 1977b; Henn et al., 1976; Gulevick & Bourne, 1970).

Fritz Henn and his colleagues (1976) conducted an extensive investigation of defendants referred for psychiatric or psychological assessment by the state courts in St. Louis over a period of years. The researchers found that crazy people (psychotics) were no more likely to be represented in criminal activity than "normal" people. For example, of the nearly 2,000 persons arrested for homicide between 1964 and 1973, only about one percent qualified as crazy (or psychotic). Comparable data have also been reported by Häfner and Böker (1973) in Germany and by Zitrin et al. (1975) and Rappeport and Lassen (1965) in the United States.

In another sample of 1,195 defendants accused of a variety of criminal offenses, Henn found that the most frequent psychiatric diagnosis was "personality disorder." It accounted for nearly forty percent of all the diagnoses provided by clinical teams. Two-thirds of those categorized "personality disorder" were specified as "antisocial personality." A sizeable number of the defendants were also diagnosed "alcoholic" or "drug addicted," which under the psychiatric classification scheme being used at the time (DSM-II) qualified as personality disorders.

"Personality disorders" are not what a vast majority of clinicians or the general population consider "crazy behavior," however. "Troublesome behavior," perhaps— troublesome toward family and society—but not "crazy." People with personality disorders do not characteristically demonstrate hallucinations, delusions, or extensive or even minor loss of contact with reality. The psychopath, for example, is likely to be classified as a personality disorder.

Moreover, the diagnostic label "personality disorder—antisocial type" is conceptually circular. People are diagnosed "antisocial" because they were, in fact, antisocial toward society; they are antisocial toward society (criminal) because they are plagued by an antisocial personality disorder. The major problem with this circularity is that the judicial system and society in general quickly associate "crazy" with a psychiatric diagnosis of any kind.

It is interesting to note that ninety-three percent of those defendants referred to a psychiatric clinic in the St. Louis projects were diagnosed something. This probably reflects, in part, the biases of the court interlocking with the apparent obligation of the evaluation team to tag onto the defendant a diagnosis of some sort. The courts apparently perceive that anyone committing certain crimes under certain conditions must be mentally disordered. Clinicians often possess the same prejudices. For a lack of a definitive mental disorder, clinicians glady embrace "antisocial personality disorder," since the individual has acted in a deviant, antisocial manner.

In summary, the research literature fails to support the widespread and enduring myth that crazy people are killers or are involved disproportionately in criminal activity. Part of this myth is fueled and maintained by the traditional medical model which pervades the judicial system and asserts that criminal behavior is "sick" and "crazy" behavior originating from disordered and primitive motivations. The myth is also partly maintained by the lack of understanding of criminal behavior and of why individuals engage in crime. Failure to comprehend the cognitive, behavioral, and situational interplay involved generally leads to oversimplification. "If I cannot identify the reason why he committed the crime, the guy must be sick or crazy; I can't understand it; he must be nuts."

Criminal behavior occurs because the actor expects some gain or change from a current predicament. The behavior might be directed at gaining stimulation and excitement (e.g., in the case of the psychopath) or at acquiring personal control over the perpetrator's life (e.g., some skyjackings and apparently motiveless offenses). Even criminal behavior engaged in by mentally disordered persons involves some expectancies. The paranoid schizophrenic might wish to terminate imagined tormentors. The list of possible motives continues indefinitely. The depressed mother may kill her infant so he will not suffer the psychological pain and distress she perceives as inevitable. The robber not only obtains immediate material gain but also may elicit praise from peers. The point is that criminal behavior is learned behavior with personal intent. We should not be too eager to ascribe crazy behavior to what we perceive as motiveless actions.

## ■ Forcible Rape

There would be little value in attempting to examine each type of criminal offense at this time, since only cursory treatment would be possible. Instead, we will focus upon one offense, examine the statistics, and consider the psychological theory and research surrounding it. Rape is chosen because it is permeated with misconceptions and myths, it engenders considerable statutory reform and legal attention, and it has drawn a fair amount of psychological research directed at both the offender and the victim. Also, rape is an offense that is particularly sensitive to the moral, social, and political climate of a society, and therefore there are some interesting trends reported in law enforcement statistics in comparison to victimization studies. Overall, the study of forcible rape exemplifies many of the points we have stressed concerning the interface between psychology and law.

According to the FBI *Uniform Crime Reports*, forcible rape is "the carnal knowledge of a female, forcibly and against her will" and includes rape by force, assault to rape, and attempted rape. *Forcible* rape is to be contrasted with *statutory* rape, where the age of the female is the crucial distinction, regardless of whether she gives her consent to engage in sexual intercourse. The age limit appears to be an arbitrary legal cutoff considered to be the age at which the person has the cognitive and emotional maturity to give her meaningful consent and understand the consequences. Although age limits vary from state to state, most cutoff points are age sixteen or eighteen. Therefore, if it can be determined to the satisfaction of the court that an adult male has engaged in sexual relations with a female who was under the legal age at the time, he can be convicted of statutory rape. *Rape by fraud* refers to the act of having sexual relations with a consenting adult female under fraudulent conditions, such as when a physician or psychotherapist has sexual intercourse with a patient under the guise of effective treatment. The legal scope of forcible rape is typically confined to imposed sexual contact or assault of adolescent and adult females who are not related to the offender. Thus, most legal definitions exclude rape of a wife by her husband, despite strong opposition by proponents of new legislation (LEAA, 1978a).

The *Uniform Crime Reports—1979* (Webster, 1980) finds that approximately 76,000 rapes were reported that year, an increase of about 12 percent over the 1978 figures when adjusted for the growth of the U.S. population. The statistic 76,000 would result in a victimization rate of .67 per 1,000 females. In the earlier part of this chapter, we saw that the NCS reported a victimization rate of between one and two per 1,000 females, suggesting that one out of every two or three forcible rapes is reported to authorities.

Between 1975 and 1979, reported rapes increased 31 percent, but this figure is misleading. Victimization studies conducted by NCS have not found significant increases in rape offenses. Rather, the victimization rate has consistently hovered between 1.5 and 2.0 per 1,000 during the 1970s. Increases in FBI statistics imply, therefore, that in recent years there may be less victim resistance to report the crime than in previous years. This observation is supported by the NCS finding that victims have reported increasing numbers of rapes to the police since 1973.

The figures reported in the *Uniform Crime Reports* (UCR) are influenced by a variety of factors. For example, many police agencies and jurisdictions do not follow the UCR instructions and often have their own classification systems. In an extensive survey done by LEAA (1977a), most law enforcement agencies reported that evidence of vaginal penetration was the minimum requirement for an alleged offense to qualify as rape. In addition, over one-half of these agencies required, as a minimum, evidence of both penetration and force; another one-third required additional evidence of either a weapon or resistance by the victim or both. As might be expected, the number of rapes reported to those police agencies requiring more evidence was significantly less than the number reported to agencies with less stringent requirements.

Prosecutors were generally more demanding about minimum requirements than the law enforcement agencies. A majority of the 150 prosecutors polled indicated that minimum requirements for filing a complaint of forcible rape were (1) evidence of penetration, (2) lack of victim consent, (3) threat of force, and (4) female sex of the victim (adult male victims were considered high legal risks for successful prosecution). The survey revealed that these requirements did not necessarily reflect legal statutes or guidelines. Rather, they were indicative of the prosecutor's own personal judgments about what elements were necessary before a successful prosecution could result. It is interesting to note that a vast majority of the prosecutors believed that there has been a dramatic increase in rape in recent years, and that this increase reflects a "general pattern of increased violence" in the United States—even though the victimization statistics do not bear this out. Some prosecutors also felt the increase was due to a change in the public attitudes toward rape, as well as the heightened "sensitivity" of the criminal justice system.

## THE VICTIM: SOCIOLOGICAL CORRELATES

According to the NCS, victims reported offenders used weapons in nearly one-third of all rape incidents; this was especially true when the offender was a stranger. The most commonly used weapon was a knife (45.6 percent), followed by a firearm (34.8 percent). The remainder was classified as "other." Victims who reported the rapes stated that in over two-thirds of the incidents, the offender threatened or used force against them. About one-fourth of the victims sustained injury serious enough to warrant medical treatment or hospitalization (LEAA, 1979c). Treatment or hospitalization is subject to varying interpretations. The NCS found that 27 percent of the rape victims sustained injury serious enough to incur expenses in excess of $250. Another 60 percent required medical expenses ranging from $50 to $249, suggesting that physical injury of some sort is extremely common for rape victims.

It appears that a majority of women resist the sexual assault, either through verbal or physical means or both (LEAA, 1978b). Initial resistance was usually verbal, and it fell into one of three strategies. In the first, the victim would try to make herself unattractive to the assailant, indicating she was pregnant, sick, diseased, virginal, or menstruating. A second strategy consisted of threats that the victim would report the incident to authorities or seek retaliation with the help of family or friends if the assailant continued. A third type of verbal resistance was to feign consent, with the stipulation that the victim be given the opportunity to use a rest room, change clothes, or call a friend. Overall, however, verbal resistance alone was an ineffective method for thwarting sexual assaults. Crying was also an ineffective method.

The survey revealed that the most effective method of thwarting a sexual assault was by screaming or using some noise device, such as a whistle, to attract attention. In some cases, however, this form of resistance could cause some offenders to become more violent, as we will see below. Physical resistance—struggling, biting, hitting, scratching, kicking—seldom terminated the attack, although some victims were able to escape by using these tactics. In general, however, the evidence suggests a direct relationship between physical resistance and physical injury sustained by the victim.

## THE VICTIM: LEGAL CONSIDERATIONS

The rape victim is frequently twice victimized—by the sexual assailant and by exposure to the judicial process (Borgida, 1980). Rape cases require thorough investigation and attention to detail, which demand keen recall and the description of intimate, stressful sexual events. Victims are also required to undergo a medical examination to establish physical evidence of penetration and use of physical force.

If the victim is able to withstand these stressful conditions, which are often exacerbated by negative reactions from parents, husband, and friends, and sometimes by threats from the assailant, the next step requires the preparation and successful prosecution of the case in court. Ninety-two percent of the prosecutors surveyed by LEAA

(1977b) asserted that the credibility of the victim was one of the most important elements in convincing juries to convict for forcible rape. Therefore, the defense often has concentrated upon the victim's prior sexual history to destroy credibility and to portray her as a demirep.

The procedure of derogating the victim by using her sexual history has come under attack in recent years, and a number of states have revised their evidentiary rules in an effort to limit this tactic. Most states (approximately forty) have enacted "rape shield" reform statutes which restrict, to varying degrees, the admissibility of the victim's sexual history into the courtroom (Borgida, 1980).

In addition to impeaching the victim's credibility via sexual history, some defense attorneys can invoke corroboration rules, which require evidence other than the victim's testimony before a person can be charged with rape. In recent years, many states have relaxed the type of evidence required to corroborate the victim's testimony, while others have abolished the requirement altogether.

A third practice peculiar to rape law is the judge's cautionary instructions to the jury, which stress that a rape charge can be easily levied by a woman and is often difficult to prove. Therefore, the jury is told that the victim's testimony should be viewed with caution.

All three of the above practices center on the credibility of the victim and exist in varying degrees in different jurisdictions. In addition, and closely aligned to victim credibility, the degree of victim consent must be established in deciding what level of guilt, if any, is to be ascribed to the defendant. These determinations of credibility and degree of consent of the victim are among the peculiar aspects of rape law in comparison to other criminal laws.

Eugene Borgida and his colleagues (1980) tested the validity of rape reforms in relation to juror interpretations of two elements: the amount of consent given, or implied, by the victim and the perceived guilt of the defendant. Borgida divided state rape laws into three categories, depending upon the amount of judge discretion allowed and the statutory restrictions on the admissibility of prior sexual activity.

Statutes permitting comparatively unlimited sexual history evidence, when offered on the issue of the victim's consent, were labeled *common law rules*. A second division consisted of the *moderate reform exclusionary rules*. State statutes in this category permitted a partial limitation on the admissibility of sexual history. While these moderate reform rules allowed trial judges considerable discretion in deciding whether sexual history evidence could be admitted, it was required that any history allowed be directly relevant to a fact at issue and that it did not induce unreasonable prejudicial effects on the jury. A third category, comprising the *radical reform exclusionary rules*, included statutes which required total exclusion of prior sexual activity when offered on the issue of consent. However, a qualifier is applied. The rules pertain only to sexual history involving third parties and not necessarily to the victim's past sexual conduct with the defendant. The primary purpose of the radical reform rules was to relieve the trial judge of discretionary power in decisions involving sexual behavior with third parties. The admissibility of evidence about sexual behavior with the defendant was left to the judge's discretion.

Borgida and his colleagues were interested in the effects of these three types of evidentiary rules on the amount of victim consent perceived by jurors. The overriding hypothesis was that the more extensive a woman's sexual history, the greater the like-lihood that jurors would believe she had given, or implied, her consent to sexual activity with the defendant. This would result in jurors finding the defendant innocent of forcible rape.

Over a three-month period, Borgida and his group administered questionnaires to 180 male and female jurors serving their last day of jury duty in a state district court. The questionnaires included the condensed case facts of a hypothetical rape trial involving a consent defense. The jurors were asked to render a personal verdict on the guilt or innocence of the defendant, as well as to rate the degree of victim consent (dependent variables).

The independent variables comprised a three-by-three experimental design. Since there were nine conditions in all, twenty jurors were assigned to each condition. The rape trial description given to each juror was governed either by the evidentiary rules found in common law, moderate reform, or radical reform categories. That is, de-pending upon the condition the juror was assigned to, he or she would receive consid-erable, partial, or no sexual history. In addition, again depending upon which condi-tion the subject was assigned to, each would read case material conveying a low probability of victim consent, an ambiguous probability, or a high probability of con-sent.

Borgida hypothesized that the jurors in the common law condition would be more likely to acquit the defendant than the jurors in the radical reform condition. Verdicts in the moderate reform condition were expected to be somewhat between. Presumably, the juror who learned the victim had a sexual history would be more likely to believe she gave her consent to the assault than the juror who had no such information. Borgida expected similar findings for those conditions where jurors were given high probability of victim consent compared to those given low probability. Raped women who gave some indication of consent brought the assault onto them-selves, the jurors were hypothesized to believe, and thus the defendant was less likely to be convicted.

Exclusionary rules were expected to interact with probability of consent condi-tions. High probability of consent interacting with common law (unlimited sexual history) would most likely lead to an acquittal for the defendant.

The results showed that under a radical reform rule the likelihood of conviction was increased. As expected, likelihood of conviction also increased when the proba-bility of the victim's consent was low. On the other hand, the lowest conviction rate was obtained under the common law rule when the case description conveyed high probability of consent. Under the moderate reform rule, however, the results were not quite so clear-cut. Overall, the moderate reform rule elicited the same conviction rate as the common law rule. More specifically, in both the common law and moderate reform conditions, twenty jurors found the defendant guilty and forty found him not guilty. Under the radical reform rule (no sexual history) thirty-two jurors found the defendant guilty and twenty-eight found him not guilty.

The above patterns exist only when we do not take into account the probability of consent, however. Under low probability of consent, jurors in the moderate reform condition were no more likely to find the defendant guilty than jurors in the radical reform condition. The overall differences reported above existed for both moderate and common law rules compared to radical reform, but only under high and ambiguous probability of consent conditions.

The second dependent measure—degree of perceived victim consent—proved to be more straightforward. There were no significant differences in the juror's perception of consent under common law and moderate reform rules. The major differences were found to be in relation to radical reform rules. Specifically, significantly less consent by the victim was believed to have taken place in the sexual assault when jurors did not receive prior sexual history of the victim.

Altogether, these simulation-based results suggest that third-party evidence of the victim's sexual history will have a prejudicial effect on the outcome of a rape trial. Jurors tend to be overly influenced by such evidence; they appear more willing to base their verdicts on judgments about the victim's past than on facts concerning the case in question. Furthermore, it also appears that the radical reform exclusionary rules will have the greatest impact in limiting this prejudicial tendency.

## THE RAPIST: SOCIOLOGICAL CORRELATES

Fewer than 5 percent of rape complaints are ultimately disposed of as forcible rape convictions (LEAA, 1978b). Therefore, over 95 percent of the potential offenders are never arrested, never charged, or never convicted of rape, and thus they are not the subjects of research on sexual assaults. Whether the small sample of offenders covered by the conviction statistics is representative of all rapists is debatable. The convicted are more likely to be the powerless, or at least the less powerful members of society.

Statistics continually show that arrested and convicted (LEAA, 1978b) and "victim-estimated" (LEAA, 1979) offenders are young. Most are between the ages of 18 and 25. In addition, minority males are consistently overrepresented in the arrested and convicted offender population. Victims in the NCS studies reported that 40 percent of the offenders were members of minority groups, figures which agree substantially with those of FBI *Uniform Crime Reports* for that year (1977).

Arrested and convicted offenders have frequently been in conflict with the law prior to the rape incident. About one-fourth of those arrested for forcible rape have raped previously, and about one-third have a prior arrest history of violent offenses other than rape (LEAA, 1977b).

One-half of the people arrested for rape apparently come from the blue-collar working class (about 50 percent) and another sizeable portion (approximately 30 percent) are unemployed (LEAA, 1977b). Few persons from the professional and other white-collar occupational fields are arrested for rape.

About two-thirds of the victims said their assailants were strangers. In addition, as mentioned earlier, strangers were much more likely to use weapons than nonstrangers. Eighty percent of the rapes were committed by a single assailant. In most instances (about 75 percent), the offender released the victim immediately after the assault. Some (22 percent) engaged the victim in a conversation for an hour or more after the assault, and the remainder drove the victim to a less accessible spot before letting her go.

One-third of a sample of convicted rapists said they would rape the same woman twice if given the opportunity (LEAA, 1978b). These assailants based their reasons for return on the following (in order of importance): victim responded well, they were invited back, a good relationship was established, they had a desire to humiliate the woman even more, and the woman agreed not to report the rape to the police.

When they were asked how a woman could best prevent a rape, the above sample of convicted assailants sounded like law enforcement officers. Women were advised by these assailants not to go out alone (32 percent), not to hitchhike (36 percent), to learn self-defense (16 percent), to buy a dog (8 percent), to carry weapons (6 percent), to dress conservatively (6 percent), and not to drink alone (2 percent). These suggestions, of course, represent gross impingements on the basic freedoms of women, and they imply that the victims brought the attacks upon themselves.

## THE RAPIST: PSYCHOLOGICAL CORRELATES

Several attempts have been made to classify rapists into groups. Such classification systems, either based on personality traits or behavioral patterns of individuals, are called typologies, and they have been moderately successful in their ability to add to our understanding of criminal behavior. A group of researchers at the Bridgewater Treatment Center in Bridgewater, Massachusetts (Cohen, Seghorn & Calmas, 1969; Cohen et al., 1971) developed a useful typology based on the behavioral patterns of convicted rapists, including the appearance of aggressive and sexual patterns in the sexual assaults.

One group of rapists demonstrated a predominance of violent and aggressive behaviors with a minimum or total absence of sexual feeling in their attacks. It appears that these men used the act of rape to harm, humiliate, and degrade women. The victims were brutally assaulted and subjected to sadistic acts such as biting, cutting, or tearing of breasts, genitals, or other parts of the body. In most instances, the victims were complete strangers and only served as the best available objects for the rapists' aggression. The assaults were not usually sexually arousing for the assailants, who often began to masturbate to become tumescent. From the information gained about these rapists' behavior during the assaults, it appears that physical resistance only made them more violent.

Although many of these rapists were married, their relationships with women were often characterized by periodic irritation and violence, and they probably qualified as wife abusers. These men generally perceived women as demanding, hostile, and unfaithful. They sometimes selected their victim because they perceived something in her behavior or appearance which communicated assertiveness, independence, and professional activity. The attacks typically followed some incident which had made them angry about women and their behavior.

The type of rapist described above is labeled the *displayed aggression* rapist, because the victim of the assault rarely has played any direct role in generating the violent attack. His occupational history is usually stable and often reveals some level of success. More often than not, his occupation is a "masculine" one, such as truck driver, carpenter, mechanic, or plumber.

A second group of offenders rape, or attempt to rape, because of an intense sexual arousal prompted by specific stimuli in the environment. Aggression and violence are not significant features in the attack, although victims certainly may perceive them to be. Rather, the fundamental motivation is the desire to prove sexual prowess and adequacy. Behaviorally, these men tend to be unusually passive, withdrawn, and lacking in social skills. They live in a world of fantasy oriented around themes of how victims will yield eagerly under attack, submit to pleasurable intercourse, and find their skill and performance so outstanding that the victims will plead for a return engagement. These rapists fantasize that they will at last be able to prove their masculinity and sexual competence.

Acquaintances often describe these men as quiet, shy, submissive, and lonely. Although they are dependable workers, their poor social skills and resulting low self-esteem prevent them from succeeding at occupational advancement. Because their sexual attacks are an effort to compensate for overwhelming feelings of inadequacy, these offenders are called *compensatory* rapists.

The victim of such a rapist is most often a stranger, but the rapist has probably watched and followed her for some time. Certain stimuli about her have drawn his attention and excited him. For instance, he may be attracted to wealthy college women who usually would pay him little attention. If the victim physically resists this offender he is likely to flee the scene. During the attack, there are few additional indicators of violence. Moreover, this sexually excited passive assailant will often ejaculate spontaneously, even upon mere physical contact with the victim. Generally, he confines his illegal activity to sexual assault and is not involved in other forms of antisocial behavior.

A third type of offender exhibits both sexual and aggressive elements in his assault. Victim pain is a prerequisite for sexual excitement. He believes women enjoy being abused, forcefully raped, aggressively dominated, and controlled by men. Therefore, this type of rapist interprets the victim's resistance and struggle as a game, and the more the victim resists, the more excited and aggressive he becomes. As a result, there is often a direct relationship between physical and verbal resistance by the victim and the amount of injury she sustains.

These offenders are frequently married, but show little commitment to marriage. Their backgrounds often are replete with antisocial behavior beginning during adolescence or before and ranging from truancy to rape murder. On occasion, this type of rapist engages in sexual sadism much like the displaced aggression rapist; in its extreme, the woman is viciously violated and murdered. This assailant is classified as the *sexual-aggressive* rapist.

The *impulsive rapist*, the fourth type, engages in sexual assault because opportunities present themselves. The rape usually occurs within the context of some other antisocial act, such as a robbery or burglary. The victims happen to be available, and they are sexually assaulted with little aggressive or sexual feeling.

Although human beings rarely fit neatly into typologies, the Cohen typology is useful in understanding rape. It takes into consideration behavioral patterns, rather than simply personality traits, as well as the context within which the behavior patterns occur. In this way the Cohen categories represent an interactionist approach more than a trait or situationism approach, and they provide a good beginning framework for theory development.

One feature which is apparent from the research on rapists is that they tend to be unusually sexually naive and socially immature (Goldstein, 1977; Eysenck, 1972). In a series of studies, Michael Goldstein found that rapists as a group had fewer contacts with erotica during their formative years than other males, and were brought up in a highly repressive and punitive atmosphere with regard to sexual curiosity. This immaturity hypothesis stems from restrictions and misinformation acquired during socialization, a developmental process influenced by the media, peers, and parents.

This section of the chapter has described one type of criminal behavior, outlining statistical, sociological, and psychological data available on both the victim and the offender. A solid, testable theory of criminal behavior will require careful analysis and integration of each sector partially described here. Theoretical integration of statistical data or frequencies requires a keen understanding of the limitations and pitfalls that accompany tabulation. Criminal behavior theory building also requires careful consideration of the knowledge available from several disciplines, especially those of sociology and psychology.

The chapter will end with a topic that is relevant to criminal behavior but has yet to be integrated within mainstream criminology. Moral behavior encompasses many issues, but traditional research has focused upon the development of moral judgment rather than upon moral behavior interacting with a variety of social situations. We will confine our presentation to cognitive and cognitive-social perspectives on moral judgment, in keeping with the cognitive-social approach to the study of criminal behavior.

# ■ Cognitive Theories of Moral Judgment

## COGNITIVE PERSPECTIVES

**Piaget.** The seeds of contemporary empirical investigations of moral reasoning were sown by Swiss psychologist Jean Piaget (1932), who claimed that moral reasoning evolved through cognitive stages in a manner similar to the development of intellectual skills. After studying children between the ages of 3 and 12, Piaget theorized that two major stages of moral development existed: the stage of *moral realism* and the stage of *moral independence*.

In the stage of moral realism, also called the morality of constraint, the child accepts the rules as dictated by parents and other authority figures. These rules are regarded as absolute, unchangeable, and not to be questioned. The child also perceives that if one breaks rules one should be punished, regardless of one's intentions. Therefore, the violation of rules and the extent of the damage done are more important in deciding punishment than the motive or whether the act was even accidental. In this sense, the child at this stage is more objective than subjective in his or her appraisal of misdeeds. In legal terms the child interprets the act to the "letter of the law," rather than the "spirit of the law."

In the second stage, moral independence, the child (or adult) begins to believe in modifying the rules to fit the situation and the offender's intention. For example, it is now worse to break a glass on purpose than to break one accidentally. This cognitive development comes gradually, and the learning comes not so much from interaction with parents or other adults as from interaction with one's peers. In addition, moral independence is a result of being able to put oneself in the place of others, an ability not ordinarily reached until early adolescence.

Although these two Piagetian stages are extensively cited in the psychological literature, Piaget himself was exceedingly cautious and guarded about his use of the term "stage" in the development of moral reasoning (Flavell, 1963). He continually emphasized that individual differences in moral judgment are very great at each age level studied.

In *The Moral Judgment of the Child*, the book in which he summarized his major concepts, Piaget discussed the child's idea of justice. Children develop ideas about how violators of rules should be punished, ideas which fall under the rubric "retributive justice." Two broad categories of punishment are involved: expiatory punishment and punishment by reciprocity.

Expiatory punishment is characterized by the belief that wrongdoers should suffer a punishment that is painful in proportion to the seriousness of the offense they committed, but not necessarily related to why the misdeed was done or the nature of the situation surrounding it. Absolute punishment or sentencing, where offenders receive a mandatory sentence regardless of the circumstances, follows the principles of expiatory punishment. For example, some states have enacted statutes that dictate a mandatory jail sentence of one year for possession of an unauthorized firearm, regardless of the offender's explanations as to why he or she was carrying it.

In the second form of punishment, by reciprocity, punishment is logically set in accordance with the nature of an offense and the wrongdoer's intentions. By making the punishment fit the crime, it is assumed that the wrongdoer will understand the implications of what he or she has done.

Piaget found a tendency for younger children to favor expiatory punishment, while older children favored punishment by reciprocity. He also discovered that younger children were more likely to believe in "immanent justice," which is the idea that nature or some unknown force will punish misdeeds. For example, children would often conclude that a girl who fell in the process of "stealing" cookies had suffered the mishap because she was doing something wrong.

In addition to retributive and immanent justice, Piaget introduced the concept of distributive justice, which refers to the distribution of rewards and punishments among members of a group responsible for certain behavior. According to Piaget, ideas about distributive justice proceeds through three different stages. In the first, the child regards as "just" or "fair" whatever rewards or punishments an authority figure metes out, regardless of the equity of the distribution. This first stage concept is most apparent among children younger than seven or eight years old. In stage 2, the child becomes a "rapid egalitarian," believing all persons must be treated equally, regardless of the circumstances (Flavell, 1963). This stage appears in children between the ages of 7 and 12. In stage 3, the child begins to "temper" equality with equity. Justice requires a balancing between what is just for one person and what is just for others in the group.

*The Moral Judgment of the Child* is a small beginning in the empirical search for moral judgment and the cognitive development of concepts of justice. Piaget's theories were not well conceptualized or clearly organized, but they have been heuristic enough to generate further theoretical development and research.

**Kohlberg.** The individual most credited with advancing Piaget's ideas of morality is the psychologist Lawrence Kohlberg, who began improving Piaget's methods of inquiry and theoretical framework in the early 1960s. Kohlberg added depth to the analysis by incorporating information from the study of ethics and moral philosophy, and he extended the study of moral development to include adolescents and adults as well as children. Kohlberg's usual methodology was to present his subjects with story problems that constituted moral dilemmas. Using this technique, he was able to delineate six stages of moral development.

Kohlberg's six stages follow an invariant, hierarchical sequence. That is, an individual must develop the characteristics and adopt the principles of one moral stage before attaining a higher one. There are three major or primary stages—the preconventional, the conventional, and the postconventional stages of morality—and within each there are two substages, early and late. Development through the stages moves from an endorsement of principles reflecting a self-centered, selfish orientation (early preconventional) to an endorsement of principles prescribed by society (conventional) to principles developed personally and which exhibit a deep understanding of individual rights of others (late postconventional). According to Kohlberg, a sizeable majority of adults in American society have not developed much beyond stages 3 or 4, the conventional morality stages.

During the early preconventional stage, behavior is dictated solely by a desire to obtain rewards and avoid punishment. Individuals at this stage have not yet developed any notion of right or wrong and basically have no sense of "morality." Behavior is independent of its effect upon others. The stage is characterized by unquestioning deference and blind obedience to authority.

In the late preconventional stage, the person continues to be highly self-centered but begins to understand that actions may be used to manipulate others. Human relationships are viewed as mediums through which to gain something. Fellow humans do not deserve loyalty, gratitude, or justice, they are merely objects to be used for one's purpose. The "principles" of morality represented by this stage follow the orientations toward others that characterize most psychopaths and Machiavellians.

The early conventional stage is referred to as the "good boy" or "good girl" orientation. Here, the "right" behavior is controlled by attempts at gaining social approval and acceptance. The behavior conforms to stereotyped images of what the majority regards as appropriate or good behavior. To obtain social rewards and to avoid punishment, one must conform. Guilt begins to develop at this stage, emerging primarily in response to perceived transgressions of the "good" code of behavior.

During the late conventional stage, principles of morality reflect a belief that one should do things out of duty and responsibility and out of respect for the authority of social institutions. The person at this stage becomes aware that rules and regulations are necessary to ensure the smooth functioning of society. The "right" behavior is motivated by anticipation of dishonor and blame if one is derelict in performing one's duty. Guilt feelings arise out of doing concrete, tangible harm to others and being discovered doing this harm. The late conventional stage is sometimes labeled the "law and order" morality, because of the strong orientation toward unquestioning respect for authority, conventionalism, and a rigid adherence to rules of conduct. Violators should be prosecuted because "it's the law."

Kohlberg believes that the final and highest stage of moral development—the early and late postconventional—are reached by only a small sector of the population. To reach these stages one must have a certain cognitive ability requiring abstraction and the perception of issues in "grays" rather than in blacks and whites. During the early postconventional stage, correct action is determined by principles which show an understanding of the general rights of the individual compared to the standards which have been examined critically and agreed upon by the society. This requires balancing individual and societal rights. In addition to taking into consideration what is constitutionally and democratically agreed upon, one must also ponder the rightness or wrongness of behavior in relation to one's own personal standards and values. These personal values may not be in agreement with those of society.

Kohlberg contends that this highest stage of morality reflects considerable emphasis upon the "legal point of view," where laws are made by persons with political, religious, and social motivations and where they can be changed if they violate basic human rights. Ideally, legislators and jurists should be at this stage when statutes are enacted and adjudication is required. Actually, few individuals qualify for this sixth stage of moral development. It is characterized by principles that reflect an orientation "toward the decisions of conscience and toward self-chosen ethical principles appealing to logical comprehensiveness, universality, and consistency" (Kohlberg, 1977, p. 63). The principles are abstract and display concern for universal principles of justice and the reciprocity and quality of human rights. The person at this stage relies on his or her own personally developed ethical principles, and as long as the dignity of human beings is preserved, the principles may be in opposition to those laid down by society. In other words, the individual lives by personally developed principles, regardless of the pressures placed by peers and society and regardless of the consequences.

According to Kohlberg people develop into these stages at different ages. In many cases a person is not at any particular stage, but is clustered at two or more stages. Kohlberg's theory has been criticized liberally, and it has often not withstood empirical inquiry (e.g., Wrightsman & Deaux, 1981). In the long run, it may need considerable revision, but it remains provocative and not to be discarded.

**Rawls.** The legal philosopher John Rawls (1971) also postulated a three-stage sequence of moral development, and the stages correspond closely to those advanced by Kohlberg. In the *morality of authority*, the only morality is derived from what agents of authority say, without critical thought from the recipient of the dicta. "The prized virtues are obedience, humility, and fidelity to authoritative persons; the leading vices are disobedience, self-will, and temerity" (Rawls, 1971, p. 466). In the *morality of association*, common sense rules of morality are developed along conventional, traditional ways of thinking. One is taught the virtues of "good" behavior and their appropriateness in relation to one's roles and position in life. At the *morality of principles* stage, the person develops "highest order principles themselves, so that just as during the earlier phase of the morality of association he may want to be a good sport, say, he now wishes to be a just person" (p. 473).

A commonality running through Piaget's, Kohlberg's, and Rawls' moral stages is that people develop from a rather selfish-but-obedient orientation, through a conforming orientation which accepts traditional values, and finally to a self-developed set of principles which hold human rights and freedoms in highest regard. All three men approach moral development in subjective terms; the highest order of morality is achieved when the individual has identified natural laws through sagacious development of abstract principles of "liberty and justice for all."

## COGNITIVE-SOCIAL PERSPECTIVES

The cognitive-social learning theorists are less lofty in their proclamations. Bandura (1977) argues that cognitive stages of morality do not have to follow an invariant ordering of progressive steps toward a natural law of wisdom favoring human dignity and respect. Rather, moral judgments and behavior are learned in the course of socialization, by the modeling and reinforcement of behaviors and cognitions that are respected by a given culture. In large part, this socialization process requires abstract modeling, where "observers extract the common attributes exemplified in diverse modeled responses and formulate rules for generating behavior with similar structural characteristics" (Bandura, 1977, p. 41). General principles of what is right and wrong are learned through environmental agents (models) who are respected and imitated. Therefore, cognitive-social learning theorists do not believe that there are developing cognitive structures that, through living experiences, will lead one to arrive at general principles for human existence. Rather, people can skip to the "highest" stage without much if any travel through "lower" stages simply by identifying with and modeling others who exemplify the principled behavior associated with ultimate moral development.

Cognitive-social learning theorists do not believe in the universality of certain principles of morality. Instead, they believe individuals make moral judgments and exhibit related behaviors on the basis of particular experiences applicable to some situations, but perhaps not to others. Under some conditions the person will exhibit a certain behavioral pattern of morality; in others the person may show a different pattern which will reflect a much higher or lower stage of morality. This is similar to the belief that persons act consistently in similar situations (cross-situational consistency) but do not invariably display the same behavior over time (temporal consistency).

Level of moral development obviously plays a significant role in influencing decisionmaking in various situations. It would also appear that level of morality influences who will engage in criminal behavior; individuals at higher levels would be less likely to become involved in transgressions against others. However, in many cases, we might expect that individuals who violate or transgress against institutions and social systems they consider wrong or repressive will also be at a high level of moral development. Persons at the law-and-order and nice-boy, nice-girl levels respect authority blindly and are less likely to violate societal expectations. However, the lower-level individuals also would be most likely to engage in criminal action against other individuals. These seeming inconsistencies in what can be expected at the various stages illustrate the need for carefully executed research stimulated by testable theory. Only then can we begin to assess with confidence the viability of moral development as a partial explanation of crime.

## ■ Summary and Conclusions

The position taken in this chapter is that criminal behavior defies easy explanations or pat solutions. Crime cannot be explained by external referrals to poverty, low socioeconomic status, prejudice, and unemployment compounded by poor job training and education. Nor can crime be explained by internal referrals to psychological deficiencies in the superego, emotional maturity, mental balance, or allusions to neat typologies of criminal personalities. Criminal behavior must be perceived as unique behavior which is a result of each individual's conditioning, instrumental learning, and cognitive-social learning processes in reciprocal relation to the situation. Each crime must be seen as subjectively adaptive for each individual, for a particular set of circumstances. Understanding criminal behavior, therefore, will require at the very least an individualized appraisal of how the antisocial individual perceives his or her predicament. Assessment, theories, and empirical study which fail to take into consideration the cognitive, subjective value of the acts for the individual are destined to provide fragmentary, "outside" perspectives. Moreover, the reciprocal nature of crime renders predictions of dangerousness and future criminal behavior exceedingly difficult and prone to unacceptable levels of accuracy.

Unfortunately, this approach does not allow for easy application to the criminal justice system, and it is likely to be labeled too complex to be of value in developing policies for the reduction and control of crime. People have argued that criminal behavior may be reduced by changing the socialization process of children, reducing the amount of aggressive and violent models available throughout society, and substantially reducing the reinforcement value and personal gain achieved through criminal behavior. But any proposals of this magnitude are unrealistic and, with our present knowledge about criminal behavior, they are also unwarranted. Criminal behavior is too deeply interwoven into the fabric of our society to be substantially reduced by these measures short of establishing a powerful dictatorship that requires massive "experimental" changes in child-rearing practices, censorship of the entertainment media, total elimination of firearms, and substantial changes in the democratic process.

We cannot end on this pessimistic note, however. The greatest avenue of social change lies within the judicial system, and there lies the potential to alter the course of increasing criminal activity. We can identify the mechanism for change, but the problem then becomes, "Where do we go from there?"

As mentioned above, changes in parenting, massive reduction of criminal models portrayed through the entertainment media, and reduction in the reinforcement gain of criminal behavior is not only an idealistic solution, it would also require massive curtailment of liberties and rights by a repressive, authoritarian government. A more realistic, potentially attainable goal is to develop a rational, consistent, economical, and comprehensible judicial system, including at the juvenile justice level. What we seek is a system with considerable sophistication in its understanding of criminal behavior, and one which handles each case with sensitivity toward the uniqueness of individual behavior, devoid of dogmatic, simplistic generalizations. In many respects, this too is an idealistic proposal, but if we are to take control of the crime problem, improvement of the judicial system appears to be the best alternative available.

The courts, however, are currently hampered by many of their own problems. In spite of the historical observation that they have established a strong reputation as fair and impartial arbiters, congestion and lack of resources are having a deleterious effect on their work product (Bork, 1977, pp. 242–254). In addition, recent surveys have indicated that the public is becoming increasingly disenchanted with the judiciary and its capacity to "effectively" handle personal disputes and social problems. For example, only 29 percent of the general public expressed a high degree of confidence in the federal courts, and only 23 percent had great faith in the state courts, according to one survey (Kastenmeier & Remington, 1979). So far in this book we have seen the inequities prompted by the political and social forces which pervade the judicial system, and these realities are not going to be altered easily. Therefore, concluding that the best place to begin stemming the tide of criminal conduct rests with the judicial system appears to be a position fraught with unrealism.

It can be done one step at a time, however. One place to begin is to urge courts to avoid seeking psychiatric or psychological opinions about criminal behavior which are not tempered with empirical caution and judicial skepticism. Many psychiatric or psychological statements about criminal behavior are philosophical, theoretical, or moral opinions and not usually based upon scientific information. Often, these statements may have no more validity than the layperson's opinions and speculations. If the judicial system intends to use the behavioral sciences, then it appears crucial that it understand their methods and develop a good understanding of scientific philosophy. Courts must appreciate, for example, that the behavioral science of criminal behavior is likely to lead to a bewildering set of conceptual and statistical labyrinths which may require enormous intellectual energy to apply in the enactment of statutes and the disposition of cases.

From this book's perspective, the most effective approach toward the reduction and partial control of criminal behavior is to first understand it. This understanding can emerge not only from continued psychological research activity directed at the learning, maintenance, and extinction processes of criminal behavior, but also at theoretical development, which ultimately could translate into policies and procedures to be adopted "realistically" by the judicial system. Therefore, in the spirit of the psychology *and* law relationship, it behooves the science of psychology to pursue empirical investigations that may help lead to the formulation of legal policies that insure the safety of the members of society, without massive curtailment of freedom.

## ■ Key Concepts and Principles, Chapter 10

Sociological, psychiatric, and
    psychological criminology
Dark figure
National crime survey

Personal and household crimes
Twin and adoption studies and crime
Concordance
Eysenckian theory of crime

Psychopathy
Cognitive-social learning theory
Reciprocal determinism
Deindividuation
Escalation
Mental illness and criminal behavior
Personality disorders
Forcible rape, statutory rape, and rape-
    by-fraud
Common law rules

Moderate reform exclusionary rules
Radical reform exclusionary rules
Displaced aggression rapist
Compensatory rapist
Sexual-aggressive rapist
Impulsive rapist
Moral realism and moral independence
Stages of moral development
Distributive, immanent, and retributive
    justice

# 11

# The Psychology of Institutional Confinement, Punishment, and Treatment

☐ This chapter is concerned with the effects on human behavior of two major, legally relevant institutions in American society—the prison and the mental hospital, which have many similarities. With reference to mental hospitals, we are most interested in involuntary commitment of persons by order of the judicial system, either for the persons' treatment, for society's protection, or both. We will scrutinize what happens to involuntarily committed persons and the philosophical and legal doctrines that are offered to support the "remedies" tried.

We will also examine some of the practices and philosophies of the correctional system, particularly in relation to rehabilitation and deterrence from a psychological perspective. The psychological effects of institutional confinement, including solitary confinement, crowding, death row, and prisonization, will also be reviewed. We begin by scanning briefly the typical responsibilities and roles of the correctional psychologist.

## ■ Correctional Psychology

The two services most frequently provided by psychologists in the correctional system are psychological assessment and treatment (Clingempeel, Mulvey & Reppucci, 1980). Psychological assessment has the longest history, beginning with intellectual assessment of offenders to place them in educational and vocational programs. Today, assessment is usually needed at three points (Brodsky, 1980):

1. At the entry level, when the offender enters the correctional system
2. When decisions are to be made concerning the offender's exit into the community
3. At times of psychological crisis

As a matter of institutional or system-wide policy, correctional facilities often require entry-level assessments so that inmates can bé "psychologically processed" and classified. In many states, an offender is initially sent to a classification and reception center, which may or may not be within the correctional institution. Theoretically, an inmate may spend several days or even many weeks in this assessment center, separated from the inmates already in-system, until assigned to an institution or a specific wing. Realistically, as crowding increases, these neat flow charts begin to break down. In far too many instances, entry level assessments are mere rituals directed at appeasing any potential public concern about rehabilitation and treatment. In general, the assessment process becomes institutionalized; classifications are made rigidly, and inmates are treated impersonally and are processed through the system.

The "reception unit" usually consists of psychologists, psychiatrists, social workers, and other personnel, who are expected to make diagnostic conclusions and treatment recommendations. The chief concern of many correctional systems, however, is to use the classification for management purposes; therefore, estimates of dangerousness and potential escape risks become very important. Reports typically are submitted to administrative authorities, who may or may not follow the recommendations or even read the reports. Even if high-quality assessments are provided, the recommendations may not be followed because the reports do not link up adequately with ongoing or available programs. In some cases, administrators do not know how to apply the results or know what they want from classification programs, because they have not clarified their own goals or the goals of the institution (Bartollas, 1981). In addition, in many state correctional systems, there is no research person or group checking on whether the process or classification procedure is fulfilling its purpose.

Psychological assessments for exit decisions are usually prepared at the specific request of parole boards (Brodsky, 1980). In many cases, the board asks specific questions, centered on concerns about the value of further imprisonment, the extent to which the inmate will be a risk to the community, and the probability of recidivism. It is highly debatable, however, whether psychology has advanced to a level where it can satisfactorily answer these questions, as we have seen in previous chapters.

The third area requiring the assessment skills of correctional psychologists is crisis intervention. Suicide attempts, emotional agitation, psychotic behaviors, and refusal to eat or to participate in programs may precipitate a request for psychological assessment. Prison officials are interested in obtaining from the psychologist both immediate solutions to the crisis and long-range solutions which will help avoid a similar problem in the future.

The second major function of the psychologist in the correctional system is to provide psychological treatment, a term that encompasses numerous variants. Among the most common are psychodrama, group therapy, transactional analysis (TA), reality therapy, behavior modification, Erhard Seminars Training (est), Emotional Maturity Institution (EMI), and traditional psychotherapy. The method used depends on the professional training and orientation of the psychologists (or psychiatrists) at each institution. In correctional settings, where the professional staff is limited and overwhelmed by the number of inmates requesting or being forced to receive treatment, group therapy is often the norm. In the typical group session, inmates talk about their concerns, experiences, and anxieties about a variety of topics, while the psychologist controls and directs the topic flow.

During the past two decades, behavior modification was popular both because it was an empirically solid procedure for changing specific behaviors and because it aided facility management for prison authorities. However, troubling questions regarding prisoner rights and behavior modification's general effectiveness once an offender had left the institution were raised. This was compounded by widespread misunderstanding about what behavior modification is, with the result that this type of therapy has lost favor with correctional authorities.

A wide spectrum of philosophies and a great variety of treatment techniques are now practiced throughout the correctional system. Although we do not have the space here to detail and evaluate the many therapies, we will examine the effectiveness of treatment and rehabilitation as global concepts. The reader should also realize that the discussion will focus on prisons as they are popularly conceived and may oversimplify the many responsibilities of correctional psychologists. There exist community-based corrections programs, halfway houses, reentry programs, and an assortment of juvenile facilities and programs for specific classes of offenders, none of which will be evaluated here.

# ■ Rehabilitation

Prisons often are brutal, demeaning places which promote isolation, helplessness, and subservience through the use of overwhelming power and often through fear. This is especially true of state maximum-security facilities. Nearly 300,000 prisoners are held in the custody of state and federal correctional institutions (LEAA, 1979b). Large increases in prisoner populations have precipitated extensive overcrowding and deteriorating conditions. For example, a class-action suit was filed in 1974, attacking conditions in the prisons of Oklahoma's State Penitentiary System, where 4,600 inmates were housed in facilities designed to accommodate 2,400 (*Battle v. Anderson*, 1974). Groups of four men were regularly confined in six-by-six-foot cells, with no ventilation, no hot water, and sewage leaks. During a three-year period, there were forty stabbings, forty-four serious beatings, and nineteen violent deaths.

A similar suit was filed against the Mississippi State Penitentiary at Parchman (*Gates v. Collier*, 1972). In this instance, dead rats surrounded the barracks, broken windows were stuffed with rags to keep out the cold and rain, and eighty men shared three wash basins, which were recycled oil drums. Milk of magnesia was forceably administered to inmates as a disciplinary measure, and cattle prods were used to keep inmates moving. Inmates placed in solitary confinement were banished to six-by-six-foot cells without clothing, light, toilet facilities, sink, bed, or mattress for three days.

Four fundamental rationales are usually in operation when offenders are sentenced to prison:

1. Protection of other members of society
2. Retribution
3. Rehabilitation or behavioral correction
4. Deterrence

We will examine each of these rationales from a psychological perspective.

## PROTECTION OF SOCIETY

The first rationale is the most straightforward justification for incarceration or confinement. If the criminal is believed dangerous to society, it is obvious that he or she must be isolated to prevent future societal harm or damage to property. Temporary banishment does eliminate further infractions of the criminal code by the individual— unless he or she still can operate behind prison walls through cohorts on the outside. In this sense, an argument can be made that imprisonment is the most effective method for the eradication of crime in society. However, the problem is that the concept of dangerousness is vague, its implementation is highly imprecise, and it can be molded to dovetail into almost any social or political purpose. Although it would be too repetitive to list again the many objections to predictions of dangerousness, we cannot forget that we simply cannot predict with comfortable accuracy over a broad collection of offenders who will continue to perpetrate substantial injury or loss to society. There are exceptions, of course, like the offender who promises to get back at persons or at society, and who perhaps already has a violent or long criminal record. Generally speaking, however, "the concept of dangerousness for sentencing purposes is an equivocal principle that leads to gross injustice" (Morris, 1974, p. 63). Sentences and prolongations of confinement by parole boards on the basis of presumed dangerousness are largely unwarranted and without predictive validity.

## RETRIBUTION

The second rationale embodies the principle that a wrongful act must be "repaid" by a punishment that is as severe as the wrongful act. Therefore, the offender should receive what he or she rightfully deserves ("just deserts"), no more, no less.

The just-deserts model has received the endorsements of a Task Force on the Role of Psychology in the Criminal Justice System (1978). The APA-commissioned group concluded that this model was the most conducive to the ethical use of psychologists in corrections. Noting that a just-deserts approach was not without its conceptual difficulties, the task force decided that it was more acceptable than the rehabilitative approach, because of the proven ineffectiveness of the treatment methods thus far employed.

> While it [just-deserts approach] will not ameliorate the horrendous human degradation that is part of many prisons—and *nothing* an offender has done could "deserve" the physical and sexual violence rampant in American "correctional" institutions—it has the important virtue of placing an upper limit on the power of the state to expose persons to such conditions. . . .
>
> Even in the unlikely event that substantial improvements in the prediction of criminal behavior were documented, there would still be reason to question the ethical appropriateness of extending an offender's confinement beyond the limits of what he or she morally "deserves" in order to achieve a utilitarian gain in public safety [Task Force, 1978, pp. 1109–1110].

The third and fourth rationales are of major concern here since one involves psychotherapy and psychological change, and one centers on the effects of punishment—threatened or applied—on behavior. The rationales of rehabilitation and de-terrence, therefore, each merit careful scrutiny.

## REHABILITATION AS A RATIONALE

Rehabilitation is a vague concept surrounded by controversy and misunderstand-ing. As noted by many other writers, the debate about the effectiveness of rehabilita-tion and psychological treatment became particularly heated when R. M. Martinson (1974) claimed that his extensive review of the literature revealed that "nothing works." "With few and isolated exceptions, the rehabilitative efforts that have been reported so far have had no appreciable effect on recidivism," Martinson charged (p. 25). His wide-sweeping statement has been attacked on several fronts, but it appears basically true that rehabilitative and psychological treatment have not produced more psycho-logically and socially adaptive members of society.

The above pessimistic conclusion requires two major qualifications, however.

1. The research conducted to evaluate the effectiveness of prison rehabilitation has often been flawed, making generalizations difficult to proffer.
2. Regardless of the type of treatment used or the method adopted to evaluate its effectiveness, rehabilitation is destined to fail, given our present correctional system.

Let us examine each of these qualifiers carefully.

## EVALUATION OF REHABILITATION

It is impossible to evaluate treatment properly unless the researcher carefully de-lineates the type of treatment and assures that the therapists being studied are using the same techniques. This is necessary because therapy comes in so many varieties in the correctional system. Many studies have neglected to include these preliminary steps, however (Quay, 1977).

Studies evaluating effectiveness also have not explored the integrity of the treat-ment program. Were the services outlined in the program actually delivered? Far too often, the written treatment plans are nothing more than symbolic gestures to appease society. In reality, the "extensive" program being offered to inmates may be fragmented and may show little resemblance to the "on paper" version. Another factor in the program's integrity has to do with whether inmates actually attend the treatment ses-sions or any part of them. Again, evaluation studies often fail to address this question.

Evaluation of the program's integrity must also consider the specific goals of the particular therapy. Was it designed to alter some specific habit pattern (e.g., fear of small spaces), or was it intended to change the individual's life style (e.g., criminal behavior in general)? The narrowly focused goal will probably have minimal effect on posttreatment criteria (recidivism rate, for example). The broader goal, although far more difficult to achieve, could produce notable changes in the inmate's approach to life situations.

The training and supervision of the personnel servicing the program are important considerations. Untrained, unsupervised paraprofessional staffs are likely to provide a different quality of treatment than highly trained staff who have access to competent supervision and consultation. State correctional systems differ widely in this feature, and this aspect must be considered in any treatment-evaluation project.

Other crucial components of therapy include the duration (two years or six months?) and the intensity (fifty minutes interspersed with a game of backgammon and directionless chatter or fifty minutes of purposeful conversation and therapy?).

Treatment evaluation studies often struggle with the criteria to be used to determine effectiveness. Many researchers favor a recidivism index as the most sensitive measure of effectiveness. However, they fail to agree upon whether it is more useful to measure the proportion of pre- to postincarceration arrests or simply the incidence of postincarceration arrest and conviction.

## REHABILITATION AND THE CORRECTIONAL SETTING

Regardless of the methodology or the results of evaluation studies, however, the problem remains that, under the present correctional system in American society, rehabilitation is destined to fail. This ill fate can be attributed to four factors.

**Coercion.** First, institutional treatment suffers from the faulty logic that psychological change can be coerced. Traditional forms of psychological treatment have been successful only when subjects were willing and motivated to participate. This basic principle applies regardless of whether the person is living in the community or within the walls of an institution which has overwhelming power over the lives of its inmates. Coercive treatment which involves temporary or permanent alterations of the nervous system, however, like psychosurgery, electroconvulsive therapy (ECT), and specific drug regimens, is a different story. Coerced or not, these modes of treatment do effect psychological change, although it is not clear whether they produce change primarily through punishment principles or through modifications of the neurological mechanisms responsible for certain cognitive and emotional processes. The ethical and constitutional ramifications of these approaches have rendered them highly questionable and, for many institutions, against policy.

Therefore, any sentencing process that forces an individual to engage in psychotherapy for the expressed purpose of ameliorating his or her criminal behavior is destined not to succeed. If early release is inexorably dependent upon the prisoner's apparent commitment to a treatment program, the prisoner enters into a perpetual game of conning those who can open the doors to freedom. It is an open secret among inmates that one of the consequences of not committing oneself to treatment may be longer confinement. Part of the rationale behind indeterminate sentencing—which establishes minimum and maximum sentences—is to elicit cooperation from inmates in the treatment process. Sentences based on the dictum that a person "should remain in custody until cured" not only perpetuate the tremendous coercive power of the institution, but also promote the inmates' behavioral appeasement rites.

This is not to say that treatment and rehabilitation programs should not be offered in the prison system. As Norval Morris (1974) so elegantly argued, treatment programs not only should be offered, but should also be substantially expanded and improved for those inmates who voluntarily seek them. Moreover, participation should be independent of early parole, so that therapeutic "con games" are reduced. Coerced re-habilitation and treatment, however, do not belong in the judicial system.

**Motivation.** A second reason why rehabilitation is destined to fail in most prison settings is closely allied with the first. Many prisoners do not want to be changed in accordance with societal standards. They are happy the way they are, and they are more interested in recreational opportunities outside their prison obligations than they are with regular group-therapy sessions. On the other hand, many prisoners do want to be more gainfully employed, have better social relationships with family and friends when they get out, and eliminate some troubling habits or emotional problems. Meaningful services should be provided for those inmates, but the services should be independent of the possibility of an early parole decision.

The belief that prisoners generally want to improve themselves derives from the medical model that criminal behavior is sick behavior that needs to be eradicated from the individual's repertoire. As we learned in Chapter 10, it might be better to conceive of much criminal behavior as deviant and adaptive rather than as deviant and mentally sick behavior. From the criminals' perspective, their behavior has provided them with the most adaptive responses under their circumstances, and until something better comes along, they feel it is wise to continue with their current behavior patterns.

Prisoners often do not want the rehabilitation the prison has to offer because they appraise it, realistically, as a farce that serves, at best, to placate society. Despite the fact that prisoners are disproportionately undereducated and intellectually limited by middle-class standards, they learn very quickly that the present rehabilitation programs are almost invariably flawed. Although the point to be made here is specifically rele-vant to vocational rehabilitation, it is offered because it dramatizes very well the gen-eralized viewpoint of most inmates to all attempts at so-called treatment. Prisoners who become "ex-cons" in society know all too well that the sheet-metal skills they have acquired in prison do not assure them of gainful employment outside of prison walls. As Daniel Glaser (1964) writes, "unemployment may be among the principal causal factors involved in the recidivism of adult male offenders" (p. 329). Moreover, it is estimated that unemployment rates for ex-offenders are three times the rate for the general public, and that most who received vocational training are not able to use it (Dale, 1976). "An opportunity to live a normal, noncriminal productive life is denied the ex-offender immediately upon his release from the penal institution. We effectively preclude his rehabilitation by failing to train and educate him, by refusing to hire him, by allowing the private bonding industry to intimidate employers, and by enact-ing restrictive occupational licensing requirements at the behest of self-serving eco-nomic groups" (Dale, 1976, p. 336).

**Environment.** The third factor promoting rehabilitative failure revolves around the unusual nature of the prison environment itself. Prison behavior does not predict community behavior. This topic is especially pertinent to behavior therapy, which attempts through learning principles to modify specified behavioral patterns exhibited within the confines of the prison. The zeitgeist of behavior therapies within correc-tional facilities over the past two decades has frequently merged with the idea of in-stitutional management. That is, behavior modification programs were more often designated to promote the smooth operations of the institutions than long-term ame-liorative effects outside the prison. Almost all the behavioral programs reported con-centrated upon eradicating undesirable or unmanageable behaviors within the system (Bartol, 1980). Bedmaking, room cleaning, personal hygiene, social appropriateness, eye-contact when spoken to, washing hands before eating—all were behaviors that rapidly and impressively improved after behavior therapy, but whether these behaviors continued in the natural environment—or whether indeed they matter—and whether they have significant effects on criminal behavior is questionable. Ideally, rehabilita-tion and treatment should have the overall effect of producing more socially desirable behaviors in the community. To date, there has been no conclusive documentation that behaviors coerced in the prison environment continue in the community (Rep-pucci & Saunders, 1974; Burchard & Harig, 1976; Johnson, 1977).

**The system.** The fourth reason for the failure of rehabilitation is the undefined pur-pose and goals of the criminal justice system, a giant rudderless bureaucracy whose deeply entrenched political forces continually obstruct change. Scholars and practi-tioners generally agree that the system is a social embarrassment and is ineffective in much of what it tries to do, but there are no shared principles about what it should do. Sentencing is often arbitrary, discriminatory, and without clearly specified pur-poses of the incarceration. Each judge has his or her own reasons or principles for mandating confinement. Despite the injection of competent personnel into the sys-tem, its procedures rarely change and its goals seldom become clearly defined. Under these conditions, rehabilitation and treatment, whatever these concepts mean, take a secondary role in the institution's day-to-day operations. As Norval Morris (1974) as-serts, in this restrictive setting it is impossible to build a rational and humane prison system.

In sum, under the present working conditions that exist in the prison setting, effective rehabilitation and psychological treatment are destined to fail. It should come as no surprise that the track record of psychological change for confined offenders has been less than impressive. The focus of this section has been upon prisons as com-monly conceived—both minimum and maximum security institutions that confine offenders and isolate them from the community. There are, of course, gradients of confinement. However, the success of these programs will still depend upon the level of coercion and commitment exerted and the extent to which evaluation studies con-sider the crucial variables outlined above.

# ■ Deterrence

Any discussion of the precise meaning of deterrence as a rationale for sentencing leads to a jungle of heavy conceptual foilage. It is sometimes wise to divide the concept into two categories, as Andenaes (1968) suggests: *general deterrence* and *specific deterrence*.

General deterrence refers to the threat of punishment or, more broadly, the threat of law. Presumably, the anticipation of unpleasant consequences for specified behavior will discourage or deter someone from engaging in that behavior. Many people are deterred from cheating on their income tax returns by the threat of social embarrass-ment or even imprisonment. In fact, the Internal Revenue Service is probably the government agency that utilizes general deterrence for its fullest impact on the population, discouraging people from exaggerating their income or not reporting large portions.

Special deterrence is a term reserved for the actual experience of punishment, which presumably will deter the punished individual from engaging in future transgressions. In evaluating the effectiveness of special deterrence, we ask, do certain forms of punishment reduce or suppress certain behaviors? Much of the psychological research relevant to deterrence has concentrated upon this question, with the result that broad "principles" of punishment have been developed. Unfortunately but understandably, psychology has developed the principles primarily after studying the behavior of subhumans, such as rats, dogs, pigeons, or monkeys. The critical drawback to such research, of course, is that it cannot take into account the powerful and awesome features of the human cognitive processes. Humans have attitudes, expectancies, values, and experiential histories which do not approximate the cognitive equation found in subhumans. We will discuss these and other aspects shortly, but first let us return briefly to the topic of general deterrence.

## GENERAL DETERRENCE

This type of deterrence is concerned not with the effect of punishment on the specific person being punished, but rather with the overall symbolic impact punishment has on the population as a whole. Therefore, determinations of the effectiveness of general deterrence require an analysis of the behavioral patterns of large aggregates of people in relation to changes in statutes or legal policy. Statutory changes might include the abolition (or inclusion) of capital punishment, or the escalation of mandatory penalties, like one year sentences for the possession of unregistered firearms. Legal policy changes might include increased active detection of and arrests for certain offenses, in hope that this will have extended impact on the general population, discouraging others from participating in the targeted behavior.

It makes good sense to assume that general deterrence has an effect on certain sectors of the population, but the question remains: how much of an effect, and to what sectors? The elementary data we have gathered thus far do not provide clear answers (Nagin, 1978). Some trends suggest that crime rates decrease as certainty of imprisonment increases. However, the relationship between sentence severity and crime rates remains equivocal. In fact, it appears that the longer the sentence the higher the crime index in the region stipulating stiffer sentences (Ehrlich, 1973; Logan, 1971, 1972).

Two lines of empirical inquiry emerging from the psychological laboratory are pertinent here. One research line focuses on the effects of *vicarious* punishment on subsequent behavior; the other, on *threats of punishment* on subsequent behavior.

**Vicarious punishment.** Research examining vicarious punishment generally has involved a modeling situation, where subjects first observe the punishment of another person (a model), and are then observed to see if they engage in similar behavior under tempting or permissive conditions. The research in this area has relied almost exclusively on children as subjects.

An exemplary study was that conducted by Walters and Parke (1964), who used six-year-old boys as subjects. Each child was shown some toys but was forbidden by an adult from touching them. "Now these toys have been arranged for someone else, so you'd better not touch them," the adult warned. Each subject was then assigned to one of four experimental conditions. In one, the boys saw a three-minute film depicting a female adult, presumably a mother, who warned the child that he should not play with the toys placed on the table. The mother then sat the child down at the table, handed·him a book, and left the room. After the mother left the room, the boy in the film put down the book and began to play with the toys for about two minutes. When the mother returned to the room, she snatched the toys from the child, shook him, and sat him down once more in the chair with the book. This sequence was referred to as the model-punished condition. In another experimental condition, boys saw the same sequence, but here the mother returned, handed the child some toys, and played with him in an affectionate manner—the model-rewarded condition. In a third condition, the three-minute film was shortened to two minutes, and the mother did not return—the no-consequence condition. A control group, where the children saw no film, was condition four.

After the subject had seen the film, the adult researcher found an excuse to leave the room, gave the boy a book to read, and left the room. The child was then observed for fifteen minutes.

Boys in the model-punished condition played with the toys less quickly, less often, and for shorter periods of time than the boys in the model-rewarded and no-consequence conditions. However, subjects in the model-punished situation did not play with the toys any less quickly, less often, or for shorter periods than the subjects in the control group, who did not see the film at all. When compared to the model-rewarded condition, the model-punished condition "got the message across" to its subjects, and this would indicate that vicarious punishment was an effective method for reducing wrongdoing. However, the acid test was whether vicarious punishment made a difference in the behavior of subjects who had seen the film when compared with subjects who had not. If vicarious punishment is an effective procedure, we would predict that the children who observed the model punished for transgressions would demonstrate significantly less toy-play behavior than the children who did not see the film at all. This did not happen in the Walters-Parke study. It would be more accurate to conclude, therefore, that vicarious reinforcement encourages subsequent behavior, but vicarious punishment does not appear to discourage it. Subjects in the model-rewarded group, who saw the film character receive affectionate attention from a mother figure, played much more with the forbidden toys than subjects in each of the other two conditions.

Bandura, Ross, and Ross (1963) showed nursery school children films depicting an adult model using considerable physical and verbal aggression against another adult. In one condition the aggressive model received severe punishment for his behavior, while in the other the model was rewarded for the behavior. There were two control conditions: one in which the children saw a film where the models engaged in vigorous but nonaggressive play, and another where there was no model. The children in the model-punished condition did not demonstrate less aggressive behavior than the children in the two control conditions.

Bandura (1965) also conducted an often-cited study in which an adult model behaved aggressively toward an inflated rubber doll. In one film sequence, the adult was punished for the behavior; in another, he was rewarded; in a third, there were no consequences for the behavior. Results revealed that children who saw the model punished for aggression showed less aggressive behavior in a later test condition than children in both the rewarded and no-consequence conditions. However, this experiment is not really a test case for the effects of vicarious punishment, because there was no control group which did not observe an aggressive model at all. While the experiment does demonstrate the power of modeling and vicarious reinforcement on the acquisition of behavior, it does not show the effects of vicarious punishment on behavior.

The numerous limitations of these studies (e.g., using children as subjects) make them of questionable value in drawing conclusions about the effects of vicarious punishment and its relationship to general deterrence. However, they are among the very few studies available. Some researchers and commentators have ventured to conclude tentatively that watching models being punished does not deter observers from engaging in the punished behavior at a later time, particularly if the behavior was in the observer's behavioral repertoire prior to watching the model (Hoffman, 1970; Rosenkoetter, 1973; Walters & Grusec, 1977). The preliminary data available to us suggest that media portrayals of models being punished do not deter a majority of the population fron engaging in that particular conduct at a later date.

**Threats of punishment.** The second line of empirical study has dealt with the effects of threats of punishment, without the subject's direct observation of some ill-fated model. The threat of punishment corresponds closely to Andeneas' (1974) *threat of law* concept, since there is an explicit or implicit, clear or ambiguous threat of what might happen if one transgresses. Preliminary evidence indicates that threatened punishment may deter antisocial or illegal behavior, but only under specific, restricted conditions. Most of the research on this topic has focused on aggressive or violent behavior, again often with children as subjects.

In an extensive review of the research literature, Robert Baron (1977) has identified four specific conditions which significantly influence the effects of punitive threats on aggressive behavior. The first condition involves the level of emotional arousal (e.g., anger) the aggressor is experiencing. Under relatively low levels of emotional arousal, the impact of threatened punishment remains at full strength. The individual apparently continues to think rationally of the consequences of his or her behavior. However, as the arousal level increases, the power of threatened punishment diminishes. A person extremely provoked and emotionally agitated is very apt to think less rationally about the consequences of behavior and engage in the antisocial, aggressive, or prohibited behavior, regardless of the consequences.

A second condition identified by Baron is the apparent probability or perceived certainty that the threatened punishment will actually be delivered. Threats that are perceived as having little chance of being enacted have minimal effects as a deterrent. If the public realizes that there is a law on the books, but also that the law is rarely enforced or punishment rarely delivered, the deterrent influence of that law will be small or virtually nonexistent.

A third condition centers on the magnitude of the punishment expected. Psychological experiments on human aggressive behavior have found that threatened punitive measures, if severe, have greater impact than threatened mild reprimands. While this relationship is clear-cut in the experimental setting, it has not been reported with consistency outside the laboratory. As reported above, increasing the sentences for certain offenses does not generally have the effect of reducing the crime rates. It may be that the relationship between the intensity of threatened punishment and prohibited behavior is curvilinear. That is, allusions to punishment severity may have a diminishing effect after a certain point. Many violations of criminal law are already severely punished by years of imprisonment; adding a few years is likely to have limited effect.

A fourth condition concerns the amount of gain a person expects from prohibited behavior. If the perceived gain is substantial, it is possible that regardless of the magnitude or certainty of threatened sanction, the person will be willing to take the risks involved.

Baron correctly observes that "together, these apparent limitations on the influence of threatened punishment seem to offer unsettling implications for our present system of criminal justice. In particular, they suggest that existing conditions, under which the probability of being both apprehended and convicted of a single violent crime is exceedingly low, may be operating largely to nullify the potential influence of the penalties established for such crimes" (1977, p. 234).

In summary, the limited psychological literature does not support the concept of general deterrence as having a powerful influence on illegal behavior except under very restricted conditions, and rarely are these conditions met by the criminal justice system. Neither the symbolism of vicarious punishment nor the presumed fear generated by threatened punishment have any significant impact on subjects except under the conditions outlined above. However, the data are in a very preliminary stage of theoretical development, and the few experiments that have studied vicarious or threatened punishment do not allow generalizations to adults in society in relation to criminal law and its sanctions.

## SPECIAL DETERRENCE

The empirical data on the psychology of special deterrence, or the effects of actual punishment on subsequent behavior, is far more extensive than that on general deterrence, but it too has its limitations. Empirical studies on general deterrence were few and most were conducted with children as subjects. Psychological investigations of the effects of punishment, by contrast, have been largely confined to subhumans. Therefore, generalizations to society and the criminal justice system must be applied only with caution. However, certain principles have been gained from the research and can be related to human behavior in institutional settings as well as outside prison walls.

Although studies have been conducted with regularity in recent years, prior to the late 1950s psychological research on the effects of punishment was dormant. The psychologists Edward Lee Thorndike, B. F. Skinner, and William Estes postulated that punishment was for the most part an ineffective procedure for the suppression of undesirable behavior. Instead, rewarding desirable behavior and not rewarding undesirable behavior was far more effective. Undesirable behavior, if not rewarded, would eventually be extinguished. This, in combination with the deliberate rewarding of desirable, alternate behaviors, would produce desired results. Many psychologists subscribed to this position and punishment had very few proponents.

However, during the late 1950s N. H. Azrin and his colleagues reexamined the concept of punishment under a wide range of experimental conditions (Azrin & Holt, 1966). They discovered that the application of punishment was not only a highly complicated process, but also that it could be an effective method of behavioral suppression under certain conditions. Azrin's experiments stimulated further research by numerous other investigators, and the experimental literature on punishment began to build on a more solid, scientific platform.

Punishment is generally defined in one of two ways: (1) presentation of an aversive or painful stimulus when a certain behavior occurs; and (2) presentation of any event that reduces the probability of responding (Walters & Grusec, 1977). The administration of a verbal reprimand, a shock, or a slap are obvious examples of the first definition. Therefore, there is no distinction made as to whether the punishment is physical, psychological (withdrawal of love), or social (embarrassment). The second definition is more functional, in that it refers to any situation or event which reduces the occurrence of a behavior. The research literature has favored the former definition, and most designs have employed some form of aversive or painful stimulus, physical or psychological.

Psychological experiments have delineated three major principles with relation to the effectiveness of punishment—magnitude, consistency, and immediacy. The magnitude or the intensity of punishment has been found to affect substantially the occurrence of behavior in both humans and animals. The level of punishment delivered to humans, however, has been relatively mild, for obvious ethical and humane reasons. Generally speaking, the more severe the punishment, the greater its impact on behavioral suppression, at least with experimental animals. The situation is not this clear-cut with humans, however, because of the matrix of cognitive variables which radically distinguish human subjects from animal ones, and because "intense" punishments for humans are relatively mild compared to those administered to animals.

A second principle developed in the laboratory is the consistency of the punitive delivery. Punishment that is administered regularly, rather than occasionally or haphazardly, is highly effective in suppressing targeted behavior. For example, punishment delivered only periodically or at whim communicates to the person that the punishment is not contingent upon anything that he or she is doing, but rather is due to chance or fate. On the other hand, if the person receives immediate, consistent punishment contingent upon the performance of a specified act, the act will be quickly suppressed, or at least an association between the act and an aversive event will be established. In general, the research with both animals and humans indicates that we may have considerably more faith in accepting the consistency principle than the intensity principle.

Studies have often reported that parents of delinquents often administer erratic discipline, characterized by a random combination of punitiveness and permissiveness (Bartol, 1980). Our present system of criminal justice, where adult delinquents are punished by the courts, continues this pattern. Inconsistent applications of law and apparently random sentencing procedures mean that clearly defined links between behavior and consequences are rarely in evidence.

The third principle that must be considered in discussing the effectiveness of punishment is immediacy, which refers to the time interval between an act and its punishment. Overall, it appears that the shorter the time between the behavior and the contingent punishment, the more effective the suppression of the targeted behavior. While there are exceptions, in many studies using subhumans this immediacy principle has been supported across a variety of situations (Mowrer, 1960). However, the results are far less clear when human subjects are involved.

The cognitive mediation process between the act and the anticipated punishment in human subjects accounts for the discrepancy in findings. Consider the effect of the often-employed stern statement, "Just wait till your father gets home!" Teenage son becomes highly vulnerable to the emotional effects produced by the anticipation of punishment, which actually may be temporally removed from the transgression. In fact, the anxious anticipation may be far worse than the eventual punishment itself. One often hears the argument that legal punishment is ineffective because of the time lag, which is almost inevitable, between detection and adjudication. The anxiety generated between the time of arrest and the final disposition may be immediate punishment in itself. This, in fact, is one of the points made by champions of due process; the person ultimately found innocent does not deserve this interim punishment. Thus, extensive delays in seeing a case through the system are undesirable, but not for the reasons so often advanced. It is not that passage of time ameliorates the effect of eventual punishment; it is that passage of time becomes the punishment, often unjustifiably.

As a whole, the results of psychological studies that have some applicability to questions about the effectiveness of general or specific deterrence have not provided many clear answers. However, in fairness to the researchers who conducted them, they were not intended to. Almost all the studies were designed to examine the effects of direct or vicarious punishment on child development, or to develop theories of punishment vis-à-vis theories of learning. We have tried to take the data out of context and relate them to an applied setting of enormous magnitude—the criminal justice system and criminal law. Although we have been able to suggest possible connections between punishment and behavior, the area is drastically underresearched and needs much more attention before additional conclusions can be drawn.

# ■ Psychological Effects of Imprisonment

Craig Haney, Curt Banks, David Jaffe, and Philip Zimbardo (1973) conducted an experiment to try to understand what it means psychologically to be a prisoner or a guard. The researchers created their own prison in the basement of the Stanford University psychology department. Small rooms were arranged to simulate six-by-nine-foot cells, a small "yard" was provided, and the researchers even added a solitary confinement "hole" (actually a closet). The "prison" had all the physical and psychological markings of an actual security institution: bars, prison drab, identification numbers, uniformed guards, and other features which not only closely approximated a prison environment but also encouraged identity slippage.

The participants in the mock prison were young male middle-class students who responded to a newspaper ad for volunteers for a psychological experiment. In all, seventy volunteers answered the ad, but through careful screening twenty-one were selected because of their maturity, emotional stability, and other indicators of normalcy. None had criminal records.

The experiment required two roles—guard and prisoner. About half the subjects were arbitrarily designated each role by a flip of a coin. Guards were allowed to develop their own formal rules for maintaining law, order, and respect, and they were relatively free to improvise new rules during their eight-hour, three-man shifts. Prisoners were unexpectedly picked up at their homes by "police," were spread-eagled and frisked, handcuffed, taken to a police station, and booked. They were then led blindfolded to the mock prison, where they were stripped, deloused, issued a uniform and an identification number, and placed into a cell where they were to live with two other prisoners for the next two weeks. All subjects understood ahead of time what the experiment would entail; they were paid fifteen dollars a day.

The uniformed guards carried various symbols of power: a nightstick, keys to cells, whistles, and handcuffs. Prisoners were required to obtain permission from the guards to do even routine things, like writing letters or smoking cigarettes. Prisoners were referred to only by number, their toilet visits were supervised, and they were lined up three times a day for a count. In addition, they were required to do pushups, clean toilets, and memorize sixteen rules and recite them on demand.

The events that occurred in the prison were observed and recorded on videotape, and the guards and prisoners were interviewed at various points throughout the project. Although the study was intended to continue for two weeks, it had to be terminated within six days because the behavior of the college men degenerated rapidly. Zimbardo (1973, p. 163) states:

> In less than a week the experience of imprisonment undid (temporarily) a lifetime of learning; human values were suspended, self-concepts were challenged and the ugliest, most base, pathological side of human nature surfaced. We were horrified because we saw some boys (guards) treat others as if they were despicable animals, taking pleasure in cruelty, while other boys (prisoners) became servile, dehumanized robots who thought only of escape, of their own individual survival and of their mounting hatred for the guards.

During the early stages of the experiment, prisoners were rebellious and even attempted to take over the prison. However, the uprising was thwarted by the guards, and prisoners began to display increasing passivity and depression. Three prisoners had to be released during the first days because of hysterical crying, confusion in thinking, and severe depression. Many others begged to be paroled, and most were willing to forfeit all the money earned if released. However, when the prisoners' requests for parole were denied, they had absorbed their prisoner roles so well that they returned docilely to their cells. During the later stages, prisoners began to adopt a personal, self-centered philosophy of "each man for himself." Some of the guards, on the other hand, were becoming increasingly brutal and sadistic, enjoying their control over the prisoners. Some of the guards performed their role with toughness and fairness, a few were even friendly, but none interfered with commands issued by one of the most brutal, demeaning guards. In summary, the simulated prison became a "real prison" with "prisoners" acting like prisoners and "guards" acting like guards.

The experiment was stopped by Zimbardo because of the deterioration he saw in the subjects. For obvious reasons, no attempts have been made to replicate the Stanford study.

Zimbardo's experiment does reveal vividly the power and pervasiveness of situations over individual behavior. It demonstrates what confinement, monitored and controlled by persons who have been given awesome power over the behavior of those confined, can do to the psychological functioning of both prisoners and guards. A valid critique of the study is that the subjects might have been merely playing roles they thought they should be playing. Therefore, while situational properties may have had considerable impact on behavior, expectancies were also involved. On the other hand, we can asume that expectancies also play a part in the behavior of the participants in the real prison system.

In the following sections we will consider some of the probable psychological effects of imprisonment on those persons confined. Imprisonment will refer to the confinement of individuals in an institutional setting due to an arrest or court adjudication, including the confinement of persons in mental institutions, against their will.

## EFFECTS OF SOLITARY CONFINEMENT

Solitary confinement refers to complete social isolation of persons for specified or unspecified periods of time, with other necessities of life being provided. Most of the psychological studies in this area have used volunteers, who submit to social isolation for varying periods of time, usually in cells similar to those used in correctional settings. Generally, the methodology has been sound, and some relevant conclusions can be drawn (Bukstel & Kilmann, 1980).

The research has found that individuals respond differently to solitude; some are glad to be away from the noise and activity of everyday living, while others demonstrate behavioral indicators of stress and frustration. Solitary confinement of a week or less does not appear to produce significant changes in motor behavior or perceptual or cognitive functioning (Walters, Callagan & Newman, 1963; Weinberg, 1967). Additional data suggest that, for most persons, solitary confinement does not generate more stress than would be expected in normal prison life (Ecclestone et al., 1974; Gendreau et al., 1972). It seems, therefore, that social isolation of inmates from other inmates for relatively short periods of time (a week or less) does not significantly affect their motor, perceptual, or intellectual functions, nor does it produce undue stress. These data are based on situations in which the primary focus was on social isolation for brief periods of time, and not on sensory deprivation or the deprivation of necessities of life. The introduction of additional deprivations, like cutting off food supplies or any sounds, are known to produce substantial changes in a number of psychological functions (Zubek, 1969).

## EFFECTS OF CROWDING

The issue of crowding is becoming increasingly important as correctional institutions are forced to house far more inmates than they were designed to hold. Not only does crowding reduce the personal physical and psychological space available, but it also means that the already marginally adequate work and activity programs are offered to fewer inmates or for shorter time periods, thereby increasing inmate confinement and time spent with nothing to do. Crowding brings increases in noise "pollution," and it reduces the opportunity for inmates to remove themselves from constant view and surveillance. The problem of crowding is particularly relevant in the dormitory arrangements now common in many prisons, where as many as sixty prisoners may be jammed into one large room, spending twenty or more hours together. It is no wonder that prisoners prefer nine-by-six-foot cells, which provide some privacy and considerable protection (Clements, 1979).

One psychological study found that diastolic and systolic blood pressure were significantly higher among dormitory inmates than among other prisoner populations at three different institutions (D'Atri, 1975). In addition, more illness complaints are found among inmates living in dormitories than among those in one- or two-person cells (McCain, Cox & Paulus, 1976). These studies strongly suggest that prison crowding is stressful, especially under dormitory conditions.

Some researchers have suggested that disruptive behavior in prison increases as available space decreases (Megargee, 1976; Nacci, Prather, & Teitelbaum, 1977). This relationship is especially strong in youthful offender institutions (Megargee, 1976).

The available evidence implies that crowding generates stress, which further instigates behavior of trying to cope with it by any available means. Carl Clements (1979) observes that in a New Mexico state penitentiary of 2,000 inmates, 300 were fortunate enough to "earn" solitary confinement for twenty-three hours per day, foregoing programs and many other "privileges." Clements found that these single cells were a sought-after premium, despite the fact that inmates confined to them would be the subjects of disciplinary reports sent to parole boards.

Overcrowding also taxes the correctional staff to the point where it is safest for all if inmates are kept in cells and dormitories as much as possible, except for meal calls. There are fewer constructive jobs for inmates, little exercise, and less access to therapeutic programs, all of which generates inactivity and boredom and, consequently, stress. The forced idleness also engenders a lowering of self-esteem and feelings of incompetence, hardly conducive to any form of rehabilitation or self-improvement.

## PRISONIZATION

In 1940, Clemmer defined prisonization as "the taking on in greater or less degree of the folkways, mores, customs, and general culture of the penitentiary" (p. 299). Prisonization means that inmates adopt and internalize the prisoner subculture within any particular institution. It is hypothesized that the longer one is incarcerated, the more deeply ingrained the attitudes and behavioral patterns endorsed by this subculture become. The inmate who rejects the protective covering of this subculture is rendered physically and psychologically vulnerable. The process by which an inmate leaves or detaches from the subculture is often called "resocialization," and it appears to occur with some regularity near the end of the confinement period and just before the inmate is about to return to the community.

Wheeler (1961) recommended an index of conformity to staff expectations as a barometer of prisonization—the lower the conformity, the higher the prisonization. Wheeler also hypothesized that the prisonization process would change according to which segment of the sentence was being served by the inmate. An inmate beginning a sentence would embrace the prison subculture somewhat differently than he or she would at the midpoint of the sentence.

The research examining the validity of the prisonization concept has been contradictory and inconclusive (Bukstel & Kilmann, 1980). The findings suggest that some mixture of personality differences, postprison expectations, and the nature of the institution is operating in the prisonization process. In other words, prisonization is not a unitary concept that can be applied across all prisoner populations. Rather, it appears more likely that "prisoner clubs" vary from institution to institution. The extent to which an inmate incorporates the subculture values, codes, and social hierarchies will depend not only on the orientation of the particular prison but also on individual needs and expectancies.

Institutions for juveniles and youthful offenders tend to be somewhat less regimented than adult facilities. In three studies designed to examine the effects of institutionalization (prisonization) on the behavior of delinquents, similar results emerged (Buehler, Patterson & Furniss, 1966; Duncan, 1974; Furniss, 1964). Delinquent peers strongly reinforced one another for such behaviors as rule breaking, criticizing adults, aggressive actions, and other anti-institution maneuvers. On the other hand, actions that deviated from the delinquent subculture were met with peer disapproval. These findings suggest the existence of a fairly generalizable delinquent subgroup, although it may be restricted to anti-authority behavioral patterns rather than to any all-encompassing subcultural code of conduct or value system.

Simha Landau (1978) cites some interesting data on prisonization among youthful offenders (ages 17.5 to 21) serving time in an Israeli prison (Tel-Mond). Wheeler (1961) had hypothesized a U-shaped trend for prisonization, meaning that at the beginning and at the end of imprisonment, inmates are less influenced by or less in need of a prison subculture. Landau found that the content of inmate thinking processes reflected a similar function. Early during the imprisonment, the prisoner is still close to the outside world, thinks about it regularly, and does not display a high degree of involvement in the prisoner subculture. As the inmate approaches the midpoint of his sentence, however, fellow inmates become his main social support and reference group. As release approaches, the inmate again begins to think about the outside world and gradually detaches himself from the prisoner subculture, which no longer fulfills the supportive and protective functions it did during the middle phase of incarceration.

The beginning and end of incarceration serve as crucial temporal guideposts for prisoners, a finding that has been reported with consistency in the research literature

(Bukstel & Kilmann, 1980). The middle of a sentence becomes a cognitive fog of existence and behavioral helplessness.

## PSYCHOLOGICAL EFFECTS OF SENTENCE PHASE

The U-shaped behavioral trends have also emerged in studies of stress reactions in prisoners. At the beginning of confinement, many inmates exhibit behavioral indicators of stress and anxiety (Fraas, 1973; Steininger, 1959; Jacobs, 1974; Kiehlbauch, 1968). During the middle segments, anxiety reduces and resignation sets in. However, as inmates approach the time of release, anxiety levels again increase. These reactions near release time have been referred to as the "short-timer's syndrome" (Agus & Allen, 1968). They reflect a sense of concern and incompetence about ability to adjust again to the outside world.

Some researchers have probed the psychological effects of death row. Inmates not surprisingly were found to exhibit various indicators of resentment, distrust, frustration, and a strong sense of helplessness and failure (Panton, 1976). A similar finding was reported by Gallemore and Panton (1972). Both studies concluded that life on death row is highly stressful and would be detrimental to adequate functioning in society if the inmate were to be released.

Overall, the results indicate that each individual who experiences confinement reacts to the situation in an idiosyncratic manner. Some find the experience extremely stressful, while others who are dependent, passive, and generally incompetent may find the structure of the prison a positive experience.

Much of the literature on the psychological effects of prison life neglects the important variable of offense conviction. In most correctional facilities, there exists a social hierarchy determined by individual criminal histories and types of crimes committed. For example, prisoners often despise fellow inmates who were convicted of certain sexual crimes, such as child rape or molestation. These offenders not only are placed at the bottom of the prisoner hierarchy, but they are also harassed to the point where they must seek protection from other inmates. Material acquisition offenses— e.g., robbery and burglary—are status offenses, particularly if performed ingeniously. Therefore, the nature of one's offense can either add to one's confinement woes or make them lighter.

The fact that prison life is stressful to many individuals is reflected in the suicide rates. Between 1950 and 1969, 41 suicides were committed in federal prisons, and another 160 were recorded in 100 major state prisons between 1952 and 1972 (Bartollas, 1981). Suicide is usually committed by young, unmarried white males during the early stages of confinement, and the usual method is hanging. Other inmates try to mutilate themselves with razor blades, fragments of metal, glass, or wire, or even eating utensils.

Bartollas (1981) notes that prison suicides can be roughly grouped into several categories. One includes those offenders who are embarrassed by the disgrace they have brought upon themselves and their families and find their guilt and debased self-esteem intolerable. A second group is represented by those inmates who find that the sense of helplessness and lack of control over their lives are intolerable. A third group exhibit suicidal behavior to manipulate others. Although they usually select methods that insure their survival or detection, they sometimes die accidentally.

# ■ Treatment in Mental Institutions

To this point, this chapter has focused upon issues surrounding rehabilitation and treatment in the prison system. What we know about the psychological effects of prison overcrowding, forced treatment, and solitary confinement can be extended to any institutional confinement. Fortunately, however, some psychologists have directed attention at mental institutions, providing us with additional information that can be applied to confinement in those settings. The remainder of the chapter will examine the results of that research.

### EVALUATION

The adequacy and effectiveness of civil institutional treatment has traditionally been evaluated by one of three methods: (1) structural analysis; (2) process method; and (3) effectiveness method (Schwitzgebel, 1977). Structural analysis focuses upon the structure of the institution and uses criteria such as staff-patient ratios and per capita expenditure to determine the adequacy of treatment. The process method investigates the type and amount of treatment delivered to the patients. Patient records are examined to determine how often the patients were seen, by whom, and for what purposes. The third method, the effectiveness method, focuses on outcome and actual change in the patient's affect, thinking processes, and actions. Here, information is collected about the results or effects of the treatment provided.

Courts in general have relied upon structural criteria for assessing and enforcing patient care and treatment, primarily because they are the easiest to document en masse (see, e.g., *Wyatt v. Stickney*, 1972). This is also the method most commonly used by social scientists in determining the effectiveness of treatment provided by correctional and mental institutions (Quay, 1977). However, it is also the least useful method for deciding whether treatment works and whether it is thus a justification for involuntary criminal or civil commitment. As we mentioned in discussing prison treatment programs, even an adequate staff-patient ratio or sufficient funding tell us little about the performance of the staff in implementing and achieving treatment goals. The case of *Whitree v. State* (1968), where an institution was fully staffed and funded, illustrates this point. The following excerpt from Schwitzgebel (1977, p. 141) outlines the case:

> Whitree received a suspended sentence for third-degree assault, violated probation, and was sent to Matteawan State Hospital, where he was evaluated as being unable to understand the proceedings aginst him. He spent the next 14½ years awaiting trial. During this time, he received no psychotherapy. What he did receive, however, was a fractured nose, a fractured right tibia, a fracture of the eighth and ninth ribs, and injury of two cervical vertebrae. Whitree also sustained other injuries, including a permanent peritonitis of the right shoulder [sic], which resulted from beatings by patients and hospital personnel. He suffered untreated rectal bleeding and headaches.

He was burned on his face and chest when a patient poured hot coffee on him. In spite of this, his prescription record for the 14 years of his confinement showed only that he received vaseline and rectal suppositories.

The hospital finally discharged Whitree as "improved." To this the court commented, "We consider the final diagnosis and the use of the word 'improve' the epitome of cynicism and a symbol in one word of the medical and psychiatric nontreatment received by this man over the greater part of 14½ years." The court awarded Whitree $300,000 in damages. There was a later out-of-court settlement for $200,000.

The second method of evaluating treatment, the process approach, focuses upon how much treatment is actually received. The methodology usually entails an examination of treatment plans, detailed records of treatment, and periodic review of patient records. The assessment is done strictly on the basis of what appears on the record. Thus, if a person received thirty minutes of "therapy" five days a week, it is presumed that he or she is receiving more treatment than a person receiving fifteen minutes, three days per week. The inadequacies of this approach need little further comment.

The third and probably most revealing method of evaluating treatment and psychotherapy has been used very infrequently (Coleman, 1976; Ennis & Emery, 1978; Kittrie, 1971). It is the most adequate method of studying treatment effect, because it is primarily concerned with the outcome and results of therapy, an orientation the courts should be taking when referring persons for treatment (Schwitzgebel, 1974). Contemporary research using this third method to assess the treatment provided in mental institutions indicates that the recovery rates for groups who receive various regimens of drugs, psychotherapy, or nothing at all are about the same (Schwitzgebel, 1974; Katz, 1969; Ennis & Litwack, 1974; Chambers, 1972; May, 1968; Eysenck, 1963; Hoffer & Osmond, 1966). "Although there appears to be a widely prevalent assumption among legislatures and courts that psychotherapeutic treatment as it is customarily practiced in institutions is generally effective in changing behavior, the available research data do not support this conclusion. . . . The evidence . . . tends to indicate that psychotherapy as traditionally practiced fails to produce demonstrable improvement . . . among involuntarily committed patients" (Schwitzgebel, 1974, pp. 938, 942). On the other hand, there is a small but growing number of studies which show that treatment provided in a community setting or on an outpatient basis is more effective than that provided in a hospital or institutional setting (see, generally, Ennis & Litwak, p. 718, note 80). These studies demonstrate that persons treated in the community recover faster, have fewer relapses, deteriorate less from dependency fostered by hospitalization, maintain employment better, and cost the state about half as much money as similar patients treated in hospitals.

## POTENTIAL ABUSES

Elimination of the institution and development of community centers would not mitigate the dangers of *parens patriae* power and its potential abuse, however. Although forced outpatient treatment under *parens patriae* justifications appears to be at least a better, more viable alternative than the traditional inpatient treatment of institutions, a disconcerting fact about outpatient programs must be considered. The major tool of community psychiatry is pharmacotherapy (Davis, 1975, 1976), which is increasing at exponential rates and is claimed to be a truly preventive approach to mental illness (Coleman & Solomon, 1976, p. 360). Increasing numbers of patients are being diagnosed "bipolar depressives," for which the highly toxic lithium carbonate is the preferred treatment (Davis, 1976). Clinics are being established whose sole function is to deliver maintenance doses of lithium on a lifetime prophylactic basis (Fieve, 1975). This type of drug maintenance is also increasingly used for those diagnosed "schizophrenic" (Davis, 1975).

The development of "depot" forms of psychoactive drugs, in which the drug is suspended in a medium that the body absorbs slowly, has been considered a great breakthrough by community psychiatrists (Ayd, 1975). Given by injection, the drugs may continue to exert their effect for several weeks and, with technological advances, for months or potentially even years. Depot drugs are especially useful for patients who resist taking medication on a regular basis. Ayd (1975, p. 491) even considers patients who resist taking forced medication "drug defectors." He adds that injectable, long-acting drugs are "a most important step forward" because they "remove responsibility for taking medicine from patients unable to assume it."

It is widely recognized, however, that the various forms of psychochemical treatment have serious limitations (Groves & Schlesinger, 1979). In most cases they merely alleviate some of the symptoms, and drug withdrawal can result in relapses without significant changes in the disordered behavior. Continuous treatment with drugs can also produce numerous serious side effects (Groves & Schlesinger, 1979).

Although radical forms of treatment, such as psychosurgery, are practiced infrequently today, there was a point in the history of psychiatry when involuntary frontal lobotomies were tried for every type of mental disorder from sexual deviancy to psychosis (Groves & Schlesinger, 1979). As more experience with this surgical procedure was gained, it became apparent that early reports of success were exaggerated and misleading. In many patients, the extensive destruction of the frontal lobes did not result in improvement, and in some patients with psychosis the condition was made worse (Freeman & Watts, 1942). Many disturbing side effects were noted several months after surgery, often involving substantial changes in personality and moods (Groves & Schlesinger, 1979). More recent studies have demonstrated that adequately matched lobectomized patients and non-operated-upon control patients showed no differences in improvement when rate of discharge from mental hospitals was used as a criterion of improvement (Robin & McDonald, 1975).

The gross psychosurgical techniques reported in the earlier years of psychiatry have given way to the more refined methods of stereotaxic surgery, where minute electrodes can be placed into various parts of the brain with precision. Electrical current or chemicals can be directed at different "centers" of the brain responsible for a wide assortment of behaviors. Potentially, this form of surgery can control a wide variety of thought processes, behaviors, and feelings (Mark & Ervin, 1970), although many claims appear to be overstated (Valenstein, 1973). The far-reaching effects of stereotaxic psychosurgery are as frightening as were those of lobotomy, because the treatments are undertaken with the same *parens patriae* justification. Society assumes these measures are being taken in the patient's best interest and does not require demonstrations of proven effectiveness.

# ■ The Right to Treatment

The right of involuntarily and voluntarily committed patients to receive treatment has generated considerable interest in recent years (e.g., Bassiouni, 1965; Drake, 1972; Goodman, 1969). It is pertinent here, because if the state is to exercise its *parens patriae* power there should be a concomitant justification for that exercise. If the treatment that would produce a "more adjusted" and "happier" human being does not exist, the individual's liberty has been denied unjustly. As an appeals court concluded in 1974, "Persons committed under what we have termed a parens patriae ground for commitment must be given treatment lest the involuntary commitment amount to an arbitrary exercise of government power proscribed by the due process clause" (*O'Connor v. Donaldson*, 1974).

In *Rouse v. Cameron* (1966), Judge David Bazelon declared that a right to treatment did indeed exist, at least in the District of Columbia. He noted, however, that the right did not include a right to a cure, or even to an improvement. Rather, all that was needed was a "bona fide" effort to provide patients with an individualized treatment program that includes periodic evaluation.

Another judge, in another case, declared that patients who are committed involuntarily to a state mental hospital "have a constitutional right to receive such individual treatment as will give each of them a realistic opportunity to be cured or to improve his or her mental condition" (*Wyatt v. Stickney*, 1971, pp. 784–785). This ruling was made in spite of an Alabama statute which permitted the commitment of persons to state institutions simply "for safekeeping." The court reasoned that "to deprive any citizen of his or her liberty upon the altruistic theory that the confinement is for humane therapeutic reasons and then fail to provide adequate treatment violates the very fundamentals of due process."

In the landmark U.S. Supreme Court case on the right to treatment, *O'Connor v. Donaldson* (1975), the Court acknowledged the inadequacy of treatment in mental institutions, but it did not resolve the question of whether there was a constitutional right to treatment. Although a federal appeals court succinctly outlined what it considered the constitutional basis for such a right, the Supreme Court stopped short of agreeing. Instead, it focused upon existing limitations of treatment.

The opinion, written by Justice Potter Stewart, asserted that a finding of "mental illness" alone cannot justify involuntary "custodial" confinement, nor can "mere public intolerance or animosity" constitutionally justify the deprivation of physical liberty. Donaldson had been confined to a mental institution for fifteen years, upon the recommendations of two nonpsychiatrist physicians and with the approval of the patient's father.

A concurring opinion offered by Chief Justice Warren Burger was more revealing about judicial understanding of psychiatric treatment and diagnosis. "The Court appropriately takes notice of the uncertainties of psychiatric diagnosis and therapy, and the reported cases are replete with evidence of the divergence of medical opinion in this vexing area," Burger noted. Further, "despite many recent advances in medical knowledge, it remains a stubborn fact that there are many forms of mental illness which are not understood, some of which are untreatable in the sense that no effective therapy has yet been discovered for them, and the rates of cure are generally low."

Hence, the issue of the constitutional right to treatment could not be broached, since the question of what constitutes adequate treatment could not be articulated.

In another observation, Justice Burger commented that "one of the few areas of agreement among behavioral specialists is that an uncooperative patient cannot benefit from therapy and that the first step in effective treatment is acknowledgement by the patient that he is suffering from an abnormal condition" (*O'Connor v. Donaldson,* 1975, p. 579). Most therapists and clinicians would agree that psychotherapy is destined to fail if it initially and continually eliminates the person's sense of control and freedom. This is precisely what happens when individuals are committed involuntarily, either to civil or criminal institutions. Even under the guise of *parens patriae* concerns, the fact remains that control and freedom have been removed from the individual.

The hallmark of successful therapy, no matter what perspective or school of thought we are considering, is the reestablishment of the person's sense of control and the elimination of inhibiting dependency and rigid social restraints. Committing individuals against their will into a regimented or choice-reducing institution ultimately defeats the purpose of treatment. Since most forms of psychotherapy are largely unsuccessful, involuntary confinement is certainly more a form of punishment than of treatment (Packer, 1968). Persons released as "improved" by hospital officials are usually nothing more than persons attempting to escape the punishment and freedom-reducing conditions of the institution. It remains clear that claims of successful treatment are empirically unfounded, and even statements of adequate treatment are suspect. Therefore, involuntary commitment for treatment purposes should be recognized for what it is: a form of social control for deviant behavior.

Unchecked, the concept of *parens patriae* will lead to total intrusion by the state into the personal lives of its citizens. The most pervasive and influential vanguard of the power in mental health law is psychiatry, although clinical psychology and social work are not far behind. To the extent that society looks the other way when persons are committed to mental institutions against their will, it too is an accomplice in allowing the expansion of *parens patriae* philosophy. The legal profession, however, often encourages this apathy. Too many lawyers have taken strong, nonadversary stances toward the medical-psychiatric profession, refusing to question its determinations of mental illness, dangerousness, and amenability to and effectiveness of treatment. The following discussion of selected state statutes illustrates this point.

## ▪ Attempts at Statutory Regulation of Parens Patriae

In 1975 the state of Iowa enacted legislation designed to limit the number of persons potentially subject to civil commitment through passage of rigorous commitment laws (Bezanson, 1975). The primary intention was to restrict the *parens patriae* elements in commitment proceedings and place greater emphasis on police power justifications. The new Iowa law mandated that, prior to involuntary civil commitment, courts must find by clear and convincing evidence that individuals are (1) mentally ill; (2) incapable of making a decision regarding treatment; (3) amenable to treatment; and (4) likely to be dangerous to selves or to others (Stier & Stoebe, 1979). The statute also advocated that defense attorneys challenge the credentials of medical experts, question their diagnoses, offer rebutting expert testimony, and submit factual evidence refuting expert opinions (Stier & Stoebe, 1979).

Despite the establishment of these more stringent requirements, an extensive study of the implementation of the new Iowa law found virtually no change in commitment proceedings from the pre-1975 practice of automatic involuntary commitment based on a recommendation by a physician or psychiatrist (Stier & Stoebe, 1979). From the precustody hearing to the hospitalization proceedings, court officials and defense attorneys continue to display nearly complete deference to the recommendations of medical experts. In most cases, the medical expert who examined the individual was not present during the hearings, but merely submitted a written report, often including nothing but a diagnosis of mental illness. Furthermore, fewer than one percent of the cases adjudicated after the statute went into effect included a second opinion.

The Iowa study also revealed that nearly 75 percent of the hospitalization hearings were conducted in a nonadversary manner. The decisionmaking power was given to the medical profession, while the defense attorneys and hearing officers assumed a ceremonial function. Court officials and psychiatrists justified this deviation from the adversary process by claiming it was in the best interest of the affected individual, since challenges and arguments would upset the person. Actually, when adversary hearings were used, no such reaction on the part of the subject occurred (Stier & Stoebe, 1979). Most defense attorneys concluded that medical testimony should not be rebutted. More disconcerting, however, was the finding that many of the defense lawyers viewed their clients as incompetent, because of their own stereotypes of "crazy" behavior. They not only decided that medical opinion should not be questioned, but also felt they should "help" their clients by obtaining treatment for them, regardless of the client's expressed wishes. Despite the alleged intent of the 1975 statute, therefore, the *parens patriae* rationale continues to influence the decisionmaking process in that state.

The Iowa study also found that very rarely were the four necessary components outlined by the new statute followed. In most involuntary commitment cases, the diagnosis of mental illness, as solely determined by one psychiatrist, was justification for commitment. Although there is widespread recognition that mental illness is not synonymous with mental incapacity, the component of judgmental capacity was usually ignored by psychiatrists and court officials. Amenability to treatment was also ignored.

The major innovation of the new Iowa law is the requirement that the individual be "dangerous" as well as mentally ill. A finding of dangerousness requires a showing that the person is likely to inflict physical harm upon himself or herself or others, or is likely to inflict serious emotional injury on those who lack reasonable opportunity to avoid contact with the person (e.g., one's children).

Again, this major innovation was not implemented in actual practice. Most members of the legal profession remained convinced that dangerousness should be determined by psychiatrists, and they seldom scrutinized the basis of those determinations. Yet, in about half of the commitments reviewed, the hearing record contained no evidence of dangerousness.

A study of California's Lanterman-Petris-Short Act further illustrates legal deference to medical experts and confusion of *parens patriae* with police power (Warren, 1977). The cases of 100 persons involuntarily committed to mental institutions on a 72-hour basis were studied. Although the California law establishes various commitment stages which differ in length, Warren was concerned with the initial stages of commitment and the transition between the initial temporary stage and a more permanent long-term commitment.

The LPS Act dichotomizes the committable mentally ill into "gravely disabled" and "imminently dangerous" categories (Welfare and Institutions Code sections 5300–5306). Thus, the statute allows a *parens patriae* rationale for use with individuals who are assessed as gravely disabled, while requiring a police power rationale for those considered dangerous to selves or others. Gravely disabled persons are those demonstrating inability to provide basic needs of food, clothing, and shelter for themselves. "Dangerousness" is not clearly specified, but reference is made to acts which are likely to lead to "physical harm."

Warren (1977) reports a wide discrepancy between the intention and language of the LPS Act and its administration. "Gravely disabled" determinations, she found, were not based on inability to provide basic necessities. They were based strictly on medical conclusions that took into account refusal to take medicine, prior hospitalization record, a tendency to deny mental illness to the psychiatrist, cooperation with mental health personnel, and the amount of rejection expressed by the patient's family. All of these determinations were based on the *parens patriae* rationale, "We know what is best."

Many of the criteria used to arrive at grave disability were also used as a basis for dangerousness. In almost all the cases, there was a notable failure by the court and the medical expert to try to ascertain the imminence and seriousness of danger to others. It is interesting to note also that in a majority of cases, the initial commitment on the ground of danger to others was bargained down to grave disablement as a basis for continued commitment. This suggests the influence of medical experts and their greater comfort with *parens patriae* than with police power rationales.

North Carolina has also rewritten its mental commitment statutes, ostensibly to reduce the number of involuntary commitments. A 1973 law permits commitment only when an individual is both "mentally ill" and imminently dangerous to self or others (Hiday, 1977). Although Hiday found some evidence that courts in that state have shown slightly less deference to psychiatrists in the implementation of the reformed statutes, "we still find numerous instances of deference and commitment where a preponderance of evidence does not support imminent danger to self or others." The primary reason seems to be the lack of knowledge of judges and lawyers about psychiatrists and mental illness which "allows psychiatrists to become the effective decision makers, often in absentia" (Hiday, 1977, p. 655). Ennis and Litwack (1974) and Morse (1978b) have made similar observations.

Studies of commitment decisions in other states have shown that courts follow psychiatric recommendations in more than 94 percent of all cases (Wexler & Scoville, 1971; Rock, Jacobson & Janopaul, 1968; Wenger & Fletcher, 1969; Zander, 1976; Pfrender, 1965). Moreover, the length of the commitment hearings ranged from 1.9 minutes in Texas (Cohen, 1966) and 4.7 minutes in Arizona (Wexler & Scoville, 1971) to 18.4 minutes in North Carolina (Hiday, 1977).

In Wisconsin, a federal court rejected the *parens patriae* argument in favor of police power requirements. The case, *Lessard v. Schmidt* (1972) (see box), has been referred to as the "first comprehensive federal court ruling on the substantive and procedural constitutional limitations on civil commitment" (Zander, 1976, p. 504). It has also functioned as precedent for the formation of numerous other state statutes, although as we have seen, a statute on the books does not mean its intent will be carried out. Subsequently, the state adopted a new mental health statute which dictated substantial changes and safeguards in procedures for involuntary commitment, including allowance for a jury trial at the original commitment hearing and at each subsequent reexamination.

The Wisconsin law was intended to exclude from commitment the nondangerous mentally ill and dilute the power of the *parens patriae* rationale (Zander, 1976; Bartol, 1981). Due process guarantees were to be assured, and commitment was to be based on standards of dangerousness. Shortly after the law was enacted, however, "incompetency commitments" began to increase—in fact, they rose 42 percent in the one-year period following the new statute (Dickey, 1980). According to Wisconsin statutes, persons suspected of crimes are committed to mental institutions for a sixty-day psychiatric examination and may ultimately be confined for up to twenty-four months if determined incompetent.

Since the state has restricted the incidences of unwarranted commitment with its new Mental Health Act, the legal system began to make more use of the back door—the incompetency hearing. Bizarre but nontroublesome persons must still be kept off the streets. Since a criminal charge is necessary for an incompetency determination, however, courts have resorted to using minor misdemeanors, like disorderly conduct, as a justification to commit bothersome individuals against their will. Dickey (1980) found that, in all the misdemeanor incompetency commitments he studied, the criminal charges were dropped once commitment time had been served.

Therefore, despite attempts by the Wisconsin legislature and courts to restrict commitment to a dangerousness standard, some courts, with the very necessary assistance of the medical profession, continue to commit the unwanted and the bizarre on the basis of a misused *parens patriae* power and a thinly veiled social-sanction rationale. Unable to establish dangerousness beyond a reasonable doubt, some Wisconsin courts have resorted to minor criminal charges to circumvent due process requirements, presumably believing it is both in the individual's and ultimately in society's best interest.

# ■ Summary and Conclusions

In this chapter we have been concerned with the two best known American institutions of confinement—the prison and the so-called mental hospital. We have examined the effects of deterrence, prison overcrowding, forced treatment, and solitary confinement in the correctional system from a psychological perspective. Although the data are widely scattered throughout a variety of topics and were acquired with a spectrum of methodological soundness, some preliminary, cautious statements can be made about trends in these areas. Deterrence appears to be effective only under certain limited conditions. Psychotherapy as often practiced in the current correctional system is destined to fail for a variety of reasons. Individual differences in observed ability to handle prison stress and solitary confinement emerge with some consistency, although situational factors (such as time left to serve) continue to exert powerful forces on prisoner behavioral patterns.

We then discussed confinement based on civil commitment. Given our present

---

## ☐ LESSARD v. SCHMIDT

The police and judicial actions that were to result in a precedent-setting case having implications for mental health law in Wisconsin began in late October, 1971, when Alberta Lessard was taken by two police officers to an emergency detention center for mental observation. Ten days later, still in custody after she had been examined without warning by two physicians and interviewed by a judge, she decided she had better contact an attorney. By this time, the label "paranoid schizophrenic" had been entered on her record by physicians. Despite legal representation, on November 24 she was ordered committed for another thirty days. The presiding judge gave no reason for his ruling other than to state he found her "mentally ill." The thirty-day period was extended each month for ninety days, and the law offered no provision for an interim hearing.

Subsequently, a class action suit was filed on behalf of Lessard and other persons held involuntarily either on a permanent, temporary, or emergency basis. They alleged that due process had been violated in a number of areas, including failure to describe a standard for commitment, failure to make hearings mandatory, and failure to provide access to a psychiatric exam by a physician of the person's choosing.

In upholding the petitioners' claims, the Wisconsin state district court noted that state commitment procedures have not traditionally assured due-process safeguards against unjustified deprivation of liberty, under the assumption that states were acting in a person's best interest—not to punish but to treat. Although the court noted that the right to treatment was not at issue, the well-documented difficulties in enforcing such a right were pertinent.

"No significant deprivation of liberty can be justified without a prior hearing on the necessity of detention," the court ruled. The court did, however, allow emergency detention of persons threatening violence to themselves or others, provided a hearing before a neutral judge were arranged. The maximum time of such detention was 48 hours. Therefore, involuntary commitment could continue if the potential for harm were great. The court resisted defining harm other than to assert that if there was an "extreme likelihood that if a person is not confined he will do immediate harm to himself or others . . . dangerousness is based upon a finding of a recent overt act, attempt or threat to do substantial harm to oneself or another." The court also said that the state "must prove *beyond a reasonable doubt* all facts necessary to show that an individual is mentally ill *and* dangerous" (italics added).

state of knowledge about human behavior and our ability to change it "for the better" in institutional settings, *parens patriae* as a justification for involuntary commitment of persons exhibiting nondangerous deviant or unusual behavior does not appear to be a viable doctrine. Despite some claims to the contrary, commitment of the unwanted and the bizarre for their "best interest" appears to be in most cases restrictive warehousing.

A commonality reported in many studies examining the civil commitment process is the rejection of the subject by the family. For instance, Warren (1977) found that the family, directly or indirectly, was the source of almost half of the commitments in her sample and, more importantly, rejection by the family was a principal factor in sustaining involuntary commitment under all three California criteria. Stone (1975, p. 46) refers to the frequent practice of family warehousing of one or more members considered bothersome as the "convenience function." He notes this function has "seldom been explicitly acknowledged, rather it has been hidden behind a promise of technical treatment, although at some points during the past century it has been the only goal actually achieved" (p. 46). Stone adds that this convenience function is "a typical instance of the clandestine decisionmaking role of mental health practitioners which allows society to do what it does not want to admit to doing, i.e., confining unwanted persons cheaply."

On the other hand, there are persons in society who are mean, brutal, and potentially dangerous to others. Society wants, and undoubtedly needs, to confine these individuals for its protection. However, confinement of these persons should be based on a police power rationale of dangerousness, with a clear understanding of the primitive art of behavioral prediction and the lack of adequate treatment methods in institutions to alter dangerous, violent behavior.

We found that the legal system's heavy reliance and strong deference to the medical profession on questions of human behavior is unwarranted. There are many other professionals and potential expert witnesses who can provide substantially more information on questions related to legally relevant behavior than medicine and psychiatry. Most legal questions concerning assessment and predictions of human behaviors call for many types of expertise, and there is no reason to believe that any one expert is able to answer all of them in a given case. The relevant expertise may come from many disciplines, including non-mental-health disciplines. By qualifying only physicians, psychiatrists, and sometimes psychologists as experts, the courts have lost the valuable services of other professionals. Such restriction has prompted the mistaken view that abnormal behavior and its consequences are uniquely medical or quasi-medical matters.

# ■ Key Concepts and Principles, Chapter 11

| | |
|---|---|
| Four fundamental rationales for criminal punishment | Three principles of effectiveness of punishment |
| Reasons for failure of rehabilitation | Stanford prison simulation |
| General and special deterrence | Prisonization |
| Vicarious punishment | U-shaped function of sentence phase |
| Threats of punishment | Right to treatment |

# ■ Psychology and the Law: A Summing Up

□ | This text has been critical of both law and psychology. The empirical results and theoretical formulations of psychology should be viewed with as much skepticism as the fireside inductions about human behavior promoted by law and the judicial system. Scientific data and conclusions advanced by psychology should be approached as cautiously as some of the glib and dogmatic generalizations offered by the legal profession.

We also should not forget that psychology and law are different from one another in philosophy, historical foundation, and general approach to human problems and issues. As one of the disciplines which deal with living organisms, scientific psychology—particularly academic psychology—is interpolated between the biological sciences and the social sciences. It relies heavily upon the scientific method for the accumulation of knowledge. The science of psychology stresses the scientific attitude of objectivity, methods of controlling situations and variables to discern what variables are affecting target behaviors, and the quantification and measurement of human variables. Hypotheses are tested and theories are developed from the collection of consistent and supporting data. Since pieces of information do not always fit together, multiple interpretations result, controversies emerge, and debates are common.

Testable theories replace other testable theories which have failed to account adequately for empirical findings. Multiple theories may arise from the data, and these theories may have to be modified to encompass still further empirical findings. Generally, what was hypothesized as a simple relationship soon mushrooms into increasing complexity, and researchers become less certain and less willing to draw firm conclusions about the nature of a relationship. Answers to questions become progressively qualified. Well-trained and knowledgeable psychologists often answer specific questions about behavior with a variant of "it depends."

Innovative and novel ways of looking at and integrating the scientific data are usually rewarded in psychology, which in a sense may be considered a "fad science."

Psychology always looks for new areas to explore but rarely completely explores all the many niches in each area. New ground is broken when someone proposes relatively simple hypotheses, but these inevitably become discouragingly complex. As the topic under study becomes a bewildering array of interactions and relationships, a majority of the once-interested researchers leave the fold in search of a new frontier, leaving a lingering few to "settle" the issue.

Law is conservative and traditional in its approach to human behavior and societal concerns. It operates on the precedential or *stare decisis* principle, in which past decisions often dictate the current ones (Haney, 1980). When statutes do not apply or are ambiguous, decisions are usually made on the basis of previous opinions and decisions of appellate courts of distinction or authority. Law cannot respond to every fad or zeitgeist on the horizon; to do so would create the uncomfortable risk of the legal system losing its cultural, traditional, and moral bearings. Responsive innovation and excessive creativity would promote legal fluidity, which would raise havoc with the little consistency, structure, and orderliness currently existing in the system. Therefore, lawyers and judges are taught to be intellectually conservative, but able to weave legal tapestry based upon previous decisions, which may be completely subjective interpretations of the intent and opinion of previous rulings. The intent of statutes or doctrines (such as the Constitution) is also interpreted subjectively. There is little to prevent a judge, especially at the appellate level, from interpreting precedent, statutes, or legal doctrines in a unique fashion. Statutes enacted by legislatures are often written not only to accommodate divergent interests and opinions within the legislative body, but also to allow multiple interpretations and applications to the variety of subsequent cases at which the statutes are directed.

There is both subjectivity and traditional thinking at work in case law and to a large extent in statutory and constitutional law. However, precedent also perpetuates fireside induction and gross biases and misconceptions about human behavior. The high status of precedence in law draws attention away from current scientific inquiry and achievements and builds pyramids of inaccuracy about human behavior, all based on the authority of some distinguished judge or group of judges who may know law but often know little about the science of behavior.

As we noted in earlier chapters, psychology and law arrive at "truth" in decidedly different ways. Truth for psychology is gained through the scientific methods of hypotheses testing, sound methodological construction, quantification and measurement, and objective interpretations of the data. Truth is, of course, an ideal which is seldom reached. Our travels through the research literature throughout the text remind us of this. However, there is a concerted attempt by behavioral scientists to approximate the ideal as much as possible.

Law, by contrast, relies on the adversarial process to discover truth. The ambiguity of the law encourages participants to present their best case in a combative fashion, since both sides have expectations of "winning." If the law were clear and concise, the adversarial or combative process would be severely undermined. Lawyers selectively choose precedent and current folklore or science to build their case and present their clients in the most favorable light.

The combative method of truth derivation encourages highly subjective interpretations of legal data. Lawyers can pick and choose what segment of the research litera-ture to present and what to avoid. In the behavioral sciences, it is likely that for every collection of data presented in favor of one side, there exists a contradictory collection of data related to the same issue. Hence, psychologists armed with one set of empirical information testify on behalf of one side, while their colleagues appear on the opposite side of the courtroom with their own contradictory research. This process often por-trays psychology as a muddled and fickle art, not sure of anything and convincing no one. In reality, lawyers are taking advantage of the inconclusive, suggestive nature of science, especially the behavioral and social sciences. Dogmatic and conclusive state-ments are shunned and often intellectually punished by the science community, but authoritative statements are expected and rewarded by the legal process.

Law emphasizes the individual case; psychology focuses upon trends in groups. Law moves from specific case to case with interpretations of law applied to each situa-tion, at least in the litigious and adjudicative process. The science of psychology at-tempts to discover lawful relationships which develop into sound theory as general explanations of human behavior across situations and personalities. As Craig Haney (1980) notes, to some degree clinical psychologists are more inclined toward the in-dividualized (idiographic) perspective, which may account for the greater frequency with which clinicians have been called to testify in legal settings.

The courts are reluctant to admit empirical generalizations into evidence, because the case at hand is more relevant than global statements about probabilities and trends. Therefore, lawyers and judges acquire their incomplete knowledge about behavioral science in a piecemeal and fragmented manner and rarely have an opportunity to consider theories and supportive data.

As stressed throughout the book, law is a social and moral enterprise hinged on political and economic realities. The science of psychology is an objective enterprise, presumably independent of social or moralistic premises and only minimally linked to political and economic realities. Theoretically, psychology can do as it damn well pleases; the law cannot. Law must answer to societal and religious concerns, teach the lessons of criminal law, and respond to political and financial interests. It is an insti-tution of high visibility and authority.

Psychologists who believe that law's refusal to place great faith on psychological experiments is based primarily on inertia do not understand the differences in respon-sibilities and viewpoints of the two disciplines. Moreover, as we have discovered, psy-chology's contributions to law have hardly been spectacular. When viewed cautiously and skeptically, however, psychological literature can be seen making small, step-by-step, valid contributions to the legal process. Psychological data should be afforded tentative status, with acknowledgement from both disciplines that expansive and valu-able contributions are yet to come.

Psychologists who testify in court should continue to present evidence in the most scientific and cautious way, regardless of the badgering or pressures applied by lawyers trying to elicit broad conclusions or dogmatic statements. Whenever possible, it should be communicated to the decisionmakers that the results are tentative and suggestive of different interpretations, and that this is the nature of science. The danger with tentativeness, of course, is that "unlike law, the authority of science evaporates when immersed in controversy" (Haney, 1980, p. 183). A lawyer who cannot elicit firm conclusions from his or her expert witness is at a disadvantage. Tentativeness bodes ill for one's case.

On the other hand, law resists the science of human behavior when information is clear-cut. Law thrives on ambiguity, because this allows wide latitude in discretion and ultimately cultivates power and control. Clear, undisputable scientific evidence would have overwhelming impact in the courtroom on the traditional process of law. The validity of lie-detection equipment is a case in point. If the science of behavior eventually becomes able to provide conclusive evidence on a number of legally relevant behaviors and issues, judges and lawyers may no longer be able to describe human behavior in and on their own terms.

The legal system likes to manipulate psychology, which as we have seen is characteristic of the psychology *in* law relationship. Firm conclusions are not wanted unless they can be used to the advantage of one's client. As long as psychologists persist in playing the lawyers' game by the lawyers' rules, the potential contributions of psychology to law will not be realized.

Another problem which interferes with the communication and understanding between psychology and law is that psychology is not a single or coherent discipline, but a disordered spectrum of many disciplines all claiming the banner "psychology" as their logo. Freudians claim that their perspective is the first and true religion, humanists argue that they are the vanguard of the human spirit, and behaviorists assert that they are the self-anointed true believers of the science of behavior. To compound the problem, each of these major schools embraces numerous internal subdivisions which differ in basic methods and conceptual ordering of human behavior. The heterogeneous viewpoints engender considerable misunderstanding about what psychology is and what it can do. On the other hand, although there are many specialties and different emphases in law, it is fundamentally a relatively single and coherent discipline following the "time-proven" methods of the profession.

This book has concentrated upon psychology as the science of behavior and has tried to extend some of the empirical findings to the practice of law. Science is a slow, gradual process which requires concise and precise conceptual ordering of events. Law is largely an art which is based upon the political, social, moral and economic perspectives and forces of society. The legal profession seems to resist or even fear the finality and conclusiveness of science and its discipline. As the legal scholar Laurence Tribe (1971) concludes: "In an era when the power but not the wisdom of science is increasingly taken for granted, there has been a rapidly growing interest in the conjunction of mathematics and the trial process. . . . Surely the time has come for someone to suggest that the union would be more dangerous than fruitful" (p. 1391).

Science rarely provides firm conclusions. Rather, it offers building blocks, limited in scope, toward knowledge. A science imposes limits on itself and makes its gradual progress by examining that which it is fitted to investigate by existing knowledge and methods (Hebb, 1974), and it must stay limited in scope to insure its progress. The reader has undoubtedly found that the science of behavior offers only segmented, partial answers to complicated puzzles. With patience and a very high tolerance for ambiguity, psychology has become and can continue to be an increasingly valuable source of knowledge for the law. Law, on the other hand, is impatient and anxious not so much for resolution of human affairs as a settlement of human conflict.

# ■ The Future of Psychology and Law

If the reader has arrived at this point with little closure about psychology and its relationship to law, we have been successful at portraying accurately the current state of affairs. Psychology's contributions to the judicial system form a midnight landscape, with events and objects poorly defined and only vaguely understood. Psycholegal research is being conducted, but theoretical integration of this fact-gathering activity is weak or nonexistent. What theories are available are borrowed from the other fields of psychology, such as social psychology and learning and memory, and they do not relate directly to the psychology-law interface. The new and developing field of psychology *and* law lacks testable theory of its own. In fact, the field of psychology in general lacks unifying, testable theory.

The scarcity of testable theory is hardly unique to psychology, however. It is a characteristic of all developing sciences (Kuhn, 1970). Still, the student of psychology finds the science of human behavior a bewildering morass of disconnected data. Donald O. Hebb (1974, p. 71), a long-time observer and master of psychology, summarizes it well:

> For a quarter century or more, ever since the end of World War II, psychology has been growing fast in ideas, methods, knowledge—data all over the place. To maintain perspective is difficult enough, but the difficulty is increased by our publications. It is bad not to see the wood for the trees, but worse not even to get to see a real tree because you're lost in the bushes, the undergrowth of insignificant detail and so-called replications, the trivial, the transient, the papers that haven't an idea anywhere about them.

Therefore, the future of psychology and law as a viable discipline will proceed most productively not simply by the further proliferation of data urged on by the shopworn call for more and better research, but by the creation and development of unifying, testable theories. As Fred Kerlinger (1973, p. 8) has convincingly asserted: "The basic aim of science is theory." In psychology, this aim extends to psychological assessment as well as judicial decisionmaking. Without some guiding idea for determining what is relevant and what is not, the advancement of our knowledge will be severely restricted.

As we have seen, much psycholegal research has used the simulation paradigm, which for a new discipline with few theoretical underpinnings presents some critical problems in the acquisition of knowledge about an intact, functioning social system. Valdimir Konečni and Ebbe Ebbesen (1981) have argued that the key to understanding the judicial system is natural research and archival methodology. In other words, it is paramount that psychologists do *in situ* research, where data are collected from the real world of the legal process. Proponents of the simulation paradigm contend, however, that access to the judicial system is generally highly limited and that the laboratory is the best place to test theories under systematically controlled conditions. It does appear that, considering the rather primordial stage at which the psychology *and* law field finds itself, observation, hypothesis development, and theory building could be best accomplished by studying the natural operations of the judicial system rather than by conducting research in the artificial surroundings of the psychological laboratory. Once testable theories are constructed, it might be wise to test certain nuances of a theory under simulated conditions. Without some theoretical idea of what we are seeking, however, data gathered by simulation will take us nowhere.

Access to many facets of the judicial system and process is limited, and this reality is used as another argument for the value of simulation research. As we have already noted, however, the external validity of simulation research is questionable, and the information gained through these procedures may be misinformation about the judicial system and the law. The data may not represent legal operations at all, and it may be better that this inaccurate material not be communicated to society and the legal profession in the first place.

Studying the legal process from a psychological perspective is likely to require creative ideas and ingenious strategies, some of which have yet to be conceived of or tried. Ultimately, the most fruitful investigation of human behavior may even be something beyond the current scientific method.

As we stated in Chapter 1, the science of human behavior is an extremely fragile enterprise. Perhaps one of the greatest challenges in the future of psychology and law will lie with the realization that, while knowledge can be gained through logic, common sense, and authority, the method which promises to provide resolutions of complex problems is the scientific one—at least until something better comes along. It is a common occurrence for students of the behavioral sciences to flip out of the scientific, empirical orientation of studying human behavior to more humanistic, metaphysical leanings, and then back again. The science of human behavior must be cultivated and nourished continually in our society. As Loren Eisley (1973, p. 33) has astutely observed: "Science does not come easily to men; they must be made to envision its possibilities." And further, "Even today, when scientific achievements surround us on every hand and the textbooks of our schools bulge with illustrative experiments, men are, in the mass, still emotional and resistant to fact, particularly in their political and social thinking" (p. 19).

Students of the psychology *and* law relationship will be called upon to educate society and the legal profession about psychology as a scientific enterprise that in its infancy has far more limitations and incompetencies than it does skills and competencies. As we have seen, psychologists are not outstanding predictors of dangerousness and other legally relevant future behavior. Trait and psychodynamic psychologists have led us too long in believing that individual differences in personality account for most of the behavior found in all situations. In reaction against these schools of thought, situationism has swayed us too far in the other direction. Perhaps interactionism presents the best balance. The science of judicial-legal psychology has an extremely promising future, but it demands a commitment to creative, persistent theory building.

The aim of the science of behavior is not necessarily to make possible a better society through the continuous improvement of the human condition. The aim of scientific psychology is theory, which leads to an understanding and prediction of human behavior. The aim of psycholegal research is to discover theories relevant to the legal process, which may or may not be used by its participants.

Finally, the material presented in this book will soon be dated. New findings will modify and replace old findings, and in view of the present rate of psycholegal research, this is likely to occur very quickly. If the research is well designed, it will produce a change in the degrees of probability and confidence psychologists will be able to offer. However, the underlying problems, issues, and goals of psychology and law will remain the same.

# ■ Ethical Issues

Psychologists working in the judicial system face a number of ethical or moral dilemmas which do not lend themselves to straightforward solutions. Although these dilemmas occur at all levels of the legal system, most occur within criminal justice. Since about 70 percent of psychologists in criminal justice are employed within the correctional system, we can expect that a sizeable proportion of these moral dilemmas will be encountered by correctional psychologists. The most common revolve around issues of confidentiality, competence, and professional roles.

### CONFIDENTIALITY

According to APA-endorsed ethical principles (APA, 1981, p. 636),

> Psychologists have a primary obligation to respect the confidentiality of information obtained from persons in the course of their work as psychologists. They reveal such information to others only with the consent of the person or the person's legal representative, except in those unusual circumstances in which not to do so would result in clear danger to the person or to others. Where appropriate, psychologists inform their clients of the legal limits of confidentiality.

It is also recommended that every effort be made to avoid undue invasion of privacy, and this is especially true with reference to court-ordered interviews and assessments, repeated orally and in writing. Information provided to the courts should be germane only to the purpose of the evaluation.

In *Tarasoff v. Regents of the University of California* (1976), the California State Supreme Court twice heard a case involving a mental health outpatient who confided to his therapist his intention to kill an individual—a threat which he eventually carried out (see box). Amicus curiae briefs filed by various professional organizations contended, among other points, that therapists do not possess special professional expertise in gauging their patients' level of dangerousness. However, the court majority rejected that argument. Realizing the limitations of predictions of dangerousness, the justices said, "the therapist is free to exercise his or her own best judgment without liability" (p. 345). Nevertheless, the court held that "once a therapist does in fact determine, or under applicable professional standards should have determined, that a patient poses a serious danger of violence to others, he bears a duty to exercise reasonable care to protect the forseeable victims of that danger" (p. 345).

Alan Stone (1976) finds the *Tarasoff* decision potentially destructive and intolerably intrusive into the confidentiality of the therapist-patient alliance which depends so much upon trust and secrecy. On the other hand, David Wexler (1981) sees considerable value in the decision, because it "has the clear-cut potential of prompting and prodding practicing therapists to terminate their continual clinging to an outmoded 'individual pathology' model of violence, and to accept the paradigm of 'interactional' or 'couple' violence already endorsed by the professional literature" (p. 160). Wexler argues, therefore, that *Tarasoff* will encourage therapists to look beyond the isolationist view of the internal states of individuals and into the social milieu in which they function.

Although a plethora of commentary has been generated by *Tarasoff*, much of the commentary wondering about its implications, it appears that determining what constitutes "clear and imminent danger" will be left largely to the discretion of the individual psychologist. Most puzzling to the professional is the question, "What probability cutoff point should I use in deciding when to contact potential victims or authorities?" Assume, for instance, that a psychologist is 10 percent sure that a patient is lethally dangerous to a specific victim. Should the psychologist contact anyone, or should he or she wait until the probability is higher, say 25 percent? And what about

---

## ☐ TARASOFF v. REGENTS

In late 1969 a young California woman was murdered by a man who two months earlier had confided his intention to kill her to his psychologist. Although the psychologist, who was employed by the University of California, notified campus police of the death threat, he informed no one else but his supervisor. Police questioned the patient but did not detain him. At that point the supervisor directed that no further action be taken. After the murder, the woman's parents sued the University, the psychologists, and the police for failing to confine the man and for not warning the family.

Following are excerpts from the decision by the California Supreme Court, which ruled that the therapist did not exercise reasonable care to protect the woman. Police, on the other hand, were not held responsible.

We shall explain that defendant therapists cannot escape liability merely because [the woman] herself was not their patient. When a therapist determines, or pursuant to the standards of his profession should determine, that his patient presents a serious danger of violence to another, he incurs an obligation to use reasonable care to protect the intended victim against such danger. The discharge of this duty may require the therapist to take one or more of various steps, depending upon the nature of the case. Thus it may call for him to warn the intended victim or others likely to apprise the victim of the danger, to notify the police, or to take whatever other steps are reasonably necessary under the circumstances. . . .

As a general principle, a "defendant owes a duty of care to all persons who are foreseeably endangered by his conduct, with respect to all risks which make the conduct unreasonably dangerous." . . .

Defendants contend . . . that imposition of

situations in which clients admit to having already committed a serious crime, like arson? Under what conditions would it be proper for psychologists to breach a confidential relationship, if there is no indication that lives are at stake? Unless answers to perplexing questions surrounding confidentiality are carved out in court decisions, psychologists have little choice other than to rely upon their own subjective judgments.

## COMPETENCE

A cardinal rule repeatedly stressed by the American Psychological Association in its ethical standards (1981) is that the psychologist must recognize the boundaries of his or her competence and the limitations of techniques. This standard requires psychologists to be familiar with the research literature in areas in which they are working and are likely to testify about. In addition, psychologists should have a thorough knowledge of the system in which they are operating. If a psychologist is doing research on jury selection, it is incumbent upon the researcher to become as knowledgeable as possible about the judicial process of jury selection. As we saw in the chapter on jury research, this does not always happen.

---

a duty to exercise reasonable care to protect third persons is unworkable because therapists cannot accurately predict whether or not a patient will resort to violence. In support of this argument amicus representing the American Psychiatric Association and other professional societies cites numerous articles which indicate that therapists, in the present state of the art, are unable reliably to predict violent acts; their forecasts, amicus claims, tend consistently to overpredict violence, and indeed are more often wrong than right. Since predictions of violence are often erroneous, amicus concludes, the courts should not render rulings that predicate the liability of therapists upon the validity of such predictions. . . .

We recognize the difficulty that a therapist encounters in attempting to forecast whether a patient presents a serious danger of violence. Obviously we do not require that the therapist, in making that determination, render a perfect performance; the therapist need only exercise "that reasonable degree of skill, knowledge, and care ordinarily possessed and exercised by members of [that professional specialty] under similar circumstances."

Within the broad range of reasonable practice and treatment in which professional opinion and judgment may differ, the therapist is free to exercise his or her own best judgment without liability; proof, aided by hindsight, that he or she judged wrongly is insufficient to establish negligence.

In the instant case, however, the pleadings do not raise any question as to failure of defendant therapists to predict that [the patient] presented a serious danger of violence. On the contrary, the present complaints allege that defendant therapists did in fact predict [he] would kill, but were negligent in failing to warn.

We realize that the open and confidential character of psychotherapeutic dialogue encourages patients to express threats of violence, few of which are ever executed. Certainly a therapist should not be encouraged routinely to reveal such threats; such disclosures could seriously disrupt the patient's relationship with his therapist and with the persons threatened. To the contrary, the therapist's obligations to his patient require that he not disclose a confidence unless such disclosure is necessary to avert danger to others, and even then that he do so discreetly, and in a fashion that would preserve the privacy of his patient to the fullest extent compatible with the prevention of the threatened danger.

At all levels of the judicial system, psychologists must take pains to point out the limitations of psychological knowledge and make appropriate qualifications about psychological generalizations. For example, they should be frank about predictions of dangerousness and violence, the effectiveness of coerced treatment, the problems in determining mental competency, and the enormous difficulties inherent in evaluating criminal responsibility. They should be exceedingly cautious in offering predictions of criminal behavior when these predictions will be used to make determinations about imprisonment, release, or treatment.

Finally, psychologists should be aware of the extensive intrusion of personal values and biases into the assessment and treatment process. Neither psychological assessment nor therapy can be provided value-free. This involves recognizing the limitations of traditional emphases on testing, classification, and prediction—individual factors—to the exclusion of economic, social, political, and other situational forces. The mutual interaction of individual and situational forces must be reckoned with if behavioral assessments are to be offered.

## PROFESSIONAL ROLES

Ethical issues surrounding roles are related to the question, "Who is (or should) the psychologist be working for and be loyal to?" Should correctional psychologists be committed to their individual clients—the offenders—or should their loyalties reside with society, the system, or the profession of psychology? Should they conceive of their functions as primarily custodial or as treatment based? If psychologists believe that treatment under the coercive and repressive atmosphere of the institution is largely ineffective, should they become advocates of noncoercive treatment and adversaries of the present system? The best solution may be to conceptualize one's professional role with regard to priorities rather than absolutes. That is, it may be necessary to clarify one's role by establishing a conceptual role hierarchy, identifying top loyalties and conditions to which they are limited.

Listing priorities may be the best approach to take, because in most cases the roles of psychologists within a system are multidimensional, and they are expected to serve multiple clients. The psychologist is often asked to assess, diagnose, and predict dangerousness and violence for society and the system; to conduct research and evaluative studies for the profession; and, simultaneously, to provide treatment and rehabilitative services to individuals whose freedom often depends upon their responsiveness to the coerced treatment.

Hand in hand with priority listing of roles comes a general clarification of one's own goals, goals which are apt to change with experience in the system. Each individual psychologist should ask himself or herself, "Am I in this for the money? To make society better? Or to make life slightly more tolerable for inmates?"

When roles, priorities, and goals have been identified, clear communication of these positions should be offered to clients. If the psychologist's primary loyalty is to the correctional system and the institution, the client should be made aware of this. This communication is especially appropriate in court-ordered preadjudication interviews, tests, or treatment.

Clarification of roles and loyalties also may help the individual psychologist identify unrecognized pressures that are forcing acceptance of a given way of perceiving and doing. For example, with experience in the correctional system, a psychologist may find that he or she is beginning to accept unquestioningly philosophies and procedures that conflict with personal values.

This section has touched only briefly upon the ethical considerations that are relevant to psychological practice in legal settings. The interested student should consult APA ethical standards, the "Report of the Task Force on the Role of Psychology in the Criminal Justice System" (1978), and the APA-published book, *Who Is the Client?* (1980), edited by John Monahan.

# List of Cases Cited

Albemarle Paper Company v. Moody, 474 F.2d 134, vac, 95 S. Ct. 2362, 45 L. Ed. 2d 298 (1975).

Apodaca, Cooper and Madden v. Oregon, 406 U.S. 404 (1972).

Baldwin v. New York, 399 U.S. 66 (1970).

Ballew v. Georgia, 435 U.S. 223 (1978).

Battle v. Anderson, 376 F. Supp. 402 (E.D. Okla. 1974).

Curtis v. Loether, 451 U.S. 189 (1974).

Carter v. United States, 252 F.2d 608 (D.C. Cir. 1957).

Chandler v. Florida, 49 USLW 4141 (1981).

Colgrove v. Battin, 413 U.S. 149 (1973).

Commonwealth v. Lykus, 327 N.E.2d 671 (Mass. Supreme Jud. Ct. 1975).

Duncan v. Louisiana, 391 U.S. 145 (1968).

Durham v. United States, 214 F.2d 862 (D.C. Cir. 1954).

Director of Patuxent Institute v. Daniels, 243 Md. 16, 221 A.2d 397, cert. denied, 385 U.S. 940 (1966).

Escobedo v. Illinois, 378 U.S. 478 (1964).

Estes v. Texas, 381 U.S. 532 (1965).

Fare v. Michael C., 440 U.S. (1979).

Gates v. Collier, 349 F. Supp. 881 (N.D. Miss. 1972), aff'd, 501 F.2d 1291 (5th Cir. 1974).

Gilbert v. California, 388 U.S. 263 (1967).

Griggs v. Duke Power Company, 401 U.S. 424; 91 S. Ct. 849 (1971).

Harris v. New York, 401 U.S. 222 (1971).

Hobson v. Hansen, 269 F. Supp. 401 (D.D.C. 1967).

In re Oakes, Monthly Law Reporter (Mass.) 1845, 8, 122–129.

Irvin v. Dowd, 366 U.S. 717 (1961).

Jackson v. Indiana, 406 U.S. 715 (1972).

Jacobson v. Massachusetts, 197 U.S. 11 (1905).

Jenkins v. United States, 307 F.2d 637 (D.C. Cir. 1962 en banc).

Johnson v. Louisiana, 40 USLW 4524 (1972).

Larry P. v. Riles, 343 F. Supp. 1306 (N.D. Cal. 1972) (order granting preliminary injunction), aff'd, 502 F.2d 963 (9th Cir. 1974), No. C–71–2270 R.F.P. (N.D. Cal. Oct. 1979) (decision on the merits), appeal docketed, No. 80–4027 (9th Cir. Jan. 17, 1980).

Lessard v. Schmidt, 349 F. Supp. 1078 (E.D. Wisc. 1972), vacated and remanded on other grounds, 94 S. Ct. 713 (1974), reinstated 413 F. Supp. 1318 (E.D. Wisc. 1976).

Merriken v. Cressman, 364 F. Supp. 913 (E.D. Pa. 1973).

Michigan v. Tucker, 417 U.S. 433 (1974).

Miranda v. Arizona, 384 U.S. 218 (1973).

Nebraska Press Association v. Stuart, 427 U.S. 539 (1976).

Neil v. Biggers, 409 U.S. 188 (1972).

O'Connor v. Donaldson, 422 U.S. 563 (1975).

PASE v. Hannon, 506 F. Supp. 831 (N.D. Ill. 1980).

*Pate v. Robinson*, 383 U.S. 375 (1966).

*People v. Davis*, 151 Neb. 368, 37 N.W.2d. 593 (1949).

*People v. Davis*, 62 Cal.2d 791, 402 P.2d 142 (1965).

*People v. Sinclair*, 300 Mich. 562, 2N.W.2d 503 (1942).

*Pernell v. Southall Realty*, 416 U.S. 363 (1974).

*Ross v. Bernhard*, 396 U.S. 531 (1970).

*Rouse v. Cameron*, 373 F.2d 451 (D.C. Cir. 1966).

*Santobello v. New York*, 404 U.S. 257 (1971).

*Sheppard v. Maxwell*, 384 U.S. 333 (1966).

*Simmons v. United States*, 390 U.S. 377 (1968).

*State ex rel. Hawks v. Lazaro*, 202 S.E.2d 109 (W. Va. 1974).

*State v. Andretta*, 269 A.2d 644 (N.J. 1972).

*State v. Bohmer*, Va. Sup. Ct. (10/11/71).

*Stovall v. Denno*, 388 U.S. 293 (1967).

*Suzuki v. Quisenberry*, 411 F. Supp. 1113 (D. Ha. 1976).

*Tarasoff v. Regents of University of California*, 529 P.2d 553 (Cal. 1974), *vac.*, *reheard in bank*, & *aff'd*. 131 Cal. Rptr. 14, 551 P.2d 334 (1976).

*United States v. Baller*, 519 F.2d 463 (4th Cir. 1975).

*United States v. Brawner*, 471 F.2d 969 (D.C. Cir. 1972).

*United States v. Franks*, 511 F.2d 25 (6th Cir. 1975).

*United States v. Freeman*, 357 F.2d 606 (2d Cir. 1966).

*United States v. Frye*, 293 F. 1013 (D.C. Cir. 1923).

*United States v. Hearst*, 412 F. Supp. 873 (N.D. Cal. 1976).

*United States v. Mandujano*, 425 U.S. 564 (1976).

*United States v. Riggelman*, 411 F.2d 1190 (4th Cir. 1969).

*United States v. Urquidez*, 356 F. Supp. 1363, 13 CLR 1251 (C.D. Calif. 1973).

*United States v. Wade*, 388 U.S. 218 (1967).

*Washington v. Davis*, 426 U.S. 229 (1976).

*Whitree v. State*, 56 Misc. 2d 693, 290 N.Y.S.2d 489 (Ct. Cl. 1968).

*Wilderness v. Morton*, 479 F.2d 842 (D.C. Cir. 1973).

*Williams v. Florida*, 399 U.S. 78 (1970).

*Williams v. United States*, 312 F.2d 862 (D.C. Cir. 1962).

*Wyatt v. Stickney*, 325 F. Supp. 781 (M.D. Ala. 1971), enforced in 334 F. Supp. 1341 (M.D. Ala. 1971), 344 F. Supp. 373, 379 (M.D. Ala. 1972).

# References

Abraham, H. J. *The judicial process*. 2d ed. New York: Oxford University Press, 1968.

Abrahamsen, D. *The psychology of crime*. New York: Columbia University Press, 1960.

Abrams, S. *A polygraph handbook for attorneys*. Lexington, Mass.: Lexington Books, 1977.

Adams, G. W. Towards the mobilization of the adversary process. *Osgoode Hall Law Journal*, 1974, *12*, 569–594.

Adelstein, R. P. Negotiated guilty plea: A framework for analysis. *New York University Law Review*, 1978, *53*, 783–834.

Adorno, J., Frenkel-Brunswik, E., Levinson, D., & Sanford, R. *The authoritarian personality*. New York: Harper & Row, 1950.

Agus, B., & Allen, T. E. The effect of parole notification on somatic symptoms in federal prisoners. *Corrective Psychiatry*, 1968, *14*, 61–67.

Allport, G. W. *Personality: A psychological interpretation*. New York: Holt, Rinehart and Winston, 1937.

Allsopp, J. F. Criminality and delinquency. In H. J. Eysenck & G. D. Wilson (eds.), *A textbook of human psychology*. Baltimore: University Park Press, 1976.

Allyn, J., & Festinger, L. The effectiveness of unanticipated persuasive communications. *Journal of Abnormal and Social Psychology*, 1961, *62*, 35–40.

Alschuler, A. W. The prosecutor's role in plea bargaining. *University of Chicago Law Review*, 1968, *36*, 50–74.

Alschuler, A. W. The defense attorney's role in plea bargaining. *Yale Law Journal*, 1975, *84*, 1179–1191.

Alschuler, A. W. Plea bargaining and its history. *Law & Society Review*, 1979, *13*, 211–245.

American Bar Association. *A review of legal education in the United States—Fall, 1978*. Chicago: American Bar Association, 1979.

American Law Institute. *Model penal code, proposed official draft*. Philadelphia: American Law Institute, 1962.

American Psychological Association. Ethical principles of psychologists. *American Psychologist*, 1981, *36*, 633–638.

American Psychological Association. Report of the task force on the role of psychology in the criminal justice system. *American Psychologist*, 1978, *33*, 1099–1113.

Anastasi, A. *Psychological testing*. 3d ed. New York: Macmillan, 1968.

Andenaes, J. Does punishment deter crime? *Criminal Law Quarterly*, 1968, *11*, 76–93.

Andenaes, J. *Punishment and deterrence*. Ann Arbor, Michigan: University of Michigan Press, 1974.

Appley, M. H., & Trumbull, R. *Psychological stress*. New York: Appleton-Century-Crofts, 1967.

Argyle, M., & Little, B. R. Do personality traits apply to social behavior? *Journal of Theory of Social Behavior*, 1972, *2*, 1–35.

Arnold, T. W. *The symbols of government.* New Haven: Yale University Press, 1935.

Aronson, E., Turner, J., & Carlsmith, J. M. Communicator credibility and communicator discrepancy as determinants of opinion change. *Journal of Abnormal and Social Psychology,* 1963, *67,* 31–136.

Arther, R. O. *The scientific investigator.* Springfield, Ill.: C. C. Thomas, 1965.

Asch, S. E. *Social psychology.* Englewood Cliffs, N.J.: Prentice-Hall, 1952.

Aubry, A. S., & Caputo, R. R. *Criminal interrogation.* Springfield, Ill.: C. C. Thomas, 1965.

Ayd, F. J. The depot fluephenazines: A reappraisal after 10 years' clinical experience. *American Journal of Psychiatry,* 1975, *132,* 491–500.

Azen, S., Snibbe, H., & Montgomery, H. K. A longitudinal predictive study of success and performance of law enforcement officers. *Journal of Applied Psychology,* 1973, *57,* 190–192.

Azrin, N. H., & Holtz, W. C. Punishment. In W. K. Honig (ed.), *Operant behavior: Areas of research and application.* New York: Appleton-Century-Crofts, 1966.

Bachrach, A. J. Speech and its potential for stress monitoring. In C. E. G. Lundgren (ed.), *Proceedings, workshop on monitoring vital signs in the diver.* Bethesda, Md.: Undersea Medical Society and Office of Naval Research, 1979.

Baehr, M. E., Saunders, D. R., Froemel, E. C., & Furcon, J. E. The prediction of performances for black and for white police patrolmen. *Professional Psychology,* 1971, *2,* 46–57.

Bakal, D. A. Headache: A biopsychological perspective. *Psychological Bulletin,* 1975, *82,* 369–382.

Balch, R. W., Griffiths, L. T., Hall, E. O., & Winfree, L. T. The socialization of jurors: The voir dire as a rite of passage. *Journal of Criminal Justice,* 1976, *4,* 271–283.

Bales, R. F., & Borgatta, E. F. Size of group as a factor in the interaction profile. In A. P. Hare, E. F. Borgatta & R. F. Bales (eds.), *Small groups.* New York: Knopf, 1955.

Bandewehr, L. J., & Novotny, R. Juror authoritarianism and trial judge partiality: An experiment in jury decision making. *Journal of Experimental Study in Politics,* 1976, *5,* 28–33.

Bandura, A. Influence of models' reinforcement contingencies in the acquisition of imitative responses. *Journal of Personality and Social Psychology,* 1965, *1,* 589–595.

Bandura, A. *Aggression: A social learning analysis.* Englewood Cliffs, N.J.: Prentice-Hall, 1973.

Bandura, A. Behavior theory and the models of man. *American Psychologist,* 1974, *29,* 859–869.

Bandura, A. *Social learning theory.* Englewood Cliffs, N.J.: Prentice-Hall, 1977.

Bandura, A. The self system in reciprocal determinism. *American Psychologist,* 1978, *33,* 344–358.

Bandura, A., Ross, D., & Ross, S. A. Vicarious reinforcement and imitative learning. *Journal of Abnormal and Social Psychology,* 1963, *67,* 601–607.

Banton, M. *Police in the community.* New York: Basic Books, 1964.

Barber, T. X., Spanos, N. P., & Chaves, J. F. *Hypnosis, imagination, and human potentialities.* New York: Pergamon Press, 1974.

Barland, G. H., & Raskin, D. C. Detection of deception. In W. F. Prokasy & D. C. Raskin (eds.), *Electrodermal activity in psychological research.* New York: Academic Press, 1973.

Baron, R. A. *Human aggression.* New York: Plenum Press, 1977.

Baron, R. A., & Byrne, D. *Social psychology: Understanding human interaction,* 3d ed. Boston: Allyn & Bacon, 1977.

Baron, R. A., & Byrne, D. *Social psychology: Understanding human interaction* 3d ed. Boston: Allyn & Bacon, 1981.

Bartol, C. R. *Criminal behavior: A psychosocial approach.* New York: Prentice-Hall, 1980.

Bartol, C. R. *Parens patriae:* Poltergeist of mental health law. *Law & Policy Quarterly,* 1981, *3,* 191–208.

Bartol, C. R. Psychological characteristics of small-town police officers. *Journal of Police Science and Administration,* 1982, *10,* 58–63.

Bartol, C. R., & Holanchock, H. A test of Eysenck's theory on an American prison population. *Criminal Justice and Behavior,* 1979, *6,* 245–249.

Bartollas, C. *Introduction to corrections.* New York: Harper & Row, 1981.

Bartos, O. J. Determinants and consequences of toughness. In P. Swingle (ed.), *The structure of conflict.* New York: Academic Press, 1970.

Bassiouni, T. M. The right of the mentally ill to cure and treatment: Medical due process. *DePaul Law Review*, 1965, *15*, 281–315.

Bauchner, J. E., Brandt, D. R., & Miller, G. R. The truth/deception attribution: Effects of varying levels of information availability. In B. D. Ruben (ed.), *Communication yearbook I*. New Brunswick, N.J.: International Communication Association, 1977.

Bazelon, D. L. Psychiatrists and the adversary process. *Scientific American*, 1974, *230*, 18–23.

Bedrosian, R. C., & Beck, A. J. Cognitive aspects of suicidal behavior. *Suicide and Life-Threatening Behavior*, 1979, *9*, 87–96.

Bem, D. J. Self-perception: An alternative interpretation of cognitive dissonance phenomena. *Psychological Review*, 1967, *74*, 183–200.

Bem, D. J. Self-perception theory. In L. Berkowitz (ed.), *Advances in experimental social psychology*. Vol. 6. New York: Academic Press, 1972.

Bem, D. J., & Allen, A. On predicting some of the people some of the time: The search for cross-situational consistencies in behavior. *Psychological Review*, 1974, *81*, 506–520.

Bennett-Sandler, G., Frazier, R. L., Torres, D. A., & Waldron, R. J. *Law enforcement and criminal justice: An introduction*. Boston: Houghton Mifflin, 1979.

Berg, K. S., & Vidmar, N. Authoritarianism and recall of evidence about criminal behavior. *Journal of Research in Personality*, 1975, *9*, 147–157.

Berk, S. F., & Loseke, D. R. "Handling" family violence: Situational determinants of police arrest in domestic disturbances. *Law & Society Review*, 1980–81, *15*, 315–346.

Bermant, G. *Conduct of the voir dire examination: Practices and opinions of federal district judges*. Washington, D.C.: Federal Judicial Center, 1977.

Bermant, G., & Shapard, J. The voir dire examination, juror challenges, and adversary advocacy. In B. D. Sales (ed.), *Perspectives in law and psychology*. Vol. 2, *The trial process*. New York: Plenum, 1981.

Bersh, P. J. A validation of polygraph examiner judgments. *Journal of Applied Psychology*, 1969, *53*, 399–403.

Bersoff, D. N. Regarding psychologists testily: Legal regulation of psychological assessment in the public school. *Maryland Law Review*, 1979, *39*, 27–120.

Bersoff, D. N. Testing and the law. *American Psychologist*, 1981, *36*, 1047–1056.

Bezanson, R. P. Involuntary treatment of the mentally ill in Iowa: The 1975 legislation. *Iowa Law Review*, 1975, *61*, 261–396.

Black, D. The social organization of arrest. *Stanford Law Review*, 1971, *23*, 1087–1111.

Black, T. E., & Higbee, K. L. Effects of power, threat, and sex on exploitation. *Journal of Personality and Social Psychology*, 1973, *27*, 382–388.

Blackmore, J. Are police allowed to have problems of their own? *Police Magazine*, 1978, July, 47–55.

Bloch, M. (ed.). *Political language and oratory in traditional society*. London: Academic Press, 1975.

Block, R. *Violent crime*. Lexington, Mass.: Lexington Books, 1977.

Blum, R. H. *Police selection*. Springfield, Ill.: C. C. Thomas, 1964.

Blunk, R., & Sales, B. D. Persuasion during the voir dire. In B. D. Sales (ed.), *Psychology in the legal process*. New York: Spectrum, 1977.

Bochner, S., & Insko, C. A. Communicator discrepancy, source credibility, and opinion change. *Journal of Personality and Social Psychology*, 1966, *4*, 614–621.

Boehm, V. Mr. prejudice, Miss sympathy, and the authoritarian personality: An application of psychological measuring techniques to the problems of jury bias. *Wisconsin Law Review*, 1968, 734–750.

Borgida, E. Evidentiary reform of rape laws: A psycholegal approach. In P. D. Lipsitt & B. D. Sales (eds.), *New directions in psycholegal research*. New York: Van Nostrand Reinhold, 1980.

Bork, R. H. Testimony given in hearings before the Subcommittee on Courts, Civil Liberties, and the Administration of Justice of the Committee on the Judiciary, House of Representatives. In *State of the judiciary and access to justice*. Washington, D.C.: U.S. Government Printing Office, 1977.

Bourne, L. E., Dominowski, R. L., & Loftus, E. F. *Cognitive processes*, Englewood Cliffs, N.J.: Prentice-Hall, 1979.

Bourne, L. E., & Ekstrand, B. R. *Psychology: Its principles and meanings*. 2d ed. New York: Holt, Rinehart & Winston, 1976.

Bowers, K. Situationalism in psychology: An analysis and a critique. *Psychological Review*, 1973, 80, 307–336.

Brandreth, D. Stress and the policeman's wife. *Police Stress*, 1978, 1, 41–42.

Bray, R. M., & Kerr, N. L. Use of simulation method in the study of jury behavior: Some methodological considerations. *Law and Human Behavior*, 1979, 3, 107–120.

Bray, R. M., & Noble, A. M. Authoritarianism and decisions of mock juries: Evidence of jury bias and group polarization. *Journal of Personality and Social Psychology*, 1978, 36, 1424–1430.

Bray, R. M., Struckman-Johnson, C., Osborne, M. D., McFarlane, J. B., & Scott, J. The effects of defendant status on decisions of student and community juries. *Social Psychology*, 1978, 41, 256–260.

Brehm, J. W. *A theory of psychological reactance*. New York: Academic Press, 1966.

Brehm, J. W. *Responses to loss of freedom: A theory of psychological reactance*. Morristown, N.J.: General Learning Press, 1972.

Brigham, J. C. Perspectives on the impact of lineup composition, race, and witness confidence on identification accuracy. *Law and Human Behavior*, 1980, 4, 315–321.

Brodsky, S. L. *Psychologists in the criminal justice system*. Urbana, Ill.: University of Illinois Press, 1972.

Brodsky, S. L. The mental health professional on the witness stand: A survival guide. In B. D. Sales (ed.), *Psychology in the legal process*. New York: Spectrum Publications, 1977.

Brodsky, S. L. Criminal and dangerous behavior. In D. Rimm & J. Somervill (eds.), *Abnormal psychology*. New York: Academic Press, 1977.

Brodsky, S. L. Ethical issues for psychologists in corrections. In J. Monahan (ed.), *Who is the client? The ethics of psychological intervention in the criminal justice system*. Washington, D.C.: American Psychological Association, 1980.

Brodsky, S. L. Introduction. In J. Monahan, *Predicting violent behavior: An assessment of clinical techniques*. Beverly Hills, Calif.: Sage Publications, 1981.

Broeder, D. W. The University of Chicago jury project. *Nebraska Law Review*, 1958, 38, 744–761.

Broeder, D. W. Voir dire examination: An empirical study. *Southern California Law Review*, 1965, 38, 503–528.

Brooks, A. D. *Law, psychiatry and the mental health system*. Boston: Little, Brown & Co., 1974.

Brown, E., Deffenbacher, K., & Sturgill, W. Memory for faces and the circumstances of encounter. *Journal of Applied Psychology*, 1977, 62, 311–318.

Buckhout, R. Eyewitness testimony. *Scientific American*, 1974, 321, 23–31.

Buckhout, R. Eyewitness identification and psychology in the courtroom. *Criminal Defense*, 1977, 4, 5–10.

Buehler, R. E., Patterson, G. R., & Furniss, J. M. The reinforcement of behavior in institutional settings. *Behaviour Research and Therapy*, 1966, 4, 157–167.

Bukstel, L. H., & Killmann, P. R. Psychological effects of imprisonment on confined individuals. *Psychological Bulletin*, 1980, 88, 469–493.

Burchard, J., & Harig, P. T. Behavior modification and juvenile delinquency. In H. Leitenberg (ed.), *Handbook of behavior modification and behavior therapy*. Englewood Cliffs, N.J.: Prentice-Hall, 1976.

Byrne, D. *The attraction paradigm*. New York: Academic Press, 1971.

Byrne, D. *An introduction to personality*. 2d ed. Englewood Cliffs, N.J.: Prentice-Hall, 1974.

Byrne, D., & Nelson, D. Attraction as a linear function of proportion of positive reinforcement. *Journal of Personality and Social Psychology*, 1965, 1, 659–663.

Cain, M. *Society and the policeman's role*. London: Routledge & Kegan Paul, 1973.

Caplan, R. D., Cobb, S., French, J. R. P., Harrison, R. V., & Pinneau, S. R. *Job demands and worker health*. Washington, D.C.: U.S. Department of Health, Education & Welfare, 1975.

Carnevale, P. J. D., Pruitt, C. G., & Britton, S. D. Looking tough: The negotiator under constituent surveillance. *Personality and Social Psychology Bulletin*, 1979, 5, 118–121.

Carroll, J. S. Judgments of recidivism risk: Conflicts between clinical strategies and base-rate information. *Law and Human Behavior*, 1977, 1, 191–198.

Carroll, J. S. Judgments of recidivism risk: The use of base-rate information in parole decisions. In P. D. Lipsitt & B. Sales (eds.),

*New directions in psycholegal research.* New York: Van Nostrand Reinhold, 1980.

Carter, L. H. *Reason in law.* Boston: Little, Brown, 1979.

Cavior, N., & Howard, L. R. Facial attractiveness and juvenile delinquency among black offenders and white offenders. *Journal of Abnormal Child Psychology,* 1973, 1, 202–213.

Cavoukian, A., & Heslegrave, R. J. The admissibility of polygraph evidence in court: Some empirical findings. *Law and Human Behavior,* 1980, 4, 117–131.

Chambers, C. C. Alternative to civil commitment: Practical guides and constitutional imperatives. *Michigan Law Review,* 1972, 70, 1108–1152.

Chance, J., & Goldstein, A. G. Recognition of faces and verbal labels. *Bulletin of the Psychonomic Society,* 1976, 7, 384–386.

Chance, J., Goldstein, A. G., & McBride, L. Differential experience and recognition memory for faces. *Journal of Social Psychology,* 1975, 97, 243–253.

Chandler, E. V., & Jones, C. S. Cynicism: An inevitability of police work? *Journal of Police Science and Administration,* 1979, 7, 65–71.

Chappell, D., & Meyer, J. C. Cross-cultural differences in police attitudes: An exploration in comparative research. *Australian and New Zealand Journal of Criminology,* 1975, 8, 5–13.

Chenoweth, J. H. Situational tests: A new attempt at assessing police candidates. *The Journal of Criminal Law, Criminology, and Police Science,* 1961, 52, 232–238.

Chertkoff, J. M., & Conley, M. Opening offer and frequency of concessions as bargaining strategies. *Journal of Personality and Social Psychology,* 1967, 7, 181–185.

Christie, G. C. Vagueness and legal language. *Minnesota Law Review,* 1964, 48, 888–1029.

Christie, R., & Geis, F. L. (eds.). *Studies in Machiavellianism.* New York: Academic Press, 1970.

Church, T. W. In defense of "bargain justice." *Law & Society Review,* 1979, 13, 509–526.

Claridge, G. Final remarks. In G. Claridge, S. Canter, & W. I. Hume (eds.), *Personality differences and biological variations.* Oxford: Pergamon Press, 1973.

Cleckley, H. *The mask of sanity.* 5th ed. St. Louis: Mosby, 1976.

Clements, C. B. Crowded prisons: A review of psychological and environmental effects. *Law and Human Behavior,* 1979, 3, 217–225.

Clemmer, D. *The prison community.* Boston: Christopher, 1940.

Clifford, B. Police as eyewitnesses. *New Society,* 1976, 22, 176–177.

Clifford, B. R., & Hollin, C. R. Effects of the type of incident and the number of perpetrators on eyewitness memory. *Journal of Applied Psychology,* 1981, 66, 365–370.

Clifford, B. R., & Scott, J. Individual and situational factors in eyewitness testimony. *Journal of Applied Psychology,* 1978, 63, 352–359.

Clingempeel, W. G., Mulvey, E., & Reppucci, N. D. A national study of ethical dilemmas of psychologists in the criminal justice system. In J. Monahan (ed.), *Who is the client? The ethics of psychological intervention in the criminal justice system.* Washington, D.C.: American Psychological Association, 1980.

Clore, G. L., & Byrne, D. A reinforcement-affect model of attraction. In T. L. Huston (ed.), *Foundations of interpersonal attraction.* New York: Academic Press, 1974.

Cocozza, J., & Steadman, H. The failure of psychiatric prediction of dangerousness: Clear and convincing evidence. *Rutgers Law Review,* 1976, 29, 1084–1101.

Cogan, N. H. Juvenile law before and after the entrance of "parens patriae." *South Carolina Law Review,* 1970, 22, 147–181.

Cohen, B., & Chaiken, J. *Police background characteristics and performance: Summary report.* No. R–999–DOJ. New York: Rand Institute, 1972.

Cohen, I. The function of the attorney and the commitment of the mentally ill. *Texas Law Review,* 1966, 44, 424–459.

Cohen, M. E., & Carr, W. J. Facial recognition and the von Restorff effect. *Bulletin of the Psychonomic Society,* 1975, 6, 383–384.

Cohen, M. L., Garafalo, R., Boucher, R., & Seghorn, T. The psychology of rapists. *Seminars in Psychiatry,* 1971, 3, 307–327.

Cohen, M. L., Seghorn, T., & Calmas, W. Sociometric study of the sex offender. *Journal of Abnormal Psychology,* 1969, 74, 249–255.

Cohen, R. L., & Harnick, M. A. The susceptibility of child witnesses to suggestions: An empirical study. *Law and Human Behavior,*

1980, *4*, 201–210.

Cole, G. F. *The American system of criminal justice.* North Scituate, Mass.: Duxbury, 1975.

Coleman, J. C. *Abnormal psychology and modern life.* 5th ed. Glenview, Ill.: Scott, Foresman, 1976.

Coleman, L., & Solomon, T. Parens patriae "treatment": Legal punishment in disguise. *Hastings Constitutional Law Quarterly,* 1976, *3*, 345–362.

Comment. Police power in Illinois: The regulation of private conduct. *University of Illinois Law Forum,* 1972.

Committee on Psychiatry and Law. *Misuse of psychiatry in the criminal courts: Competency to stand trial.* New York: Group for Advancement of Psychiatry, 1974.

Cooper, C. L., & Marshall, J. Occupational sources of stress: A review of the literature relating to coronary heart disease and mental ill health. *Journal of Occupational Psychology,* 1976, *49*, 11–28.

Cross, A. C., & Hammond, K. R. Social differences between "successful" and "unsuccessful" state highway patrolmen. *Public Personnel Review,* 1951, *12*, 159–161.

Cross, J. F., Cross, J., & Daly, J. Sex, race, age and beauty as factors in recognition of faces. *Perception and Psychophysics,* 1971, *10*, 393–396.

Dahlstrom, W. G. Whither the MMPI? In J. N. Butcher (ed.), *Objective personality assessment,* New York: Academic Press, 1972.

Dale, M. W. Barriers to the rehabilitation of ex-offenders. *Crime and Delinquency,* 1976, *22*, 322–337.

Dalessio, D. J. *Wolff's headache and other head pain.* New York: Oxford University Press, 1972.

Danet, B. Language in the legal process. *Law & Society Review,* 1980, *14*, 445–564.

Danto, B. L. Police suicide. Paper presented at the American Association of Suicidology, Los Angeles, 1976.

Darley, J. M., & Latane, B. Bystander intervention in emergencies: Diffusion of responsibility. *Journal of Personality and Social Psychology,* 1968, *8*, 377–383.

Dash, J., & Reiser, M. Suicide among police in urban law enforcement agencies. *Journal of Police Science and Administration,* 1978, *6*, 18–21.

D'Atri, D. A. Psychophysiological responses to crowding. *Environment and Behavior,* 1975, *7*, 237–252.

Davies, G., Ellis, H., & Shepherd, J. Face recognition accuracy as a function of mode of representation. *Journal of Applied Psychology,* 1978, *63*, 180–187.

Davis, J. Protecting consumers from overdisclosure and gobbledygook: An empirical look at the simplification of consumer-credit contracts. *Virginia Law Review,* 1977, *63*, 841–888.

Davis, J. H., Bray, R. M., & Holt, R. W. The empirical study of decision processes in juries: A critical review. In J. L. Tapp & F. J. Levine (eds.), *Law, justice, and the individual in society: Psychological and legal issues.* New York: Holt, Rinehart & Winston, 1977.

Davis, J. H., Kerr, N. L., Atkin, R. S., Holt, R., & Meek, D. The decision processes of 6- and 12-person mock juries assigned unanimous and two-thirds majority rules. *Journal of Personality and Social Psychology,* 1975, *32*, 1–14.

Davis, J. M. Overview: Maintenance therapy in psychiatry: I. Schizophrenia. *American Journal of Psychiatry,* 1975, *132*, 1237–1241.

Davis, J. M. Overview: Maintenance therapy in psychiatry: II. Affective disorders. *American Journal of Psychiatry,* 1976, *133*, 1–13.

Deffenbacher, K. A. Eyewitness accuracy and confidence. Can we infer anything about their relationship? *Law and Human Behavior,* 1980, *4*, 243–260.

Delgado, R. Religious totalism: Gentle and ungentle persuasion under the first amendment. *Southern California Law Review,* 1977, *51*, 1–55.

Delgado, R. Ascription of criminal states of mind: Toward a defense theory for the coercively persuaded ("brain-washed") defendant. *Minnesota Law Review,* 1978, *63*, 1–33.

Dent, H. R. Stress as a factor influencing person recognition in identification parades. *Bulletin of the British Psychological Society,* 1977, *30*, 339–340.

Dershowitz, A. M. The origins of preventive confinement in Anglo-American law. Part 2, The American experience. *University of Cincinnati Law Review,* 1974, *43*, 781–846.

Deutsch, A. *The mentally ill in America.* New York: Columbia University Press, 1949.

Developments in the Law: Civil commitment of the mentally ill. *Harvard Law Review,*

1974, 87, 1190–1406.

Dickey, W. Incompetency and the nondangerous mentally ill client. *Criminal Law Bulletin*, 1980, *16*, 25–40.

Dillman, E. G. Role-playing as a technique in police selection. *Public Personnel Review*, 1963, *24*, 116–118.

Dion, K. Physical attractiveness and evaluations of children's transgressions. *Journal of Personality and Social Psychology*, 1972, *24*, 207–213.

Dion, K. K., Berscheid, E., & Walster, E. What is beautiful is good. *Journal of Personality and Social Psychology*, 1972, 24, 285–290.

Doob, A. N., & Kirshenbaum, H. M. Bias in police lineups—Partial remembering. *Journal of Police Science and Administration*, 1973, *1*, 287–293.

Dowdle, M., Gillen, H., & Miller, A. Integration and attribution theories as predictors of sentencing by a simulated jury. *Personality and Social Psychology Bulletin*, 1974, *1*, 270–272.

Drake, C. Enforcing the right to treatment. *American Criminal Law Review*, 1972, *10*, 587–600.

Dressler, J. Professor Delgado's "Brainwashing" defense: Courting a determinist legal system. *Minnesota Law Review*, 1979, *63*, 335–365.

Dubois, P. H., & Watson, R. I. The selection of patrolmen. *Journal of Applied Psychology*, 1950, *34*, 90–95.

Duncan, D. F. Verbal behavior in a detention home. *Corrective and Social Psychiatry and Journal of Behavior Technological Methods and Therapy*, 1974, 20, 38–42.

Duval, S., & Wicklund, R. A. Effects of objective self-awareness on attribution of causality. *Journal of Experimental Social Psychology*, 1973, *9*, 1–6.

Easterbrook, J. A. The effect of emotion on cue utilization and the organization of behavior. *Psychological Review*, 1959, *66*, 181–201.

Easterbrook, J. A. *The determinants of free will: A psychological analysis of responsible, adjustive behavior*. New York: Academic Press, 1978.

Ebbesen, E. B., & Konečni, V. J. Decision making and information integration in the courts: The setting of bail. *Journal of Personality and Social Psychology*, 1975, *32*, 805–821.

Ecclestone, C. E., Gendreau, P., & Knox, C. Solitary confinement of prisoners: An assessment of its effects on inmates' personal constructs and adrenocortical activity. *Canadian Journal of Behavioral Science*, 1974, *6*, 178–191.

Edelman, M. *Political language: Words that succeed and policies that fail*. New York: Academic Press, 1977.

Efran, M. G. The effect of physical appearance on the judgment of guilt, interpersonal attraction, and severity of recommended punishment in a simulated jury task. *Journal of Research in Personality*, 1974, 8, 45–54.

Eiseley, L. *The man who saw through time*. New York: Charles Scribner's Sons, 1973.

Eisenberg, T. Labor-management relations and psychological stress—View from the bottom. *The Police Chief*, 1975, 42, 54–58.

Ekman, P., & Friesen, W. Nonverbal leakage and clues to deception. *Psychiatry*, 1969, 32, 88–106.

Ekman, P., & Friesen, W. Detecting deception from the body and face. *Journal of Personality and Social Psychology*, 1974, 29, 288–298.

Ekman, P., Friesen, W. V., & Scherer, K. R. Body movement and voice pitch in deceptive interaction. *Semiotica*, 1976, *16*, 23–27.

Elion, V., & Megargee, E. I. Validity of the MMPI *Pd* scale among black inmates. *Journal of Consulting and Clinical Psychology*, 1975, *43*, 166–172.

Elliot, E. S., Wills, E. J., & Goldstein, A. G. The effects of discrimination training on the recognition of white and oriental faces. *Bulletin of the Psychonomic Society*, 1973, 2, 71–73.

Ellis, H. D., Deregowski, J. B., & Shepherd, J. W. Descriptions of white and black faces by white and black subjects. *International Journal of Psychology*, 1975, *10*, 119–123.

Ellison, K. W., & Buckhout, R. *Psychology and criminal justice*. New York: Harper & Row, 1981.

Elwork, A., Sales, B. D., & Alfini, J. J. Juridic decisions: In ignorance of the law or in light of it? *Law and Human Behavior*, 1977, *1*, 163–189.

Elwork, A., & Sales, B. D. Psycholegal research on the jury and trial process. In W. Curran, L. McGarry & D. Petty (eds.), *Modern legal medicine, psychiatry and forensic sci-*

*ence*. Philadelphia: F. A. Davis, 1980.

Endler, N. S. The person versus the situation—a pseudo issue? *Journal of Personality*, 1973, *41*, 287–303.

Endler, N. S., & Hunt, J. McV. Generalizability of contributions from sources of variance in the S-R inventories of anxiousness. *Journal of Personality*, 1969, 37, 1–24.

Endler, N. S., & Magnusson, D. *Interactional psychology and personality*. New York: Wiley, 1976.

Ennis, B. J., & Emery, R. D. *The rights of mental patients*. New York: Avon Books, 1978.

Ennis, B. J., & Litwack, T. J. Psychiatry and the presumption of expertise: Flipping coins in the courtroom. *California Law Review*, 1974, *62*, 693–752.

Eysenck, H. J. Behavior therapy, spontaneous remission and transference in neurotics. *American Journal of Psychiatry*, 1963, *119*, 867–871.

Eysenck, H. J. *The biological basis of personality*. Springfield, Ill.: C. C. Thomas, 1967.

Eysenck, H. J. Obscenity—officially speaking. *Penthouse*, 1972, November, 95–102.

Eysenck, H. J. *The inequality of man*. San Diego, Calif.: Edits Publishers, 1973.

Eysenck, H. J. *Crime and personality*. London: Routledge & Kegan Paul, 1977.

Farr, J. L., & Landy, F. G. The development and use of supervisory and peer scales for police performance appraisal. In C. D. Spielberger (ed.), *Police selection and evaluation: Issues and techniques*. Washington, D.C.: Hemisphere Publishing, 1979.

Feeley, M. The concept of laws in social science: A critique and notes on an expanded view. *Law and Society Review*, 1976, *10*, 497–523.

Feeley, M. M. Perspectives on plea bargaining. *Law & Society Review*, 1979a, *13*, 199–209.

Feeley, M. M. Pleading guilty in lower courts. *Law & Society Review*, 1979b, *13*, 461–466.

Feinman, S., & Entwisle, D. R. Children's ability to recognize other children's faces. *Child Development*, 1976, *47*, 506–510.

Feldman, M. P. *Criminal behavior: A psychological analysis*. London: John Wiley, 1977.

Fenster, C. A., Wiedemann, C. F., & Locke, B. Police personality—Social science folklore and psychological measurement. In B. D. Sales (ed.), *Psychology in the legal process*. New York: Spectrum, 1977.

Festinger, L., & Maccoby, N. On resistance to persuasive communications. *Journal of Abnormal and Social Psychology*, 1964, *68*, 359–366.

Festinger, L., Pepitone, A., & Newcomb, T. Some consequences of deindividuation in a group. *Journal of Abnormal and Social Psychology*, 1952, *47*, 382–389.

Fieve, R. R. The lithium clinic: A new model for the delivery of psychiatric services. *American Journal of Psychiatry*, 1975, *132*, 1018–1022.

Fisher, J., Epstein, L., & Harris, M. Validity of the psychiatric interview: Predicting the effectiveness of the first Peace Corps volunteers in Ghana. *Archives of General Psychiatry*, 1967, *17*, 744–750.

Flavell, J. H. *The developmental psychology of Jean Piaget*. Princeton, N.J.: D. Van Nostrand, 1963.

Forston, R. F. Judges' instructions: A quantitative analysis of jurors' listening comprehension. *Today's Speech*, 1970, *18*, 34–38.

Fraas, L. A. Effects of incarceration as measured by the Taylor-Johnson Temperament Analysis. *Psychological Reports*, 1973, *32*, 1033–1034.

Frank, J. *Courts on trial: Myth and reality in American justice*. Princeton, N.J.: Princeton University Press, 1949.

Freedman, M. Professional responsibilities of the civil practitioner. In D. Weckstein (ed.), *Education in the professional responsibilities of the lawyer*. Charlottesville, Va.: University Press of Virginia, 1970.

Freeman, W., & Watts, J. W. *Psychosurgery*. Springfield, Ill.: C. C. Thomas, 1942.

Friedman, L. M. Law and its language. *George Washington Law Review*, 1964, *33*, 563–613.

Friedman, L. M. Plea bargaining in historical perspective. *Law & Society Review*, 1979, *13*, 247–259.

Friedman, M., & Rosenman, R. H. *Type A behavior and your heart*. New York: Knopf, 1974.

Friedman, P. Suicide among police. In E. Schneidman (ed.), *Essays in self-destruction*. New York: Science House, 1967.

Friend, R. M., & Vinson, M. Leaning over backwards: Jurors' responses to defendants' attractiveness. *Journal of Communication*,

1974, 24, 124–129.

Fuller, L. The adversary system. In H. Berman (ed.), *Talks on American law*. New York: Vintage Books, 1961.

Fuller, L. Two principles of human association. In J. Pennock & J. Chapman (eds.), *Voluntary association*. New York: Lieber-Atherton, 1969.

Furniss, J. M. Peer reinforcement of behavior in an institution for delinquent girls. Unpublished master's thesis, Oregon State University, 1964.

Galanter, M. Why the "haves" come out ahead: Speculations on the limits of legal change. *Law and Society Review*, 1974, 9, 95–160.

Gallagher, T. Discretion in police enforcement. In L. E. Abt & I. R. Stuart (eds.), *Social psychology and discretionary law*. New York: Van Nostrand Reinhold, 1979.

Gallemore, J. L., & Panton, J. H. Inmate responses to lengthy death row confinement. *American Journal of Psychiatry*, 1972, 129, 167–172.

Gearing, M. L. The MMPI as a primary differentiator and predictor of behavior in prison: A methodological critique and review of the recent literature. *Psychological Bulletin*, 1979, 86, 929–963.

Gendreau, P., Freedman, N., Wilde, G. J. S., & Scott, G. D. Changes in EEG alpha frequency and evoked response latency during solitary confinement. *Journal of Abnormal Psychology*, 1972, 79, 54–59.

Gentry, W. D., Shows, W. D., & Thomas, M. Chronic low back pain: A psychological profile. *Psychosomatics*, 1974, 15, 174–177.

Gerbasi, K. D., Zuckerman, M., & Reis, H. T. Justice needs a new blindfold: A review of mock jury research. *Psychological Bulletin*, 1977, 84, 323–345.

Gerber, S. R., & Schroeder, O. *Criminal investigation and interrogation*. Cincinnati: W. H. Anderson, 1962.

Gettman, L. R. Aerobics and police fitness. *Police Stress*, 1978, 1, 22–25.

Gibbons, D. Society, crime and criminal careers. 3d ed. Englewood Cliffs, N.J.: Prentice-Hall, 1977.

Gilbert, C., & Bakan, P. Visual asymmetry in perception of faces. *Neuropsychologia*, 1973, 11, 355–362.

Glaser, D. *The effectiveness of a prison and parole system*. Indianapolis, Ind.: Bobbs-Merrill,

1964.

Glass, D. C. *Behavior patterns, stress, and coronary disease*. Hillsdale, N.J.: Lawrence Erlbaum Associates, 1977.

Glick, H. R., & Vines, K. N. *State court systems*. Englewood Cliffs, N.J.: Prentice-Hall, 1973.

Going, M., & Read, J. D. Effects of uniqueness, sex of subject, and sex of photograph on facial recognition. *Perceptual and Motor Skills*, 1974, 39, 109–110.

Goldberg, L. R. Simple models or simple processes? Some research on clinical judgments. *American Psychologist*, 1968, 23, 483–496.

Goldberg, L. R. Man vs. model of man: A rationale, plus some evidence for a method of improving on clinical inferences. *Psychological Bulletin*, 1970, 73, 422–432.

Goldberg, L. R., & Werts, C. E. The reliability of clinician's judgments: A multitrait-multimethod approach. *Journal of Consulting Psychology*, 1966, 30, 199–206.

Golden, M. Some effects of combining psychological tests on clinical inferences. *Journal of Consulting Psychology*, 1964, 28, 440–446.

Goldkamp, J. S., & Gottfredson, M. R. Bail decision making and pretrial detention. *Law and Human Behavior*, 1979, 3, 227–249.

Goldstein, A. G. The fallibility of the eyewitness: Psychological evidence. In B. D. Sales (ed.), *Psychology in the legal process*. New York: Spectrum Publications, 1977.

Goldstein, A. G., & Chance, J. E. Recognition of children's faces. *Child Development*, 1964, 35, 129–136.

Goldstein, A. G., & Chance, J. E. Visual recognition memory for complex configurations. *Perception and Psychophysics*, 1970, 9, 237–241.

Goldstein, A. G., & Chance, J. Measuring psychological similarity of faces. *Bulletin of the Psychonomic Society*, 1976, 7, 407–408.

Goldstein, A. G., & Chance, J. Judging face similarity in own and other races. *Journal of Psychology*, 1978, 98, 185–193.

Goldstein, B. *Screening for emotional and psychological fitness in correctional officer hiring*. Resource Center on Correctional Law and Legal Services, 1975.

Goldstein, J. H. *Aggression and crimes of violence*. New York: Oxford University Press, 1975.

Goodman, N. Right to treatment: The responsibility of the courts. In D. S. Burris (ed.), *The right to treatment*. New York: Springer Publishing, 1969.

Gordon, G. C. *Perspectives on law enforcement. 1. Characteristics of police applicants.* Princeton, N.J.: Educational Testing Service, 1969.

Gordon, M. E., Kleiman, L. S., & Hanie, C. A. Industrial-organization psychology: Open thy ears O house of Israel. *American Psychologist*, 1978, 33, 893–905.

Gorenstein, G. W., & Ellsworth, P. C. Effect of choosing an incorrect photograph on a later identification by an eyewitness. *Journal of Applied Psychology*, 1980, 65, 616–622.

Gorer, G. Modification of national character: The role of the police in England. *Journal of Social Issues*, 1955, 11, 24–32.

Gottesman, J. *The utility of the MMPI in assessing the personality patterns of urban police applicants.* Hoboken, N.J.: Stevens Institute of Technology, 1975.

Gough, H. G. A leadership index on the California Psychological Inventory. *Journal of Counseling Psychology*, 1969, 16, 283–289.

Greenaway, W. K. & Brickley, S. L. (eds.). *Law and social control in Canada*. Scarborough, Ont.: Prentice-Hall of Canada, 1978.

Grenick, J. M. *The psychological fitness of deputies assigned to the patrol functions and its relationship to the formulation of entrance standards for law enforcement officers.* Law Enforcement Assistance Administration Grant, Final Report, Washington, D.C., June 1973.

Griffitt, W., & Jackson, T. Simulated jury decisions: The influence of jury-defendant attitude similarity-dissimilarity. *Social Behavior and Personality*, 1973, 1, 1–7.

Groves, P., & Schlesinger, K. *Introduction to biological psychology*. Dubuque, Iowa: Wm. C. Brown, 1979.

Guion, R. M. Content validity: Three years of talk—What's the action? *Public Personnel Management*, 1977, 6, 407–414.

Gusfield, J. *Illusions of authority*. Chicago: University of Chicago Press, 1980.

Haas, K. *Abnormal psychology*. New York: D. Van Nostrand, 1979.

Häfner, H., & Böker, W. Mentally disordered violent offenders. *Social Psychology*, 1973, 8, 220–229.

Hageman, M. J. C. Occupational stress and marital relationships. *Journal of Police Science and Administration*, 1978, 6, 402–409.

Hagerty, T. J. Police union studies job stress. *Wisconsin Law Enforcement Journal*, 1976, 16, 9, 35.

Halleck, S. L. *Psychiatry and the dilemmas of crime*. New York: Harper & Row, 1967.

Halpern, A. L. Use and misuse of psychiatry in competency examination of criminal defendants. *Psychiatric Annals*, 1974, 8, 3–17.

Haney, C. Psychology and legal change: On the limits of a factual jurisprudence. *Law and Human Behavior*, 1980, 4, 147–200.

Haney, C., Banks, W., & Zimbardo, P. Interpersonal dynamics in a simulated prison. *International Journal of Criminology*, 1973, 1, 69–97.

Hardisty, J. H. Mental illness: A legal fiction. *Washington Law Review*, 1973, 48, 735–762.

Hare, R. D. *Psychopathy: Theory and research.* New York: John Wiley, 1970.

Hare, R. D., & Schalling, D. (eds.). *Psychopathic behaviour: Approaches to research.* Chichester, England: Wiley, 1978.

Harmon, L. D. The recognition of faces. *Scientific American*, November 1973, 71–82.

Hart, H. M. Jr., & Sacks, A. M. *The legal process: Basic problems in the making and application of law* (Harvard University, 1958).

Harvard Laboratory of Community Psychiatry. *Competency to stand trial and mental illness.* New York: Jason Aronson, 1974.

Harvey, J. H., & Smith, W. P. *Social psychology: An attribution approach.* St. Louis: C. V. Mosby, 1977.

Hayden, R. M., & Anderson, J. K. On the evaluation of procedural systems in laboratory experiments: A critique of Thibaut and Walker. *Law and Human Behavior*, 1979, 3, 21–38.

Hebb, D. O. What psychology is about. *American Psychologist*, 1974, 29, 71–79.

Heider, F. *The psychology of interpersonal relations.* New York: Wiley, 1958.

Heiman, M. F. Police suicides revisited. *Suicide*, 1975, 5, 5–20.

Heinz, J. P., & Laumann, E. O. The legal profession: Client interests, professional roles, and social hierarchies. *Michigan Law Review*, 1978, 6, 1111–1142.

Henderson, N. D. Criterion-related validity of personality and aptitude scales. In C. D. Spielberger (ed.), *Police selection and evaluation: Issues and techniques.* Washington, D.C.: Hemisphere Publishing, 1979.

Henn, F. A., Herjanic, M., & Vanderpearl, R. H. Forensic psychiatry: Diagnosis of criminal responsibility. *The Journal of Nervous and Mental Disease,* 1976, *162,* 423–429.

Hess, J. H., & Thomas, H. E. Incompetency to stand trial: Procedures, results and problems. *American Journal of Psychiatry,* 1963, *119,* 713–720.

Hess, L.R. Police entry tests and their predictability of score in police academy and subsequent job performance. *Dissertation Abstracts International,* 1973, 33-B, 5552.

Hetherington, E. M., & Parke, R. D. *Child psychology: A contemporary viewpoint.* New York: McGraw-Hill, 1975.

Heumann, M. A note on plea bargaining and case pressure. *Law & Society Review,* 1975, 9, 515–520.

Heumann, M. *Plea bargaining: The experiences of prosecutors, judges, and defense attorneys.* Chicago: University of Chicago Press, 1978.

Hiday, V. A. Reformed commitment procedures: An empirical study in the courtroom. *Law and Society Review,* 1977, *11,* 651–666.

Hilgard, E. R. *Hypnotic susceptibility.* New York: Harcourt Brace Jovanovich, 1965.

Hilton, J. Psychology and police work. In J. C. Anderson and P. J. Stead (eds.), *The police we deserve,* 93–105. London, Wolfe Publishers, 1973.

Hoffer, A., & Osmond, H. *How to live with schizophrenia.* New York: University Books, 1966.

Hoffman, M. L. Moral development. In H. Mussen (ed.), *Carmichael's manual of child psychology.* Vol. 2. New York: Wiley, 1970.

Hogan, R. Personality characteristics of highly rated policemen. *Personnel Psychology,* 1971, *24,* 679–686.

Hollien, H. Vocal indicators of psychological stress. In F. Wright, C. Bahn, & R. W. Rieber (eds.), *Forensic psychology and psychiatry.* Annals of the New York Academy of Sciences, vol. 347. New York: New York Academy of Sciences, 1980.

Holmes, J. G., & Miller, D. T. Interpersonal conflict. In J. W. Thibault, J. T. Spence & R. C. Carson (eds.), *Contemporary topics in social psychology.* Morristown, N.J.: General Learning Press, 1976.

Holmes, T. H., & Masuda, M. Life change and illness susceptibility. In B. S. Dohrenwend & B. P. Dohrenwend (eds.), *Stressful life events: Their nature and effects.* New York: Wiley, 1974, 45–72.

Holmes, T. H., & Rahe, R. H. The social readjustment rating scale. *Journal of Psychosomatic Research,* 1967, *11,* 213–218.

Holt, R. R. Clinical and statistical prediction: A reformulation and some new data. *Journal of Abnormal and Social Psychology,* 1958, *56,* 1–12.

Horvath, F. S. The effect of selected variables on interpretation of polygraph records. *Journal of Applied Psychology,* 1977, *62,* 127–136.

Houlden, P. Impact of procedural modifications on evaluations of plea bargaining. *Law & Society Review,* 1980–81, *15,* 267–292.

Houlden, P., LaTour, S., Walker, L., & Thibaut, J. Preference for modes of dispute resolution as a function of process and decision control. *Journal of Experimental Psychology,* 1978, *14,* 13–22.

Hovland, C. I., & Janis, I. L. *Personality and persuasibility.* New Haven, Conn.: Yale University Press, 1959.

Hovland, C. I., Janis, I. L., & Kelley, H. H. *Communication and persuasion.* New Haven, Conn.: Yale University Press, 1953.

Howells, T. H. A study of ability to recognize faces. *Journal of Abnormal and Social Psychology,* 1938, 33, 124–127.

Hunt, Y. C., Jr. *Minority recruiting in the New York City Police Department. Part 1, The attraction of candidates.* New York: New York City–Rand Institute, 1971.

Hutchings, B., & Mednick, S. A. Criminality in adoptees and their adoptive and biological parents: A pilot study. In S. A. Mednick & K. A. Christiansen (eds.), *Biological bases of criminal behavior.* New York: Gardner Press, 1977.

Ichheiser, G. Misinterpretations of personality in everyday life and the psychologist's frame of reference. *Character and Personality,* 1943, 12, 145–160.

Inbau, F. E., & Reid, J. E. *Criminal interrogation and confessions.* Baltimore: Williams & Wilkins, 1967.

Inwald, R. E., Levitt, D. B., & Knatz, H. F. Preemployment psychological evaluation as a predictor of correction officer job performance. Paper presented at APA Convention, Montreal, Sept. 1–5, 1980.

Izzett, R., & Fishman, L. Defendant sentences as a function of attractiveness and justification for actions. *Journal of Social Psychology*, 1976, *100*, 285–290.

Izzett, R., & Leginski, W. Group discussion and the influence of defendant characteristics in a simulated jury setting. *Journal of Social Psychology*, 1974, *93*, 271–279.

Jaccard, J. Toward theories of persuasion and belief change. *Journal of Personality and Social Psychology*, 1981, *40*, 260–268.

Jacob, H. *Justice in America: Courts, lawyers, and the judicial process.* 2d ed. Boston: Little, Brown, 1972.

Jacobi, H. Reducing police stress: A psychiatrist's point of view. In W. H. Kroes & J. Hurrell (eds.), *Job stress and the police officer.* Washington, D.C.: U.S. Department of Health, Education and Welfare, 1975.

Jacobs, J. R. Psychopathology as a function of time with institutionalized male offenders. Doctoral dissertation, University of Northern Colorado, 1973. *Dissertation Abstracts International*, 1974, *34*, 5681B (University Microfilms No. 74–9, 756).

James, F., Jr. *Civil procedure.* Boston: Little, Brown, 1965.

James, R. Status and competence of jurors. *American Journal of Sociology*, 1959, *64*, 563–570.

James, W. *Essays on faith and morals.* New York: New American Library, 1962.

Jirak, M. Alienation among members of the New York City Police Department of Staten Island. *Journal of Police Science and Administration*, 1975, *3*, 149–161.

Johnson, C., & Scott, B. Eyewitness testimony and suspect identification as a function of arousal, sex of witness, and scheduling of interrogation. Paper presented at meeting of the American Psychological Association, Washington, D.C., 1976.

Johnson, H., & Steiner, I. Some effects of discrepancy level on relationships between authoritarianism and conformity. *Journal of Social Psychology*, 1967, *9*, 179–183.

Johnson, R. N. *Aggression in man and animals.* Philadelphia: W. B. Saunders, 1972.

Johnson, V. S. Behavior modification in the correctional setting. *Criminal Justice and Behavior*, 1977, *4*, 397–428.

Jones, C., & Aronson, E. Attribution of fault to a rape victim as a function of respectability of the victim. *Journal of Personality and Social Psychology*, 1973, *26*, 415–419.

Jones, R. A. *Self-fulfilling prophecies: Social, psychological, and physiological effects of expectancies.* Hillsdale, N.J.: Lawrence Erlbaum, 1977.

Joos, M. *The five clocks: A linguistic excursion into the five styles of English usage.* New York: Harcourt, Brace & World, 1961.

Jurow, G. L. New data on the effect of a "death-qualified" jury on the guilt determination process. *Harvard Law Review*, 1971, *84*, 567–611.

Kahneman, D., & Tversky, A. On the psychology of prediction. *Psychological Review*, 1973, *80*, 237–251.

Kairys, D., Schulman, J., & Harring, S. *The jury system: New methods for reducing prejudice.* Philadelphia: National Jury Project and National Lawyers Guild, 1975.

Kalven, H. Jr., & Zeisel, H. *The American jury.* Boston: Little, Brown & Co., 1966.

Kanno, C. K., & Scheidemandel, P. L. *The mentally ill offender: A survey of treatment programs.* Washington, D.C.: Joint Information Service, 1969.

Kaplan, J. *Criminal justice: Introductory cases and materials.* Mineola, N.Y.: Foundation Press, 1973.

Kaplan, M. F. Discussion polarization effects in a modified jury decision paradigm: Informational influences. *Sociometry*, 1977, *40*, 262–271.

Kaplan, M. F., & Kemmerick, G. D. Juror judgments as information integration: Combining evidential and nonevidential information. *Journal of Personality and Social Psychology*, 1974, *30*, 493–499.

Kaplan, M. F., & Miller, L. E. Reducing the effects of juror bias. *Journal of Personality and Social Psychology*, 1978, *36*, 1443–1455.

Kaplan, M. F., & Schersching, C. Reducing juror bias: An experimental approach. In P. Lipsitt & B. Sales (eds.), *New directions in psycholegal research.* New York: Van Nostrand Reinhold, 1980.

Kaplan, M. F., & Schersching, C. Juror deliberation: An informational integration analysis. In B. D. Sales (ed.), *Perspectives in law and psychology.* Vol. 2, *The trial process.* New York: Plenum, 1981.

Kasl, Q. V., & Mahl, G. F. The relationship of disturbances and hesitations in spontaneous speech to anxiety. *Journal of Personality and Social Psychology*, 1965, *1*, 425–433.

Kassin, S. M., & Wrightsman, L. S. On the requirements of proof: The timing of judicial instruction and mock juror verdicts. *Journal of Personality and Social Psychology*, 1979, *37*, 1877–1887.

Kastenmeier, R. W., & Remington, M. J. Court reform and access to justice: A legislative perspective. *Harvard Journal on Legislation*, 1979, *16*, 301–342.

Katz, J. The right to treatment—An enchanting legal fiction. *University of Chicago Law Review*, 1969, *36*, 755–788.

Katz, L. S., & Reid, J. F. Expert testimony on the fallibility of eyewitness identification. *Criminal Justice Journal*, 1977, *1*, 177–206.

Katz, M. M., Cole, J. O., & Lowery, H. A. Studies of the diagnostic process: The influence of symptom perception, past experience, and ethnic background on diagnostic decision. *American Journal of Psychiatry*, 1969, *125*, 937–947.

Keeton, R. E. *Trial, tactics, and methods*. 2d ed. Boston: Little, Brown, 1973.

Kelly, H. H. Attribution theory in social psychology. In D. Levine (ed.), *Nebraska symposium on motivation, 1967*. Lincoln, Neb.: University of Nebraska Press, 1967.

Kenrick, D. T., & Stringfield, D. O. Personality traits and the eye of the beholder: Crossing some traditional philosophical boundaries in the search for consistency in all of the people. *Psychological Review*, 1980, *87*, 88–104.

Kent, D. A., & Eisenberg, T. The selection and promotion of police officers: A selected review of recent literature. *The Police Chief*, 1972, *39*, 20–29.

Kerlinger, F. N. *Foundations of behavioral research*. 2d ed. New York: Holt, Rinehart & Winston, 1973.

Kerr, N. L., Nerenz, D., & Herrick, D. Role playing and the study of jury behavior. *Sociological Methods and Research*, 1979, *7*, 337–355.

Kiehlbauch, J. B. Selected changes over time in internal-external expectancies in a reformatory population. Doctoral dissertation, Kansas State University, 1968. *Dissertation Abstracts International*, 1968, *29*, 371B (University Microfilms No. 68–9, 912).

Kimmel, M. J., Pruitt, D. G., Magenau, J. M., Konar-Goldband, E., & Carnevale, P. J. D. Effects of trust, aspiration, and gender on negotiation tactics. *Journal of Personality and Social Psychology*, 1980, *38*, 9–22.

Kirscht, J. P., & Dillehay, R. C. *Dimensions of authoritarianism: A review of research and theory*. Lexington: University of Kentucky Press, 1967.

Kittrie, N. N. *The right to be different: Deviance and enforced therapy*. Baltimore: Johns Hopkins University Press, 1971.

Klatzky, R. L. *Human memory: Structures and processes*. San Francisco: W. H. Freeman & Co., 1975.

Knapp, M. L. *Nonverbal communication in human interaction*. 2d ed. New York: Holt, Rinehart & Winston, 1978.

Knapp, M. L., Hart, R. P., & Dennis, H. S. An exploration of deception as a communication construct. *Human Communication Research*, 1974, *1*, 15–29.

Kohlberg, L. The child as a moral philosopher. In CRM, *Readings in developmental psychology today*. New York: Random House, 1977.

Kole, D. M. A study of intellectual and personality characteristics of medical students. Unpublished master's thesis, University of Oregon, 1962.

Komorita, S. S., & Barnes, M. Effects of pressure to reach agreement in bargaining. *Journal of Personality and Social Psychology*, 1969, *13*, 245–252.

Komorita, S. S., & Brenner, A. R. Bargaining and concession-making under bilateral monopoly. *Journal of Personality and Social Psychology*, 1968, *9*, 15–20.

Konečni, V. J., & Ebbesen, E. B. External validity of research in legal psychology. *Law and Human Behavior*, 1979, *3*, 39–70.

Konečni, V. J., & Ebbesen, E. B. A critique of theory and method in social-psychological approaches to legal issues. In B. D. Sales (ed.), *The trial process*. New York: Plenum, 1981.

Kostlan, A. A method for the empirical study of psychodiagnosis. *Journal of Consulting Psychology*, 1954, *18*, 83–88.

Kozol, H. L., Boucher, R. L., & Garofalo, P. F. The diagnosis and treatment of dangerousness. *Crime and Delinquency*, 1972, *8*, 371–392.

Kroes, W. H. *Society's victim—the policeman: An analysis of job stress in policing*. Springfield, Ill.: C. C. Thomas, 1976.

Kroes, W. H., Hurrell, Jr., & Margolis, B. Job stress in police administrators. *Journal of Police Science and Administration*, 1974, 2, 381–387.

Kubis, J. *Comparison of voice analysis and polygraph as lie detection procedures*. Aberdeen Proving Ground, Md.: U.S. Army Land Warfare Laboratory, 1973.

Kubis, J. F. Experimental and statistical factors in the diagnosis of consciously suppressed affective experience. *Journal of Clinical Psychology*, 1950, 6, 12–16.

Kuhn, T. S. *The structure of scientific revolutions*. 2d ed. Chicago: University of Chicago Press, 1970.

Kulka, R. A., & Kessler, J. B. Is justice really blind?—The influence of litigant physical attractiveness on juridical judgment. *Journal of Applied Social Psychology*, 1978, 8, 366–381.

Labovitz, S., & Hagedorn, R. An analysis of suicide rates among occupational categories. *Sociological Inquiry*, 1971, 41, 67–72.

Lachman, J. A., & McLauchlan, W. P. Models of plea bargaining. In S. S. Nagel (ed.), *Modeling the criminal justice system*. Beverly Hills, Calif.: Sage, 1977.

Lakoff, R. Language and woman's place. *Language and Society*, 1973, 2, 45–79.

Landau, S. F. Thought content of delinquent and nondelinquent young adults: The effect of institutionalization. *Criminal Justice and Behavior*, 1978, 5, 195–210.

Landy, D., & Aronson, E. The influence of the character of the criminal and his victim on the decisions of simulated jurors. *Journal of Experimental Social Psychology*, 1969, 5, 141–152.

Landy, F. J. The validity of the interview in police officer selection. *Journal of Applied Psychology*, 1976, 61, 193–198.

LaTour, S. Determinants of participant and observer satisfaction with adversary and inquisitorial modes of adjudication. *Journal of Personality and Social Psychology*, 1978, 36, 1531–1545.

LaTour, S., Houlden, P., Walker, L., & Thibaut, J. Procedure: Transnational perspectives and preferences. *The Yale Law Journal*, 1976, 86, 258–290.

Laughery, K. R., Alexander, J. E., & Lane, A. B. Recognition of human faces: Effects of target exposure time, target position, pose position, and type of photograph. *Journal of Applied Psychology*, 1971, 55, 477–483.

Laughery, K. R., Duval, G. C., & Fowler, R. H. An analysis of procedures for generating facial images. University of Houston Mug File Project, Report No. UHMUG-2, 1977.

Laughery, K. R., Fessler, P. K., Lenorovitz, D. R., & Yoblick, D. A. Time delay and similarity effects in facial recognition. *Journal of Applied Psychology*, 1974, 59, 490–496.

Laughery, K. R., & Fowler, R. H. Factors affecting facial recognition. University of Houston Mug File Project, Report No. UHMUG-3, 1977.

Laughery, K. R., & Fowler, R. H. Analysis of procedures for generating facial images. Paper presented at the annual meeting of the American Psychological Association, Toronto, 1978.

Lavrakas, P. J., Buri, J. R., & Mayzner, M. S. A perspective on the recognition of other-race faces. *Perception and Psychophysics*, 1976, 20, 475–481.

Law Enforcement Assistance Administration. *Forcible rape: A national survey of the response by police*. Washington, D.C.: U.S. Government Printing Office, 1977a.

Law Enforcement Assistance Administration. *Forcible rape: A national survey of the response by prosecutors*. U.S. Government Printing Office, 1977b.

Law Enforcement Assistance Administration. *Forcible rape: An analysis of legal issues*. Washington, D.C.: U.S. Government Printing Office, 1978a.

Law Enforcement Assistance Administration. *Forcible rape: Final project report*. Washington, D.C. U.S. Government Printing Office, 1978b.

Law Enforcement Assistance Administrator's State Court Caseload Statistics: Annual Report, 1975. Washington, D.C.: U.S. Government Printing Office, 1979a.

Law Enforcement Assistance Administration. *Prisoners in state and federal institutions on December 31, 1977*. Washington, D.C.: U.S. Government Printing Office, 1979b.

Law Enforcement Assistance Administration. *Criminal victimization in the United States 1977*. U.S. Government Printing Office: Washington, D.C., 1979c.

Lazarus, R. S. *Psychological stress and the coping process*. New York: McGraw-Hill, 1966.

Lazarus, R. S., Averill, J. R., & Opton, E. M.,

Jr. The psychology of coping: Issues of research and assessment. In G. V. Coelho, D. A. Hamburg & J. E. Adams (eds.), *Coping and adaptation*. New York: Basic Books, 1974.

Lefcourt, H. M. Internal versus external control of reinforcement: A review. *Psychological Bulletin*, 1966, 65, 206–220.

Lefkowitz, J. Attitudes of police toward their job. In J. R. Snibbe & H. M. Snibbe (eds.), *The urban policeman in transition*. Springfield, Ill.: C. C. Thomas, 1973.

Lefkowitz, J. Psychological attributes of policemen: A review of research and opinion. *Journal of Social Issues*, 1975, 31, 3–26.

Lefkowitz, J. Industrial-organizational psychology and the police. *American Psychologist*, 1977, 5, 346–364.

Leifer, R. The psychiatrist and tests of criminal responsibility. *American Psychologist*, 1964, 19, 825–830.

Leippe, M. R. Effects of integrative memorial and cognitive processes on the correspondence of eyewitness accuracy and confidence. *Law and Human Behavior*, 1980, 4, 261–274.

Leippe, M. R., Wells, G. L., & Ostrom, T. M. Crime seriousness as a determinant of accuracy in eyewitness identification. *Journal of Applied Psychology*, 1978, 63, 345–351.

Lempert, R. D. Uncovering "nondiscernible" differences: Empirical research and the jury-size cases. *Michigan Law Review*, 1975, 73, 643–708.

Lerner, M. J. The desire for justice and reactions to victims. In J. Macaulay and L. Berkowitz (eds.), *Altruism and helping behavior*. New York: Academic Press, 1970.

Lerner, M. J. The justice motive: Some hypotheses as to its origins and forms. *Journal of Personality*, 1977, 45, 1–52.

Lerner, M. J. *The belief in a just world: A fundamental delusion*. New York: Plenum Press, 1980.

Lerner, M. J., & Simmons, C. H. Observer's reaction to the "innocent victim": Compassion or rejection? *Journal of Personality and Social Psychology*, 1966, 4, 203–210.

Levy, R. J. Predicting police failures. *Journal of Criminal Law, Criminology and Police Science*, 1967, 58, 265–276.

Levy, R. J. *Investigation of a method for identification of the high risk police applicant*. Berkeley: Institute for Local Government, 1971.

Lewis, R. W. Toward an understanding of police anomie. *Journal of Police Science and Administration*, 1973, 1, 484–490.

Liggett, J. *The human face*. London: Constable, 1974.

Lind, E. A., & O'Barr, W. M. The social significance of speech in the courtroom. In H. Giles & R. St. Clair (eds.), *Language and social psychology*. Oxford, England: Blackwell, 1978.

Lind, E. A., Thibaut, J., & Walker, L. Discovery and presentation of evidence in adversary and nonadversary proceedings. *Michigan Law Review*, 1973, 71, 1129–1144.

Lind, E. A., & Walker, L. Theory testing, theory development, and laboratory research on legal issues. *Law and Human Behavior*, 1979, 3, 5–19.

Lindsay, R. C. L., & Wells, G. L. What price justice? Exploring the relationship of lineup fairness to identification accuracy. *Law and Human Behavior*, 1980, 4, 303–313.

Lindsay, R. C. L., Wells, G. L., & Rumpel, C. M. Can people detect eyewitness identification within and across situations? *Journal of Applied Psychology*, 1981, 66, 79–89.

Little, K. B., & Schneidman, E. S. Congruencies among interpretations of psychological test and anamnestic data. *Psychological Monographs*, 1959, 73 (6, Whole No. 47).

Littlepage, G., & Pineault, T. Verbal, facial, and paralinguistic cues to the detection of truth and lying. *Personality and Social Psychology Bulletin*, 1978, 4, 461–464.

Loftus, E. F. Leading questions and the eyewitness report. *Cognitive Psychology*, 1975, 7, 560–572.

Loftus, E. F. Shifting human color memory. *Memory and Cognition*, 1977, 5, 696–699.

Loftus, E. F. *Eyewitness testimony*. Cambridge, Mass.: Harvard University Press, 1979.

Loftus, E. F. Impact of expert psychology testimony on the unreliability of eyewitness identification. *Journal of Applied Psychology*, 1980, 65, 9–15.

Loftus, E. F., & Loftus, G. R. On the permanence of stored information in the human brain. *American Psychologist*, 1980, 35, 409–420.

Loftus, E. F., Miller, D. G., & Burns, H. J. Semantic integration of verbal information into a visual memory. *Journal of Experi-*

mental Psychology: Human Learning and Memory, 1978, 4, 19–31.

Loftus, G R. Eye fixations and recognition memory. Cognitive Psychology, 1972, 3, 525–557.

Loftus, G. R., & Loftus, E. F. Human memory: The processing of information. Hillsdale, N.J.: Erlbaum Press, 1976.

Loh, W. D. Psychology and law: A coming of age. Contemporary Psychology, 1979, 24, 164–166.

Lott, A. J., & Lott, B. E. The role of reward in the formation of positive interpersonal attitudes. In T. Huston (ed.), Foundations of interpersonal attraction. New York: Academic Press, 1974.

Lotz, R., & Regoli, R. M. Police cynicism and professionalism. Human Relations, 1977, 30, 175–186.

Luce, R. D., & Raiffa, N. Games and decisions. New York: Wiley, 1958.

Luft, J. Implicit hypotheses and clinical predictions. Journal of Abnormal and Social Psychology, 1950, 45, 756–759.

Lunde, D. T. Murder and madness. San Francisco: San Francisco Book Co., 1976.

Lykken, D. T. A study of anxiety in the sociopathic personality. Journal of Abnormal and Social Psychology, 1957, 55, 6–10.

Lykken, D. T. Psychology and the lie detector industry. American Psychologist, 1974, 29, 725–739.

Lykken, D. T. The psychopath and the lie detector. Psychophysiology, 1978, 15, 137–142.

Lykken, D. T. The detection of deception. Psychological Bulletin, 1979, 86, 47–53.

McCain, G., Cox, V. C., & Paulus, P. B. The relationship between illness complaints and degree of crowding in a prison environment. Environment and Behavior, 1976, 8, 283–290.

McClearn, G. E., & DeFries, J. C. Introduction to behavioral genetics. San Francisco: W. H. Freeman, 1973.

McClintock, C. G., & Hunt, R. C. Nonverbal indicators of affect and deception in an interview setting. Journal of Applied Social Psychology, 1975, 5, 54–67.

MacDonald, J. M. Psychiatry and the criminal. 3d ed. Springfield, Ill.: C. C. Thomas, 1976.

McDonough, L. B., & Monahan, J. The quality control of community caretakers: A study of mental health screening in a sheriff's department. Community Mental Health Journal, 1975, 11, 33–44.

McGarry, A. L. The fate of psychiatric offenders returned for trial. American Journal of Psychiatry, 1971, 127, 1181–1184.

McGinnies, E., & Ward, C. D. Persuasibility as a function of source credibility and locus of control: Five cross-cultural experiments. Journal of Personality, 1974, 42, 360–371.

McGuire, W. J. Inducing resistance to persuasion. In L. Berkowitz (ed.), Advances in experimental social psychology. Vol. I. New York: Academic Press, 1964.

McKinney, T. S. The criterion-related validity of entry level police officer selection procedures. Phoenix, Ariz.: City of Phoenix Personnel Department, 1973.

MacLaughlin, G. H. The lie detector as an aid in arson and criminal investigation. Journal of Criminal Law and Criminology, 1953, 43, 693–694.

McLean, P. D. Depression as a specific response to stress. In I. G. Sarason & C. D. Spielberger (eds.), Stress and anxiety. Vol. 3. Washington, D. C.: Hemisphere Publishing, 1976.

MacNitt, R. D. In defense of the electrodermal response and cardiac amplitude as measures of deception. Journal of Criminal Law and Criminology, 1942, 33, 266–275.

Maloney, M. P., & Ward, M. P. Psychological assessment: A conceptual approach. New York: Oxford University Press, 1976.

Malpass, R. S., & Kravitz, J. Recognition for faces of own and other race. Journal of Personality and Social Psychology, 1969, 13, 330–334.

Malpass, R. S., Lavigueur, H., & Weldon, D. E. Verbal and visual training in face recognition. Perception and Psychophysics, 1973, 14, 285–292.

Margolis, B. L. Stress is a work hazard too. Industrial Medicine, Occupational Health and Surgery, 1973, 42, 20–23.

Marin, B. V., Holmes, D. L., Guth, M., & Kovac, P. The potential of children as eyewitnesses: A comparison of children and adults on eyewitness tasks. Law and Human Behavior, 1979, 3, 295–306.

Mark, V. H., & Ervin, F. R. Violence and the brain. Hagerstown, Md.: Harper & Row, 1970.

Marlowe, D., Gerben, K. J., & Doob, A. N. Opponent's personality, expectation of social interaction and interpersonal bargaining. *Journal of Personality and Social Psychology*, 1966, 3, 206–213.

Marsh, S. H. Validating the selection of deputy sheriffs. *Public Personnel Review*, 1962, 23, 41–44.

Marshall, J. *Law and psychology in conflict*. New York: Bobbs-Merrill, 1966.

Marshall, J. *Intention in law and society*. New York: Minerva Press, 1968.

Marshall, J. Trial, testimony and truth. In S. S. Nagel (ed.), *The rights of the accused*. Vol. 1. Beverly Hills, Ca.: Sage Publications, 1972.

Martin, M. J. Muscle-contraction headache. *Psychosomatics*, 1972, 13, 16–19.

Martinson, R. M. What works—questions and answers about prison reform. *Public Interest*, 1974, 35, 22–54.

Matarazzo, J. D., Allen, B. V., Saslow, G., & Wiens, A. Characteristics of successful policemen and firemen applicants. *Journal of Applied Psychology*, 1964, 48, 123–133.

May, P. R., et al. *Treatment of schizophrenia: A comparison study of five treatment methods*. New York: Aronson, 1968.

Mazer, D. Mental illness and the law. In W. K. Greenaway & S. L. Brickley (eds.), *Law and social control in Canada*. Scarborough, Ont.: Prentice-Hall of Canada, 1978, 94–104.

Mears, F., & Gatchel, R. J. *Fundamentals of abnormal psychology*. Chicago: Rand McNally, 1979.

Mechanic, D. *Mental health and social policy*. 2d ed. Englewood Cliffs, N.J.: Prentice-Hall, 1980.

Mednick, S. A., & Christiansen, K. O. (eds.). *Biosocial bases of criminal behavior*. New York: Gardner Press, 1977.

Meehl, P. E. *Clinical versus statistical prediction*. Minneapolis: University of Minnesota, 1954.

Meehl, P. E. Some ruminations on the validation of clinical procedures. *Canadian Journal of Psychology*, 1959, 13, 102–128.

Meehl, P. E. Seer over sign: The first good example. *Journal of Experimental Research in Personality*, 1965, 1, 27–32.

Meehl, P. E. Law and the fireside inductions: Some reflections of a clinical psychologist. *Journal of Social Issues*, 1971, 27, 65–100.

Megargee, E. I. Population density and disruptive behavior in a prison setting. In A. K.

Cohen, F. G. Cole, & R. G. Bailey (eds.), *Prison violence*. Lexington, Mass.: Lexington Books, 1976.

Megargee, E. I. (ed.). A new classification system for criminal offenders. *Criminal Justice and Behavior*, 1977, 4, 107–216.

Mehrabian, A. Nonverbal betrayal of feeling. *Journal of Experimental Research in Personality*, 1971, 5, 64–73.

Mehrabian, A., & Williams, M. Nonverbal concomitants of perceived and intended persuasiveness. *Journal of Personality and Social Psychology*, 1969, 13, 37–58.

Messick, S. Test validity and the ethics of assessment. *American Psychologist*, 1980, 35, 1012–1027.

Miller, G. R., Bauchner, J. E., Hocking, J. E., Fontes, N. E., Kaminski, E. P., & Brandt, D. R. ". . . and nothing but the truth." How well can observers detect deceptive testimony? In B. D. Sales (ed.), *Perspectives in law and psychology*. Vol. 2, *The trial process*. New York: Plenum, 1981.

Miller, H. L., Lower, J. S., & Bleechmore, J. The clinical psychologist as an expert witness on questions of mental illness and competency. *Law and Psychology Review*, 1978, 4, 115–125.

Miller, H. S., McDonald, W. F., & Cramer, J. A. *Plea bargaining in the United States*. Washington, D.C.: U.S. Government Printing Office, 1978.

Mills, C. J., & Bohannon, W. E. Personality characteristics of effective state police officers. *Journal of Applied Psychology*, 1980, 65, 680–684.

Mills, J. Opinion change as a function of the communicator's desire to influence and liking for the audience. *Journal of Experimental Social Psychology*, 1966, 2, 152–159.

Mills, J., & Jellison, J. Effect on opinion change of how desirable the communication is to the audience the communicator addressed. *Journal of Personality and Social Psychology*, 1967, 6, 98–101.

Mills, R. B. Use of diagnostic small groups in police recruit selection and training. *Journal of Criminal Law, Criminology, and Police Science*, 1969, 60, 238–241.

Mills, R. B. Simulated stress in police recruit selection. *Journal of Police Science and Administration*, 1976, 4, 179–186.

Mills, R. B., McDevitt, R. J., & Tonkin, S. Situational tests in metropolitan police recruit selection. *Journal of Criminal Law, Criminology, and Police Science*, 1966, 57, 99–104.

Miron, M. S. Issues of psychological evidence: Discussion. In F. Wright, C. Bahn, & R. W. Rieber (eds.), *Forensic psychology and psychiatry*. Annals of the New York Academy of Sciences, vol. 347. New York: New York Academy of Sciences, 1980.

Mischel, W. *Personality and assessment*. New York: Wiley, 1968.

Mischel, W. Toward a cognitive social learning reconceptualization of personality. *Psychological Review*, 1973, 80, 252–283.

Mischel, W. *Introduction to personality*. 2d ed. New York: Holt, Rinehart & Winston, 1976.

Mischel, W. On the interface of cognition and personality: Beyond the person-situation debate. *American Psychologist*, 1979, 34, 740–754.

Mischel, W. *Introduction to personality*. 3d ed. New York: Holt, Rinehart & Winston, 1981.

Mischel, W., & Mischel, H. N. *Essentials of psychology*. New York: Random House, 1977.

Mitchell, H. E., & Byrne, D. The defendant's dilemma: Effects of jurors' attitudes and authoritarianism on judicial decisions. *Journal of Personality and Social Psychology*, 1973, 25, 123–129.

Monahan, J. Abolish the insanity defense? Not yet. *Rutgers Law Review*, 1973, 26, 719–740.

Monahan, J. Violence prediction. *Virginia Law Review*, 1976, 27, 179–183.

Monahan, J. Social accountability: Preface to an integrated theory of criminal and mental health sanctions. In B. D. Sales (ed.), *Perspectives in law and psychology*. Vol. 1, *The criminal justice system*. New York: Plenum, 1977.

Monahan, J. The prediction of violent criminal behavior: A methodological critique and prospectus. In A. Blumstein et al. (eds.), *Deterrence and incapacitation: Estimating the effects of criminal sanctions on crime rates*. Washington, D.C.: National Academy of Sciences, 1978.

Monahan, J. (ed.). *Who is the client? The ethics of psychological intervention in the criminal justice system*. Washington, D.C.: American Psychological Association, 1980.

Monahan, J. *Predicting violent behavior: An assessment of clinical techniques*. Beverly Hills, Calif.: Sage Publications, 1981.

Monson, T. C., & Snyder, M. Actors, observers, and the attribution process: Toward a reconceptualization. *Journal of Experimental Social Psychology*, 1977, 13, 89–111.

Morris, N. *The future of imprisonment*. Chicago and London: The University of Chicago Press, 1974.

Morse, S. J. Crazy behavior, morals, and science: An analysis of mental health law. *Southern California Law Review*, 1978a, 51, 527–654.

Morse, S. J. Law and mental health professionals: The limits of expertise. *Professional Psychology*, 1978b, 9, 389–399.

Mowrer, O. H. *Learning theory and behavior*. New York: Wiley, 1960.

Mullineaux, J. E. An evaluation of the predictors used to select patrolmen. *Public Personnel Review*, 1955, 16, 84–86.

Munsterberg, H. *On the witness stand*. New York: Doubleday, Page, 1908.

Murphy, J. J. Current practices in the use of psychological testing by police agencies. *The Journal of Criminal Law, Criminology and Police Science*, 1972, 63, 570–576.

Murray, H., et al. *Assessment of men: Selection of personnel for the Office of Strategic Services*. New York: Rinehart & Co., 1948.

Myers, D. G., & Kaplan, M. F. Group-induced polarization in simulated juries. *Personality and Social Psychology Bulletin*, 1976, 2, 63–66.

Myers, D. G., & Lamm, H. The group polarization phenomenon. *Psychological Bulletin*, 1976, 83, 602–627.

Nacci, P. L., Prather, J., & Teitelbaum, H. E. Population density and inmate misconduct rates in the federal prison system. *Federal Probation*, 1977, 41, 26–31.

Nagel, S. S. *The legal process from a behavioral perspective*. Homewood, Ill.: Dorsey, 1969.

Nagin, D. General deterrence: A review of the empirical evidence. In A. Blumstein, J. Cohen, & D. Nagin (eds.), *Deterrence and incapacitation: Estimating the effects of criminal sanctions on crime rates*. Washington, D.C.: National Academy of Sciences, 1978.

Narrol, H. G., & Levitt, E. E. Formal assessment procedures in police selection. *Psychological Reports*, 1963, 12, 691–694.

Nemeth, C., & Sosis, R. M. A simulated jury: Characteristics of the defendant and the jurors. *Journal of Social Psychology*, 1973, 90, 221–229.

Nemeth, C., & Wachtler, J. Creating the perceptions of consistency and confidence: A necessary condition for minority influence. *Sociometry*, 1974, 37, 529–540.

Niederhoffer, A. *Behind the shield: The police in urban society*. New York: Doubleday, 1967.

Nimmer, R. T. The system impact of criminal justice. In J. L. Tapp & F. J. Levine (eds.), *Law, justice, and the individual in society*. New York: Holt, Rinehart & Winston, 1977.

Nisbett, R. E., & Borgida, E. Attribution and the psychology of prediction. *Journal of Personality and Social Psychology*, 1975, 32, 932–943.

Nisbett, R. E., Borgida, E., Crandall, R., & Reed, H. Popular induction: Information is not necessarily informative. In J. S. Carroll & J. W. Payne (eds.), *Cognition and social behavior*. Hillsdale, N.J.: Erlbaum, 1976.

Noonan, J. T. The purposes of advocacy and the limits of confidentiality. *Michigan Law Review*, 1966, 64, 1485–1492.

O'Brien, M. D. Cerebral blood change in migraine. *Headache*, 1971, 10, 139–143.

O'Brien, M. D. The haemodynamics of migraine—A review. *Headache*, 1973, 12, 160–162.

O'Hara, C. E. *Fundamentals of criminal investigation*. Springfield, Ill.: C. C. Thomas, 1970.

Olson, B. T. Police opinions of work: An exploratory study. In J. R. Snibbe & H. M. Snibbe (eds.), *The urban policeman in transition*. Springfield, Ill.: C. C. Thomas, 1973.

Opinion Research Corporation. *Police-community relations: A survey among New York City patrolmen*. Ann Arbor, Mich.: University Microfilms, 1968.

Orne, M. T. Hypnosis, motivation and the ecological validity of the psychological experiment. In W. J. Arnold & M. M. Page (eds.), *Nebraska symposium on motivation*. Lincoln: University of Nebraska Press, 1970.

Packer, H. L. *The limits of the criminal sanction*. Stanford: Stanford University Press, 1968.

Padawer-Singer, A. M., & Barton, A. H. The impact of pretrial publicity on jurors' verdicts. In R. J. Simon (ed.), *The jury system in America*. Beverly Hills, Ca.: Sage Publishing, 1975.

Padawer-Singer, A. M., Singer, A. N., & Singer, R. L. J. Voir dire by two lawyers: An essential safeguard. *Judicature*, 1974, 57, 386–391.

Panton, J. H. Personality characteristics of death row prison inmates. *Journal of Clinical Psychology*, 1976, 32, 306–309.

Partridge, A., & Bermant, G. *The quality of advocacy in the federal courts*. Washington, D.C.: Federal Judicial Center, 1978.

Passingham, R. G. Crime and personality: A review of Eysenck's theory. In V. D. Nebylitsyn & J. A. Gray (eds.), *Biological bases of individual behavior*. New York: Academic Press, 1972.

Pei, M. *Double-speak in America*. New York: Hawthorn, 1973.

Pennington, N., & Hastie, R. Juror decision-making models: The generalization gap. *Psychological Bulletin*, 1981, 89, 246–287.

Penrod, S., & Hastie, R. Models of jury decision making: A critical review. *Psychological Bulletin*, 1979, 86, 462–492.

Perlin, M. L. The legal status of the psychologist in the courtroom. *Journal of Psychiatry and Law*, 1977, 5, 41–54.

Petty, R. E., & Cacioppo, J. T. *Attitudes and persuasion: Classic and contemporary approaches*. Dubuque, Iowa: Wm. C. Brown, 1981.

Phares, E. J. *Locus of control in personality*. Morristown, N.J.: General Learning Press, 1976.

Piaget, J. *The moral judgment of the child*. London: Routledge & Kegan Paul, 1932.

Platt, A., & Pollock, R. Channeling lawyers: The careers of public defenders. In G. Bermant, C. Nemeth & N. Vidmar (eds.), *Psychology and the law: Research frontiers*. Lexington, Mass.: Lexington Books, 1976.

Podlesny, J. A., & Raskin, D. C. Physiological measures and the detection of deception. *Psychological Bulletin*, 1977, 84, 782–799.

Poland, J. M. Police selection methods and the prediction of police performance. *Journal of Police Science and Administration*, 1978, 6, 374–393.

Popper, K. *Conjectures and refutations: The growth of scientific knowledge*. New York: Basic Books, 1962.

Poythress, N. G. A proposal for training in forensic psychology. *American Psychologist*, 1979, 34, 612–621.

Prentky, R. A. Creativity and psychopathology:

A neurocognitive perspective. In B. Maher (ed.), *Progress in experimental research*. Vol. 9. New York: Academic Press, 1979.

President's Commission on Law Enforcement and Administration of Justice. *The challenge of crime in a free society*. Washington, D.C.: U.S. Government Printing Office, 1967.

Pruitt, D. G., & Johnson, D. F. Mediation as an aid to face saving in negotiation. *Journal of Personality and Social Psychology*, 1970, 14, 239–246.

Pruitt, D. G., & Lewis, S. A. Development of integrative solutions in bilateral negotiation. *Journal of Personality and Social Psychology*, 1975, 31, 621–633.

Pruitt, D. G., & Lewis, S. A. The psychology of integrative bargaining. In D. Druckman (ed.), *Negotiation: A social psychological perspective*. New York: Halsted, 1977.

Pruitt, D. G., Kimmel, M. J., Britton, S., Carnevale, P. J. D., Magenau, J. M., Peragallo, J., & Engram, P. The effect of accountability and surveillance on integrative bargaining. In H. Savermann (ed.), *Contributions to experimental economics*. Vol. 7. Tubingen, West Germany: Mohr, 1978.

Quay, H. C. The three faces of evaluation. What can be expected to work. *Criminal Justice and Behavior*, 1977, 4, 341–354.

Rabin, R. L. Lawyers for social change: Perspectives on public interest law. *Stanford Law Review*, 1976, 28, 207–261.

Rafky, D. M. My husband the cop. *Police Chief*, 1974, 41, 62–65.

Rafky, D. M., Lawley, T., & Ingram, R. Are police recruits cynical? *Journal of Police Science and Administration*, 1976, 4, 352–360.

Rahe, R. H., Mahan, J. L., & Arthur, R. J. Prediction of near-future health changes from subject's preceding life changes. *Journal of Psychosomatic Research*, 1970, 14, 401–406.

Rankin, J. H. Psychiatric screening of police recruits. *Public Personnel Review*, 1959, 20, 191–196.

Rappeport, J., & Lassen, G. Dangerousness-arrest rate comparisons of discharged patients and the general population. *American Journal of Psychiatry*, 1965, 121, 776–783.

Raskin, D. C. Scientific assessment of the accuracy of detection of deception: A reply to Lykken. *Psychophysiology*, 1978, 15, 143–147.

Raskin, D. C., & Hare, R. D. Psychopathy and detection of deception in a prison population. *Psychophysiology*, 1978, 15, 126–136.

Rawls, J. *A theory of justice*. Cambridge, Mass.: Belknap Press of Harvard University Press, 1971.

Refsum, S. Genetic aspects of migraine. In P. J. Vinken & G. W. Bryn (eds.), *Handbook of clinical neurology*. Vol. 5. New York: Wiley, 1968.

Regan, D. T., & Cheng, J. B. Distribution and attitude change: A resolution. *Journal of Experimental Social Psychology*, 1973, 9, 138–147.

Regoli, R. M. The effects of college education on the maintenance of police cynicism. *Journal of Police Science and Administration*, 1976, 4, 340–351.

Reiser, M. *Practical psychology for police officers*. Springfield, Ill.: C. C. Thomas, 1973.

Reiss, A. J. Career orientations, job satisfaction and the assessment of law enforcement problems by officers. *Studies in crime and law enforcement in major metropolitan areas*. Vol. 2. Washington, D.C.: U.S. Government Printing Office, 1967.

Reppucci, N. D., & Sanders, T. J. Social psychology of behavior modification. *American Psychologist*, 1974, 29, 649–660.

Reynolds, E. D., & Saunders, M. S. The effects of defendant attractiveness, age, and injury on severity of sentence given by simulated jurors. Paper presented at the meeting of the Western Psychological Association, San Francisco, April 1973.

Reynolds, E. D., & Sanders, M. S. Effect of defendant attractiveness, age and injury on severity of sentence given by simulated jurors. *Journal of Social Psychology*, 1975, 96, 149–150.

Rhead, C., Abrams, A., Trasman, H., & Margolis, P. The psychological assessment of police candidates. *American Journal of Psychiatry*, 1968, 124, 1575–1580.

Richard, W. C., & Fell, R. D. Health factors in police job stress. Paper presented at the symposium on job stress and the police officer. National Institute for Occupational Safety and Health, Cincinnati, Ohio, May 1975.

Roberts, E. F. Paradoxes in law enforcement. *Journal of Criminal Law, Criminology and Police Science*, 1961, 52, 224–228.

Robin, A., & Macdonald, D. *Lessons of leucotomy*. London: Henry Kimpton, 1975.

Rock, R. S., Jacobson, M. A., & Janopaul,

R. M. *Hospitalization and discharge of the mentally ill.* Chicago: University of Chicago Press, 1968.

Roper, R. Jury size and verdict consistency: "A line has to be drawn somewhere"? *Law & Society Review*, 1980, *14*, 977–995.

Rosenfeld, H. M. Approval-seeking and approval-inducing functions of verbal and nonverbal responses in the dyad. *Journal of Personality and Social Psychology*, 1966, *4*, 597–605.

Rosenkoetter, L. I. Resistance to temptation: Inhibitory and disinhibitory effects of models. *Developmental Psychology*, 1973, *8*, 80–84.

Rosenthal, D. *Genetic theory and abnormal behavior.* New York: McGraw-Hill, 1970.

Rosenthal, D. *Genetics of psychopathology.* New York: McGraw-Hill, 1971.

Ross, L. The intuitive psychologist and his shortcomings: Distortions in the attribution process. In L. Berkowitz (ed.), *Advances in experimental social psychology.* Vol. 10. New York: Academic Press, 1977.

Rothman, D. J. *The discovery of the asylum: Social order and disorder in the new republic.* Boston: Little, Brown, 1971.

Rotter, J. B. *Social learning and clinical psychology.* Englewood Cliffs, N.J.: Prentice-Hall, 1954.

Rotter, J. B. Generalized expectancies for internal versus external control of reinforcement. *Psychological Monographs*, 1966, *80* (Whole No. 609).

Rotter, J. B. Beliefs, social attitudes and behavior: A social learning analysis. In J. B. Rotter, J. E. Chance, & E. J. Phares (eds.), *Applications of social learning theory of personality.* New York: Holt, Rinehart & Winston, 1972.

Rotter, J. B., Chance, J. E., & Phares, E. J. (eds.). *Applications of a social learning theory of personality.* New York: Holt, Rinehart & Winston, 1972.

Rottschaefer, W., & Knowlton, W. A cognitive social learning theory perspective on human freedom. *Behaviorism*, 1979, *7*, 17–21.

Rubin, B. Predictions of dangerousness in mentally ill criminals. *Archives of General Psychiatry*, 1972, *27*, 397–407.

Rubin, Z., & Peplau, A. Belief in a just world and reactions to another's lot: A study of participants in the national draft lottery. *Journal of Social Issues*, 1973, *29*, 73–93.

Rubin, Z., & Peplau, A. Who believes in a just world? *Journal of Social Issues*, 1975, *31*, 65–89.

Rumsey, M. G., & Castore, C. H. The effect of group discussion on juror sentencing. Paper presented at the annual meeting of the Midwestern Psychological Association, Chicago, 1974.

Rychlak, J. F. *A philosophy of science for personality theory.* Boston: Houghton Mifflin Co., 1968.

Rychlak, J. F. *Discovering free will and personal responsibility.* New York: Oxford University Press, 1979.

Sadoff, R. L. *Forensic psychiatry.* Springfield, Ill.: C. C. Thomas, 1975.

Saks, M. J. Ignorance of science is no excuse. *Trial*, 1974, *10*, 18–24.

Saks, M. J. *Jury verdicts.* Lexington, Mass.: Lexington Books, 1977.

Saks, M. J., & Hastie, R. *Social psychology in court.* New York: Van Nostrand Reinhold, 1978.

Saks, M. J., & Kidd, R. F. Human information processing and adjudication: Trial by heuristics. *Law & Society Review*, 1980–81, *15*, 123–160.

Saks, M. J., & Miller, M. A systems approach to discretion in the legal process. In L. E. Abt & I. R. Stuart (eds.), *Social psychology and discretionary law.* New York: Van Nostrand Reinhold, 1979.

Saks, M. J., & Ostrom, T. M. Jury size and consensus requirements: The laws of probability vs. the laws of the land. *Journal of Contemporary Law*, 1975, *1*, 163–173.

Sales, B. D., Elwork, A., & Alfini, J. Improving comprehension for jury instructions. In B. D. Sales (ed.), *Perspectives in law and psychology: The criminal justice system.* New York: Plenum, 1977.

Sandy, J. P., & Devine, D. A. Four stress factors unique to rural patrol. *Police Chief*, 1978, *9*, 42–44.

Sarason, I. G., & Stoops, R. Test anxiety and the passage of time. *Journal of Consulting and Clinical Psychology*, 1978, *46*, 102–108.

Sawyer, J. Measurement and prediction, clinical and statistical. *Psychological Bulletin*, 1966, *66*, 178–200.

Schein, E. H. *Coercive persuasion.* New York: Norton, 1971.

Schoenfeld, C. G. Recent developments in the law concerning the mentally ill—"A cornerstone of legal structure laid in mud." *University of Toledo Law Review*, 1977, 9, 1–29.

Schwitzgebel, R. K. The right to effective mental treatment. *California Law Review*, 1974, 62, 936–956.

Schwitzgebel, R. K. Professional accountability in the treatment and release of dangerous persons. In B. D. Sales (ed.), *Perspectives in law and psychology*. Vol. 1, *The criminal justice system*. New York: Plenum Press, 1977, 139–150.

Schwitzgebel, R. L., & Schwitzgebel, R. K. *Law and psychological practice*. New York: Wiley, 1980.

Scott, J. Civil commitment statutes in the courts today. In *The health policy center. Paper victories and hard realities: The implementation of the legal and constitutional rights of the mentally disabled*, 1976.

Selye, H. *The stress of life*. 2d ed. New York: McGraw-Hill, 1976.

Selye, H. The stress of police work. *Police Stress*, 1978, 1, 7–8.

Shaffer, T. L. Introduction. *Santa Clara Lawyer*, 1973, 13, 369–376.

Shapiro, M., & Tresolini, R. J. *American constitutional law*. 5th ed. New York: Macmillan, 1979.

Shepherd, J. W., & Ellis, H. D. The effect of attractiveness on recognition memory for faces. *American Journal of Psychology*, 1973, 86, 627–633.

Sheppard, B. H., & Vidmar, N. Adversary pretrial procedures and testimonial evidence: Effects of lawyer's role and Machiavellianism. *Journal of Personality and Social Psychology*, 1980, 39, 320–332.

Sherman, M. *Personality: Inquiry and application*. New York: Pergamon Press, 1979.

Shoemaker, D. J., South, D. R., & Lowe, J. Facial stereotypes of deviants and judgments of guilt or innocence. *Social Forces*, 1973, 51, 427–433.

Shook, H. C. Pitfalls in policing. *The Police Chief*, 1978, 5, 8–10.

Shure, G. H., Meeker, R. J., & Hansford, E. A. The effectiveness of pacifist strategies in bargaining games. *Journal of Conflict Resolution*, 1965, 9, 106–117.

Siegel, S., & Fouraker, L. E. *Bargaining and group decision making*. New York: McGraw-Hill, 1960.

Sigall, H., & Landy, D. Effects of the defendant's character and suffering on juridic judgment: A replication and clarification. *Journal of Social Psychology*, 1972, 88, 149–150.

Sigall, H., & Ostrove, N. Beautiful but dangerous: Effects of offender attractiveness and nature of the crime on juridic judgment. *Journal of Personality and Social Psychology*, 1975, 31, 410–414.

Silving, H. Testing of the unconscious in criminal cases. *Harvard Law Review*, 1956, 69, 683–705.

Simon, R. J. (ed.). *The jury system in America*. Beverly Hills, Ca.: Sage Publishing, 1975.

Skolnick, J. A sketch of the policeman's working personality. In A. Niederhoffer & A. S. Blumberg (eds.), *The ambivalent force*. San Francisco: Rinehart Press, 1973.

Slater, P. E. Contrasting correlates of group size. *Sociometry*, 1958, 21, 129–139.

Slovenko, R. The developing law on competency to stand trial. *Journal of Psychiatry and Law*, 1977, 5, 165–200.

Smigel, E. O. *The Wall Street Lawyer*. New York: Free Press, 1964.

Smith, D. H., & Stotland, E. A new look at police officer selection. In J. R. Snibbe & H. M. Snibbe (eds.), *The urban policeman in transition*. Springfield, Ill.: Charles C. Thomas, 1973.

Snibbe, H. M., Fabricatore, J., Azen, S. P., & Snibbe, J. R. Race differences in police patrolmen: A failure to replicate the Chicago study. *American Journal of Community Psychology*, 1975, 3, 155–160.

Sobeloff, S. G. From M'Naghten to Durham and beyond. In P. W. Nice (ed.), *Crime and insanity*. New York: Philosophical Library, 1958.

Solomon, M. R., & Schopler, J. The relationship of physical attractiveness and punitiveness: Is the linearity assumption out of line? *Personality and Social Psychology Bulletin*, 1978, 4, 483–486.

Somodevilla, S. A. The role of psychologists in a police department. In W. Taylor & M. Braswell (eds.), *Issues in Police and Criminal Psychology*. Washington, D.C.: University Press of America, 1978.

Soskin, W. F. Influence of four types of data on diagnostic conceptualization in psychological testing. *Journal of Abnormal and Social Psychology*, 1959, 58, 69–78.

Spencer, G., & Nichols, R. A study of Chicago

police recruits: Validation of selection procedures. *The Police Chief*, 1971, 38, 50–55.

Spielberger, C. D. (ed.), *Police selection and evaluation: Issues and techniques*. Washington, D.C.: Hemisphere Publishing, 1979.

Spielberger, C. D., Spaulding, H. C., & Ward, J. C. *Selecting effective law enforcement officers: The Florida police standards research project*. Tampa, Fla.: Human Resources Institute, 1978.

Spielberger, C. D., Ward, J. C., & Spaulding, H. C. A model for the selection of law enforcement officers. In C. D. Spielberger (ed.), *Police selection and evaluation: Issues and techniques*. Washington, D.C.: Hemisphere Publishing, 1979.

Spielberger, R. D. The effects of anxiety on complex learning and academic achievement. In C. D. Spielberger (ed.), *Anxiety and behavior*. New York: Academic, 1966.

Spitzer, R. L., & Fleiss, J. A re-analysis of the reliability of psychiatric diagnosis. *British Journal of Psychiatry*, 1974, 125, 341–347.

Staub, E. *Positive social behavior and morality: Social and personal influences*. Vol. 1. New York: Academic Press, 1978.

Steadman, H. J. Predicting dangerousness. In D. J. Madden & J. R. Lion (eds.), *Rage-hate-assault and other forms of violence*. New York: Spectrum Publishers, 1976.

Steadman, H. J., & Cocozza, J. J. *Careers of the criminally insane*. Lexington, Mass.: Lexington Books, 1974.

Steininger, E. M. Changes in the MMPI profiles of first prison offenders during their first year of imprisonment. Doctoral dissertation, Michigan State University, 1959. *Dissertation Abstracts International*, 1959, 19, 3394–3395 (University Microfilms No. 59–1, 341).

Stephan, C., & Tully, J. C. The influence of physical attractiveness of a plaintiff on the decisions of simulated jurors. *Journal of Social Psychology*, 1977, 101, 149–150.

Stever, A. Legal vocabulary—its uses and limitations. *Practical Lawyer*, 1969, 15, 39–55.

Stier, S. D., & Stoebe, K. J. Involuntary hospitalization of the mentally ill in Iowa: The failure of the 1975 legislation. *Iowa Law Review*, 1979, 64, 1284–1458.

Stone, A. *Mental health and law: A system in transition*. U.S. Government Printing Office, Washington, 1975.

Stone, A. The *Tarasoff* decisions: Suing psychotherapists to safeguard society. *Harvard Law Review*, 1976, 90, 358–388.

Stoner, J. A. F. A comparison of individual and group decisions involving risk. Unpublished master's thesis, School of Industrial Management, MIT, 1961.

Storms, M. D. Videotape and the attribution process: Reversing actors' and observers' points of view. *Journal of Personality and Social Psychology*, 1973, 27, 165–175.

Stotland, E., & Berberich, J. The psychology of the police. In H. Toch (ed.), *Psychology of crime and criminal justice*. New York: Holt, Rinehart & Winston, 1979, 24–67.

Stratton, J. G. Police stress: An overview. *The Police Chief*, 1978, 5, 58–62.

Strawn, D. U., & Buchanan, R. W. Jury confusion: A threat to justice. *Judicature*, 1976, 5, 478–483.

Strodtbeck, F. L., & Hook, L. H. The social dimensions of a twelve-man jury table. *Sociometry*, 1961, 24, 397–415.

Strodtbeck, F. L., James, R., & Hawkins, C. Social status in jury deliberation. *American Sociological Review*, 1957, 22, 713–719.

Strodtbeck, F. L., & Mann, R. Sex role differentiation in jury deliberations. *Sociometry*, 1956, 29, 3–11.

Suggs, D., & Sales, B. D. The art and science of conducting the voir dire. *Professional Psychology*, 1978, 9, 367–388.

Szasz, T. S. The myth of mental illness. *American Psychologist*, 1960, 15, 113–118.

Szasz, T. S. *Law, liberty and psychiatry*. New York: Collier Books, 1968.

Tagatz, G. E., & Hess, I. R. *Police entry tests and their predictability of score in police academy and subsequent job performance*. Milwaukee: The Center for Criminal Justice, 1972.

Tapp, J. L. Psychology and law: Look at interface. In B. D. Sales (ed.), *Psychology in the legal process*. New York: Spectrum, 1977.

Tapp, P. W. Who is the criminal? *American Sociological Review*, 1947, 12, 100–110.

Tedeschi, J. T., & Lindskold, S. *Social psychology: Interdependence, interaction, and influence*. New York: Wiley, 1976.

Terman, L. M. A trial of mental and pedagogical tests in a civil service examination for policemen and firemen. *Journal of Applied Psychology*, 1917, 1, 17–29.

Thibaut, J., & Walker, L. *Procedural justice: A psychological analysis*. Hillsdale, N.J.: Lawrence Erlbaum Associates, 1975.

Thibaut, J., & Walker, L. A theory of procedure.

*California Law Review*, 1978, 66, 541–566.

Thomas, N. H. The use of biofeedback training in alleviation of stress in the police officer. In W. Taylor & M. Braswell (eds.), *Issues in police and criminal psychology*. Washington, D.C.: University Press of America, 1978.

Thurstone, L. L. The intelligence of policemen. *Journal of Personnel Research*, 1922, *1*, 64–74.

Tribe, L. H. Trial by mathematics: Precision and ritual in the legal process. *Harvard Law Review*, 1971, *84*, 1329–1393.

Trovillo, P. V. A history in lie detection. *Journal of Criminal Law and Criminology*, 1939, 29, 848–881.

Truax, C. B., & Mitchell, K. M. Research on certain therapist interpersonal skills in relation to process and outcome. In A. E. Bergin & S. I. Garfield (eds.), *Handbook of psychotherapy and behavior change*. New York: Wiley, 1971.

Ubrich, L., & Trumbo, D. The selection interview since 1949. *Psychological Bulletin*, 1965, *63*, 100–116.

Unikovic, C. M., & Brown, W. R. The drunken cop. *The Police Chief*, 1978, April, 18–20.

Ursin, H., Baade, E., & Levine, S. *Psychobiology of stress: A study of coping men*. New York: Academic Press, 1978.

U.S. House of Representatives, Committee on the Judiciary. *State of the judiciary and access to justice*. Washington, D.C.: U.S. Government Printing Office, 1977.

U.S. Senate, Committee on the Judiciary, *Criminal Code Reform Act of 1977*. Washington, D.C., U.S. Government Printing Office, 1977.

Valenstein, E. S. *Brain control*. New York: John Wiley, 1973.

Vander Zanden, J. W. *Social psychology*. New York: Random House, 1977.

Vago, S. *Law and society*. Englewood Cliffs, N.J.: Prentice-Hall, 1981.

Verinis, J. S., & Walker, V. Policemen and the recall of criminal details. *Journal of Social Psychology*, 1970, *81*, 217–222.

Vidmar, N. The other issues in jury simulation research: A commentary with particular reference to defendant character studies. *Law and Human Behavior*, 1979, 3, 95–106.

Walbert, D. F. The effect of jury size on the probability of conviction: An evaluation of *Williams v. Florida. Case Western Research*

*Law Review*, 1971, 22, 529–554.

Walker, T. G., & Main, E. C. Choice-shifts in political decision making: Federal judges and civil liberties cases. *Journal of Applied Social Psychology*, 1973, 2, 39–48.

Wall, P. M. *Eye-witness identification in criminal cases*. Springfield, Ill.: C. C. Thomas, 1965.

Wallerstein, J. S., & Wyle, J. Our law-abiding law breakers. *Probation*, 1947, 25, 107–112.

Walters, G. C., & Grusec, J. E. *Punishment*. San Francisco: W. H. Freeman, 1977.

Walters, R. H., Callagan, J. E., & Newman, A. F. Effects of solitary confinement on prisoners. *American Journal of Psychiatry*, 1963, *119*, 771–773.

Walters, R. H., & Parke, R. D. Emotional arousal, isolation, and discrimination learning in children. *Journal of Experimental Child Psychology*, 1964, *1*, 269–280.

Warren, C. Involuntary commitment for mentally disordered: The application of California's Lanterman-Petris-Short Act. *Law & Society Review*, 1977, *11*, 629–649.

Webster, W. H. *Uniform Crime Reports for the United States*. Washington, D.C.: U.S. Government Printing Office, 1980.

Weinberg, M. M. Effects of partial sensory deprivation on involuntary subjects. Doctoral dissertation, Michigan State University, 1967. *Dissertation Abstracts International*, 1967, 28, 2171B (University Microfilms No. 67–14, 558).

Weiss, J. M. Effects of coping response on stress. *Journal of Comparative and Physiological Psychology*, 1968, 65, 251–260.

Weiss, J. M. Somatic effects of predictable and unpredictable shock. *Psychosomatic Medicine*, 1970, 32, 397–409.

Weiss, J. M. Effects of coping behavior in different warning signal conditions on stress pathology in rats. *Journal of Comparative and Physiological Psychology*, 1971, 77, 1–13.

Weiten, W., & Diamond, S. S. A critical review of the jury simulation paradigm: The case of defendant characteristics. *Law and Human Behavior*, 1979, 3, 71–94.

Wells, G. L. Applied eyewitness testimony research: System variables and estimator variables. *Journal of Personality and Social Psychology*, 1978, 36, 1546–1557.

Wells, G. L., Leippe, M. R., & Ostrom, T. M. Guidelines for empirically assessing the fairness of a lineup. *Law and Human Be-*

*havior,* 1979, *3,* 285–294.

Wells, G. L., Lindsay, R. C. L., & Ferguson, T. J. Accuracy, confidence, and juror perceptions in eyewitness identification. *Journal of Applied Psychology,* 1979, *64,* 440–448.

Wenger, D. L., & Fletcher, C. R. The effect of legal counsel on admissions to a state mental hospital: A confrontation of professions. *Journal of Health and Social Behavior,* 1969, *10,* 66–80.

Wenk, E. A., Robison, J. O., & Smith, G. W. Can violence be predicted? *Crime and Delinquency,* 1972, *18,* 393–402.

West, S. T., Gunn, S., & Chernicky, P. Ubiquitous Watergate: An attribution analysis. *Journal of Personality and Social Psychology,* 1975, *32,* 55–65.

Westin, A. *Privacy and freedom.* New York: Atheneum, 1967.

Westley, W. A. Secrecy and the police. *Social Forces,* 1956, *34,* 254–257.

Wexler, D. B. *Mental health law: Major issues.* New York: Plenum Press, 1981.

Wexler, D. B., & Scoville, S. E. The administration of psychiatric justice theory and practice in Arizona. *Arizona Law Review,* 1971, *13,* 1–250.

Wheeler, S. Socialization in correctional communities. *American Sociological Review,* 1961, *26,* 697–712.

Widacki, J., & Horvath, F. S. An experimental investigation of the relative validity and utility of the polygraph technique and three other common methods of criminal investigation. *Journal of Forensic Sciences,* 1978, *23,* 596–601.

Wiggins, J. S. *Personality and prediction: Principles of personality assessment.* Reading, Mass.: Addison-Wesley Publishing, 1973.

Wilkins, L. T. Policy control, information, ethics, and discretion. In L. E. Abt & I. R. Stuart (eds.), *Social psychology and discretionary law.* New York: Van Nostrand Reinhold, 1979.

Williams, G. *The proof of guilt.* 3d ed. London: Stevens & Sons, 1963.

Williams, G. R., England, J. L., Farmer, L. C., & Blumenthal, M. Effectiveness in legal negotiation. In G. Bermant, C. Nemeth, & N. Vidmar (eds.), *Psychology and the law.* Lexington, Mass.: Lexington Books, 1976.

Wilson, J. Q. *Varieties of police behavior: The management of law and order in eight communities.* Cambridge, Mass.: Harvard University Press, 1968.

Winick, C. The psychology of the courtroom. In H. Toch (ed.), *Psychology of crime and criminal justice.* New York: Holt, Rinehart & Winston, 1979.

Wootton, B. *Crime and the criminal law.* London: Stevens & Sons, 1963.

Worchel, S., & Cooper, J. *Understanding social psychology.* Rev. ed. Homewood, Ill.: Dorsey Press, 1979.

Wrightsman, L. S. *Social psychology.* 2d ed. Monterey, California: Brooks/Cole, 1977.

Wrightsman, L. S., & Deaux, K. *Social psychology in the 80's.* 3d ed. Monterey, California: Brooks/Cole, 1981.

Yarmey, A. D. *The psychology of eyewitness testimony.* New York: The Free Press, 1979.

Yarmey, A. D., & Kent, J. Eyewitness identification by elderly and young adults. *Law and Human Behavior,* 1980, *4,* 359–371.

Yuille, J. C. A critical examination of the psychological and practical implications of eyewitness research. *Law and Human Behavior,* 1980, *4,* 335–346.

Yukl, G. A. Effects of situational and opponent concessions on a bargainer's perception, aspirations, and concessions. *Journal of Personality and Social Psychology,* 1974, *29,* 227–236.

Zander, M. *Legal services for the community.* London: Temple Smith, 1978.

Zander, T. K. Civil commitment in Wisconsin: The impact of *Lessard v. Schmidt. Wisconsin Law Review,* 1976, *26,* 503–562.

Zeisel, H. . . . And then there were none: The diminution of the federal jury. *University of Chicago Law Review,* 1971, *38,* 710–724.

Zeisel, H. Twelve is just. *Trial,* 1974, *10,* 13–15.

Zeisel, H., & Diamond, S. The effect of peremptory challenges on the jury and verdict. *Stanford Law Review,* 1978, *30,* 491–531.

Zeisel, H., Kalven, H., Jr., & Buchholz, R. *Delay in the court.* Boston: Little, Brown, 1959.

Zilboorg, G. Legal aspects of psychiatry. In American Psychiatric Association (ed.), *One hundred years of American psychiatry.* New York: Columbia University Press, 1944, 507–584.

Zimbardo, P. G. The psychological power and pathology of imprisonment. In E. Aronson and R. Helmreich (eds.), *Social psychology.* New York: Van Nostrand, 1973.

Zitrin, A., Hardesty, A., Burdock, E., & Drossman, A. Crime and violence among mental patients. *Scientific Proceedings of the 128th Annual Meeting of the American Psychiatric Association, Abstracts,* 1975, *142,* 140–141.

Zubek, J. P. (ed.). *Sensory deprivation: Fifteen years of research.* New York: Appleton-Century-Crofts, 1969.

Zuckerman, M., & Gerbasi, K. C. Belief in internal control or belief in a just world: The use and misuse of the I-E scale in prediction of attitudes and behavior. *Journal of Personality,* 1977, *45,* 356–378.

# Author Index

# Subject Index

Please remember that this is a library book,
and that it belongs only temporarily to each
person who uses it. Be considerate. Do
not write in this, or any, library book.